Cloud Security:

Concepts, Methodologies, Tools, and Applications

Information Resources Management Association
USA

Volume I

Published in the United States of America by
    IGI Global
    Engineering Science Reference (an imprint of IGI Global)
    701 E. Chocolate Avenue
    Hershey PA, USA 17033
    Tel: 717-533-8845
    Fax: 717-533-8661
    E-mail: cust@igi-global.com
    Web site: http://www.igi-global.com

Library of Congress Cataloging-in-Publication Data

Names: Information Resources Management Association, editor.
Title: Cloud security : concepts, methodologies, tools, and applications /
  Information Resources Management Association, editor.
Description: Hershey, PA : Engineering Science Reference, [2019] | Includes
  bibliographical references.
Identifiers: LCCN 2018048047| ISBN 9781522581765 (hardcover) | ISBN
  9781522581772 (ebook)
Subjects: LCSH: Cloud computing--Security measures.
Classification: LCC QA76.585 .C5864 2019 | DDC 004.67/82--dc23 LC record available at https://lccn.loc.gov/2018048047

British Cataloguing in Publication Data
A Cataloguing in Publication record for this book is available from the British Library.

The views expressed in this book are those of the authors, but not necessarily of the publisher.

For electronic access to this publication, please contact: eresources@igi-global.com.

List of Contributors

Table of Contents

Volume I

Section 1
Fundamental Concepts and Theories

John Gyang Chaka, University of Kwazulu-Natal, South Africa
Mudaray Marimuthu, University of Kwazulu-Natal, South Africa

Kowsigan Mohan, Sri Krishna College of Technology, India
P. Balasubramanie Palanisamy, Kongu Engineering College, India
G.R. Kanagachidambaresan, Veltech Rangarajan Dr Sagunthala R&D Institute of Science
and Technology, India
Siddharth Rajesh, Sri Krishna College of Technology, India
Sneha Narendran, Sri Krishna College of Technology, India

Chiba Zouhair, Hassan II University of Casablanca, Morocco
Noreddine Abghour, Hassan II University of Casablanca, Morocco
Khalid Moussaid, Hassan II University of Casablanca, Morocco
Amina El Omri, Hassan II University of Casablanca, Morocco
Mohamed Rida, Hassan II University of Casablanca, Morocco

Marcus Tanque, Independent Researcher, USA

Section 2
Development and Design Methodologies

Section 4
Utilization and Applications

Section 5
Organizational and Social Implications

Volume IV

Section 6
Managerial Impact

Section 7
Critical Issues and Challenges

Section 8
Emerging Trends

Preface

The constantly changing landscape of Cloud Security makes it challenging for experts and practitioners to stay informed of the field's most up-to-date research. That is why Engineering Science Reference is pleased to offer this four-volume reference collection that will empower students, researchers, and academicians with a strong understanding of critical issues within Cloud Security by providing both broad and detailed perspectives on cutting-edge theories and developments. This reference is designed to act as a single reference source on conceptual, methodological, technical, and managerial issues, as well as to provide insight into emerging trends and future opportunities within the discipline.

Cloud Security: Concepts, Methodologies, Tools, and Applications is organized into eight distinct sections that provide comprehensive coverage of important topics. The sections are:

1. Fundamental Concepts and Theories;
2. Development and Design Methodologies;
3. Tools and Technologies;
4. Utilization and Applications;
5. Organizational and Social Implications;
6. Managerial Impact;
7. Critical Issues and Challenges; and
8. Emerging Trends.

The following paragraphs provide a summary of what to expect from this invaluable reference tool.

Section 1, "Fundamental Concepts and Theories," serves as a foundation for this extensive reference tool by addressing crucial theories essential to the understanding of Cloud Security. Introducing the book is "Curtailing the Threats to Cloud Computing in the Fourth Industrial Revolution?" by John Gyang Chaka and Mudaray Marimuthu: a great foundation laying the groundwork for the basic concepts and theories that will be discussed throughout the rest of the book. Section 1 concludes and leads into the following portion of the book with a nice segue chapter, "Approaches to Cloud Computing in the Public Sector" by Jeffrey Chang and Mark Johnston.

Section 2, "Development and Design Methodologies," presents in-depth coverage of the conceptual design and architecture of Cloud Security. Opening the section is "A Multi-Dimensional Mean Failure Cost Model to Enhance Security of Cloud Computing Systems" by Mouna Jouini and Latifa Ben Arfa Rabai. Through case studies, this section lays excellent groundwork for later sections that will get into present and future applications for Cloud Security. The section concludes with an excellent work by Rekha Kashyap and Deo Prakash Vidyarthi, "A Secured Real Time Scheduling Model for Cloud Hypervisor."

Section 3, "Tools and Technologies," presents extensive coverage of the various tools and technologies used in the implementation of Cloud Security. The first chapter, "CCCE: Cryptographic Cloud Computing Environment Based on Quantum Computations" by Omer K. Jasim, Safia Abbas, El-Sayed M. El-Horbaty, and Abdel-Badeeh M. Salem, lays a framework for the types of works that can be found in this section. The section concludes with "Keystroke Dynamics Authentication in Cloud Computing" by Basma Mohammed Hassan, Khaled Mohammed Fouad, and Mahmoud Fathy Hassan. Where Section 3 described specific tools and technologies at the disposal of practitioners, Section 4 describes the use and applications of the tools and frameworks discussed in previous sections.

Section 4, "Utilization and Applications," describes how the broad range of Cloud Security efforts has been utilized and offers insight on and important lessons for their applications and impact. The first chapter in the section is "Cloud Computing and Cybersecurity Issues Facing Local Enterprises" written by Emre Erturk. This section includes the widest range of topics because it describes case studies, research, methodologies, frameworks, architectures, theory, analysis, and guides for implementation. The breadth of topics covered in the section is also reflected in the diversity of its authors, from countries all over the globe. The section concludes with "Necessity of Key Aggregation Cryptosystem for Data Sharing in Cloud Computing" by R. Deepthi Crestose Rebekah, Dhanaraj Cheelu, and M. Rajasekhara Babu, a great transition chapter into the next section.

Section 5, "Organizational and Social Implications," includes chapters discussing the organizational and social impact of Cloud Security. The section opens with "Impact of Technology Innovation: A Study on Cloud Risk Mitigation" by Niranjali Suresh and Manish Gupta. This section focuses exclusively on how these technologies affect human lives, either through the way they interact with each other or through how they affect behavioral/workplace situations. The section concludes with "Trust Management in Cloud Computing" by Vijay L. Hallappanavar and Mahantesh N. Birje.

Section 6, "Managerial Impact," presents focused coverage of Cloud Security in a managerial perspective. The section begins with "The Collaborative Use of Patients' Health-Related Information: Challenges and Research Problems in a Networked World" by Fadi Alhaddadin, Jairo A. Gutiérrez, and William Liu. This section serves as a vital resource for developers who want to utilize the latest research to bolster the capabilities and functionalities of their processes. The chapters in this section offer unmistakable value to managers looking to implement new strategies that work at larger bureaucratic levels. The section concludes with "Smart Healthcare Administration Over Cloud" by Govinda K. and S. Ramasubbareddy.

Section 7, "Critical Issues and Challenges," presents coverage of academic and research perspectives on Cloud Security tools and applications. The section begins with "A Comparative Study of Privacy Protection Practices in the US, Europe, and Asia" by Noushin Ashrafi and Jean-Pierre Kuilboer. Chapters in this section will look into theoretical approaches and offer alternatives to crucial questions on the subject of Cloud Security. The section concludes with "Privacy Preserving Public Auditing in Cloud: Literature Review" by Thangavel M., Varalakshmi P., Sridhar S., and Sindhuja R.

Section 8, "Emerging Trends," highlights areas for future research within the field of Cloud Security, opening with "Advances in Information, Security, Privacy, and Ethics: Use of Cloud Computing for Education" by Joseph M. Woodside. This section contains chapters that look at what might happen in the coming years that can extend the already staggering amount of applications for Cloud Security. The final chapter of the book looks at an emerging field within Cloud Security in the excellent contribution "Emerging Cloud Computing Services: A Brief Opinion Article" by Yulin Yao.

Although the primary organization of the contents in this multi-volume work is based on its eight sections, offering a progression of coverage of the important concepts, methodologies, technologies, applications, social issues, and emerging trends, the reader can also identify specific contents by utilizing the extensive indexing system listed at the end of each volume. As a comprehensive collection of research on the latest findings related to using technology to providing various services, *Cloud Security: Concepts, Methodologies, Tools, and Applications* provides researchers, administrators, and all audiences with a complete understanding of the development of applications and concepts in Cloud Security. Given the vast number of issues concerning usage, failure, success, policies, strategies, and applications of Cloud Security in countries around the world, *Cloud Security: Concepts, Methodologies, Tools, and Applications* addresses the demand for a resource that encompasses the most pertinent research in technologies being employed to globally bolster the knowledge and applications of Cloud Security.

Section 1
Fundamental Concepts and Theories

Chapter 1
Curtailing the Threats to Cloud Computing in the Fourth Industrial Revolution

John Gyang Chaka
University of Kwazulu-Natal, South Africa

Mudaray Marimuthu
University of Kwazulu-Natal, South Africa

ABSTRACT

Cloud computing enables end users to make use of third party's resources to support their computing needs. The services offered by cloud computing make the technology very critical to the fourth industrial revolution. The benefits include cost minimization, scalability of services, speed, integration and higher data management, low innovation risk, and quicker response to organizational needs, among others. However, these benefits have been threatened by a number of security threats. This chapter seeks to curtail the effects of these threats by enlightening and educating users on the current ways to mitigate them. The chapter first defines cloud computing and highlights its relevance or benefits to businesses in the fourth industrial revolution. In addition, various security threats that are associated with cloud computing are brought to the fore. Thereafter, various measures that are used to mitigate the threats are discussed. The chapter concludes that with adequate enlightenment, the full benefits of cloud computing in industry 4.0 would be better enjoyed by users.

INTRODUCTION

The fourth industrial revolution, also known as Industry 4.0 has been viewed as an era where technology will play a major role like never before in the way that people live and relate to one another (Schwab, 2015). This era builds on the third industrial revolution, which had electronics and information technology at its centre. It combines information technology (dealing with business process and office automations) with operational technology (dealing with industrial process and factory automations). Since the fourth industrial revolution, which integrates various computational systems including sensor networks, Internet

DOI: 10.4018/978-1-5225-8176-5.ch001

communication infrastructure, intelligent real-time processing management, automated management of systems, and advanced robotics, will involve Big Data it requires a scalable data processing, which single individuals or organizations may not be able to handle in isolation. Thus, the Internet serves as the core in this era (Bloem et al., 2014). In other words, the fourth industrial revolution is expected to further tilt the world into a digitized entity – cyberspace, where human activities are more driven or dependent on centralized use of information and mechanical systems.

The Internet, the core of the fourth industrial revolution, serves as the converging point and superhighway on which every operation depends. It is estimated that Industry 4.0 will consist of about 50 billion connected devices. By implication, interdependence and shareability of resources among organizations are the top features of the fourth industrial revolution. This makes cloud computing a critical component of the fourth industrial revolution since the backbone of this era, which is the Internet, will mainly function by utilizing cloud computing services (Moavenzadeh, 2015). No wonder Alcorta (2017), the director, Policy, Research and Statistics, United Nations Industrial Development Organization (UNIDO), mentions cloud computing as one of the technological breakthroughs that will play a vital role in transforming manufacturing in the Industry 4.0 era.

However, while it is obvious that cloud computing will play a vital role in the fourth industrial revolution, as more resources will tend to be interconnected and shared, one major concern is the security of cyberspace (Alcorta, 2017; Bigger, 2015). Cyberspace, specifically cloud computing is witnessing some security challenges, or different forms of attacks, which seem to threaten the efficacy of the fourth industrial era if mitigating measures are not taken. Therefore, as part of measures to ensure a safer use of cyberspace and promote the success of the fourth industrial revolution, this chapter highlights some cyber threats that are detrimental to cloud computing and more importantly educates the audience on various ways by which the threats can be curtailed or mitigated.

BACKGROUND

Cloud computing signifies or represents a deviation from the traditional storage and management of computing resources which are limited by factors such as size, space and cost among others. Cloud computing describes an environment where computing resources can be accessed on a larger scale by users through the Internet and the Web (Chappell, 2011; Stair & Reynolds, 2016). It is simply a way of maximizing the use of resources while minimising cost. Perhaps a clearer description of cloud computing is provided by Rao, Leelaran, and Kumar (2013, p. 3390) who simply see cloud computing as "using the Internet to access someone else's software running on someone else's hardware in someone else's datacenter". Among resources that can be shared in a cloud are hardware, data storage and data management facilities, applications, and many other services (Hatwar & Chavan, 2015). These resources are not only shared simultaneously by multiple users but can be used in turns by re-allocation to users in different time zones. This way, less demand is made on the environment since less power, air conditioning and space would be required for the same services. Typical examples of cloud services include iCloud, Google drive, and Dropbox. Other services include those provided by social networking sites such as Facebook and LinkedIn (Kazim & Zhu, 2015). The most common example of cloud services that is used by most people is the electronic mail (e-mail) service provided by Google, Yahoo and other providers (Chou, 2013).

Origin of Cloud Computing, Cloud Services and Deployment Models

Origin of Cloud Computing

There seems to be no agreement on the origin of cloud computing. For instance while some authors (Bartholomew, 2009; Bogatin, 2006) believe that cloud computing was first coined by Eric Schmidt – chief executive officer of Google™ in 2006, Kaufman (2006) attributes the origin of cloud computing to use of virtual private networks (VPN) by telecommunications networks in the 1990s. In another dimension, the origin of cloud computing has been linked to the application of large-scale mainframe computers in academia and corporations in the 1950s. In the academia and corporations, client or terminal computers which were known as "dumb terminals" were used to connect to the mainframes, which had the sole computational or processing capability. The concept of cloud computing became clearer and defined in 2007. Amazon.com played a key role in advancing the technology through the modernization of its data centre, which provided access to their Web services (Rao et al., 2013). Since then, many organizations including Google, IBM, and universities have found cloud computing very beneficial in view of its scalability, ability to manage large sets of data and the fact that it reduces operational costs among others (Hatwar & Chavan, 2015). Cloud computing can be provided or deployed in the form of services. The three main services include Infrastructure as a Service (IaaS), Platform as a Service (PaaS), and Software as a Service (SaaS) (Bhadauria & Sanyal, 2012; Chou, 2013).

Cloud Computing Services

Infrastructure as Service (IaaS) refers to the provision or deployment of computing facilities, specifically hardware, by a third party. IaaS provides facilities such as servers, data processing and storage supports, networks and other vital infrastructure for the use of a consumer or user through the Internet by someone else (Rao et al., 2013). In this case, the user neither has control of the resources that he is using nor does he know their exact location. In fact, in most cases, the different cloud infrastructures being used by a user might be provided or controlled by different individuals or groups (IBM, 2009). Subsets of IaaS are applicable to different industries. For example, Communication as a Service (CaaS) is more peculiar to IP telephony services. Some examples of infrastructural services in the cloud include Google's Compute Engine, Amazon's Elastic Compute Cloud, Dropbox, and Microsoft Windows Azure storage (Dekker, Livery, & Lakka, 2013).

Platform as a Service (PaaS) is a service that provides an environment for applications to be developed or run (Chappell, 2011). The service provides tools and libraries that are essential for the development and running of applications. This service relieves users of the cost of buying tools that are needed to develop applications as well as configuration settings (Chou, 2013). Platforms that can be provided as a service could include Web servers, database servers, and applications servers (Bhadauria & Sanyal, 2012). Examples of Platform services include Amazon Web Services (AWS), Microsoft Azure, and SalesForce among others (Oredo & Njihia, 2014).

Software as a Service (SaaS) enables users to run complete applications which are hosted on the Internet (Cloud) through a sort of renting arrangement. Computer applications are not only expensive to purchase, but they are often updated regularly. This service relieves users of the burden of buying, installing, and maintaining in their local computers any application that they require to use. In order to achieve this goal, two servers – Main Consistence and Domain Consistence Servers are deployed. The security of the Main Consistence Server (MCS) is crucial as any damage to it amounts to a loss in control to the cloud environment (Bhadauria & Sanyal, 2012). The Web or online versions of Microsoft office applications and GoogleApps are typical examples of SaaS.

Deployment Models

A number of deployment models for cloud computing exist. The four common deployment models are private, public, hybrid, and community clouds (Backe & Lindén, 2015; Rao et al., 2013; Stair & Reynolds, 2016).

Private cloud deployment refers to a situation where the sharing of resources is restricted to individuals within the confine of a private network. Resources in a private cloud can be managed either internally by the user organization or by a third party. Furthermore, the resources can be hosted either internally or externally. A typical example is an organizational data centre which houses resources such as database servers, mail servers and other resources that are centrally used by all individuals within an organization.

Public cloud deployment refers to a deployment method in which the sharing of resources is open to the general public. Resources on public cloud may be freely shared and the users of resources can be individuals or companies. In terms of architecture, the difference between private and public clouds is very slim. However, substantial differences may exist in terms of security. An example of public cloud providers is the Amazon Web Services (AWS).

Hybrid cloud deployment is a deployment method which allows businesses to combine the services of two or more cloud models. The different clouds maintain their distinct individual identities but are bound together through the offering of benefits of the different models to the same client. Simply put, hybrid cloud deployment crosses isolation and provider boundaries such that it is not simply identified as falling into any specific deployment model. An example is a situation where an organization stores its sensitive data in its private network but interconnects the application using this data locally to another application (such as a business intelligence application) that is provided in a public cloud and runs as software service (Moore, 2014).

Community clouds allow several businesses to form a specific community with common concerns to share cloud computing resources. The needs or concerns of the community may be in relation to security, compliance, jurisdiction or any other issue. Community clouds can be managed internally or by a third party. They can also be hosted internally or externally to the user community.

Benefits of Cloud Computing to Industry 4.0

Considering the various services that can be provided in the cloud as already discussed, and the emerging trends in the application of new technologies, the benefits of cloud computing to industry 4.0 are numerous (Saint-Marc, 2014). Macias and Thomas (2011) see the benefits of cloud computing as comparable to the use of common public utilities in place of individual ones. For example, the use of public power in place of a personal generator, or the choice of using a public transport system instead of personal cars by people are relevant scenarios. Although this is not the main focus of the chapter, a brief discussion on some of the benefits of cloud computing is considered vital in providing a good background to the chapter. On this basis, a few of the benefits, which span across different businesses or industries are briefly highlighted below.

Cost Minimisation

As already mentioned, cloud computing enables businesses to minimise their expenditure. It saves businesses the cost of buying and maintaining infrastructure such as networking and storage facilities; application development platforms such as servers and operating system; and relevant application software. In other words, businesses are liberated from worrying about purchases of new computing facilities, revaluation of existing facilities, or the monthly review of the level of utilization of facilities. One important cost benefit of cloud computing is found in business start-ups. Cloud computing can be very beneficial in the starting up of businesses through the provision of access to facilities that may be very expensive to acquire. This is particularly important for small businesses that may not be able to afford facilities that can support advanced processes. Another way in which cloud computing minimises cost is through labour optimisation. Since most of the organization's services are virtual, their labour requirements are drastically reduced to only mission critical activities (Macias & Thomas, 2011). Furthermore, most cloud providers operate on a pay-as-you-go basis, thus users are charged only for services that they use (Chappell, 2011). By implication, the expenditures of most business is reduced to mainly operational expenditures as they are relieved of the heavier burdens of capital expenditure (Saint-Marc, 2014).

Choice and Scalability

With cloud computing, businesses are offered the benefit of making choices that are based on their needs and operational budgets at any particular time. This suggests that cloud computing provides the opportunity for every business to operate within the confines of their operational budgets (Saint-Marc, 2014). Another implication is that businesses in the fourth industrial revolution have the choice and opportunity of expanding easily to any level depending on their needs (Chou, 2013). Businesses can simply scale up their services by exploring the services of a cloud provider that are appropriate for their needs (Chappell, 2011).

Speed and Faster Rollout Capability

Cloud computing offers businesses the fastest means to rollout new capabilities and innovations. This is because organizations sometimes take a lot of time to finalize arrangements towards deploying IT infrastructure internally. This situation in most cases results in huge losses of revenue to the organizations (Chappell, 2011). Additionally, advertisements and information about products can be accessed by unlimited numbers of people irrespective of location and distance (Saint-Marc, 2014). Therefore, with cloud computing, businesses have the opportunities to cope with the expected market demands of Industry 4.0.

Integration and Big Data Management

Being host to several databases and applications which are properly organized, cloud computing serves as a good means of integrating various data components. In other words, cloud computing has opened the doors for effective generation and management of Big data (Chou, 2013; Saint-Marc, 2014). In this regard, Saint-Marc (2014) states that the cloud has the ability to provide countless application program interfaces (APIs) to be used by third party services; coordinate access to various database components (OData, JSON, JSONP, XML) by APIs; and also ensure flexible and easier access to traditional databases including SQL and NoSQL databases.

Low Innovation Risk

Every business tries to stay ahead of others by way of rolling out regular innovations. However, each innovation has a risk of failure associated with it. Chappell (2011) states that the extent of the risk that is attached to an innovation is proportional to the financial obligation associated with the innovation. He maintains that the benefit of cloud computing to businesses is that it makes innovations less expensive and thus less risky. No doubt, this is a good motivation for businesses in the fourth industrial revolution as businesses are sure of rolling out more innovations with fewer risks.

Flexibility

Cloud computing makes room for high flexibility in terms of the use of resources. Organizations are not tied to the use of resources for life. Businesses can withdraw from the use of resources at any time when they no longer require such resources. Since these resources can be reallocated to other users, wastages due to redundant resources are minimised.

Business Continuity Planning and Centralizing Volatility of Businesses

This point serves as one of the major benefits of cloud computing. Business continuity planning or management refers to an organizational approach or approaches towards preventing or responding to situations that may affect the organizational assets negatively. It involves the implementation of measures that provide quick response to contingencies or crises of different origins so that at least vital business processes continue to run. Business continuity planning considers events such as malfunctioning of equipment, contingencies and crises. Traditionally, business continuity and disaster recovery techniques require the purchase and maintenance of a complete set of hardware that can mirror an enterprise's critical systems. For example, sufficient storage systems may be required to back up the complete set of a company's data. The maintenance fee and cost of regular replication of data on the mirror systems can be very high. Added to this cost is the cost of ensuring that the application software in use synchronizes all data locations. Cloud computing provide opportunities for companies to ensure the continuity of their businesses through adequate and cost effective disaster planning and recovery management. In the event of a disaster, business continuity planning is not hampered through the application of disaster recovery measures including cold or hot backups, high-redundancy, and data duplication backups among others, which are provided by different cloud service providers (Saint-Marc, 2014). Most cloud providers invest heavily towards ensuring the safety and resilience of their infrastructure to attacks. The Microsoft Cloud platform – Azure for example is ISO 27001 certified thus, it provides disaster recovery as a service. The implication is that in the unlikely event of any data loss, data recovery is guaranteed (Petrowisch, 2017). Therefore cloud computing assures organizations in Industry 4 of business continuity as they are relieved of the burdens and complexities associated with disaster planning and recovery.

Improved Agility and Adaptability

Two important potentials that cannot be detached from the fourth industrial revolution are effectiveness and efficiency in relation to organizational operations or business agility. Cloud computing promotes these potentials in organizations through the deployment of IT resources such as applications that support user requirements in real time (Oredo & Njihia, 2014). Most resources in the cloud are virtual, suggesting that cloud computing is built with mobile productivity in mind (Bigger, 2015). Thus, employees of organisations, especially ICT experts, are provided with better opportunities to quickly respond to the needs of their jobs using a variety of personal devices irrespective of their locations (Macias & Thomas, 2011). In other words, as long as Internet connection is available, job performance of employees or the services that organizations render to customers, are not limited to any time zone or geographic location (Apostu, Puican, Ularu, Suciu, & Todoran, 2014). Furthermore, the efficiency of organizations' IT departments is enhanced since their operations will no longer be limited by on-site infrastructure. Additionally, the IT departments are no longer concern about software upgrades and other major issues of the organization except minor ones that may pop up occasionally (Bigger, 2015).

Drawbacks or Challenges Associated With Cloud Computing and Implications for Industry 4.0

Although the benefits of cloud computing in relation to Industry 4.0 are enormous, a number of challenges have been identified which may be acting against the successful deployment and use of cloud computing services. Some of these challenges are presented below.

Technical Issues/Availability

Although a major benefit of cloud computing is that it promotes business agility, there must be moments when systems fail. In other words, no technology can be perfect. Apostu et al. (2014) state that even the best cloud service providers experience outages from time to time. Since organizations that utilize cloud services may not have control over the resources that they use, the organizations are helpless and their operations are truncated when cloud services become unavailable perhaps due to technical faults in the cloud. This suggests that businesses or organizations must embrace industry 4.0 with some caution and vigilance.

Security Issues

Security has been identified as one of the greatest concerns in cloud computing (Chou, 2013; CSA, 2016; Liu, Sun, Ryoo, Rizvi, & Vasilakos, 2015). Organizations or individuals that use cloud computing services surrender sensitive data to the cloud service providers which are mostly third parties (Oredo & Njihia, 2014). Information that is hosted in the cloud is subjected to different forms of external attacks which places organization that utilize cloud services in some form of danger. Without critically weighing all options before choosing cloud service providers by businesses, the benefits of cloud computing may be undermined (Apostu et al., 2014). This puts the success of Industry 4.0 on shaky ground.

Cost

As was discussed earlier, cost is considered to be one of the benefits of cloud based on the reasoning that organizations incur costs for only services that they use. However, it has been observed that the situation may not always be the same across all service providers. In some cases, cloud service providers present a predetermined suite of services to clients as a single contract irrespective of usage (Apostu et al., 2014). Indirectly, clients still pay for services that they do not use.

Inflexibility/Vendor Lock

Using cloud computing services makes business operations sort of inflexible. The choice of a cloud computing vendor by an organization is as good as restricting the operations of the organisation to the proprietary applications or formats of the cloud computing vendor (Oredo & Njihia, 2014). Apostu et al. (2014) cite the difficulty or restriction in inserting a document that has been created in a different application into a Google Docs spreadsheet as a typical example.

Inadequate Support

Poor support in terms of lack of prompt response to the needs of customers has been viewed as a challenge in cloud computing. For most businesses, a halt or a little delay in operations can result in significant losses. Therefore poor support emanating from long delays in responding to customers on the part of cloud service providers surely have negative consequences for businesses (Campbell, 2010). These consequences could have negative implications for Industry 4.0.

Cultural Resistance

In line with Isaac Newton's law of motion, people always develop some form of resistance when changes occur. Shifting from traditional computing to cloud computing may result in a change in the roles of members of an organization especially the IT department. In addition, uncertainties and inadequate preparations towards the changes may result in high resistance to the adoption of cloud computing.

Limited Scope for Customisation

The joy of most users or organizations is to use applications that fit adequately into their operations. Most cloud solutions are generic. This means that they may not completely satisfy the yearnings of users in terms of fitting tightly into their specific business (Oredo & Njihia, 2014).

Lack of Investment on Infrastructure/Big Data Management

The success of cloud computing and by extension, Industry 4.0 depends on accessibility to high quality, reliable, and ubiquitous broadband connectivity to infrastructure. Following Cisco's projection that Internet traffic may reach a monthly estimate of 14.1 zettabytes in 2020, investments in vital infrastructure such as broadband connectivity, data storage facilities that will ensure uninterrupted Internet access to all businesses information, remain a big challenge (Access_Partnership, 2017). This explosive growth in data traffic no doubt places a higher demand on already strained existing infrastructure. Thus, unless a corresponding response in terms of large investments on appropriate infrastructure is ensured, the success of the fourth industrial revolution may be limited. New technologies and platforms which may offer better services are emerging. Some of the new technologies include "5G mobile systems, new satellite broadband networks, TV White Space radios" among others (Access_Partnership, 2017, p. 7). However, the ability to handle or manage the amount of data that may be generated through emerging technologies remains a challenging task.

Lack of Appropriate Incentives for Adoption/Regulatory and Compliance Restrictions

The full benefits or positive impact of cloud computing on businesses and by implication Industry 4.0 can only be felt in the presence of policies that enable users to leverage its capabilities. However, policies that for example ensure respect for privacy rights which are considered critical components of trust in the digital economy have either not been properly put in place or need to be addressed. Further compounding the situation are laws which seek to restrict international transfer of data (Access_Partnership, 2017). A number of countries particularly European countries have regulations in place that seek to serve as bottle necks in the international transfer of personal information (Oredo & Njihia, 2014). Such regulations prohibit personal information and any sensitive data from being physically located outside their States or countries. Although the intention behind such rules may be 'good', the regulations pose a challenge to the deployment of cloud computing services. Cloud services providers have to consider setting up data centres exclusively for such countries in order to comply with such regulations. This development negates the cost benefits of cloud computing which in turn impacts negatively on Industry 4.0 to a large extent.

Inadequate Workforce Skills

Cloud computing and by extension Industry 4.0 place more demands on individuals and organizations in terms of IT skills. Access Partnership (2017) reports that cloud computing and Industry 4.0 will require a shift in workforce skills to areas such as digital literacy and perhaps data science, which have been reported to have a massive skills gap.

TOP SECURITY THREATS ASSOCIATED WITH CLOUD COMPUTING

Hatwar and Chavan (2015) classified the top security threats that are associated with cloud computing to include those identified by Cloud Security Alliance, those inherited from networking perspectives, and other additional security threats.

The main threats that were identified by Cloud Security Alliance (CSA, 2016) include but are not limited to abuse and nefarious use of cloud computing, insecure interfaces and application program interfaces (APIs), malicious insiders, shared technology issues, data loss or leakages, account or service hijacking, and unknown risk profiles. Some other threats are not peculiar to cloud computing alone, but occur due to shared resources used in the cloud. Examples of these include cross sites scripting (XSS) attacks, sniffer attacks, SQL injection attacks, denial of service (DoS) attacks, man-in-the-middle attacks, distributed denial of service (DDoS) attacks, re-used IP addresses, hypervisor related security issues, google hacking, cookie poisoning, and cracking CAPTCHA (Arif & Shakeel, 2015; Dunn, 2009; Liu et al., 2015; Lua & Yow, 2011). These threats have become a great concern to most users of the technology as they appear to have downgraded the benefits of the technology (Stair & Reynolds, 2016). To ease understanding, a brief discussion on the top security threats to cloud computing and by extension, Industry 4.0 is presented in three categories – data security threats, network security threats, and cloud environment security threats.

Data Security Threats

Data Breaches

A data breach is a situation where vital information belonging to an individual or organization is leaked to an unauthorised individual or group (Bhadauria & Sanyal, 2012; Kazim & Zhu, 2015; Racuciu & Eftimie, 2015). A data breach may occur as a result of a deliberate attack on the target or due to human error, application vulnerability and/or improper security practices (CSA, 2016; Hatwar & Chavan, 2015). Depending on the value of such information to the interested party (attacker), a data breach in the cloud has no limit to the kind of information that it affects. It can involve different kinds of information including personal, financial, trade secret and intellectual property. The most worrisome data breach is that which originates from unauthorized insiders who may not be detected easily. Hence, data breaches are rated among the top security threats in organizations' clouds (CSA, 2016). The main sources of data breaches are cloud provider personnel and their devices as well as third party partners of the cloud providers.

The impact of data breaches on organizations will vary depending on the sensitivity of the data involved. The impact may include large fines incurred by companies, lawsuits or litigations, cost for investigations, and perhaps criminal charges. Damage to reputation which may result in loss of business opportunities is another dimension to the impact of data breaches. Industry 4.0 is based on the principles of cloud computing. Data breaches will serve as a set-back to the fourth industrial revolution because most organizations are still not confident in moving to the cloud (Bhadauria & Sanyal, 2012).

A practical example of a data breach as reported by CSA (2016) is the case of an antivirus firm – Bit-Defender which had the usernames and passwords of some of its customers stolen in 2015 as a result of a security vulnerability in its public cloud application that was hosted by Amazon Web Services (AWS).

Data Loss

Apart from malicious attacks and data breaches, there are other actions or events that can result in permanent loss of data in organizations or clouds. Some of these actions or events include accidental deletion of data by a service provider or a physical disaster like fire or earthquake, data corruption, loss of encryption keys, and perhaps faults in storage equipment (CSA, 2016; Kazim & Zhu, 2015). As already mentioned, data remains the most valuable asset to organizations, hence its permanent loss can be terrifying. Kazim and Zhu (2015) state that 44% of cloud service providers faced challenges due to brute force attacks which led to data loss and leakages in 2013. The attack on Sony, which resulted in the leaking of confidential information such as email exchanges in November, 2014; the hacking of Code Spaces (an online hosting and code publishing provider) in June, 2014, which led to the compromise and complete destruction of most customers' data are practical examples of attacks that have resulted in huge data losses (CSA, 2016). In view of this development, threats that result in data loss are considered as top threats.

System Vulnerability

System vulnerabilities result from bugs in programs which are exploited by attackers to infiltrate computer systems. The aim of an attacker may be to steal the organizations data, take entire control of the system or disrupt the services of the organization. Data is the most valuable asset of organizations, thus, system vulnerabilities can cost organizations a lot. With networks and cloud computing, the risk associated with system vulnerability is extended to remote attacks (CSA, 2016). In industry 4.0, more data is expected to be generated, systems and resources are expected to be shared by more organizations, and thus the impact of system vulnerability may be higher if not mitigated.

Network Security Threats

Account Hijacking

Account or service hijacking involves methods that are used to steal the credentials of users with the aim of gaining access to their accounts or other computing services. Attack methods include phishing, fraud, cross site scripting and exploiting of software vulnerabilities (CSA, 2016; Kazim & Zhu, 2015). Account or service hijacking results in access to critical cloud computing services thereby compromising the confidentiality, integrity, and availability of these services and the data to which the services relate. Account hijacking can also result in damaging the reputations of organizations as well as their clients. A practical example is the hijacking of credentials from the Amazon site in 2010 due to a cross-site scripting (XSS) bug. A more recent example is the compromise in Code Space's account with Amazon AWS in June, 2014 which saw the failure of the system to shield the administrative console with multifactor authentication. This attack is reported to have put the company out of business as virtually all their assets were destroyed (CSA, 2016).

Denial of Service Attacks (DoS)

DoS attacks are forms of attacks that deny legitimate users access to services that they should ideally have access to. These services could include the users' data, applications, storage facilities, cloud network and other services (CSA, 2016; Kazim & Zhu, 2015). Denial of service attacks tend to consume excessive amounts of critical system resources, for example processor power, memory, and bandwidth thereby causing unnecessary slowdown in terms of the system response to the needs of legitimate users (Racuciu & Eftimie, 2015). In Distributed Denial of Service (DDoS) attacks, which are more common in cloud environments, the attacker sends a large number of requests from multiple sources in the network. These requests consume critical resources which should provide services to users. The result is that requests from legitimate users either do not get access to these system resources or are responded to very slowly or inappropriately. Some types of attacks that relate to DDoS include DNS amplification attacks, malformed UDP and TCP packets, and asymmetric application-level attacks among others (CSA, 2016; Racuciu & Eftimie, 2015, p. 106). These attack mostly exploit vulnerabilities in Web-based services (Kazim & Zhu, 2015). The impact of DoS attacks has been compared with being in a rush-hour traffic gridlock with no way forward or backwards (CSA, 2016).

Shared Technology Vulnerabilities

As discussed earlier, cloud services are delivered to customers through the sharing of resources (infrastructure, platforms and applications). These services are sometimes deployed using off-the-shelf hardware and/or software (for instance CPUs and GPUs) which do not meet the security requirements for cloud computing environments. For example, the components that are used to deploy various services may not have been designed with isolation properties which can enable multiple clients to share infrastructure or platforms securely. This situation exposes the cloud providers to newer threats resulting from the vulnerabilities of shared technologies (Kazim & Zhu, 2015; Racuciu & Eftimie, 2015). The impact of shared technology vulnerability can be high because it extends to the entire cloud environment. For instance, any attack on the hypervisor – a computer software that runs virtual machines specifically in the cloud - will expose the entire cloud environment to risk. The CSA 2016 (p.33) mentions the "construction of an access-driven side-channel attack by which a malicious virtual machine (VM) extracts fine-grained information from a victim VM running on the same physical computer" as a typical example.

Malicious Insiders

The malicious insider threat is a threat that emanates from someone who may have vital information relating to an organization. It is a threat that is associated with current or former employees of organizations, contractors or other business partners who may have access to vital resources (network, system, data) of the organization and decide to misuse privileges in a manner that affects the organization negatively (CSA, 2016; Kazim & Zhu, 2015). The impact of a malicious insider can be high. For example, an insider such as a system administrator or cloud administrator could have access to critical systems of organizations. The risks can be higher in clouds since they provide services to several organizations. A hobbyist hacker is another type of malicious insider. The intention of a hobbyist hacker is to have access to sensitive information just for fun (Kazim & Zhu, 2015). By implication, malicious insiders constitute a big threat to Industry 4.0 where virtually all aspects of organizations are expected to be driven by centralized machines. CSA (2016) reports that the insider threat is not always related to malicious activities. The negative action(s) of the insider could just be accidental. For example, uploading a customer's data into a public database (CSA, 2016).

Advanced Persistent Threats (APTs)

An APT is a kind of parasitical threat which usually infiltrates a system in order to establish a sort of base in targeted organizations' computing infrastructure. The attackers then use the foothold or base that they have established to smuggle or steal data and intellectual property from such organizations (CSA, 2016). Advanced persistent threats operate in an environment for an extended period of time in order to study and adapt to various security measures that have been set against them. Attack techniques and common points of entry for APTs include "spear phishing, direct hacking systems, delivering attack code through USB devices, penetration through partner networks and use of unsecured or third party networks" (CSA, 2016, p. 22). They achieve this objective by blending with normal traffic in organisations or cloud networks. CSA (2016) reports that typical examples of APTs are the 'Carbanak' gang which targets banks, and Chinese Cyber-Espionage which has stolen data amounting to hundreds of terabytes from several organisations since 2006.

Cloud Environment Security Threats

Insufficient Identity, Credential and Access Management

Another top security concern in cloud computing emanates from the lack of a scalable identity access management system, lack of multifactor authentication techniques, use of weak passwords, and the lack of ongoing automated rotation of cryptographic keys, among other issues (Hatwar & Chavan, 2015). CSA (2016) reports that these threats can be responsible for numerous forms of attacks such as the data breach that was discussed previously. Embedding of credentials and cryptographic keys in source code or their distribution in repositories such as GitHub, which are accessible by the public constitute a big threat to information in the cloud since such keys can be discovered and misused.

Insufficient identity, credential and access management may provide the opportunity for malicious actors to masquerade as legitimate users to modify and/or delete data, assume control of management functions; snoop on data or inject malicious software that appears to be coming from a genuine source (CSA, 2016). In other words, insufficient identity, credential and access management makes room for unauthorised access to data resulting in a huge damage to organizations and end users. The fourth industrial revolution involves an unprecedented number of users and interconnected and shared resources. Therefore, the impact of insufficient identity, credential and access management may be catastrophic.

A practical example of an attack that results from insufficient identity, credential and access management is the cloud-based Password Cracking Service launched by Paetorian – a Texas-based information security solutions provider. CSA (2016) reports that the service leverages the computing power of Amazon Web Services in order to crack passwords.

Insecure Interfaces and Application Program Interfaces (APIs)

Users interact with cloud services via software known as User Interfaces or Application Program Interfaces (APIs) which are provided by the cloud service providers. Since cloud providers manage their services through these interfaces, it implies that the security and availability of the various services that are provided in the cloud depends on the security of these interfaces (CSA, 2016; Racuciu & Eftimie, 2015). Organizations and third parties also make use of these interfaces by building on them in order to provide services to their own customers. Thus the new APIs that have been introduced result in increased risk since the organizations that are involved may be required to disclose their credentials to the third party in order to ensure smooth interoperability. Weak APIs have been associated with a number of risks which concern confidentiality, integrity, availability and accountability of organizations' data (CSA, 2016; Racuciu & Eftimie, 2015). A typical example is the exposure of about 300,000 records of the US internal revenue service via unsecured APIs in 2015 (CSA, 2016).

Insufficient Due Diligence

Due diligence refers to deliberate attempts or efforts by individuals or organizations to have a complete understanding in terms of what is needed to assess risks that may be associated with the use of certain business services prior to using such services (Kazim & Zhu, 2015). For example, an organization's attempt to understand all aspects of cloud computing and the risks that are associated with its services before adopting any of the services can be described as due diligence (Racuciu & Eftimie, 2015). On the other hand, an organization which rushes into adopting cloud services without a prior in-depth assessment of such services (insufficient due diligence) may be exposing itself to a myriad of risks such as financial, commercial, technical and compliance risks (CSA, 2016). Risks associated with insufficient due diligence are capable of jeopardizing the entire success of an organisation, hence they are considered among the top security risks in cloud computing. A practical example is the challenge that was experienced in 2013 by Nirvanix – a company which provided cloud services to IBM, Dell, and other services. The challenge led to Nirvanix operations being shuttered and clients were given a two week period to relocate their data to other services. This development had the potentials of leading to situations such as data losses, operational disruptions, security breaches and issues of non-compliance especially for clients that had not envisaged such challenges (CSA, 2016).

Abuse and Nefarious Use of Cloud Services

This threat relates to the inappropriate delivery of cloud services to consumers and/or the misuse of cloud services by consumers through illegal or unethical behaviours in the cloud. Activities that can be associated with the abuse and nefarious use of cloud services include deployment of poorly secured cloud services, free cloud service trials, and fraudulent account sign-ups (CSA, 2016), and using cloud network addresses for spam by malicious users (Kazim & Zhu, 2015). These actions provide room for malicious users (attackers) to leverage cloud computing resources to target individual customers, organizations, and even other cloud service providers. Examples of attacks that are associated with misuse of cloud resources include "distributed denial of service attacks (DDoS); email spam and phishing campaigns; 'mining' for digital currency; large-scale automatic click fraud; brute-force compute attacks of stolen credential databases; and hosting of malicious or pirated content" (CSA, 2016, p. 29; Kazim & Zhu, 2015). One major impact of abuse and nefarious use of cloud services is inefficiency on the part of the cloud service provider. In other words, it results in a drastic reduction in available capacity to respond to legitimate customers that the cloud service provider is hosting. A typical example is the attack on Amazon's Elastic cloud computing division in July, 2014, where the attackers created an easily accessible backdoor into the organization's "massive bank of available processing power" (CSA, 2016, p. 30).

SECURITY MEASURES FOR CLOUD COMPUTING

As already highlighted previously, the Internet is the main platform that allows for data communication and application accessibility in a cloud computing environment. Hence, the Internet can be subjected to many types of attacks. It is therefore vital that various security measures are implemented to protect data and applications over the Internet (Jose & Sajeev, 2011; Musa & Sani, 2016; Patidar & Bhardwaj, 2011). The measures are presented in three broad categories as discussed below.

Data Security

Data Encryption

Data encryption using secure socket layer (SSL) and transport layer security (TLS) is one measure that can be used to encrypt data as they flow over the Internet (Dua, 2013). SSL which was developed by Netscape allows for secured communications between a web browser and a web server. It allows a web browser to authenticate a web server. The secured hypertext transfer protocol (HTTPS) allows encrypted information to flow between devices on the Internet. This is done using a RSA algorithm which is a public key for encryption and decryption of data (Dua, 2013). To establish whether devices on the Internet are interacting with trusted devices, SSL and TLS make use of Certificate Authorities that issue certificates to communicating devices. These authorities then verify the authentic identify of devices in the cloud (Dua, 2013).

To keep the data secure during the communication, TLS/SSL uses cryptographic techniques. Confidentiality, integrity, authentication and non-repudiation are amongst the four aims of cryptography. Three (confidentiality, integrity, and authentication) of these four aims are successfully implemented in TLS/SSL protocols in two steps. The first step uses asymmetric cryptography and X509 digital certificates (Dua, 2013). These certificates use the internationally accepted X.509 public key infrastructure (PKI) standard that ensures that the public key belongs to the device identity contained within the certificate. This step allows for entities involved in data exchange to be authenticated. The second step guarantees confidentiality through the use of message authentication code (MAC) and symmetric encryption. Packets transmitted are also verified in this step to assure confidentiality (Dua, 2013).

However, some drawbacks have been associated with encrypting data for storage in the cloud. One such is that it is difficult to disseminate decryption keys to authorised users, thus efficient key management techniques are required (Wan, Liu, & Deng, 2012). Remote key management service helps with this drawback by allowing clients to maintain the key management systems (KMS) solution on-premises. In this scenario, clients own, maintain and support their own KMS, thereby leaving hosting and processing to the cloud providers and ownership and control of KMS to the customer (CSA, 2012). Another drawback to encryption is that, as the number of legitimate users becomes greater, the solution becomes inefficient since it lacks scalability and flexibility. If a valid user needs to be withdrawn, re-encryption of related data needs to occur and all existing valid users must be supplied with new keys again. For this process to successfully occur, all data owners must encrypt or re-encrypt data and new keys supplied to authorised users.

Internet Protocol Security (IPSec) is a transmission protocol that also can be utilised to secure data over a cloud network. It works by ensuring that each and every packet in the communication session is encrypted and authenticated. IPsec's can act as data protectors between host pairs and also between security gateway pairs. They can additionally provide data protection between a host and a security gateway. IPSec also has a replay protection function that avoids hackers making changes to a packet as it travels between source and destination (Alhumrani & Kar, 2016). Hence, IPSec supports data confidentiality, data integrity, data origin authentication and anti-play capability.

Encryption and authentication discussed above can be used to secure data in transit and at rest. Apart from these, stored data can be protected by users' ensuring that data is stored on backup drives and verified that key words in files remain unchanged. Before upload into servers, the hash of the file is calculated to guarantee that the data is not altered (Raoa & Selvamanib, 2015). Data stored in the cloud can also be filtered before storing. Since large amount of data that is stored consists of important and unimportant data and it is difficult to encrypt all the data, data therefore needs to be filtered to determine the important data that needs to be encrypted and then stored (Matloob & Siddiqui, 2017). "Content address storage can be used instead of physical storage like physical drives etc., because the physical device consists of a physical address which can be copied whereas content address storage stores the information with a unique identity which is unique to the stored information and cannot be copied" (Matloob & Siddiqui, 2017, p. 1493). It is also vital that private and sensitive data not be stored in the public cloud but stored by the client in private clouds thus making is more difficult to be accessed by unauthorised individuals.

Robust Access Control

Access control is another measure that can be used to protect data in the cloud. Access control can be defined as an action that denies, restricts or disallows users' entry to a system. It can also record and monitor all attempts that are made to gain entry to a system, as well as identify unauthorized users who are attempting to access a system. It is a very useful protection mechanism in computer security. There are numerous access control models that are in use including Discretionary and Mandatory Access Control, Role Based Access Control (RBAC) and Attribute Based Access Model (ABAC), to name a few. These models are identity based access control models since users (subjects) and resources (objects) are identified using unique names. The identification can be done directly or via roles assigned to the subjects. These types of access control methods work best in distributed systems that do not change and where the users and services are known (Khan, 2012).

An Identification Based Access Control (IBAC) model allows users into the system by verifying their user's identity. However, as the number of networks and users increases IBAC becomes limited in scalability and problematic for distributed systems. To overcome the limitation of this model, the Role Based Access Control (RBAC) model was introduced. This model allowed users to access the system based on their roles. RBAC uses the minimum amount of permissions required to complete their tasks. However, this model has proved to be difficult when trying to determine user roles across administrative domains (Khan, 2012). To address this difficulty, Varsha and Patil (2015) propose trust models that enable roles of individuals to be determined by data owners and users using cryptographic role-based access control (RBAC) schemes. The model guarantees that data is accessible only by those documented in access policies. This development improves the security of data stored in the cloud and removing the weaknesses of other RBAC models.

Attribute based access control is considered to be better. It was developed to address the problems of some RBAC models. In this model the user is granted access based on attributes that can be proved. An example of such attributes is identity number or date of birth (Khan, 2012). Most of the access controls that implement attribute-set-based encryption (ASBE) are inflexible in implementing access controls that have complex policies. To have access controls that have scalability, flexibility and fine-grained access control so as to provide a high level of privacy, a hierarchical attribute set based encryption (HASBE) is suggested. This measure is achieved by "extending ciphertext-policy attribute-set-based encryption (ASBE) with a hierarchical structure of users" Wan et al. (2012, p. 743). This model combines the flexibility and fine-gained access control that is part of ASBE with a hierarchical structure of users, achieving scalability, flexibility and fine-gained access control. It also deals more efficiently with user revocation by having access expiration time assigned in numerous value assignments.

Cloud computing is used to host data and applications from multiple customers, known as tenants. Hence, in order to protect data and applications from being accessible by other tenants, it is important to separate this data and applications into different compartments for each tenant. Therefore this security ability must be supported by the cloud. This is achieved using the Multi-tenancy based control model (MTACM) which implements the security duty separation principle by incorporating a two granule level access control mechanism. One granule is to compartmentalize different customers and the other granule is for client applications so that clients can control access to their own applications only. Li, Shi, Guo, and Ma (2011) revealed that the implementation of MTACM show a good performance and is technically and practically feasible.

Intrusion Detection Systems

In cloud computing it is important to distinguish between authorised and unauthorised users. Intrusion detection systems (IDS) incorporate behaviour based and knowledge based techniques in the detection of unauthorised users (Pathak, 2015). For these techniques to be effective, an Intrusion Detection System Agent component is needed that will gather information about users, and all activities of the users are tracked and forwarded to the IDS system for further analysis (Narwane & Vaikol, 2012).

Behaviour based analysis involves analysing previous behaviour patterns of users in the cloud with the current behaviour. This method automatically or manually builds a profile of users that describes normal activity which will serve as a baseline profile. When a deviation to this baseline profile occurs the system administrator is informed of possible suspicious activity (Narwane & Vaikol, 2012).

Knowledge based techniques make use of information accumulated from previous attacks and system vulnerabilities. When an intrusion occurs that meets the profile of previous attacks, an alarm is activated and the system administrator is informed (Narwane & Vaikol, 2012).

Protection Against Data Loss

The ways in which data, information and applications are stored have changed tremendously since the introduction of cloud computing. This development allows users to access their applications, information and documents, anytime and anywhere using different types of devices (Wu, Ping, Ge, Wang, & Fu, 2010).

Availability and reliability are some of the benefits offered by cloud storage. Cloud providers continually backup data, ensuring reliability of data (Kamara & Lauter, 2010; Kazim & Zhu, 2015). Data is also duplicated across multiple physical machines to ensure that information and data stored within the cloud is protected from accidental deletion and hardware crashes. By so doing, the cloud is operational regardless if one or more machines are offline since the data is duplicated on other machines within the cloud (Kamara & Lauter, 2010). Nate (2016) states that in cloud environments, daily backup and off-site storage of data is critical to protect against data loss.

Isolation of Virtual Machines

Cloud computing is made possible through virtualization. Virtualization is the simulation of a device or resource to one or more client devices. A virtual machine (VM) is an operating system or a software program that portrays the behaviour of a computer and also is able to run applications and programs like a separate computer.

VMs provide cost effective security, since virtualization utilizes one physical machine to the fullest by running multiple VMs on it. This measure allows only for perimeter security mechanisms to be implemented on one physical server rather than multiple servers, thereby reducing the cost of security (Randell, 2006).

Despite this advantage VM poses some security risks such as attack on hypervisor, virtual library checkout, migration attack and encryption attack (Zheng & Jain, 2011).

Isolation of virtual machines is a resilient defence characteristic of virtualization. Basically, each virtual machine can run without knowing any information about other virtual machines. This process makes it complicated for a malicious attacker to access other virtual machines from a compromised virtual machine since only the hypervisor knows about the existence of other virtual machines (Zheng & Jain, 2011).

Cloud service providers aim to uphold a high level of isolation between virtual machine (VM) instances, including isolation between inter user processes. A robust isolation between virtual machines could be able to restrict an attacker from integrating malicious code in a neighbouring virtual machine. Isolation of virtual machines is helpful in alleviating metadata spoofing attacks and backdoor channel attacks (Modi, Patel, Borisaniya, Patel, & Rajarajan, 2013).

Network Security

Preventing Account and Service Hijacking

The stealing or hijacking of a user's account or service is referred to as account or service hijacking. For this to be successfully executed, perpetrators need to obtain personal and confidential information. Exploitation of software vulnerabilities, phishing, spoofed emails, social engineering, and guessing of passwords are some of the techniques that criminal hackers use to obtain this personal and confidential information. When illegal access to network resources is successfully gained, the integrity, availability and confidentiality of services are compromised. To reduce account hijacking, two-factor authentication approaches can be used (Racuciu & Eftimie, 2015). The process uses the user name and password as one factor of authentication and a personal piece of information that only the user knows as the second factor (Racuciu & Eftimie, 2015). To make authentication more reliable for its cloud applications, multi-factor authentication is implemented in Microsoft's Windows Azure Active Directory. Three authentication factors are used. These are one-time password, an automated phone call, and a text message (SMS) (Dasgupta, Roy, & Nag, 2016). To reduce the dependency on passwords, Fast Identity Online (FIDO) alliance developed a framework for online authentication that uses biometric authentication and PIN-codes. This framework supports multi-factor authentication without the use of conventional passwords (Dasgupta et al., 2016).

Other techniques that can be used to prevent account hijacking are encryption management systems, prohibiting the sharing of account credentials between users and services, and employing an identification management system to detect unauthorised activity (Christina, 2015; Racuciu & Eftimie, 2015). In addition, non-technical techniques also need to be used to prevent service hijacking. According to Pereira et al. (2016), the user also needs to play a role to prevent hackers from obtaining the credentials to hijack services. Therefore users need to be aware of social engineering and phishing attacks that hackers use to obtain information.

Protection Against Denial of Service Attacks

Stopping of cloud services by flooding the server with illegitimate requests leading to damage of hardware or data is caused by a denial of service (DoS) attack and a distributed denial of service attack (DDoS). A DoS attack is carried out by a single device whereas a DDoS attack can be carried out by multiple devices. Bakshi and Yogesh (2010) propose a method for securing cloud services from attacks using DDoS and an Intrusion Detection System (IDS). "In this method, a Snort based Network Intrusion Detection System (NIDS) tool is connected on a virtual machine to detect if any untrusted activity is occurring. If such activity happens, the IP address of that activity is determined and all data from that IP address is blocked. If a DDoS attack is established, the service running on the attacked virtual machine is moved to another virtual machine.

Sullivan (2014) mentions that a DDoS attack can also be prevented by measures such as deep data checking and using hardware situated on the network to examine data. Khalil, Khreishah, and Azeem (2014) observed that the most dangerous attacks in cloud computing are accounted for by denial of service attacks (DoS) especially HTTP, XML or Representational State Transfer (REST) based DoS attacks. These attacks, according to Khalil et al. (2014) start off with the attacker initiating requests in XML which are sent through the HTTP protocol. Attackers construct the system interface using REST protocols such as those used in Microsoft Azure and Amazon EC2. In view of the vulnerability of the system-interface, it is difficult for cloud security experts to overcome these forms of denial of service attacks. Denial of service attacks caused by XML or HTTP are the hardest to overcome (compared to traditional attacks) because there are no measures put in place to avoid them from occurring. Implementing security over these protocols is therefore important in cloud computing in order to ensure the secured development of the cloud. As a way forward Karnwal, Sivakumar, and Aghila (2012) propose a five staged framework called "cloud defender" that attempts to countermeasure denial of service attacks. The first four stages of the framework detect HTTP-based DoS attacks whereas the fifth stage detects XML-based DoS attacks. REST-based attacks are not catered for in this framework as they are mainly an attack on the user interface which varies for different users and systems.

The solutions proposed by the framework of Karnwal et al. (2012) are as follows:

1. **Sensor:** Detects the incoming requests and if it identifies an increase in the number of requests from the same user it flags a warning where it marks the user as suspicious.
2. **HOP Counter Filter:** Counts the number of hops (the number of nodes the request went through) and compares this to the pre-defined hop count. The request is marked as suspicious if there is a difference between these values as it may indicate that the header of the message was altered by the attack's system
3. **IP Frequency Divergence:** Marks a request message suspicious if it detects the same frequency of IP messages.
4. **Puzzle Solver:** It helps in identifying a legitimate request by determining the ability of the requester to solve a puzzle.
5. **Double Signature:** Doubles the number of XML signatures such that if there is an attack, both XML signatures need to be validated.

Puzzle Solver involves the solving of complex puzzles where the solution of the puzzle is inserted into the header of a Simple Object Access Protocol such that if the cloud suspects a possible attack, it will send the puzzle to the IP from which it received the messages. If the solved puzzle is sent back to the cloud, then the user is identified as not a threat, otherwise the message is identified as a HTTP DoS attack (Khalil et al., 2014). An example of puzzle solver is Graphical Turing Tests, which distinguish between human users and robots. CAPTCHA (Completely Automated Public Turing Tests to Tell Computers and Humans Apart) is used for a Graphical Turing Test. Furthermore, Yadav and Sujata (2013) recommend a Two-Tier CAPTCHA. The method is described as Two-Tier CAPTCHA in the sense that a cloud attack defence system known as a CLAD node needs to generate two things – first an alphanumeric CAPTCHA code and second a query related to that CAPTCHA code. In this method, a human can provide input according to a query that is not easy for software bots.

Another form of preventive mechanism against DDoS is to guard web services right at the application level (Vissers, Somasundaram, Pieters, Govindarajan, & Hellinckx, 2014). The suggested method is aimed at guarding against Oversized XML, Oversized Encryption, HTTP flooding and so on, through the use of a reverse proxy which serves as a sieve to interrupt all service requirements.

The most severe denial of service attacks on cloud computing are XML based Denial of Service (X-DoS) and HTTP-based Denial of Service (H-DoS). Using countermeasures such as firewalls, updates to patches and intrusion detection systems is inefficient in preventing these attacks (Alotaibi, 2015). On this note, a neural network to find and remove X-DoS and H-DoS attacks was proposed (Chonka, 2011). The system discovers attacks immediately using Cloud TraceBack (CTB) and identifies and removes these attacks using Cloud Protector. Furthermore, Sarhadi (2013) developed a cloud defender system known as Cloud Service Queuing Defender (CSQD) which increases the effectiveness and efficiency in the detection and elimination of XML weaknesses in web services. It is also capable of determining the source of an attack and prevents future attacks by self-learning from previous attacks.

Protecting Against Shared Technology Vulnerabilities

According to Ashktorab and Taghizadeh (2012), various steps can be taken to confront this threat. The first step is to implement security best practices during the installation and configuration of hardware and software components. The environment should also be monitored for unauthorised changes and activities. Strong authentication and access control must be promoted for administrative access and operations. Service level agreements should also be enforced with cloud vendors that will create agreements for patching and vulnerability remediation and to perform regular vulnerability testing and configuration audits (Ashktorab & Taghizadeh, 2012).

The hypervisor plays a crucial role in the cloud architecture since it is responsible for facilitating interactions between virtual machines and the physical hardware. Hence to allow for optimal functioning of all virtualization components, the hypervisor must be secured and isolation between VMs must be implemented (Kazim & Zhu, 2015). It is important to develop and implement a strategy to prevent shared technology threats for all the service models that includes infrastructure, platform, software and user security. When creating the strategy, it is suggested that all cloud components must have baseline requirements established and these requirements must be used in the design of the cloud architecture (Kazim & Zhu, 2015).

Protecting Against Advanced Persistent Threats (APTs)

Security awareness training is important in preventing advanced persistent threats. This will assist in combating social engineering techniques like spear-phishing emails (Musa & Sani, 2016). In addition, organizations can deploy traditional defence mechanisms measures such as patch management, anti-virus software, firewalls, and intrusion detection systems among others (Chandra, Challa, & Hussain, 2014; Hudson, 2014). Advanced malware detection using sandboxing execution can assist with the identification of advanced unknown malware (Hudson, 2014). Anomaly detection methods can be utilized to detect suspicious network traffic and system activities. Confidential data while in use, in motion and at rest can be monitored and blocked by using a Data Loss Prevention system that detects and prevents possible data breach (Chen, Desmet, & Huygens, 2014). Chen et al. (2014, p. 8) further state that "since APT actors typically launch repeated attacks against the target, defenders can create an intelligence feedback loop, which allows them to identify patterns of previous intrusion attempts, understand the adversaries' techniques, and then implement countermeasures to reduce the risk of subsequent intrusions".

Cloud Environment Security

APIs

Clients use application program interfaces (APIs) to access services on the cloud. The API of a cloud is responsible for observing and managing the various services offered by a cloud so it is therefore important to validate the details of the user. As such, unprotected APIs constitute a major security risk to the cloud environment (Gonzalez et al., 2012). One way of mitigating this threat is to restrict access to the cloud environment by ensuring that APIs are provided with robust authentication, encryption, as well as reliable activity monitoring mechanisms (Hatwar & Chavan, 2015; Modi et al., 2013). According to Gunjan, Tiwari, and Sahoo (2013), the most common way of securing APIs is by having passwords to check if the identity of the user attempting to access the cloud application is valid. For this measure to be more successful, it is required that clients and service providers must work in collaboration with one another (Shaikh & Haider, 2011). Thus, the *Confidentiality*, *Integrity*, and *Availability* (CIA) of data in the cloud environment can be guaranteed. In this case, the cloud service provider must offer security features that include tested encryption of schema which ensures that all data on the shared environment is guarded; stringent access controls that will help prevent unauthorized users from gaining access to the data; scheduled data backup and ensuring safe storage of backed-up data (Kaufman, 2009).

Musa and Sani (2016), suggest that security-focused code reviews and penetration testing during application development are also reliable countermeasures to this type of attack.

Preventing Abuse of the Cloud

A number of measures can be adopted to negate or prevent the risk of abuse of cloud computing. The first prevention method relates to cloud service providers obscuring the internal structure of the cloud to complicate any abusive attempts on the cloud. Secondly, the use of blinding techniques will reduce the data or information that can be retrieved by external or unethical sources. This requires that all side-channels should be recorded and be blinded (Ristenpart, Tromer, Shacham, & Savage, 2009). These decisions are believed to be the best ways to prevent the abuse of the cloud (Ristenpart et al., 2009).

Furthermore, various technical and non-technical measures can be implemented to prevent abuse in the cloud environment. The technical measures include measures such as intrusion prevention systems (IPS), network traffic filtering and logging. The non-technical measures on the other hand include measures such as acceptable use policies, account verifications and financial incentivisation (Lindemann, 2015). Service level agreement between user and service provider can incorporate policies to protect critical assets of organizations. From these policies users can be aware of the legal recourse organization can pursue if they violate this agreement (Kazim & Zhu, 2015).

IPS is an extension of intrusion detection systems (IDS). However, similar to IDS, IPS may generate false reports which, if acted upon, may result in incorrect clients being removed from the cloud. This situation can result in disruptions of the clients' operations which may expose the cloud vendor to litigation due to a breach in service level agreement. Acceptable use policies between client and vendor can also assist to deter abuse. Although this measure may not completely protect against abuse, it will make users aware that certain types of use will not be tolerated. The measure is especially important since previously, cloud users were allowed trial use of cloud services without proper verification thereby increasing the possibility of abuse. Account verification by requesting users' phone numbers and sending a verification code to them via SMS can also help to verify the trustworthiness of users. Another useful measure is financial incentivisation which allows clients to make a deposit (Bit coin) and if a client commits any form of abuse in the cloud, the deposit is forfeited (Lindemann, 2015).

Malicious Insiders

According to Kandias, Virvilis, and Gritzalis (2011) two types of insiders pose a threat to the cloud. The first is an insider that works for the cloud service and can cause large amounts of damage to the user as well as service provider. The second is an insider that is part of the organization that decides to outsource the cloud service (Kandias et al., 2011).

Some countermeasures that can be used to address the threat of malicious insiders include; Cloud Service Provider and Client Identity, Access Management, Multi factor authentication, Log analysis and auditing, IDS/IPS and Insider prediction/detection models (Kandias et al., 2011). Another measure is to implement a strict supply chain management which conveys a complete supplier assessment (Hatwar & Chavan, 2015). cloud providers can supply information to clients on how their data and services are secured by providing them information on security and management practices as well as enlightening them on security breaches (Claycomb & Nicoll, 2012). Other security measures that can be taken to protect clouds against insiders that are looking to take advantage of cloud services' flaws include implementing basic security controls such as data loss prevention, separation of duties, limiting access based on job role and consistent auditing just to mention a few (Claycomb & Nicoll, 2012; Rashid, 2016). Attacks on local and external resources by employees can also be prevented by limiting employee's access to external resources or by using host based controls such as firewalls and proxies (Claycomb & Nicoll, 2012).

Overcoming Insufficient Due Diligence

It is critical that the risks associated with cloud implementation be fully understood by organization before shifting their business and critical assets like data to the cloud (Kazim & Zhu, 2015). Furthermore, the type of cloud services that organizations will be using together with their risk tolerance levels must be determined (Mahajan & Giri, 2014). "Data security measures combined with risk transfer in the form of insurance coverage and the acceptance of taking risk from the cloud service providers is the major solution to this problem" (Kumar & Padmapriya, 2014, p. 624).

cloud providers must disclose to customers the infrastructure such as firewall, or methods such as encryption, that will be used to protect data (CSA, 2017). Also, cloud vendors should use industry standards when implementing cloud applications and services. Both quantitative and qualitative risk assessments need to be periodically conducted to examine the storage, flow and processing of data (Kazim & Zhu, 2015). Organizations can also follow the record of self-assessed security practices maintained by the Cloud Security Alliance (Mahajan & Giri, 2014).

DISCUSSION

The fourth industrial revolution represents a paradigm shift from the traditional way of processing and storing data. This shift is masterminded by the principles of cloud computing technology which allows individuals or organisations to share resources (infrastructure and software) over the Internet. This provides room for greater availability of IT resources and decrease costs.

However, while laudable, cloud computing is perceived to entail a high degree of risk owing to new security threats that are being launched on cyberspace regularly. No doubt, the consequences of these threats, if unchecked, can be grievous in view of the multitenancy nature of cloud computing. In this case, it will not be out of place to state that the success of cloud computing is dependent on the implementation of proper security measures as the success of the fourth industrial revolution depends on cloud computing. Therefore, user enlightenment on mitigating the various security threats, which forms the basis of this chapter, remains critical to the success of the fourth industrial revolution.

The chapter has brought to the fore benefits of cloud computing services, security threats and security measures that are currently used to mitigate these threats. As already mentioned, creating awareness of the various measures that can be used to curtail the security threats to cloud computing is considered imperative. This is because the fourth industrial revolution is centred on the principles of cloud computing thus, threats to cloud computing imply threats to the fourth industrial revolution. For example, threats to data such as data breaches, data losses and system vulnerabilities may result in loss of confidence on cloud service providers. This implies that industries would rather be sceptical towards the integration and use of shared resources which industry 4.0 leans on. Similarly, the Internet constitutes a superhighway for the transmission and sharing of resources. This makes its role vital in the fourth industrial revolution, especially in the coordination of inter-organizational operations. Despite the importance of this infrastructure, threats such as account hijacking, denial of service attacks, shared technologies vulnerabilities, malicious insiders and advanced persistent threats appear to be acting against its efficacy. However, with the appropriate security measures put in place as already discussed, the impact of most of the threats on the fourth industrial revolution can be minimised. Furthermore, the cloud environment itself results in some security threats. Most of the cloud environment threats are associated with inappropriate decisions and/or improper use of various cloud services. Some of the cloud environment threats which have been discussed include insufficient identity, credentials and access management; insecure interfaces and application program interfaces; insufficient due diligence; and abuse and nefarious use of cloud services.

The measures that have been discussed cannot be said to be perfect. For example, during encryption, the storing of these certificates on the vendor sever can result in a problem because the data of various clients can be compromised if the certificates are stolen. Although remote key management is suggested as another way of handling this situation, the best security measure will be to prevent any attempt from occurring in the first place. This is achievable using intrusion detection systems. However, as earlier highlighted, one of the main disadvantages of intrusion detection systems is false alarms. For instance if the response to all alarms results in the automatic removal of a client from the cloud and a client is removed as a result of a false alarm, then the cloud vendor may breach the service level agreement. An important consideration in this situation is to determine the nature of an alarm before any action is taken. This must be done within a reasonable timeframe, otherwise delaying may allow time for malicious hackers to gain entry into the cloud.

Furthermore, due to the multitenancy of the cloud, any infiltration of the cloud network will result in many clients being affected. Therefore the isolation of virtual machines is considered key to reducing the impact of malicious hackers since it will hide the identity of other virtual machines in the cloud.

Apart from looking for technical vulnerabilities such as open ports on a network, hackers also try to hijack the accounts and services of users by using various social engineering techniques. Therefore, the awareness of clients about the different ways in which they can be scammed becomes vital. While the two key authentication techniques that have been discussed can be effective against preventing access to the network, including the verification code sent via SMS, the possibility that the codes can be hijacked may not be ruled out. Therefore, it is important that clients be aware of social engineering techniques that are continuously being devised by hackers. In addition, the multifactor method of authentication as implemented in Microsoft's Windows Azure Active Directory combined with biometrics may also go a long way in mitigating the threats of account hijacking.

In another dimension, Puzzle Solvers make use of Graphical Turing Tests such as Two-Tier CAPTCHA to help to distinguish between machines and humans that are trying to access the network. The Solvers rely on human intelligence to distinguish between numeric characters and alpha characters. However, with rapid advancements in artificial intelligence, methods that use human intelligence to distinguish humans from machines are under threat since robots will have the intelligence of humans and will be able to make similar decisions as humans. Fortunately, advances in biometric authentication methods can help to distinguish between humans and machines.

CONCLUSION

This chapter has highlighted the potential threats to cloud computing and the potential measures that can be implemented to counter these threats. From the discussion above, it is clear that there are however inherent weaknesses in some of the current measures. As yet there is no silver bullet to securing the cloud computing infrastructure from malicious hackers and insiders. Therefore, in order for cloud computing to be secure a variety of measures must be implemented. It is therefore vital for businesses, cloud designers and implementers to be aware of the array of measures available and how to use these measures to secure the cloud.

REFERENCES

Access_Partnership. (2017). *Delivering the fourth industrial revolution: The role of government.* Retrieved from Washington, DC: Author.

Alcorta, L. (2017). *Manufacturing the Future: the 4th Industrial Revolution and the 2030 Development Agenda.* Retrieved from http://unctad.org/meetings/es/Presentation/cstd2016_p23_Alcorta_en.pdf

Alhumrani, S. A., & Kar, J. (2016). Cryptographic Protocols for Secure Cloud Computing. *International Journal of Security and Its Applications, 10*(2), 301–310. doi:10.14257/ijsia.2016.10.2.27

Alotaibi, K. H. (2015). Threat in Cloud- Denial of Service (DoS) and Distributed Denial of Service (DDoS) Attack, and Security Measures. *Journal of Emerging Trends in Computing and Information Sciences, 6*(5), 241–244.

Apostu, A., Puican, F., Ularu, G., Suciu, G., & Todoran, G. (2014). New Classes of Applications in the Cloud. Evaluating Advantages and Disadvantages of Cloud Computing for Telemetry Applications. *Database System Journal, 5*(1), 3–14.

Arif, M., & Shakeel, H. (2015). Virtualization Security: Analysis and Open Challenges. *International Journal of Hybrid Information Technology, 8*(2), 237–246. doi:10.14257/ijhit.2015.8.2.22

Ashktorab, V., & Taghizadeh, S. R. (2012). Security Threats and Countermeasures in Cloud Computing. *International Journal of Application or Innovation in Engineering & Management, 1*(2), 234–245.

Backe, A., & Lindén, H. (2015). *Cloud computing security: A systematic review.* Uppsala University.

Bakshi, A., & Yogesh, B. (2010). Securing cloud from DDOS Attacks using Intrusion Detection System in virtual machine. *ICCSN '10 Proceedings of the 2010 Second International Conference on Communication Software and Networks*, 260-264.

Bartholomew, D. (2009). *Cloud rains opportunities for software developers.* Retrieved from http://career-resources.dice.com/articles/content/entry/cloud_rains_opportunities_for_software

Bhadauria, R., & Sanyal, S. (2012). Survey on Security Issues in Cloud Computing and Associated Mitigation Techniques. *International Journal of Computers and Applications, 47*(18), 47–66. doi:10.5120/7292-0578

Bigger, J. (2015). *5 Benefits of Cloud Computing for the Financial Services Industry.* Retrieved from https://blog.marconet.com/blog/5-benefits-of-cloud-computing-for-the-financial-services-industry

Bloem, J., Doorn, M., Duivestein, S., Excoffier, D., Maas, R., & Ommeren, E. (2014). *The Fourth Industrial Revolution: Things to tighten the link between IT and OT*. Retrieved from Online: https://www.fr.sogeti.com/globalassets/global/downloads/reports/vint-research-3-the-fourth-industrial-revolution

Bogatin, D. (2006). *Google CEO's new paradigm: Cloud computing and advertising go hand-in-hand*. Retrieved from http://www.zdnet.com/blog/micro-markets/google-ceos-new-paradigmcloud-computing-and-advertising-go-hand-inhand/369

Campbell, A. (2010). *These issues need to be resolved before Cloud computing becomes ubiquitous*. Retrieved from https://www.openforum.com/articles/these-issues-need-to-be-resolvedbefore-cloud-computing-becomesubiquitous-1

Chandra, J. V., Challa, N., & Hussain, M. A. (2014). Data and Information Storage Security from Advanced Persistent Attack in Cloud Computing. *International Journal of Applied Engineering Research*, *9*(2), 7755–7768.

Chappell, D. (2011). *The Benefits and Risks of Cloud Platforms - A Guide for Business Leaders*. Retrieved from http://www.storm.ie/PublishingImages/Documents/Azure%20for%20Business%20Leaders.pdf

Chen, P., Desmet, L., & Huygens, C. (2014). Lecture Notes in Computer Science: Vol. 8735. *A Study on Advanced Persistent Threats*. Berlin: Springer.

Chonka, A. X. Y., Zhou, W., & Bonti, A. (2011). Cloud security defence to protect cloud computing against HTTP-DoS and XML-DoS attacks. Elsevier.

Chou, T. (2013). Security threats on cloud computing vulnerabilities. *International Journal of Computer Science & Information Technology*, *5*(3), 79–88. doi:10.5121/ijcsit.2013.5306

Christina, A. A. (2015). Proactive Measures on Account Hijacking in Cloud Computing Network. *Asian Journal of Computer Science and Technology*, *4*(2), 31–34.

Claycomb, W. R., & Nicoll, A. (2012). *Insider threats to cloud computing: Directions for new research challenges*. Paper presented at the Computer Software and Applications Conference (COMPSAC), 2012 IEEE 36th Annual. 10.1109/COMPSAC.2012.113

CSA. (2012). *SecaaS Implementation Guidance, Category 8: Encryption*. CSA.

CSA. (2016). *The Treacherous 12: Cloud Computing Top Threats in 2016*. CSA.

CSA. (2017). *Security Guidance - For Critical Areas in Cloud Computing v4.0*. CSA.

Dasgupta, D., Roy, A., & Nag, A. (2016). Toward the design of adaptive selection strategies for multi-factor authentication. *Computers & Security, 63*, 85-116.

Dekker, M., Livery, D., & Lakka, M. (2013). *Cloud security incident reporting*. Academic Press.

Dua, I. V. (2013). Data Security in Cloud Oriented Application Using SSL/TLS Protocol. *International Journal of Application or Innovation in Engineering & Management*, *2*(12), 79–85.

Dunn, J. E. (2009). *Spammers break Hotmail's CAPTCHA yet again*. Retrieved from NetworkWorld website: http://www.networkworld.com/article/2262871/lan-wan/spammers-break-hotmail-s-captcha-yet-again.html

Gonzalez, N., Miers, C., Redigolo, F., Simplicio, M., Carvalho, T., Näslund, M., & Pourzandi, M. (2012). A quantitative analysis of current security concerns and solutions for cloud computing. *Journal of Cloud Computing: Advances. Systems and Applications, 1*(11), 1–18.

Gunjan, K., Tiwari, R. K., & Sahoo, G. (2013). Towards Securing APIs in Cloud Computing. *International Journal of Computer Engineering & Applications, 2*(2), 27-34.

Hatwar, S. V., & Chavan, R. K. (2015). Cloud Computing Security Aspects, Vulnerabilities and Countermeasures. *International Journal of Computers and Applications, 119*(17), 46–53. doi:10.5120/21163-4218

Hudson, B. (2014). *Advanced Persistent Threats: Detection, Protection and Prevention*. Retrieved from http://resources.idgenterprise.com/original/AST-0112935_sophos-advanced-persistent-threats-detection-protectionprevention.pdf

Jose, G. J. A., & Sajeev, C. (2011). Implementation of Data Security in Cloud Computing. *International Journal of P2P Network Trends and Technology*, 18-22.

Kamara, S., & Lauter, K. (2010). *Cryptographic Cloud Storage*. Paper presented at the Financial Cryptography and Data Security, Tenerife, Canary Islands, Spain. 10.1007/978-3-642-14992-4_13

Kandias, M., Virvilis, N., & Gritzalis, D. (2011). *The insider threat in cloud computing*. Paper presented at the International Workshop on Critical Information Infrastructures Security.

Karnwal, T., Sivakumar, T., & Aghila, G. (2012). *A Comber Approach to Protect Cloud Computing against XML DDoS and HTTP DDoS attack*. Paper presented at the 2012 IEEE Students' Conference on Electrical, Electronics and Computer Science, Bhopal, India.

Kaufman, L. M. (2006). Data security in the world of cloud computing. *IEEE Security and Privacy*, 61–64.

Kazim, M., & Zhu, S. Y. (2015). A survey on top security threats in cloud computing. *International Journal of Advanced Computer Science and Applications, 6*(3), 109–113. doi:10.14569/IJACSA.2015.060316

Khalil, I. M., Khreishah, A., & Azeem, M. (2014). Cloud Computing Security: A Survey. *Computers, 3*(4), 1–35. doi:10.3390/computers3010001

Khan, A. R. (2012). Access control in cloud computing environment. *Journal of Engineering and Applied Sciences (Asian Research Publishing Network), 7*(5), 613–615.

Kumar, S. V. K., & Padmapriya, S. (2014). A Survey on Cloud Computing Security Threats and Vulnerabilities. *International Journal of Innovative Research in Electrical, Electronics, Instrumentation and Control Engineering, 2*(1), 622–625.

Li, X.-Y., Shi, Y., Guo, Y., & Ma, W. (2011). *Multi-Tenancy Based Access Control in Cloud*. Paper presented at the Computational Intelligence and Software Engineering (CiSE).

Lindemann, L. (2015). *Towards Abuse Detection and Prevention in IaaS Cloud Computing.* Paper presented at the Availability, Reliability and Security (ARES), 10th International Conference on. 10.1109/ARES.2015.72

Liu, Y., Sun, Y., Ryoo, J., Rizvi, S., & Vasilakos, A. V. (2015). A Survey of Security and Privacy Challenges in Cloud Computing: Solutions and Future Directions. *Journal of Computing Science and Engineering: JCSE, 9*(3), 119–133. doi:10.5626/JCSE.2015.9.3.119

Lua, R., & Yow, K. (2011). Mitigating DDoS attacks with transparent and intelligent fast-flux swarm network. *IEEE Network, 25*(4), 28–33. doi:10.1109/MNET.2011.5958005

Macias, F., & Thomas, G. (2011). *Cloud Computing Advantages in the Public Sector.* Retrieved from http://www.cisco.com/c/dam/en_us/solutions/industries/docs/c11-687784_cloud_omputing_wp.pdf

Mahajan, H., & Giri, N. (2014). Threats to Cloud Computing Security. *International Journal of Application or Innovation in Engineering & Management.*

Matloob, G., & Siddiqui, F. (2017). Data at rest and it's security solutions-A survey. *International Journal of Advanced Research in Computer Science, 8*(5), 1491–1493.

Moavenzadeh, J. (2015). *The 4th Industrial Revolution: Reshaping the Future of Production.* Paper presented at the DHL Global Engineering & Manufacturing Summit, Amsterdam.

Modi, C., Patel, D., Borisaniya, B., Patel, A., & Rajarajan, M. (2013). A Survey on Security Issues and Solutions at Different Layers of Cloud Computing. *The Journal of Supercomputing, 63*(2), 561–592. doi:10.100711227-012-0831-5

Moore, J. (2014). *Business tntelligence takes to Cloud for small businesses.* Retrieved from https://www.cio.com/article/2375744/business-intelligence/business-intelligence-takes-to-cloud-for-small-businesses.html

Musa, F. A., & Sani, S. M. (2016). Security Threats and Countermeasures In Cloud Computing. *International Research Journal of Electronics & Computer Engineering, 2*(4), 22–27.

Narwane, S. V., & Vaikol, S. L. (2012). *Intrusion Detection System in Cloud Computing Environment.* Paper presented at the International Conference on Advances in Communication and Computing Technologies (ICACACT).

Nate, L. (2016). *Data Security Experts Reveal The #1 Information Security Issue Most Companies Face with Cloud Computing & Storage.* Retrieved from https://digitalguardian.com/blog/27-data-security-experts-reveal-1-information-security-issue-most-companies-face-cloud

Oredo, J. O., & Njihia, J. (2014). Challenges of Cloud computing in business: Towards new organizational competencies. *International Journal of Business and Social Science, 5*(3), 150–160.

Pathak, P. K. (2015). Integrated Intrusion Detection System in Cloud Computing Environment. *International Journal of Innovations & Advancement in Computer Science, 4*, 206–210.

Patidar, P., & Bhardwaj, A. (2011). Network Security through SSL in Cloud Computing Environment. *International Journal of Computer Science and Information Technologies, 2*(6), 2800–2803.

Pereira, N., Elvitigala, V., Athukorala, M., Fernando, P., Ehelepola, D., Sameera, K., & Dhammearatchi, D. (2016). Secure User Data in Cloud Computing through Prevention of Service Traffic Hijacking and Using Encryption Algorithms. *International Journal of Scientific and Research Publications, 6*(4), 350–355.

Petrowisch, J. (2017). *The benefits of cloud computing in the manufacturing industry*. Retrieved from http://www.techpageone.co.uk/industries-uk-en/benefits-cloud-computing-manufacturing-industry/

Racuciu, C., & Eftimie, S. (2015). Security threats and risks in Cloud computing. *Mircea cel Batran. Naval Academy Scientific Bulletin, 18*, 105–108.

Randell, R. (2006). *Virtualization Security and Best Practices*. Retrieved from http://www.cpd.iit.edu/netsecure08/ROBERT_RANDELL.pdf

Rao, C., Leelaran, M., & Kumar, Y. R. (2013). Cloud: Computing Services And Deployment Models. *International Journal Of Engineering And Computer Science, 2*(12), 3389–3392.

Raoa, R. V., & Selvamanib, K. (2015). Data Security Challenges and Its Solutions in Cloud Computing. *Procedia Computer Science, 48*, 204–209. doi:10.1016/j.procs.2015.04.171

Rashid, F. Y. (2016). *The dirty dozen: 12 cloud security threats*. Retrieved from http://www.infoworld.com/article/3041078/security/the-dirtydozen-12-cloud-security-threats.html

Ristenpart, T., Tromer, E., Shacham, H., & Savage, S. (2009). Hey, you, get off of my cloud: exploring information leakage in third-party compute clouds. *Proceedings of the 16th ACM conference on Computer and communications security*. 10.1145/1653662.1653687

Saint-Marc, E. (2014). *7 benefits of cloud from an enterprise architect point of view*. Retrieved from IBM Cloud Computing News website: https://www.ibm.com/blogs/cloud-computing/2014/03/seven-benefits-of-cloud-from-an-enterprise-architect-point-of-view/

Schwab, K. (2015). *The Fourth Industrial Revolution: What It Means and How to Respond*. Retrieved from http://www.vassp.org.au/webpages/Documents2016/PDevents/The%20Fourth%20Industrial%20Revolution%20by%20Klaus%20Schwab.pdf

Shaikh, F. B., & Haider, S. (2011). *Security Threats in Cloud Computing*. Paper presented at the 6th International Conference on Internet Technology and Secured Transactions, Abu Dhabi, UAE.

Stair, R. M., & Reynolds, G. W. (2016). *Principles of information systems* (12th ed.). Boston: Cengage Learning.

Sullivan, D. (2014). *Protecting cloud networks against DDoS and DoS attacks* Retrieved from http://searchcloudcomputing.techtarget.com/answer/Protecting-cloud-networks-against-DDoS-and-DoS-attacks

Varsha, M., & Patil, P. (2015). A Survey on Authentication and Access Control for Cloud Computing using RBDAC Mechanism. *International Journal of Innovative Research in Computer and Communication Engineering, 3*(12), 12125–12129.

Wan, Z., Liu, J., & Deng, R. H. (2012). HASBE: A hierarchical attribute-based solution for flexible and scalable access control in cloud computing. *IEEE Transactions on Information Forensics and Security, 7*(2), 743–754. doi:10.1109/TIFS.2011.2172209

Wu, J., Ping, L., Ge, X., Wang, Y., & Fu, J. (2010). *Cloud Storage as the Infrastructure of Cloud Computing*. Paper presented at the 2010 International Conference on Intelligent Computing and Cognitive Informatics. 10.1109/ICICCI.2010.119

Yadav, P., & Sujata. (2013). Security Issues in Cloud Computing Solution of DDOS and Introducing Two-Tier CAPTCHA. [*International Journal on Cloud Computing: Services and Architecture, 3*(3), 25–40.

Zheng, M., & Jain, R. (2011). *Virtualization security in data centers and clouds*. Retrieved from http://www.cse.wustl.edu/~jain/cse571-11/ftp/virtual.pdf

Chapter 2
Role of Security Mechanisms in the Building Blocks of the Cloud Infrastructure

Kowsigan Mohan
Sri Krishna College of Technology, India

P. Balasubramanie Palanisamy
Kongu Engineering College, India

G.R. Kanagachidambaresan
Veltech Rangarajan Dr Sagunthala R&D Institute of Science and Technology, India

Siddharth Rajesh
Sri Krishna College of Technology, India

Sneha Narendran
Sri Krishna College of Technology, India

ABSTRACT

This chapter describes how security plays a vital role in cloud computing, as the name itself specifies the data can be stored from any place and can be owned by anyone. Even though the cloud offers many benefits such as flexibility, scalability and agility, security issues are still backlog the cloud infrastructure. Much research is being done on cloud security equal to the scheduling problems in the cloud environment. The customers under the cloud providers are very concerned about their data, which has been stored in the cloud environment. In this regard, it is essential for a cloud provider to implement some powerful tools for security, to provide a secure cloud infrastructure to the customers. Generally speaking, there are some foundational needs to be attained and some actions to be combined to ensure data security in both cloud, as well as, non-cloud infrastructure. This book chapter concentrates only on the security issues, security measures, security mechanisms, and security tools of the cloud environment.

DOI: 10.4018/978-1-5225-8176-5.ch002

INTRODUCTION

The Internet is definitely one of the greatest inventions in the history of humankind, if not the greatest invention. It is a fact everyone agrees on as it has made our lives simpler and has made the entire world, a global village. The Internet has ensured that we enjoy the privileges offered by it such as fast and efficient communication, access to knowledge at our fingertips and so many offers that are more exciting. Today there are more than a billion devices connected to the World Wide Web (www), i.e., the Internet that shows its growth and the number of computers or so-called nodes is destined to increase in the upcoming years.

Since the advent of the Internet, storage and accessibility of data have been two major factors bothering the users and hence storage of files on the internet, which could be accessible by only the allowed users, was an idea, before it became reality in the 1960's. Robnett Licklider is the inventor of Cloud Computing, which allows users to store files online in storages called Clouds. These files, which were stored in the cloud, could be accessed later on any time thus saving the space on the physical hard disk of the user's computer.

Cloud Computing

Cloud Computing (Armbrust et al., 2010) is the term used to describe the delivery of computing services such as servers, storage, software and more, all over the Internet. Companies which provide such services are called cloud computing vendors. Some of the major vendors are Amazon (EC2), Google (Google Cloud Storage, Drop box), HP (Enterprise Services Cloud-Compute), IBM (SmartCloud), Microsoft (Azure), etc. Many of the scheduling problems in the cloud environment can be solved by using soft computing techniques such as auto associative memory network (Kowsigan, Balasubramanie, 2016). Metaheuristic approaches can also be used to solve scheduling problems in the cloud environment (Kowsigan et al., 2017). Probability distribution was used to schedule the jobs in a cloud environment (Kowsigan et al., 2017).

Cloud computing is being used by almost all the users of the Internet. Even the simplest and most often used tasks such as sending emails, editing documents, listening to songs online, etc., use cloud computing behind the scenes. Here are a few uses of cloud computing:

- Making new services and applications
- Storing and retrieving data
- Analyzing data to make predictions
- Hosting websites and blogs
- To provide software on demand
- Streaming the videos and audio clips

Cloud Security

The worldwide cloud computing market is expected to grow to $191 billion by the year 2020. Although it is universally known and agreed that cloud computing has numerous advantages, there is no denial that there are absolutely no disadvantages. Despite the number of advantages far outnumbering the disadvantages, it is necessary to keep in mind that the disadvantages have to be taken care of. A breach in the data displays the inefficiency of the cloud security and can damage and/or manipulate the data of the user(s) of that cloud service. The most particularly troubling breach is the LastPass breach, which has concerned IT departments throughout the world. In this type of breach, the hacker can access the user's entire website and cloud service passwords. With knowledge of these passwords, especially those belonging to administrators of an enterprise with extensive permissions of an organization's critical infrastructure, a cyber-criminal could launch a devastating attack (Kandukuri, et al., 2009).

There are various cloud-computing security risks faced by IT organizations. A few of them are:

- Loss of intellectual property
- Violation of compliance
- Account hijacking
- Injection of malware
- Data breaches
- Diminished customer trust
- Revenue losses
- Hacked interfaces and APIs

Information Security

Information security is a term that includes a set of practices, which protect information from unauthorized access (Loeb, Gordon, 2002). In short, it means the practices meant to keep the user data safe by preventing unauthorized access to it, which can manipulate or destroy the data.

The sole purpose of information security is to provide us:

- Confidentiality
- Integrity
- Availability

Key Information Security Terminology

- Confidentiality, integrity and availability (CIA)
- Authentication, authorization and auditing (AAA)
- Defense-in-depth
- Velocity of attack
- Information assurance
- Data privacy
- Data ownership

Confidentiality

Confidentiality is one of the most essential goals of information security. It along with integrity and availability is usually known as the security triad. Confidentiality provides the required data secrecy and ensures granting access to only authorized users. If there were no confidentiality of data, any person in an organization would be access the data stored and easily manipulate/destroy it which would be a data breach. Data confidentiality is a term, which usually refers to the user's agreement to store and share data to a group of authorized individuals.

Integrity

While data confidentiality prevents unauthorized users from accessing the data, integrity, as the name suggests, keeps all the data together and ensures that any unauthorized user is not able to modify the contents or delete the data. Integrity also checks when an authorized user accesses the data and makes unauthorized changes to its contents, and prevents it from happening. The main objective of ensuring integrity is to detect and protect against unauthorized alteration or deletion of information. It is also referred to as "data quality".

Availability

Availability ensures that the unauthorized users do not have any kind of access to the compute, storage, network and data resources. Data availability can be described as a term, which refers to the process of ensuring that the information is always available to the authorized users, whenever and wherever they need it. Availability itself refers to the condition that the stored data can be accessed by its authorized users whenever and wherever they need to. If any authorized user is unable to access the data at any point, it directly indicates a flaw in the cloud management system.

Data availability is done usually by implementing data redundancy such that authorized users during both normal and disaster recovery operations can access the data. Storage area networks (SAN), Network attached storage (NAS) and RAID-based (Redundant array of independent disks) storage systems are popular storage management technologies for ensuring data availability.

Authentication

Authentication (Dinesha & Agrawal, 2002) in an ATM money withdrawal process is to ensure the identity of the person making that transaction. It is a mandatory safety regulation. Similarly, authentication in data is a process to ensure that the users are who they claim to be. There has to be authentication/verification for all users to check if they are who they claim to be and not some outsider who is trying to access the data under the name of an authorized person. In fact, there have been such malicious attacks by highly skilled persons who have used the identity and information of authorized persons to access their data by either phishing or using Trojan viruses on their computers and then modify/delete the data. Authentication process asks credentials, which are compared to the ones, stored on a file in the database or within an authentication server and if they match, access is granted.

Single-factor and multi-factor are the two types of authentication. Single-factor authentication involves the usage of only one factor, such as a password. Example: email login process, which requires a password. Multi-factor authentication uses more than one factor to authenticate a user. It is also known as "two step verification" and provides an extra layer of security to the data.

Authorization

Authorization (Ronald L. Krutz, Russell Dean Vines, A Comprehensive guide to secure Cloud Computing) can be defined as the process of determining what type of access privileges is offered to an authorized user for a particular resource. There are different levels of authorization depending upon the data. Authorization is done only after authentication. Only an authenticated user is subjected to authorization. The most common authentication and authorization mechanisms used in data centers and cloud environments are

- Windows Access Control List (ACL)
- UNIX Permissions
- Kerberos
- Challenge-Handshake Authentication Protocol (CHAP)

Auditing

Auditing refers to the logging of all transactions for assessing the effectiveness of security mechanisms. It helps to validate the behavior of the infrastructure components and to perform forensics, debugging and monitoring activities.

Defense-in-Depth

Defense in depth is a strategy in which there are numerous layers of security deployed throughout the entire cloud infrastructure in order to protect the data (Byres, 2012). Even if one layer of security is compromised, there will be various other security layers a hacker will have to pass through before he or she can access the data protected. Defense in depth strategy is also called "layered approach" and mainly relies on the efficiency of multiple firewalls between the protected computer systems and the internet. There are many different layers such as data, application, host, and internal network, and perimeter, physical and procedural layer.

Velocity of Attack

Velocity-of-attack (Chang, Kuo, 2016, pp. 24-41) refers to a situation, where there is already an existing security threat in the cloud infrastructure that can spread rapidly and have a greater impact. A typical cloud environment features homogeneity and standardization in terms of the components such as hypervisors, virtual machine file formats and guest operating systems. Since a cloud environment has numerous components, hence sometimes a minor breach in any random system goes unnoticed. This minor breach then can grow quickly and access data from other systems and then lead to data loss or data corruption. Security threats can be amplified and allowed to spread quickly when there are too many components in an environment.

Mitigating Velocity-of-Attack

Mitigating velocity-of-attack in a cloud infrastructure is a herculean task as there are numerous components in the cloud. The only way to mitigate is by employing strong and robust security enforcement mechanisms, which will scan the entire cloud infrastructure for even minor breaches.

Information Assurance

All cloud consumers need an assurance that all the other consumers operating on that cloud are given permission to access the data which only they have the rights to, and not any random user's data (Chakraborty et al., 2010). In simple words, IA ensures the confidentiality, integrity and availability of the user's data stored in the cloud. Confidentiality restricts access by placing restrictions on classified corporate data. Integrity ensures that those who are authorized to do so can only access the data. Availability ensures that the data stored is ready for usage by the user(s) who are permitted to access it.

Data Privacy

Data privacy is one of the major problems of cloud users (Chen & Zhao, 2012). All cloud consumers fear their personal data being stolen or misused, hence making all cloud vendors give major importance to data privacy. It is also known as Information privacy. Data privacy can be controlled by employing data encryption at all levels and through data shredding. Data security is also required in wireless sensor network, which has been managed by cloud computing nowadays (Kowsigan et al., 2017). The companies can define data privacy as the appropriate usage of data, where the user's data is entrusted to them. Data Security can be defined as the act of ensuring the confidentiality, availability and integrity of data.

Data Ownership

Data ownership can be described as the act of having legal rights and full control over a single piece or set of data (Subashini, Kavita, 2011). He/she has the legal rights over the data and it is the user's right to access and modify the data. While creating data, which is to be stored on a cloud environment, the determination on who owns the data depends upon:

- Terms of service, as defined in the service contract
- Type of information
- Name of the country in which it is created and stored

Security Threats in a Cloud Environment

According to the Cloud Security Alliance (CSA), the top threats in a cloud environment in the world right now are as follows:

- Data leakage
- Data loss
- Account hijacking

- Insecure APIs
- Malicious insiders
- Denial of service
- Abuse of cloud services
- Insufficient due diligence

Data Leakage

Data leakage is a term used to describe unauthorized access of any confidential data by a hacker (Clark, Hunt & Malacaria, 2012). Unauthorized user in case of a breach can access the data, which is stored on the cloud infrastructure and then that confidential data once accessed by a hacker can be very easily manipulated and even destroyed from the cloud infrastructure. Unauthorized access to confidential data of a user can be obtained by any of the following:

- Exploitation of poor application design
- Poor encryption implementation on the cloud infrastructure
- Using a Trojan virus to compromise the password database and get the details
- Through a malicious insider who knows the security protocols well

Although data leakage is definitely a nuisance for both the user and the cloud vendor, there are control measures to avoid data leakage. Although there are many ways to prevent data leakage, the best way is data encryption. The converted form is known as a ciphertext, which is difficult to interpret and therefore increasing security and making it impossible for unauthorized users (attackers) to access the data. Data encryption at both ends makes the data very secure by converting it as a ciphertext rather than the conventional plaintext.

Data Loss

Data loss can happen in the cloud infrastructure due to various reasons also including malicious attacks (Pearson, Benameur, 2010). It is an error condition in information system. Data loss occurs mostly due to system or hardware malfunctions in the storage infrastructure, which produces changes (unintended) to the original data, which destroys the data. Data corruption is also known to be one of the causes of data loss, which occurs during storage and produces unintended changes to the original data. Luckily, there are ways to protect the data from data loss such as data backup and replication. The original data, which is stored on the cloud, can be stored in various storages including physical memory banks as a backup in case there is any data loss. In addition, it is very essential to replicate the data stored on the cloud infrastructure as it can be destroyed during a natural disaster. Here data redundancy using RAID-based (Redundant Array of Independent Disks) mechanisms can be used to replicate the original data. It is a very efficient way to replicate data and store it in various locations, which can be easily retrieved later in case of any data loss.

Account Hijacking

It is possible for accounts on any cloud infrastructure to be hijacked once the attacker has the necessary security credentials to create a breach. In cloud account hijacking, (Khorsed et al., 2012) the account(s) of a single user or an entire organization is stolen by an attacker. The account once hijacked, can be used by the attacker to access its data to perform malicious activity. Account hijacking is one of the major concerns for data security provided by the cloud vendor and can be devastating as it depends on what the hijacker(s) can use the stolen data for. It destroys the reputation and company integrity of the organization and the confidential data stored can be leaked or manipulated which will significantly cost the business and lose them many of their customers. There are also legal implications for organizations. For example, account hijacking in a healthcare organization will lead to the exposure of confidential data of their clients and patients, which would be a disaster for that organization. Phishing is a type of account hijacking attack using the principles of social engineering where the user is deceived. It is done typically be spoofing emails, which appear as genuine addresses but are in fact a link to fake addresses, which ask for login details. Once the details are given, they are captured by the attacker which can be used later to take over the user's account(s).

Insecure APIs

Application Programming Interfaces (APIs) are extensively used in cloud infrastructures in order to perform resource provisioning and orchestration activities. There are two types of APIs. They are:

- Open
- Closed

Open APIs are also known as public APIs. APIs allow the network owner to grant universal access to customers, mostly developers. A closed API is not openly accessible anywhere on the internet and is known as a private API.

Denial of Service (DOS) Attack

A denial of service attack (Kevin J. Houle & George M. Weaver, Trends in Denial of Service Attack Technology) prevents the users from accessing the services of the network infrastructure. DOS attacks can be targeted against computer systems, networks and storage resources. In simple words, DOS attacks are attacks on online services and making them unavailable to the users by flooding it with traffic from multiple sources. It is possible to determine when a DOS attack is underway through the following indications:

- Inability to reach a particular website, even in multiple attempts
- Decrease in the network performance when trying to open websites
- Higher than usual volume of spam email

Distributed Denial of Service (DDOS) Attack

Distributed denial of service (DDOS) is a variant of DOS attack. DDOS attack (Felix Lau & Stuart H. Rubin, "Distributed Denial of Service Attacks") occurs when multiple systems flood the bandwidth and/or resources of a targeted system. An example of DDOS attack is a botnet flooding a web server with traffic from multiple sources. DDOS attacks cannot be avoided or escaped from without employing high capacity, stable and secure internet channels and distributed hardware equipment, which is clearly unaffordable by small businesses making these attacks un-avoidable as they are very expensive. Typical targets of DDOS attacks include financial institutions, e-commerce sites, news and media sites, public sectors and even entire countries.

Malicious Insiders

Cloud vendors are well aware of the number of threats issued by attackers, which are mostly outside the company, however insider attacks also occur, which are known as malicious attacks and are much more difficult to contain, as the insider would know the cloud infrastructure, required passwords, etc. Countermeasures such as firewalls and malware protection systems can minimize the risk of attacks from outsiders but it does not pose any kind of risk for an insider as he or she is familiar with the countermeasures and can easily pass through them and access the data. The various control measures to prevent such insider attacks are:

- Strict access control policies
- Regular security audit
- Disabling employee accounts immediately after contract termination
- Data encryption on both sides
- Role based access control
- Performing background checks on candidate before hiring them (Background investigation)

Abuse of Cloud Services

Cloud computing is indeed a boon to both customers and service providers, due to the several advantages it offers. However, individuals who perform illegal or unauthorized activities (Krutz & Vines, 2010) can misuse the services provided. Certain users who do not intend to use it for good purposes can use cloud services nefariously, which makes it one of the top threats identified by the Cloud Security Alliance (CSA). Cloud resources are often misused by performing unauthorized activities such as cracking an encryption key and by distributing pirated software. Many users mostly use the trial services offered by cloud vendors for their products and then use pirated software instead of buying original licensed software. In most cases, pirated software is not just used but also distributed which severely affects the sales of the original software, as most people in the world prefer to use free pirated software instead of paying for it when it is available free of cost.

Insufficient Due Diligence

Cloud Vendors must pay due diligence towards understanding the complete scope of the undertaking, while offering the customers with the cloud services. For example, in a hybrid cloud environment, where a cloud service provider connects to one or more cloud infrastructure(s) to leverage their capabilities, complete understanding of operational responsibilities is required. These responsibilities include incident response, encryption, governance, compliance, and security monitoring. Insufficient due diligence towards understanding these responsibilities may increase risk levels. Similarly, understanding operational responsibilities is very essential when a service provider may act as a broker by connecting to multiple cloud service providers to integrate their capabilities and offer services to the consumers. This risk can be reduced by thoroughly understanding and evaluating the cloud providers' services and their terms, and ensuring they provide security controls that can satisfy the consumers' security need. Further, it is important to understand the consumers' risk profile to ensure that the risks involved are within acceptable levels.

Case Study on Cloud Security Threats

Attack on Amazon EC2 cloud (Mosca, Wang, Zhang, 2014). Amazon's EC2 cloud was attacked in the year 2009. The Zeus Trojan horse was used to infect the machines and gain access through some other vulnerable domain. The cybercriminals behind the attack also plugged into Amazon's RDS (Relational Database Service) as backend alternative in case they failed to gain access to the original domain. Google, Facebook, Twitter, etc. have also experienced similar threats.

Existing Technologies in Cloud Security

RSA is a computer and network security company, founded in the year 1982. It is known for its security products like SecureID, which has experienced a phenomenal change in the last decade. Its products include threat detection and response, RSA SecureID suite, fraud prevention system, etc. Similarly, many other companies also provide cloud security services.

RSA SecureID

Identity and access management is an important assessment tool in order to permit or restrict an authority from accessing the data. The solution for this problem is provided by RSA SecureID suite. The fact that makes it stand apart is that it separates the concepts of access management and authentication. To access a resource, a user must combine both security PIN and a token code. This gives double assurance in terms of checking the identity of the authority trying to access the data.

RSA Adaptive Authentication

It is an authentication system, which measures the login as well as post-login activities by evaluating risk indicators. It provides transparent authentication by protecting online web portals, mobile applications, browsers, ATM's, SSL's and web-access management applications.

VMware Vcloud Networking and Security

It virtualizes networking and security to a greater agility, efficiency and extensibility in the data centre. It delivers software-defined networks and security with a broad range of services. The services include virtual firewall, virtual private network, load balancer and VXLAN.

Cloud Access Security Broker

A Cloud Access Security Broker (CASB) is cloud-based software, which sits right in-between the cloud service users and the cloud infrastructure, monitors all the activities, and enforces various security policies. A CASB can provide security services or management services as well as both.

IBM Dynamic Cloud Security

IBM Dynamic Cloud security offers protection from threats in the cloud environment through a range of solutions. It spans SaaS, IaaS and PaaS, which is designed to work together with the organisation's existing security system and provide extra protection to the data. It also offers identity and access management, application, data security and security intelligence.

McAfee Cloud Security

McAfee allows organisations to customise their own security protocols. This further enables clarity, transparency and consistency. Constant data monitoring ensures regular checks on the critical data transfers. Deployment of this security mechanism could take place in a public, private or a hybrid cloud.

CipherCloud

Data transfer is made more secure through various approaches like malware detection, encryption, tokenisation, data loss prevention etc. Keys are generated and stored which provides authentication, which is further useful in businesses, which may encounter a series of risks. Thus, sensitive data could be safeguarded from threats.

Importance of Security Mechanisms at Various Levels of the Cloud Infrastructure

The Security Mechanisms are classified as administrative and technical. Administrative security is one, which is enabled by default and comprises of the standard procedures and policies to control the safe execution of operations. It activates the settings that enable a protection to the servers from an unauthorized access. Technical security also highlights the protection and authentication of sensitive data, which is prone to theft and is usually implemented through tools or devices deployed on computer systems, networks or storage. Security mechanisms in cloud infrastructure is deployed at three levels (Saini & Saini, 2014). They are:

- Compute level

- Network level
- Application level

Security mechanism at compute level includes security at a physical level i.e. to a server or a hypervisor. Security is provided to the hypervisor, as it is vulnerable to an attack. Security measures also include VM isolation and hardening which involves the changing of default settings. Antivirus should be implemented as well as updated.

Security mechanism(s) at network level includes a virtual firewall, which establishes a secure link between the VM's. This also ensures a secure traffic between the machines. An internal network could be vulnerable to attacks if exposed to an external network. Thus, a Demilitarized Zone (DMZ) is deployed which sets an additional logical or physical layer of security. Full disk encryption could be a method to provide security to the data-at-rest that resides at a particular location.

At application level, security of hardware and software must never be compromised. An intrusion detection system could be implemented which can be server-based, network-based or even an integrated system, which implements both a server based and network-based detection system.

Key Security Mechanisms

The key security mechanisms can broadly be classified as the following:

- Physical security
- Identity and access management
- Role-based access systems
- Network monitoring and analysis
- Firewall
- Intrusion detection and prevention system
- Port binding and fabric binding
- Virtual private network
- Virtual LAN and Virtual SAN
- Zoning and iSNS discovery domain
- Security hypervisor and management server
- Virtual machine hardening
- Securing operating systems and applications
- LUN masking
- Data encryption
- Data shredding

Authorization

Different types of job functions or entities access different type of data. However, each application service is logically separated from each other. Thus, should provide an efficient mechanism for accessing and control. Different entities are authenticated which further restricts accessibility and sharing of files and folders by other anonymous users. Types of authorization include Windows ACLs, UNIX permissions and OATH.

Windows ACLs

Access Control Lists (Yu et al., 2010) comprise of the set of rules that specify the access permissions given to users. A list involving the access control entries (ACEs) further identifies the trustees and highlights the rights given to them respectively. It can contain two types of ACLs: a DACL and a SACL.

If an object has a discretionary access control lists, access permissions are allowed explicitly by the access control entries in the DACLs. If the system does not have DACLs, the access permission is granted to everyone i.e. full access is given. If there are no ACEs in the DACLs, no permission is given to access to anyone. SACLs are used for implementing wider security policies for actions such as logging or auditing resource access. It creates an audit record when there is the access attempt either is successful or fails.

UNIX Permissions

These common permissions (Allison et al., 1998) depict whether a group, an owner and everyone else have the permission to read, write or execute a file. The access rights given to the users allow them to view, modify and also execute the contents of the file system.

OAuth

It (Hammer-Lahav, 2010) is an open authorization mechanism that allows a client to access protected resources from a resource server rather than accessing it from the resource owner. The entities that are involved in authorization are the resource owner, the resource server, the client and the authorization server. The resource owners can authorize a third-party access to the information without exchanging any other credentials.

Figure 1. OAuth pictorial description

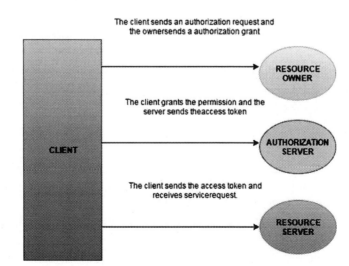

Authentication

It is a mechanism, which determines the user's credentials are compared to those given in a database. The process is carried out, if the credentials match otherwise the process is halted. It enables authentication among the clients and the servers. The types of authentication used are multi-factor authentication, CHAP, Kerberos, etc. Authentication is essential in order to safeguard data and to monitor its usage.

Multi-Factor Authentication

It is the process of granting access to a user by extracting several pieces of evidence depicting their identity. It can be something they know, something they own or something they are broadly classified as knowledge, possession and inherence (Quian, Lu, 2012).

Kerberos

It was created by MIT. It provides a solution to network security issues. A strong authentication is provided by using a secret-key cryptology. It is generally used for a client-server application. Encryption of communication is done in order to ensure private and secure data transmissions. A client and a server prove their identity using Kerberos. It can also be useful between server-server transmissions. Kerberos is very flexible, efficient and secure (Neumann, 1994).

Challenge Handshake Authentication Protocol

CHAP is a method, which is used to authenticate a user or a network to an authenticating entity by utilizing a private code. It is used periodically to verify the identity by a 3-way handshake.

A link is established between the initiator and the target. The initiator sends a "challenge message "or asks to initiate the login. The target sends a CHAP challenge (Simpson, 1994). The initiator reciprocates with a value calculated using "one-way hash" function and returns to the target. The target checks and compares with a calculated value of its own. If the hash values match, the authentication is acknowledged else the connection is terminated. At random intervals, the target sends a new challenge and this cycle is repeated.

The CHAP algorithm requires the password to be the length of at least one octet and also it should be a strong one, which cannot be easily guessed by anyone. A central server can be established in order to examine the responses and values.

OpenID

It is promoted by a non-profit foundation named OpenID Foundation. It is a mechanism in which one existing account can be used to sign in multiple websites. It does not require creation of new passwords for different websites. It is an open and standardized authentication protocol. The user has to create an account by selecting an OpenID identity provider. It is also a decentralized protocol i.e. it does not rely on any central authority to authenticate user's ID.

Role Based Access Control

This mechanism is useful in multiuser computing function. It is an approach where permission is given based on the individual's roles or job function (Sandhu, 1994). In an organization, roles are created based on qualification, responsibility and other criteria. Additionally, these roles can also be reassigned. Permissions and restrictions both are assigned to the specific roles as the system is upgraded or new system or applications are incorporated. Separation of duties is used to ensure that no single individual is able to specify an action as well as carry it out at the same time. Only certain roles are assigned certain privileges of performing the task associated with that role. Roles are considered a more stable concept in an organization than a task or a function.

Network Monitoring and Analysis

Network monitoring and analysis is a mechanism in which provides a detection of network failure or performance problems and further protect from such problems (Anderson et al., 2006). It is done in order to extract information about the type of data packets being transmitted, the uploading and downloading speeds, the data utilization etc. Any activity or transmission of malicious data packets can be identified and stopped from harming the system. This can be performed in two ways. They are:

- Active monitoring
- Passive monitoring

Active monitoring includes tools that can transmit data between two monitored ends. Passive monitoring depicts the information about a link or a device collected by probing the link or device. Active monitoring injects "test" traffic into the network whereas passive monitoring system is more of an observational test to analyze the already established network. Mechanisms used to monitor, detect and prevent the attacks are Firewalls, IDPS and network analysis systems.

Firewall

It is a security mechanism which is used to examine the data packets traversing a network and compare them with a set of filtering rules. It can either be hardware, software, or both. It is an essential part of the intranet security and is deployed at network level, compute level or a hypervisor level. It can also be used for the internal portion of organization's internal network, which implies protection from internal attacks. Its main function is to analyze the incoming packets and permit/restrict them, according to the configuration.

Intrusion Detection and Prevention System (IDPS)

IDPS is a process, which analyses the events of intrusion and prevents them. It is in fact, a security tool, which is used to automate the entire process of detecting and preventing events that can compromise the confidentiality, integrity, or availability of resources. There are two detection techniques. They are signature-based detection technique and anomaly-based detection technique. The signature-based detection technique scans for signatures to detect an intrusion event but is only effective for known threats. Anomaly-based detection technique scans and analyses events to detect if there are any abnormal events taking place. It can detect various events such as multiple login failures, excessive network bandwidth consumed by an activity. An anomaly based detection technique is able to detect most of the new attacks as these new attacks deviate from the already existing protocols. IDPS is implemented at three levels i.e. compute system level, network level and hypervisor level. The components of an IDPS include a sensor or an agent, a management server, a database server and a console. IDPS at network levels is used to monitor and analyze the network traffic, network devices and application protocol behavior. It is deployed in the form of appliance or software on the computer system and is usually isolated from malicious applications on computer systems. IDPS at hypervisor levels is used to monitor anomalies in a hypervisor.

Port Binding and Fabric Binding

Port binding limits the devices that can be attached to a specific switch port. It is rather the configuration, which determines the timing, and the destination of the message sent or received. It is supported in two environments. Firstly, FC SAN which maps a WWPN to a switch port. The WWPN login is rejected when illegitimate host is connected. Secondly, the Ethernet maps MAC and IP address of a computer system to a switch port. Fabric binding allows binding at the switch level. Additionally, it can used along with port and port-type locking capabilities.

Virtual Private Network (VPN)

It is the process, which provides an encrypted tunneling of the traffic. It can used to privatize and encrypt the flow until destination is reached. It extends a consumer's private network across a public network such as the Internet and enables the consumer to apply their internal network's security to the data transferred over the VPN connection (Ledesma, 2004).

There exist two methods to establish a VPN connection. They are:

- Remote access VPN connection
- Site-to-site VPN connection

In a remote access VPN connection, the remote client works by initiating a remote VPN connection request, which is gradually authenticated by the VPN server that grants access to the cloud network. In a site-to-site VPN connection, the remote site works by creating a site-to-site VPN connection and then access to the cloud network is granted by the server. There are two types of site-to -site VPN connection. They are:

- Intranet based
- Extranet based

Virtual LAN and SAN

A Virtual LAN (Yuasa, 2000) is software used to provide multiple networks in a single hub. VLAN has many advantages over LANs such as performance, simplicity, cost and security. They are widely used as they promise scalability and better security policies. Virtual SAN is provided by VMware, which gives the freedom of pooling our storage capabilities. VSAN is used as it reduces the cost and facilitates an easier storage and better management.

Zoning and iSNS Discovery Domain

The logical segmentation of node ports into groups is referred to as Zoning. Port zoning is used to reduce the risk of WWPN spoofing as it also provides higher security levels. In port zoning, we only work with switch domain or port number implying an efficient and easier use of it.

Internet Storage Name Service (iSNS) is a protocol that is used for automated configuration, management and discovery of iSCSI on any network. It functions identically to FC zones and enables a grouping of devices in an IP-SAN. Few benefits of iSNS include centralized management, scalability and flexibility.

Securing Hypervisor and Management Server

The security of the cloud depends upon the security of the hypervisors, which support their VMs. Compromising the hypervisor security places all VMs at risk. An attacker can access the information by attacking the hypervisor, as it is the backbone of any cloud infrastructure.

The control measures are given below as follows:

- Install security-critical hypervisor updates
- Harden hypervisor using specifications provided by CSI and DISA
- Restrict core functionality to only few selected administrators

Virtual Machine Hardening

It is a process used to change the default configuration of a VM. It removes or disables the devices that are not required. For example, disabling of the USB ports or CD/DVD drives. It is used to tune the configuration of VM features to operate in a secure manner such as disallowing changes to MAC address. In order to know the security baselines, VM templates should be hardened.

Securing Operating Systems and Applications

- Hardening OS and application
- Sandboxing

Hardening OS and Applications

Though anti-viruses and other protections cater to the needs of the system's security, they do not fulfill the complete needs of the operating system, in terms of protection. The main aim of system hardening is to provide better security and to prevent attacks. This is mainly done by the removal of unimportant or non-essential software, which may act as a gateway for the attackers to exploit the system. It may include reformatting the disks, configuring the components as per a hardening checklist provided by CIS and DISA. Benefits of hardening of OS include cost reduction as removal of non-essential software or hardware results to saving of money.

Sandboxing

Sandboxing is a mechanism, which tests non-trusted codes. It provides a tightly controlled set of resources on which the application executes. By implementing this, we can reduce or eliminate various risks, as it concentrates on damage containment. Most of the codes we run are sandboxed, for example, the web pages, the browser plug-in content, the mobile apps, etc.

LUN Masking

Logical Unit Numbering masking (H. Yoshida," LUN Masking", 1999) is a process, which deals with the assignment of numbers to ports. Thus, access is authorized to certain ports and unauthorized to the other. It refers to the assignments of LUNs to specific host bus adapter worldwide. However, more commonly at Host Bus Adapters (HBA) ports and are vulnerable to attacks. It improves management levels. Stronger variant of LUN masking uses source Fiber Channel address. In FC SAN, access controls done through zoning. These are used to identify the ports. In a cloud infrastructure, LUN masking can set policies at physical storage array and prevent data loss or intrusion.

Data Encryption

It is very important to protect our confidential data from hackers as there lays a threat of manipulation as misuse of it. Therefore, data is encrypted. Encryption (D. Coppersmith, "Data Encryption", 1994) simply means conversion of data. It is a cryptographic method by which data is encoded and made indecipherable to eavesdroppers or hackers. It is done for confidentiality and security reasons.

Data Shredding

It is impossible to also recover data from deleted files and folders. In order to prevent this, data shredding is implemented. Even emptying the system's recycle bin does not solve the issue of data theft. Data shredding is the process of deleting files and making them unrecoverable. Techniques for shredding data stored on tapes include overwriting tapes with invalid data. This primarily highlights the conversion of bit patterns i.e. 0's and 1's. This would make the recovery of the data stored previously in the disk hard.

Upcoming Security Mechanism Trends in Cloud Computing

Physical security deals with the implementation of measures to secure sensitive data. Deployment of these physical controls is useful in order to safeguard data from theft and provide an easy surveillance. It is rather the foundation of IT security strategy. The upcoming technological trends in cloud computing promise better security. They are:

- **Securing Server-less Processes:** It involves the implementation of micro-services and virtual machines.
- **Security Through AI and Automation:** Artificial Intelligence and automation could be used to leverage the security by implementing predictive security postures across public, private and SaaS cloud infrastructure.
- **Micro-Segmentation:** It involves the usage of an identity management strategy to locate the end-point before it has any network visibility.

Security as a Service

Along with data comes the responsibility to secure it, efficiently and widely. This should also include the cost effectiveness and making it less vulnerable to attacks. According to the "Cloud Security Alliance", Security as a Service refers to the provision of security services via the cloud either to the cloud-based infrastructure and the software or from the cloud to the customer's on-premise systems. It enables the consumer to reduce the capital expenditure on security deployments and they also have a control on the security policies that are to be implemented.

Introduction to GRC

Data integrity can be maintained only by the trust between a Cloud Service provider (CSP) and a Cloud Service user (CSU). There need to be an appropriate check and maintenance of the information provided. GRC is the term which helps the organization ensure that its acts are ethically correct.

Governance

Cloud Governance highlights the implementations of policies by which an institution can be directed. Governance ensures the policies are agreed-upon and that the data is maintained properly and managed well. IT governance not only maintains a good database but also develops the understanding between the strategies set in by the providers and the infrastructure provided. The basic IT governance principle is to focus on policies related to managing and consuming cloud service.

Risk Management

Any business objective is accompanied by risks or an uncertainty. It is not possible to eliminate risks, but they can be managed. A systematic process needs to be followed to evaluate the consequences of each step, which is followed. This process is known as risk management. It includes the mechanism to assess the assets or data, evaluating its worth and creating a risk profile that is rationalized for each information asset across the business. The outages restrict the user to access the data for a certain amount of time but can cost the user heavily. Therefore, a framework needs to be designed to evaluate the cloud computing risks. The four key steps of risk management include risk identification, risk assessment, monitoring and risk mitigation. Risk identification is used to identify the source of the threat. Once the risk is identified, it is essential to assess and analyze the risk. Further, there are measures to be taken to minimize its impact. Thus, mitigating the risk is an important step that involves planning and deploying security mechanisms. After the securing of the system, it is necessary that we monitor the risk and its affects.

Compliance

The act of adhering to the laws, regulations and procedures is known as compliance. It demonstrates the act of embracement of the policies and demands of the service provider, the consumer 's demand and/or the demands of participating cloud providers. These policies may vary from one type of cloud to another i.e. public, private and hybrid. The primary purpose of compliance is to analyze the provider's policies so that it understands the controlling of it. There are two types' compliance policies that control IT operations i.e. internal policy compliance and external policy compliance. The internal policy compliance controls the nature of IT operations within an organization, whereas the external policy compliance controls the nature of the IT operations outside the organization. The compliance levels may differ based upon the type of information, business and so on.

CONCLUSION

The essence and the need for Cloud Security is discussed in this book chapter. The inclination of enterprises to the cloud for data storage is growing exponentially. This comes only with the trust that the data stored would be secure. Though there are many advantages of cloud computing, a breach in the data displays the inefficiency of the cloud security. Security threats like data leakage, data loss, account hijacking, abuse of cloud service exist which can be tackled only by implementing the above said and proven mechanisms. These mechanisms include identity and access management, role based access systems, firewalls, zoning, encryption, IDPS etc. Deployment of these security mechanisms ensure that the data will be stored in a secure manner in the cloud. The vulnerability to data theft can be reduced.

Figure 2. Four corner stones of risk management

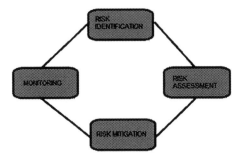

The concept of GRC and its importance in Cloud Security has also been explained briefly in this book chapter. Concisely, the maintenance and security of data is the responsibility of the user who needs to choose the appropriate mechanism to safeguard it.

REFERENCES

Allison, B., Hawley, R., Borr, A., Muhlestein, M., & Hitz, D. (1998). File System Security: Secure Network Data Sharing for NT and UNIX. *Network Appliance, 16.*

Anderson, B. D. O., & Vongpanitlerd, S. (1973). *Network Analysis and synthesis.* Prentice-Hall.

Armbrust, M., Fox, A., Griffith, R., Joseph, A. D., Katz, R., Konwinski, A., ... Zaharia, M. (2010). A view of cloud computing. *Communications of the ACM, 53*(4), 50–58.

Byres, E. J. (2012). *Defense in Depth. InTech Magazine.* Nov-Dec.

Chakraborty, R., & Reddy, S. (2010, March). The Information Assurance Practices of Cloud Computing Vendors. *IT Professional, 12*(4), 29–37. doi:10.1109/MITP.2010.44

Chang, V., Kuo, Y. H., & Ramachandran, M. (2016). Cloud computing adoption framework: A security framework for business clouds. *Future Generation Computer Systems, 57*, 24–41.

Chen, D., & Zhao, H. (2012). Data Security and Privacy Protection issues in Cloud Computing. In *International Conference on Computer Science and Electronics Engineering.* 10.1109/ICCSEE.2012.193

Clark, D., Hunt, S., & Malacaria, P. (2002). Quantitative Analysis of the leakage of Confidential Data. Elsevier Electronic Notes in Theoretical Computer Science, 59(3), 238-251.

Coppersmith, D. (1994). The Data Encryption Standard (DES) and its strength against attacks. IBM journal of research and development, 38(3), 243-250. doi:10.1147/rd.383.0243

Dinesha, H. A., & Agrawal, V. K. (2012, February). Multi-level authentication technique for accessing cloud services. In *2012 International Conference on Computing, Communication and Applications (ICCCA).* IEEE. doi:10.1109/ICCCA.2012.6179130

Gordon, L. A., & Loeb, M. P. (2002). The economics of information security investment. *ACM Transactions on Information and System Security, 5*(4), 438–457.

Hammer-Lahav, E. (2010). *The OAuth 1.0 Protocol.* Internet Engineering Task Force.

Houle, K. J., & Weaver, G. M. (2001). *Trends in Denial of Service Attack Technology (v1.0).* Carnegie Mellon University.

Kandukuri, B. R., & Rakshit, A. (2009, September). Cloud security issues. In *IEEE International Conference on Services Computing SCC '09* (pp. 517-520). IEEE. doi:10.1109/SCC.2009.84

Khorshed, M. T., Ali, A. S., & Wasimi, S. A. (2012). A survey on gaps, threat remediation challenges and some thoughts for proactive attack detection in cloud computing. *Future Generation Computer Systems, 28*(6), 833–851.

Kowsigan, M., & Balasubramanie, P. (2016). An Improved Job Scheduling in Cloud Environment using Auto-Associative-Memory Network. *Asian Journal of Research in Social Sciences and Humanities*, *6*(12), 390–410.

Kowsigan, M., Kalicharan, S., Karthik, P., Manikandan, A., & Manikandan, R. M. (2017). An Enhanced Job Scheduling in Cloud Environment Using Probability Distribution. *IACSIT International Journal of Engineering and Technology*, *9*(2), 1374–1381.

Kowsigan, M., Rajkumar, S., Seenivasan, P., & Kumar, C. V. (2017). An Enhanced Job Scheduling in Cloud Environment using Improved Metaheuristic Approach. *International Journal of Engineering Research and Technology*, *6*(2), 184–188.

Kowsigan, M., Rubasri, M., Sujithra, R., & Banu, H. S. (2017). Data Security and Data Dissemination of Distributed Data in Wireless Sensor Networks. *International Journal of Engineering Research and Applications*, *7*(3 part 4), 26–31.

Krutz, R. L., & Vines, R. D. (2010). *Cloud security: A comprehensive guide to secure cloud computing*. Wiley Publishing.

Krutz, R. L., & Vines, R. D. (2010). Cloud security: A comprehensive guide to secure cloud computing. Wiley Publishing.

Lau, F., Rubin, S. H., Smith, M. H., & Trajkovic, L. (2000). Distributed denial of service attacks. In *2000 IEEE International Conference on Systems, Man, and Cybernetics* (Vol. 3, pp. 2275-2280). IEEE. doi:10.1109/ICSMC.2000.886455

Ledesma, S., Aviña, G., & Sanchez, R. (2008). Practical considerations for simulated annealing implementation. In *Simulated Annealing*. InTech.

Lu, H. K. (2014). U.S. Patent Application No. 13/729,070.

Mosca, P., Zhang, Y., Xiao, Z., & Wang, Y. (2014). Cloud Security: Services, Risks, and a Case Study on Amazon Cloud Services. *International Journal of Communications. Network and System Sciences*, *7*(12), 529.

Neuman, B. C., & Ts'o, T. (1994, September). Kerberos: An authentication service for computer networks. *IEEE Communications Magazine*, *32*(9), 33–38. doi:10.1109/35.312841

Pearson, S., & Benameur, A. (2010). Privacy, Security and Trust Issues Arising from Cloud Computing. In *IEEE Second International Conference on Computer Science and Technology*. 10.1109/CloudCom.2010.66

Rajeshkumar, J., & Kowsigan, M. (2011). Efficient Scheduling in Computational Grid with an Improved Ant Colony Algorithm. International Journal of Computer Science and Technology, 2(4), 317-321.

Saini, H., & Saini, A. (2014). Security Mechanisms at different Levels in Cloud Infrastructure. International Journal of Computer Applications, 108(2).

Sandhu, R. S., Coyne, E. J., Feinstein, H. L., & Youman, C. E. (1996). Role-based access control models. *Computer*, *29*(2), 38–47.

Simpson, W. A. (1996). *PPP challenge handshake authentication protocol*. CHAP.

Subashini, S., & Kavita, V. (2011). *A survey on security issues in service delivery models of cloud computing. Elsevier Journal of Network and Computer Applications*.

Yoshida, H. (1999). *LUN security considerations for storage area networks (Paper-XP, 2185193)*. Hitachi Data Systems.

Yu, S., Wang, C., Ren, K., & Lou, W. (2010, March). *Achieving secure, scalable, and fine-grained data access control in cloud computing. In 2010 proceedings IEEE Infocom*. IEEE.

Yuasa, H., Satake, T., Cardona, M. J., Fujii, H., Yasuda, A., Yamashita, K., . . . Suzuki, J. (2000). U.S. Patent No. 6,085,238. Washington, DC: U.S. Patent and Trademark Office.

KEY TERMS AND DEFINITIONS

Authentication: The process of validating someone's identity.

Authorization: An act of granting permission to somebody.

Cloud Security: The set of rules, regulations and policies that are created to adhere to compliance rules to protect enterprises assets like data, information associated with cloud.

Data Encryption: The translation of the data into another form so that a third party cannot understand or extract it.

Data Loss: The information stored is destroyed, due to various reasons in an error condition.

Data Privacy: An aspect which considers the fact whether the data could be shared a third party or not.

Integrity: The maintenance and the assurance of the accuracy and the consistency of data.

This research was previously published in Applications of Security, Mobile, Analytic, and Cloud (SMAC) Technologies for Effective Information Processing and Management edited by P. Karthikeyan and M. Thangavel, pages 1-23, copyright year 2018 by Engineering Science Reference (an imprint of IGI Global).

Chapter 3
A Review of Intrusion Detection Systems in Cloud Computing

Chiba Zouhair
Hassan II University of Casablanca, Morocco

Noreddine Abghour
Hassan II University of Casablanca, Morocco

Khalid Moussaid
Hassan II University of Casablanca, Morocco

Amina El Omri
Hassan II University of Casablanca, Morocco

Mohamed Rida
Hassan II University of Casablanca, Morocco

ABSTRACT

Security is a major challenge faced by cloud computing (CC) due to its open and distributed architecture. Hence, it is vulnerable and prone to intrusions that affect confidentiality, availability, and integrity of cloud resources and offered services. Intrusion detection system (IDS) has become the most commonly used component of computer system security and compliance practices that defends cloud environment from various kinds of threats and attacks. This chapter presents the cloud architecture, an overview of different intrusions in the cloud, the challenges and essential characteristics of cloud-based IDS (CIDS), and detection techniques used by CIDS and their types. Then, the authors analyze 24 pertinent CIDS with respect to their various types, positioning, detection time, and data source. The analysis also gives the strength of each system and limitations in order to evaluate whether they carry out the security requirements of CC environment or not.

DOI: 10.4018/978-1-5225-8176-5.ch003

INTRODUCTION

Cloud computing (CC) is rapidly growing computational model in today's IT world. It delivers convenient, on-demand network access to a shared pool of configurable computing resources (e.g. Networks, servers, storage, applications, etc.), "as service" on the Internet for satisfying computing demand of users (National Institute of Standards and Technology [NIST], 2011). It has three basic abstraction layers i.e. system layer (which is a virtual machine abstraction of a server), the platform layer (a virtualized operating system of a server) and application layer (that includes web applications). The characteristics of CC include:

- **Virtual:** Physical location and underlying infrastructure details are transparent to users.
- **Scalable:** Able to break complex workloads into pieces to be served across an incrementally expandable infrastructure.
- **Efficient:** Services Oriented Architecture for dynamic provisioning of shared compute resources. (Bakshi & Dujodwala, 2010).
- **Flexible:** Can serve a variety of workload types (consumer and commercial).

Cloud computing has also three service models namely Platform as a Service (PaaS), Infrastructure as a Service (IaaS) and Software as a Service (SaaS) models. IaaS model delivers services to users by maintaining large infrastructures like hosting servers, managing networks and other resources for clients. In PaaS, it offers development and deployment tools, languages and APIs used to build, deploy and run applications in the cloud, and in SaaS, systems offer complete online applications that can be directly executed by their users, making them worry free of installing and running software services on its own machines.

Threat Model for Cloud

Due to lack of control over the Cloud software, platform and/or infrastructure, several researchers stated that security is a major challenge in the Cloud (Aljawarneh, 2011). A recent survey performed by Cloud Security Alliance (CSA) and IEEE, indicates that enterprises across sectors are eager to adopt cloud computing but that security are needed both to accelerate cloud adoption on a wide scale and to respond to regulatory drivers (Jouini & Ben Arfa Rabai, 2014). One of major security issues in Cloud is to detect and prevent network intrusions since the network is the backbone of Cloud, and hence vulnerabilities in network directly affect the security of Cloud. Martin from Cyber Security division stated that main concern after data security is an intrusion detection and prevention in the Cloud (Martin, 2010).

There are principally two types of threats; insider (attackers within a Cloud network) and outsider (attackers outside the Cloud network) considered in Cloud Network (Chiba, Abghour, Moussaid, El omri, & Rida, 2016).

- **Insider Attackers:** Authorized Cloud users may attempt to gain (and misuse) unauthorized privileges. Insiders may commit frauds and disclose information to other (or modify information intentionally). This poses a serious trust issue. For example, an internal DoS attack demonstrated against the Amazon Elastic Computer Cloud (EC2) (Macro, 2009).

- **Outsider Attackers:** Can be called as the network attackers who are able to perform different attacks as IP spoofing, Address Resolution Protocol (ARP spoofing), DNS poisoning, man-in-the-middle, Denial of Service (Dos)/Distributed Denial of service (DDoS) attacks, phishing attack, user to root attack, Port scanning, attack on virtual machine (VM) or hypervisor such BLUEPILL and DKSM through which hackers can be able to compromise installed-hypervisor to gain control over the host, Backdoor channel attacks etc.

These attacks affect the integrity, confidentiality, and availability of Cloud resources and offered services. To address above issues, major Cloud providers (like Amazon ECC, Window Azure, Rack Space, Eucalyptus, Open Nebula etc.) use the firewall. Firewall protects the front access points of system and is treated as the first line of defense. As firewall sniffs the network packets only at the boundary of a network, insider attacks cannot be detected by it (Modi, Patel, Borisaniya, Patel, Patel, & Rajarajan, 2012a). Few DoS or DDoS attacks are too complex to detect using traditional firewall. For example, if there is an attack on port 80 (web service), firewall cannot differentiate normal and legitimate traffic from DoS attack traffic ("Denial-of-service attack", 2017). Thus, use of only traditional firewall to block all the intrusions is not an efficient solution. To overcome such problems, an intrusion detection system (IDS) comes into play. Originally, the concept of intrusion detection was proposed by Anderson in 1980 (Sangve & Thool, 2017).The IDS plays very important role in the security of cloud since it acts as additional preventive layer of security (Modi, Patel, Patel, & Muttukrishnan, 2012b) and apart from detecting only known attacks, it can detect variants of many known attacks and unknown attacks. According to the guidance from National Institute of Standards and Technology (NIST), intrusion detection is defined as "the process of monitoring the events occurring in a computer system or network and analyzing them for signs of possible incidents, which are violations or imminent threats of violation of computer security policies, acceptable use policies, or standard security practices" (Aminanto, HakJu, Kyung-Min, & Kwangjo, 2017). An intrusion detection system (IDS) could be software, hardware or a combination of both that monitors network or system activities for malicious activities or policy violations and notifies network manager by mailing or logging the intrusion event (Oktay & Sahingoz, 2013).

The rest of this chapter is structured as follows: The following section presents the Cloud architecture. Then, we describe concisely several possible intrusions in the Cloud and we discuss the challenges and essential features of Cloud IDS. Afterwards, we present the detection techniques used by IDS, followed by a description of the different types of IDS in the Cloud and later, we give detailed analysis of various existing Cloud IDS. Finally, we conclude our work with references at the end.

CLOUD ARCHITECTURE

The architecture of Cloud involves multiple cloud components communicating with each other over the application programming interfaces (APIs), usually web services. Figure 1 depicts Cloud computing architecture, consisting of mainly two ends; the front end (Cloud users and Cloud Manager) and the back end (Host machine, virtual network and virtual machines (VM)). The front end is the part seen by the client, i.e. the customer. This includes the client's network or computer, and the applications used to access the Cloud through a user interface such as a web browser. The back end of the cloud computing architecture is the 'cloud' itself, which contains of various computers, servers and data storage devices (Dhage et al., 2011).

Figure 1. Architecture of Cloud Computing

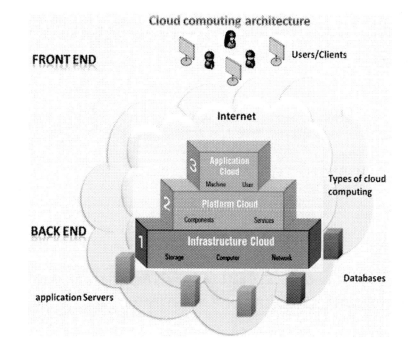

Using the front end, Cloud users demand the instances offered services via internet. The Cloud controller manages Cloud applications through their entire life cycle, from provisioning to monitoring, metering and billing. Host machine consists of computer hardware and software, which handles the user's query and executes it for allowing to access VM instances, where Cloud application is running. It queries and controls the system software on its node (E.g. Host operating system and Hypervisor) in response to queries and control request coming from the front end. Virtual network (Internal network) is designated for VM instance interconnectivity (Modi & Patel, 2013).

CHALLENGES AND ESSENTIAL CHARACTERISTICS OF CLOUD IDS

Objective

Main purpose is to design and integrate an effective IDS that can detect intrusions in traditional as well as virtual network in Cloud Environment, while reducing false positives and false negatives, with affordable computational cost and higher detection accuracy.

Challenges to Cloud IDS

Cloud IDS has some main challenges that are as follows:

- **Attacks on Virtual Environment:** In a virtualized environment, VMs communicate over hardware backplane rather than a network. As a result, the standard network security controls are blind to this traffic, and cannot execute security control for supervising and in-line blocking. In fact, a malicious user having a VM instance can perform several attacks like (Rubens, 2010; Kenneth, 2010) Hyper jacking, VM escape, VM hopping, VM migration to gain control of other's VM or host machine. Cloud NIDS should be able of monitoring and detecting intrusions from network traffic between VM and the host.

- **High Network Traffic:** Not long ago, Cloud is a rapidly growing computing model that provides various advantages in economic and business aspects. Thus, Cloud users are augmenting at very high rate. This generates heavy network traffic from a great number of Cloud users. IDS should handle such traffic quickly. Otherwise, it will be resulting into high probability of packet dropping.
- **NIDS Deployment:** In Cloud, the major challenge is to monitor both external and internal traffic for securing and protecting front end and back end of Cloud. This is due to the distributed and visualized nature of Cloud. Therefore, IDS should be deployed in the manner that they can detect internal attacks, external attacks and distributed attacks like DDoS attacks in the overall Cloud network.

Moreover, traditional IDS challenges should be considered before integrating IDS in Cloud environment such false positives, false negatives, detection accuracy and detection rate.

Essential Characteristics of IDS for the Cloud

IDS should have the following characteristics for integrating it in the cloud.

- **Detection of Attacks on Each Layer:** IDS should be able to detect intrusions at each component of Cloud architecture, either at the front end or at the back end. It should be capable of detecting known attacks as well as unknown attacks.
- **Low Computational Cost and Faster Detection Rate:** In Cloud, great number of users is involved. So, high number of requests may turn into high traffic rate in Cloud. Thus, IDS should have faster detection at lower cost.
- **Low False Positives and Low False Negatives:** The term false positive describes a situation, in which an IDS triggers a false alarm, but it is a wrong alarm, in fact, there is no attack. Whereas, false negative can be defined as an inability of IDS to detect the true intrusion; in other words, malicious activity is not detected or alerted. We need to keep very low false negatives and false positives in the Cloud, to let pass legitimate network packets and to protect network against malicious traffic. Fortunately, there are some actions that can be taken to reduce the chance of false negative conditions without increasing the number of false positives (Zhao & Huang, 2002; Yurcik, 2002).

Intrusions in Cloud

Cloud computing (CC) is an emerging technology and the rapidly growing field of IT. Most of the organizations are moving their IT systems and uploading their huge quantity of sensitive data into the cloud computing paradigm because of its encouraging features, such as easy to usage, reliability, availability and cost efficiency. Regardless of its advantages, the transition to CC raises security concerns; the sensitive data moved to the cloud data centers is vulnerable to security risks such confidentiality, integrity and availability. Moreover, the uninterrupted service of cloud technology attracts the intruders to gain access and misuse services and resources provided by Cloud service provider. The attacks that may affect cloud computing system are: Insider attack, Denial of service (DOS) attack, User to root attack, Port scanning, Attacks on virtualization, and Backdoor channel attacks.

Insider Attack

An insider attack (Duncan, Creese, & Goldsmith, 2014) can be defined as the intentional misuse of computer systems by users who are authorized to access those systems and networks. The attackers may attempt to gain and misuse the privileges that are either assigned or not assigned to them officially. Consequently, they may commit frauds, modify information intentionally or reveal secrets to opponents. For example, Amazon Elastic Compute Cloud (EC2) suffered from an internal DoS attack (Macro, 2009).

Denial of Service (DOS) Attack

In this attack also called flooding attack, attacker tries to flood virtual machine by sending huge amount of packets continuously from innocent hosts (zombies) in the network. Also, a hacker can cause denial of system services by consuming the bandwidth of the network by means of the Worms for example, which replicate themselves and spread within minutes to a large number of computers, leading to network congestion (Aljawarneh, 2016).Packets can be of type UDP, TCP, ICMP or a mix of them. The aim of this attack is to deny access for legitimate users and hack the cloud resources. By attacking a single server providing a certain service, attacker can cause a loss of availability of the intended service. Such an attack is called direct DoS attack. If the server's hardware resources are completely exhausted by processing the flood requests, the other service instances on the same hardware machine are no longer able to perform their intended tasks. Such type of attack is called indirect DoS attack (Modi et al., 2012a). This attack is very difficult to detect and filter, since packets that cause the attack are very much similar to legitimate traffic. DoS attack is considered as the biggest threat to IT industry, and intensity, size and frequency of the attack are observed to be increasing every year (Gupta & Badve, 2017).

Attacks on Hypervisor or Virtual Machines

An attacker may successfully control the virtual machines by compromising the lower layer hypervisor. For e.g. SubVir, BLUEPILL, and DKSM are well-known attacks on virtual layer. Through these attacks, hackers can be able to compromise installed-hypervisor to gain control over the host. Attackers easily target the virtual machines to access them by exploiting the zero-day vulnerabilities in virtual machines, this may damage the several websites based on virtual server (Kene & Theng, 2015).

Port Scanning

Attackers can use port scanning method to obtain list of open, closed, and filtered ports. Through this technique, attackers can determinate the open ports and attack the services running on these ports. Different techniques of port scanning are SYN scanning, ACK scanning, TCP scanning, Windows scanning, FIN scanning, UDP scanning etc. They reveal the entire network related information such MAC address IP address, router and gateway filtering and firewall rules. In cloud system, port scanning attack may cause loss of confidentiality and integrity on cloud.

User to Root Attack

User to Root exploits (Massachusetts Institute of Technology MIT Lincoln Laboratory [MIT Lincoln Laboratory], 2016) are a class of exploit in which the attacker starts out with access to a normal user account on the system (perhaps gained by sniffing passwords, a dictionary attack, or social engineering) and is able to exploit some vulnerability to gain root access to the system. There are several different types of User to Root attacks like buffer overflow attack, perl, xterm, etc. For example, Buffer overflows are used to generate root shells from a process running as root. It occurs when application program code overfills static buffer. The mechanisms used to secure the authentication process are a frequent target. There are no universal standard security mechanisms that can be used to prevent security risks like weak password recovery workflows, phishing attacks, keyloggers, etc. In case of Cloud, attacker acquires access to valid user's instances which enables him/her for gaining root level access to VMs or host.

Backdoor Channel Attacks

A backdoor in a computer system (or cryptosystem or algorithm) is a method of bypassing normal authentication, securing illegal remote access, obtaining access to plaintext, and so on, while attempting to remain undetected. It may take the form of an installed program or may subvert the system through a Rootkit. For example, default passwords can be a backdoor. It allows an attacker to gain remote access over the compromised system. An attacker can make the victim system as a zombie so that it can be used to perform a DDoS attack (Modi & Acha, 2016). It can also be used to disclose the confidential data of the victim (Kashif & Sellapan, 2012). As result, compromised system confronts difficulty in performing its regular tasks. In Cloud environment, attacker can get access and control Cloud user's resources through backdoor channel and make VM as Zombie to launch DoS/DDoS attack.

DETECTION TECHNIQUES USED BY IDS

As it can be seen in Figure 2, there are two main intrusion detection techniques used by IDS; anomaly detection (based on behavior of users) and signature detection (based on signatures of known attacks). To improve the performance of IDS, it is better to use a combination of these techniques, which called Hybrid detection.

Each technique is described in the following sub sections:

Signature Based Detection

Signature based detection is performed by comparing the information collected from a network or system against a database of signatures. A signature is a predefined set of patterns or rules that correspond to a known attack. This technique is also recognized as misuse detection. These signatures are composed by several elements that allow identifying the traffic. For instance, in Snort, the parts of a signature are the header (e.g. source address, destination address, ports) and its options (e.g. payload, metadata). To decide whether or not the network traffic corresponds to a known signature, the IDS uses pattern recognition techniques. Some IDS that use this approach are Snort, Network Flight Recorder, Network Security Monitor and Network Intrusion Detection, etc. It can efficiently detect known attacks with

Figure 2. Detection techniques used by IDS

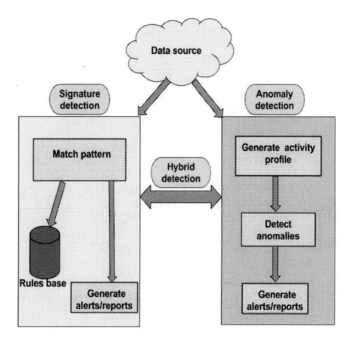

negligible false alarms. Signature based method helps network managers with average security expertise to identify intrusions accurately. It is a flexible approach since new signatures can be added to database without modifying existing ones. However, it is unable to detect unknown attacks (Mehmood, Habiba, Shibli, & Masood, 2013). Any new attack pattern or a change in the previous attack pattern with attack signature known will remain undetected (Zeeshan, Javed, & Ullah, 2017).

Anomaly Based Detection

An anomaly-based IDS tries to find suspicious activity on the system. The focus in this technique is on normal behavior rather than attack behavior (Lekha & Ganapathi, 2017). It assumes that the attacker behavior differs to that of a normal user, and so, any significant deviations or exceptions from the normal behavior model is considered anomaly (Zeeshan, Javed, & Ullah, 2017). This approach consists of comparing current user activities against preloaded profiles of users or networks to detect abnormal or unusual behavior that may be intrusions. The profiles may be dynamic or static and correspond to the expected or legitimate behavior of users. To build a profile, regular activities of users, network connections, or hosts are supervised for a specific period of time called training period (NIST, 2007). Profiles are developed using different features such failed login attempts, number of times a file is accessed by a particular user over a particular time duration, CPU usage etc. Anomaly based detection is efficacious against unknown attacks. The researchers use many detection techniques to determine what a normal activity is. Some of these methods are IDES (Intrusion Detection Expert System) that uses a knowledge-based system, ISA-IDS which is based on statistical methods, Audit Data Analysis and Mining which is based on automatic/machine learning methods, etc. In spite of their capability in detecting novel attacks, anomaly based intrusion detection systems suffer from high false positive rate (Tesfahun & Bhaskari, 2015).

Hybrid Detection

The efficacy of IDS can be significantly improved by combining signature based and anomaly based techniques which is called Hybrid detection technique. The idea behind the implementation of hybrid detection is to detect both known and unknown attacks based on signature and anomaly detection techniques (Kene & Theng, 2015).

TYPES OF CLOUD-BASED IDS

Cloud-based IDS can be divided into four types. These types are shown in Figure 3, we will describe each of them in the following subsections.

Network Based IDS (NIDS)

NIDS captures the traffic of entire network and analyze it for signs of malicious activities or events such DoS attacks, port scanning, user to root attacks etc. Network based IDS is designed to detect unauthorized use, misuse and abuse of computer networks by both insider and external intruders (Tabatabaefar, Miriestahbanati, & Gregoire, 2017). It usually performs intrusion detection by inspecting the IP and transport layer headers of each packet. NIDS utilizes the anomaly and/or signature based detection approach to identify intrusions. For signature detection approach, it looks for the correlation of captured packet with signatures of known attacks, while for anomaly detection method; it compares the user's current behavior with previous behavior. However, it is unable to perform analysis if traffic is encrypted (NIST, 2001), and it cannot detect intrusions inside a virtual network contained by hypervisor.

Host Based IDS (HIDS)

HIDS monitors and analyzes the information collected from a specific host machine to detect unauthorized and intrusive events. HIDS detects intrusion for the machine by collecting information such as file system used, network events, system calls, etc. HIDS observes modification in host kernel, host file system and behavior of the program. Upon detection of change in behavior or change of system or program, it

Figure 3. Cloud based IDS

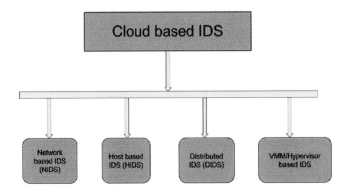

reports to network manager that system is under attack (NIST, 2001). The effectiveness of HIDS can be improved by specifying the features that provide it more information for detection. However, it requires more storage for information to be analyzed. In the case of cloud computing network, it is possible to deploy HIDS on hypervisor, VM or host to analyze the system logs, user login information or access control policies and detect intrusion events. Cloud user is responsible for monitoring and management of HIDS deployed at a VM while cloud provider is responsible for the deployment of HIDS on hypervisor. It is the responsibility of the providers that they should ensure that they are providing adequate IDS in their sides (Iqbal et al., 2017). HIDS is capable of analyzing encrypted traffic. However, it is susceptible to DoS attack and can even be disabled. HIDS is commonly used to protect the integrity of software.

Distributed IDS (DIDS)

A Distributed IDS (DIDS) contains numerous IDSs (such as NIDS, HIDS) that are deployed over a large network to monitor and analyze the traffic for intrusive detection behavior. The participant IDSs can communicate with each other or with a centralized server. Each of these individual IDSs has its own two function components: detection component and correlation manager. Detection component examines system's behavior and transmits the collected information in a standard format to the correlation manager. Correlation manager combines data from multiple IDS and generates high level alerts that keep up a correspondence to an attack. Analysis phase makes use of signature based and anomaly based detection techniques so DIDS can detect known as well as unknown attacks. In case of cloud, DIDS can be located at any of two positions: at processing server or at Host machine (Patel, Taghavi, Bakhtiyari, & Júnio, 2013).

Hypervisor-Based Intrusion Detection System

Hypervisor provides a platform to run VMs. Hypervisor based IDS is deployed at the hypervisor layer. It allows monitoring and analyzing of available information for detection of anomalous activities and events. The information is based on communication at different levels like communication between VMs and communication within the hypervisor based virtual network (Mehmood et al., 2013).

ANALYSIS OF EXISTING CLOUD BASED INTRUSION DETECTION SYSTEMS (CIDS)

In this section, we will present different CIDS and classify them into three categories based on the intrusion detection technique used by each system. The categories are Signature based, Anomaly based and Hybrid. We have studied systems from each category and analyzed them to evaluate whether or not they meet the security requirements of cloud.

Signature Based Detection

Sengaphay et al. (2016) have proposed Snort-IDS rules for intrusion behavior detection using multi-sensors in private cloud, in order to detect malicious activities and events and to protect cloud resources and services against intrusions form both inside and outside of the system. Each sensor installed in the private cloud is based on Snort IDS, and it works accordance with created snort-IDS rules installed on their own selves to catch intrusion. When intrusion behavior is detected by each snort IDS sensor, it will generate alert and store it into an alert event database. Then, a virtual machine dedicated for analysis of alerts into the alert event database, analyzes all the data from sensors to identify type of the intrusion behaviors. Finally, the detection system notifies the system Administrator. The authors have created Snort-IDS rules to detect five kinds of the intrusion behavior such as detection port scanning behavior, checking operating systems behavior, surveying IP address behavior, detection of use the application behavior, and intrusion detection of the malware and virus and behavior. In order to test the detection performance of proposed intrusion detection system of private cloud, the authors have used the data set from the MIT-DARPA and Nmap, and the results show that their system can detect 51 cases of intrusion behavior.

Santoso et al. (2016) have designed and implemented signature-based Network Intrusion Detection System (NIDS) to protect OpenStack private cloud resources and services from various kinds of threats and attacks. The proposed NIDS was placed between the OpenStack Cloud and the external network for monitoring purposes.

The NIDS modules consist of the following supporting tools:

- **Snort Engine:** The module matches every incoming network packet with rules stored in misuse base to find any correlation. In this case, it determines the nature of the attack and send alert message to "Alert or Unified Log" module. Otherwise, the incoming packet is considered as benign traffic;
- **Snort Rule:** Called also misuse base, which was generated based on predefined network attack rules; The authors set the DoS rules for detecting the possible attacks such as UDP echo+chargen bomb attack, UDP Bay/Nortel Nautica Marlin attack, etc;
- **Pulledpork:** The module updates the Snort rules when latest attack is detected;
- **Alert or Unified Log:** The module logs the detected attack in a log file;
- **Barnyard2:** The module analyzes Snort binary log file, generates the database records and inserts them into the MySQL DB.
- **Snorby:** The module interprets the result of Snort log previously transformed into the MySQL DB records to web-based interface.

The UDP flooding attack simulation performed during the experiments conducted by the authors reveal that the proposed model is functioning securely and accurately. Moreover, the real-time alert of signature-based NIDS is useful for the private cloud administrator to become aware of any possible classified attacks. However, that NIDS have exhibited some false intrusions because it falsely recognized some applications on OpenStack host and their both VMs as intrusions. Hence the false positive rate on each of the OpenStack host and both VMs. Furthermore, it is not able to detect unknown attacks because it uses signature detection approach.

Mehmood et al. (2015) have proposed a Distributed Intrusion Detection System using Mobile Agents in Cloud Computing (DIDMACC) to detect distributed attacks in Cloud. They have used mobile agents to carry intrusion alerts collected from different VMs where Suricata NIDS is deployed to the management server. In this server, the correlation module (Open Source Security Information Management (OSSIM) correlation engine) correlates intrusion alerts to generate high level alerts that correspond to a distributed attack. Then, the management server sends the signature of detected attack to all virtual machines monitored, to update the signature database of local Suricata IDS to avoid such intrusions in future. The results show that the use of mobile agents to carry intrusion-related data and code reduces network load, and correlation of intrusive events collected by those mobile agents by means of a correlation engine helps in detection of distributed intrusions. However, the proposed system can't detect zero-day attacks or unknown attacks.

Khatri and Khilari (2015) have proposed an architecture which provides implementation of Suricata IDS as network IDS in the backend of Cloud environment. The aim of Suricata IDS is to secure the virtualized servers on hypervisors in the cloud platform from attackers and various threats. The main function of Suricata IDS in the network is capturing of all coming packets from external users and destined to virtualized servers, analyzing these packets and finally sending alert if a packet is matching one of rules stored into Suricata configuration file. However, the However, the proposed model can't detect insider attacks, network intrusions in virtual network as well as known attacks.

Khaldi et al. (2014) have proposed a framework based on secure mobile agents (Bee-Gent Mobile agent) for detecting distributed intrusions and repairing the vulnerabilities in hybrid cloud. The operating of this framework is divided into three successive phases:

1. Detect distributed attacks
2. Evaluate the attack's risks
3. Repair attacks.

The proposed model is based on six actors:

1. **A HIDS (host IDS):** An IDS based Snort deployed in each virtual machine (VM) in the hybrid cloud (private and public). The IDS monitors the traffics, detects intrusions and saves it in its alert database.
2. **Correlated Mobile Agent (CMA):** It is a mobile agent dispatched to each VM in the cloud area. The CMA contains the rules to verify in each VM using the alerts saved in IDS database. In the same time, the framework supports two CMA every one, in each cloud area (public, private) to have rapidly a whole idea about the hybrid cloud intrusions.
3. **A Public Cloud Agent (PbCA):** It is a static agent deployed in the administrator node in public cloud. This agent dispatches a Correlated Mobile Agent (CMA) to detect intrusions and go back with all the results of the correlation process.
4. **A Private Cloud Agent (PvCA):** Performs the same tasks as PbCA in the private cloud.
5. **A Hybrid Cloud Agent (HCA):** It is a static agent implemented in the administrator node in hybrid cloud. This agent queries the PbCA and the PvCA to start with the detection process in order to evaluate the security level in the hybrid cloud.
6. **A Static Agent (SA):** The static agent is implemented in each VM to receive the CMA. When the HCA detects distributed intrusion, it dispatches a Reparation mobile agent (RMA) to:
   a. The vulnerable VM to repair it if there is any service to close or to reject any established communication with a malicious user.
   b. The firewall to apply new security rules to avoid intrusions detected. In this way, firewall should implement a Static to receive the RMA in order to get rules and apply them.

The IDS with Mobile Agent approach claims the less network load compared to the client/server approach, by shipping code to data instead of shipping data to code. However, it can't detect unknown attacks because it is based on Snort.

Manthira and Rajeswari (2014) have proposed security architecture for cloud, in which a virtual host based intrusion detection system was placed between router and Cloud host. The developed IDS consists of three components namely: Event Auditor, IDS service (combination of analyze system and Alert system) and CIDD (Cloud Intrusion Detection Data Sets). The analyzer system examines the content of packet against the cloud intrusion datasets signatures stored in CIDD by means of pattern matching. The experiments conducted by the authors show that the proposed IDS was able to detect 80% of random sets of cloud attacks and no false positive alarm is raised while filtering background traffic received form DARPA dataset. However, results show that latency in IDS is increasing according to background traffic, and a breaking point was identified at 2 mbps, in which, the IDS generated an error and stopped. Therefore, an unstable interval was determined between 1.5 to 2 mbps.

Modi et al. (2012c) have integrated a signature Apriori based NIDS to Cloud. Signature Apriori takes network packets and known attack signatures as input and generates new derived rules that are updated in the Snort. Therefore, Snort is able to detect known attacks and derivative of known attacks in the Cloud. This approach improves the efficiency of Snort. However, it cannot detect unknown attacks.

Alharkan and Martin (2012) have proposed an Intrusion Detection System as a Service (IDSaaS), which enables consumers to protect their virtual machines against internal and external attacks in public clouds. IDSaaS is a network and signature based IDS, and it targets the Infrastructure-as-a-Service level of the cloud. It is on-demand, elastic, portable, controllable by the cloud consumer and available through the pay-per-use cost model of the cloud. With IDSaaS, users can define a virtual private area within the cloud space for their applications that can be secured with application specific policies. The IDSaaS framework was implemented in Amazon web services using the EC2 cloud. The IDSaaS utilizes the VPC service from Amazon. In the VPC space, it was created both private and public subnets. The private subnet maintains the protected business application VMs. The public subnet hosts various IDSaaS VMs. The various components of the proposed system are:

1. **IDSaaS Manager:** It is the security administrator access point where various supervision tasks can be performed. The Event Database is also resides in the Manager VM. The Manager VM can be used as an access point to configure other VMs in both public and private subnets.
2. **IDS Core:** It is the gatekeeper to the business application VMs in the private subnet. It inspects all incoming traffic using the Intrusion Engine component. Identical replica of the IDS Core VM can be created to distribute the traffic load to prevent single point of failure situations. Based on the threat signature matching process, a request to the business application VMs can be allowed or trapped by the IDS Core VM.
3. **Load Balancer:** It increases the availability of the IDSaaS system in the cloud. It is responsible for balancing the traffic load between multiple IDS Core VMs.

The drawbacks of IDSaaS are: It is a signature based IDS, so it is not able to detect unknown attacks. Also, the current implementation of the IDSaaS is designed to work in a single public cloud and not in a distributed environment.

Anomaly Based Detection

Dildar et al. (2017) have proposed the Virtual Machines and Hypervisor Intrusion Detection System, (VMHIDS) to detect, prevent and mitigate the hypervisor attacks in the virtualized cloud environment. Although there are five exiting tools such as Virtual Firewall, Intrusion Detection and Prevention Systems (IDPS), Network based IDS, Hosted-based IDS and Hypervisor-based IDS used to protect Cloud computing, but these approaches emphasizes on defending the cloud computing instead of hypervisor attacks. Hence, VMHIDS is proposed to overcome the weakness found in the existing systems. It is placed on the hypervisor and its' virtual machines. So, new attacks or suspicious attack on hypervisor can be detected easily for faster prevention. The VMHIDS has adopted the anomaly-based detection method to automatically identify the malicious packets in real time by tracking and analyzing the network traffic and blocking the malicious events. Consequently, this approach defends both the hypervisor and virtual machines from either internal or external attack on cloud environment. Even though it is a novel approach, however, the implementation details and the results are not given to prove the concept.

Out-VM monitoring allows cloud administrator (CA) to monitor and control a VM from a secure location outside the VM. Mishra et al. (2017) have proposed an out-VM monitoring based security approach named as "Program Semantic-Aware Intrusion Detection at Network and Hypervisor Layer" (PSI-NetVisor) to deal with intrusions at network and virtualization layer in Cloud Environment. PSI-NetVisor provides two-level of defense from attackers. It is deployed at centralized Cloud Network Server (CNS) to perform network monitoring by employing behavior based intrusion detection approach (BIDA) that is based on ensemble learning algorithm which combines the power of two classifiers namely Random Forest (RF) and Logistic Regression (LR). Therefore, providing first level of defense at network level. If malicious packets are bypassed by CNS, they are again checked and analyzed by another instance of PSI-NetVisor at hypervisor layer of Cloud Compute Server (CCoS), which hosts various VMs and is the most critical security component of cloud. This instance of PSI-NetVisor incorporates semantic awareness in proposed BIDA using system call flow graph based method and VM memory introspection capability which helps to detect both network attacks and malicious processes at VMM of CCoS; assuring second level of defense at virtualization level. PSI-NetVisor has been validated with latest intrusion datasets (UNSW-NB & Evasive Malware). The experiments conducted by authors show that the traffic monitoring and process monitoring functionalities achieve accuracy of 94.54% with 2.81% of false positive rate (FPR) and accuracy of 96% with 1% FPR respectively. However, the average processing time is 1.3583 sec (min) to 649.176 sec per sample, which is relatively high-performance overhead in Cloud Environment where increasing number of Cloud users produce heavy network traffic. Intrusion detection activity in such traffic should be very fast. Otherwise, it will be resulted into high probability of packet dropping (Modi & Patel, 2013).

In the research work of Sharma et al. (2016), the authors have created an anomaly intrusion detection system for detecting Denial-of-Service attacks in Cloud using Artificial Bee Colony (ABC). For producing datasets for training and testing, the authors have generated the background traffic in CloudSim, a framework for modeling and simulation of cloud computing infrastructures and services. The proposed framework has been divided into three steps:

Step 1: It consists of applying basic feature selection on each record or network packet. Hence, basic network features are extracted, and traffic is recorded in well defined manner.

Step 2: Employ ABC and determinate its working nature.

Step 3: This final stage called decision making. It incorporates tow processes; training and testing phases. in the training stage, the ABC module generates profiles for all kinds of legitimate records and saves these generated profiles in a profile database. In the testing stage, ABC detection module is employed to detect DoS attacks.

The proposed framework was carried out in CloudSim, and the experiments conducted prove the ability of artificial bee Colony approach for detection of denial-of-service attack in cloud environment in a very short time. Besides, this approach was compared to quantum-inspired PSO (QPSO) and was found to be better. In fact, the average detection rate observed for ABC was 72.4% while that for QPSO was 68.3%.

Gupta and Kumar (2015) have proposed an approach to detect malicious program executions at client VM's in Cloud environment, with the use of a new technique of Immediate System Call signature detection. In this approach, for every unique System Call (user program or system program), the list of all Immediate System Calls following it is identified, and created from its normal execution logs, and such signatures are stored and then used as baseline for anomalous program detections. This method is based on the fact that whenever the program is subverted or is executed in a malicious way on a client, it causes a deviation in the Immediate System Call sequence pattern corresponding to each unique System Calls. This deviation can easily be detected and logged for generating alerts to Cloud Admin. Cloud admin then react on it either by uninstalling the malicious software from client or by replacing the software with its valid replica. However, the detection of malicious programs is not in real time, because of the periodic nature of the proposed anomaly detection module. In addition, the detection module can detect only subversions of programs whose the signatures of their immediate system calls are already generated, and also the reaction to an attack is not automatic, it is decided by the cloud admin.

Pandeeswari and Kumar (2015) have proposed an anomaly detection system at the hypervisor layer named Hypervisor Detector. It uses a hybrid algorithm which is a mixture of Fuzzy C-Means clustering algorithm and Artificial Neural Network (FCM-ANN) to improve the accuracy of intrusion detection system. The general procedure of FCM-ANN approach has the following three phases. In the first phase, a fuzzy clustering technique is used to divide the large dataset into small clusters or training subsets. Based on different training sets, different ANNs are trained in the second phase. Since the size and the complexity of the training set are greatly reduced, the effectiveness of the consequent ANN module can be improved so as to improve the learning capability of ANN In the third phase, in order to eliminate the errors of different ANNs, Fuzzy aggregation module is introduced to learn again and combine the resultant ANN network modules into a single ANN module. The proposed model gives high detection rate and minimum false alarm when compared to classic ANN and Naïve Bayes classifier for detecting various attacks (Dos, Probe attacks, R2L and U2R). Also, it is more efficient than those approaches.

Muthukumar and Rajendran (2015) have proposed an Intelligent Intrusion Detection System for Private Cloud Environment to satisfy the security and the performance issues of cloud computing. The proposed IDS combine combining hardware and an application to detect intrusion. The software component is implemented within virtualized servers such web server to detect intrusions, without influencing the performance of the servers. The hardware component is used to store intrusions traces and parameters of the IDS. The main goal of the proposed model is to detect the intrusion in an efficient manner, by predicting the intrusion using the previous history of intrusion given to the system during the training phase, and by self-updating the intrusion detection database in a constant manner, without any human intervention (Intelligent mechanism). The proposed IDS have three phases. Each phase has been written as an algorithm. 1. Training the intrusion detection system. 2. Testing the intrusion detection system.

3. Implementation and updating intrusion detection system. The proposed IDS was able to detect all of new types of intrusion, the result of performance testing using gives overall impression, that the implementation is much efficient in terms of time and space.

Sangeetha et al. (2015) have proposed a Signature based Semantic Intrusion Detection System on Cloud, which concentrates on the application level to detect application specific attacks. Those attacks aim to compromise the system by exploiting vulnerabilities of the protocols of the application layer such as HTTP, FTP etc..The packets transferred between cloud users and servers are captured by Cloud IDS Engine and analyzed for any maliciousness. The operation of the components of that IDS is as follow; the packets of various protocols captured by packet sniffer are forwarded to the protocol analyzer, which recognizes the protocol type and dispatches them to its corresponding parser. The parser translates a sequence of packets into protocol messages and forwards them to the parsing grammar for analysis and checking with the semantic rules. Semantic Classification tree is constructed by analyzing the specification of the protocol. The specification gives the rules and the individual patterns which will be matched in the corresponding fields of the protocol. The tree is formed in the top-down format. As each node on the path from the root to a leaf node checks with the input, if any signature does not match with the rule base then it raises alerts to the cloud IDS Interpreter which in turn alerts the Virtual Cloud Provider. The traffic is continuously monitored and analyzed for any malicious behavior and is reported to the administrator. Even though it is a novel approach, however, the implementation details and the results are not given to prove the concept.

Al –Shadaifat et al. (2015) have proposed an anomaly intrusion detection model to deal with attacks and security violations in cloud environment. The proposed approach consists of Hopefield Artificial Network and Simulating Annealing as aggregator. The framework for anomaly IDS is divided into three stages: Dataset Grouping, Hopfield Artificial Neural Network (HANN) and Simulating Annealing aggregator. According to experiments performed by authors, the proposed model provides a detection rate <=93%, which can be considered as a weak detection rate compared with methods in (Modi & Patel, 2013; Pandeeswari & Kumar, 2015). For gain better detection rate, more enhancements must be conducted by exploring the impact of network features in detection rate.

Hybrid Based Detection

Ahmad et al. (2017) have developed a prototype of Cloud IDS inspired by Dendritic Cell mechanism for detecting any threat and intrusion attempt targeting the Cloud environment. Cloud IDS model imitate the activity and process of Dendritic Cell in human immune system which is known for detecting and killing any pathogens that infected human tissue and cells. Emulating the activity of dendritic cell required this model uses two primary source of information as a primary data; antigens and signals. Cloud IDS model captures network packets gathered from the private cloud environment and at the same time, antigens will be extracted from the network packets by the selected features of the network packets. It also collects and synthesizes signals from observed events and the state of the network and guest cloud by implementing signal sensors on each Cloud node. Each Cloud node consists of three signal sensors; host monitor, network monitor and alert monitor. Each signal includes two functional elements. The first element is the antigen feature value where this designates the antigen that produces the signals. The second element is the signal level. This model consists mainly of a set of danger model signal generator, a misuse-based network intrusion detection system (NIDS) and artificial peripheral tissue (APT) where the dendritic cells, danger model signals and antigens interact. As result, this model classifies antigens as dangerous or safe and yields this information in detecting any threat or malicious event in the Cloud environment. The experiments show that this Cloud IDS was able to detect attempts to attack the Cloud environment. However, it achieves weak detection rate and moderate precision which are 59.86% and 79.43% respectively.

Raja et al. (2017) have proposed a fuzzy self-classifying clustering based cloud intrusion detection system which is intelligent to gain knowledge of fuzzy sets and fuzzy rules from data to detect intrusions in a cloud environment. The cloud intrusion detection system (CIDS) developed is designed based on a five-layered fuzzy neural network. Layers from 1 to 5 consist of the input nodes, antecedent nodes, rule nodes, consequent nodes and output nodes, respectively. The function of the first layer is to simply forward the input vector to the second layer which in turn matches antecedents of the input training value with the corresponding labels. The next layer generates the set of type 2 fuzzy TSK rules (Each fuzzy rule includes mean, deviation and the scaled deviation as its antecedent parameters and the rule weights as its consequent parameters) from the training data by measuring the overall similarity between the input training vector and the antecedent part of the fuzzy rule. The purpose of layer 4 is to extract consequent for the fuzzy rules from the input vector. The last layer generates a crisp output through defuzzification.

Implementation of the proposed CIDS goes through two phases, namely, training phase and testing phase. In the training phase, the proposed fuzzy self-classifying clustering algorithm is employed to partition the intrusion detection dataset into a number of clusters, where similar patterns are associated with the same cluster. Each of the resulting clusters is defined with the membership function by statistical mean and deviation which results in a type-2 fuzzy TSK IF-THEN rule. A fuzzy neural network is constructed accordingly and the associated parameters are refined by a type-2 fuzzy neural network through the application of a dynamical optimal learning algorithm. This phase makes Fuzzy Neural Network (FNN) to learn normal and abnormal patterns of Cloud Intrusion Detection Dataset (CIDD), in several iterations. In addition to this learning of known patterns, it also becomes capable of identifying new or mysterious patterns. In the testing phase, for each pattern (service request) of test dataset sent from a consumer to the Cloud, the fuzzy rulebase is consulted to make the decision of allowing or denying the request. With the help of knowledge which is already gained through learning/training phase, the FNN can identify various attack patterns of testing data and produces the attack type as its result. Otherwise, the service request is considered as a valid request. Practically, for a new input from the test data set, a corresponding crisp output of the system is obtained by combining the inferred results of all the rules into a type-2 fuzzy set which is then defuzzified by applying a type reduction algorithm. During experiments conducted by authors, Detection Accuracy (DA) measurements during training and testing phases are carried out for the proposed CIDS and other three systems, as to say, K means clustering based CIDS, modified K means clustering based CIDS and self-constructing clustering based CIDS. Experimental Results explained by Statistical analysis with ANOVA using Tukey post hoc method demonstrate that the proposed method achieves statistically significant performance than other methods. In fact, it attains 99.31% DA during training and 99.26% DA during testing.

The distributed and dynamic nature built-in of cloud environment leads to several issues for Cloud IDS such as to analyze enormous log files, to aggregate heterogeneous traffic and to correlate complex events. In addition, virtualization which is the base of cloud computing carries to various loopholes. To overcome these issues, and to gain secured cloud environment, Ambikavathi and Srivatsa (2016) have proposed an integrated intrusion detection approach, which is established by means of integrating both IDS models (H-IDS and N-IDS), each equipped with both SD (Signature based detection approach) and AD (Anomaly based detection approach). Moreover, a Central coordinator module is developed to in order to aggregate the results such as attacks, events and alerts from both H-IDS and N-IDS for updating the rules set for signature based detection. In the security architecture proposed, each VM is monitored by H-IDS to detect internal attacks initiated by cloud users. The H-IDS is deployed in each VM during its creation. The N-IDS is located at the entry point of the cloud environment to detect external attacks. Along with detection accuracy is improved by the combination of SD and AD methods. The main components of the proposed architecture are; OSSEC H-IDS, NI-IDS and Central Coordinator module.

- **OSSEC H-IDS:** Each VM is built-in in with OSSEC H-IDS. OSSEC is an Open Source H-IDS that functions using both anomaly based and signature based techniques. OSSEC checks the execution of system programs, memory usage, network usage, and processor usage by the VM to detect malicious activities and events. It achieves log analysis, policy monitoring, file integrity checking, rootkit detection, real-time alerting and active response.
- **Network IDS:** it is placed at the entry point of the cloud environment in order to detect outside hackers. It combines two open source N-IDS tools that are Bro-IDS for anomaly detection and Snort for signature-based detection.
- **Central Coordinator Module:** It is deployed in one of the hypervisors in the Cloud platform. Central coordinator is required in order to aggregate the results such as attacks, events, and alerts from both H-IDS and N-IDS. This aggregation is used for generating the rules set to update signature database of N-IDS and H-IDS.

Singh et al. (2016) has proposed a novel Collaborative IDS (CIDS) framework for cloud, to defend network accessible Cloud resources and services from various threats and attacks. The proposed NIDS is integrated in each cloud cluster, and a correlation Unit (CU) provides collaboration between all cluster NIDSs, is placed in any one cluster. Bully election algorithm is used to elect one best cluster for placement of CU on the basis of workload. The hybrid NIDS use Snort to detect the known stealthy attacks using signature matching, and to detect unknown attacks, anomaly detection system (ADS) is built using Decision Tree Classifier and Support Vector Machine (SVM). In the proposed model, cascading decision tree and SVM has improved the detection accuracy and system performance as they remove the limitation of each other. Use of DT makes the learning process speedy and divides the dataset into small sub datasets. Use of SVM on each sub dataset reduce the learning time of SVM and overcome the overfitting and reduce the size of decision tree to make the detection faster. For frequent attacks detected by ADS, signature generation process generates a Snort based signature. Once the signature is generated, local knowledge base is updated, and this signature is sent to the central correlation unit. It receives the signature sent by all the NIDSs in the Cloud network and calculates the value of a criterion to make a decision on the bases of how much part of total NIDSs send the similar signature. If calculated value for an attack signature is higher than a threshold, thereafter, correlation unit multicasts this signature to all the IDSs. They receive this signature and update their knowledge base. By this way, collaboration between NIDSs prevents the coordinated attacks against cloud infrastructure and knowledge base remains up-to-date. The performed experiments by the authors show that the proposed ADS outperform both SVM and decision tree in terms of accuracy and computation time when they are used separately.

In order to detect and prevent distributed attacks and other malicious activities at the virtual network layer of the Cloud environment, Modi (2015) has proposed and implemented a Network IDS sensor on each host machine of the Cloud, which uses Snort to detect known attacks and an associative classifier to detect unknown attacks. The main components of the proposed NIDS are: Packet capture, Signature detection, Network traffic profile generation, Anomaly detection, Severity calculation and Alert system. The Signature detection module is based on snort, which checks the content of a captured packet with the predefined rules or patterns to find any correlation. If no correlation found, the network packet is forwarded to the Network traffic profile generation module, which derives network profile by extracting the network features from that packet. Therefore, the anomaly detection module based on an associative classifier, predicts the class label of the generated network profile. Upon detection of an intrusion, it sends alert of intrusive connection to severity calculation module, which identify distributed attack from the detected intrusions by calculating the Majority_vote (intrusion) indicator. The value of Majority_Vote indicator is equal to the quotient of dividing the number of sensors sending same alert by the number of sensors installed in whole Cloud. If the value of Majority_vote parameter is greater than a threshold, then given profile is mentioned as a profile of distributed attack. The alert system products alert messages of intrusions, which are stored in network traffic profile log base, for further learning of Associative classifier. By cascading signature detection module and anomaly detection module, using a central base of intrusion logs and a severity calculation module, the capability of the proposed framework in term of detection intrusion is improved. In fact, it can detect 96% non-distributed and 95% distributed attacks in real time.

Ghosh et al. (2015) has proposed an Intrusion Detection System for protecting the Cloud environment against intrusions, based on the collaboration of multi-threaded Network Intrusion Detection System (NIDS) and Host Intrusion Detection System (HIDS). The multi-threaded NDIS is placed at the bottleneck position of the Cloud, to monitor the requests send by the Cloud users. The multi-threaded approach is performed to overcome the large network traffic and for easy process. As the request passes NIDS for getting access to the Cloud infrastructure, it is again monitored by HIDS deployed in each hypervisor server. In the proposed system, the multi-threaded NIDS consists of three modules; Capture and Query module, Analysis module and Reporting module. The capture module performs the task of capturing and receiving inbound and outbound (ICMP, TCP, IP, UDP) data packets. As large amount of data packets entered into the NIDS, the Capture and Query module first allocates and arrange them in an ordered manner and place them into a shared queue for analysis. The analysis of packets is done using K-Nearest Neighbor and Neural Network (KNN-NN) hybrid classifier. For any incoming packet, a number of relevant features are extracted (feature selection) to decrease memory space and time, therefore, anomaly detection using K-Nearest Neighbor algorithm (KNN) is performed. KNN acts as a binary classifier and classifies a packet as 'normal' or 'abnormal'. For all the packets classified as abnormal, an Artificial Neural Network (ANN) is used to perform misuse detection and sub classifies them into specific attack types (Dos, Probe, U2R and R2L). If any packet is classified as an attack by cloud IDS, an intrusion report is generated and sent to the Administrator, which first alerts the user about intrusion and with that it also maintains the IP log list for the affected client requests. Further the logged intrusion is processed by the Administrator. For each intrusion, the occurrence counter value is incremented by 1. The occurrence counter value is checked with respect to a threshold value. If the counter value doesn't exceed the threshold value, the access is denied for the particular user. If the counter value is greater than the threshold value, further IP is made blocked for all operations. Also, a revised restore point is also proposed for quick revival of previous state of the user after network or system reoccurrence. Experimental results show the proposed Hybrid Multilevel classifier gives high detection accuracy than KNN and ANN, when they are used as classifier modules separately.

Ambikavathi and Srivatsa (2015) have developed an Intelligent Intrusion Detection System (I-IDS) to improve the security of virtual machine (VM), which is the base for cloud computing model. The proposed model works at virtualization layer, it improves security of VM by creating VM profiling, packet flow monitoring and conducting centralized periodic automated vulnerability scans for infected VMs. A management Schema is centralized to ensure all virtual machines offer in the same level of protection. VM profile is created for each virtual machine with its details such as OS type, CPU, RAM size, IP address, login credentials, which are stored as a profile in database, and used later by the vulnerability scanner to identify the vulnerable and exploited VMs. Packet monitoring is assuring by an intelligent IDS, it is done for all incoming packets to check whether the packet contains any malicious code or data, by means of combining of tow techniques, signature-based and anomaly-based. Signature based IDS identify known attacks by comparing an incoming packet with database of selected rules/ signatures. If a match occurs, the IDS declare that packet as infected packet and the node as infected node, and it notifies the vulnerability scanner. The Anomaly based IDS analyses network for unknown or new attacks. It works by comparing the sending data rate of each machine with a threshold value. If the sending data rate is more than the threshold then that machine is declared as suspect, and the vulnerability scanner is informed. Scanning of only infected VM is done periodically in centralized manner by means of OpenVAS tool. It reports the list of VMs which are stable, vulnerable and exploited.

Modi and Patel (2013) have proposed a hybrid-network intrusion detection system (H-NIDS) deployed on each host machine, to detect internal and external network attacks in Cloud Computing environment. The architecture of proposed H-NIDS consists of mainly seven successive modules; Packet capture, Signature based detection, Anomaly detection, Score function, Alert system and Central log. Signature based detection module uses Snort and signature Apriori algorithm, which generates derived attack rules, thereby, Snorts can detect known attacks and derivative attacks. Anomaly based detection module uses a combination of multiple classifiers; Bayesian, Associative rule and Decision tree. They predict the class label of given network packets and send the result to score function. The score function uses weighted averaging method to determine whether the predicted intrusion is really intrusion or not. Moreover, it determines whether the detected intrusion is a type of distributed attack or not, by checking the central log of malicious packets and applying a majority vote method. The Alert system raises alerts about intrusion that is determined either by Sort or score function, and stores alerted intrusion in the central log base. Further to the experiments realized by the authors, proposed H-NIDS has capability of detecting known and known attacks efficiently with high accuracy and low false alerts. Moreover, that system has lower computational and communication overhead than agent based approaches.

Table 1, Table 2, and Table 3 give analysis of cloud IDS using signature detection technique, anomaly detection technique and hybrid detection technique respectively.

CONCLUSION

The security of Cloud Computing paradigm must be considered primarily for its success. In this chapter, we have described several intrusions which can threat confidentiality, integrity and availability of Cloud resources and services. Firewall only may not be able sufficient to defend the Cloud against those threats. In fact, it is not able to detect insider attacks, either over physical network or over virtual network within hypervisors. Also, few DoS or DDoS attacks are too complex to detect using traditional firewall. To address this issue, incorporating the Intrusion Detection System (IDS) in Cloud Environment may enhance the security by acting as a second line of defense after the firewall. The IDS is a needful component to detect cyber-attacks. Afterwards, we have emphasized the challenges and essential characteristics

Table 1. Analysis of cloud based IDS using signature detection technique

Work	IDS Type	Position	Detection Time	Data Source	Characteristics/ Strengths	Limitations/ Challenges
Integrating signature Apriori based network intrusion detection system (NIDS) in cloud computing (Modi Patel, Patel,& Rajarajan, 2012c)	NIDS	At the processing servers	Real time	Network traffic, signatures of known attacks	Can detect known attacks and derivative of known attacks.	Can't detect unknown attacks.
IDSaaS: Intrusion Detection System as a Service in Public Clouds (Alharkan & Martin, 2012)	NIDS	In the public subnet of VPC Amazon Cloud	Real time	Network traffic, signatures of known attacks	IDS as service is on-demand, elastic, portable, controllable by the cloud consumer and available through the pay-per-use cost model of the cloud.	It is not able to detect unknown attacks, and the current implementation of the IDSaaS is designed to work with single public cloud and not with a distributed environment.
Framework to detect and repair distributed intrusions based on mobile agent in hybrid cloud (Khaldi, Karoui, & Ben ghezala, 2014)	HIDS	At each VM	Real time	Audit data, known intrusions patterns, system logs, alert database of IDS, reports of intrusions	• Less network load compared to the client/server approach. • Distributed correlation for detection of distributed intrusions. • Secure communication between mobile agents. • It can detect known attacks.	Test the effectiveness of this framework in detecting DDOS attacks in the cloud is not done.
Virtual Host based Intrusion Detection System for Cloud (Manthira & Rajeswari, 2014)	NIDS	Placed between router and Cloud host	Real time	• Network traffic, CIDD (Cloud Intrusion Detection Data Sets; which contains attack signatures based on port that are opened in cloud for communications) • New rules are generated for intrusion detection by mean of Genetic algorithm	Detection rate is 80% and no false positive alarm.	• Latency in IDS is increasing according to background traffic, and a breaking point was identified at 2 mbps, in which, the IDS generated an error and stopped. • Can't detect unknown attacks.
Advancement in Virtualization Based Intrusion Detection System in Cloud Environment (Khatri & Khilari, 2015)	NIDS	On separate machine in the back end of cloud environment, between virtualized servers an cloud users	Real time	Network traffic, rules configured into Suricata configuration file	Can detect known attacks.	Can't detect unknown attacks, and rules of intrusion detection are configured manually.
Creating Snort-IDS Rules for Detection Behavior Using Multi-sensors in Private Cloud (Sengaphay, Saiyod, & Benjamas, 2016)	NIDS	On multi-sensors deployed in private cloud	Real time	Network packets, alert event database, Snort-IDS rules	The created Snort-IDS rules allow detecting 51 cases of intrusion behavior, such port scan, IP scan, OS scan, application scan, intrusion virus and malware.	• The proposed system cannot detect unknown attacks. • To evaluate performance of proposed system, the performance measurements of IDS are not used such as TP, TN, FP, FN, DR (Detection Rate) and FPR (False Positive Rate).
Distributed intrusion detection system using mobile agents in cloud computing environment (Mehmood, Shibli, Kanwal, & Masood, 2015)	NIDS	At each VM	Real time	Network traffic, Signature database of intrusion patterns, Suricata logs, correlation rules, vulnerability base, audit data	• Helps to detect distributed attacks. It detects vulnerable software in VMs and apply patch to software. • It detects vulnerable ports in VMs and closes those ports. - Mobile agents reduce the network load by carrying intrusion-related data and code.	• The proposed model cannot detect unknown attacks or zero day attacks. • It has high rate of false positive of 93%, as result, the IDS may drop or reject normal packets.
Designing Network Intrusion and Detection System Using Signature-Based Method for Protecting OpenStack Private Cloud (Santoso, Idrus, & Gunawan, 2016)	NIDS	Placed between the OpenStack Cloud and the external network	Real time	Network traffic, Snort rules	Can detect known attacks accurately. In fact, for known attacks, it attains 100% of Detection rate.	It is not able to detect unknown attacks

Table 2. Analysis of cloud based IDS using anomaly detection technique

Work	IDS Type	Position	Detection Time	Data Source	Characteristics/Strengths	Limitations/ Challenges
Immediate System Call Sequence Based Approach for Detecting malicious Program Executions in Cloud Environment (Gupta & Kumar, 2015)	HIDS	At each VM	Periodic and scheduled by the Cloud Admin	Program activities (immediate System call sequences), System call signature database, audit data	• It has low cost in deployment and it is independent to platform in cloud environment. • It has 98% accuracy in intrusion detection with a negligible amount of false positive.	• The detection of malicious programs is not in real time, detect subversions of programs whose their signatures are already generated. • The reaction to an attack is not automatic.
Anomaly Detection System in Cloud Environment Using Fuzzy Clustering Based ANN (Pandeeswari & Kumar, 2015)	VMM based	At each VMM	Real time	Virtual network traffic (Network based events on multiple VMs over VMM), anomaly database	Offer higher detection rate and lower false alarm rate than the Naïve Bayes and the classic ANN algorithms.	• Can't detect attacks when network traffic is encrypted, there is no cooperation between IDS in the cloud environment. • Performance has not been considered.
Intelligent Intrusion Detection System for Private Cloud Environment (Muthukumar & Rajendran, 2015)	HIDS	On each virtualized server at application level	Real time	Audit data, anomaly database	Can detect known attack and all new types of attack (100%), without causing error to protect or influence response time.	Require multiple IDS pour multiple VM over the same VMM.
Detection Signature Based Semantic Intrusion System on Cloud (Sangeetha, Devi,Ramya, Dharani, & Sathya, 2015)	NIDS	Between cloud users and cloud platform	Real time	Network packets, semantic rule base	Can help CPS to detect application specific attacks exploiting vulnerabilities of the protocols of the application layer.	The proposed idea is theoretical, no implementation provided.
Applying Hopfield Artificial Network and Simulating Annealing for Cloud Intrusion Detection (Al-Shdaifat, Alsharafat, & El-bashir, 2015)	Not specified	Not specified	Real time	Network packets, anomaly database	It has an acceptable detection rate <=93%.	Weak detection rate compared to other methods cited in (Al-Shdaifat et al., 2015) and need enhancement by exploring the impact of network features.
An Intrusion Detection System for Detecting Denial-of-Service Attack in Cloud Using Artificial Bee Colony (Sharma, Gupta, & Agrawal, 2016)	Not specified	Not specified	Real time	Network traffic, profile database	• The proposed approach is able to detect DoS attacks in Cloud in a very short period of time. • It outperforms QPSO in term of detection rate; its average rate was 72.4% while that for QPSO was 68.33%.	• To evaluate the performance of proposed anomaly IDS, alarm rate is not considered, whereas it is an important performance criteria for anomaly IDS. • To ensure experimental persuasiveness, the proposed system should further use the KDD datasets of DRPA, which are standard benchmarks for evaluation of IDSs.
Effective Way to Defend the Hypervisor Attacks in Cloud Computing (Dildar, Khan, Abdullah, & Khan, 2017)	DIDS	On each VM and on hypervisor	Real time	Network traffic	• VMHIDS protects both of the hypervisor and virtual machines from either insider or external attack on cloud environment. • It adopts anomaly based intrusion detection. So, it is can detects both known and unknown threats.	The implementation details and the results are not given to prove the concept.
PSI-NetVisor: Program semantic aware intrusion detection at network and hypervisor layer in cloud (Mishra, Pilli, Varadharajan, & Tupakula, 2017)	DIDS	At the network layer of centralized Cloud Network Server (CNS) and at the hypervisor layer of Cloud Compute Server (CCoS)	Real time	System call and network traces	Perform network monitoring at network layer of CNS by employing behavior based intrusion detection approach (BIDA). Also, it provides network monitoring and process monitoring at the hypervisor layer of Cloud Compute Server (CCoS) by incorporating semantic awareness in BIDA approach with Virtual Machine Introspection (VMI).	The average processing time is 1.3583 sec (min) to 649.176 sec per sample, which is relatively high performance overhead in Cloud Environment.

Table 3. Analysis of cloud based IDS using hybrid detection technique

Work	IDS Type	Position	Detection Time	Data Source	Characteristics/Strengths	Limitations/ Challenges
A novel Hybrid-Network Intrusion Detection System (H-NIDS) in Cloud Computing (Modi & Patel, 2013)	NIDS	On each host machine	Real time	Network packets, knowledge base, derived attack rule base, behavior base, alerts stored in central log of malicious packets	• Can detect internal and external attacks, secure whole cloud from distributed attacks. • It has high detection rate, high accuracy and low false alerts.	• Complexity increased due to integration of Snort, Signature Apriori algorithm, tree classifiers (Bayesian, Associative and Decision tree). • The Latency in IDS needed to be evaluated, because if it increases, the IDS will be detectable to attackers, as result, it will be itself a target to attacks.
Improving virtual machine security through intelligent intrusion detection system (Ambikavathi & Srivatsa, 2015)	VMM based	At each VMM	Real time	Network packets, profile database, signature database, vulnerabilities database	Detect infected VMs, and help cloud administrator to identify vulnerable and exploited VMs, thereafter, administrator can take corrective actions.	Evaluation by various metrics of the proposed model is not performed and the results are not given.
An Efficient Cloud Network Intrusion Detection System (Ghosh, Mandal, & Kumar, 2015)	DIDS	HIDS in hypervisor servers and NIDS at bottleneck position of the cloud network	Real time	Network packets, Behavior base, misuse base, system activities, audit data	• Feature selection makes analysis of the IDS fast, accurate and saves memory storage. • It has high accuracy than KNN and ANN, when they are used as classifier modules separately.	• For evaluating the performance of the proposed IDS, others evaluation criteria are not used like detection rate, false alarms rate, precision, Recall and F-value. • The interest of use of Artificial Neural network misuse classifier for classifying abnormal packets is not shown. • By blocking IP of a user if the number of intrusions from that IP exceeds the threshold value, the IDS can block IP of legitimate user in case of IP spoofing attack.
Network Intrusion Detection in Cloud (Modi, 2015)	NIDS	on each host machine of Cloud	Real time	Virtual network traffic, Known attack patterns, Network traffic profile log, Central log of intrusion Alerts.	• It can detect known and unknown attacks. • It identifies distrusted attacks by means of severity calculation module of proposed NIDS • In other works, for identifying the distributed attack n × (n − 1) messages are exchanged between sensors (n is number of sensors), while in proposed approach, only n messages are exchanged since each alert is stored in central log. • It reduces computational cost by applying signature detection prior to anomaly detection. • It can detect 96% non-distributed and 95% distributed attacks in real time.	• The proposed IDS does not monitor physical network that can be source of insider attacks which may compromise host machines and VM running over them. • The central log server presents a point of failure of the proposed architecture that must be protected by means of Host IDS. • The centralized approach of central log base represents a single point of failure.
Integrated intrusion detection approach for cloud computing (Ambikavathi & Srivatsa, 2016)	DIDS	H-IDS deployed at each VM and N-IDS placed the entry point of the cloud network.	Real time	User activities, audit data, system logs, signature database, network packets, anomaly database, alerts from both H-IDS and N-IDS.	• Integrating H-IDS and N-IDS in cloud allows monitoring the attacks initiated internally and externally. • Combination of both SD and AD detection method in each IDS improves detection accuracy.	• Experimental results are not given. • Performance evaluation of the proposed system by means of evaluation criteria such detection rate and alarm rate was not done.

continued on following page

Table 3. Continued

Work	IDS Type	Position	Detection Time	Data Source	Characteristics/Strengths	Limitations/ Challenges
Collaborative IDS framework for cloud (Singh, Patel, Borisaniya, & Modi, 2016)	NIDS	At each cloud cluster (NIDS sensors in all node controllers on the virtual bridge, and a NIDS on separate connected with the cluster) and a correlation unit is placed in the best cluster selected by using Bully algorithm	Real time	Captured packets, network traffic base, knowledge base	• Anomaly detection system proposed (Decision Tree (DT) + Support Vector Machine (SVP)) outperforms both SVM and DT in terms of accuracy, computation time, and false alarms. • Automatic Generating of Snort signature for frequent detected unknown attacks to keep knowledge base up-to-date.	The Centralized approach adopted for correlation Unit is less scalable. The limitations of Bully algorithm adopted are the number of stages to decide the new leader and the huge number of messages exchanged due to the broad-casting of election and OK messages. In contract, Modified Bully algorithm is more efficient than the Bully algorithm with fewer messages passing and fewer stages (Soundarabai, Sahai, Thriveni, Venugopal, & Patnaik, 2013).
CloudIDS: Cloud Intrusion Detection Model (Ahmad, Idris, & Kama, 2017)	DIDS	At each Cloud node (hypervisor) and at NIDS sensor	Real time	Knowledge base, anomaly database, state of guest cloud, captured packets, antigens and signals	The experiments show that this Cloud IDS was able to detect attempts to attack the Cloud environment.	It achieves weak detection rate and moderate precision which are 59.86% and 79.43% respectively.
An efficient fuzzy self-classifying clustering based framework for cloud security (Raja, Jaiganesh, & Ramaiah, 2017)	Not specified	Between Consumers and IaaS layer of a Cloud platform	Real time	Cloud Intrusion Detection dataset, consumer's activity patterns, fuzzy rulebase	• The proposed model attains 99.31% of Detection Accuracy (DA) during training phase and 99.26% of DA during testing phase. • It outperforms three other CIDS; K means clustering based CIDS, modified K means clustering based CIDS and self constructing clustering based CIDS.	To evaluate the performance of proposed IDS, alarm rate (FPR) and Detection rate (DR) are not considered, whereas, they are important performance criteria for an IDS.

of Cloud based IDS. Then, we have presented different intrusion detection techniques used by IDS in a comprehensive and illustrated way, in the form of figure and definitions that are helpful to in easy understanding of the whole scenario of cloud computing. A detailed description of various types of IDS in cloud environment is also provided. Finally, we have analyzed some latest research works that have been proposed to enhance the cloud security using IDS. The analysis shows that although different IDS techniques help in detection of intrusions, but they don't give complete security. The hybrid intrusion detection approach is certainly the best detection technique used by the IDS, but the most Cloud based IDS (CIDS) don't take in consideration the performance challenges of the cloud computing. So, to have an effective and efficient CIDS, we recommend use the hybrid approach to detect intrusions and satisfy both security issues and performance challenges of cloud computing.

REFERENCES

Ahmad, A., Idris, N. B., & Kama, M. N. (2017). CloudIDS: Cloud intrusion detection model inspired by dendritic cell mechanism. *International Journal of Communication Networks and Information Security*, *9*(1), 67–75.

Al-Shdaifat, B., Alsharafat, W. S., & El-bashir, M. (2015). Applying hopfield artificial network and simulating annealing for cloud intrusion detection. *Journal of Information Security Research*, *6*(2), 49–53.

Alharkan, T., & Martin, P. (2012). Idsaas: Intrusion detection system as a service in public clouds. In *Proceedings of the 12th IEEE/ACM International Symposium on Cluster, Cloud and Grid Computing (CCGrid)* (pp. 686-687). Ottawa, Canada: IEEE. 10.1109/CCGrid.2012.81

Aljawarneh, S. A. (2011). Cloud security engineering: Avoiding security threats the right way. *International Journal of Cloud Applications and Computing*, *1*(2), 64–70. doi:10.4018/ijcac.2011040105

Aljawarneh, S. A., Moftah, R. A., & Maatuk, A. M. (2016). Investigations of automatic methods for detecting the polymorphic worms signatures. *Future Generation Computer Systems*, *60*, 67–77. doi:10.1016/j.future.2016.01.020

Ambikavathi, C., & Srivatsa, S. K. (2015). Improving virtual machine security through intelligent intrusion detection system. *Journal of Computing Science and Engineering: JCSE*, *6*(2), 33–39.

Ambikavathi, C., & Srivatsa, S.K. (2016). Integrated intrusion detection approach for cloud computing. *Indian Journal of Science and Technology Computing*, *9*(22), 1-5.

Aminanto, M. E., HakJu, K. I. M., Kyung-Min, K. I. M., & Kwangjo, K. I. M. (2017). Another fuzzy anomaly detection system based on ant clustering algorithm. *IEICE Transactions on Fundamentals of Electronics Communications and Computer Sciences*, *E100-A*(1), 176–183.

Bakshi, A., & Dujodwala, Y. B. (2010). Securing cloud from ddos attacks using intrusion detection system in virtual machine. In *Proceedings of Second International Conference on Communication Software and Networks* (pp.260-264). Singapore: IEEE. 10.1109/ICCSN.2010.56

Chiba, Z., Abghour, N., Moussaid, K., omri, A. E., & Rida, M. (2016). A cooperative and hybrid network intrusion detection framework in cloud computing based on snort and optimized back propagation neural network. *Procedia Computer Science*, *83*, 1200–1206. doi:10.1016/j.procs.2016.04.249

Denial-of-service attack. (2017). Retrieved from Wikipedia: https://en.wikipedia.org/wiki/Denial-of-service_attack

Dhage, S. N., Meshram, B. B., Rawat, R., Padawe, S., Paingaokar, M., & Misra, A. (2011). Intrusion detection system in cloud computing environment. *In Proceedings of International Conference and Workshop on Emerging Trends in Technology (ICWET)* (pp.235-239). New York, NY: Association for Computing Machinery (ACM). 10.1145/1980022.1980076

Dildar, M. S., Khan, N., Abdullah, J. B., & Khan, A. S. (2017). Effective way to defend the hypervisor attacks in cloud computing. In *Proceedings of 2nd IEEE International Conference on Anti-Cyber Crimes (ICACC)* (pp.154-159). Abha, Saudi Arabia: IEEE. 10.1109/Anti-Cybercrime.2017.7905282

Duncan, A., Creese, S., & Goldsmith, M. (2014). An overview of insider attacks in cloud computing. *Concurrency and Computation*, *27*(12), 2964–2981. doi:10.1002/cpe.3243

Ghosh, P., Mandal, A. K., & Kumar, R. (2015). An efficient network intrusion detection system. In J. Mandal, S. Satapathy, M. Kumar Sanyal, P. Sarkar, & A. Mukhopadhyay (Eds.), *Information systems design and intelligent applications* (pp. 91–99). New Delhi, India: Springer.

Gupta, B. B., & Badve, O. P. (2017). Taxonomy of dos and ddos attacks and desirable defense mechanism in a cloud computing environment. *Neural Computing & Applications*, *28*(12), 3655–3682. doi:10.100700521-016-2317-5

Gupta, S., & Kumar, P. (2015). Immediate system call sequence based approach for detecting malicious program executions in cloud environment. *Wireless Personal Communications*, *81*(1), 405–425. doi:10.100711277-014-2136-x

Iqbal, S., Kiah, M. L. M., Dhaghighi, B., Hussain, M., Khan, S., Khan, M. K., & Choo, K. R. (2017). On cloud security attacks: A taxonomy and intrusion detection and prevention as a service. *Journal of Network and Computer Applications*, *74*, 98–120. doi:10.1016/j.jnca.2016.08.016

Jouini, M., & Ben Arfa Rabai, L. (2014). Surveying and analyzing security problems in cloud computing environments. In *Proceedings of Tenth IEEE International Conference on Computational Intelligence and Security (CIS)* (pp. 689-693). Kunming, China: IEEE. 10.1109/CIS.2014.169

Kashif, M., & Sellapan, P. (2012). Security threats/attacks present in cloud environment. *International Journal of Computer Science and Network Security*, *12*(12), 107–114.

Kene, S. G., & Theng, D. P. (2015). A review on intrusion detection techniques for cloud computing and security challenges. In *Proceedings of IEEE 2nd International Conference on Electronics and Communication Systems (ICECS 2015)* (pp. 227-232). Coimbatore, India: IEEE. 10.1109/ECS.2015.7124898

Kenneth, V. S. (2010). *A comprehensive framework for securing virtualized data centers*. Retrieved from http://virtualization.info/en/news/2010/12/paper-a-comprehensive-framework-for-securing-virtualized-data-center.html

Khaldi, A., & Karoui, K., & Ben Ghezala, H. (2014). Framework to detect and repair distributed intrusions based on mobile agent in hybrid cloud. In *Proceedings of the International Conference on Parallel and Distributed Processing Techniques and Applications (PDPTA'14)* (pp. 471-476). Las Vegas, NV: CSREA Press.

Khatri, J. K., & Khilari, G. (2015). Advancement in virtualization based intrusion detection system in cloud environment. *International Journal of Science Engineering and Technology Research*, *4*(5), 1510–1514.

Lekha, J., & Ganapathi, P. (2017). Detection of illegal traffic pattern using hybrid improved cart and multiple extreme learning machine approach. *International Journal of Communication Networks and Information Security*, *9*(2), 164–171.

Macro. (2009, August 9). *Black hat presentation demo vids: Amazon* [series of video files]. Retrieved from https://www.sensepost.com/blog/2009/blackhat-presentation-demo-vids-amazon/

Manthira, S. M., & Rajeswari, M. (2014). Virtual host based intrusion detection system for cloud. *IACSIT International Journal of Engineering and Technology*, *5*(6), 5023–5029.

Martin, L. (2010). *Trust and security to shape government cloud adoption*. Retrieved from http://www.lockheedmartin.com/content/dam/lockheed/data/corporate/documents/Cloud-Computing-White-Paper.pdf

Massachusetts Institute of Technology Lincoln Laboratory. (2016). Intrusion detection attacks database [Data file]. Retrieved from https://www.ll.mit.edu/ideval/docs/attackDB.html#u2r

Mehmood, Y., Habiba, U., Shibli, M. A., & Masood, R. (2013). Intrusion detection system in cloud computing: Challenges and opportunities. In *Proceedings of 2nd National Conference on Information Assurance (NCIA)* (pp. 59-66). Rawalpindi, Pakistan: IEEE. 10.1109/NCIA.2013.6725325

Mehmood, Y., Shibli, M. A., Kanwal, A., & Masood, R. (2015). Distributed intrusion detection system using mobile agents in cloud computing environment. In *Proceedings of EEE 2015 Conference on Information Assurance and Cyber Security (CIACS)* (pp.1-8). Rawalpindi, Pakistan: IEEE. 10.1109/CIACS.2015.7395559

Mishra, P., Pilli, E. S., Varadharajan, V., & Tupakula, U. (2017). PSI-netvisor: Program semantic aware intrusion detection at network and hypervisor layer in cloud. *Journal of Intelligent & Fuzzy Systems, 32*(4), 2909–2921. doi:10.3233/JIFS-169234

Modi, C., Patel, D., Borisaniya, B., Patel, H., Patel, A., & Rajarajan, M. (2012a). A survey of intrusion detection techniques in cloud. *Journal of Network and Computer Applications, 36*(1), 42–57. doi:10.1016/j.jnca.2012.05.003

Modi, C. N. (2015). Network intrusion detection in cloud computing. In N. R. Shetty, N. H. Prasad, & N. Nalini (Eds.), *Emerging Research in Computing, Information, Communication and Applications* (pp. 289–296). New Delhi, India: Springer India. doi:10.1007/978-81-322-2550-8_28

Modi, C. N., & Acha, K. (2016). Virtualization layer security challenges and intrusion detection/prevention systems in cloud computing: A comprehensive review. *The Journal of Supercomputing, 73*(3), 1192–1234. doi:10.100711227-016-1805-9

Modi, C. N., & Patel, D. (2013). A novel hybrid-network intrusion detection system (H-NIDS) in cloud computing. In *Proceedings of IEEE Symposium on Computational Intelligence in Cyber Security (CICS)* (pp. 23-30). Singapore: IEEE. 10.1109/CICYBS.2013.6597201

Modi, C. N., Patel, D. R., Patel, A., & Muttukrishnan, R. (2012b). Bayesian classifier and snort based network intrusion system in cloud computing. In *Proceedings of Third International Conference on Computing, Communication and Networking Technologies. (ICCCNT 2012)* (pp. 1-7). Coimbatore, India: IEEE. 10.1109/ICCCNT.2012.6396086

Modi, C. N., Patel, D. R., Patel, A., & Rajarajan, M. (2012c). Integrating signature apriori based network intrusion detection system (NIDS) in cloud computing. *Procedia Technology, 6*, 905–912. doi:10.1016/j.protcy.2012.10.110

Muthukumar, B., & Rajendran, P. K. (2015). Intelligent intrusion detection system for private cloud environment. In J. Abawajy, S. Mukherjea, S. Thampi, & A. Ruiz-Martínez (Eds.), *Security in Computing and Communications* (pp. 54–65). Cham, Switzerland: Springer.

National Institute of Standards and Technology (NIST). (2001). Intrusion detection systems (Publication No. 800-31). Gaithersburg, MD: National Institute of Standards and Technology (NIST).

National Institute of Standards and Technology (NIST). (2007). Guide to intrusion detection and prevention systems (IDPS) (Publication No. 800-94). Gaithersburg, MD: National Institute of Standards and Technology (NIST).

National Institute of Standards and Technology (NIST). (2011). The NIST definition of cloud computing (Publication No. 800-145). Gaithersburg, MD: National Institute of Standards and Technology (NIST).

Oktay, U., & Sahingoz, O. K. (2013). Proxy network intrusion detection system for cloud computing. In *Proceedings of International Conference on Technological Advances in Electrical, Electronics and Computer Engineering (TAEECE)* (pp. 98-104). Konya, Turkey: IEEE. 10.1109/TAEECE.2013.6557203

Pandeeswari, N., & Kumar, G. (2015). Anomaly detection system in cloud environment using fuzzy clustering based ANN. *Mobile Networks and Applications, 21*(3), 494–505. doi:10.100711036-015-0644-x

Patel, A., Taghavi, M., Bakhtiyari, K., & Júnio, J. C. (2013). An intrusion detection and prevention system in cloud computing: A systematic overview. *Journal of Network and Computer Applications, 36*(1), 25–41. doi:10.1016/j.jnca.2012.08.007

Raja, S., Jaiganesh, M., & Ramaiah, S. (2017). An efficient fuzzy self-classifying clustering based framework for cloud security. *International Journal of Computational Intelligence Systems, 10*(1), 495–506. doi:10.2991/ijcis.2017.10.1.34

Rubens, P. (2010). *3 ways to secure your virtualized data center*. Retrieved from http://www.serverwatch.com/trends/article.php/3895846/3-Ways-to-Secure-Your-Virtualized Data-Center.htm

Sangeetha, S., Devi, B. G., Ramya, R., Dharani, M. K., & Sathya, P. (2015). Signature based semantic intrusion detection system on cloud. In J. Mandal, S. Satapathy, M. Kumar Sanyal, P. Sarkar, & A. Mukhopadhyay (Eds.), *Information Systems Design and Intelligent Applications* (pp. 657–666). New Delhi, India: Springer India. doi:10.1007/978-81-322-2250-7_66

Sangve, S. M., & Thool, R. C. (2017). ANIDS: anomaly network intrusion detection system using hierarchical clustering technique. In *Proceedings of the International Conference on Data Engineering and Communication Technology* (pp. 121-129). Pune, India: Springer. 10.1007/978-981-10-1675-2_14

Santoso, B. I., Idrus, M. R. S., & Gunawan, I. P. (2016). Designing network intrusion and detection system using signature-based method for protecting Openstack private cloud. In *Proceedings of IEEE 6th International Annual Engineering Seminar (InAES)* (pp. 61-66). Yogyakarta, Indonesia: IEEE. 10.1109/INAES.2016.7821908

Sengaphay, K., Saiyod, S., & Benjamas, N. (2016). Creating Snort-ids rules for detection behavior using multi-sensors in private cloud. In K. Kim & N. Joukov (Eds.), *Information Science and Applications (ICISA)* (pp. 589–601). Singapore: Springer. doi:10.1007/978-981-10-0557-2_58

Sharma, S., Gupta, A., & Agrawal, S. (2016). An intrusion detection system for detecting denial-of-service attack in cloud using artificial bee colony. In: S. Satapathy, Y. Bhatt, A. Joshi, & D. Mishra (Eds.), *Proceedings of the International Congress on Information and Communication Technology* (pp. 137-145). Singapore: Springer. 10.1007/978-981-10-0767-5_16

Singh, D., Patel, D., Borisaniya, B., & Modi, C. (2016). Collaborative ids framework for cloud. *International Journal of Network Security*, *18*(4), 699–709.

Soundarabai, P. B., Sahai, R., Thriveni, J., Venugopal, K. R., & Patnaik, L. M. (2013). Improved bully election algorithm for distributed systems. *International Journal of Information Processing*, *7*(4), 43–54.

Tabatabaefar, M., Miriestahbanati, M., & Gregoire, J. C. (2017). Network intrusion detection through artificial immune system. In *Proceedings of 2017 Annual IEEE International Systems Conference (SysCon)* (pp. 1-6). Montreal, Canada: IEEE. 10.1109/SYSCON.2017.7934751

Tesfahun, A., & Bhaskari, D. L. (2015). Effective hybrid intrusion detection system: A layered approach. *International Journal of Computer Network and Information Security*, *7*(3), 35–41. doi:10.5815/ijcnis.2015.03.05

Yurcik, W. (2002). Controlling intrusion detection systems by generating false positives: Squealing proof-of-concept. *In Proceedings of 27th Annual IEEE Conference on Local Computer Networks* (pp.134-135). Tampa, FL: IEEE. 10.1109/LCN.2002.1181776

Zeeshan, M., Javed, H., & Ullah, S. (2017). Discrete r-contiguous bit matching mechanism appropriateness for anomaly detection in wireless sensor networks. *International Journal of Communication Networks and Information Security*, *9*(2), 157–163.

Zhao, J. Z., & Huang, H. K. (2002). An intrusion detection system based on data mining and immune principles. In *Proceedings of IEEE International Conference on Machine Learning and Cybernetics* (Vol. 1, pp.524-528). Beijing, China: IEEE. 10.1109/ICMLC.2002.1176811

KEY TERMS AND DEFINITIONS

Accuracy: Can be defined as the proportion of the total number of the correct predictions to the actual test set size.

Detection Rate (DR): Also called as true positive rate (TPR), recall, or sensitivity. It is defined as the number of intrusion records detected as attacks by the IDS divided by the total number of intrusion records present in the test set.

False Negative (FN): Are attack events incorrectly classified as normal events.

False Positive (FP): Normal events being classified as attacks.

False Positive Rate (FPR): Also called false alarm rate (FAR), is the ratio of the number of legitimate instances detected as attack instances divided by total normal (legitimate) instances included in the test set. If this value is consistently elevated, it causes the administrator to intentionally disregard the system warnings, which makes the system enter into a dangerous status. Thus, it should be as minimum as possible.

Precision: It indicates the percentage of intrusions that have occurred, and the IDS detects them correctly. It is calculated by the number of correctly classified positive (intrusion) examples divided by the number of examples labeled by the system as positive.

Snort: It is a popular open source IDS that uses a signature-based approach for detecting attacks. Snort is free, widely used, can run on multiple platforms (i.e., .GN U/Linux, Windows), configurable, and is constantly updated. It captures network data packets and checks their content with the predefined known attack patterns for any correlation (pattern matching process). The detection engine of Snort allows registering, alerting, and responding to any known attack. Snort in inline mode is most used to prevent system from known attacks.

Suricata: It is an open source next generation intrusion detection and prevention engine that can be used to monitor events in the Cloud and detect attacks. Suricata has different modes that can be used, but the main function of Suricara for IDS in networks is capturing all incoming packets, analyzing these packets, and finally, giving alert if a packet matches the configured rules.

True Negative (TN): Events that are actually normal and are successfully labeled as normal.

True Positive (TP): Events that are actually attacks and are successfully labeled as attacks.

This research was previously published in Security and Privacy in Smart Sensor Networks edited by Yassine Maleh, Abdellah Ezzati, and Mustapha Belaissaoui, pages 253-283, copyright year 2018 by Information Science Reference (an imprint of IGI Global).

Chapter 4
Cloud-Based Platforms and Infrastructures:
Provisioning Physical and Virtual Networks

Marcus Tanque
Independent Researcher, USA

ABSTRACT

Cloud computing consists of three fundamental service models: infrastructure-as-a-service, platform-as-a service and software-as-a-service. The technology "cloud computing" comprises four deployment models: public cloud, private cloud, hybrid cloud and community cloud. This chapter describes the six cloud service and deployment models, the association each of these services and models have with physical/virtual networks. Cloud service models are designed to power storage platforms, infrastructure solutions, provisioning and virtualization. Cloud computing services are developed to support shared network resources, provisioned between physical and virtual networks. These solutions are offered to organizations and consumers as utilities, to support dynamic, static, network and database provisioning processes. Vendors offer these resources to support day-to-day resource provisioning amid physical and virtual machines.

INTRODUCTION

In recent years, cloud computing has transformed the way information technology organizations and consumers conduct business. This technology revolution is attributable to the Information Technology (IT) democratization of physical and virtual platforms or network infrastructure solutions. Cloud computing is a pervasive technology that many organizations and consumers continue to adopt. In the cloud, deployment models are adopted as integrated solution architecture to interface with other cloud-based technologies: virtualization, cyber-physical systems, data analytics, big data, Internet of things, artificial-predictive intelligence, cybersecurity. In this chapter other useful solutions required to make more efficient the production time, enhance productivity and improve operation's performance are discussed. The integration of cloud computing with other technology solutions has improved the consumption of

DOI: 10.4018/978-1-5225-8176-5.ch004

technology services i.e., forecasting, aggregating hardware and software performance for emergency response time, and the adoption of innovative business models. Vendors examine the transformation of traditional IT systems to leading-edge cloud-based, as a complex process for enhancing involved policy implementation. The adoption of cloud solutions is often supported by analytical and practical procedures needed to balance all-inclusive cloud implementation processes (Buyya, Ranjan, Rodrigo, & Calheiros, 2010; Gartner, 2012; Buyya, Ramamohanarao, Leckie, Calheiros, Dastjerdi, & Versteeg). In recent times, the provisioning of cloud service and deployment models has advanced significantly. Despite vendor's adoption of database-as-a-Service/DBaaS, the industry has developed assorted methods to support enterprise IT network infrastructure solutions (Ko, Ahn, & Shehab, 2009; Vozmediano, Montero, & Llorente, 2011). Aside from these developments, more security solutions are developed to protect organizations and consumers' IT resources (Stanton et al., 2005; Ko, Ahn, & Shehab, 2009; Al-hazmi, & Shami, 2014). IT experts continue to research on measures to enable the integration of native computer solutions with cloud computing systems i.e., hardware, software, data and user-users (Grance & Mell, 2011; Ross, 2010; Buyya, Ranjan, Rodrigo, & Calheiros, 2010; Ko, Ahn, & Shehab, 2009; Vozmediano, Montero, & Llorente, 2011). The transformation of these solutions is vital for leveraging day-to-day IT operations and provide essential strategies organizations need for adopting, configuring and deploying integrated computer systems (Lease, 2005). The adoption and implementation of cloud-based solutions are key of deploying IT resources for diverse enterprises (Grance & Mell, 2011; Gentry, 2009). In general, Service level agreements (SLAs) are fundamental business methods every organization would require, to assess its economic growth (Alhazmi & Shami, 2014). Lacking proper security standards commonly can affect the adoption/deployment of cloud computing resources. This could also expose network infrastructure solutions to cyber related vulnerabilities (Lease, 2005; Buyya, Ranjan, Rodrigo, & Calheiros, 2010; Gartner, 2012; Gartner, 2009; Alhazmi & Shami, 2014). Vendors must to develop customized solutions, to properly mitigate malicious cyber-attacks. Besides, this chapter aims to emphasize on areas affecting the virtualization and provisioning of cloud-based services. These services comprise: IaaS, SaaS, PaaS, DBaaS, public cloud, private cloud and hybrid cloud. The three NIST certified cloud computing services discussed in this chapter are: PC, PC and HC (Ross, 2010; Gartner, 2012; Amazon, 2012; Bruening & Treacy, 2009; Ko, Ahn, & Shehab, 2009; Alhazmi & Shami, 2014).

BACKGROUND

For nearly a decade, industry has implemented XaaS or EaaS as "anything/everything-as-a-service" service model. XaaS and/or EaaS is an emerging cloud service model developed to interact with related technology-based services and business processes. This cohesive model is designed to interact with cloud computing services: infrastructure-as-a-service, platform-as-a-service and software-as-a-service. These solutions are carefully selected to interface with the following deployment models: public cloud, private cloud, hybrid cloud and community cloud (Grance & Mell, 2011). The need for industry to adopt XaaS/EaaS is to supplement organization and customer's cloud platform specifications (Grance & Mell, 2011; Toosi, Calheiros, & Buyya, 2014). XaaS/EaaS is defined as a collection of cloud services: IaaS, IaaS and SaaS. This term includes other industry-based cloud services i.e., communication as a service, monitoring-as-a-Service. Vendors have developed software/hardware products and related XaaS capabilities/services to interact with related service-centric solutions (Buyya, Ranjan, Rodrigo, & Calheiros, 2010; Toosi, Calheiros, & Buyya, 2014). This include a variety of capabilities needed to enable XaaS/EaaS solutions as delivered utilities (Toosi, Calheiros, & Buyya, 2014). Vendors designed XaaS/EaaS solutions to serve the customer's needs, address any deficiencies between legacy network infrastructure solutions and state-of-the-art cloud business models (Buyya, Ramamohanarao, Leckie, Calhieros, Dastjerdi, & Versteeg, 2015). Vendors define public cloud as pay-as-you-go or pay-per-use model. XaaS features consist of (Toosi, Calheiros, & Buyya, 2014; Alhazmi & Shami, 2014):

- High Scalability
- Multitenancy
- Online Provisioning
- Automated Provisioning
- Try and Purchase
- Device Independence (e.g., which in numerous instances, allows users to acquire software despite the type of device they are using)
- Location Independence
- Term-based Billing
- Pay-per-use Models

XaaS/EaaS services consist of: (Buyya, Ranjan, Rodrigo, & Calheiros, 2010; Gartner, 2012; Toosi, Calheiros, & Buyya, 2014)

- **Business Process**: Offered by third party cloud or managed service providers
- **Communication**: Type of service offerings Cisco, Hewlett-Packard, Microsoft, usually deliver to many customers, as a service utility
- **Identify**: Cloud services that (OpenID, Google, FB, Salesforce), deliver to many clients
- **Security**: Defined as Symantec cloud services deployed to enterprise IT infrastructure solutions
- **Software**: Delivered by Salesforce, Workday and Netsuite
- **Database**: Service made available to customers (e.g., MongoDB, Clustrix)
- **Platform**: Cloud services provided by VMforce, Google AppEngine, Salesforces
- **Infrastructure**: Provided by Amazon, Rackspace
- **Monitor**: Often delivered by Logic Monitor

XaaS/EaaS model is a business enabler offering agile cloud solutions to support organization and customer's requirements as well as enhance business values (Buyya, Ramamohanarao, Leckie, Calhieros, Dastjerdi, & Versteeg, 2015). These characteristics are based on cloud-based platforms, infrastructure solutions and/or process elements required for supporting dynamic, static, network and database provisioning processes (Buyya, Ranjan, Rodrigo, & Calheiros, 2010; Buyya, Ramamohanarao, Leckie, Calhieros, Dastjerdi, & Versteeg, 2015; Toosi, Calheiros, & Buyya, 2014). The process also redefines the crucial method for multi-tier server operation, virtualization, sustainability, scalability and load balancing. Analytical and responsive procedures are needed to support these processes when deployed to the cloud. The provisioning of these resources has altered the way physical and virtual machines frequently interface, distribute and process data (Ross, 2010; Gartner, 2012; Amazon, 2012; Lease, 2005; Stanton et al., 2005; Alhazmi & Shami, 2014). Besides, this chapter explains different concepts of cloud computing service and deployment models, benefits and limitations. Thereby the manuscript aims to provide measures for supporting the adoption of cloud architecture solutions in support of the public and private sector. The chapter also explains the benefits and limitations cloud computing presents, to organizations, consumers, data center evolutions & trends, continuous monitoring of network infrastructure services (Lease, 2005; Stanton et al., 2005). These cloud-based solutions are selected to provide optimal research directions and recommendations for the body of knowledge (Buyya, Ranjan, Rodrigo, & Calheiros, 2010; Buyya, Ramamohanarao, Leckie, Calhieros, Dastjerdi, & Versteeg, 2015). The improvement of storage, data, protection and privacy preservation, yet has elevated interest among software developers, IT engineers and management (Lease, 2005; Toosi, Calheiros, & Buyya, 2014; Messmer, 2009). These analyses are associated with multidisciplinary technical procedures. These processes are developed to minimize and/ or address any security threats, affecting the public and private sector (Grance & Mell, 2011). Such level of threats can influence how organizations and customers conduct business (Stanton et al., 2005; Lease, 2005; Ko, Ahn, & Shehab, 2009).

MAIN FOCUS OF THE CHAPTER

The chapter focuses on topics affecting the provisioning of cloud computing platform solutions (Buyya, Ranjan, Rodrigo, & Calheiros, 2010; Gartner, 2012; Alhazmi, & Shami, 2014). Each of these sections/ subsections are viewed as accentuated areas supporting service and deployment models. The chapter also different aspects such as the database systems, virtualization technology, security techniques and how physical and virtual systems can easily scale (Ross, 2010; Buyya, Ranjan, Rodrigo, & Calheiros, 2010; Buyya, Ramamohanarao, Leckie, Calhieros, Dastjerdi, & Versteeg, 2015). Cloud technology solutions are key factors affecting the provisioning of physical, virtual server infrastructure and data (Lease, 2005; Stanton et al., 2005; Alhazmi & Shami, 2014).

Cloud Architecture Models and Key Areas of Functionality

Cloud-based technology is an emerging technology built with key capability solutions to increase productivity (Stanton et al., 2005). Cloud-based solutions consist of: cloud-based services, dynamic and static provisioning. These solutions are frequently deployed to increase organization and consumer's productivity (Grance & Mell, 2011; Messmer, 2009). The following is a set of cloud architectural models and functional concepts (Gartner, 2009; Gartner, 2012; Buyya, Ramamohanarao, Leckie, Calhieros, Dastjerdi, & Versteeg, 2015):

- **Amazon ECS**: Simple storage and relational databases services for enterprises
- **Cloud Service Alliance**: Enterprise security based
- **Cisco**: IT data centers and networks
- **IBM**: Cloud service management
- **Storage Networking Industry Association**: IT cloud storage
- **Windows Azure**: Microsoft data center applications

For many years, cloud computing technology has played a major role in fulfilling IT organizations and consumers requirements. Below are commercial benefits cloud computing offers to various organizations and customers. These services are provided by major vendors (Alhazmi & Shami, 2014):

- **Amazon** (e.g., Amazon EC2)
  - *Infrastructure-as-a-Service*
- **Microsoft** (i.e., Window Azure, Google App Engine)
  - *Platform-as-a-Service*
- **Google** (e.g., Google Apps)
  - *Software-as-a-Service*
- **SalesForce** (e.g., SalesForce.com)
  - *Software-as-a-Service*

Virtualization and Migration

The term "virtualization" was originally introduced in 1960s. At that juncture this term "virtualization" was adopted, to define virtual machines also known as pseudo-machines. The activities executed by virtualization technology are called platform or server virtualization. Vendors describe virtualization as a technology developed to support software, operating systems, performing parallel activity(ies), independently from other programs and/or applications. In general, platform virtualization is described as a process through which various activities are performed by the computer hardware over a host and/ or control program. In platform virtualization, a computer software is responsible for assigning a host machine. As a consequence, the role host machine is to emulate events within the network infrastructure environments. In platform virtualization, VMs are designed to perform several process activities for the guest software, despite independent ability these machines have, to support any functions/requests beyond the user's applications. Thereby host computers are designed to provide operating systems with a wide -range of activities. In VM environment the software component is responsible for directly perform any required computing activities. These applications often run on a physical machine. There is a set of strict registration cloud administrators must enforce when initiating requests/transactions between virtual and physical machines. The following functions: network access, display of any applications, keyboard request/related activities to disk storage are managed and restricted to various security levels e.g., those performed by host processor or system-memory (Oracle, 2016; Cisco, 2011; RedHat, 2016). All guest machines are restricted from retrieving computer applications or related peripheral devices. This includes any subclass of system built-in capabilities lacking hardware access policy for the virtualization host (Oracle, 2016; Cisco, 2011; RedHat, 2016). The following are important details involving virtualization technology as relate to IT organizations: server or hardware consolidation/migration, reduction of energy consumption/ratio, adequate control or inspection of VMs from assigned external entity, instead of internal administrator, who often are responsible for provisioning existing VMs without acquiring new hardware/software. These actions can be performed by relocating/migrating single/multiple VMs from physical to virtual environments, physical-to-physical, virtual-to-virtual, etc (Oracle, 2016; Cisco, 2011; RedHat, 2016). Vendors such as Red Hat, Cisco, Oracle have also adopted virtualization technology as a utility to support data centers/network infrastructure solutions. This includes the adoption of cutting-edge hypervisor hardware and software (Oracle, 2016; Cisco, 2011; RedHat, 2016).

The technology industry, refer to hypervisor as an interface application layer designed to support other hardware devices on the network i.e., server, storage, applications as well as related operating systems e.g., "guest" system (Oracle, 2016; Cisco, 2011). If associated activities are performed on computer/ machine residing in the same physical system environment, either the operating system or guest is described as a "host" computer. For many years, there has been false technical impression in the public and public sector which led to whether the process of virtualizing machines between physical to virtual environments is cost-effective or not (Oracle, 2016; Cisco, 2011; RedHat, 2016). Such conjectures have concluded that virtualization can be a complex solution to implement. Since then, vendors have encouraged decision makers to conduct a wide-ranging analysis of alternatives on IT organizations' anticipated return-on-investment/ROI, prior to deciding whether it is reasonable migrating their physical resources i.e., applications, storages, servers and database systems to virtual environments (Cisco, 2011; Oracle, 2016; RedHat, 2016). Other studies similarly have provided cost savings benefits for virtualizing platforms and network infrastructure solutions from physical to virtual locations. When conducting the ROI analysis, decision makers should consider the following factors e.g., decide whether it is feasible making a compelling management decision, to support an organization's business requirements: less power consumption, minus maintenance, adequate lifecycle of installed software or applications, forecast cost association and space limitation. Similar studies have also confirmed that virtualization involves numerous procedures. These processes can be determined as follows (Oracle, 2016; Cisco, 2011; RedHat, 2016):

- **Full Virtualization**: The practice which includes hardware capabilities initiated by a single or various processor(s). This allows guest(s) operating systems to access resources running on the host physical system. Through this concept new virtual system(s) also can be created known as "virtual machines" (Oracle, 2016; Cisco, 2011; RedHat, 2016). VMs are designed to provide guest operating system(s) and support required to perform further activities, whether the guest VM systems are aware or not of any other instances running on a virtual environment. In Red Hat Enterprise Linux environment hypervisor(s) are designed to support full-virtualization events
- **Para-Virtualization**: A set of applications and information patterns, available to the virtualized guest system. This process requires modification of software running on a particular machine e.g., guest. The process generally allows the guest machine to consume para-virtualized settings. A complete Kernel is required in virtualized-environment e.g., Xen para virtualized guest system, drivers for the input/out devices (Oracle, 2016)
- **Software Virtualization**: There is a degree of limitation in virtualization technology, which consist of machine activities and performance degradation. This is attributable to binary translation/resolution forcing the system to perform leisurely. The Red Hat Enterprise Linux does not support software virtualization

Migration

Migration is a practice of relocating guest virtual systems from single-to-single or single-to-multiple host computers. This method requires that VMs often run in a simulated/physical environment. In VM environment the migration process involves (Oracle, 2016; Cisco, 2011; RedHat, 2016):

- **Off-Line Migration**: The guest virtual machine(s) does/do not perform its/their activities on the network, while the off-line migration is in progress. Any machine selected as part of the off-line migration must immediately be removed or its activities should be suspended from execution of normal operations within the network. The complete process of migration is thereafter performed by the image of virtual machines' memory, to assigned host destination machine(s) (Oracle, 2016; Cisco, 2011; RedHat, 2016). As a result, the designated VM restarts its activities, after the migration process is complete; in so doing deployed system(s) will automatically resume their typical operations. The memory attached to a particular VM will independently restart its activities within the network

- **Live Migration**: The process which begins by migrating an active VM from physical to virtual network environment or assigned destination host. Then the migration process is selected to move VM memory onto disk volumes residing in a particular machine (Oracle, 2016; Cisco, 2011; RedHat, 2016). During the migration process, live blocks are required to support all systems activities

Virtualization Security Features

For many years, both the public and private sectors have developed security solutions to protect physical and virtual machines. Listed are software security tools already available in industry for IT organizations use: SELinux, sVirt. Following are limitless advantages of migrating virtual machines: load balancing, upgrades of host machines, energy-saving, geographic relocation of VMs (Oracle, 2016; Cisco, 2011; RedHat, 2016).

Capacity Planning and Management

The need for planning and managing cloud-based services is crucial on how customers commonly adopt and/or deploy these models. The deployment of cloud services normally is designed to determine, how responsive computer processes can be (Buyya, Ranjan, Rodrigo, & Calheiros, 2010; Gartner, 2012). SLAs are key for an effective deployment of cloud technology solutions (Buyya, Ranjan, Rodrigo, & Calheiros, 2010; Buyya, Ramamohanarao, Leckie, Calheiros, Dastjerdi, & Versteeg, 2015; Gartner, 2012). The cloud capacity and infrastructure management encompass the following characteristics or models (Gartner, 2009; Gartner, 2012):

- Network Model
- Compute Model
- Storage Model
- Data Center Facilities
- Cloud Platform Capacity
- Demand Forecasting
- Procurement

Cloud computing has altered how IT and business resources are managed (Leighton, 2009). According to Gartner survey, cloud computing is a paradigm that advances IT and business operations (Gartner Hype-Cycle, 2012; Oracle, 2016). These resources are required to balance capital and operational expenditures. Infrastructure management and platform are indispensable when deploying IT resources (Price, 2008; Oracle, 2016; Cisco, 2011; Oracle, 2016). Quite the opposite, cloud computing is a technology developed for delivering software applications and processes, needed to support platform provisioning (Badger, Grance, Patt-Corner, & Voas, 201; Price, 2008; Alhazmi & Shami, 2014). Cloud computing services are designed to interact with virtualization technology: hypervisors, VMware, vSphere and Hyper-V provide resourceful, flexible management and load balancing for virtual machines (Oracle, 2016; Cisco, 2011). Commodity hardware and software appliances are fundamental cloud resources designed to support the enterprise deployment of cloud resources (Alhazmi, Abusharkh, Ban, & Shami, 2014). Both hardware and software solutions are designed to provide a flexible and efficient management between legacy and modern systems (Buyya, Ranjan, Rodrigo, & Calheiros, 2010; Grance & Mell, 2011; Buyya, Ramamohanarao, Leckie, Calhieros, Dastjerdi, & Versteeg, 2015).

In the 1990s vendors began adopting open-source software to support organization and consumer's operation requirements (Buyya, Ranjan, Rodrigo, & Calheiros, 2010; Gartner, 2012; Buyya, Ramamohanarao, Leckie, Calhieros, Dastjerdi, & Versteeg, 2015; Oracle, 2016). In consequence of deployment of open-source software as a product, now organizations have the option to acquire and customize desired applications, required to interact with other IT infrastructure capabilities (Lease, 2005; Grance & Mell, 2011; Alhazmi, et al, 2014). In part, integrated solutions are simplified applications designed to provisioning and enabling dynamic computer as well as server scalability (Lease, 2005; Alhazmi & Shami, 2014; Alhazmi & Shami, 2014; Oracle, 2016; Cisco, 2016). Server virtualization and infrastructure performance are technologies developed to provide self-regulating automation process, multi-tenancy and system resiliency for delivering results to the end-users. Network infrastructure solutions are deployed to provide data centers virtualized network resources, strengthen IT organizations' effectiveness and productivity (Grance & Mell, 2011; Bruening & Treacy, 2009; Oracle, 2016; Cisco, 2011; RedHat, 2016).

PROVISIONING PHYSICAL AND VIRTUAL NETWORKS

Physical and virtual networks concepts date back to traditional and interconnected complex systems deployed to various geographic locations. There are two types of virtual network provisioning: adaptive and initial virtual network provisioning (Oracle, 2016). Adaptive virtual network provisioning is the process of maintaining and managing agile computer resources residing on various network systems (Alhazmi & Shami, 2014; Oracle, 2016). This concept is adopted to support virtual network topologies required to parsing/distributing resources for various physical or virtual computer systems (Vaquero et al., 2009; Vouk, 2008; Chowdhury, Rahman, & Boutaba, 2012; Metzler, 2011; Oracle, 2016; Oracle, 2016; Cisco, 2011; RedHat, 2016).

Database Provisioning

Provisioning is a process that enables agility of IT systems for organizations and consumers. This method is designed to satisfy organizations and customers' requirements. Database provisioning consist of several network resources residing between physical and virtual machines (Badger et al., 2011; Garfinkel, & Shelat, 2003). Thus resource pooling is a major factor in the provisioning of cloud assets (Badger et al., 2011; Alhazmi & Shami, 2014). There are two types of provisioning (dynamic and static). Dynamic provisioning is a self-governing process developed to increase system capacity for multi-layer cloud-based applications. These applications allow for increased system performance (Sen & Sengupta, 2005; Garfinkel & Shelat, 2003; Alhazmi & Shami, 2014; RedHat, 2016). Despite various methods required to support the performance process for larger disk state, database provisioning remains a complex practice. Virtual machines can create a bottleneck when performing functional/intensive compute workload if not correctly configured (Biggs & Vidalis, 2009; Amazon, 2012). There is a difference between database and the legacy web server provisioning. Thereby the need for replicating large workload manually is one of the reasons why database provisioning has transformed from the traditional to automated concept (Badger et al., 2011; Alhazmi & Shami, 2014). A successful provisioning of database requires that system administrators, first define the amount of time required to replicate/synchronize disk state and imagine each replica online. This is attributable to the workload being processed and storage engine configuration (Sen & Sengupta, 2005; Bruening & Treacy, 2009; Alhazmi & Shami, 2014). The following areas are fundamentals for system administrators to know during database, network, dynamic, and static provisioning in the cloud (Biggs & Vidalis, 2009; Buyya, Ranjan, Rodrigo, & Calheiros, 2010; Gartner, 2012; Alhazmi & Shami, 2014; Oracle, 2016; RedHat, 2016; Cisco, 2011):

- When to provision
- How to provision
- Prototype implementation
- Evaluating public, private cloud, hybrid cloud, community cloud platforms

In database provisioning replication is a crucial concept that organizations and consumers must comply with. How data is backed up, restored and/or snapshot could determine the homogenous configuration of database systems in interconnected clusters (Biggs & Vidalis, 2009; Gartner, 2012; Buyya, Ranjan, Rodrigo, & Calheiros, 2010; Badger et al., 2011; Chor et al., 1998).

Network Function Virtualization

Network Function Virtualization (NFC) is a process that commonly manages and supports virtualized technology solutions. In NFV, middleboxes resources are distributed to various networks through software versa hardware-based solutions. In recent years, vendors have designed middleboxes technology to replace NFV (Chowdhury, Rahman, & Boutaba, 2012; Oracle, 2016). In essence, the software was developed to take precedency of provisioning network solutions through commoditized and hardware-based solutions (Chowdhury, Rahman, & Boutaba, 2012; Alhazmi, et al, 2014; Oracle, 2016). These functions are designed to reducing cost and providing responsive processes. Despite the fact much research has been conducted as part of NFV, cloud vendors have elected new technology solutions such as service functions chains and software-defined network solutions (Oracle, 2016; Alhazmi, & Shami, 2014). New investigations indicate that the number of middleboxes deployed to various networks i.e., Internet service providers and data centers parallels to that of physical routers dispersedly in the enterprise (Chowdhury, Rahman, & Boutaba, 2012; Oracle, 2016; Houidi et al., 2010).

Network Provisioning

Provisioning is a process that integrates network infrastructure solutions and streamlines the time system administrators need to deploy, configure, maintain and manage services within the multi-tenancy cloud environments. The main goals for network provisioning are (Oracle, 2016; Cisco, 2011; RedHat, 2016): Reducing latency, increasing throughput and allowing for effective, efficiency, automated and repeatable infrastructure management (Biggs & Vidalis, 2009; Leighon, 2009; Buyya, Ranjan, Rodrigo, & Calheiros, 2010; Oracle, 2016). In these scenarios, the traditional network security systems i.e., firewall, intrusion detection/protection systems, web application firewalls can be displayed as middleboxes (Alhazmi, et al, 2014; Oracle, 2016). The configuration of these systems frequently occurs inside and outside network boundaries. Attributable to continuous adoption of cloud computing technology, innovated network systems are deployed to support the migration of enterprise IT and related multi-tenancy solutions (Chowdhury, Rahman, & Boutaba, 2012; Alhazmi & Shami, 2014; Oracle, 2016). Both physical or virtual networks are designed to perform provisioning process of resources for user's specifications. In physical and virtual networks, the provisioning process involves (Alhazmi, et al, 2014; Chowdhury, Rahman, & Boutaba, 2012; Alhazmi & Shami, 2014; Oracle, 2016):

- Resource and Advertisement
- Resource Discovery and Matching
- Physical and Virtual Network Embedding
- Physical and Virtual Network Binding

Physical and virtual networks are generally deployed and managed as cloud computing technology solutions (Alhazmi & Shami, 2014). These technology solutions 'physical and virtual networks' are designed to satisfy the consumer and organization's requirements. Generally, these networks are divergently distributed via a dynamic provisioning process (Vaquero et al., 2009; Vouk, 2008; Houidi, Louati, Zeghlache, Papadimitriou, & Mathy, 2010). Such activities are attributable to asymmetrical deviations, which could conceivably affect the following: stream of traffics and physical assets. The below Figure 1 outlines different specifications of the virtual network provisioning (Chowdhury, Rahman, & Boutaba, 2012; Alhazmi, et al, 2014; Alhazmi & Shami, 2014; Houidi et al., 2010).

Service Function Chaining

Service Function Chaining (SFC) is a technology that still in its emerging phase. Generally, Service Function Chains (SFCs) are deployed to support the functionality of network devices: firewalls, load balancers are logical functioning (Chowdhury, Rahman, & Boutaba, 2012; Oracle, 2016; Houidi et al., 2010). By and large, SFCs are central technology solutions developed to defining and instantiating network systems as well as interacting with the network (Chowdhury, Rahman, & Boutaba, 2012; Oracle, 2016). SFCs provides data traffic flows through selected service functions. The delivery of end-to-end

Figure 1. Provisioning of virtual networks
Source: https://orbi.ulg.ac.be/bitstream/2268/126822/1/adaptive_embedding_VISA10.pdf

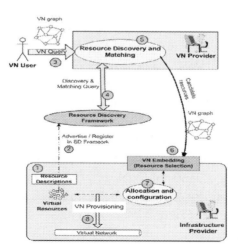

services can only be processed through the aid of several provision functions. Application-specific service functions are illustrated as hypertext transfer protocols/HTTP header manipulation (Alhazmi & Shami, 2014; Oracle, 2016). Tenants are responsible for delivering service functions (Chowdhury, Rahman, & Boutaba, 2012). This process is described as shared concept involving several groups or users assigned to a single or multiple networks (Vaquero et al., 2009; Vouk, 2008; Chowdhury, Rahman, & Boutaba, 2012; Alhazmi & Shami, 2014; Houidi et al., 2010).

Software-Defined Networking

This network function is a utility designed to streamline SFC embedded technologies (Oracle, 2016). In recent years, vendors have designed software-defined networking/SDN technology as technology to balance NFV and SFC features. The main purpose of this new technology discovery aim at providing efficiency for the flow of data being transported over end-to-end physical and virtual networks (Chowdhury, Rahman, & Boutaba, 2012; Oracle, 2016). In the cloud, NFV and SDN technology solutions are designed with flexible, responsive and sustainable solutions. These solutions are intended to guarantee that instances of virtual network functions are deployed into diverse enterprise IT infrastructures. The end-to-end paths are preconfigured within network systems, to expedite data flow through various network functions (Chowdhury, Rahman, & Boutaba, 2012; Alhazmi, et al, 2014; Houidi et al., 2010).

Network Virtualization Forces

System architects use network virtualization forces to re-examine assumptions when designing network topologies (Houidi et al., 2010). In virtualized network traffic flow and server performance occur faster than in usual external network hardware environment i.e., physical server network interface controller/card, physical switches and routers (Cisco, 2016). The ability to set up and modify virtualized network topologies may disrupt organizational structures dedicated to separate computer, storage and network management (Oracle, 2016; Cisco, 2011; Houidi et al., 2010).

Topology Dependencies

Topology dependencies are services required to deploy single or multiple networks. The process of various cloud services is often by specific, physical and virtual networks. These solutions are called hybrid network topologies. In the virtual local area network or vLANs the firewalls are deployed to normalize the flow of network traffic (Chowdhury, Rahman, & Boutaba, 2012; Alhazmi, et al, 2014). If a firewall is deployed or positioned on a particular network segment through the process of vLAN foundation, data flow is predetermined by the selected path required to balance the traffic flow in the direction of the firewall device. This topology dependence is needed to further enforce upon certain restrictions on functions such as service delivery mechanisms (Chowdhury, Rahman, & Boutaba, 2012; Alhazmi & Shami, 2014). Network operator is prevented from making use of its service resources or decreasing elasticity (Chowdhury, Rahman, & Boutaba, 2012; Houidi et al., 2010). New service functions, such as firewalls are designed with other collation of topology variations tagged to the front and back of each service function. This model allows for complex network changes and device configuration. If properly configured, the firewall will guarantee all traffics sent through meet certain security measures (Chowdhury, Rahman, & Boutaba, 2012; Alhazmi, et al, 2014; Oracle, 2016).

Vendor's Contribution

In recent years, the public and private sectors have experienced seismic shift in operation's activities. Business owners are now able to deploy additional cloud services with better cost-savings. Customers prefer to adopt leased, customized commodity hardware, and application appliances in IT infrastructure environment (Amazon, 2012; Buyya, Ranjan, Rodrigo, & Calheiros, 2010; Buyya, Ramamohanarao, Leckie, Calhieros, Dastjerdi, & Versteeg, 2015; Badger et al., 2011).

CLOUD COMPUTING

The National Institute for Standards and Technology, describes cloud computing as (Badger, Grance, Patt-Corner, & Voas, 2011; Grance & Mell, 2011; Buyya, Ramamohanarao, Leckie, Calhieros, Dastjerdi, & Versteeg, 2015): "a model for enabling convenient, on-demand network access to a shared pool of configurable computing resources (e.g., networks, servers, storage, applications and services) that can be provisioned and released with economical management efforts or service interaction". The advancement of cloud computing solution architecture comprises the following asymmetrical process: networks, inter-networks "Internet", world wide web, grid computing and cloud computing ((Badger, Grance, Patt-Corner, & Voas, 2011). See Figure 2.

BENEFITS OF PUBLIC AND PRIVATE CLOUD COMPUTING SERVICES

In the public and private sector cloud service providers and/or managed service providers' responsibilities aim to provide key solutions for supporting IT organizations and consumers' day-to-day operations. These service/product offerings are based on selected paradigms organizations and consumers require to achieve business or market demands. Public cloud comprises larger scale services focusing on broader technical standards such as open source solutions (Buyya, Ranjan, Rodrigo, & Calheiros, 2010; Buyya, Ramamohanarao, Leckie, Calhieros, Dastjerdi, & Versteeg, 2015; Pearson, & Charlesworth, 2009; Torry Harris, n.d.). Public cloud services focus on rapid and effective deployment. Cloud service providers are responsible for hardware maintenance and application pooling in support of platform deployment and infrastructure delivery service (Buyya, Ranjan, Rodrigo, & Calheiros, 2010; Gartner, 2015; Gartner, 2012; Blaze et al., 2009). Private cloud services are deployed to specific organizations, where services are directed to organization's capabilities and business trends (Pearson & Charlesworth, 2009; Oracle,

Figure 2. Cloud computing evolution and trends
Source: http://ir.lib.uwo.ca/cgi/viewcontent.cgi?article=3713&context=etd

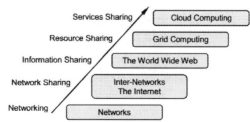

2016; Cisco, 2011; RedHat, 2016). Organizations have far-reaching proprietorship of private cloud and their services (Torry Harris, n.d.). This allows private cloud service providers to specifically tailor their services to conform with customer's requirements. Despite the need for more bandwidth, organizations and consumers are doubting of deploying resources to the cloud, due to security and privacy (Buyya, Ranjan, Rodrigo, & Calheiros, 2010; Buyya, Ramamohanarao, Leckie, Calhieros, Dastjerdi, & Versteeg, 2015; Zhang & Joshi, 2009; Torry Harris, n.d.).

Cloud-Based Architecture

Cloud computing is one of the fastest growing technology developed to support cloud-based service and delivery models (Lease, 2005). The need for resource-sharing, scalability, responsiveness, availability, real-time disposition of resources in the cloud is essential. This process has significant impact on the way IT organizations determine their operations, system performances and upgrades (Ross, 2010; Buyya, Ranjan, Rodrigo, & Calheiros, 2010). Each of these components can be managed, provisioned, deployed and decommissioned through utility-based consumption and allocation model. Cloud architectures are designed to support compute modules (Sen & Sengupta, 2005). These solutions are deployed to data centers for enhancing performance and streamlining provision time as well as restrict access to unauthorized individuals (Buyya, Ramamohanarao, Leckie, Calhieros, Dastjerdi, & Versteeg, 2015; Gartner, 2012; Buyya, Ranjan, Rodrigo, & Calheiros, 2010). There are six key cloud technology features that describe the resource management between cloud services and legacy computing systems: (CSA Security Guidance, 2009)

- Abstraction of Infrastructure(s)
- Resource Democratization
- Service-oriented Architecture
- Elasticity
- Dynamism
- Utility Model of Consumption, Allocation

The basics of cloud-based architecture discussed in this chapter are envisioned to leverage cloud deployment models (Lease, 2005). Cloud deployments models are designed to integrate resources and maintain some level of data provisioning with assigned service models (i.e., IaaS, PaaS, SaaS, DaaS). These analytical solutions entail (Lease, 2005; Buyya, Ramamohanarao, Leckie, Calhieros, Dastjerdi, & Versteeg, 2015; Alhazmi & Shami, 2014):

- Ability to define infrastructure, deployment, skill reduction, capital and operational expenditures, prior to deploying IT resources
- Understanding of data elasticity and resource-processing to determine deployment demands, maintenance and improve bandwidth allowing for scalable system performance
- How to mitigate internal resource capabilities, to sustain compliance, threat management, governance, and related security requirements
- The need to systems with more resources and processes required to support data sources
- Design agile and faster IT solutions, procurement of enhanced prototypes with cost-effective processes

Public Network Systems

Public network systems are technology specifications that can be integrated with public network systems via the Internet. This includes assorted data sources, application services and users. Public network systems consist of exterior bases such as the N data collected to support big data analytics efforts on the Internet. The functions in these components are comprise of: domain network system servers, firewalls, content delivery networks (Gartner, 2012; Buyya, Ranjan, Rodrigo, & Calheiros, 2010; Buyya, Ramamohanarao, Leckie, Calhieros, Dastjerdi, & Versteeg, 2015).

Cloud Data Sources

There are several data sources in the cloud. These data sources include big data systems and data analytics solutions. How investment and risk management can be evaluated often can influence the deployment of cloud data sources in the enterprise. These components comprise the three original characteristics: velocity, volume, variety, and data discrepancy. The data resources, enterprise applications, and cloud user capabilities comprise (Buyya, Ramamohanarao, Leckie, Calhieros, Dastjerdi, & Versteeg, 2015; Gartner, 2009; Gartner, 2012):

- Machine and Sensor Data
- Image and Video
- Social Data
- Internet Data
- Third Part Data
- Self-service
- Visualization
- Edge Services
- Domain Name System Server
- Content Delivery Networks
- Firewalls
- Load Balancer

Cloud Service Providers

For numerous years, cloud service providers have played a vital role in the management of cloud resources. The decision to provisioning resources over the cloud is determined by the administrators assigned to data centers. These components comprise the following (Buyya, Ramamohanarao, Leckie, Calhieros, Dastjerdi, & Versteeg, 2015; Gartner, 2009; Ross, 2010; Amazon, 2012; Alhazmi, & Shami, 2014):

- Data Integration
- Data Repositories
- Streaming Computing
- Transformation, Connectivity

Cloud Elasticity, Fast Provisioning and Scalability

Public and private clients are now able to deploy IT resources needed, to support the enterprise IT infrastructure community at a viable, scalable and reasonably priced rates, without experiencing any system downtime. Storage capacity, allocated time, unlimited demand of resources and data availability are key factors that decide the adoption and/or deployment of resources in the cloud (Ross, 2010; Buyya, Ranjan, Rodrigo, & Calheiros, 2010; Buyya, Ramamohanarao, Leckie, Calhieros, Dastjerdi, & Versteeg, 2015; Everett, 2009). A fast provisioning between physical and virtual servers reduces capital and operational expenditures. Attributable to the implementation of cloud-based solutions, users now appreciate the self-autonomy of data, continuous availability of resources, accessibility of information, fast provisioning, enhanced security, et al (Amazon, 2012; Biggs & Vidalis, 2009; Everett, 2009; Alhazmi & Shami, 2014).

Cloud Elasticity

In cloud elasticity computers are programmable to interact with any changes that can be made affecting the workloads. These changes are expected when an autonomous resource provisioning and de-provisioning process occur within the network infrastructure environments. Autonomous resource provisioning and de-provisioning process occur to guarantee data is extracted and/or processed allowing for computer resources to be distributed consistent with the user's needs.

Cloud Provisioning

Cloud provisioning is a process that selects which applications and services to be made available in the public cloud. This process comprises the resources that stay on-premises behind the firewall or in the private cloud. The method is designed to share resources stored on the service provider's data center and make these assets accessible to customers at the same time (Molnar & Schechter, 2010; Alhazmi & Shami, 2014). In cloud provisioning, providers are responsible for evaluating and determining any acceptance of requests made by customers (Alhazmi & Shami, 2014). Such processes are done by creating a number of virtual machines to support the client's requests. This method is needed to deliver an array of cloud computing services to customers (Molnar & Schechter, 2010; Alhazmi & Shami, 2014). In the provisioning sequence, desired solutions or methods are targeted at arraying and incorporating cloud services as well as deployment models (Gellman, 2009, Leavitt, 2009; Alhazmi & Shami, 2014). Cloud computing provisioning comprises: server, user, database, network, self-service mobile subscriber, Internet access and mobile content provisioning (Zetter, 2010; Grance & Mell, 2011; Gruschka & Iacono, 2009; Molnar & Schechter, 2010; Zimory, 2009). The provisioning of cloud computing solutions helps integrating policies, techniques and IT objectives for related sourcing cloud services, along with other technology solutions. These services or solutions are provided by both cloud service provider and managed service provider (Ross, 2010; Badger, Grance, Patt-Corner, & Voas, 2011; Pearson, 2009; Shacham & Waters, 2009). Cloud computing provisioning consists of tagging, dispensing and making available IT assets to support organizations' day-to-day operations (Pearson, 2009). When customers initiate requests to cloud service providers or managed service providers and these requests are accepted; for that reason, an applicable number of virtual machines and resources must be identified and made accessible to support such an operation (Ross, 2010; Gartner, 2012; Badger, Grance, Patt-Corner, & Voas, 2011; Grance & Mell, 2011; Gellman, 2009; Alhazmi & Shami, 2014).

Cloud provisioning is the provisioning or sharing of requested resources from the Internet service provider to IT organizations or customers. These activities are performed when the customer and/ or an IT organization submits the request to the ISP for approval. Once the approval is reviewed and processed, the provisioning of data or resources is granted. Cloud provisioning is performed through a proportionate assistance of virtual provisioning cloud administrators and/or virtual provisioning operators, who are responsible to monitor and regulate user requests. VMs are responsible for provisioning or distributing resources between ISPs and identified customers, from whom respective requests were generated. Vendor's Technologies such as Amazon EC2, Microsoft Azure, Google Engine Manager and IBM SoftLayer are used to provisioning or distributing data from several ISPs to elected IT organizations or customers. During cloud provisioning the following specifications are monitored: virtualization system abstraction; VM reuse and configuration, controlled lease time, programmed cost regulation, improved service catalog interface, role-based access, the need for dedicated service portals, complete integration of serviceNow platform.

CRITERIA FOR EFFECTIVE PUBLIC AND PRIVATE SECTOR CLOUD ADOPTION

The adoption of cloud computing services is a major topic in many public and private sectors. The adoption of cloud computing consists of the below six major criteria. These point of reference underline the main criteria for effective public and private sector cloud computing adoption (Buyya, Ranjan, Rodrigo, & Calheiros, 2010; Buyya, Ramamohanarao, Leckie, Calhieros, Dastjerdi, & Versteeg, 2015; Sims, 2009; Grance & Mell, 2011; Ristenpart et al., 2009). The six criteria comprise (Grance & Mell, 2011; Gartner, 2012):

- **Agility:** A service that is applied to dynamic infrastructure management "orchestration". The service allows agile deployment and system scalability. Agile services are designed to reduce the deployment of solutions, while providing sustained time management
- **Security:** Consist of trusted and secure cloud-based services required to apply the defense-in-depth measures. These measures are vital in preventing information disclosure to unauthorized users. This service is provided to prevent, repudiate and minimize data tampering and guarantee infrastructure integrity
- **Dependability:** This service guarantees for streamlined performance and reliability, compliance and service level agreement
- **Open:** This service is designed to implement benchmarks needed to advance interoperability, portability, through mixed conditions
- **Transparent:** This service offers the public and private sector alongside stakeholders, the ability to parallel, monitor, and audit balancing books
- **Aware:** Designed for capitalizing on several embedded service offerings in the cloud infrastructure. These services are hosted and provisioned to assorted computing systems. When provisioned, users are able to access these services in real-time

Enterprise Network Systems

Enterprise networks are applications required to transport complex business solutions over the Internet. These systems support IT platforms and network infrastructure solutions. The services are designed to support data storage and network systems in the enterprise. Comparatively, enterprise network systems involve the following components (Ross, 2010; Gartner, 2012; Buyya, Ramamohanarao, Leckie, Calhieros, Dastjerdi, & Versteeg, 2015; Amazon, 2012):

- Reference Data
- Master Data
- Transitional Data
- Application Data
- Log Data
- Enterprise Content Data
- Historical Data

Cloud Computing Service Models

Consistent with NIST the following are three government approved cloud computing service models (Badger, Grance, Patt-Corner, & Voas, 2011; Bruening & Treacy, 2009):

- **IaaS**: A method through which vendors could manage the system performance 'power' and the amount of storage, to support customers in the public and private sector. This service is capable of providing the performance and storage required to house data
- **PaaS**: Services to users via the cloud services. These services can be developed and provisioned in real-time and/or through a configuration-based system
- **SaaS**: Pay-per-use application services to diverse IT and business communities. This application can be leased from cloud service providers. Users benefit by leasing the services from cloud service providers, rather than managing application resources in-house. Salesforce, Zoho, Google, Amazon, Yahoo are demonstrated examples of SaaS

Managing IT resources is challenging and requires continuous planning, sustainable capital resources and operational assets necessary, to scale cloud-based infrastructure and platforms. IT issues must be resolved prior to adopting cloud-based solutions (Armbrust et al., 2009; Buyya, Ramamohanarao, Leckie, Calhieros, Dastjerdi, & Versteeg, 2015). These models influence application, server and network provisioning. These models enable users the tools necessary to forecast the provisioning of computing resources, needed to produce desirable results in the workplace (Lease, 2005; Torry Harris, n.d.). Technical experts select the best strategies, to support enterprise IT infrastructure. These strategies are key in reducing redundancy other business and technical constraints (Armbrust et al., 2009; Buyya, Ranjan, Rodrigo, & Calheiros, 2010; Torry Harris, n.d.). The below Figure 3 describes the cloud service models and respective characteristics (Alhazmi & Shami, 2014).

Figure 3. Cloud service models
Source: http://www.thbs.com/downloads/Cloud-Computing-Overview.pdf

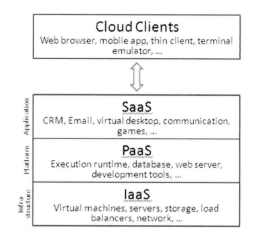

CLOUD DEPLOYMENT

Cloud Computing Deployment Models

models are infrastructure-based. The models are developed to store and protect data. When engineered with service models, these solutions are capable of storing, provisioning and supplying larger data loads from/to various data center end points in real-time (Armbrust et al., 2009; Buyya, Ranjan, Rodrigo, & Calheiros, 2010; Buyya, Ramamohanarao, Leckie, Calhieros, Dastjerdi, & Versteeg, 2015; Torry Harris, n.d.):

- **Private Cloud**: The cloud-based solutions are delivered to single or multiple organizations exclusively. As such, every organization has the autonomous right to manage its provisioned solutions
- **Public Cloud**: This cloud-based technology allows users the ability to manage resources via the cloud service providers. Cloud-based services may be sold individually, despite the availability of these solutions that can be provisioned to enterprises and their respective users
- **Hybrid Cloud**: These are cloud-based solutions provisioned from physical and virtual data centers. The data stored in private servers is shared with several users residing in the public domain to guarantee end-users have the policy and rights to access data through selective provisioning
- **Community Cloud**: Cloud-based solutions provisioned to support single or multiple communities. Despite complex provisioning, this service is offered to support the public and private sector users. These services are frequently monitored by a single and/or multiple cloud service providers

Cloud Computing and Database Platforms

These cloud-based database central mechanisms are key in providing the public and private sector with assets needed to support their day-to-day operations. Below is a list of vendor's approved cloud-based platforms (Gartner, 2009; Gartner, 2012):

- Amazon Web Services - Elastic Compute Cloud
- Oracle Cloud Solutions
- Hewlett Packard Cloud Services
- IBM Cognitive Cloud
- Cisco Platforms
- Microsoft Cloud Services
- Intel Cloud Services
- Google Cloud Services
- Yahoo Cloud Services
- Government Cloud
- Dell Cloud

The below Figure 4 illustrates the four cloud computing deployment models.

Public Sector

Cloud computing technology has transformed how public sector adopts and deploys cloud services. Such technical deviations have affected the way cloud services are delivered in both physical and virtual environments. How cloud services are deployed often guarantees the availability, agility, scalability, reliability, dependency, sustainability and overall security of network infrastructure solutions (Grance & Mell, 2011). Lacking such services could influence how resources are deployed in various organizations (Lease, 2005). These resources consist of: servers, compute nodes, network appliances, applications, storage and network systems. Public clouds comprise broad-spectrum computing systems (Buyya, Ranjan, Rodrigo, & Calheiros, 2010; Gartner, 2012; Buyya, Ramamohanarao, Leckie, Calhieros, Dastjerdi, & Versteeg, 2015). Apart from these adoptions and security barriers, vendors believe that improved security best practices are required to address any level of threats or vulnerability concerns, minimize capital expenditures and operational expenditures (Grance & Mell, 2011; Gartner, 2012; Buyya, Ramamohanarao, Leckie, Calhieros, Dastjerdi, & Versteeg, 2015). The benefits cloud computing offers to information technology engineers and managers in the public-sector are fundamental to organizations' mission-critical and operational posture (Buyya, Ranjan, Rodrigo, & Calheiros, 2010; Gartner, 2012; Buyya, Ramamohanarao, Leckie, Calhieros, Dastjerdi, & Versteeg, 2015). In an organization the adop-

Figure 4. Cloud computing deployment models
Source: www.csrc.nist.gov/groups/SNS/cloud-computing/index.html

	Infrastructure Managed By	Infrastructure Owned By	Infrastructure Located	Accessible and Consumed By
Public	Third Party Provider	Third Party Provider	Off-Premise	Untrusted
Private/ Community	Organization *Or* Third Party Provider	Organization Third Party Provider	On-Premise Off-Premise	Trusted
Hybrid	Both Organization & Third Party Provider	Both Organization & Third Party Provider	Both On-Premise & Off-Premise	Trusted & Untrusted

tion of virtual desktop services is envisioned to redefine the posture and how the public sector may benefit from this technology. The provisioning of agile, available, scalable, reliable and secure desktop applications encourages probe of new practical solutions. On occasion Chief Information Officers (CIOs) benefit from the deployment of cloud-based solutions. The solutions are designed to administrate the trade-offs and balance IT resources after being deployed to the cloud (Buyya, Ranjan, Rodrigo, & Calheiros, 2010; Stanton et al., 2005; Buyya, Ramamohanarao, Leckie, Calhieros, Dastjerdi, & Versteeg, 2015; Golden 2009). Cloud computing technology guarantees the scalability of systems in multi-tenant environments. Public sector requires more bandwidth to support the provisioned workload (Grance & Mell, 2011; Stanton et al., 2005; Buyya, Ranjan, Rodrigo, & Calheiros, 2010; Buyya, Ramamohanarao, Leckie, Calhieros, Dastjerdi, & Versteeg, 2015). Capital and operational expenditures are key factors for determining bandwidth cost apportionment in the cloud. The lack of suitable asset scalability in the cloud is critical to how systems respond and execute each task in the physical and virtual environment (Grance & Mell, 2011; Golden, 2009).

Private Sector

The adoption or deployment of cloud services in the private sector is essential to several IT organizations. The benefits can be determined by the economic growth opportunities, trade-offs, cost-effectiveness, enhanced security, economies of scale and new policies. Cloud computing offers information technology engineers, managers and organizations an integrated computing architecture. This architecture is designed to support system interoperability and dependency. Integrated computing architecture is the model through which consumers in the private sector describe the need to select several resources from several distributed computing environments (Buyya, Ranjan, Rodrigo, & Calheiros, 2010; Gartner, 2012; Buyya, Ramamohanarao, Leckie, Calhieros, Dastjerdi, & Versteeg, 2015). This model allows for provisioning and balancing management resources and ensures these solutions are central factors on how resources are deployed and secured. How such resources are distributed to consumers is based on higher provisioning practices required to support multiple-tier cloud platforms. Users are able to access and share data from virtual sources via the Internet (Buyya, Ranjan, Rodrigo, & Calheiros, 2010; Buyya, Ramamohanarao, Leckie, Calhieros, Dastjerdi, & Versteeg, 2015; Lease, 2005). Aside from several advantages customers have in the private sector, managers are inclined to reevaluate capital and operational expenditures, when adopting cloud services. How much budget an organization has would certainly determine the agility, reliability, scalability and dependability of services in the cloud. Security, agility, reliability, scalability and reliability always regulate the level of complexity designers, developers, information technology engineers and managers would need, when adopting/deploying cloud services (Alhazmi & Shami, 2014). Cloud computing technology is designed and deployed to support small, medium and large scale business communities. With cloud computing technology, businesses could scale to larger computer environments without significant capital and operational costs (Grance & Mell, 2011).

Data Integrity and Protection

Data integrity involves the complexity and consistency required to attribute a validity and accurateness of data composition. This process involves data back-ups and archives. Customers in the public and private sectors seek solutions to maintain record retention trends. These trends include the metadata needed to reconstruct attributes. Record-keeping procedures are accentuated concepts, which organizations implement to protect data from being corrupted or compromised (Buyya, Ramamohanarao, Leckie, Calhieros, Dastjerdi, & Versteeg, 2015; Sen & Sengupta, 2005; Alhazmi & Shami, 2014). In the public and private sector decision markers, put into effect security policies and procedures to protect organizations' data. Such procedures are necessary to protect IT infrastructure resources in the public private sector.

In recent years, there has been significant issues affecting data integrity and how organizations must conform to security requirements (Sen & Sengupta, 2005; Gartner, 2009; Gartner, 2012). Lacking security best practices in customized commodity e.g., hardware and software peripherals is a key factor to infrastructure security (Badger et al., 2011). Both the public and private sector are facing numerous challenges, when preparing to adapt new cloud computing solutions in on-premises or off-premises. Vendors working on optimum solutions required to redefine these security issues. The provisioning of physical and virtual machine systems is an essential topic to public and private customers (Sen & Sengupta, 2005; Buyya, Ranjan, Rodrigo, & Calheiros, 2010; Buyya, Ramamohanarao, Leckie, Calhieros, Dastjerdi, & Versteeg, 2015). Prior studies indicate the need for vendors to develop advanced solutions to moderate these technology limitations is fundamental. To attract a large number of customers in the public and private sectors an important determination in industry must be adopted whether by researching, developing solutions, and upgrading the existing hardware/software to attract the client's interest (Ross, 2010; Buyya, Ranjan, Rodrigo, & Calheiros, 2010; Buyya, Ramamohanarao, Leckie, Calhieros, Dastjerdi, & Versteeg, 2015). The primary tasks of data centers comprise the following (Buyya, Ramamohanarao, Leckie, Calhieros, Dastjerdi, & Versteeg, 2015; Amazon, 2012; Biggs & Vidalis, 2009; Buyya, Ranjan, Rodrigo, & Calheiros, 2010; Alhazmi & Shami, 2014):

- **Provisioning**: A process of deploying network equipment, via virtualized servers
- **Management**: A method that could influence on both strategic and operational decisions. After selected hardware is deployed and/or configured system administrators and engineers must begin monitoring or maintaining the management of the IT environment
- **Orchestration**: A process for managing data center infrastructure explicitly, servers, storage and others. The synchronization of computing systems for example storage and associated network equipment is what defines the orchestration process in the network environment

DATA CENTER EVOLUTION AND TRENDS

In recent decades, data centers experienced legacy "client-server" technology transformations. Business needs increased, due to the adoption of physical and virtual data centers (Grance & Mell, 2011; Song, Wagner, & Perrig, 2000; Kant, 2009). Data centers are designed to fulfil business or client requirements. The process involves agility, efficiency, scalability, availability, fast provisioning and virtualization (Kant, 2009). Server virtualization is designed to provide IT managers with the tool needed to tackle various IT challenges such as minimize capital and operational expenditures (Grance & Mell, 2011; Shin & Ahn, 2005; Takabi, Joshi, & Ahn, 2005; Kant, 2009). The integration of compute infrastructure, self-governing tools, and management systems has yield significant effects between services and infrastructure (Grance & Mell, 2011; Buyya, et al, 2015; Petry, 2007; Song, Wagner, & Perrig, 2000). Figure 5 describes the data center evolution and trends (Alhazmi & Shami, 2014; Kant, 2009).

Aside from these trends in cloud technology, data centers require high performance computing infrastructure to operate (Golden, 2009). Despite these processes and configuration theories, programing

Figure 5. Data center evolution and trends
Source: http://bnrg.cs.berkeley.edu/~randy/Courses/CS294.S13/1.3.pdf

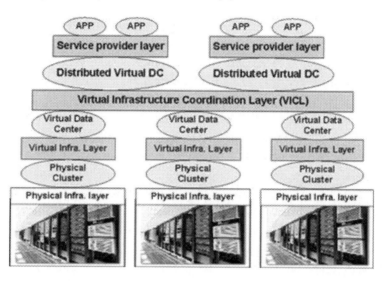

developers, engineers and managers in both public and private sectors are concerned about the lack of expertise to support the IT network infrastructure (Grance & Mell, 2011; Lease, 2005; Golden, 2009; Kant, 2009). To improve the IT infrastructure performance, reduce any constraints in data center operations, vendors must develop enterprise solutions, responsive processes and best practices (Grance & Mell, 2011; Gartner, 2012; Buyya, Ranjan, Rodrigo, & Calheiros, 2010; Buyya, Ramamohanarao, Leckie, Calhieros, Dastjerdi, & Versteeg, 2015; Oracle, 2016; Cisco, 2011; Kant, 2009).

Data Center Automation

In recent years, data center automation has regained its market presence in the public and private sectors (Ross, 2010). Vendors are committed to develop optimal cloud-based platforms that is, virtualization, provisioning and synchronization to sustain such enterprise transformation. For instance, demilitarized zones in the cloud environment have proven automated data centers are more agile, secure, reliable, scalable and cost-effective (Leighon, 2009; Badger et al., 2011). Virtualization occurs at (Grance & Mell, 2011; Gartner, 2012; Ross, 2010; Alhazmi & Shami, 2014; Kant, 2009):

- System Level (i.e., Java Virtual Machine or .NET CLRs)
- Machine Level (e.g., VMware, Citrix)
- Network Level (e.g., Virtual Private Networks)
- Database Level (e.g., Delphix)
- Entire data center level (e.g., Nutanex)
- Cloud Computing level (i.e., public, private and hybrid cloud; IaaS, PaaS, SaaS)

Data Center Security Challenges

Lacking security procedures to protect data centers' core infrastructure and resources could result in major challenges for organizations and customers. Data centers are one of the major targets hackers could launch cyber-attacks against. There are many methods hackers or intruders use to gain access beyond organization's security perimeters. Such process can be accomplished by a series of exploitations intruders frequently perform in an effort to increase access to the network infrastructure solutions (Lease, 2010; Takabi, Joshi, & Ahn, 2005). As a result of these types of threats, decision makers in the public and private sector urge vendors, to improve their solutions designed to deter, retract and defend organizations' vital resources (Gartner, 2012; Buyya, Ranjan, Rodrigo, & Calheiros, 2010; Buyya, Ramamohanarao, Leckie, Calhieros, Dastjerdi, & Versteeg, 2015; Sinclair, & Smith, 2008). Vendors are designing front-line solutions e.g., VMware NSX, to support customer's enterprise IT resources. VMware NSX is a tool required to provide network virtualization resources on data centers. Thus VMware is a trusted solution designed to provide detection, analytics and responsive controls required for protecting the infrastructure network resources. In part, VMware is a tool designed with cutting-edge features and/or capabilities to thwart vulnerabilities and threats. Additionally, the features are needed to detect and prevent malware propagation inside data centers and related cloud-based platforms (Sen & Sengupta, 2005): hypervisors, virtual switches. The NSX distributed firewalls are programmable applications that inspect horizontal traffic (end-to-end) amid VMware systems deployed in the data centers (Sinclair & Smith, 2008).

Data Center Virtualization

In recent years, VMware products have transformed virtualization. As a consequence, virtualization is a theory that has existed for many decades (Oracle, 2016; Cisco, 2011, RedHat, 2016). In the past VMware technology was incorporated by industry, to ensure that high performance computers can process large quantity of data (Oracle, 2016; Cisco, 2011). Nearly ten years ago, industry reinstated the virtualization technology, to guarantee for system, storage and network convergence as well as real-time resource provisioning. The lack of improved security measures has encouraged vendors to adopt newer solutions to improve the security of IT platform and infrastructures (Buyya, Ranjan, Rodrigo, & Calheiros, 2010). For instance, virtualization technology is a modeling for which virtualized systems are adopted (Alhazmi & Shami, 2014; Oracle, 2016; Cisco, 2011). These virtualized systems were designed to support analytic performance models: server consolidation, virtual machine monitor, transaction processing monitor, batching, testing, hardware performance, mapping of virtual to physical disks, central processing unit/ CPU processing, workload variance, load balancing, legacy application stance (Biggs & Vidalis, 2009). The management and optimization of virtualization systems i.e., oracle/Sun Microsystems virtual box, IBM, and VMware products is/are essential on how customers manage IT resources (Biggs & Vidalis, 2009). Virtualization is an enabling platform that simplifies IT resources. This process mostly provides a higher level of abstraction (Leighon, 2009). Abstraction simplifies system's operation, while disconnecting physical dependences (Buyya, Ranjan, Rodrigo, & Calheiros, 2010; Oracle, 2016; Cisco, 2011).

Desktop Virtualization

The outright concept involving desktop virtualization remains a major challenge to numerous IT organizations and consumers. In desktop virtualization the limited management of applications through IT enterprise is prodigious to cloud administrators and developers. Such challenges are prone to significant increase of applications needed to preserve IT organizations' production, business continuity operations and corporate growth opportunities and/or margins (Metzler, 2011; Oracle, 2016; Cisco, 2011; RedHat, 2016). The operational constraints have compelled IT organizations to implement daily project/operational functions that are outside of their regular business missions and scopes. Beneath is a list of extra activities that organizations need perform to sustain their operational postures (Metzler, 2011; Oracle, 2016; Cisco, 2011):

- Provisioning new requests or desktop systems
- Repairing desktop machines along with random updates of software
- Guarding platforms and complex infrastructure from unsolicited users
- Providing continuous service desk support to sustain infrastructure environment and platform performance
- Conforming with inner organization requirements, code of practice and guidelines as relating to the PC environment & measurability or continuous monitoring against both inside and outside threats

Network Virtualization

The integrated method network virtualization offers to public and private sectors is key in defining organization success. The benefit of the operating system provisioned techniques allows for the creation and configuration of virtual networks that can be separated from regular physical network. Physical networks are used as a backbone to forward packets on the networks (Oracle, 2016; Cisco, 2011; RedHat, 2016). In essence, virtual networks are comprised of a single or multiple systems using VMs and zones with one or more network interface(s). These interface(s) are configured through a physical network interface card or vNIC (Oracle, 2016). Whether are located on the same network or dispersed locations vNIC are capable to seamlessly communicate. This process allows VMs to talk to each other, while connected to a same host machine (Oracle, 2016; Cisco, 2011). In network virtualization the convergence of hardware and software resources e.g., physical and virtual resources is vital to the organization's day-to-day operations (Oracle, 2016). In network virtualization multiple VMs have the ability to perform multiple or simultaneous activities in a single physical machine (Oracle, 2016). The concept also allows for VMs to run independently on several instances as well as performing functions on a single physical machine (Oracle, 2016; Cisco, 2011). Virtualization technology provide servers, firewalls, routers, switches the ability to run independently. This exempts organizations from acquiring or procuring extra network hardware (Metzler, 2011; Oracle, 2016; Cisco, 2011). For several decades, network virtualization has been used in the following technology scenarios (Oracle, 2016; Cisco, 2011): production, testing, prototyping, designing, and deployment of novel solutions. Network virtualization consists of the following (Metzler, 2011; Oracle, 2016; Cisco, 2011):

- **Platform Virtualization**: (e.g., assert and network virtualization)

- **Network Virtualization**: (e.g., virtualized process that supports external and internal compute methods)
- **Wireless Virtualization**: (e.g., spectrum distribution, infrastructure and air crossing point virtualization). This process is parallel to network virtualization. In the wired virtualization, many Internet service providers are accountable for the day-to-day operations of their corresponding physical network infrastructure solutions. Wireless network virtualization includes physical wireless systems, for instance radio assets, which can be abstracted or secluded to support frequent virtual machines
- **Peripheral "External" Virtualization**: Single or multiple local networks known as LANs. Generally, the LANs are segmented into virtual network platforms needed to perform various activities in support of larger network systems e.g., data centers
- **Inner "Internal" Virtualization**: Designed to syndicate one or more software containers (e.g., Xen hypervisor control programs or quasi crossing points); for example, the virtual network interface controllers. The goal is to interact with physical networks with software. Internal virtualization is designed to augment one or multiple systems' performance through the process of segregating applications to various dispersed containers or virtual crossing points

In recent years, vendors e.g., Citrix, Microsoft, Vyatta have manufactured computer-generated systems and protocol stacks. The purpose of these virtual networks and protocol stacks is designed to converge complex solutions: routers, firewalls and virtual private network utilities (Buyya, Ranjan, Rodrigo, & Calheiros, 2010). These functions are then combined with Citrix NetScaler load balancer, outlet repeaters e.g., Wide Area Networks (WAN) optimizers as well as Secure Socket Layers (SSLs) for virtual private network systems (Buyya, Ranjan, Rodrigo, & Calheiros, 2010). OpenSolaris networks comprise virtualized systems designed to providing load balancing between VPNs, LANs and WANs. This model is described as "network in a box" technique designed to support the x86 systems. Any of these containers can seamlessly perform in wide-ranging operating systems/machines (i.e., Microsoft windows, Linux). These operating systems are also designed to interact with network interface controllers. This process is performed through a sustained availability, applicability and operation computerization of resources deployed to the physical and virtual environments (Lease, 2005; Oracle, 2016; Cisco, 2011). VMware solutions are designed to provide the industry, public and private sector customers with the capability needed, to redefine virtualized infrastructure-based technology postures. In general, VMware is a reliable solution that delivers scalable support to diverse clients in the public and private sectors (Buyya, Ranjan, Rodrigo, & Calheiros, 2010; Grance & Mell, 2011; Gartner, 2012; Buyya, Ramamohanarao, Leckie, Calhieros, Dastjerdi, & Versteeg, 2015; Oracle, 2016; Cisco, 2011).

Virtualization Challenges

In modern days, server infrastructure, resource-enablement, optimization, and dynamic dataload management are perceived as key challenges for the overall process (Buyya, Ranjan, Rodrigo, & Calheiros, 2010; Buyya, Ramamohanarao, Leckie, Calhieros, Dastjerdi, & Versteeg, 2015; Ross, 2010). Virtualization overhaul occurs when the network fails to perform its activities (Oracle, 2016; Cisco, 2011). This also arises when hardware components require immediate remediation to prevent further outage. Such activities include the reliability, cost-effectiveness (Oracle, 2016; Cisco, 2011). There are five types of hardware virtualization: complete virtualization/virtual machine model, partial virtualization, storage virtualization and client virtualization. The following is a list of some of the challenges that virtualization technology poses to IT organizations (Oracle, 2016; Cisco, 2011; Rajalakshmi, Srinandhini, & Uma, 2015):

- **Argumentative Management of vSwithes**: A method of managing vSwitch systems or virtualized network assets. This concept comprises a single or multiple application-based computergenerated switches. Yet this model is designed to boost one or more network layers to data center or local area network settings. The overall process can be challenging when assigned to administrators its yielding a degree of system anomalies e.g., from planning, executing and system degradation

- **Failure of System Structure and Monitoring Tools**: The range of tasks or activities assigned to the administrators can be prodigious to network configuration and divergences. Often such deviations, can range from system configuration process that administrators require to ensure/guarantee for data center's agility and optimum performance. Lacking such practical network functions could result in noticeable dynamic network degradation and/or virtual machine performance

- **Multiple Hypervisors and Difference in Functionality**: For several years, VMware was the main vendor for hypervisors in wide-reaching technology or computer/hardware industry. VMware remains one of the few technology leading companies in the designing of hypervisor hardware/ software. Recently, there has been other vendors i.e., Citrix, Red Hat and Microsoft that also have launched similar versions of hypervisor hardware and storage systems. In recent years, some of these vendors have designed and transformed their respective versions of hypervisor hardware and software applications i.e., Xen, Kernel-based virtual machines and Hyper-V

- **Virtual Machine-to-Virtual Device Traffic Flow Discernibility**: The initial product of vSwitches was designed with limited or inadequate network traffic flow features. By contrast, the physical access switches are designed with limited features. Such technical limitations are due to the lack of security features, to support all server-domain activities within the virtualized network environment

- **Dynamic Infrastructure Management**: The process encompassing the dynamic virtualized network settings. Active infrastructure administration is a process which administrators bank on from complex scalability vantage point, to unified domain name system, dynamic host configuration protocol and Internet process address management solutions. DNS, DHCP or IPAM are protocols designed to aggregate database resources. The process is designed to prevent system administrators from managing records located in various sites without prior permission

- **Multiple Troubleshootings on a Per-Virtual Device Source**: In recent years, IT organizations have adopted other computing performances known as "n-tier" applications. The four-tier application consist of: web servers, application servers, database servers and web browsers. In the past, the performance of these applications was infrequent to the organization's efficiency. Lacking collaboration among cloud administrators, end-users and/or managers could affect the organization's day-to-day operations and productivity

- **Distributed Virtual Switching**: This process includes vSwitches built with merged system boards. This process also allows for the adaptation and administration of vSwitches' control planes with contiguous alterations with virtual server systems

- **Planning and Provisioning**: In planning and provisioning of resources adaptive and provisioning methods are required to support everyday tasks performed manually. Some of these tasks are now provisioned through a unique physical or dynamic controller. This is also viewed as a capacity designed to support virtualization services. Yet, more than half of IT organizations are beginning to espouse desktop virtualization in their respective industries. The concept further advances organization's productivity, and lessening capital or operational expenditures e.g., procedures, policies, and security specifications needed to maintain data center functionality, while providing robust information protection. Consequently, there are two rudiments of desktop virtualization processes: client-side application to desktop virtualization and server-side application to desktop virtualization

- **Server Resources Over Subscription**: As virtual machines escalate, the return-on-investment aligned with the server virtualization has an affinity to spiral as well. This is viewed as a balanced flow of both virtual machines and the CPU sequences allowing for the increase of traffic flow via application-based virtual switches: the complex the percentage rotation of physical machines or CPUs with ability to sustain the VMs application performance
- **Edge Virtual Bridges**: Eccentric procedures developed to support this model and sustain the edge virtual bridges. This method further segments multiple network devices through various virtual software-based topology
- **Physical Network Reconfiguration to Provision VM Migration**: The dependency of on-demand computing staging for virtual machines and/or physical servers can be resolute by data centers' dispersed locations. Recently, vendors have designed better virtual server management systems, to support the migration process of virtual machines. In recent decade, pervasive challenges in the quality of service, access control lists and firewalls have resulted in insufficient transferal of VM systems, to new locations. Yet cloud administrators are concerned with the amount of time required to physically configure and/or migrate VMs
- **Varying Network Plan Enforcement**: Traditional vSwitches are designed with limited hardware/software specifications, needed to support large data capacities and traffic flow as well as providing suitable computational mechanisms between segmented and virtual data centers. This includes VLANs, the quality of service and/or far-reaching access control lists. In the event that some of these capabilities are to be supported by vSwitches, administrators are responsible for physically configuring each machine. The process is performed through virtual server management application console. The anticipated features must be configured and/or attuned to support the physical access switches. This diagram (Figure 6) displays a wide-ranging virtualization processes.

In the network infrastructure layer, virtualization process is performed beyond the server hardware (Gorelik, 2013). The migration of CC technology enables data centers, the ability to interact with multi-tenant virtual systems (Grance & Mell, 2011; Buyya, Ranjan, Rodrigo, & Calheiros, 2010; Buyya, Ramamohanarao, Leckie, Calhieros, Dastjerdi, & Versteeg, 2015). Virtualization management overhaul is a range of architecture solutions that consists of: (Grance & Mell, 2011; Ross, 2010; Grance & Mell, 2011; Buyya, Ranjan, Rodrigo, & Calheiros, 2010; Buyya, Ramamohanarao, Leckie, Calhieros, Dastjerdi, & Versteeg, 2015; Cisco, 2011; Oracle, 2016; RedHat, 2016; Rajalakshmi, Srinandhini, & Uma, 2015)

- VMware ESX/GSX Server(s)
- VMware Virtual Machine File System(s)
- VMware Virtual Symmetric Multi-Processing
- VirtualCenter Management Server(s)
- Virtual Infrastructure Client

Figure 6. Hardware virtualization process
Source: http://www.ijircce.com/upload/2015/october/69_A%20Technical.pdf

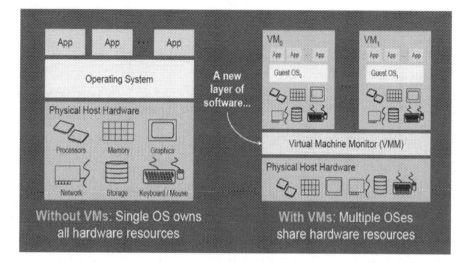

- Virtual Infrastructure Web Access
- VMware VMotion
- VMware High Availability
- VMware Distributed Resource Scheduler
- VMware Consolidated Backup(s)
- VMware Infrastructure SDK
- Citrix–Xen
- Citrix (i.e., Xenserver and Xensource)
- Microsoft (i.e., Microsoft Hyper-V "formerly known as windows server virtualization")
- Oracle (i.e., Virtual Machines)
- Novel
- Read Hat
- Parallels
- Amazon
- GoGrid
- IBM
- Joyent
- Carpathia
- Rackspace
- Hewlett Packard
- NetApp
- Cisco

In recent decades, vendors have developed security solutions to address challenges affecting the day-to-day performance of both private and public sector's data centers (Sen & Sengupta, 2005; Gorelik, 2013). These security solutions are developed to scan, detect and analyze any connections between processes and hypervisors (Takabi, Joshi, & Ahn, 2005). The solutions consist of the following components

(Gartner, 2012; Buyya, Ramamohanarao, Leckie, Calhieros, Dastjerdi, & Versteeg, 2015; Rajalakshmi, Srinandhini, & Uma, 2015; Chen, n.d.; Gorelik, 2013):

- Secure Virtual Machine(s)
- Analysis and Inspection Engine
- Centralized Management Components

The below Figure 7 describes the core architecture concept of VMware NSX virtualization architecture (Chen, n.d.; Gorelik, 2013).

Dynamic Applications

Dynamic applications are programing languages designed to perform several tasks on the network. Dynamic applications consist of: server, network, platform, container-level and database scalability (Buyya, Ranjan, Rodrigo, & Calheiros, 2010; Gartner, 2012; Gorelik, 2013). Scalability is a capability that consists of networks, systems and processes. This capability is deployed to support customer's day-to-day operations. These capabilities are developed to support large amount of workloads (Gartner, 2012; Buyya, Ranjan, Rodrigo, & Calheiros, 2010; Buyya, Ramamohanarao, Leckie, Calhieros, Dastjerdi, & Versteeg, 2015). Dynamic applications are defined as the base of advanced network computing resources. In the cloud, scalability plays a key role; particularly on how services, platforms and infrastructure share data in real-time (Itani, Kayssi, & Chehab, 2009). The following is a list that integrates numerous scalability models involving dynamic applications (Gartner, 2012; Ross, 2010; Buyya, Ramamohanarao, Leckie, Calhieros, Dastjerdi, & Versteeg, 2015; Gorelik, 2013):

- Server Scalability
- Network Scalability
- Platform Scalability

Figure 7. VMware NSX virtualization architecture
Source: http://www.mit.edu/~caoj/pub/doc/jcao_j_netsec.pdf

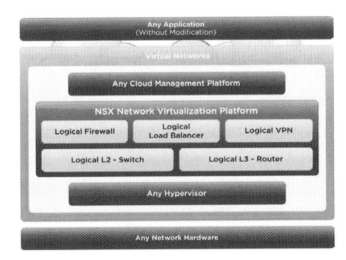

- Container-level Scalability
- Database Scalability

Dynamic scalability was added to the evolution of virtual machine technology. While scalability resource management is the process that emphasizes the application program interface unchanging activities, protocol dependency and the need for other toolkits is/are necessary to develop software applications designed to balance network, server and storage workload. Cloud services: IaaS, PaaS, SaaS cannot provide system performance to assigned platforms: public cloud, private cloud, hybrid cloud and cloud computing. Customers in the public and private sector must invest in prime IT solutions, required to perform cloud services that is, agile, reliable, scalable and sustainable.

Cloud Security and Privacy

Advanced solutions to support security of cloud infrastructure and platforms are key resources to public and private sectors (Sen & Sengupta, 2005). Lacking these solutions could affect the overall functionality of IT network infrastructure. Grance & Mell (2011) argued that vendors must develop viable technical solutions to moderate existing security breaches in the enterprise. In the public and private sector, security challenges are paramount (Takabi, Joshi, & Ahn, 2005). There is a lack of security solutions, to address the level of threats affecting the cloud service providers, services, and infrastructure (Buyya, Ranjan, Rodrigo, & Calheiros, 2010; Sen & Sengupta, 2005; Buyya, Ramamohanarao, Leckie, Calhieros, Dastjerdi, & Versteeg, 2015; Itani, Kayssi, & Chehab, 2009). IT vendors must discuss these security challenges affecting the physical and virtual infrastructure (Sen & Sengupta, 2005). In the public and private sector customers are skeptical in granting cloud service providers complete access, to data stored in their enterprise IT infrastructure e.g., the physical and virtual servers, networks or storage systems. This uncertainty is due to frequent security threats organizations have dealt with over the course of years (Sen & Sengupta, 2005; Gartner, 2012; Buyya, Ranjan, Rodrigo, & Calheiros, 2010). There is a need for trusted connectivity between physical and virtual infrastructure. This need consists of end-to-end 'trusted' encryption solutions, designed to avert or minimize security breaches in the cloud (Sen, 2010b; Oracle, 2016). When vendors develop security solutions, cloud service providers have equal responsibility to improve security measures i.e., policies and guidelines necessary to secure data in the cloud (Takabi, Joshi, & Ahn, 2005). There is a need for vendors to develop robust data-mining applications systems (Buyya, Ranjan, Rodrigo, & Calheiros, 2010; Buyya, Ramamohanarao, Leckie, Calhieros, Dastjerdi, & Versteeg, 2015; Gartner, 2012). These systems can be used to detect and prevent malware from disseminating in the cloud. Apache Hadoop is an open source software application designed to support storage and distributed provisioning of data to various compute clusters. In this instance, commodity hardware act as independent frameworks designed to support, prevent any latency, during hardware performance (Sen, 2010c; Sen, 2010b; Buyya, Ranjan, Rodrigo, & Calheiros, 2010; Buyya, Ramamohanarao, Leckie, Calhieros, Dastjerdi, & Versteeg, 2015; Itani, Kayssi, & Chehab, 2009). In the cloud, legacy security methods and network firewalls do not interact (Sen, 2010b). Elastic perimeters or 'boundaries' are needed in the enterprise in tandem with outside legacy firewalls (Alhazmi, & Shami, 2014). Cloud devices are designed to provide seamless access and share data located in the outer boundary of the demilitarized zone and firewalls (Armbrust et al., 2009; Takabi, Joshi, & Ahn, 2005). The use of these advanced security models or controls is designed to guarantee security for the physical and virtual infrastructure (Buyya, Ranjan, Rodrigo, & Calheiros, 2010; Gartner, 2012; Alhazmi, & Shami, 2014). The security of physical infrastructure requires a broader concept and newer solutions, benchmarks and end-to-end multi-tier infrastructure encryption methods. The need for policies, new methods and security controls is necessary to protect data, applications, services, end-point devices and related infrastructure (Armbrust et al., 2009; Buyya, Ranjan, Rodrigo, & Calheiros, 2010; Buyya, Ramamohanarao, Leckie, Calhieros, Dastjerdi, & Versteeg, 2015). For many years, vendors have developed security solutions to satisfy customer's technical and business demands. These demands include, but are not limited to the following areas (Sen, 2010c; Sen, 2010b; Alhazmi, et al, 2014; Alhazmi & Shami, 2014):

- Security of data stored in data centers worldwide
- Developing encryption, security solutions or techniques to guarantee for continuity of operations on the physical and virtual networks
- Security of transitory data between single and multiple network systems
- Authentication of users, application, network, server, and storage systems
- Develop proven security solutions, to detect, prevent, and repudiate any vulnerabilities or threats found on the physical and virtual IT infrastructure
- Develop methods for data aggregation in several storage systems
- Address any regulatory, policy, and other related legal issues affecting the public and private sector enterprise IT infrastructure
- Data sanitization between cloud service providers and customer's physical or virtual systems i.e., servers, networks, applications and storage
- Develop measures to address, prevent, repudiate, deter and/or manage incident response issues

The need for training, retaining and employing other security experts is crucial. In view of that, any current or imminent threats to the cloud can be mitigated, if vendors invest more resources, to research and come with robust security solutions (Sen, 2010c; Buyya, Ramamohanarao, Leckie, Calhieros, Dastjerdi, & Versteeg, 2015).

Virtualized Cloud-Based Platforms and Applications

In the cloud, the virtual process allows for elastic and balanced utilization of resources in real-time. Overall, public and private sector customers benefit from the adoption and deployment of virtualized solutions in IT infrastructure environment. The consumption of electricity and space-cooling are core factors users often seek to deploy virtualized on physical and virtual data centers (Amazon, 2012; Gartner, 2012). Subsequent to the adoption of 'virtualization' there has been shifts in IT infrastructure and applications (Sen & Sengupta, 2005; Gartner, 2012). These are integral and/or enabling processes through which services and platforms benefit from the unified and/or distributed IT environment. Vendors developed virtualization technology to support and augment cloud solutions. Virtualization is designed to transform applications and network platforms' interaction in real-time. This technology is also designed to provide load balancing and resource sharing. Virtualization allows for the incorporation of physical and virtual servers in a unique operational disposition (Ross, 2010). Virtualization and cloud technology are key resources to support the customer's IT infrastructure. This technology permits the migration of legacy physical servers to modern virtual single or multiple server farms physically dispersed throughout the world (Amazon, 2012; Alhazmi & Shami, 2014).

Virtual Disks Structures

Virtual disks are categorized as virtual drives are applications mechanisms designed to compute such system functions/actions. These activities are supported by disk storage devices. Disk storages are hardware components or peripheral devices e.g., electronic, magnetic, optical disk, virtual disk or hard disk drives designed to store, record and process data. Often virtual disks are stored inside of virtual machines/computer hardware virtualization (Metzler, 2011; Oracle, 2016; Cisco, 2011). As hardware platforms virtual drives provide consistent abstractions needed to boot up operating systems. In virtualization, the physical description of any computer hardware platform is hidden from the actual end-users. Such activity, provides the user with an abstraction of computer platform. Virtual drives comprise of: disk image, logical disk, and random-access memory/RAM disk (Metzler, 2011; Oracle, 2016; Cisco, 2011). In hardware virtualization, virtual drives are implemented by VMs. This process duplicates the function a physical machine would require to implement (e.g., ordinary computer). Alike physical computer, VMs require virtual disks or a disk image to run. By contrast, in network boot administrators must add more virtual drives for any computer activity to initiate. Virtual optical drives are used to transfer data between optical and hard disk drives. System administrators have the choice to use optical disk drives, as these devices provide faster disk transfer time than CDs or DVDs (Metzler, 2011; Oracle, 2016; Cisco, 2011).

Cloud Storage

Cloud storage involves virtual machines that are physically dispersed through several data centers in the world. These virtual machines share data storage pools. As such, virtualized storage systems are hosted by cloud service providers, and in large data centers throughout the world. Cloud service providers must require users to store data in leased data centers. Virtual machines access data from servers located in multiple infrastructures (Buyya, Ranjan, Rodrigo, & Calheiros, 2010; Buyya, Ramamohanarao, Leckie, Calhieros, Dastjerdi, & Versteeg, 2015; Gartner, 2012). In the public and private sectors, customers must lease the amount of storage needed to support the day-to-day business and IT operations. Whether in the public or private cloud, organizations are not required to deploy additional servers in respective premises (Gorelik, 2013). Instead, these storage devices are deployed to data centers that are sustained by the cloud service providers. Even with the geographic locations that cloud storages are located, the off-shore costs are much lower than the leasing rates in the United States (Buyya, Ramamohanarao, Leckie, Calhieros, Dastjerdi, & Versteeg, 2015; Gartner, 2012; Gorelik, 2013). Faster storage systems allow users to conduct incremental and regular backups of data. In the event that users are in need of more storage, proper requests must be made to cloud service providers for approval (Gorelik, 2013). Cloud service providers are responsible for allocating extra space to accommodate their customers' needs. This gives users the flexibility needed to divert their attention to other business missions (Gartner, 2012; Buyya, Ranjan, Rodrigo, & Calheiros, 2010). Figure 8 describes virtualized cloud-based platforms and applications (Gorelik, 2013).

Data Model

The two types of cloud database systems discussed are: relational database management system, non-relational and/or NoSQL databases among others are very prevalent to how organization provision and share data. Each vendor adapts to its zest of database systems, which are supported in the cloud (Buyya,

Figure 8. Virtualized cloud-based platforms and applications
Source: http://web.mit.edu/smadnick/www/wp/2013-01.pdf

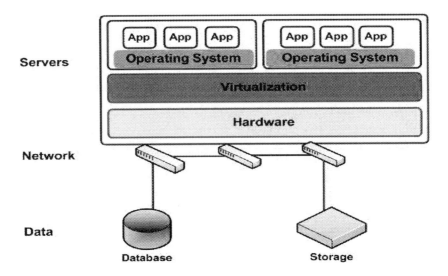

Ranjan, Rodrigo, & Calheiros, 2010; Gartner, 2012). These database systems contain the following (Gartner, 2009; Gartner, 2012; Gorelik, 2013):

- Oracle Database
- Microsoft Database
- Apache Cassandra
- IBM DB2
- Sybase

These databases are deployed in the cloud as virtual machine images or DaaS to support the customer-based infrastructure. Databases are difficult to maintain and/or scale, due to complexity and performance that are not suited to cloud environments. Non-relational databases otherwise known as NoSQL consist of: (Gartner, 2012; Gorelik, 2013).

- Apache Cassandra
- CouchDB
- MariaDB
- MongoDB

These databases are capable to scale over cloud platforms and infrastructure. NoSQL databases have compatible features, to support heavy read/write workloads. NoSQL databases are scaled without any point of failure or interruption through performance (Gartner, 2012). The embedded rewrite of application code is designed around SQL data models. NoSQL are scalable with complete rewritable application code to boost databases' performance (Buyya, Ramamohanarao, Leckie, Calhieros, Dastjerdi, & Versteeg, 2015; Amazon, 2012; Itani, Kayssi, & Chehab, 2009).

CONTINUOUS MONITORING

Implementing defensive security methods in the cloud, poses greater challenges to public and private sector (CPNI Security Briefing, 2010; Biggs & Vidalis, 2009). Despite numerous security perimeters between cloud-based systems and users, there are numerous other types of vulnerabilities and threats affecting IT platforms and infrastructure (CPNI Security Briefing, 2010). Cloud services and applications are exposed to external and internal attacks. These attacks and threats may be minimized, prevented and repudiated, if vendors invest adequate resources to support public and private sector customers (Biggs & Vidalis, 2009; Badger et al., 2011). Continuous development or integration of security tools is found in the trusted solutions. These trusted solutions include: vulnerability scans, cyber risk management, identity management access/risk and end-to-end security. Such solutions are designed provide layers of security to physical and virtual platforms (Sen & Sengupta, 2005; Emig et al., 2007; Schubert, Kipp, & Wesner, 2009). The need for federated and integrated cloud-based solutions is designed to provide management security tools, needed to obviate and deter unauthorized/authorized individuals' from accessing private-private sector IT assets/resources (CPNI Security Briefing, 2010). In the public and private sector customers are concerned on how cloud service providers/vendors secure consumers' data (Sen & Sengupta, 2005); CPNI Security Briefing, 2010; Schubert, Kipp, & Wesner, 2009). These concerns are as follows (Biggs & Vidalis, 2009; Gartner, 2012; Ross, 2010):

- Define security benchmarks and related policy requirements
- Conduct routine due-diligence and due-process on platforms and infrastructure
- Manage cloud-based supplier's risks, network vulnerabilities and system threats

The following security fundamentals are critical to public and private sector's IT infrastructure and platforms (Amazon, 2012; Biggs & Vidalis, 2009; Buyya, Ranjan, Rodrigo, & Calheiros, 2010; Buyya, Ramamohanarao, Leckie, Calhieros, Dastjerdi, & Versteeg, 2015; Badger et al., 2011; Bruening & Treacy, 2009):

- Legacy security issues and concerns
- Current and imminent issues
- Cloud service provider's data access, security and monitoring

This Figure 9 illustrates the theoretical method of database management systems.

Figure 9. Process for database management system
Source: https://www.google.com/search

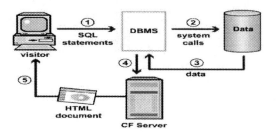

These applications and/or platforms are designed to reduce redundancy, fault-tolerance, scalability, latency, machine-image, federation, enhanced encryption methods, democratization, self-autonomy, real-time data sharing, fast provisioning, system agility, no single point of failure, backup/disaster recovery, security, clustering, and elasticity solutions (Amazon, 2012; Biggs & Vidalis, 2009; Buyya, Ranjan, Rodrigo, & Calheiros, 2010; Joshi et al., 2004).

Database Management Systems

In recent years, cloud database systems have gained a lot of attention in the public and private sector (Amazon, 2012). The adoption of amazon web services-elastic compute cloud has spun web-based applications and integrated solutions. Web-based applications and network platforms are easy to deploy, due to such evolution (Badger et al., 2011).

Database System Replication

In databases, replication is defined as a process/component that shares data between computers and servers (Badger et al., 2011). Redundant resources are software and hardware components. These computer resources are deployed to improve, maintain and orchestrate the fault-tolerance posture and display data in real-time. In the replicated environment, data is stored in several computers for continuous task processing (Sen & Sengupta, 2005). Replication is a very fundamental concept for all database systems (Joshi et al., 2004). IT professionals and vendors agree that the process of replicating database systems is a very complex task (Biggs & Vidalis, 2009; Amazon, 2012; Gartner, 2012; Gartner, 2009). For many years, vendors have designed database solutions to support the replication process between instances and incremental business environments. In essence, database tables are separated from several objects to allow data residing in the back-end database and/or network server environment (i.e., network-based, Internet, and intranet). This process is developed to guarantee that database queries, forms, reports, macros and modules activities are executed in the front-end database and/or end-user computer (Sen, 2010c; Biggs & Vidalis, 2009; Badger et al., 2011; Chen et al., 2010).

Oracle Cloud-Based Enterprise Solutions

Enterprise manager is a solution platform that provides engineering and infrastructure concepts needed, to optimize IT customer services and operational capacities. These IT solution architectures, though, are required to decrease cost complexity, capital and operational outlays (Sen & Sengupta, 2005; Gartner, 2012; Buyya, Ranjan, Rodrigo, & Calheiros, 2010; Buyya, Ramamohanarao, Leckie, Calhieros, Dastjerdi, & Versteeg, 2015). These solutions are incorporated as enterprise manager, virtual machine and real application cluster or architecture. Both the enterprise manager and backbone-platform yet are designed to support many Oracle technologies (Badger et al., 2011; Oracle, 2016).

SOLUTIONS AND RECOMMENDATIONS

Cloud computing technology offers a range of advantages to current and/or future adopters (Biggs & Vidalis, 2009; DeCandia et al., 2007). Attributable to such benefits, vendors are committed to researching and improving existing cloud solutions and security best practices, to meet organizations and customers' business/operation's requirements (Lease, 2005; Buyya, Ranjan, Rodrigo, & Calheiros, 2010; Badger et al., 2011). IT and cloud experts anticipate that continued research in cloud computing technology will give rise to diverse discoveries of topics such as, data science, big data/predictive analytics, data mining, data-warehousing and others. Any advent research areas including cyber security and computer forensics must benefit from basis of prior cloud computing research findings (Grance & Mell, 2011; Buyya, Ramamohanarao, Leckie, Calhieros, Dastjerdi, & Versteeg, 2015; Biggs & Vidalis, 2009; Badger et al., 2011; Garfinkel & Shelat, 2003).

FUTURE RESEARCH DIRECTIONS

The future direction of this research aims to produce significant conclusions for the academic, public and private sectors. This study builds on the body of knowledge required, to advance the functionality of cloud solutions, improve physical, virtual machine performance, software, hardware scalability and the way programming language (i.e., *PHP, Python, HTML, Java, Visual Basic, C Shell, C++)* interaction in the enterprise. In essence the goal of this chapter is to provide fundamental or depth of expertise for technology novices, junior, expert IT professionals and/or vendors (CPNI, 2010). The chapter further delineates and/or improves on parallel technology essentials necessary, to support the deployment of cloud solutions (Sen & Sengupta, 2005; Buyya, Ramamohanarao, Leckie, Calhieros, Dastjerdi, & Versteeg, 2015). The ability to solve daily management and technical issues organizations and consumers deal with will be determined by different trends of cloud computing technology (Bruening & Treacy, 2009; Chen et al., 2010). These trends include big data analytic solutions, storage capacity, agility, robust of IT systems and program language solutions needed to leverage the performance of physical and virtual machines (Sen & Sengupta, 2005; Biggs & Vidalis, 2009; Buyya, Ranjan, Rodrigo, & Calheiros, 2010; Badger et al., 2011; Blaze et al., 2009; CPNI, 2010; Chen et al., 2010; Lowensohn & McCarthy, 2009).

CONCLUSION

In present years, cloud computing transformed the way customers in the public and private sector view IT technology. Presently, more organizations are adopting and deploying cloud computing solutions (Leighon, 2009; Bruening & Treacy, 2009; Chow et al., 2009). The flexibility, scalability, fast provisioning, elasticity, availability, encryption-based solutions, sustainability, improved security, reliability, redundancy, fault tolerance no single point of failure and latency encouraged customers to migrate enterprise IT resources from the legacy to modern data center infrastructure and platforms (Sen & Sengupta, 2005; Biggs & Vidalis, 2009; Chor et al., 1998; Chow et al., 2009; Gajek et al., 2009). Cloud computing is the next technology frontier in the innovation of information and communications technology (ICT). Vendors define cloud computing as a transformative leap for the physical and virtual network systems besides data centers. Cloud services and deployment models are selected as crucial service assets (Chor et al., 1998; DeCandia et al., 2007). While CIOs measure cloud computing as a progressing paradigm, customers need its resources, to support business transformation and system scalability (Lease, 2005; Sen & Sengupta, 2005; Buyya, Ranjan, Rodrigo, & Calheiros, 2010; Biggs & Vidalis, 2009; Chor et al., 1998).

REFERENCES

Alhazmi, K., Abusharkh, M., Ban, D., & Shami, A. (2014). A map of the clouds: Virtual network mapping in cloud computing data centers. *IEEE Canadian Conference on Electrical and Computer Engineering.* 10.1109/CCECE.2014.6901053

Alhazmi, K., Abusharkh, M., Ban, D., & Shami, A. (2014). *Drawing the Cloud Map: Virtual network embedding in cloud computing Environment. IEEE Systems Journal.*

Alhazmi, K. M. (2014). *Online Virtual Network Provisioning in Distributed Cloud Computing Data Centers*. Electronic Thesis and Dissertation Repository. Paper 2319. Retrieved from: http://ir.lib.uwo.ca/cgi/viewcontent.cgi?article=3713&context=etd

Alhazmi, K., & Shami, A. (2014). *A Greener Cloud: Energy Efficient Provisioning for Online Virtual Network Requests in Cloud Data Centers*. IEEE International Conference on Communications (ICC).

Alliance for Telecommunications Industry Solutions. (n.d.). Retrieved from: http://www.atis.org

Amazon S3 Availability Event. (2008). Retrieved from: http://status.aws.amazon.com/s3-20080720.html

Amazon Auto Scaling. (n.d.). Retrieved from: http://aws.amazon.com/autoscaling/

Armbrust, M., Fox, A., Griffith, R., Joseph, A. D., Katz, R. H., Konwinsky, A., . . . Zaharia, M. (2009). *Above the Clouds: A Berkley View of Cloud Computing*. Technical Report No. UCB/EECS-2009-28, Department of Electrical Engineering and Computer Sciences, University of California at Berkley. Retrieved from: http://www.eecs.berkeley.edu/Pubs/TechRpts/2009/EECS-2009-28.pdf

Association for Retail Technology Standards (ARTS). (n.d.). Retrieved from: http://www.nrf-arts.org

Badger, L., Grance, T., Patt-Corner, R., & Voas, J. (2011). *Draft Cloud Computing Synopsis and Recommendations*. National Institute of Standards and Technology (NIST) Special Publication 800-146. US Department of Commerce. Retrieved from: http://csrc.nist.gov/publications/drafts/800-146/Draft-NIST-SP800-146.pdf

Bertion, E., Paci, F., & Ferrini, R. (2009). *Privacy-preserving digital identity management for cloud computing. IEEE Computer Society Data Engineering Bulletin.*

Biggs & Vidalis. (2009). Cloud Computing: The Impact on Digital Forensic Investigations. *Proceedings of the 7th International Conference for Internet Technology and Secured Transactions* (ICITST'09), 1-6.

Blaze, M., Kannan, S., Lee, I., Sokolsky, O., Smith, J. M., Keromytis, A. D., & Lee, W. (2009). Dynamic Trust Management. *IEEE Computer, 42*(2), 44–52. doi:10.1109/MC.2009.51

Bruening, P. J., & Treacy, B. C. (2009). *Cloud Computing: Privacy, Security Challenges*. Bureau of National Affairs.

Buyya, R., Ramamohanarao, K., Leckie, C., Calhieros, N., Dastjerdi, A., & Versteeg, S. (2015). *Big Data Analytics-Enhanced Cloud Computing: Challenges, Architectural Elements, and Future Directions*. Retrieved from: http://arxiv.org/abs/1510.06486

Buyya, R., Ranjan, R., Rodrigo, N., & Calheiros, R. N. (2010). InterCloud: Utility-oriented federation of cloud computing environments for scaling of application services. In *Proceedings of the 10th International Conference on Algorithms and Architectures for Parallel Processing, 6081*, 13–31.

Center for the Protection of Natural Infrastructure. (2010). *Information Security Briefing on Cloud Computing, March 2010*. Retrieved from: http://www.cpni.gov.uk/Documents/Publications/2010/2010007-ISB_cloud_computing.pdf

Chen, Y., Paxson, V., & Katz, R. H. (2010). *What's New About Cloud Computing Security? Technical Report UCB/EECS-2010-5*. Berkeley, CA: EECS Department, University of California. Retrieved from http://www.eecs.berkeley.edu/Pubs/TechRpts/2010/EECS-2010-5.html

Chen, Z., Dong, W., Li, H., Cao, L., Zhang, P., & Chen, X. (n.d.). *Collaborative network security in multi-tenant data center for cloud computing*. Retrieved from: http://www.mit.edu/~caoj/pub/doc/jcao_j_netsec.pdf

Chor, B., Kushilevitz, E., Goldreich, O., & Sudan, M. (1998). Private Information Retrieval. *Journal of the ACM, 45*(9), 965–981. doi:10.1145/293347.293350

Chow, R., Golle, P., Jakobsson, M., Shi, E., Staddon, J., Masuoka, R., & Molina, J. (2009). Controlling Data in the Cloud: Outsourcing Computation without Outsourcing Control. In *Proceedings of the ACM Workshop on Cloud Computing Security (CCSW'09)*. ACM Press. 10.1145/1655008.1655020

Chowdhury, M., Rahman, R. M, & Boutaba, R. (2012). Vineyard: Virtual network embedding algorithms with coordinated node and link mapping. *IEEE/ACM Transactions on Networking, 20*(99), 206–219.

Cisco. (2011). *Virtual Machine Networking: Standards and Solutions*. San Jose, CA: Cisco.

Cloud Security Alliance (CSA)'s Security Guidance for Critical area of Cloud Computing. (2009). CSA. Retrieved from: https://cloudsecurityalliance.org/csaguide.pdf

DeCandia, G., Hastorun, D., Jampani, M., Kakulapati, G., Lakshman, A., Pilchin, A., ... Vogels, W. (2007). Dynamo: Amazon's Highly Available Key-Value Store. *Proceedings of the 21st ACM SIGOPS Symposium on Operating Systems Principles*, 205-220. 10.1145/1294261.1294281

Desisto, R. P., Plummer, D. C., & Smith, D. M. (2008). *Tutorial for Understanding the Relationship between Cloud Computing and SaaS*. Stamford, CT: Gartner.

Emig, C., Brandt, F., Kreuzer, S., & Abeck, S. (2007). Identity as a Service- Towards a Service-Oriented Identity Management Architecture. *Proceedings of the 13th Open European Summer School and IFIP TC6.6 Conference on Dependable and Adaptable Network and Services*, 1-8.

Everett, C. (2009). Cloud Computing- A Question of Trust. *Computer Fraud & Security,* (6), 5-7.

Gajek, S., Jensen, M., Liao, L., & Schwenk, J. (2009). Analysis of Signature Wrapping Attacks and Countermeasures. *Proceedings of the IEEE International Conference on Web Services*, 575-582. 10.1109/ICWS.2009.12

Garfinkel, S., & Shelat, A. (2003). Remembrance of Data Passed: A Study of Disk Sanitization Practices. *IEEE Security and Privacy, 1*(1), 17–27. doi:10.1109/MSECP.2003.1176992

Gartner. (2009). *Gartner Says Cloud Consumers Need Brokerages to Unlock the Potential of Cloud Services*. Retrieved from http://www.gartner.com/it/page.jsp?id=1064712

Gartner Hype-Cycle. (2012). *Cloud computing and Big data*. Retrieved from http://www.gartner.com/technology/research/hype-cycles/

Gellman, R. (2009). *Privacy in the Clouds: Risks to Privacy and Confidentiality from Cloud Computing*. World Privacy Forum (WPF) Report. Retrieved from: http://www.worldprivacyforum.org/cloudprivacy.html

Gentry, C. (2009). Fully Homomorphic Encryption Using Ideal Lattices. *Proceedings of the 41st Annual ACM Symposium on Theory of Computing, 169-178. 10.1145/1536414.1536440

Golden, B. (2009). *Capex vs. Opex: Most People Miss the Point about Cloud Economics*. Retrieved from: http://www.cio.com/article/484429/Capex_vs._Opex_Most_People_Miss_the_point_About_Cloud_Economic

Gorelik, E. (2013). *Cloud computing models* (Master's Thesis). Massachusetts Institute of Technology, MIT Sloan School of Management. Retrieved from: http://web.mit.edu/smadnick/www/wp/2013-01.pdf

Grance, T., & Mell, P. (2011). *The NIST definition of cloud computing. (NIST Publication No. NIST SP- 800-145)*. Washington, DC: US Department of Commerce. Retrieved from http://csrc.nist.gov/publications/drafts/800-146/Draft-NIST-SP800-146.pdfhttp://www.nist.gov/manuscript-publicationsearch.cfm?pub_id=909616

Gruschka, N., & Iacono, L. L. (2009). Vulnerable Cloud: SOAP Message Security Validation Revisited. *Proceedings of IEEE International Conference on Web Services, 625-631. 10.1109/ICWS.2009.70

Harris, T. (n.d.). *Cloud computing. An Overview*. Retrieved from: http://www.thbs.com/downloads/Cloud-Computing-Overview.pdf

Houidi, I., Louati, W., Zeghlache, D., Papadimitriou, P., & Mathy, L. (2010). *Adaptive virtual network provisioning*. Retrieved from: https://orbi.ulg.ac.be/bitstream/2268/126822/1/adaptive_embedding_VISA10.pdf

Itani, W., Kayssi, A., & Chehab, A. (2009). Privacy as a Service: Privacy-Aware Data Storage and Processing in Cloud Computing Architectures. *Proceedings of the 8th IEEE International Conference on Dependable, Automatic and Secure Computing, 711-716. 10.1109/DASC.2009.139

Joshi, J. B. D., Bhatti, R., Bertino, E., & Ghafoor, A. (2004). Access Control Language for Multi-domain Environments. *IEEE Internet Computing, 8*(6), 40–50. doi:10.1109/MIC.2004.53

Kant, K. (2009). *Data center evolution. A tutorial on state of the art, issues, and challenges.* Intel Corporation. Retrieved from: http://bnrg.cs.berkeley.edu/~randy/Courses/CS294.S13/1.3.pdf

Kaufman, L. M. (2009). Data Security in the World of Cloud Computing. *IEEE Security and Privacy, 7*(4), 61–64. doi:10.1109/MSP.2009.87

Ko, M., Ahn, G.-J., & Shehab, M. (2009). Privacy-Enhanced User-Centric Identity Management. *Proceedings of IEEE International Conference on Communications,* 998-1002.

Lease, D. R. (2005). *Factors influencing the adoption of biometric security technologies by decision-making information technology and security managers (Capella University).* ProQuest Dissertations and Theses. Retrieved from http://search.proquest.com/docview/305359883?accountid=27965

Leavitt, N. (2009). Is Cloud Computing Really Ready for Prime Time? *IEEE Computer, 42*(1), 15–20. doi:10.1109/MC.2009.20

Leighon, T. (2009). *Akamai and Cloud Computing: A Perspective from the Edge of the Cloud.* White Paper. Akamai Technologies. Retrieved from http://www.essextec.com/assets/cloud/akamai/cloudcomputing-perspective-wp.pdf

Lowensohn, J., & McCarthy, C. (2009). *Lessons from Twitter's Security Breach.* Retrieved from: http://news.cnet.com/8301-17939_109-10287558-2.html

Messmer, E. (2009, October 21). Gartner on Cloud Security: 'Our Nightmare Scenario is Here Now'. *Network World.* Retrieved from: http://www.networkworld.com/news/2009/102109-gartner-cloud-security.html

Metzler, J. (2011). *Virtualization: Benefits, Challenges and Solutions.* Riverbed Technology. Retrieved from: http://www.stotthoare.com.au/sites/default/files/files/1_16100_WhitePaper_VirtualizationBenefits_by_Webtorials.pdf

Molnar, D., & Schechter, S. (2010). Self-Hosting vs. Cloud Hosting: Accounting for the Security Impact of Hosting in the Cloud. *Proceedings of the Workshop on the Economics of Information Security.* Retrieved from: http://weis2010.econinfosec.org/papers/session5/weis2010_schechter.pdf

Oracle. (2016). *Management Network Virtualization and Network Resources in Oracle Solaris* (11.3 ed.). Reston, VA: Oracle.

Pearson, S. (2009). Taking Account of Privacy when Designing Cloud Computing Services. *Proceedings of the ICSE Workshop on Software Engineering Challenges of Cloud Computing,* 44-52. 10.1109/CLOUD.2009.5071532

Pearson, S., & Charlesworth, A. (2009). Accountability as a Way Forward for Privacy Protection in the Cloud. *Proceedings of the 1st International Conference on Cloud Computing,* 131-144. 10.1007/978-3-642-10665-1_12

Petry, A. (2007). *Design and Implementation of a Xen-Based Execution Environment* (Diploma Thesis). Technische Universitat Kaiserslautern.

Price, M. (2008). The Paradox of Security in Virtual Environments. *IEEE Computer, 41*(11), 22–38. doi:10.1109/MC.2008.472

Rajalakshmi, A., Srinandhini, S., & Uma, R. (2015). *A technical review on virtualization technology.* Retrieved from: http://www.ijircce.com/upload/2015/october/69_A%20Technical.pdf

RedHat. (2016). *Advantages and Misconceptions of Virtualization.* Raleigh, NC: RedHat.

Ristenpart, T., Tromer, E., Shacham, H., & Savage, S. (2009). Hey, You, Get Off of My Cloud: Exploring Information Leakage in Third-Party Compute Clouds. *Proceedings of the 16th ACM Conference on Computer and Communications Security,* 199-212. 10.1145/1653662.1653687

Rochwerger, R., Caceres, J., Montero, R. S., Breitgand, D., & Elmroth, E. (2009). The RESERVOIR Model and Architecture for Open Federated Cloud Computing. *IBM Systems Journal, 53*(4), 4:1–4:11. doi:10.1147/JRD.2009.5429058

Ross, V. W. (2010). *Factors influencing the adoption of cloud computing by Decision making manager.* (Capella University). ProQuest Dissertations and Theses. Retrieved from http://search.proquest.com/docview/305262031?accountid=27965

Schubert, L., Kipp, A., & Wesner, S. (2009). Above the Clouds: From Grids to Service- Oriented Operating Systems. In Towards the Future Internet- A European Research Perspective (pp. 238-249). Amsterdam: IOS Press.

Sen, J. (2010b). An Intrusion Detection Architecture for Clustered Wireless Ad Hoc Networks. *Proceedings of the 2nd IEEE International Conference on Intelligence in Communication Systems and Networks,* 202-207. 10.1109/CICSyN.2010.51

Sen, J. (2010c). A Robust and Fault-Tolerant Distributed Intrusion Detection System. *Proceedings of the 1st International Conference on Parallel, Distributed and Grid Computing,* 123-128. 10.1109/PDGC.2010.5679879

Sen, J., Chowdhury, P. R., & Sengupta, I. (2006c). A Distributed Trust Mechanism for Mobile Ad Hoc Networks. *Proceedings of the International Symposium on Ad Hoc and Ubiquitous Computing,* 62-67. 10.1109/ISAHUC.2006.4290649

Sen, J., Chowdhury, P. R., & Sengupta, I. (2007). A Distributed Trust Establishment Scheme for Mobile Ad Hoc Networks. *Proceedings of the International Conference on Computation: Theory and Applications,* 51-57. 10.1109/ICCTA.2007.3

Sen, J., & Sengupta, I. (2005). Autonomous Agent-Based Distributed Fault-Tolerant Intrusion Detection System. *Proceedings of the 2nd International Conference on Distributed Computing and Internet,* 125-131. 10.1007/11604655_16

Sen, J., & Sengupta, I. (2005). Autonomous Agent-Based Distributed Fault-Tolerant Intrusion Detection System. In *Proceedings of the 2nd International Conference on Distributed Computing and Internet Technology,* 125-131. 10.1007/11604655_16

Sen, J., Sengupta, I., & Chowdhury, P. R. (2006a). A Mechanism for Detection and Prevention of Distributed Denial of Service Attacks. *Proceedings of the 8th International Conference on Distributed Computing and Networking,* 139-144. 10.1007/11947950_16

Sen, J., Sengupta, I., & Chowdhury, P. R. (2006b). An Architecture of a Distributed Intrusion Detection System Using Cooperating Agents. *Proceedings of the International Conference on Computing and Informatics,* 1-6. 10.1109/ICOCI.2006.5276474

Sen, J., Ukil, A., Bera, D., & Pal, A. (2008). A Distributed Intrusion Detection System for Wireless Ad Hoc Networks. *Proceedings of the 16th IEEE International Conference on Networking,* 1-5. 10.1109/ICON.2008.4772624

Shacham, H., & Waters, B. (2008). Compact Proofs of Retrievability. *Proceedings of the 14th International Conference on the Theory and Application of Cryptology and Information Security, 5350,* 90-107. 10.1007/978-3-540-89255-7_7

Shin, D., & Ahn, G.-J. (2005). Role-Based Privilege and Trust Management. *Computer Systems Science and Engineering, 20*(6), 401–410.

Shin, D., & Ahn, G. J. (2005). Role-Based Privilege and Trust Management. *Computer Systems Science and Engineering, 20*(6), 401–410.

Sims, K. (2009). *IBM Blue Cloud Initiative Advances Enterprise Cloud Computing.* Retrieved from: http://www-03.ibm.com/press/us/en/pressrelease/26642.wss

Sinclair, S., & Smith, S. W. (2008). Preventive Directions for Insider Threat Mitigation Using Access Control. In Insider Attack and Cyber Security: Beyond the Hacker. Springer.

Song, D., Wagner, D., & Perrig, A. (2000). Practical Techniques for Searches on Encrypted Data. *Proceedings of the IEEE Symposium on Research in Security and Privacy,* 44-55.

Song, D., Wagner, D., & Perrig, A. (2000). Practical Techniques for Searches on Encrypted Data. *Proceedings of the IEEE Symposium on Research in Security and Privacy,* 44-55.

Sotomayor, B., Montero, R. S., Llorente, I. M., & Foster, I. (2009). Virtual Infrastructure Management in Private and Hybrid Cloud. *IEEE Internet Computing, 13*(5), 14–22. doi:10.1109/MIC.2009.119

Stanton, J. M., Stam, K. R., Mastrangelo, P., & Jolton, J. (2005). Analysis of end user security behaviors. *Computers & Security, 24*(2), 124–133. doi:10.1016/j.cose.2004.07.001

Takabi, H., Joshi, J. B. D., & Ahn, G.-J. (2010). Security and Privacy Challenges in Cloud Computing Environments. *IEEE Security and Privacy, 8*(6), 24–31. doi:10.1109/MSP.2010.186

Toosi, A. N., Calheiros, R. N., & Buyya, R. (2014). Interconnected Cloud Computing Environments: Challenges, Taxonomy, and Survey. *ACM Comput. Surv., 47*(1), Article 7.

Vaquero, L. M., Rodero-Merino, L., Caceres, J., & Linder, M. (2009). A Break in the Clouds: Towards a Cloud Definition. *Computer Communication Review, 39*(1), 50–55. doi:10.1145/1496091.1496100

Vouk, M. A. (2008). Cloud Computing – Issues, Research and Implementations. *Proceedings of the 30th International Conference on Information Technology Interfaces,* 31-40.

Vozmediano, R. M., Montero, R. S., & Llorente, I. M. (2011). Multi-Cloud Deployment of Computing Clusters for Loosely-Coupled MTC Applications. *IEEE Transactions on Parallel and Distributed Systems*, *22*(6), 924–930. doi:10.1109/TPDS.2010.186

Zetter, K. (2010). Google hackers Targeted Source Code of More Than 30 Companies. *Wired Threat Level*. Retrieved from: http://www.wired.com/threatlevel/2010/01/google-hackattack/

Zhang, Y., & Joshi, J. (2009). Access Control and Trust Management for Emerging Multidomain Environments. In S. Upadhyay & R. O. Rao (Eds.), *Annals of Emerging Research in Information Assurance, Security and Privacy Services* (pp. 421–452). Emerald Group Publishing.

Zimory Gmb, H. (2009). *Zimory Distributed Cloud-Whitepaper*. Retrieved from: http://www.zimory.de/index.php?eID=tx_nawsecuredl&u=0&file=fileadmin/user_upload/pdf/Distributed_Clouds_Whitepaper.pdf&t=1359027268&hash=93c5f42f8c91817a746f7b8cff55fbdc68ae7379

KEY TERMS AND DEFINITIONS

Cloud Provisioning: A process that selects applications and services to be made available in the public cloud.

Full Virtualization: The practice which includes hardware capabilities initiated by a single or various processor(s).

Migration: A practice of relocating guest virtual systems from single-to-single or single-to-multiple host computers.

Network Virtualization: The method of delivering hardware and software network resources and software into an exclusive, application-based or physical as well as virtual network solutions.

Provisioning: A process of deploying network equipment and/or making available network resources via virtualized servers.

Para-Virtualization: Best described as a set of applications and information patterns that are made available to the virtualized guest system.

Software Virtualization: The limitation of software virtualization is that, all machine activities/performance degrade, due to binary translation or resolution that force the system to run slowly.

Virtual Machines: A process that takes place on physical machines that use applications designed to provide functioning background. The software is designed to run or host a guest operating system.

Virtualization: A central physical configuration of several technologies. This includes the method of building virtual rather than physical system(s) in the network e.g., hardware platform, operating system, storage device or other related network resources.

This research was previously published in Advancing Cloud Database Systems and Capacity Planning With Dynamic Applications edited by Narendra Kumar Kamila, pages 47-90, copyright year 2017 by Information Science Reference (an imprint of IGI Global).

Chapter 5
A Comprehensive Survey on Trust Issue and Its Deployed Models in Computing Environment

Shivani Jaswal
Chandigarh University, India

Gurpreet Singh
Chandigarh University, India

ABSTRACT

Cloud computing is growing with a giant pace in today's world. The speed with which it is growing, the same speed is taken over by the insecure data transfer over the cloud. There are many security issues that are underlying in cloud computing. This chapter presents how a trust is built between any user and a cloud service provider. Various techniques have been adopted to calculate the value of trust and further how it can be strength. This chapter has also explained various trust models based on the necessities of a user. This chapter has also thrown some light over the concept of TTP, i.e., Trusted Third Party which further helps in maintaining trust over the cloud environment.

INTRODUCTION

By the growing era of various computing techniques, resources have become cheaper in cost, powerful and available more than required without any hindrance or disturbance. This computing technology has enabled the world of realization that denotes a Cloud Computing model.

In Cloud Computing environment, resources are provided that can be leased on demand and then can be released by the users when their need is over. This Cloud Computing has made an impact on the IT industry over the past few years. Some of the examples of cloud services are Google, Amazon and Microsoft that provide the most powerful, trustworthy and cost efficient services.

DOI: 10.4018/978-1-5225-8176-5.ch005

The cloud works on the "Pay-as-you-go" model that supports storage and network bandwidth services, whereas computation slightly depends on virtualisation level. While talking about Google AppEngine, it automatically scales in or scales out their services as required by the user. Amazon Web Services (AWS) charges the by number of instances that a user occupy per hour (even if the user's machine is idle) (Mell et al, 2009).

Cloud Computing providers provide various techniques for optimum use of resources. By imposing technique of per-hour or per-byte costing, a user can pay attention to his/her efficiency i.e. they need to release and acquire resources only when highly required by them.

VARIOUS DEFINITIONS OF CLOUD COMPUTING

A style of figuring where greatly versatile IT-related abilities are given as an administration over the Internet to different outside clients (Zissis et al, 2012).

A pool of disconnected, exceedingly versatile, and oversaw framework fit for facilitating end-client applications and charged by utilization.

The fantasy of vast processing assets accessible on request, the disposal of in advance responsibilities by cloud clients, and the capacity to pay for utilization of figuring assets on a fleeting premise as required.

Distributed computing grasps digital foundation, and expands on virtualisation, dispersed figuring, framework registering, utility processing, systems administration, and Web and programming administrations (Singh et al, 2015).

A kind of parallel and disseminated framework comprising of an accumulation of interconnected and virtualised PCs that are progressively provisioned and exhibited as at least one bound together figuring assets in light of administration level assentions built up through transaction between the specialist co-op and customers.

An expansive pool of effectively usable and available virtualised assets, (for example, equipment, improvement stages as well as administrations). These assets can be progressively reconfigured to acclimate to a variable load (scale), permitting additionally for an ideal asset use. This pool of assets is normally misused by a compensation for every utilization display in which ensures are offered by the framework supplier by methods for tweaked SLAs (Singh et al, 2016).

A model for empowering advantageous, on-request organize access to a mutual pool of configurable figuring assets (e.g. systems, servers, stockpiling, applications, and administrations) that can be quickly provisioned and discharged with negligible administration exertion or specialist co-op collaboration (Subashini et al, 2011).

TRUST IN CLOUD COMPUTING

Security is considered as one of the most important field that needs to be handled in the emerging area of cloud computing. If security is not handled as per requirement, then there are high chances of failing of cloud computing environment as it involves management of personal sensitive information in a public network. The security which is provided by service a provider becomes an important factor to protect the network and its resources so as to fulfil the feature of vigorous and trustworthiness.

For the proper administration of cloud system and its services to take place, trust management models the trust based on various elements and entities. Several leading research groups both in academia and the industry are working in the area of trust management in cloud computing (Kumar et al, 2012).

Many researchers have studied the issue of trust from user's perspective. Also, some of them have analysed various other issues related to trust from what an expectation is expected by the user in terms of privacy and security. Many techniques have been undertaken by the service providers to enhance the trust of the user in cloud and its services. Particularly, in this context, many parameters have been identified such as control, ownership, prevention and security etc. Decreasing control and absence of straightforwardness have distinguished as the issue that lessens the client trust on cloud frameworks. The creators have anticipated that remote get to control offices for assets of the clients, straightforwardness concerning cloud suppliers activities as programmed traceability offices, affirmation of cloud security properties and abilities through an autonomous confirmation expert and giving security enclave to clients could be utilized to improve the trust of clients in the administrations and specialist organizations (Shaikh et al, 2012).

A mechanism has been proposed separate software which can further create a trust binding between them. This mechanism introduces an involvement of four parties, namely those shown in Figure 1.

Here, the resource provider helps in hosting data and software both which further provides platform to execute that software on data. The software providers are the respective owners of software and data. The coordinator helps in coordinating all the resources in a better away. It also provides some of the important services such as searching for a specific resource or providing an interface to execute some applications.

The operation of the model is as follows:

The software provider and data provider can save their resources to the specific resource provider. Now, the uploaded resources can go through the encryption technique before they are used for the communication by various users. A coordinator i used by the data provider for a searching of a specific software. After the execution, an ID is generated for a individual requests which is forwarded to the data provider. After the usage is over, results are displayed on the data provider's interface which can be further printed or viewed anytime. In this due course, a log of operation is also prepared for the future reference. This is done so that it can be known that the product has been used and for the amount of time it was used (Huan et al, 2013).

Despite the fact that the creators guarantee that this model isolates the product and information, there is no affirmation that the product can't make a duplicate while the information is being prepared as just the calculation or depiction of the product is given to the information proprietor. Without the source code, there is no confirmation that the code won't contain any malevolent code covered up inside. Ad-

Figure 1. Components of trust software proposed

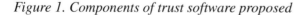
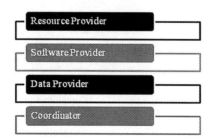

ditionally, since the product keeps running on information proprietor's rights and benefits, the product would have finish control over information. This is a security danger and the review trail regardless of the possibility that it is accessible, won't identify any security breaks.

TRUST ISSUE

At the time of origin, trust was usually used in the subjects of social science in constructing relationships and now its is considered as one of the important entity to make decisions.

Figure 2 interprets various features of developing a trust on an individual entity.

Basically, evaluation of trust includes the answering of a question, "That while interacting in a system, which nodes a user should interact and which should not?

Suppose there are two parties A & B.

B is using a service X.

Then A will trust on party B by the honesty of service X being used by the party B.

Traditionally, encryption and authorization plays a vital role in providing a strong foundation but now they are failing in case of cloud system as it provides scalability feature with it. Now, here trust acts as a security barrier and can fight against threats by limiting their interactions in a cloud computing environment.

Broadly, trust issues can be divided into three sections:

1. How to evaluate trust and which parameters to be taken into an account.
2. How to handle with fake information provided to generate a good value of trust.
3. How different level of security to be provided when a relationship based on trust in always dynamic in nature.

TRUST THIRD PARTY

We guarantee that utilizing Trusted Third Party benefits inside the cloud, prompts the foundation of the vital Trust level and gives perfect answers for safeguard the classification, honesty and credibility of information and correspondence. In cryptography, a Trusted Third Party (TTP) is a substance which encourages secure connections between two gatherings who both put stock in this outsider. The extent of

Figure 2. Parameters (benefits) of trust

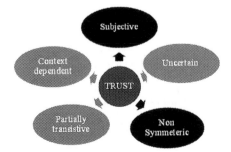

a TTP inside an Information System is to give end-to-end security administrations, which are adaptable, in light of norms and valuable crosswise over various spaces, land zones and specialization divisions. The foundation and the affirmation of a trust connection between two executing parties might be finished up because of particular acknowledgments, systems and components. The Third Party surveys all basic exchange interchanges between the gatherings, in view of the simplicity of making false computerized content. Presenting a Trusted Third Party can particularly address the loss of the customary security limit by creating confided in security spaces (Srujan, 2012).

''A Trusted Third Party is a fair association conveying business certainty, through business and specialized security highlights, to an electronic exchange. It supplies in fact and lawfully solid methods for completing, encouraging, creating autonomous proof about and additionally mediating on an electronic exchange. Its administrations are given and guaranteed by specialized, lawful, budgetary or potentially basic means''. This framework use an arrangement of advanced testament dissemination and a component for partner these authentications with known source and target destinations at each taking an interest server. TTP administrations are given and guaranteed by specialized, as well as by legitimate, money related, and auxiliary means. TTPs are operationally associated through chains of put stock in (more often than not called declaration ways) with a specific end goal to give a web of trust framing the idea of a Public Key Infrastructure (PKI). Open Key Infrastructure gives actually stable and lawfully adequate intends to actualize (Figure 3).

The trusted third party can be relied upon for:

- Low and High level confidentiality.
- Server and Client Authentication.
- Creation of Security Domains.
- Cryptographic Separation of Data.
- Certificate-Based Authorization.

Figure 3. Public key infrastructure (PKI)

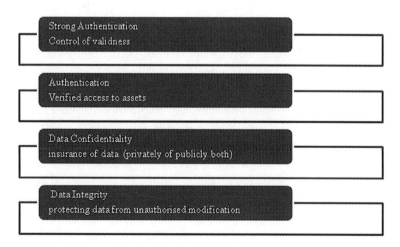

LOW AND HIGH LEVEL CONFIDENTIALITY

The technique of securing information going over the system is a hard and a complex issue, while the danger of information adjustment and information intrusion is ceaselessly rising. A cloud situation expands this unpredictability as it doesn't just require security of activity towards the cloud yet also between cloud has, as they do not have a customary physical association. PKI empowers executing IPSec or SSL for secure interchanges. IPSec is an IP layer convention that empowers the sending and getting of cryptographically secured bundles of any sort (TCP, UDP, ICMP, and so forth.) with no change. IPSec gives two sorts of cryptographic administrations. In view of need, IPSec can give privacy and realness, or it can give credibility as it were. IPsec clients can confirm themselves to the companion substance, utilizing PKI authentications in a way that upgrades versatility, on the grounds that exclusive the trusted CA certificate(s) should be transmitted in advance. SSL convention creates end-to-end encryption by interfacing amongst applications and the TCPIP conventions to give client–server verification and a scrambled correspondences channel between client–server. Because of the cloud conditions interesting qualities, interchanges are required to be secured amongst clients and has yet in addition from have to-have. Picking IPSec or SSL relies upon the various needs and security necessities. IPSec is good with any application however requires an IPSec customer to be introduced on every remote gadget (PC, PDA, and so forth.) to include the encryption. Conversely, SSL is incorporated with each program, so no unique customer programming is required. As the cloud condition advances use by heterogeneous stages it is unsatisfactory to expect clients to introduce an IPSec customer for encryption. Also as cloud administrations are for the most part gotten to through programs, SSL has many advantages for customer to have interchanges. Then again, IPSec underpins utilizing pressure settling on it a more productive decision for have to-have interchanges. This paper proposes actualizing IPSec for scrambling correspondences for have to-have interchanges and SSL for Client-to Cloud interchanges (Aljawarneh et al, 2017).

SERVER AND CLIENT AUTHENTICATION

In a cloud situation a Certification expert is required to ensure elements associated with cooperations, these incorporate confirming physical foundation servers, virtual servers, conditions clients and the systems gadgets. The PKI accreditation specialist is in charge of creating these required endorsements while enrolling these inside the put stock in work. At the end of the day, a Certification Authority constructs the important solid qualifications for all the physical or virtual elements associated with a cloud and it along these lines assembles a security space with particular limits inside the generally fluffy arrangement of elements of a cloud. Advanced marks in mix with SSO and Ldap, execute the

most grounded accessible confirmation process in appropriated conditions while ensuring client versatility and adaptability. The marking private key can be utilized to validate the client naturally and straightforwardly to different servers and gadgets around the system at whatever point he/she needs to build up an association with them. While the cloud is turning into the normal working stage, each administration will require a protected confirmation and approval process. As the calculated limit between an associations claim administration's and outsourced administrations moves toward becoming ''fluffy'', the need to embrace Single-Sign-On arrangement is basic. Clients require to make utilization of uses sent on their virtual ''"office"'' without repeating the confirmation procedure on each administration (application) supplier or keep up various passwords, yet make utilization of a solitary solid validation process that approves them to utilize benefits crosswise over confided in parties. ''Eight years back, it was tied in with securing applications inside the venture through character administration (Kalpana et al, 2017). Today we discuss securing applications in the cloud with characters beginning inside the endeavor''. Shibboleth is benchmarks based, open source middleware programming which gives Web Single Sign On (SSO) crosswise over or inside authoritative limits. It enables locales to settle on educated approval choices for singular access of ensured online assets in a security protecting way. Shibboleth innovation depends on an outsider to give the data about a client, named properties. In the proposed framework design, this is performed by the TTP LDAP archive. It is basic to recognize the verification procedure from the approval procedure. Amid the confirmation procedure a client is required to explore to his home association and validate himself. Amid this stage data is traded between the client and his home association as it were. After the fruitful validation of a client, as indicated by the client traits/qualifications, authorization to get to assets is either allowed or dismissed. The procedure in which the client trades his properties with the asset server is the approval procedure amid which no individual data is released and must be performed after fruitful confirmation. To boost interoperability between conveying parties, it is a need to receive broadly utilized benchmarks (Aljawarneh et al, 2016).

CREATION OF SECURITY DOMAINS

Presenting alliances, in relationship with PKI and Ldap innovation, will prompts proficient confide seeing someone between included substances. An organization is a gathering of lawful substances that offer an arrangement of concurred approaches and leads for access to online assets. An alliance gives a structure and a legitimate system that empowers validation and approval crosswise over various associations. Cloud frameworks can be sorted out in particular security areas (an application or gathering of utilizations that all trust a typical security token for validation, approval or session administration) empowering ''Federated mists''. Combined Clouds are a gathering of single Clouds that can interoperate, i.e. trade information and processing assets through characterized interfaces. As indicated by fundamental organization standards, in a Federation of Clouds each single Cloud stays autonomous, yet can interoperate with different Clouds in the league through institutionalized interfaces. A league gives a structure and a lawful system that empowers verification and approval crosswise over various associations (Armbrust et al, 2010).

CRYPTOGRAPHIC SEPARATION OF DATA

The assurance of individual data or/and delicate information, inside the structure of a cloud domain, constitutes a urgent factor for the effective arrangement of SaS and AaS models. Cryptographic Separation in which procedures, calculations and information are hidden such that they seem impalpable to pariahs (Aljawarneh et al, 2017). Classification and trustworthiness, yet additionally security of information can be ensured through encryption. Utilizing a mix of deviated and symmetric cryptographic (frequently alluded to as crossover cryptography) can offer the productivity of symmetric cryptography while keeping up the security of hilter kilter cryptography.

CERTIFICATE-BASED AUTHORIZATION

A cloud situation is a virtual net of a few free areas. In a cloud situation, the connection amongst assets and clients is all the more specially appointed and dynamic, asset suppliers and clients are not in a similar security area, and clients are typically recognized by their qualities or properties instead of predefined personalities. Along these lines, the conventional personality based get to control models are not powerful, and get to choices should be made in view of properties. An illustration is the utilization of an expanded X.509 authentication that conveys part data about a client. These endorsements are issued by a confirmation specialist that goes about as a put stock in focus in the worldwide Web condition. Characteristic authentications contain an attribute–value combine and the essential to whom it applies (Aljawarneh et al, 2017). They are marked by quality experts that have been determined in an utilization condition testament. Characteristic based get to control, settling on get to choices in light of the qualities of requestors, assets, and nature, gives the adaptability and versatility that are fundamental to huge scale conveyed frameworks, for example, the cloud.

A trusted declaration fills in as a solid electronic ""international ID"" that builds up an element's personality, accreditations and duties. Trust can be seen as a chain from the end client, to the application proprietor, who thusly puts stock in the foundation supplier (either at a virtual or equipment level as indicated by the chose benefit demonstrate). A Trusted Third Party can give the required trust by ensuring that imparting parties are who they claim to be and have been examined to hold fast to strict prerequisites. This procedure is performed through the affirmation procedure, amid which an element requiring accreditation is required to accommodate with an arrangement of approaches and necessities.

Some of the key factors that are common in front of various disciplines and researchers in field of trust are:

- Trust plays a role only when the environment is uncertain and risky.
- Trust is the basis based on which certain decisions are made.
- Trust is built using prior knowledge and experience.
- Trust is a subjective notion based on opinion and values of an individual.
- Trust changes with time and new knowledge while experience will have overriding influence over the old ones.
- Trust is context-dependent.
- Trust is multi-faceted.

VARIOUS TRUST MODELS

Cuboid Trust

CuboidTrust is a worldwide notoriety based trust display for distributed systems. It takes three factors in particular, commitment of the companion to the framework, associate's reliability in giving input and nature of assets to assemble four relations. At that point it makes a cuboid utilizing little solid shapes whose directions (x,y,z) where z – nature of asset, y – peer that stores the esteem and x – the associate which appraised the asset and indicated by Px,y,z. The rating is parallel, 1 showing credible and (–1) demonstrating inauthentic or no evaluating. Worldwide trust for each associate has been figured utilizing power emphasis of the considerable number of qualities put away by the companions.

Eigen Trust

EigenTrust relegates each associate a one of a kind worldwide trust an incentive in a P2P document sharing system, in light of the companion's history of transfers. This reduces the downloading of inauthentic records. Nearby trust esteem Sij has been characterized

$$Sij = sat\left(i,j\right) - unsat\left(i,j\right)$$

where sat(i,j) indicates the tasteful downloads by i from j and unsat(i,j) is the inadmissible downloads by i from j. Power cycle is utilized to process the worldwide trust for each associate.

AntRep

AntRep calculation depends on swarm insight. In this calculation, each companion keeps up a notoriety table like separation vector steering table. The notoriety table somewhat varies from the directing table as in

1. Each associate in the notoriety table compares to one notoriety content;
2. The metric is the likelihood of picking each neighbour as the following jump while in the steering table it is the bounce tally to goals. Both forward ants and in reverse ants are utilized for discovering notoriety esteems and proliferating them.

In the event that the notoriety table has a neighbour with the most astounding notoriety, a unicast subterranean insect is sent toward that path. On the off chance that no inclination exists, communicate ants are sent along every one of the ways.

Once the required notoriety data is discovered, a retrogressive subterranean insect is produced. At the point when this subterranean insect goes back, it refreshes all the notoriety tables in every hub on its way.

Figure 4. Cuboid trust i.e. associatively P(x,y,z)

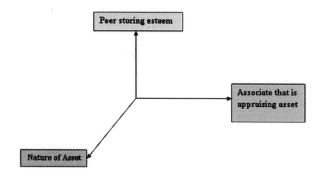

Peer Trust

This is notoriety based put stock in supporting structure. This incorporates a rational versatile put stock in display for measuring and looking at the reliability of associates in light of an exchange based input framework. It presents three fundamental trust parameters to be specific input an associate gets from different companions, the aggregate number of exchanges a companion plays out, the believability of the criticism sources and two versatile components that are exchange setting factor and the group setting factor in processing dependability of associates, at that point it consolidates these elements to figure a general trust metric.

TRUST EVOLUTION

Also, trust advancement display for Peer to Peer Systems have been introduced. This model uses two basic measurements, experience and setting to assemble confide seeing someone among peers. It fabricates two sorts of trust: coordinate trust and suggestion trust measures trust inside the interim.

Coordinate trust (CT) between two companions is processed utilizing the keep going n associations between those substances. Prescribed trust is ascertained utilizing proposals from different associates and the past collaborations with the suggesting peers.

TRUST ANT COLONY SYSTEM (TACS)

TACS depends on the bio-enlivened calculation of insect settlement framework. In this model pheromone follows are related to the measure of trust a companion has on its neighbours when providing a particular administration. It processes and chooses both the most dependable hub to associate and the most reliable way prompting that companion. Each associate needs to monitor the present topology of the system as each companion has its own particular pheromone follows for each connection. Ants go along each way looking building the most reliable way prompting the most trustworthy server.

Ants stop the hunt once they discover a hub that offers the administration asked for by the customer and the pheromone follows having a place with the present way prompting it are over the preset limit, else they would take after on additionally choosing a neighbor that has not been gone to yet.

Figure 5. Interface between substances via coordinate trust

CONCLUSION

Nowadays, lots of security issues are arising while using any service of Cloud. Similarly, the issue of trust is the biggest issue which is hindering user to use various services of cloud required as per their needs. This chapter has thrown light that why trust is considered as threat in communicating over the cloud. Also, this Chapter has elaborated the issue of trust in detail by taking various perspectives in detail. Also, some of the various trust models have been explained which are used for calculating trust strength and other parameters. In the end, various other trust models have been discussed in detail that takes various parameters of security into an account.

REFERENCES

Aberer, K., & Despotovic, Z. (2001). Managing trust in a peer-2-peer information system. *Proc. of 10th International Conference on Information and Knowledge Management*, 310-317. 10.1145/502585.502638

Ahmed, Xiang, & Ali. (2010). Above the Trust and Security in Cloud Computing: A Notion towards Innovation. *IEEE/IFIP International Conference on Embedded and Ubiquitous Computing*. doi:10.1109/CSCWD.2010.5471954

Aljawarneh, S., Aldwairi, M., & Yassein, M. B. (2017). Anomaly-based intrusion detection system through feature selection analysis and building hybrid efficient model. *Journal of Computational Science*. doi:10.1016/j.jocs.2017.03.006

Aljawarneh, S., Yassein, M.B. & Talafha, W.A. (2017). A multithreaded programming approach for multimedia big data: encryption system. *Multimed Tools Appl*. doi:10.100711042-017-4873-9

Aljawarneh, S. A., Alawneh, A., & Jaradat, R. (2017). Cloud security engineering: Early stages of SDLC. *Future Generation Computer Systems*, *74*, 385–392. doi:10.1016/j.future.2016.10.005

Aljawarneh, S. A., Moftah, R. A., & Maatuk, A. M. (2016). Investigations of automatic methods for detecting the polymorphic worms signatures. *Future Generation Computer Systems*, *60*, 67–77. doi:10.1016/j.future.2016.01.020

Aljawarneh, S. A., Vangipuram, R., Puligadda, V. K., & Vinjamuri, J. (2017). G-SPAMINE: An approach to discover temporal association patterns and trends in internet of things. *Future Generation Computer Systems*, *74*, 430–443. doi:10.1016/j.future.2017.01.013

Armbrust, M., Stoica, I., Zaharia, M., Fox, A., Griffith, R., Joseph, A. D., ... Rabkin, A. (2010). A view of cloud computing. *Communications of the ACM*, *53*(4), 50–58. doi:10.1145/1721654.1721672

Barsoum & Hasan. (2012). Enabling Dynamic Data and Indirect Mutual Trust for Cloud Computing Storage Systems. *IEEE Transactions on Parallel and Distributed Systems*.

Beth, T., Borcherding, M., & Klein, B. (1994). Valuation of trust in open networks. In *Proc. of the 3rd European Symposium on Research in Computer Security*. Springer-Verlag.

Bonatti, P. A., & Olmedilla, D. (2005). Driving and monitoring provisional trust negotiation with metapolicies. In *IEEE 6th International Workshop on Policies for Distributed Systems and Networks (POLICY)*. Stockholm, Sweden: IEEE Computer Society. 10.1109/POLICY.2005.13

Boukerche & Ren. (2008). A trust-based security system for ubiquitous and pervasive computing environments. *Computer Communications*.

Buyya, R., Yeo, C. S., Venugopal, S., Broberg, J., & Brandic, I. (2009). Cloud computing and emerging IT platforms: Vision, hype, and reality for delivering computing as the 5th utility. *Future Generation Computer Systems*, 25(6), 599–616. doi:10.1016/j.future.2008.12.001

Canedo. (2012). Trust Model for Private Cloud. *IEEE International Conference on Cyber Security, Cyber Warfare and Digital Forensic (CyberSec)*.

Grandison, T., & Sloman, M. (2002). Specifying and analysing trust for internet applications. In *Towards the Knowledge Society: eCommerce, eBusiness, and eGovernment, The Second IFIP Conference on E-Commerce, E-Business, E-Government (I3E 2002), IFIP Conference Proceedings*. Lisbon, Portugal: Kluwer.

Huang, J., & Nicol, D. M. (2013). *Trust mechanisms for cloud computing*. Retrieved from http://www.journalofcloudcomputing.com/content/2/1/9

Kalpana, G., Kumar, P. V., Aljawarneh, S., & Krishnaiah, R. V. (2017). Shifted Adaption Homomorphism Encryption for Mobile and Cloud Learning. *Computers & Electrical Engineering*. doi:10.1016/j.compeleceng.2017.05.022

Kotikela & Gomathisankaran. (2012). CTrust: A framework for Secure and Trustworthy application execution in Cloud computing. *International Conference on Cyber Security*.

Li, N., Mitchell, J. C., & Winsborough, W. H. (2002). Design of a role-based trust-management framework. *Security and Privacy, 2002. Proceedings. 2002 IEEE Symposium on*.

Li, T., Lin, C., & Ni, Y. (2010). Evaluation of User Behavior Trust in Cloud Computing. *International Conference on Computer Application and System Modeling*.

Mell, P., & Grace, T. (2009). *The NIST Definition of Cloud Computing*. National Institute of Standards and Technology.

Microsystems, S. (2009). *Introduction to Cloud Computing Architecture*. White paper.

Muchahari & Sinha. (2012). A New Trust Management Architecture for Cloud Computing Environment. *IEEE International Symposium on Cloud and Services Computing (ISCOS)*.

Pearson, S., & Benameur, A. (2010). Privacy, security and trust issues arising from cloud computing. *Proceedings of the 2nd IEEE International Conference on Cloud Computing Technology and Science*, 693-702. 10.1109/CloudCom.2010.66

Putri & Mganga. (2011). *Enhancing Information Security in Cloud Computing Services using SLA Based Metrics*. School of Computing, Blekinge Institute of Technology.

Shaikh, R., & Sasikumar, M. (2012). Trust Framework for Calculating Security Strength of a Cloud Service. *IEEE International Conference on Communication, Information & Computing Technology (ICCICT)*, 1-6. 10.1109/ICCICT.2012.6398163

Shaikh & Sasikumar. (2012). Cloud Security issues: A Survey. *International Journal of Computers and Applications*.

Shekarpour, S., & Katebi, S. D. (2010). Modeling and evaluation of trust with an extension in semantic web. *Journal of Web Semantics*, *8*(1), 26–36. doi:10.1016/j.websem.2009.11.003

Singh, A., Juneja, D., & Malhotra, M. (2015). A Novel Agent Based Autonomous Service Composition Framework for Cost Optimization of Resource Provisioning in Cloud Computing. In JKSU-CIS. Elsevier.

Singh, A., & Malhotra, M. (2015). Evaluation of a Secure Agent based optimized Resource Scheduling Framework in Cloud Environment. IJCAR, 188-198.

Singh, A., & Malhotra, M. (2016). Hybrid Two Tier Framework for Improved Security in Cloud Environment. India-Com., 1601-1606.

Singh, A., & Malhotra, M. (n.d.). A Novel Agent Based Framework for Cost Optimization in Cloud Computing Environment. *International Journal of Cloud Applications*, 53–61.

Subashini, S., & Kavitha, V. (2011). A survey on security issues in service delivery models of cloud computing. *Journal of Network and Computer Applications*, *34*(1), 1–11. doi:10.1016/j.jnca.2010.07.006

Takabi, H., Joshi, J. B. D., & Ahn, G.-J. (2010). Security and privacy challenges in cloud computing environments. *IEEE Security and Privacy*, *8*(6), 24–31. doi:10.1109/MSP.2010.186

Yang, Jia, Ren, Zhang, & Xie. (2013). DAC-MACS: Effective Data Access Control for Multiauthority Cloud Storage Systems. *IEEE Transaction on Information Forensics and Security*.

Yang, Z., Qiao, L., Liu, C., Yang, C., & Guangming, W. (2010). A Collaborative Trust Model of Firewall-through based on Cloud Computing. *14th International Conference on Computer Supported Cooperative Work in Design*.

Zhang, Q., Cheng, L., & Boutaba, R. (2010). *Cloud computing: state-of-the-art and research challenges* (Vol. 7). Springer.

Zissis, D., & Lekkas, D. (2012). Addressing cloud computing security issues. *Future Generation Computer Systems*, *28*(3), 583–592. doi:10.1016/j.future.2010.12.006

This research was previously published in Critical Research on Scalability and Security Issues in Virtual Cloud Environments edited by Shadi Aljawarneh and Manisha Malhotra, pages 150-166, copyright year 2018 by Information Science Reference (an imprint of IGI Global).

Chapter 6
Anomaly Detection in Cloud Environments

Angelos K. Marnerides
Liverpool John Moores University, UK

ABSTRACT

Cloud environments compose unique operational characteristics and intrinsic capabilities such as service transparency and elasticity. By virtue of their exclusive properties as being outcomes of their virtualized nature, these environments are prone to a number of security threats either from malicious or legitimate intent. By virtue of the minimal proactive properties attained by off-the-shelf signature-based commercial detection solutions employed in various infrastructures, cloud-specific Intrusion Detection System (IDS) Anomaly Detection (AD)-based methodologies have been proposed in order to enable accurate identification, detection, and clustering of anomalous events that could manifest. Therefore, in this chapter the authors firstly aim to provide an overview in the state of the art related with cloud-based AD mechanisms and pinpoint their basic functionalities. They subsequently provide an insight and report some results derived by a particular methodology that jointly considers cloud-specific properties and relies on the Empirical Mode Decomposition (EMD) algorithm.

INTRODUCTION

Undoubtedly, cloud computing has evolved as a critical asset regarding the adequate deployment of large-scale, always-on services that are nowadays considered as a necessity within a range of important socio-economical ICT environments (e.g. online banking, high frequency trading systems, e-health databases/services). In practice, cloud computing is a paradigm that enables the deployment of dynamic and scalable virtualized resources to the end user through the Internet. Throughout recent years, a plethora of companies such as Google, Microsoft, Amazon and eBay have placed enormous efforts and investments towards the development, maintenance and upgrade of data-centers in order to improve their cloud-based services and further provide the best Quality of Service (QoS) as well as Quality of Experience (QoE) to the end user as indicated by Chengwei et al. (2010). Hence, their thorough analysis and proposition of

DOI: 10.4018/978-1-5225-8176-5.ch006

sufficient frameworks that support the various dimensions (e.g. security, availability, resilience) of the aforementioned domains of QoS and QoE has been prioritized in the agenda of the research community. An extremely core design element towards the healthy operation of virtualized cloud environments is regarded as the provision of mechanisms that may sufficiently confront security challenges that are likely to emerge due to the highly complex and inter-connected persona that persists in such environments.

By virtue of the intra-cloud hardware and software multi-layered nature of several components as well as the direct dependency with the Internet, the cloud composes a number of unique security concerns that need to be efficiently addressed. Apart from the networking aspect in regards to functionality and security, the cloud encompasses many technologies ranging from databases, resource scheduling, transaction management, load balancing up to operating systems and concurrency control. Thus, cloud networks trigger diverse security concerns such as storage security, data security, network security and secure virtualization. Moreover, in contrast with distributed systems as deployed over the Internet in the past where data owners had a full control over their data, their successors which are formulated by cloud environments hold intrinsic beneficial properties such as service transparency and elasticity which at the same time hold a complete control of the original owners' data. Hence, despite the end-user benefits gained by the virtual components that constitute the basis of such systems do also come with a range of threats that exploit the security holes on virtual machines (e.g. rootkit attacks on virtual machines investigated by Christodorescu et al. 2009) as well as with mutated cloud-specific Internet-based attacks that aim to compromise cloud networks (e.g. malware as studied by Gruschka et al. 2010; Marnerides et al. 2013), DDoS attacks on cloud services by Gruschka et al. 2010). According to Chen et al. (2010), blackhat hackers have already identified the potentials of the cloud since the manifestation, maintenance and operation of botnets seems to be much more efficient under a cloud paradigm in comparison with how it was in the past.

Furthermore, due to the aforementioned transparency and shared resource environment offered by the virtualized nature of the cloud, the work in Ristenpart et al. (2009), has demonstrated that hacker techniques have also transformed and evolved. In particular, it was noticed that attackers could easily construct side channels that could allow passive eavesdropping in the intra-cloud network as well as they could create covert channels that in practice send malicious data through the network. These vulnerabilities were achieved by exploiting the Virtual Machine (VM) placing method conducted by the cloud management software by allocating the attacking VM on a physical machine of the underlying datacenter and further by initiating an SSH keystroke timing attack (Song et al. 2001). Hence, the operational architecture and design of the cloud has indirectly aided the construction of new types of attacks that need to be adequately faced.

Hence, there has been a rapid development of cloud-specific security solutions that target to proactively and reactively detect cloud-specific threats either by adjusting the attack signatures of Intrusion Detection/Prevention Systems (i.e. IDS and IPS) or with statistical methods that encompass the notion of anomaly detection. IDS and IPS systems have been the main commercial solution for a number of years in the traditional Internet security domain as well as in current cloud environments and their efficiency has been questioned in several cases (Chengwei et al. 2011; Marnerides et al. 2013). Due to their signature-based concept and their full dependency on monitoring already known threats, such solutions tend to not be in a position at efficiently detecting new types of attacks that may manifest. However, the research community achieved to address this issue by suggesting a number of techniques that go beyond traditional rule and signature-based systems by implementing sophisticated statistical models that perform anomaly detection. Hence, such models have been incorporated in some IDS/IPS formulations (e.g. Snort.AD 2005).

Anomaly detection has been witnessed as a good asset in several disciplines since it has exhibited sufficient prediction, detection and forecasting accuracy in a number of scenarios as pointed in the comprehensive survey by Chandola et al. (2009). The properties embodied within anomaly detection frameworks as used in traditional IP networks (e.g. Lakhina et al. 2004; Zhang et al. 2005) have also led the research community to aim at employing such mechanisms within cloud-specific scenarios. As shown in previous works, it's considered as a good candidate at detecting and adapting in to new types of anomalies that might be caused by either legitimate (e.g. utility anomalies caused by operator errors, hardware/software misconfigurations studied by Chengwei et al. 2010) or malicious intent (e.g. malware analysis by Marnerides et al. 2013). In particular, the studies by Marnerides et al. (2013) and Shirazi et al. (2013) report that techniques derived by anomaly detection methodologies have proven to be much more effective than traditional rule-based approaches. The main reason for the latter statement is related with the fact that the statistical modeling embodied within such models allows the design of robust and holistic normal behavior models that consider a range of operational system and network features in order to be in a position at pinpointing any known and unknown anomalous patterns.

Therefore, in this chapter we initially aim at providing a brief survey on the state of the art in anomaly detection techniques as proposed for virtualized cloud infrastructures[1]. The target behind this survey is to provide a reader with the basic mindset regarding the design and deployment of anomaly detection methodologies in cloud-specific scenarios. Hence, via this comprehensive survey we aim at enlightening the reader on the applicability of anomaly detection techniques for the cloud scenery as well as to pinpoint on how each proposed methodology from the literature was formulated in order to meet cloud-specific requirements. Nonetheless, in order to facilitate an even more robust understanding to the general audience with respect to the usage of anomaly detection in such problems, this chapter is also dedicated at presenting a case study regarding an exemplar anomaly detection technique employed within a controlled experimental cloud test-bed. In particular, the demonstrated anomaly detection approach is mainly concerned with the security domain and particularly for the explicit task of detecting the Kelihos malware that was initially investigated by Garnaeva (2012) under the cloud-specific functionality of VM "live" migration that constitutes the basis on all commercial cloud management software (e.g. VMWare VSphere, 2012). The backbone of this technique is derived by the properties of the *non-parametric* Ensemble Empirical Mode Decomposition (E-EMD) algorithm that is proven to be an effective data-driven method for adequately decomposing highly non-stationary and non-linear signals as it happens with the network and system-wise measurements gathered within a cloud infrastructure.

BACKGROUND ON ANOMALY DETECTION IN CLOUD ENVIRONMENTS

By virtue of the exploding information and the demand of cloud-based online services with respect to processing data with high frequency rates by multiple clusters (i.e. datacenters), anomaly detection in computing and networked environments has gained momentum. The suitability of anomaly detection techniques is not necessarily restricted within the security domain as done by Christodorescu et al. (2009) but also applies for the domains of fault/failure management (Chengwei et al. 2010; 2011; Guan et al. 2013) and network/system resilience (Marnerides et al. 2013; Shirazi et al. 2013; Watson et al. 2013).

The main property of an online or offline anomaly detection technique is to establish a threshold of "normal" behavior based on past observations on a given system(s) or network(s) in order to detect any deviations which are considered as anomalous. In general, there are two categories of anomaly detection techniques; i) *parametric,* ii) *non-parametric.* In contrast with parametric techniques, non-parametric approaches do not have *a priori* assumption regarding the distributional behavior of the observed features. Both categories have been employed for a number of problems experienced in cloud environments and they have both shown some promising outputs.

Nevertheless, in order to better structure the various anomaly detection approaches proposed in past and current literature we consider as important to define the notion of the cloud for the purposes of this chapter. Hence, we consider the "cloud" to be the both the application layer services offered to the end-user (e.g. Software as a Service – SaaS) [2] as well as the underlying virtualized layer that is supported by hardware and software that defines the datacenter. Hence, for the remaining of this section we will navigate through a number of anomaly detection techniques that aimed to address security as well as fault management challenges the aforementioned layers.

As already mentioned, regardless of the various and differing cloud computing systems (e.g. Amazon EC2, 2006; Google App Engine, 2008) there have been a number of anomaly detection approaches that mainly aimed to address the various operational and security challenges on the multiple layers that determine the cloud. For instance, the work by Chengwei et al. (2010) placed a strong effort at the online detection of anomalous characteristics on utility clouds using multiple types of metrics from the system components in their investigated cloud (e.g. CPU utilization on server racks, memory utilization, read/write counts on the OS, etc.). In particular their proposed Entropy-based Anomaly Testing (EbAT) system was operating under observations with respect to the Shannon entropy timeseries resulted by the distribution of the measured raw metrics. They have explicitly used the Shannon's entropy formulation (Shannon, 1948) in order to capture the degree of dispersal or concentration of the metric distributions and further aggregate entropy timeseries from each hardware components of the cloud for further processing under wavelets (Cencay et al. 2001). Thus, the explicit anomaly detection aspect was achieved using the online implementation of wavelets as well as with visual inspection of the finalized timeseries (i.e. spike detection). As demonstrated, the EbAT system had promising outcomes with respect to scalability with minimal real-time computational overhead since while the volume of the gathered metrics was growing, their online scheme could scale extremely well with respect to the detection alarm time as well as with the computational complexity invoked.

Within a similar range of objectives with respect to the adequate online detection of anomalous patterns in the cloud, the work by Chengwei et al. (2011) proposed two statistical techniques. The aim behind that study was to demonstrate the effectiveness of the point-threshold-based Tukey algorithm and the windowing-based Relative Entropy approach over captured data from a cloud-based production environment and from a cloud test-bed for multi-tier web applications running on server class machines. In particular, the authors had the objective to illustrate how their two proposed algorithms could overcome the limitations of techniques that implement models with Gaussian assumptions. Moreover, their suggested techniques targeted the improvement of the detection accuracy as well as the system performance in order to aid towards remedies at the onset of an anomalous event caused either from a legitimate or malicious intent. Thus, their approach was directly related and adjusted to operate under scenarios of analyzing continuous measurement streams gathered from various levels of abstraction in the cloud ranging from hardware, system and software up to middleware and upper-layer applications.

Throughout the description of their methodology the authors emphasize that both algorithms operate under a non-parametric fashion, thus they do not hold any assumptions regarding the statistical distribution of the observed datasets. Hence, in contrast with some threshold-based techniques that rely on the Gaussian assumption (e.g. the Multivariate Adaptive Statistical Filtering – MASF method) in order to determine a "normal" behavior threshold the examined algorithms were data-driven without complying with any assumptions. As finally exhibited, the Tukey as well as the Relative Entropy approach managed to achieve much higher recall accuracy with a much lower False Positive Rate (FPR)[3] on the detection of various anomalies that were mainly caused by failures or performance degradations manifested in online services.

Inspired by the usage of the wavelet algorithm on detecting anomalous traffic in the Internet as demonstrated by Barford et al. (2001), the work by Guan et al. (2013) provided a novel prototype that enabled an online spatio-temporal anomaly detection scheme in a cloud scenario. Thus, Guan et al. (2013) achieved to initially formulate ad further implement a wavelet-based multi-scale anomaly detection system that relied on measured cloud performance metrics (e.g. CPU utilization, memory) gathered by multiple components (e.g. hardware, software, system) that consisted the examined institution-wide cloud environment. In order to adequately decompose and characterize the various non-stationary measurements as well as to capture the dynamicity of the cloud with respect to its internal (e.g. "live" migration of VMs) and external operations (e.g. service to end-users) there was the need to invoke several time sliding-windowing learning technologies that permitted the construction of meaningful wavelet functions. Hence, there was a coherent statistical description of the normal behavior of numerous metrics that could then be utilized for determining the deviations that could likely be caused by anomalous events. The resulted experimental outcomes were quite promising since the proposed approach reached a 93.3% of sensitivity[4] on detecting anomalous events with only just a 6.1% of the reported events to be false alarms.

Qiang et al. (2013) placed an effort towards the design and development of an autonomic anomaly detection component that could significantly aid at monitoring the health of an entire production cloud. Via tampering the commonly used Principal Component Analysis (PCA) approach the authors composed a strategy that on real-time could adaptively identify the most relevant principal components (MRPCs) for each type of a possible failure in an in-campus 362-node cloud infrastructure. Similarly with the work by Guan et al. (2013) their implementation relied on a total of 518 cloud performance metrics that described several operational aspects such as hardware, system and network performance. Throughout their experimentation the introduced prototype seemed to overcome other well-known algorithms such as Decision Trees, Bayesian Networks and Support Vector Machines (SVMs) since it achieved a rate of 91.4% for sensitivity at detecting various anomalies with an extremely low false positive rate of 3.7%. In order to empower their experimental outcomes, this study also employed the suggested algorithm on emulated datasets gathered from a Google datacenter and achieved similar detection accuracy performance.

Under a different mindset than other pieces of work, the study by Doelitzscher et al. (2013) proposed an anomaly detection methodology that did not solely aimed at characterizing the cloud-specific performance metrics but rather targeted at profiling user behavior within a SaaS cloud. Through carefully designed use case scenarios Doelitzscher et al. (2013) defined the normal behavior of a user's VM(s) based on the events monitored by the cloud management software. Thus, based on the utilization of a VM over the time period it was active they could extrapolate using a neural networks paradigm on whether a VM holds a commonly seen utilization profile or whether it was dysfunctional throughout time due to its persistent re-initiation as seen by the management software. With the development of user-specific normal behavior profiles it was subsequently feasible to create a cloud-wide normal behavior model that in practice generalized the aggregate of user-specific profiles. The implemented scheme was validated under a simulated environment and has shown reasonably good results with extremely low false alarms.

The seminal work by Bhanduri et al. (2011) produced the promising framework of Fault Detection in Cloud Systems (FDCS) that had the objective to detect faulty anomalous characteristics in a cloud setting by using cloud performance metrics under the Ganglia monitoring system (Ganglia, 2000). The FDCS algorithm was implemented in C++ using a Message Passing Interface (MPI) API and it is mainly composed by two phases; the push phase and the pull phase. Both phases synergistically allow the in-network interaction between the physical nodes that consist the clouds' underlying infrastructure (i.e. datacenter) in order to update each other regarding their local health information with respect to the local performance characteristics (e.g. CPU utilization, memory, I/O) after a comparison of the locally produced k-nearest neighbor algorithm (Altman, 1992) as resulted by the locally measured data. With the usage of a distributed version of an outlier ranking function it was feasible for this approach to initially identify locally on whether a given node experienced a fault and further notify the rest of the nodes regarding the occurred failure. Hence, the system could overall pinpoint the global outlier machines within the whole infrastructure. The experimentation conducted in this piece of work considered data from 8 physical machines that run a number of jobs for a period of 3 days and exhibited extremely good results with respect to detection accuracy.

Due to the fact that anomaly detection algorithms are prone to increase the number of flagged anomalies/events while the measured cloud performance metrics grow, Viswanathan et al. (2012) proposed a framework that allows the ranking of the severity of a reported anomaly. In particular, their framework consists of implemented parametric anomaly detection algorithms in conjunction with a ranking technique for specific false positive rates (FPRs) under an *a priori* assumption regarding the underlying distributional behavior of the measured data. With the use of the Z-score statistical metric (Kreyszig, 1979) as applied on two online anomaly detection methods that considered a Gaussian and a Bernoulli approximation respectively, the authors achieved to produce a time window-based anomaly detection and ranking approach that allowed the ranking of each reported anomaly. Through their experimentation that was conduced using synthetic as well as real datasets it was shown that their suggested framework could adequately detect several types of anomalies occurring on multiple cloud abstraction layers (e.g. hardware, system) and could further rank the threats based on the urgency required to act for remediating them. Hence, they managed to construct a system that would act as the main aid to an operator.

Pannu et al. (2012) instrumented an online adaptive anomaly detection (AAD) framework that aimed towards the autonomic detection of failures using execution and runtime cloud performance metrics. The notion of autonomic failure detection had the objective to aid towards the comprehension of emergent cloud-wide phenomena in order to ensure a level of self-management on cloud resources. Nonetheless, the proposed framework relied on an initial feature filtering and extraction process that managed to exclude useless cloud performance metrics, thus helping to increase the detection accuracy. Subsequently, all selected features were inserted within a component where the Support Vector Machine (SVM) algorithm was implemented. Their implemented SVM was based on a specially designed Gaussian kernel function and was in a position to map all the selected performance metrics on a hyper-plane where outliers were spotted as possible anomalous events on real-time. In parallel, the designed kernel function was updated on real-time, thus adapting on newly incoming testing sets. Nevertheless, under a real experimentation over a 362 –node cloud computing environment in a university campus the produced results were extremely promising since they exhibited the efficiency of the proposed scheme that reached over

91% of anomaly detection sensitivity. Moreover, the conclusive alarms flagged by the AAD framework were triggered under a small timeframe of below than 7.5 seconds and the real-time detection process was run on reasonable computational costs.

In the work by Smith et al. (2010) there was the introduction of an autonomic mechanism that was capable to detect anomalous events by the continuous analysis of noisy and multi-dimensional data gathered from compute cloud systems. In contrast with commonly used root-cause analysis tools which are in the majority of cases reliant on simple rules and event signatures, the suggested scheme was operating under a set of techniques that ensured an automatic analysis of real-time monitored data gathered from a range of cloud abstraction layers (e.g. I/O operations, memory read/writes on VMs, memory utilization, network packets). The implemented techniques could adequately transform the raw cloud features into a uniform data format that was subsequently filtered by dedicated feature selection algorithms in order to compose a meaningful dataset for the actual detection phase. In particular, the detection phase was achieved under a Bayesian network-based unsupervised learning scheme that allowed the monitoring of outliers from the normally distributed (i.e. healthy) nodes within a large-scale institutional compute cloud. During the performance evaluation of the proposed scheme it was evidenced that it was feasible to reach high detection accuracy of more than 90%.

Mi et al. (2011) constructed the Magnifier tool that in practice was dealing with the detection of real-time performance problems in large-scale cloud computing systems. By exploiting the traditional hierarchical structure of service components within a given cloud computing system the authors managed to model the user service requests under a hierarchical tree scheme. Given the performance indications by various metrics gathered from the cloud infrastructure, as well as with the usage of pre-defined empirical performance thresholds, the Magnifier tool was comparing the overall system behavior with respect to service component user requests. Thus, it was feasible to identify the most heavily consumed VM service within the examined environment and further localize the experienced anomalous events. The methodology behind the explicit anomaly localization was based on a PCA-based clustering formulation that had as the main objective functions to denote the service response latency and the total processing time for a given service that was running on a VM. The experiments conducted for evaluating the Magnifier tool revealed that in comparison with two other techniques it exhibited high detection accuracy of faults experienced on several cloud services. In addition, the Magnifier tool also demonstrated an extremely good ability at localizing the events and identifying the exact root cause of failure.

Given the wide usage of Googles' MapReduce framework by many cloud providers, the study by Kai et al. (2012) developed an online anomaly detection method explicitly for MapReduce-based cloud environments. MapReduce is a cloud computing framework firstly introduced by Dean and Chemawat (2008) that enables the distributed and parallel operation of applications over large-scale datacenters and is considered as a core software component for several commercial, utility and production cloud deployments. However, the internal scheduling of MapReduce that triggers various parallel processes within different task execution time-lags has an indirect negative impact on the granular detection of anomalous events that are likely to appear within a given datacenters' clusters. Hence, the work by Kai et al. (2012) orchestrated a density-based clustering scheme that based on peer-similarity could identify on real-time the anomalous patterns that could appear on the workload of a computing node within a cluster. In more detail, the suggested technique operates under the assumptions of peer-similarity that: a) in normal conditions the workload posed by the similar tasks is equal; b) in the scenario of an anomalous event, all tasks will indicate different characteristics. Thus, by considering measurements (e.g. disk I/O speed, CPU utilization, memory utilization per process) and with respect to the resource consumption reported by each computing node in a cluster(s) it was feasible to create similarity clusters that denote the normal behavior profile on a given time frame. Hence, any deviating outlier from the composed clusters would correspond to anomalous events. The experimentation conducted in this case was based on simulated attacks and the suggested technique exhibited a high detection accuracy of over 90%.

In parallel, Vallis et al. (2014) in Twitter Inc composed a long-term anomaly detection scheme that aimed to protect the availability and resilience of Twitter's cloud-based web services by predicting possible abnormalities that could likely manifest. With the construction of statistical learning models that were developed based on application (e.g. Tweets per second - TPS) and system metrics (e.g. CPU utilization) gathered from production Twitter cloud data it was feasible to efficiently track and detect anomalous characteristics on long-term timeseries. In particular, Vallie et al. (2014) designed a scheme that employed a generalized Extreme Student Deviate (ESD) test that aided on the decomposition of the examined timeseries. Moreover, by following a piecewise approximation with the usage of Piecewise Median and the Quantile Regression B-Spline methods on the underlying trend on each timeseries this work managed to track the changes on the timeseries trend component. In addition, by accounting for weekly timeseries seasonality this work managed to significantly reduce the number of false positive alarms. The evaluation conducted on the proposed scheme indicated that under a really small computational time it was possible to detect anomalies with high detection accuracy of over 95% with respect to the Recall, Precision and F-measure metrics [5].

Derived by a multi-level, self-organizing network resilience architecture firstly introduced by Shirazi et al. (2013) and subsequently extended by Watson et al. (2013), the technique proposed by Marnerides et al. (2013) targeted the explicit identification and detection of malware as initiated on an HTTP service running on a VM. This seminal offline technique was solely considering operational network traffic as seen on the network interfaces of each VM running on a physical node within an experimental cloud setting. Its algorithmic operation relied on the computation of a matrix that contained meta-statistics based on 13 network raw features (e.g. counts of bytes, packets, flows) that were subsequently used by a covariance analysis approach. In particular, the covariance analysis was in a position to pinpoint the most discriminant feature within the aforementioned matrix that essentially was capable at identifying the initiation and further establishment of the Kelihos malware (Bureau, 2011) over the active HTTP service. It was observed that the most discriminant feature was the energy metric derived by the packet timeseries of each active flow as computed by the Choi-Williams energy Time-Frequency (TF) distribution (Cohen, 1989). As the authors mention, this particular distribution was in a position to adequately capture the non-stationary properties of each unidirectional TCP flow (as also shown in other traffic characterization studies as in Marnerides, Pezaros et al. 2013) and they could further compose a meaningful metric that describe the evolution of transport flows on the TF plane. Hence, this granular view on each flow could effectively aid towards the sufficient construction of normal behavior profiles under the covariance approach. Based on the produced normal behavior profiles it was then feasible to monitor the change of the covariance matrix over time using the Euclidean distance between each computed matrix on every observational time snapshot and identify the malware activities.

The latter mentioned piece of work acted as the triggering point for future studies regarding the deployment of malware detection techniques in the cloud. Hence, in the next section we provide a case study that has the target to thoroughly and coherently present a malware detection scheme based on a non-parametric, data-driven technique that considers both network and system information.

CASE STUDY: MALWARE DETECTION IN THE CLOUD

Given the brief overview of cloud-specific AD techniques covered in the previous section, the aim behind this section is to present a case study on explicitly detecting the anomalous activity initiated by a particular type of malware. As already mentioned, this work was a natural evolution of earlier published work in (Marnerides et al., 2013; Shirazi et al., 2013; Watson et al., 2013) and had the objective to detect the Kelihos malware under the scenario of Virtual Machine(s) (VMs) "live" migration which is a core component within the management functionality of any cloud-based environment. In parallel, a secondary objective behind this experiment was to also answer on whether a VM that is already infected with malware would remain infected when it's migrated to another physical host. The scenario and the controlled experimental setup that we describe in subsequent sections were formulated based on discussions we had with operators from cloud providers in the UK as being part of the activities of the India-UK Advanced Technology Centre (IU-ATC) project (IU-ATC Project, 2008). We following describe the "live" VM migration process as well as the basic properties of the Kelihos malware.

VM "Live" Migration and Kelihos Malware

Due to the heavy concern of cloud operators regarding the security implications of VM "live" migration within an intra-cloud scenario we have considered as necessary to examine the detection of malware under this explicit cloud-specific property. In contrast with "cold" migration where migration occurs for powered-off VMs, live migration allows to move running VMs from one physical host to another. In practice, during this type of migration there is a real-time transfer of Operating System (OS) – related instances alongside all the memory related with all the activities of a given VM between two physical hosts. Live migration is an extremely important functionality contained within any cloud resource management strategy and is mainly executed for resource allocation purposes on real time. Thus, we have explicitly aimed to emulate live migration since the greatest majority of commercial cloud management software (e.g. VMWare VSphere, 2012) utilize this functionality by default.

As already mentioned, the malware sample used in this work is known as "Kelihos" and is regarded as an emerging threat based on investigations conducted by the studies of Bureau (2011) and Garnaeva (2012) and Marnerides et al. (2013). The Kelihos malware (also known as Hlux) is a replacement of the famous Storm worm, which was active in 2007 and replaced by Waledac in 2009.

A study presented by Garnaeva (2012) provided a thorough overview on the functionality of Kelihos and exposed its peer-to-peer network protocol. The authors highlight that the new variant that we use in our experimentation is capable of sophisticated evasion techniques both in system and network components. In practice, this malware monitors network traffic for HTTP and FTP in order to steal sensitive information and propagates through TCP port 80 where data exchange is completely encrypted. Furthermore, the initial infection vector used by Kelihos is through propagation of malicious links embedded in emails where these links are based on domains controlled by the bot master that generally use fast flux techniques.

Data Collection and Experimental Setup

Based on the earlier work of Marnerides et al. (2013) we have managed to build a measurement framework that is actually employed on the hypervisor level of every physical node. In practice, the measurement framework consists of a range of monitoring and post-processing scripts that employ Virtual Machine Introspection (VMI) using the libVMI library (2011) and the Volatility tool (2011) in order to summarize system-specific features (e.g. process list, count of threads etc.) for every VM that runs on a given physical host. In parallel, we were able to gather network traffic traces from every VMs' network interface with the usage of tcpdump (Tcpdump, 1987). Given both network and system-wise features it was then feasible to construct a joint dataset for each VM. Hence, our dataset can be seen as a joint set of a total of 55 network and system features on the hypervisor level that gives a summarizing measurement view for every VM under a sampling rate of 3 seconds for each measurement.

The experimental setup formulated in this work was achieved within a controlled Local Area Network (LAN) environment in order to have a robust ground truth regarding the normal system and network-wise behavior for all the VMs that composed the test-bed. As shown by Figure 1 the test-bed consists of two physical nodes running multiple VMs with varying resource utilization profiles (Host A and Host B), a management node (Management Host) that regulates the migration process, and some client machines. All physical nodes apart the client machines run Xen v4.1 (Xen, 2003) with the XAPI toolstack and Ubuntu 12.10 Linux as the hypervisor operating system. The VMs used for testing were running Windows XP (SP3) with some regular user activity (e.g. Internet browsing) and the VM that was infected provides HTTP service by virtualizing an HTTP Apache server. Thus, in order to generate some realistic background traffic we have written some custom scripts that enable the client machine(s) within the same LAN to randomly generate HTTP requests to the VM HTTP Apache server.

Figure 1. The experimental setup for malware detection under VM live migration

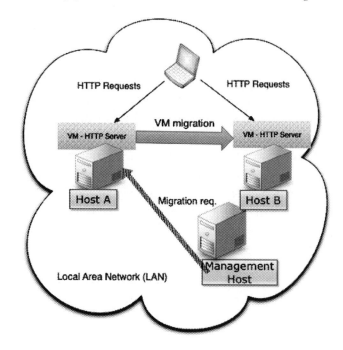

Overall, this experiment lasted for 20 minutes and we had the Kelihos malware injected on Host A around the 5th minute and the live migration to host B for the VM that run the HTTP server was initiated on the 9th minute. Based on the measurements gathered from all the running VMs of hosts A and B we subsequently constructed the joint system and network matrices for each VM and proceeded with their statistical, signal-oriented decomposition enabled by the Ensemble Empirical Mode Decomposition (E-EMD) algorithm as we describe next.

Methodology: EMD and E-EMD

A basis in the overall anomaly detection methodology is regarded as the robust non-parametric statistical characterization of the gathered measurements that was allowed by the E-EMD algorithm. The E-EMD algorithm is a variant of the EMD algorithm that was firstly proposed as a fundamental building block of the Hilbert-Huang transform (Huang, Attoh-Okine, 2005).

The EMD algorithm is a data-driven technique that allows the decomposition and description of non-linear and non-stationary data. Thus, it can naturally extract meaningful statistical insight regarding the internal properties of a given signal or timeseries that represent the data measurements. The data-driven decomposition instrumented by the EMD algorithm is achieved by considering the local characteristics (i.e. local minima, maxima and envelopes) of a signal on a given time window. The resulted decomposition based on the aforementioned characteristics is formulated with the creation of a small number of modes represented by Intrinsic Mode Functions (IMFs) that yield instantaneous frequency representations with respect to time. A given mode is considered to be a complete IMF if it complies with the following properties:

1. Equality or difference at most by one between the number of extrema and the number of zero crossings.
2. Throughout the whole signal the mean value of the upper and lower envelopes is zero.

Nevertheless, the original EMD algorithm tends to not be fully capable at decomposing signals or timeseries that hold flat properties (e.g. constant values) for long periods of time. In order to confront the aforementioned constraint, the studies by Torres et al. (2011) and Wu and Huang (2009) proposed a variant of EMD, the Ensemble-EMD that we also use in this work.

The E-EMD formulation behaves as a Noise-Assisted-Data-Analysis (NADA) technique since it considers the measurement noise factor whilst decomposing a given signal. The additive noise aids at composing a uniform reference scale distribution to facilitate the traditional EMD method and achieves to confront the "mode mixing" problem. Hence, the E-EMD initially considers a measurement signal $x(t)$ (e.g. the count of memory reads/writes on a VM, the number of captured packets etc.) to be composed as a series of observations in time t alongside a measurement random noise for each observation such as the jth "artificial" observation be defined as:

$$x_j(t) = x(t) + w_j(t) \tag{1}$$

As a following step, the E-EMD algorithm decomposes the signal $x(t)$ into a sum of IMFs as follows:

$$x(t) = \sum_{j}^{n} h_j + m_n \qquad (2)$$

The term h_j denotes a resulted IMF if it complies with the conditions of the EMD algorithm stated earlier and the term m_n defines the residue of the signal $x(t)$ after n IMFs are extracted. Overall, the decomposition of $x(t)$ that relies on the estimation of h_j and m_n is extremely dependent on an iterative sifting process that follows the following basic steps:

1. Identify the minima and maxima of a signal $x(t)$ with some measurement white noise.
2. Interpolate[6] between minima and maxima and provide the resulted envelopes of $e_{min}(t)$ and $e_{max}(t)$ respectively.
3. Calculate the mean using the envelopes: $m(t) = \dfrac{e_{max}(t) + e_{min}(t)}{2}$
4. Compute the detail of the signal $x(t)$, $h(t)$ as follows: $h(t) = x(t) - m(t)$
5. Initiate an iteration on residual $m(t)$, until $h(t)$ is zero mean and satisfies the sifting conditions until it's considered as an IMF.
6. Repeat step 1 until 5 with different noise series.
7. Derive the means (i.e. ensemble) of the corresponding final IMFs and terminate the process.

In order to demonstrate the effectiveness of E-EMD over the traditional EMD and further justify our choice on using this particular variant we provide an exemplar comparison between the resulting decompositions on a given measurement signal. Fig. 2 depicts the decomposition conducted by both EMD and E-EMD on a given measurement timeseries that describes the count of process handles on a given VM. It is clearly evidenced that the original raw signal depicted on the top plots holds flat properties and as expected the traditional EMD algorithm could not sufficiently narrow down that signal in descriptive IMFs that are terminated to a monotonic function. In particular, the EMD algorithm has produced two IMFs where the last one (plot on the bottom left of Fig.2) is not fully considered as an absolute monotonic function. Nevertheless, the decomposition resulted by the E-EMD approach exhibited a granular decomposition, hence it produced one more IMF having the last one (plot on the bottom right of Fig.2) is clearly defined as a monotonic function.

Methodology: Anomaly Detection Step

Prior to providing the precise anomaly detection formulation we feel the essence to initially provide some insight regarding the general notation used.

As already mentioned, the presented technique depends on empirical system measurements obtained at the hypervisor level for a number of running Virtual Machines (VMs) as well as the aggregated network traffic as being captured individually on the virtual network interface on each VM. The overall behavior of a hypervisor H for the full period of the experiment performed in time T is denoted by the sum of all the measurement snapshots captured from each individual VM on a given physical node where the hypervisor H runs. Thus, H is defined as:

Figure 2. Exemplar decomposition from the traditional EMD (left) and the E-EMD (right) for the count of process handles as measured on a single Virtual Machine (VM)

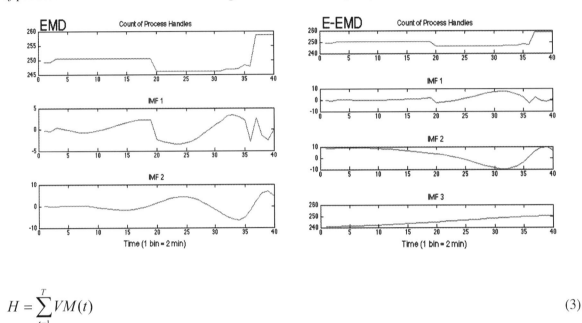

$$H = \sum_{t=1}^{T} VM(t) \tag{3}$$

where a measurements snapshot for a VM in time *t* is represented by:

$$VM(t) = \begin{bmatrix} f_1(\tau) & f_2(\tau) & \ldots & f_n(\tau) \\ \vdots & \vdots & \ddots & \vdots \\ f_1(\tau) & f_2(\tau) & \ldots & f_n(\tau) \end{bmatrix} \tag{4}$$

Given the definition in equation (4), τ is the measurements sampling rate for a feature *f* which in our case was 3 seconds, time *t* is the time taken for a full snapshot and in the presented experiment it was for a period of 2 minutes. The term *n* represents the total number of features where in our case was a total of 55 features. Hence, each column on the matrix of *VM(t)* corresponds to the timeseries of a single system or network feature *f* for a period of 2 minutes.

Due to the controlled experimental cloud test-bed described earlier it was feasible to determine and regulate normal workload activity on each VM before the activation of the Kelihos malware in order to compose a normal behavior model. The normal behavior model serves the purpose at enabling a descriptive statistical threshold that determines normal operation on the hypervisor level. Hence, we initially estimate the corresponding IMFs based on the E-EMD algorithm for each "normal" VM snapshot, and we subsequently compute the correlation matrix between them. Finally, the normal behavior threshold is defined based on the sum of the median correlation matrices. We have particularly used the median correlation matrices rather than the mean correlation matrices in order to gain a centralized average description of E-EMD on every VM snapshot.

Nonetheless, we denote μ to be the mean vector of the resulting snapshot IMFs matrix *Y(t)* for each feature column *f(t)* in a *VM(t)*. Under μ for every *f(t)* we derive a newly composed matrix

$X(t) = [\mu_1, \mu_2, \ldots, \mu_n]$, that summarizes the IMF characterization for each VM snapshot. Based on $X(t)$ we subsequently compute the reference correlation C_{ik} in order to quantify the behaviour of VM_i with VM_k in the snapshot t where they both run on the hypervisor M under normal operation. Given this quantification we subsequently compute a normal behaviour reference vector as follows:

$$R_{normal}(t) = median\left(C_{ik}\right) \tag{5}$$

Given the composition of the normal behavior profile based on "normal" VM snapshots it is feasible to proceed with the comparison of newly tested VM snapshots in order to determine on whether they pose an anomalous behavior or not. Similarly with the "normal" VM snapshots it is firstly required for every newly tested VM snapshot to get transformed and decomposed by the E-EMD algorithm. The decomposition allowed by the E-EMD algorithm enables the computation of a reference vector $R_{test}(t)$ that provides a statistical description for the tested VM snapshot. With the usage of this newly composed vector as well as with the consideration of the earlier computed $R_{normal}(t)$ we then derive the distance metric $d(t)$ that describes the deviation (or not) of the tested VM snapshot against normal behavior as follows:

$$d(t) = \left(\sum_{j=1}^{k} W_{tr}\left|C_j(t) - R_{normal}(t)\right|^{\vartheta}\right)^{\frac{1}{\vartheta}} \tag{6}$$

where k is the number of the testing VMs, ϑ is a tuning parameter[7], the term $C_j(t)$ is the correlation matrix of the jth VM snapshot and W_{tr} is a varying weight parameter denoted as:

$$W_{tr} = R_{test}(t) \Big/ R_{normal}(t) \tag{7}$$

The actual detection of malicious activity on a given VM snapshot is achieved under outlier detection allowed by the Median Absolute Deviation (MAD) test as also used by Fontugne et al. (2013). Hence, a VM is anomalous if:

$$d(t) > median\left(R_{normal}(t)\right) + \varphi MAD\left(R_{test}(t)\right) \tag{8}$$

where

$$MAD\left(R_{test}(t)\right) = \beta median\left(\left|R_{test}(t) - median\left(R_{test}(t)\right)\right|\right) \tag{9}$$

The tunable φ parameter at equation 8 seemed to work well when equal to 4 and β is always equal to 1.48.

Results

As already described earlier, the conducted experimentation aimed to address the aspect of VM live migration under the threat of the Kelihos malware. In general, this experiment had the goal to derive some answers with respect to the persistence of the infection after the migration and if it can be adequately detected by the proposed detection scheme. The actual experiment lasted for 20 minutes and it was necessary to construct in an offline mode a ground truth of normal operation from Host A by utilizing data gathered for a period of 10 minutes. As expected we observed that the Kelihos malware was transferred alongside all the other memory of the affected VM from Host A to Host B. Moreover, we have also witnessed the initiation of malicious activity (e.g. new child processes) by Kelihos right after the migration process was terminated and the VM was established on Host B. These observations are also implied by the results obtained by our anomaly detection methodology that are depicted via Figure 3.

In order to initially construct the normal behavior profile and determine the $R_{normal}(t)$ parameter that also affects the normality threshold we have used the data gathered from 5 running VMs on Host A. As evidenced via Figure 3, the introduced E-EMD-based anomaly detection method performed reasonably well on accurately detecting the malware on Host A right after its injection on the 5th minute. However, it seemed to not fully detecting the Kelihos instance on the first 5 minutes after the migration process occurred on Host B. For the first 2 post-migration minutes, the proposed technique achieved to identify that the first observational testing sample of the hypervisor snapshot[8] (i.e. $R_{test}(t)$) had an anomalous activity since it went over the pre-defined threshold. However, the subsequent snapshot was not correctly detected as anomalous regardless of the fact that the Kelihos malware was already injected.

The reason of this inaccuracy relates with the explicit behavior of Kelihos when firstly established on a VM. In particular, the Kelihos malware was rightfully detected on the first hypervisor snapshot (i.e. on the 6th time bin on Figure 3) since the majority of the activity corresponding to system processes triggered were transferred from physical host A to B. Hence, these processes consumed memory that contributed to the amplification of the measured host-specific signals in a point to be tracked by the

Figure 3. Detection of the Kelihos malware after being injected on a VM HTTP server on Host A where the VM migrates to Host B

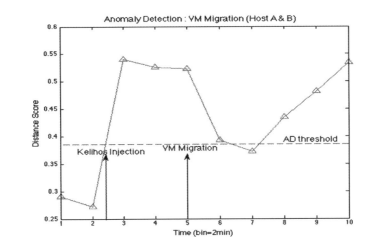

proposed detection scheme. On the other hand, during the second hypervisor snapshot the system related processes were reduced as they have been ordered by the malware executable in order to not be easily visible. At the same time, until the 14th minute there were not any networking initializations forked by the malware as it happens in the subsequent observational time bins thus the overall decomposition of all the hypervisor snapshots were still relatively close to the anomaly detection threshold. As evidenced by Figure 3, as soon as network-related processes were triggered, both system and network features contributed at amplifying the measurements and resulting to anomalous characteristics in comparison with the pre-defined normal behavior threshold.

A common approach at quantifying the detection performance of a given algorithm is the computation of the Receiver Operating Characteristic (ROC) curve that we also adopt in this work[9]. Hence, we provide Figure 4 that depicts the resulting ROC curve of our proposed detection scheme. Based on the produced ROC curve it is fairly reasonable to state that the detection accuracy rate in the presented technique is quite high. In particular, by considering the number of true positives (TPs) and false negatives (FPs) it is shown that the suggested technique has reached a 90% of overall detection accuracy. The shape of the ROC curve justifies the reported high accuracy rate where all the points hold high values of TPR and zero FPR expect one where an FPR of approximately 0.4 is attained.

Case Study: Summary and Conclusion

A critical security issue in virtualized cloud environments relates with the adequate identification and detection of malware, thus sophisticated anomaly detection approaches are required to be developed under cloud-specific settings. In this case study we have demonstrated the applicability of an anomaly detection approach that explicitly addresses the detection of malware and relies on the system and network measurements captured from each running VM at the hypervisor level. We have placed a particular focus on the scenario where VM and service migration (in our case with an HTTP server) occurs and regulated an experiment within a controlled cloud test-bed.

Due to the fact that the greatest majority of the monitored network and system features demonstrate highly non-linear and non-stationary properties, the proposed technique initially employs the non-para-

Figure 4. Receiver Operating Characteristic (ROC) curve for the proposed detection approach

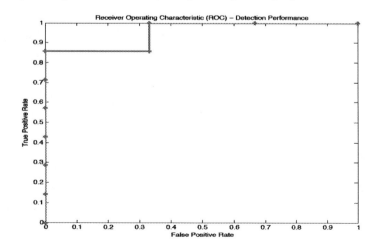

metric E-EMD algorithm in order to establish a coherent statistical characterization and decomposition of the measurement signals. The resulting outcomes of this experimentation have demonstrated that the proposed exemplar anomaly detection scheme may reach up to 90% of overall accuracy at detecting the Kelihos malware that has been reported to be an evolving threat where a range of attacks may be triggered after its initiation.

Overall, the main objective behind the presentation of this exemplar technique was to provide a practical example to the reader with respect to the design, deployment and evaluation of cloud-specific anomaly detection techniques. However, we feel the essence to clarify that the above described method is surely subject to improvement since the experimentation setup was not covering all the aspects of a real cloud but rather was restricted within specific cloud properties as VM live migration. Furthermore, the proposed technique did not consider any other types of anomalies (e.g. DDoS) or VM services with different workloads (e.g. a VM that runs a transcoding service for IPTV networks) that would surely affect the composition of the normal behavior profile as well as the anomaly detection threshold.

FUTURE RESEARCH DIRECTIONS AND ONGOING PROJECTS IN CLOUD-BASED ANOMALY DETECTION

The rapid growth of dependence by numerous online services in conjunction with the increased complexity forked by cloud deployments has definitely triggered a plethora of challenges with respect to their sufficient maintenance, management and security. As justified by the studies mentioned throughout this chapter, the particular concept of anomaly detection may adequately serve the role of a critical component within any strategy related to the sufficient resource management of a cloud environment. Hence, within the corresponding literature review in this chapter it was clearly evidenced that anomaly detection techniques have been successfully used in a number of resource management tasks that tackled a range of issues ranging from fault/failure management up to security-related problems.

By simply accounting the recent evolution of the Cloud of Things (CoT) (Parwekar et al., 2011) as resulted by the integration of ubiquitous and smart environments that compose the Internet of Things (IoT) (Atzori et al., 2010) it is anticipated to observe amplified operational as well as security concerns. Consequently, the diverse system and network characteristics alongside the intrinsic application-layer requirements posed by each involved heterogeneous environment will directly affect the mindset behind the design of future anomaly detection techniques. It is greatly anticipated that the highly demanding QoS and QoE-related requirements from the exponentially growing number of end-users or automated "smart" devices in such settings would truly place a great obstacle towards the development of real-time anomaly detection techniques due to the multidimensional datasets that need to be monitored, analyzed and further interpreted by a given algorithm. Thus, regardless of the mathematical formulation for a certain technique it would be necessary to systematically re-visit the domain of monitoring and measurements and aim to incorporate anomaly detection methods within native measurement instrumentations. Ultimately such integration will enable efficient and "lightweight" anomaly detection "on the fly" as achieved in Internet-based scenarios in the past as demonstrated by Levy-Leduc and Roueff (2009). Moreover, such formulations would also be in the position at composing situation-awareness given the implicit requirement that their analysis depends on the fusion of multiple and multi-layered metrics gathered by a range of heterogeneous environments.

Nonetheless, a number of the aforementioned topics are seen to be already under investigation by several large-scale European Union (EU) and non-EU research projects. Hence, anomaly detection for multiple aspects in the domain of cloud management (e.g. fault/failure management, security) is placed as a top priority topic in the research agenda of several academic institutions and industrial stakeholders. For instance, the multi-disciplinary EU funded SEcure Cloud computing for CRitical infrastructure IT project (EU SECCRIT, 2012) consists of 10 academic and industrial partners and has the main objective to construct mechanisms that confront the security risks invoked within real cloud deployments. In particular, the SECCRIT project aims at assessing the risks and challenges involved in cloud-based critical ICT environments (e.g. air traffic control systems) in order to identify and further implement anomaly detection components. Consequently, such components would be in a position to ensure a certain level of network and system resilience as well as to determine trustworthy high assurance policies. Moreover, a subset of the activities within the largest multi-disciplinary India-UK research initiative via the India-UK Advanced Technology Center project (IU-ATC, 2008) project targets at the development of anomaly detection techniques in cloud environments. As part of the objectives behind building resilient system and networks mechanisms, scientists involved in this project have already constructed offline and online anomaly detection frameworks (e.g. Marnerides et al. 2013; Shirazi et al., 2013; Watson et al., 2013) that are consistently evaluated over a large-scale experimental cloud test-bed that interconnects all 35 academic and industrial partners. The outcomes of this synergistic research initiative have considered a range of pragmatic scenarios that go beyond the traditional cloud management aspect and they included upper layer intrinsic requirements from areas such as e-agriculture and e-health. In parallel with the aforementioned projects, there is also a large number of other projects (e.g. EU FP7 NEMESYS, 2012, EU FP7 ANIKETOS, 2012) as well as agencies such as the European Network and Information Security Agency (ENISA) that have indicated their strong interest towards the development of anomaly detection techniques in order to target the rise of cyber-attacks (EU ENISA, 2012). Moreover, a strong initiative is also seen in the new strategic goals set by the EU regarding the security and management implications invoked by the evolution of future cloud deployments, thus a large funding scheme has been granted to the new Horizon 2020 research and innovation program (HORIZON2020, 2014).

The domains of critical cloud computing resilience and security have also reached the attraction of several projects funded by the National Science Foundation (NSF, 2010) in the USA. Prestigious institutions and companies are heavily interested towards the design and development of efficient real-time security solutions for large-scale cloud environments. As reported in the strategic plan for the federal cyber-security research and development program by the US National Science and Technology Council (NSTC) a top priority objective is the development of cyber defense mechanisms that may adequately predict and further remediate any threat seen on the national cyber grid in the USA (NSTC, 2011). Hence, there have been a number of frontier collaborative projects between US academic institutions and industrial partners under the umbrella of a total of 20 US million dollars. Thus, in alignment with the objectives established by the strategic plan of NSTC the collaborative frontier project related with Trustworthy CyberSystems for Health and Wellness (National Science Foundation, 2013) consists of a number of research institutions (e.g. Dartmouth College, John Hopkins University, University of Illinois at Urbana-Champaign) and is particularly investigating techniques that could sufficiently detect anomalous events (e.g. malware) that could manifest in mobile cloud environments that constitute the basis for a number of e-health systems. In parallel, the ongoing activities within another NSF-funded frontier project targets to re-visit the requirements behind the development of secure mechanisms in cloud computing. Hence, a number of institutions including the Stony brook University at New York, the North Carolina State University and Duke University have been allocated with the task at examining and proposing advanced techniques for anomalous incident detection, user and software authentication and secure data transportation. Furthermore, the joint NSF and CISCO-funded NEBULA project (2010) includes a multi-disciplinary team composed by prestigious institutions such as the Massachusetts Institute of Technology (MIT), Cornell University, Stanford University, Princeton University, the University of Texas, Purdue University and the University of California at Berkley in order to address current and future threats in utility cloud environments. In more detail, the consortium addresses the aspects of confidentiality, integrity and availability in such cloud sceneries via a systems approach under their developed NEBULA architecture. An extremely important element within the NEBULA future Internet architecture is considered to be the domain of anomaly detection since it has already proven to be utilized for a number of tasks ranging from cloud resilience, fault tolerance up to cloud resource management.

As shown above, the notion of anomaly detection is widely considered under several cloud-specific scenarios and is used to target issues related with the overall domain of cloud resource management. By virtue of the fact that anomaly detection methodologies depend on generic statistical formulations they hold the advantage at being flexible and adaptive on several problems. Thus, it is highly anticipated that statistical anomaly detection methods would evolve as foundational and possible native solutions in future cloud deployments.

CONCLUSION

Up to a great scale, cloud computing has already grasped and confronted the demanding needs derived by always-on, mission-critical or everyday services offered by a number of systems. IT and unified ICT networked infrastructures opt to outsource their computational tasks on cloud solutions that are proven to be cost effective, extremely optimal on hosting a number of services as well as tremendously efficient at conducting large-scale data processing tasks. Therefore the cloud is considered as a vital element within modern socio-economical ICT environments thus its optimal operation as allowed by adequate management and maintenance mechanisms is paramount. Nevertheless, the increased scalability, transparency and elasticity of services and resources as achieved by the computational and operational properties embodied within the cloud computing paradigm have consequently led to several issues with respect to security, fault diagnosis and the overall domain of cloud management. Hence, in recent years, there has been an emerging trend from both and industry and academia towards the design and development of cloud management schemes that assess the aforementioned issues.

Anomaly detection is a domain derived by data mining and statistics and as already mentioned in earlier sections it has seen a great level of success on several disciplines ranging to health informatics up to image recognition. Thus, it has naturally evolved as an important building block within several cloud management strategies and many formulations have been adjusted for cloud-specific scenarios. In contrast with rule and signature-based fault analysis or intrusion detection schemes, anomaly-based detection mechanisms tend to provide a much more holistic viewpoint with respect to the normal operation of a given network, system or infrastructure in order to become capable at observing deviations from a normal pattern. The intuition behind such schemes is not restricted at already known patterns but they rather center on a statistical baseline that apart from detecting known anomalous it also enables the identification of new types of faults or attacks. Hence, these kind of formulations do not only cover the aspect of cloud security at detecting anomalous patterns caused by malicious intent (e.g. malware,

DDoS) but they also address the discovery of events that compose anomalous system of network-wise properties that could have been caused by legitimate events (e.g. Flash Crowds) or human errors (e.g. router, switch, hypervisor misconfiguration).

Therefore, in this chapter we have initially aimed to re-visit several studies that managed to design, deploy and assess the performance of anomaly detection techniques in cloud-specific scenarios. Via a thorough and detailed description of seminal pieces of work, this chapter highlighted the contributions of anomaly detection techniques as applied in all the abstraction layers that consist cloud environments ranging from system, hardware and network-oriented issues up to application-specific problems. Through the designated literature review section, it was feasible to pinpoint the properties derived by *parametric* and *non-parametric* techniques and emphasize on the resulted outcomes produced by each approach. By assessing the conclusive experimental outputs on each of the selected studies we argued in fair of the effectiveness and high detection accuracy performance obtained by each proposed technique and further elaborated on their usefulness on a number of threats or faults that are likely to occur in a cloud scenery. The conducted investigation on each of the introduced experimentations have allowed to empower the argument regarding the applicability of anomaly-based techniques on the adequate identification and detection of not only security-related threats but also on the efficient profiling of anomalies that could directly affect the overall operation and resilience of cloud-based infrastructures.

In order to enlighten the reader on how an anomaly detection technique is instrumented within a cloud scenario, this chapter has also provided a novel anomaly detection scheme that explicitly addressed the detection of the Kelihos malware which is considered to be an emerging threat to cloud environments since it acts as the first point of initiation for several large-scale attacks (e.g. DDoS, phishing, email spam). The proposed offline and non-parametric scheme holds a high dependency on the Noise-Assisted-Data-Analysis (NADA) data-driven Ensemble-Empirical Mode Decomposition (E-EMD) algorithm that enabled the statistical profiling of the aggregated Virtual Machines (VMs) measurements gathered at the hypervisor level of a given physical node. In particular, the presented experimentation was conducted within a controlled experimental testbed and aimed to assess the detection of malware under the scenario of Virtual Machine (VM) "live" migration that is regarded as a core resource management process within any cloud environment. The evaluation of the E-EMD-based malware detection scheme revealed an accuracy of over 95% at detecting the Kelihos malware by using system and network-based features that were captured on the hypervisor level, thus highlighting the efficiency of the introduced technique.

This chapter has also managed to illustrate the importance of anomaly detection schemes in future resource management strategies by discussing on the research agenda from a number of research institutions and organizations. In particular it was briefly emphasized that the design and proposition of new cloud-specific anomaly detection components are currently placed as a top priority within many European Union (EU) and National Science Foundation (NSF) funded research projects. Hence, anomaly detection in the cloud is regarded as a crucial component by many organizations and it is already under investigation for future cloud-based deployments.

Overall, we argue that the content described herein can provide the basic means towards the comprehension of the complexity invoked behind the design and deployment of anomaly detection schemes in cloud environments. Given the thorough background literature review we targeted at a holistic overview of the trends that underpin the development of such schemes and in parallel aimed to describe some core requirements that need to be considered. Moreover, we emphasized upon the intrinsic properties of the cloud and demonstrated how such properties were included within cloud-specific anomaly detection schemes. At the same time, the exemplar E-EMD-based malware detection case study allowed the insightful view with respect to the development, instrumentation and evaluation of an anomaly detection technique. In conjunction with the discussion regarding the importance of anomaly detection as seen by several EU and NSF cloud research projects, this chapter has managed to empower the argument in favor of cloud resource management schemes that should be designed with an underlying dependency on anomaly detection methodologies.

REFERENCES

Altman, N. S. (1992). An introduction to kernel and nearest-neighbor nonparametric regression. *The American Statistician, 46*(3), 175–185.

Amazon EC2. (2006). Retrieved July 27, 2014, from http://aws.amazon.com/ec2/

Atzori, L., Iera, A., & Morabito, G. (2010). The internet of things: A survey. *Computer Networks, 54*(15), 2787-2805.

Barford, P., Kline, J., Plonka, D., & Ron, A. (2002), A signal analysis of network traffic anomalies. In *Proceedings of the 2nd ACM SIGCOMM Workshop on Internet Measurment* (IMW '02). ACM. 10.1145/637201.637210

Bhaduri, K., Das, K., & Matthews, B. L. (2011). Detecting abnormal machine characteristics in cloud infrastructures. In *Proceedings of Data Mining Workshops (ICDMW)* (pp. 137-144). ICDMW.

Bureau, P. (2011). Same botnet, same guys, new code. In *Proceedings of Virus Bulletin*. VB.

Chandola, V., Banerjee, A., & Kumar, V. (2009, July). Anomaly detection: A survey. *ACM Computing Surveys, 41*(3), 15. doi:10.1145/1541880.1541882

Chen, Y., Paxson, V., & Katz, R. (2010). What's new about cloud computing security. Technical Report. EECS Department, University of California, Berkeley.

Chengwei, W., Talwar, V., Schwan, K., & Ranganathan, P. (2010), Online detection of utility cloud anomalies using metric distributions. In *Proceedings of Network Operations and Management Symposium (NOMS)* (pp. 96-103). IEEE.

Chengwei, W., Viswanathan, K., Choudur, L., Talwar, V., Satterfield, W., & Schwan, K. (2011). Statistical techniques for online anomaly detection in data centers. In *Proceedings of Integrated Network Management (IM)* (pp. 385-392). Academic Press.

Christodorescu, M., Sailer, R., Schales, D. L., Sgandurra, D., & Zamboni, D. (2009). Cloud security is not (just) virtualization security: A short paper. In *Proceedings of the 2009 ACM Workshop on Cloud Computing Security* (CCSW '09). ACM. 10.1145/1655008.1655022

Cohen, L. (1989), Time-frequency distributions-A review, *Proceedings of the IEEE*, 77(7), 941-981. 10.1109/5.30749

Dean, J., & Ghemawat, S. (2008, January). MapReduce: Simplified data processing on large clusters. *Communications of the ACM, 51*(1), 1. doi:10.1145/1327452.1327492

Doelitzscher, F., Knahl, M., Reich, C., & Clarke, N. (2013). Anomaly detection in IaaS clouds. In *Proceedings of Cloud Computing Technology and Science (CloudCom)* (vol. 1, pp. 387-394). Academic Press.

ENISA. (2012). *Report on resilience in critical cloud computing.* Retrieved July 27, 2014, from https://resilience.enisa.europa.eu/cloud-security-and-resilience/publications/critical-cloud-computing

EU FP7 ANIKETOS. (2012). Retrieved July 27, 2014, from http://www.aniketos.eu/

EU FP7 NEMESYS. (2012). Retrieved July 27, 2014, from http://www.nemesys-project.eu//

EU SECCRIT. (2011). Retrieved July 27, 2014, from https://www.seccrit.eu/

Fawcelt, T. (2006). An introduction to ROC analysis. *Pattern Recognition Letters, 27*(8), 861–874. doi:10.1016/j.patrec.2005.10.010

Fontugne, R., Tremblay, N., Borgnat, P., Flandrin, P., & Esaki, H., (2013). Mining anomalous electricity consumption using ensemble empirical mode decomposition. In *Proceedings of IEEE ICASSP.* IEEE.

Ganglia. (2000). *The Ganglia monitoring system.* Retrieved July 27, 2014, from http://ganglia.sourceforge.net/

Garnaeva, M. (2012). Kelihos/Hlux botnet returns with new techniques. *Securelist.* Retrieved July 27, 2014, from, http://www.securelist.com/en/blog/655/Kelihos_Hlux_botnet_returns_with_new_techniques

Gençay, R., Selçuk, F., & Whitcher, B. (2001). An introduction to wavelets and other filtering methods in finance and economics. Academic Press.

Google App Engine. (2008). Retrieved July 27, 2014, from http://cloud.google.com/products/app-engine/

Gruschka, N., & Jensen, M. (2010). Attack surfaces: A taxonomy for attacks on cloud services. In *Proceedings of Cloud Computing (CLOUD).* IEEE.

Guan, Q., Fu, S., DeBardeleben, N., & Blanchard, S. (2013). Exploring time and frequency domains for accurate and automated anomaly detection in cloud computing systems. In *Proceedings of Dependable Computing (PRDC).* IEEE.

HORIZON2020. (2014). The EU framework program for research and innovation. *HORIZON, 2020.* Retrieved from http://ec.europa.eu/programmes/en

Huang, N. E., & Attoh-Okine, N. O. (2005). *The Hilbert-Huang transform in engineering.* CRC Taylor & Francis.

IU-ATC Project. (2008). Retrieved July 27, 2014, from http://www.iu-atc.com

Kai, W., Ying, W., & Bo, Y. (2012), A density-based anomaly detection method for MapReduce. In *Proceedings of Network Computing and Applications (NCA).* IEEE.

Kreyszig, E. (1979). *Applied mathematics* (4th ed.). Wiley Press.

Lakhina, A., Crovella, M., & Diot, C. (2004, August). Diagnosing network-wide traffic anomalies. *Computer Communication Review, 34*(4), 219–230. doi:10.1145/1030194.1015492

Lévy-Leduc, C., & Roueff, F. (2009). Detection and localization of change-points in high-dimensional network traffic data. *The Annals of Applied Statistics*, 3. Retrieved July 27, 2014, from http://code.google.com/p/vmitools/wiki/LibVMIIntroduction

Marnerides, A. K., Pezaros, D. P., Kim, H., & Hutchison, D. (2013). Internet traffic classification under energy time-frequency distributions. In *Proceedings of IEEE International Conference on Communications*. Budapest, Hungary: IEEE.

Marnerides, A. K., Watson, M., Shirazi, N., Mauthe, A., & Hutchison, D. (2013). Malware analysis in cloud computing: Network and system characteristics. In Proceedings of IEEE GLOBECOM CCSNA Workshop 2013. IEEE.

Mi, H., Wang, H., Yin, G., Cai, H., Zhou, Q., Sun, T., & Zhou, Y. (2011). Magnifier: Online detection of performance problems in large-scale cloud computing systems. In *Proceedings of Services Computing (SCC)*. IEEE.

NEBULA Project. (2010). *The NEBULA Project*. Retrieved July, 27, 2014, from http://nebula-fia.org/index.html

NSF. (2010). *National science foundation research project awards*. Retrieved July 27, 2014, from http://www.gov/mobile/news/news_summ.jsp?cntn_id=128679&org=NSF&from=news

NSTC. (2011). *Executive Office of the President, trustworthy CyberSpace: Strategic plan for the federal CyberSecurity research and development program*. National Science and Technology Council. Retrieved July 27, 2014, from http://www.whitehouse.gov/sites/default/files/microsites/ostp/fed_cybersecurity_rd_strategic_plan_2011.pdf

Pannu, H. S., Jianguo, L., & Song, F. (2012). AAD: Adaptive anomaly detection system for cloud computing infrastructures. In *Proceedings of Reliable Distributed Systems (SRDS)* (pp. 396-397). IEEE.

Parwekar, P. (2011). From internet of things towards cloud of things. In *Proceedings of Computer and Communication Technology (ICCCT)* (pp. 329-333). ICCCT.

Qiang, G., & Song, F. (2013). Adaptive anomaly identification by exploring metric subspace in cloud computing infrastructures. In *Proceedings of Reliable Distributed Systems (SRDS)* (pp. 205-214). Academic Press.

Ristenpart, T., Tromer, E., Shacham, H., & Savage, S. (2009), Hey, you, get off of my cloud: exploring information leakage in third-party compute clouds. In *Proceedings of the 16th ACM Conference on Computer and Communications Security* (CCS '09). ACM. 10.1145/1653662.1653687

Shannon, C. E. (1948). A mathematical theory of communication. *Mobile Computing and Communications Review, 5*(1), 3–55.

Shirazi, N., Watson, M. R., Marnerides, A., K., Mauthe, A., & Hutchison, D. (2013). A multilevel approach towards challenge detection in cloud computing. In *Cyberpatterns*. Academic Press.

Smith, D., Qiang, G., & Song, F. (2010). An anomaly detection framework for autonomic management of compute cloud systems. In *Proceedings of Computer Software and Applications Conference Workshops (COMPSACW)* (pp. 376-381). Academic Press.

Snort AD. (2005). Retrieved July 27, 2014, from http://anomalydetection.info/

Song, D. X., Wagner, D., & Tian, X. (2001). Timing analysis of keystrokes and timing attacks on SSH. In *Proceedings of the 10th conference on USENIX Security Symposium* (SSYM'01) (*Vol. 10*). USENIX Association.

Tcpdump. (1987). Retrieved July, 27, 2014, from http://www.tcpdump.org/

Torres, M.E., Colominas, M.A., Schlotthauer, G., & Flandrin, P. (2011). A complete ensemble empirical mode decomposition with adaptive noise. In *Proceedings of IEEE ICASSP*. IEEE.

Vallis, O., Hochenbaum, J., & Kejariwal, A. (2014). A novel technique for long-term anomaly detection in the cloud. In *Proceedings of the 6ᵗʰ USENIX Workshop on Hot Topics in Cloud Computing*. USENIX HotCloud.

Viswanathan, K., Choudur, L., Talwar, V., Chengwei, W., Macdonald, G., & Satterfield, W. (2012). Ranking anomalies in data centers. In *Proceedings of Network Operations and Management Symposium (NOMS), 2012 IEEE* (pp. 79-87). IEEE. 10.1109/NOMS.2012.6211885

VMWare vSphrere. (2012). Retrieved July 27, 2014, from http://www.vmware.com/uk/products/vsphere

Volatility. (2011). Retrieved July 27, 2014, from https://www.volatilesystems.com/default/volatility

Watson, M., Shirazi, N., Marnerides, A. K., Mauthe, A., & Hutchison, D. (2013). Towards a distributed, self-organizing approach to malware detection in cloud computing. In *Proceedings of 7th IFIP International Workshop on Self-Organizing Systems*. IFIP/IFISC IWSOS.

Wu, Z., & Huang, N. E. (2009). Ensemble empirical mode decomposition: A noise-assisted data analysis method. Advances in Adaptive Data Analysis, 1(1), 1-41.

Xen. (2003). *Citrix Systems, Inc*. Retrieved July 27, 2014, from http://www.xen.org/

Zhang, Y., Ge, Z., Greenberg, A., & Roughan, M. (2005), Network anomography. In *Proceedings of the 5th ACM SIGCOMM Conference on Internet Measurement* (IMC '05). USENIX Association.

KEY TERMS AND DEFINITIONS

Anomaly Detection: Detection of anomalous patterns in datasets using statistical techniques.

Cloud Networks: Networks in charge for the delivery of hosted services over the Internet to end-users.

Cloud Resilience: The ability of a cloud network or cloud-based infrastructure to maintain an acceptable level of service in the face of various challenges to its normal operation.

Cloud Security: A sub-domain of cloud resilience in charge of ensuring the secure transmission of data within a network and at the same time responsible for the detection and defense of the cloud environment from any malicious attacks.

Empirical Mode Decomposition: A signal processing technique that allows the decomposition of a given signal into different modes.

Malware Detection: Detection approaches that explicitly aim at detecting malware instances.

Virtual Machine Live Migration: The process where a running Virtual Machine is moved from one physical host to another.

ENDNOTES

[1]   By virtue of the large number of mathematical principles invoked in every reported work we do not provide the formulations employed in each study but rather direct an interested reader to the corresponding bibliography.

[2]   Several vendors may also mention SaaS under the acronyms of Platform as a Service (PaaS) or Infrastructure as a Service (IaaS) according to their products. However, for the purposes of this chapter we will only refer to SaaS as the definition for all the services offered by a given cloud to the end-user.

[3]   Recall accuracy is denoted as the rate of the number of successful detections over the number of total anomalies. The FPR is defined as the ratio of the number of false alarms over the total number of alarms.

[4]   Sensitivity or True Positive Rate (TPR) is defined as the rate of True Positives (TPs) over the sum of True Positives (TPs) with False Negatives (FNs).

[5]   The precision metric is defined as the ratio of True Positives (TP) over the sum of True Positives (TPs) with False Positives (FPs). The F-measure metric is also known as the F1 score and is defined as the harmonic mean of precision and sensitivity. For detailed formulations we refer any interested reader to Fawcelt (2006).

[6]   The analysis described in this chapter was carried out by using the cubic spline interpolation approach.

[7]   In our case the ϑ parameter worked well when equal to 2.

[8]   We remind the reader, that the hypervisor snapshot is denoted by the sum of measurements gathered by all the running VMs on a given physical node.

[9]   A ROC curve is a plot that demonstrates the evolvement of the detections' true-positive rate (TPR) against false-positive rate (FPR) where points towards the bottom left correspond to high thresholds (or low sensitivity) and those on the top right to low thresholds (or high sensitivity). The best performance is indicated by curves that reside on the top left, as these imply that sensitivity may be decreased and eliminate more False Positives (FPs) without degrading the TPR (Fawcelt, 2006).

This research was previously published in Resource Management of Mobile Cloud Computing Networks and Environments edited by George Mastorakis, Constandinos X. Mavromoustakis, and Evangelos Pallis, pages 43-67, copyright year 2015 by Information Science Reference (an imprint of IGI Global).

Chapter 7
Cloud Database Security Issues and Challenges

Ganesh Chandra Deka
Ministry of Labour and Employment, India

ABSTRACT

To get the desired benefits for the IT enterprise, NoSQL databases must be combined with proven and reliable SQL features into a single proven infrastructure meeting the manageability and security requirements of cloud computing. Various specifications, including SAML (Security Assertions Markup Language), improved interoperability across organizational boundaries are coming up. This chapter discusses some of the security issues of NoSQL databases. All the related technology used in the chapter are explained either where they appear or at the end of the chapter.

INTRODUCTION

Data collected from various sources such as social media, logs, mobile devices and sensor networks has become very sensitive as lots of organization use various cloud based applications for various transactions. Data compromise is caused by:

- Malicious attack,
- Web application vulnerabilities,
- Unauthorized access/change of data.

    Data needs security when

1. Data at rest,
2. Data in motion,
3. Data in use.

    Data security plays a vital role specifically when the data is remotely accessible in cloud. The cloud computing delivery models i.e. SaaS, PaaS, IaaS are attractive targets for attacker due to the volume of information that can be compromised.

DOI: 10.4018/978-1-5225-8176-5.ch007

Developed specifically for meeting the requirements of cloud computing NoSQL database also popularly known as "Not only SQL" databases are primarily a non-relational distributed databases. NoSQL databases support massive data storage across multiple storage clusters.

Varieties of NoSQL database having different features are available with open source and proprietary option. The very interesting fact about the NoSQL database is that, no two NoSQL database solutions are same since they are designed to meet the specific requirements of particular cloud based applications. Most NoSQL database does not offer a Data Definition Language (DDL) for specifying a global schema. There is no schema management interface that works across NoSQL systems from different providers, allowing application administrators to manage their data structure systematically (McWilliams & Ivey, 2012).

Since NoSQL has not been designed with security as a priority, protecting data stores has become a concern to organizations using NoSQL databases. For example the MongoDB Developer FAQ says "… with MongoDB we are not building queries from strings, so traditional SQL injection attacks are not a problem" (Sullivan, 2011). The lack of NoSQL security features, namely Authentication and Authorization support, means that sensitive data are safer in traditional RDBMS (Cobb, 2013). It was concluded in the proceedings of "2011 International Joint Conference of IEEE TrustCom-11/IEEE ICESS-11/FCST-11" that "The lack of encryption support for the data files, weak authentication both between the client and the servers and between server members, very simple authorization without support for RBAC or fine-grained authorization, and vulnerability to SQL Injection and Denial of Service attacks" (Factor, 2013).

The NoSQL security concerns are:

1. Authorization,
2. Authentication,
3. Confidentiality,
4. Injection [schema injection specifically in document databases].

This chapter discusses the emerging trends in NoSQL database security. Security mechanisms used by some popular NoSQL will be discussed in brief.

NoSQL SECURITY THREATS

Cloud providers offer services through Application Programming Interface (APIs) such as SOAP, REST, or HTTP with XML/JSON. Hence the security of the cloud applications depends upon the security of these application interfaces.

In comparison to SOAP-Based Web services, a REST-based approach to Web services is much easier to implement since REST simply relies on the HTTP protocol. REST uses (Lee & Mehta, 2013):

1. URIs (Uniform Resource Identifiers) to identify resources.
2. GET, PUT, POST and DELETE actions to retrieve, update, create, and delete the resources remotely through Web servers.

In addition, JavaScript Object Notation (JSON), a text-based data interchange format that is completely language independent and provides significant performance gains over XML due to its light weight nature and native support for JavaScript (Ying & Miller, 2013), is an excellent way to transport/ exchange messages between services as well as between client and servers.

Following are some of the NoSQL Vulnerabilities (Armorize Special Force):

1. **Cross-Site Scripting (XSS):** Client-side JavaScript Injection (XSS) are very common injection attack. The common source of PHP security imperfection is invalidated input leading to rise in security threats such as SQL Injection, XSS, Remote Command Execution & Local and Remote File Inclusion. For example, if the string variable filename is insufficiently sanitized, the following PHP code:

```
exec("open(".$filename.")");
```

Injecting a custom sleep code technique is used to spot injection vulnerabilities in web applications using server-side JavaScript execution. Custom Sleep Code technique works with any web system supporting Server-side JavaScript execution or NoSQL engines like MongoDB (Syhunt Cyber-Security Company, 2014).

2. **Server-Side JavaScript (SSJS):** The Server-Side JavaScript (SSJS) injection is a common injection attack. The SSJS injection is more harmful than the Cross-Site Scripting. SSJS injection does not require any intermediate victim or launch pad; instead, the attacker can attack the application directly with arbitrarily created HTTP requests. Because of this, defence against SSJS injection are also similar to SQL injection defences (myNoSQL, 2011) i.e.
   a. Avoid creating "ad-hoc" JavaScript commands by concatenating script with user input.
   b. Validate user input used in SSJS commands with regular expressions.
   c. Avoid use of the JavaScript eval (a function to evaluate a string) command. In particular, when parsing JSON (Storage format for NoSQL) input, use a safer alternative such as JSON.parse.

Server-side JavaScript injection vulnerabilities are not limited to just *eval* calls inside of node.js scripts. The bottom line is:

A. Always use authentication/authorization.
B. Firewalls alone are not sufficient, it is better to write own authorization code, a better but difficult alternative.
C. Be extremely careful with server-side script.

NoSQL database engines that process JavaScript containing user specified parameters can also be vulnerable. For instance, MongoDB permit use of JavaScript for queries and Map/Reduce operations. While the MongoDB databases have not strictly defined database schemas, using JavaScript for writing query allows developers to write arbitrarily complex queries against unrelated document structures (Sullivan, 2011).

Security experts realize the danger of relying on perimeter security, since it is possible to use JavaScript or JSON to get the access "authorized" behind the firewall to access all the databases. Some NoSQL systems allow JavaScript to run on the server leading to a potential for injection attack.

3. **Connection String Pollution:** Authentication services collect the user credentials that interact directly with the user or interface with identity federation and other web services to validate user and service client requests. There are two ways of defining an authentication system for a web application (Alonso, Fernandez, Martín & Guzmán, 2010):

   a. Create an own credential system, or
   b. Delegate it to the database engine.

In a delegated authentication environment connection string injection techniques allow an attacker to inject parameters by appending them with the semicolon (;) character. When the connection string is populated, the encryption value will be added to the previously configured set of parameters.

4. **Schema Injection:** Java is an interpreted language. Since the JavaScript are the easy target of the injection attacks, the web applications built using JavaScript are very prone to SQL injection attacks. Worse NoSQL injection attacks can be executed within a procedural language, rather than in the declarative SQL language. Hence the potential impacts of NoSQL injection attack are greater than traditional SQL injection attack. The followings are some of the injection attacks:

   a. JSON Injection,
   b. View Injection,
   c. Lightweight Directory Access Protocol (LDAP) Injection.

JSON is a way to transfer data in a structured format an alternative to XML. The JSON interactive AJAX programs are used by Yahoo and Google. JSON script can be called across domains. The tempting to directly read/write to database is possible. Attacker can use any HTTP based fuzzer to send different values in the JSON format to get the code processed at server end.

5. **Port Scanning:** If an attacker finds an open port, his job is done. The following (shown in Table 1) are some of the important port of various NoSQL database port requiring high level protection (Sullivan, 2011).

Table 1. NoSQL Ports requiring high level protection

NoSQL	Port Number
MongoDB	27017
	28017
	27080
CouchDB	5984
HBase	9000
Cassandra	9160
Neo4j	7474
Riak	8098
Redis	6379

One of the examples for prevention of port scan attack is Amazon Web Service (AWS). When AWS detects unauthorized port scanning, AWS ports are immediately stopped and blocked. Port scans of Amazon EC2 instances are generally ineffective because, by default, all inbound ports on Amazon EC2 instances are closed and are only opened by users (Amazon Web Services, 2013).

6. **Key Bruteforce:** Various studies have revealed that, many brute-force attacks are based on pre-compiled lists of usernames and passwords, which are widely shared (Owens & Matthews, 2008). The common Brute-force attacks are against remote services such as SSH, FTP and Telnet. One commonly-used method that virtually eliminates the threat of bruteforce password guessing attacks is public-key authentication. Following are some of the Key Bruteforce Prevention techniques at Application-level are:
    a. Key Size,
    b. Key Space,
    c. Unpredictable Key Generation.
7. **Web Application Vulnerabilities:** The Web applications are prone to injection vulnerabilities since they do not syntactically constrain the inputs used to construct structured output. Confidentiality and integrity have to be provided entirely by the application accessing the NoSQL data. It is not a sound practice to have the last line of defence for any valuable data at the application level. Any requests sent to a NoSQL database need to be escaped, filtered and validated, while the database itself needs to reside in a hardened environment (Bar-Yosef, 2012).

CASE STUDY

In this section security features of some NoSQL databases from ColumnFamily, Document, Graph and Key-Value store will be discussed.

All the NoSQL databases developed so far are coming under the following four categories i.e.

1. Column-Oriented Stores,
2. Document Stores,
3. Graph Stores,
4. Key-Value Stores.

HBase and Cassandra are based on Google's Bigtable, popularly known as Column Family (CF). In CF NoSQL database model, a key identifies a row containing data stored in one or more column families. Within a CF, each row can contain multiple columns. The values within each column are timestamped, so that several versions of a row-column can be available within a CF.

Document stores, such as MongoDB map a key to some document that contains structured information. These systems store documents in a JSON or JSON-like format. They store lists and dictionaries, which can be embedded recursively inside one-another. MongoDB separates the keyspace into collections, so that keys do not collide. The freedom and complexity of document stores is a double-edged sword i.e. application developers have a lot of freedom in modelling their documents, but application-based query logic can become exceedingly complex.

Figure 1. Architecture of relational and NoSQL databases

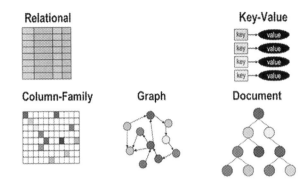

AllegroGraph and Neo4j are two popular NoSQL database for storing Graph structured data. Graph stores differ from the other stores in almost every way such as:

- Data models,
- Data traversal and querying patterns,
- Physical layout of data on disk,
- Distribution to multiple machines,
- Transactional semantics of queries.

The simplest form of NoSQL database is Key-value store where each key is mapped to a value containing arbitrary data. Around 40% of the NoSQL databases are Key-Value Stores.

1. Column Family

Cassandra brings together the distributed system technologies from Amazon DynamoDB(based on the principles of Dynamo) and the data model from Google's BigTable. "NASA uses Cassandra for security applications that track all hardware and software patches around the globe for the agency, and deals with data that is both structured and unstructured. NASA found that the flexible data model of Cassandra allowed them to insert data much more naturally than their prior RDBMS, plus query response times were reduced for retrieving the data as well" (Datastax Corporation, 2014). Cassandra is eventually consistent and based on a Peer-to-Peer (P2P) model without a single point of failure. Like BigTable, Cassandra provides a ColumnFamily based data model richer than typical key/value systems (Abramov, n.d.). Cassandra supports transaction logging and automatic replication.

1. **Data Files:** Data in Cassandra is kept unencrypted. Cassandra does not provide a mechanism to automatically encrypt the data in storage making the data vulnerable to attack. Operating system level mechanisms (file system permissions, file system level encryption, etc.) should be used to prevent access to the files by unauthorized users.
2. **Client Interfaces:** Cassandra uses the Apache Thrift framework for client communications. Thrift version 0.6 provides an SSL transport. The client interface supports a login () operation, but both username and password are sent across the network as clear text.

3. **Inter-Cluster Communication:** In general, nodes on a cluster can communicate freely and no encryption or authentication is used. No protection or authentication is provided for Fat clients. All communication between the database and its clients is unencrypted. An attacker capable of monitoring the database traffic will be able to see all of the data as the clients see it.

4. **Cassandra Query Language:** Cassandra uses a new interface called Cassandra Query Language (CQL). CQL syntax is similar to SQL. Developers familiar with SQL will be at home with CQL. CQL is compatible with the JDBC API. Being a parsed language CQL is vulnerable to injection attacks, like SQL.

5. **Denial of Service (DoS) Problem:** Cassandra uses a Thread- Per-Client model in its network code. Setting up a connection requires the Cassandra server to start a new thread on each connection. An attacker can prevent the Cassandra server from accepting new client connections by causing the Cassandra server to allocate all its resources to fake connection attempts.

A single HTTP request with an eight-byte payload is sufficient to disable a target. An alternative DoS attack would be to simply exit or kill the running process:

```
process.exit ()
process.kill (process.pid)
```

Distributed DoS (DDoS) attacks are often the source of cloud services disruptions. DDoS is launched from multiple sources from multiple locations mainly by means of Botnet. The emergence of cloud computing has make it possible for highly distributed denial of service attacks. Using Cloud the attacker can now hit their target by Cloud-based botnets, hijacking distributed processing power of cloud computing.

Some of the probable symptoms of a DDoS attack are:

1. Abrupt System slow down,
2. Spike in the number service request from a large number of users.

DDoS attacks exhaust all the Commuting/ Network resources ultimately bridging the system to a halt.

A careful monitoring of the network can help in keeping DDoS attack in control. One of the methods for detecting DDoS is to use the Intrusion Detection Systems (IDS). The chapter "Intrusion Detection and Prevention on Flow of Bigdata Using Bacterial Foraging" discusses about the intrusion detection by self learning process with characteristics of bacterial forging approach.

1. **Authentication:** Authentication is a key feature in multi-user system. Cassandra provides an IAuthenticate interface. The default implementation is one that turns off the requirement to authenticate to the database. The other provided implementation is SimpleAuthenticator class that allows setting up users and passwords via a flat Java properties file. The file is formatted as sets of password properties and the password can be specified in plain text as well. Another issue with the SimpleAuthenticator implementation is that the administrator must make sure that the flat password file available with each cluster member is synchronized with the rest of the cluster. Otherwise, the passwords used by each cluster member may not be the same for the same user.

2. **Authorization:** Authorization provides coarse and fine-grained access to various policy enforcement and decision points. Cassandra provides an IAuthority interface which is used in the Cassandra's

codebase when a keyspace is being modified, and on each column family access (read or write). The current set of permissions is an *enum* containing Read and Write permissions. The IAuthority interface provides a single method returning a set of permissions for a provided authenticated user and hierarchical list of resource names. Similar to the authorization code, Cassandra provides two implementations of IAuthority:

a.   A pass-through implementation that always allows full permissions, regardless of the user; and

b.   Using a flat Java properties file to allow matching permissions to usernames.

The weakness in the SimpleAuthority implementation is that it depends on a flat file, and not on a consistent file that is maintained across the cluster. This means that the effective permissions granted to a user are the permissions listed in the file located on the cluster member to which the connection was established. Another issue with the provided SimpleAuthority implementation is that it does not reload the file on every access. This means that the effective permissions cannot be changed without restarting the Cassandra process. Finally, it is important to note that Authorization in Cassandra is specified only on existing column families and therefore no protection is available on newly added column families and columns, and also protection at the raw (object) level is not available.

3.   **Auditing:** If auditing is required, then Cassandra does a custom implementation of IAuthority. IAuthority can be written to provide full auditing of all operations that require authorization, and a custom implementation of IAuthenticate can be written to provide a full audit trail for all login success/failure occurrences. Cassandra aims to bring the Risk Based Audit (RBA) approach to a next level. RBA approach focuses on the risks and the underlying causes of disruptions in transaction results as well as records. Therefore RBA approach shifts the attention from transaction quality to overall process quality. RBA uses information on:

a.   Business processes;

b.   Assessment methodology; and

c.   Measures for risk control.

Instead of only transaction data. Above discussed Cassandra security mechanism are summarized in Table 2.

"Fine-grained access control is the primary feature of Accumulo that differs from other similar databases. Accumulo includes cell-level security, which would allow organizations making use of it to let users' access only particular fields of the database" (Hoover, 2011).

Apache Accumulo extends the BigTable data model by adding a new element to the key called ColumnVisibility. The ColumnVisibility class stores a logical combination of security labels which are to be satisfied at query time. If the security labels are satisfied, then only the Key and Value are returned as part of a user request. This allows data of varying security requirements to be stored in the same table and allowing the user to see only those keys and values for which they are authorized. Apart from the Cell-Level Security, Apache Accumulo also provides a server-side programming mechanism called Iterators. Iterators allows user to perform additional processing at the Tablet Server. The range of operations that can be applied is equivalent to those that can be implemented within a MapReduce Combiner function for producing an aggregate value for several key-value pairs (Apache Software Foundation, 2013). Accumulo is suitable for applications where the data access is restricted on the cell level (Kovacs, 2014).

Table 2. Security features in Cassandra

Category	Status	Recommendation
Data at rest	Unencrypted	Protect with OS level mechanisms.
Authentication	The available solution isn't production ready.	Implement a custom Iauthentication provider.
Authorization	Done at the CF granularity level. The available solution isn't of production quality.	Implement a custom IAuthority provider.
Auditing	Not available Out Of The Box	Implement as part of the authentication and authorization solutions.
Intercluster Network communication	Encryption is available	Enable this using a private CA.
Client communication	No encryption is available.	Add packet-filter rules to prevent unknown hosts from connection. Re-implement the Thrift server-side to use the SSL transport in Thrift 0.6. Add timeouts for silent connections in the Thrift server side, and cap the number of acceptable client connection.
Injection attacks	Possible in CQL	If using the Java driver, prefer PreparedStatements to Statements. Always perform input validation in the application.

2. Document NoSQL

MongoDB was originally not built for single server, hence not recommended to run in replication for proper durability. MongoDB supports Master-Slave replication.

Mongo is not having methods to automatically encrypt data files, hence the data files are unencrypted be default. Hence to safeguard from unauthorized access to files the application dealing with the files must explicitly encrypt the crucial data before writing it into the database (All Answers Ltd, 2014). The Kerberos authentication system enables enterprise and government users of MongoDB Enterprise edition to integrate into standard security systems.

The authentication is "turned off" by default in MongoDB. Since MongoDB does not support authentication while running in Sharded mode, therefore there is no support for authorization. Therefore, MonogDB REST interface is not recommended for production (Mishra, 2013).

Running in standalone or replica-set mode, authentication can be enabled. In replica-set mode apart from the clients authenticating to the database, each replica server must authenticate other servers before joining the cluster.

While authentication is enabled MongoDB supports two types of users:

1. Read-only; and
2. Read-write.

Read-only users can query everything in the database on which they are defined.

Read-Write users have full access to all the data in the database on which they are defined.

Intensive use of JavaScript as internal scripting language has made the Mongo susceptible to Injection attack. Substantial number of internal commands available in the developer forum of MongoDB is basically short JavaScript. It is possible to store JavaScript functions in the database in the "db.system. js" collection which are available to the database users.

The above discussion is summarized in Table 3.

Table 3. Security features in MongoDB

Category	Status	Technique/Method for Data Security
Data at rest	Unencrypted	OS level security mechanisms.
Authentication for native connections	Available (Only in un-Sharded configuration)	Enable if possible.
Authorization for native connections	Read/ReadWrite/ Admin levels (Only in un-Sharded configuration).	Enable if possible, requires enabled authentication.
Authentication, Authorization & Auditing for RESTful connections	Externally maintained Users and Permissions	If configured available on a reverse proxy
Injection attacks	Possible, via JavaScript or String concatenation.	Intensive input Filtering/ Validation.

The common major problems with both systems are lack of encryption support for the data files, weak authentication both between the client and the servers as well as between server members.

The simple authorization without support for Role-Based Access Control (RBAC) or fine-grained authorization makes a distributed database vulnerable to SQL injection and Denial of Service attacks. Clearly the future generations of such DBMSs need considerable development and hardening in order to provide secure environment for sensitive data which is being stored by applications (such as social networks) using them (Abramov n.d.).

Sudden peaks in the CPU and memory loads of host systems and sudden high in the database indicates a Denial of Service attack. MongoDB is equipped with a variety of tools including "mongostat" and "mongotop" that can be used to monitor database (MongoDB, 2014).

3. Graph NoSQL

AllegroGraph uses the following security features to protect databases from unauthorized access and misuse.

1. Only giving access to registered users to the system;
2. Defining *roles* granting specific permissions; and
3. Assigning each user to one or more roles.

Users are *authenticated* when they access the database by providing a username and password which are known to AllegroGraph.

Authorization is privilege i.e. *role* assigned to user to *Access*, *Add* or *Modify* specific data. Roles are defined by an administrator. The users are assigned *role* having a specific list of permissions. A user may have more than one *role*.

User security depends in part on users keeping their relevant information secure. If someone other than the actual user knows the username and password and has access to other relevant information, the AllegroGraph will not be able to prevent that person from accessing data. There is support for anonymous users having single and typically limited role.

Administrators and users must understand that, security is a joint responsibility. Administrators can use the tools provided by AllegroGraph along with their own policies and intelligence to protect data from unauthorized access and to facilitate authorized users in performing their legitimate tasks (Franz Incorporated, 2014).

Security in AllegroGraph is implemented by:

1. **Defining Users:** A user is given a username and a password and can only access the system using that username and password. A Guest is allowed to log in as *anonymous* without a password with limited privileges. Each user has a set of permissions from a system-defined list of available permissions.
2. **Defining Roles:** A role is a collection of permissions. Roles are defined to make administration easier and more efficient. One could achieve the same end result by simply giving each user the permissions associated with the user's role(s). The permissions are
    a. Superuser,
    b. Start sessions,
    c. Evaluate arbitrary code, and
    d. Control replication.

Further, read, write, or read/write permission can be set for each catalog and repository. The permissions are as below.

1. **Specifying Filters:** A *security filter* prevents roles or individual users from accessing (reading and writing) triples with specified subject, object, predicate, and/or graph.
2. **Classes of Roles:** Users can be grouped in various ways. Here are some suggested broad categories (not necessarily AllegroGraph categories) are:
    a. **Trusted Expert Roles:** A trusted expert will usually be given all permissions. The administrator is a trusted expert and others may be as well. It is compulsory for persons to be the part of an organization to be trusted in the broad sense. Users with all or most permissions have the ability to cause malicious damage.
    b. **Trusted Ordinary Roles:** Some users may be fully trusted but not programming experts. These persons usually are not given permissions which would allow them accidentally compromise the system if given all sensitive permissions. The trusted ordinary users may be denied to some sensitive permission even though they are trusted.
    c. **General Internal Users:** Often members of an organization will need to access their data stored in the databases basically for reading only or sometimes for Read and Write. These users will normally give limited Read/Write permissions.
    d. **Outsider Roles:** Database to be viewable by outsiders. Some outsiders may have the ability to write data. As a rule of thumb, outsiders should never have general permissions. It is possible to enable anonymous access.
3. **Ports:** By default, the AllegroGraph server's HTTP API will open a random TCP port with a number greater than 1024 for new sessions. In order to allow a firewall more effective control over access to the AllegroGraph server, specifying a SessionPorts range in the agraph.cfg file and then filtering only these ports.
4. **Issues with Transferring Passwords etc. over the Internet:** When running an AllegroGraph server accessible from untrusted networks such as Internet, administrators need to be aware that passwords will be transferred in unencrypted form between AllegroGraph clients and the server.

To avoid exposing users' AllegroGraph passwords to malicious third parties AllegroGraph service connect to untrusted networks only on an SSLPort using the correct SSLCertificate settings or through a SSL-enabled reverse proxy such as pound or nginx.

5. **Security Filters:** A security filter can be set by an administrator (superuser). It can prevent access both read and write to triples with a specified value for subject, predicate, object and/or graph. Security filters prevents users from accessing both reading and writing privacy-sensitive data. When querying, triples filtered out by a security filter will appear as if they were not in the store in the first place. In contrast, attempts to add them or remove filtered triples will result in an error.

The administrator must take care to allow users access only to those triples that are safe for these users to see. This can be hard to accomplish with only subject/predicate/object-based filters when there is deep graph structure involved. In such cases, it is advisable to put triples that should be (or should not be) accessed by a certain set of users into their own graph. According the filter set using the graph is to be defined. Security filters can be set by a superuser in the user administration screen of AllegroGraph.

6. **WebView:** If assigned the filters to roles, these filters will be merged into a set of effective filters for each user with that role accessing a store.

Neo4j, another popular Graph NoSQL does not deal with data encryption explicitly, but supports all techniques of Java and the JVM to protect data by encrypting it before storing. Batch Inserter of Neo4j directly operates on the stored files.

Shell injection attacks occur when input is incorporated into a string to be interpreted by the shell. Neo4J "Shell" allows the execution of arbitrary code which may constitute a security to risk Server risk from un-trusted users. For security reasons Neo4j Shell may be disable the in Webadmin in the "conf/neo4j-server.properties" file. Also, the Java Security Manager <http://docs.oracle.com/javase/1.4.2/docs/api/java/lang/SecurityManager.html> can be used to secure parts of codebase. Neo4j server includes built in support for SSL encrypted communication over HTTPS. Neo4j server can be configured to Permit/Block specific IP addresses, URL patterns and IP ranges. Neo4j supports SSL encrypted communication over HTTPS (The Neo4j Team neo4j.org, 2013). Neo4j server supports administrators in Allowing/Disallowing access the specific aspects of the database based on credentials of the User/Application (The Neo4j Team neo4j.org, 2013).

4. Key-Value Store

Key-value stores are easier to configure on a per-application basis. Amazon DynamoDB is an example of Key-Value NoSQL. DynamoDB is suitable for applications that are "Write" intensive and no updates are rejected. DynamoDB is specifically built for an infrastructure within a single administrative domain where all nodes are assumed to be trusted. Since used for Amazon's internal services, the primitive version of DynamoDB does not focussed on the problem of data Integrity, Authentication, Authorization and Security (DeCandia, Hastorun, Jampani, Kakulapati, Lakshman, Pilchin, Swaminathan Vosshalln & Vogels, 2007). DynamoDB is a fully managed NoSQL database service from Amazon Web Services (AWS) providing fast and predictable performance with seamless scalability. To achieve high level of availability, DynamoDB sacrifices consistency under certain failure scenarios (Vaidya, n.d.). DynamoDB replicates data over 3 data centres minimum.

Another Key-Value NoSQL database Riak is Scalable, Highly-available, Distributed open-source database. Riak is Dynamo-based reliable adaptation of Amazon's Dynamo model. Riak is very good for single-site scalability, availability and fault-tolerance. The features of Riak includes (Gross, 2012):

1.   Elastic architecture, row clusters can be dynamically added without downtime,
2.   Master-less i.e. No single point of failure,
3.   Fault tolerant, capable of surviving outages without data loss,
4.   Multi-Data Centre Write-available, Masterless replication,
5.   Linearly scalable,
6.   Consistent hashing without any downtime,
7.   Supports Map/Reduce.

There is no inbuilt security in Riak. However, administrator can add Access/ Restrictions via Http authentication, Firewalls, etc. However, the commercial product such as Riak CS has ACLs and built-in security. JMX (Java Management Extensions, Oracle use JMX) monitoring can be enabled in the application configuration by just specifying the port.

Following are the two categories of access control for Riak (Basho Technologies, Inc., 2014):

1.   Other Riak nodes participating in the cluster,
2.   Clients making use of the Riak cluster.

The settings for both access groups are located in app.config:

1.   pb (Protocol Buffers, TCP 8087),
2.   Http,
3.   Https.

Recently some of the NoSQL projects starting to adopt RDBMS-type security features. For instance, Oracle has added transactional control over data written to one node. Oracle Key-Value NoSQL provides OS-independent, cluster-wide file based user password authentication for greater protection from unauthorized access to sensitive data. Additionally, session-level Secure Sockets Layer (SSL) encryption and network port restrictions deliver greater protection from network intrusion (Oracle Data Sheet, 2013). "Oracle Platform Security Services (OPSS) is the underlying security framework for the entire platform and is common across Oracle Fusion Middleware applications including WebLogic Server. Designed by Oracle to be portable, OPSS provides the same security services to third-party developers, including interfaces for authentication, authorization, credential management, audit and encryption" (Howarth, 2014).

Redis is another popular open source Key-value store NoSQL. Redis is a server for data structures such as Keys, Strings, Hashes, Lists and Sets / Sorted Sets etc. Designed to be accessed by trusted clients in trusted environments, Redis can be easily acceded by untrusted clients directly through TCP ports or UNIX socket. Hence, Redis port should be firewalled to prevent access from the unauthorized users' (Citrusbyte). Redis is suitable for rapidly changing data with a foreseeable database size.

DISCUSSION

NoSQL databases were built to tackle different challenges posed by the analytics world, and security was never addressed during the design stage. Developers using NoSQL databases usually embed security in the middleware. NoSQL databases do not support for explicitly enforcing security in the database. Further, clustering aspects of NoSQL databases pose additional challenges to the robustness of such security practices. Lack of security standards has caused vendors to develop bottom-up NoSQL solutions and address security issues on an adhoc basis. NoSQL uses HTTP Basic or Digest-based authentication, which are prone to man-in-the-middle attack. Although some of the existing NoSQL databases offer authentication at the local node level, they fail to enforce authentication across all the cluster nodes. Since NoSQL architecture employs lightweight protocols and mechanisms that are loosely coupled, it is susceptible to various injection attacks like JSON injection, array injection, view injection, REST injection, GQL injection, schema injection, etc. (Cloud Security Alliance, 2013)

Hiding NoSQL under the secure wrapper of middleware or accessing NoSQL using a framework like Hadoop can create a virtual secure layer around the NoSQL perimeter. Object-level security at the collection or column-level can be induced through the middleware, retaining its thin database layer. Such a methodology will ensure that there is no direct access to the data and that the data is only exposed based on the controls configured within the middleware or framework layer (Cloud Security Alliance, 2013).

Most of the middleware software comes with ready-made support for authentication, authorization and access control. In the case of Java, Java Authentication and Authorization Services (JAAS) and SpringSource (Spring Security frameworks are deployed for authentication, authorization and access control) are used. Such type architectures will ensure that any changes to schema, objects and/or data are validated for gaining better control while preserving the capabilities of NoSQL (Cloud Security Alliance, 2013).

Some of NoSQL issues are summarized in Table 4 (W. Gretzky, 2011; Sullivan, 2011).

Traditional RDBMS best practises for storing sensitive data can be applied to NoSQL based application such as (Winder, 2012):

- Sensitive database fields encryption;
- Storing the unencrypted values in sandboxed environment (sandbox is a security mechanism for separating running programs);
- Intensive input validation mechanism;
- Deployment of strong user authentication policies.

Most of the middleware software comes with ready-made support for Authentication, Authorisation and Access control. For instance, if Java is used, then the default choice is Java Authentication and Authorization Service (JAAS). Similarly, for Oracle Corporation the default choice for enterprise Java computing platform is Java Platform, Enterprise Edition (J2EE) or for VMware based cloud services the Spring Security frameworks are available for the authentication, authorisation and access control for NoSQL database implementations by SpringSource (SpringSource was initially developed based on Spring Framework, a programming model for enterprise Java applications. VMware purchased SpringSource in 2009).

Table 4. NoSQL security issues

Lack of expertise	There are very few experts who understand the security aspects of NoSQL technologies. Since there is no obvious security model that fits with NoSQL, the implementation of standard security for NoSQL has become a very intricate process. As more and more organizations are shifting their operating to cloud-based systems, security of data will be more and more crucial by every passing day. Until the third party security solutions are available and integrated with NoSQL database, the NoSQL applications have to shoulder the security load. Adding authentication and authorization processes to the application will make the application much more complex. The positions related to the Network, NoSQL and overall IT security will be of high demand.
Buggy applications	While the application needs to manage the security, it must be aware of all the other application. This will be required in order to disable access to any Non-application data. When new data types are added to the data store, the data store administrator would have to find out and ensure what application should not access which specific data. Since the Cloud APIs are frequently updated, introduced and bugs are fixed the newly introduced/ Bug fixed/ Updated API can introduce another security hole in the application.
Vulnerability-prone code	Since majority of the NoSQL are open source, the magnitude of applications and application server products are extremely high. More applications mean more varieties of code using varieties of programming languages in various platforms leading to high probability of Bugs/ Malicious codes.
Data Duplicity	In NoSQL systems data are replicated to maintain high availability in various nodes in various network clusters. Data are duplicated in many tables in for optimizing query processing. NoSQL also lack confidentiality and integrity since the databases are schema-less. The permission on a table, column or row cannot be segregated leading to multiple copies of the same data, making the data consistency, particularly in multiple tables wrapped in a transaction as a logical unit of Insert, Update or Delete operations executed as a whole very difficult (EnterpriseDB, 2011). The high availability techniques used includes Backup, Clustering, Mirroring, Log shipping and Clustering.
Privacy	Major privacy issues relate to data access Unauthorized access, Vendor Lock-in, Data Deletion, Backup Vulnerabilities, Isolation failure, Inadequate monitoring and Audit. Although the focus is on security, privacy concerns cannot be ignored. Data stored across multiple servers provides improved fault tolerance and scalability at the cost of privacy.

Graph databases provide high horizontal scalability but less powerful indexing, querying and security features. Bio4j is a high-performance cloud-enabled graph based open source bioinformatics data platform, integrating the data available in the most representative open data sources around protein information. Bio4j is a bioinformatics *graph*-based data platform integrating most data available in the most representative open data sources around protein information available today. It integrates the data available in (Pareja, 2014)

The Crypto Stick project develops Open Source USB keys for secure login in the Web to enable high secure encryption of e-mails and data. It includes a One Time Password feature which can be used with Google and many other popular websites (Assembla.com).

- Secret keys are stored securely inside the Crypto Stick. Since their extraction is not possible, the Crypto Stick protected from computer viruses and Trojan horses.
- The user-chosen PIN and the tamper-proof design protect Crypto Stick in case of loss/theft. The software stack is Open Source allowing verifying the security and integration with own applications.
- Different PCB/boards on the market can be used for development.
- Many exciting features has been implemented such as support of Google's two-factor authentication, SSH, GnuPG, Mozilla Thunderbird, OpenSC.
- Future implementation roadmap includes integration of email encryption with popular e-mail services such as Gmail.

Using Kerberos and SSL at the Same Time

Both the Kerberos and SSL libraries provide authentication, encryption, and integrity protection:

- **Kerberos:** While enabled, the Kerberos authentication, integrity protection is also enabled. However, the integrity protection can be enabled without encryption.
- **SSL:** If SSL is used, authentication, integrity protection, and encryption are all enabled or disabled. HTTP access to the DSE Search/Solr data is protected using SSL. Node-to-node encryption using SSL protects internal Solr communication. Similarly, Amazon DynamoDB is accessible via SSL-encrypted endpoints, which accessible from Internet as well as within Amazon EC2.
- **Kerberos and SSL:** It is possible to enable both Kerberos authentication and SSL together. However, this causes some overlap since the authentication is performed twice by two different schemes.

Kerberos authentication and certification are done through SSL. DataStax recommends choosing any one and using it for both encryption and authentication. These settings are described in the "dse.yaml" configuration file.

Securing DSE (DataStax Enterprise) Search Services

The security table summarizes the security features of DSE Search/Solr and other integrated components. DSE Search data is completely or partially secured by using these DataStax Enterprise security features:

- **Managing Object Permissions Using Internal Authorization:** Access to Solr documents, excluding cached data, can be limited to users who have been granted access permissions. Permission management also secures tables used to store Solr data.
- **Transparent Data Encryption:** Data at rest in Cassandra tables, excluding cached and Solr-indexed data, can be encrypted. Encryption occurs on the Cassandra side and impacts performance slightly. Data in DSE/Search Solr tables is encrypted by Cassandra. Encryption has a slight performance impact, but ensures the encryption of original documents after Cassandra permanently stores the documents on disk. However, Solr cache data and Solr index data (metadata) is not encrypted.
- **Client-to-Node Encryption:** User can encrypt HTTP access to Solr data and internal, node-to-node Solr communication using SSL. Enable SSL node-to-node encryption on the Solr node by setting encryption options in the dse.yaml file as described in Client-to-node encryption.

The TCP-communications layer for Solr supports client-to-node and node-to-node encryption using SSL, but does not support Kerberos. Cassandra commit log data is not encrypted; only at rest data is encrypted (DEMIRBAS, 2013).

Cassandra has less need for fine grained security, since all access is normally mediated by the application layer, which authenticates to the database with a single identity. However, this leaves the database vulnerable to a user within the firewall, such as a DBA or a user with ad hoc query capability. Authorization is handled in Cassandra at the Column Family granularity level. The current set of permissions includes the Read and Write permissions.

Cassandra provides two implementations of authority interface. The first one is the Pass-through implementation which always allows full permissions, regardless of the user. The second implementation uses a flat Java properties file to allow matching permissions to usernames.

Both MongoDB and Cassandra now support Kerberos authentication in their enterprise (non-free) editions, and Cassandra also supports transparent data encryption (Harrison, 2013). Companies like Google and Amazon use their own cloud-friendly NoSQL database technologies, and there are a number of commercial and open source NoSQL databases available, such as Couchbase (suitable for low-latency data access, high concurrency support and high availability requirements), MongoDB, Cassandra and Riak.

In terms of Security MongoDB is more mature than the other document databases. In MongoDB encryption is available for Intercluster Network communication but not for client communication. MongoDB is suitable for dynamic queries processing requirements and defining indexes.

By default, the Hadoop client provides the identity of the user to the Hadoop cluster, which accepts that identity without verification. However, modern versions of Hadoop can run in "secure mode" which allows Hadoop to confirm identify using the Kerberos protocol.

HDFS contains POSIX-type permissions similar to Linux or UNIX. Each file associates read/write/execute permissions with the owner, a group and the world. So, it's possible to limit modifications to a specific user while allowing read capabilities to a wider group or users and denying any access otherwise. A single HDFS file may contain information that spans the scope of a number of users. For instance, a HDFS file in a medical application may contain medical records for all patients, and there is no way to limit access to a specific doctor or medical centre. If user can read *any* data in the file, then they have permission to read *all* the data in the file. HDFS does not provide high availability, because an HDFS file system instance requires one unique server, the name node (single point of failure). Built-in HDFS security features such as Access Control List (ACLs) and Kerberos used alone are not adequate for enterprise needs.

CouchDB uses very innovative authentication handler. CouchDB is suitable for accumulating, occasionally changing data, on which pre-defined queries are to be run. Also suitable for places where versioning is important (Kovacs, 2014).

CouchDB authentication handler includes:

- HTTP basic authentication.
- Cookie-based and OAuth (Open Authorization).
- Protocol based authentication.

CouchDB provides very limited role-based access control at the database granularity level.

DataStax Security Management

DataStax Enterprise 4.0 includes advanced data protection for enterprise-grade databases. The internal authentication is done using login accounts and passwords. The object permissions are managed using internal authorization based on the GRANT/REVOKE paradigm.

The Client-to-node encryption is done using SSL for data going from the client to the Cassandra cluster. For Node to node encryption SSL is used for data transfer between nodes.

The Kerberos authentication is used by nodes to communication over a non-secure network by proving their identity to one another in a secure manner using tickets.

For configuring and using data auditing for an administrator to use to create detailed audit trails of cluster activity. Transparent data encryption that transparently encodes data flushed from the memtable in system memory to the SSTables on disk (at rest data), making the at rest data unreadable by unauthorized users. Hadoop and Solr data auditing is done at the Cassandra access level, so requests to access Cassandra data is audited. Node-to-node encryption using SSL protects communication over inter-node gossip protocol.

Similarly, all physical access to data centres by AWS employees is logged and audited routinely (Amazon Web Services, 2013).Therefore, all NoSQL databases vendors are working hard to enhance the security features of their product to grab the exponentially growing market.

Biometric Authentication Systems

Next Generation Biometric authentication systems using face, fingerprint, iris, voice, signature, vein and DNA (Deoxyribo Nucleic Acid,) recognition are being used for different applications. Out of all these types Face, Fingerprint and Iris recognition are commonly used in most of the Biometric authentication applications. Fingerprint recognition is the oldest type of biometric authentication and used by Banks, ATMs and various government offices (PR Newswire, 2014). By 2016, 30% of organisations will use biometric authentication on mobile devices (Rossi, 2014). Total revenue of the global biometric market is expected to grow at an estimated CAGR (Compound Annual Growth Rate i.e. year-over-year growth rate of an investment over a specified period of time) of 17.6% from 2014 to 2020 (Wood, 2014).

CONCLUSION

The combination of security, availability, scalability and data model flexibility will ultimately lead to development of a comprehensive high performance NoSQL database solution. Sharding technique used to partition database into multiple instances having different sets of data requires increasing security, since the database will be having multiple entry and exit points. Most middleware software includes support for authentication, authorization and access control. Furthermore, the NoSQL clusters utilizing HTTP as a transport, security can also be validated on proxy servers and load-balancers in the middle of the way.

The securities of databases are highly dependent how an application accessing data from a database is designed. Although one size does not fit all, still the security mechanisms of NoSQL are to be standardized to some extent by replacing the User ID and password approach with advanced biometrics authentication systems. Once the malicious users are blocked from accessing the databases majority of the problems are solved.

REFERENCES

Abramov, J. (n.d.). *Security issues in NoSQL Databases*. Retrieved from http://jkb.netii.net/index.php/pub/sinosqldb/introduction

All Answers Ltd. (2014). Files used in the mongo db computer science essay. *UK Essays*. Retrieved from http://www.ukessays.com/essays/computer-science/files-used-in-the-mongo-db-computer-science-essay.php

Alonso, C., Fernandez, M., Martín, A., & Guzmán, A. (2010). In N. Garbolino (Ed.), Connection string parameter pollution attacks. Arlington, VA: Black hat dc 2010.

Amazon Web Services. (2013, November). *Amazon Web Services: Overview of Security Processes*. Retrieved from http://media.amazonwebservices.com/pdf/AWS_Security_Whitepaper.pdf

Apache Software Foundation. (2013). *Apache accumulo*. Retrieved from https://accumulo.apache.org/

Assembla.com. (n.d.). *Crypto Stick*. Retrieved from https://www.assembla.com/spaces/cryptostick/wiki

Bar-Yosef, N. (2012, May 31). Examining the Security Implications of Bigdata. *Wired Business Media*. Retrieved from http://www.securityweek.com/examining-security-implications-big-data

Basho Technologies, Inc. (2014). *Security and Firewalls*. Retrieved from http://docs.basho.com/riak/latest/ops/advanced/security/

Citrusbyte. (n.d.). *Redis Security*. Retrieved from http://redis.io/topics/security

Cloud Security Alliance. (2013, April). *Bigdata Working Group Expanded Top Ten Bigdata Security and Privacy Challenges*. Retrieved from https://downloads.cloudsecurityalliance.org/ initiatives/bdwg/Expanded_Top_Ten_Big_Data_Security_and_Privacy_Challenges.pdf

Cobb, M. (2013, April). NoSQL Security: Do NoSQL Database Security Features stack up to RDBMS? *SearchSecurity.com*. Retrieved from http://searchsecurity.techtarget.com/tip/NoSQL-security-Do-NoSQL-database-security-features-stack-up-to-RDBMS

Datastax Corporation. (2014, February). *Datastax Corporation White Paper: Implementing a NoSQL Strategy*. Retrieved from http://www.datastax.com/wp-content/uploads/2013/06/DS_WP_Implementing_a_NoSQL_Strategy.pdf

DeCandia, G., Hastorun, D., Jampani, M., Kakulapati, G., Lakshman, A., Pilchin, A., et al. (2007, October). *Dynamo: Amazon's Highly Available Key-Value Store*. Retrieved from http://www.allthingsdistributed.com/files/amazon-dynamo-sosp2007.pdf

Enterprise, D. B. (2011, December 27). Re-evaluating current database infrastructure could pay dividends. *Enterprise DB Corporation*. Retrieved from http://www.enterprisedb.com/news-events/news/re-evaluating-current-database-infrastructure-could-pay-dividends

Franz Incorporated. (2014, April 11). *Allegrograph 4.13.1 Security Implementation*. Retrieved from http://franz.com/agraph/support/documentation/v4/security.html

Gross, M. (2012, May 30). *An Overview of Riak*. Retrieved from http://www.palominodb.com/blog/2012/05/31/overview-riak

Harrison, G. (2013, October 9). As nosql matures, security mechanisms evolve rapidly. *Database Trends and Applications*. Retrieved from http://www.dbta.com/Columns/Notes-on-NoSQL/As-NoSQL-Matures-Security-Mechanisms-Evolve-Rapidly-92527.aspx

Hoover, J. N. (2011). NSA submits open source, secure database to apache. *InformationWeek*. Retrieved from http://www.informationweek.com/applications/nsa-submits-open-source-secure-database-to-apache/d/d-id/1099972

Howarth, L. (2014, January). *An Oracle White Paper: Complete and Scalable Access Management*. Retrieved from http://www.oracle.com/technetwork/middleware/id-mgmt/overview/complete-and-scalable-access-mgmt-1697349.pdf

Kovacs, K. (2014). *Cassandra vs Mongodb vs CouchDB vs Redis vs Riak vs HBbase vs Couchbase vs Neo4j vs Hypertable vs Elasticsearch vs Accumulo vs Voltdb vs Scalaris comparison*. Retrieved from http://kkovacs.eu/cassandra-vs-mongodb-vs-couchdb-vs-redis

Lee, H., & Mehta, M. R. (2013). Defense Against REST-based Web Service Attacks for Enterprise Systems. *Communications of the IIMA, 13*(1), 57-68. Retrieved from http://www.iima.org/index.php?option=com_phocadownload&view=category&download=426:defenseagainstrest-basedwebserviceattacksforenterprisesystems&id=76:2013-volume-13-issue-1&Itemid=68

McWilliams, J., & Ivey, M. (2012). *Google Developers: Updating Your Model's schema*. Retrieved from https://developers.google.com/appengine/articles/update_schema

Mishra, P. (2013, December 6). *Inside India's Aadhar, the world's biggest biometrics database*. Retrieved from http://techcrunch.com/2013/12/06/inside-indias-aadhar-the-worlds-biggest-biometrics-database/

MongoDB. (2014, March). *MongoDB Security Architecture*. Retrieved from http://info.mongodb.com/rs/mongodb/images/MongoDB_Security_Architecture_WP.pdf

myNoSQL. (2011, December 19). *Attacking NoSQL and node.js: Server-Side Javascript Injection (SSJS)*. Retrieved from http://nosql.mypopescu.com/post/14453905385/attacking-nosql-and-node-js-server-side-javascript

Neo4j Team Neo4j.org. (2013, January 17). *The Neo4j Manual v1.9.M04*. Retrieved from http://cs.brown.edu/courses/csci2270/papers/neo4j.pdf

Newswire, P. R. (2014, April 09). *Next Generation Biometric Market Worth $23.54 Billion by 2020*. Retrieved from http://www.prnewswire.com/news-releases/next-generation-biometric-market-worth-2354-billion-by-2020-254579511.html

Oracle Data Sheet. (2013). *Oracle NoSQL Database, 12CR1 Version 3.0, Community Edition*. Retrieved from http://www.oracle.com/technetwork/products/nosqldb/documentation/datasheet-oracle-nosql-db-ce-1876735.pdf

Owens, J., & Matthews, J. (2008, February 12). *A Study of Passwords and Methods used in Brute-force SSH Attacks*. Retrieved from https://www.usenix.org/legacy/confadmin /leet08/papers/L12/content.pdf

Pareja, P. (2014). *Bio4j: Bigger, Faster, Leaner*. Retrieved from http://ohnosequences.com/slides/fosdem-2014/bio4j-bigger-faster-leaner

Penchikala, S. (2011, November 15). Virtual panel: Security considerations in accessing nosql databases. *InfoQ*. Retrieved from http://www.infoq.com/articles/nosql-data-security-virtual-panel

rmorize Special Force. (n.d.). *NoSQL, No Injection!? By Kuon*. Retrieved from http://www.hitcon.org/hit2010/download/8_NoSQL_No_Injection.pdf

Rossi, B. (2014, February 4). 30% of organisations will use biometric authentication for mobile devices by 2016. *Information Age*. Retrieved from http://www.information-age.com/technology/mobile-and-networking/123457684/30-organisations-will-use-biometric-authentication-mobile-devices-2016

Su, Z., & Wassermann, G. (2006, January). *The essence of command injection attacks in web applications*. Retrieved from http://www.cs.ucdavis.edu/~su/publications/popl06.pdf

Sullivan, B. (2011, July). *Server-Side Javascript Injection*. Retrieved from http://media.blackhat.com/bh-us-11/Sullivan/BH_US_11_Sullivan_Server_Side_WP.pdf

Sullivan, B. (2011). *NoSQL, but even less security* [Web log message]. Retrieved from http://blogs.adobe.com/security/files/2011/04/NoSQL-But-Even-Less-Security.pdf?file=2011/04/ NoSQL-But-Even-Less-Security.pdf

Syhunt Cyber-Security Company. (2014). *Time-based php v8js injection & nosql/ssjs injection*. Retrieved from http://www.syhunt.com/?n=Articles.NoSQLInjection

Vaidya, G. (n.d.). *Dynamo Amazon's Highly Available Key-Value Store*. Retrieved from http://www.cse.buffalo.edu/~mpetropo/CSE736-SP10/slides/seminar100226a2.pdf

Wayne Gretzky. (2011). *Hacker Intelligence Initiative, Monthly Trend Report, Security Trends 2012*. Retrieved from http://www.imperva.com/docs/HI_Security_Trends_2012.pdf

Winder, D. (2012, June). Securing nosql applications: Best practises for big data security. *Computer-Weekly.com*, Retrieved from http://www.computerweekly.com/tip/Securing-NoSQL-applications-Best-practises-for-big-data-security

Wood, L. (2014, April 16). Research and markets: Next generation biometric market 2014-2020-technology, function & applications. *Business Wire*. Retrieved from http://www.businesswire.com/news/home/20140416006128/en/Research-Markets-Generation-Biometric-Market-2014-

Ying, M., & Miller, J. (2013). Refactoring Legacy AJAX Applications to Improve the Efficiency of the Data Exchange Component. *Journal of Systems and Software, 86*(1), 72–88. doi:10.1016/j.jss.2012.07.019

ADDITIONAL READING

Brewer, E. A. (2000, July). Towards Robust Distributed Systems. PODC Keynote 2000, California. Retrieved from http://www.eecs.berkeley.edu/~brewer/cs262b-2004/PODC-keynote.pdf

F. Chang, J. Dean, S. Ghemawat, W. C. Hsieh, D. A. Wallach, M. Burrows, T. Chandra, A. Fikes, and R. E. Gruber, "Bigtable: A distributed storage system for structured data" ACM Transactions on Computer Systems (TOCS), vol. 26, pp. 4:1–4:26, June 2008.

Demirbas, M. (2013, April 23). Conflict-free replicated data types [Web log message]. Retrieved from http://muratbuffalo.blogspot.in/2013/04/conflict-free-replicated-data-types.html

Gilbert, S., & Lynch, N. (2002, June). Brewer's conjecture and the feasibility of consistent, available, partition-tolerant web services. *SIGACT News*, *33*(2), 51–59. doi:10.1145/564585.564601

Lakshman, A., & Malik, P. (2010, April). Cassandra: A decentralized structured storage system. *SIGOPS Oper. Syst. Rev.*, *44*(2), 35–40. doi:10.1145/1773912.1773922

KEY TERMS AND DEFINITIONS

Data Encryption: Data encryption is defined as the process of scrambling transmitted or stored information making it unintelligible until it is unscrambled by the intended recipient. Encryption algorithms in use for years include Secure Sockets Layer (SSL) for Internet transactions, Pretty Good Privacy (PGP), and Secure Hypertext Transfer Protocol (S-HTTP). Data must first be compressed and then it can be encrypted.

Developers Prefer Simple Authentication and Security Layer (SASL): With Kerberos via Generic Security Service Application Program Interface (GSSAPI) to authenticate users for defining the accessible services to a particular user/User group. When a user connects to a Job Tracker, the connection is mutually authenticated using Kerberos. Operating system authentication principles are also matched to a set of user and group access control lists maintained in flat configuration files.

Dynamo: Dynamo is collection of techniques that collectively forms a highly available Key-Value structured storage system or a distributed data store.

Fuzz Testing: Originally developed by Barton Miller at the University of Wisconsin in 1989, Fuzz testing or fuzzing is a software testing technique used to discover coding errors and security loopholes in software, operating systems or networks. Fuzzing software input massive amounts of random data, called fuzz, to the system in an attempt to make it crash.

Kerberos: Secret-Key Distribution Model Kerberos was originally developed by Needham & Schroeder. The basis of authentication in Kerberos is the Keys, typically a short sequence of bytes used for both encryption and decryption. Kerberos must be integrated with all important parts of a system to be effective. Kerberos only protects the messages from software that has been written or modified to use Kerberos. Kerberos itself does not provide authorization but passes authorization information generated by other services. Hence Kerberos can be used as a base for building separate authorization services.

Light Weight Directory Access Protocol (LDAP): An open network protocol standard designed to provide access to distributed directories. LDAP provides a mechanism to query or modify information that exists in a directory information tree (DIT), which may contain a broad range of information about different types of objects such as users, printers, applications, and other network resources. This document presents information on the basic models used to describe LDAP, and describes the APIs used to expose the LDAP protocol.

MD5: Designed in 1992 as an improvement of MD4 the MD5 is one of the most widely used cryptographic hash functions nowadays. The best known result so far was a semi free-start collision, in which the initial value of the hash function is replaced by a non-standard value, which is the result of the attack.

Port Scan: The port scan is the technique used by hackers on a System or Network to determine which ports is Open or in use. To collect the port status information Hackers use various tools to send data to TCP or UDP ports. Based on the response received from the port scan utility the Hackers can determine whether a port is in use/open. If a security flaw exists, hackers can register as legitimate users to carry out attacks through these ports for gaining unauthorized access of resources.

Replication Factor: Represents the number of times a KV-Value pairs is stored in NoSQL database.

Shard: A set of partitions also referred to as a partition group.

XML Common Biometric Format Technical Committee (XCBF): An XML-based system for standardising biometric data transmission is being developed by standards organisation the Organization for the Advancement of Structured Information Standards (Oasis).

This research was previously published in the Handbook of Research on Securing Cloud-Based Databases with Biometric Applications edited by Ganesh Chandra Deka and Sambit Bakshi, pages 153-173, copyright year 2015 by Information Science Reference (an imprint of IGI Global).

Chapter 8
Approaches to Cloud Computing in the Public Sector:
Case Studies in UK Local Government

Jeffrey Chang
London South Bank University, UK

Mark Johnston
Julian Campbell Foundation, UK

ABSTRACT

Cloud computing refers to a scalable network infrastructure where consumers receive IT services such as software and data storage through the Internet on a subscription basis. Potential benefits include cost savings, simpler IT and reduced energy consumption. The UK government and local authorities, like commercial organisations, are considering cloud-based services. Concerns have been raised, however, over issues such as security, access, data protection and ownership. This study attempts to investigate the likely impact of cloud computing on local government based on a conceptual framework and case studies of four London borough councils. It reveals that the concept of cloud computing is new and not clearly understood. Local authorities, who face further cuts in government funding, welcome a cloud-based IT infrastructure which may lead to considerable savings. Yet local government is conservative, so with their risk-adverse attitude local authorities are more likely to adopt a hybrid approach to implementation.

INTRODUCTION

Cloud computing is held to offer a number of advantages to the organisations which utilise it. These include cost savings, scalable computing services, simpler IT infrastructure and reduced energy consumption. Theoretically the advantages offered are as relevant to public sector organisations as they are for the private sector. Within local government there are pressures, positive and negative, from a decline in IT budgets, a lack of adequate skills in public sector employees and from the centrally imposed e -Government agenda. As a result cloud-based delivery models are rapidly gaining the attention of government. Across the public sector, many IT leaders are carefully considering the implications of cloud

DOI: 10.4018/978-1-5225-8176-5.ch008

utilisation. Software applications, hardware, infrastructure, platforms, services and storage or whether the government should develop its own cloud are issues which require careful consideration. Key concerns include issues such as the security and ownership of data, potential impact on employment within the client organisations and the structural and cultural implications of moving to cloud provision for large, complex and conservative government institutions. As yet, very little research has been carried out on the implications of utilising cloud services for local government. This study, through theoretical analysis using a conceptual framework and four case studies of London-based borough councils, attempts to explore the likely impact of cloud computing use within local authorities. Firstly, the conceptual framework is presented in the context of current literature relating to the subject. This will consider aspects such as driving and resisting forces and potential implementation issues arising within the public sector. Following on from this theoretical discussion case study data from the four boroughs will be analysed using the same framework considerations. Conclusions will be drawn and consideration given to potential next-steps in this specific field of research.

THE CONCEPT OF CLOUD COMPUTING

Cloud computing is a style of computing where IT capabilities are provided as a service delivered over the Internet to a customer's workplace, similar to utilities such as water and electricity which are 'piped' to the customer's premises. Although there is no universally agreed definition, cloud computing has five key attributes according to a group of researchers at Gartner: service-based, scalable and elastic, shared, metered by use and using Internet Technology (Plummer et al, 2009). These attributes are addressed as 'essential characteristics' by the National Institute of Standard and Technology (NIST, 2011).

The key advantages of cloud computing are held to be reduced costs, increased efficiency and a significant reduction in energy consumption leading to cost savings and greener IT (Catteddu, 2010; Armbrust et al, 2010; Foster et al, 2008; Luis et al, 2008; Aymerich et al, 2009; Grossman, 2009; Korri, 2009; Maggiani, 2009; Nelson, 2009). For potential customers cloud computing presents an attractive alternative to buying, setting up and maintaining their own in-house computing infrastructure (Korri, 2009). These advantages are theoretically as applicable to the public sector as to private organisations, and as set out in the Digital Britain (2009) report, the UK government sees the adoption of cloud computing as critical to the success of its plans to increase efficiency in the public sector.

In the private sector, concerns have been expressed both about the security of data management and loss of organisational control of a key resource (Takabi et al, 2010; Buyya et al, 2009; Grossman, 2009). Public sector clients (or potential clients) will be aware of these concerns. Given the confidential and sensitive nature of much of the data held by public institutions, this becomes a particularly important issue (Nelson, 2009).

So in considering the public sector use of cloud computing we see there are opposing forces; potential cost and efficiency savings verses potential, but difficult to quantify, risks to data security.

THE CONCEPTUAL FRAMEWORK FOR IMPLEMENTING CLOUD COMPUTING IN LOCAL GOVERNMENT

The conceptual framework (Figure 1) draws on two models for analysing the change process: Lewin's model (Lewin, 1947) and the PEST model which sorts attributes and consequences by four types: political, economical, social and technological. In the framework the key elements commonly associated with cloud computing, or commonly understood to be attributes or consequences of cloud computing implementation, are categorised using PEST. This provides a general background and sets out the relevance of cloud computing for government organisations. On top of this, through applying Kurt Lewin's change process model, driving forces and resisting forces are identified. This framework was developed as part of a theoretical paper (Chang, 2011) before the current empirical study was devised.

There are three client-side activities involved in the implementation of cloud computing; business process change, information assurance and governance, and choice of vendors, products, platform and approach. These implementation activities also form part of the conceptual framework.

Background

In the UK public sector the move towards cloud-based services is largely driven by the Westminister government's strategies for centralising ICT resources and for making more public services directly available online (Cabinet Office, 2010). It has been predicted that the adoption of the government cloud, known as the G-Cloud would result in some £3.2 billion savings. G-Cloud is considered to be an innovative development to meet demand for greater efficiency and a simpler IT infrastructure in the current

Figure 1. A conceptual framework of implementing cloud computing in local government (Chang, 2011)

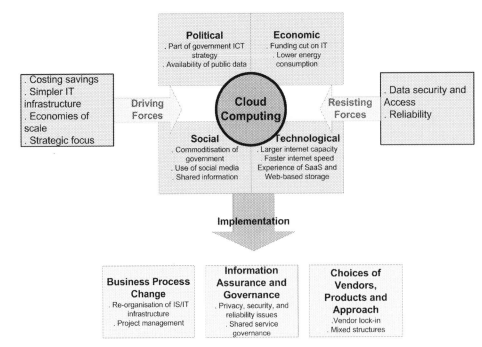

economic situation where, even as the mainstream economy recovers, it is considered prudent policy to maintain low public spending, or even reduce it further. Government agencies need to prioritise their IT services and explore shared platforms, such as the public cloud, in order to achieve the required cost savings. They will have to focus their IT spend on mission-critical business areas (Das et al, 2011; Di Maio, 2009).

Using public cloud services to host public data which can be accessed through social media is an important trend that will have a significant impact both on citizen service delivery and on the government workplace. Cloud computing and the development of G-Cloud will inevitably accelerate and open up such communication channels, and government IT leaders need to consider the associated issues such as security, potential loss of control and accountability for data recovery.

Government agencies have experienced a range of IT solutions over past years including outsourcing, grid computing, SaaS, virtualisation and Web-based storage. These form a foundation for the implementation of cloud computing. Additionally, larger internet capacity and speed nowadays will ensure reliant and appropriate cloud service delivery.

Driving Forces

There are four significant driving forces that may act on local government IT leaders, prompting them to consider cloud computing and encouraging them forward during analysis of their IT options. These driving forces are cost savings, simpler IT infrastructure and flexibity, economies of scale and strategic focus.

Cost Savings

The cloud computing client should benefit from reduced investment in IT and much smaller servicing and maintenance costs because the requirement for 'owned' or 'in house' IT hardware will drop significantly (Wyld et al, 2010; Vaquero et al, 2008). They will also benefit financially because running less hardware means reduced energy consumption (AbdelSalam et al, 2009). Cloud users can also utilise their remaining 'in house' hardware more efficiently (Aymerich et al, 2008) thus freeing up internal resources.

Simpler IT Infrastructure/Flexibility

Cloud computing services are delivered through the Internet so, as stated above, there is no need for the client organisation to own and run a large and complex IT infrastructure. There is no need for capacity for changes in usage or software/technology. The cloud is easily flexible, providing an inherent ability to scale computing power up and down according to usage (Armbust 2010; McEvoy & Schulze, 2008). With cloud-based software services clients do not need to worry about updating or maintaining software, or with licensing issues. These aspects are dealt with by the vendor (Vining & Di Maio, 2009).

Economies of Scale

Cloud vendors have typically been reputable enough to offer customers a reliable service because they are large enough to provide the necessary resilience. With their large data centres and extensive computing capacity cloud providers can enjoy economies of scale impossible for individual clients, yet the benefits can be passed on to those clients (Marston et al, 2011; Grossman, 2009).

Strategic Focus

Having realised cost savings by using cloud based computing, and with a smaller in-house IT infrastructure, local authorities are able to re-focus their attention on strategic goals. Cloud computing should free them up to make better use of limited financial, IT and human resources (Low et al, 2011; Vining & Di Maio, 2009).

Resisting Forces

At the same time there are significant resisting forces that local government must consider during analysis of their IT options, and which may ultimately prevent them from adopting cloud computing. These resisting forces are security and access, and reliability and trust.

Security and Access

Customers of cloud computing do not know where the machines they use actually are. They do not know where their data is actually stored. Everything is somewhere in the cloud. This is a significant concern for local authorities because, to meet the requirements of current privacy legislation, government agencies must know exactly where their data is being stored and who is able to access it (Mishra et al, 2013; Buyya et al, 2008).

Reliability and Trust

The successful implementation of cloud computing relies largely on the trust between buyers and vendors, so local authority clients will need reassuring as to the service they will receive. In particular the vendor has to provide assurance over data security and privacy issues, which must be carefully written into the service level agreements (SLAs) agreed between the parties (Moreno-Vozmediano et al, 2013; Kandukuri et al, 2009). The cloud supplier must use encryption technologies to protect data in shared environments (Younis and Kifayat, 2013; Vining & Di Maio, 2009).

Implementation Issues

So we see that local authorities should carefully consider the benefits and risks of adopting a cloud based service model, and this will include start-up and ongoing 'rental' costs as well as long term savings. They must also consider which of the several service models on offer is appropriate for their needs. Once the decision to proceed has been taken it is important that they implement cloud computing as a business process change project, which requires senior management support (Bojanova et al, 2013; Scholl, 2003). Concerns have already been raised that local government is not used to running large IT projects and therefore the project failure rates are high (Gilbert, 2009). In the public sector successful cloud computing implementation does not just depend on solving the technical issues, such as broadband bandwidths. It will have considerable impact on the authority's IT infrastructure, on its staff, both in terms of numbers and required skills, and on the authority's service users. These aspects all need to be addressed to achieve successful implementation, and decisions taken now will have implications for how local government provides services well into the future.

According to Armbrust et al (2010) success in implementing cloud-based infrastructure depends on a careful comparative assessment of the various types of service delivery available, and the alternative price models. IT leaders should also consider the choice of public cloud or private cloud. Some of the pricing models on the market are quite complex and therefore total service costs may be difficult to predict. Vendor lock-in could potentially be a serious concern because it can be extremely difficult to change the interface when moving from one provider to another (Silva et al, 2013; Buyya et al, 2008). This may cause problems for authorities who have to comply with stringent public sector competition and 'value for money' tests. Another significant risk consideration will be future technology change costs if the provider discontinues the service (Foster et al, 2008).

Cloud computing generally is a relatively new service model. Considering this alongside the concerns over data security and privacy already discussed has lead to the suggestion that local government is more likely to adopt a staged approach to the implementation of cloud computing and to utilise a mixed service structure built on both public and private clouds (Tsohou et al, 2014; Di Maio, 2009).

RESEARCH QUESTIONS

Chang's conceptual model (Chang, 2011) sets out in theoretical terms the principle issues local authorities must address when considering cloud computing. By discovering some of the actual views and concerns held by real life stakeholders we can develop a more realistic assessment of potential implementation problems.

There are three main research questions:

1. To what extent are local authorities aware of cloud computing and the development of the government cloud (G-Cloud)?
2. What do stakeholders see as the main benefits for local authorities of adopting cloud computing and what do they see as the main disadvantages?
3. How might cloud computing be implemented by local authorities, in terms of business process change, information assurance and vendor selection?

RESEARCH METHOD AND DESIGN

As the aim of the research was to investigate key stakeholders' perceptions of cloud computing and the relative importance of contextual factors, a qualitative approach was used (Yin, 2009; O'Donnell & Stewart, 2007). Case study analysis was undertaken at four London based local authorities to determine if they were planning to move to cloud service utilization, and if so, how they were planning to achieve this change.

Interviews were held with the head of IT and members of the IT management team at each council between October 2011 and January 2012, seeking to gain a better understanding of how they viewed cloud service provision and the nature and purposes of the G-Cloud as well as opportunities for, and constraints on, its implementation in local authorities. The local authorities selected are all sufficiently large to be at the stage of considering cloud computing and may already have some experience of shared services. They were identified from press reports and government publications. Prior to commencing the interviewees were all give assurance that no mention would be made of their name or the organisation they represent in any of the findings/published material.

The results obtained from interviewing the four case study organisations have been comparatively analysed based on the conceptual framework previously proposed and using the three main research questions addressed in the study. The findings have then been analysed to identify the level of awareness of cloud computing in local government, perceived opportunities for its use, perceived constraints and threats and then to determine if there are any organisational factors which account for differences in response from one council to another. It will also be possible to gauge differences in central government's perception of the key issues and determine what actions need to be taken to address the concerns raised.

DISCUSSION

The four local authorities will be referred to as Council A, Council B, Council C and Council D. Although these local government organisations have yet to adopt cloud computing they are fully aware of cloud services currently available and the development of government cloud (G-Cloud) from various government publications. In particular Council B has intentions to implement cloud computing with an SME cloud provider and has included this in their strategic plans.

A brief introduction to each of the participating councils is given below:

Council A: Council A serves a population of 295,532 people, of which over 60 per cent are in employment with only 2.7 per cent registered unemployed. The council had a net budget of £200 million for 2012-13. Their strategic plan is to save more than £30 million over the three years to 2015. This is in addition to the £22 million the council saved in 2011-12. Therefore in total the council will be saving £50 million over a four year period. The council has already cut staffing costs saving over £3 million. At the time of interview they were in discussion with surrounding councils to look at potential shared services.

Council B: Council B serves a population of some 247,000, according to the 2011 census data. Residents aged 25-49 count for more than 42% of this total, while residents aged 50 and over comprise a smaller amount of the whole borough population (23%). The prevailing economic climate and central government funding cuts were placing considerable pressure on the council's budget, and this is likely to continue for the next few years. Efficiency savings had been a priority in addressing the budget cuts in order to minimise the effect on front-line services. Council B claims to be one of the first local authorities to be migrating email telephony and Microsoft technology to a cloud-based solution.

Council C: Council C serves a population of over 300,000, and has seen 6% population growth per annum since 1991. In that time the number of people aged below 16 has increased by 5%. The council's diversity is high and has also increased in recent years, with over than 40% of residents being classified as minority ethnic compared with 9.1% nationally. One the council's priorities from financial year 2012-13 onwards has been to deliver value for money in response to funding cuts, with an objective to save £85 million by April 2015. The council has supported the concepts of opening up public information and providing public services online, and a range of electronic forms has been developed. The council has adopted a 24-hour automated information service with the aim of reducing the need for unnecessary customer visits, with an appointment system for complex queries.

Council D: Council D serves a population of approximately 150,000, and is one of the richest and most densely populated districts in the United Kingdom. Notwithstanding this demographic the council, in line with the rest of the public sector, has suffered cuts in central government grant. They were actively seeking means of reducing management and operational costs at the time of the interviews. A major aspect of this was seeking to establish a new relationship with surrounding boroughs in the shared delivery of council services. With an objective to reduce management costs in shared services by 50% the council was expecting to save a total of £35 million a year by 2014-15. Council D adopts a hybrid approach to IT provision. Whilst the network server is developed and maintained in-house, many departmental information systems have been outsourced, one example being the human resources information systems.

Concept of Cloud Computing

The notion that cloud computing is not clearly defined is confirmed by all four local authorities. The lack of a universally agreed definition of cloud computing is expressed by Council A, "I think the first thing is that cloud computing isn't clearly defined, what people mean by cloud computing, do they mean hosted solutions accessible via the internet? …. I think there's a lot of hype around it, without going into detail about what they actually mean by it". Similar to Council A, Council C is concerned that "different people are using that term and meaning different things" and staff in the IT department believe, from a technical point of view, that cloud computing is, in a sense, software as a service (SaaS) on a subscription basis, while Council D refers cloud computing as hosting services "with a different kind of name". Council B, sharing the same view as other participating councils, further indicates that because of the confusion about what is really meant by cloud computing it is unclear how much cloud computing and the G-Cloud will assist the council to achieve the substantial gains it promises.

Background

Political

All four councils disagreed with the notion that cloud computing is driven by Central Government's ICT strategies. The reasoning behind this is that, regardless of Government's ICT strategies and e-initiatives, local authorities have already been looking into ways of saving costs which always includes rationalisation options for their IT provision. In Council B's own words, cloud computing is driven by "the provision of more cost-effective services and the private sector responding to that business model or new business model which it is beginning to do at the minute…". Similarly Council A believes that cloud's cost-saving abilities, and the potential to be 'infrastructure-free' are major advantages in terms of transforming the way the council operates and therefore it is an area that local government has been considering anyway, whether or not the Government had it in its IT strategy.

When asked specifically whether considering cloud computing has any correlation with the government's intentions to provide information and services online (Cabinet Office, 2010) the participants again disagree to some extent. Council B states that they can supply public service data online without necessarily subscribing to a cloud-based service, so the two are not inevitably linked. This argument is supported by Council C. Council D further explains that central government strategy is that by 2005 all services could be delivered electronically and that therefore local authorities - with this timeline in mind - had done a considerable amount of work to support the strategy. So this does indicate some driving influence from central government. However, they had not actually implemented cloud computing at the time of interviews because, as Council D indicates, "we do have concerns over where our data would reside for some of our sensitive data".

There are differing opinions between the interviewees when considering if councils should specifically include moving to a cloud-based infrastructure of future IT provision in their ICT plans. Council B, in support of the government's cloud strategy, confirms that a cloud-based infrastructure is in the council's ICT strategy. Council A, on the other hand, maintains that the broader aims of reducing costs and increasing the flexibility of IT provision in future years are what are addressed in the council's strategic plans, and they are not convinced that cloud would be mature enough in the current strategic timeframe.

Of the four participants only Council D agrees with the notion that the move to cloud-based IT provision and the development of G-Cloud come as a result of the Westminster government's intention to centralise IT resources. Aside from the issue of cloud computing, councils have already experienced the advantage of shared IT provision and recognise the need for collaboration among local authorities in a belief that it will lead to significant cost reduction and economies of scale. It is evident, according to Council A, that they have achieved a lower cost through jointly tendering for IT projects with a neighbouring council. Council C also points out that most local authorities are looking at ways of sharing their infrastructure or their key applications and hosted solutions, although again they do not consider such a practice to be cloud-driven.

Economic

All the participating councils have experienced significant cuts in IT budgets as a general result of the economic downturn of 2008 onwards, and specifically because of central governments ongoing tight public spending policies. Councils are proactively seeking ways of reducing IT costs and rationalising their existing infrastructure to sit within the available funding. With regard to cloud computing, however, Council A believes that G-Cloud is not the answer to the shrinking IT budget. The move to cloud-based services will make savings but it is not the only way of driving those savings. Conversely, savings may not be the only driver for change: Council C indicates that the council would not consider cloud computing purely for cost-saving purposes.

Although local councils generally support the development of the government cloud there is a level of suspicion in local government and the general attitude is to 'wait and see'. G-Cloud has been advocated by central government as an innovative ICT strategy for tomorrow's IT infrastructure model. The councils, however, consider both the innovation and the progress of the G-Cloud disappointing. According to Council D: "…. the whole G-cloud concept has been scaled back recently and kind of distilling down more to consolidating of data centres in the public centre really. Not much emphasis on the G-app side of it as there was before shall we say. …. I've attended various seminars, heard the spiel on G-Cloud, nothing much seems to be happening is my observation really, beyond the work they seem to be doing on data centre consolidation which seems generally sensible". The suspicion is that economic considerations have got in the way of central governments ambitious aspirations.

One of the held advantages of implementing cloud computing is that it is environmentally friendly and will reduce energy consumption in IT systems, therefore leading to reduced energy servicing costs

(Vining & Di Maio, 2009; AbdelSalam et al, 2009). While greener IT is a top priority for many local authorities (Foster et al, 2008) the participating councils do not think that adopting cloud computing on its own will reduce energy consumption much more than the IT practices they are already implementing. For example, Council B points out that the third-party data centre they use has greatly enhanced efficiency both in terms of virtualisation of servers and the environmental efficiency of cooling, heating and the use of electricity. The cost savings achieved through running a highly efficient data centre is also confirmed by Council C who own their own data centre and believe that they may not achieve any further cost savings by opting for an external cloud-based data centre. When asked about the G-Cloud, Council C felt that if it is built in an energy efficient data centre using virtualisation technology then it will use less energy. However, they are not sure whether this is in fact the case, at least not yet.

Council D, taking a slightly different view, emphasises that actual realised reductions is energy consumption will depend entirely on how efficient the particular cloud provider is. It is suggested that, "yes it would reduce our energy consumption and in terms of the carbon reduction commitment that would be good for us as an organisation, it would reflect well on us, ...on the eco friendliness shall we say, of the provider, ...to watch from a purist point of view of the environmental impact of what you're delivering as a business, ...so you do need to watch the provider and make that your criteria..." This response also points to the fact that green technology issues are not just relevant to authorities as an economic factor. There are also political and social considerations.

Social

In the literature there is a general assumption that the development of cloud computing or G-Cloud is derived from the concepts of 'commoditisation of government' and 'open government data' through the use of social media (Bertot et al, 2014; Di Maio, 2009). The participating councils disagree with this assumption, arguing instead that cloud computing has nothing to do with social media. They hold that the concept of allowing the general public to access public data through the Internet had been proposed a while ago, and therefore bears no direct connection with the move to cloud services.

It has been suggested that with their previous experience of outsourcing, SaaS (Software as a Service) and virtualisation, local authorities would be well positioned to successfully implement cloud-based initiatives. From the case studies it is clear that local government does indeed have a great deal of experience in outsourcing. For example, Council A's IT infrastructure is heavily outsourced, including the IT helpdesk, servers and data networks and web-based back-up. Council C has virtually outsourced the entire IT management to a private sector service provider, and their applications run on hosted services from a variety of different vendors. When asked about implementing cloud computing from the perspective of building on their outsourcing experience, Council C said, "there's no great impediment to the council using cloud". However, as cloud computing and, more precisely, G-Cloud are still at an initial stage of development it seems from the interviewees that local authorities intend to wait until full benefits have been realised before considering implementation. As Council D comments, "We tend to be a risk averse organisation so we tend not to be on the leading edge, but we were an early adopter of virtualisation technology..."

Technological

It is held that one of the key features of cloud computing is simpler client-side infrastructure with a significantly reduced requirement for heavy IT investment, both hardware and upkeep costs (Han, 2013; Vaquero et al, 2008). This would be welcomed by local government when developing future IT strategies. After some years experience of outsourcing, the IT skills in Council B have been left undeveloped. There is therefore a 'skills gap' and the magnitude of that gap, or at least its significance as a problem, would be minimised by using cloud computing services and outsourcing various components on those services. Council D is the only one of the four case study participants to retain an in-house IT team. This team, they believe, has a lot of expert technical capability, so simpler infrastructure of itself would not be a factor to encourage them to move to cloud. That does not prevent them from considering cloud services for other reasons.

Flexibility is an important factor for local authorities when considering the cloud, specifically the ability to easily scale up and down the type and level of services provided sounds appealing (Herbst et al, 2013; McEvoy & Schulze, 2008). Scalability means that if the council buys the IT infrastructure and has it for five years, and in that time the organisation shrinks, or some specific processes in the organisation shrink, then the council would need less of that infrastructure. In practice Council A predicts that identifying the level of infrastructure takes some 'intelligence around storage'. Local councils tend not to be that flexible. Most things are known in advance, so the cloud's flexible scalability is not a significant advantage to the council. Council B reaches a similar conclusion but via a different argument: they point out that one of the selection criteria in choosing a vendor is that if the service provider is incapable of meeting the council's needs and adjust the level of services quickly the council would not consider it. As the participating councils have yet to have substantial experience of cloud computing it is unclear to them how the 'scalability' feature will work for local authorities.

Local councils have had lots of experience in appraising and choosing external IT vendors through their outsourcing and SaaS practices. For example, Council A do not own in-house developers at all; they buy packages off the shelf and the application is customised according to requirements. As Council A comments, "the biggest challenge is to modernise line of business applications and some of the suppliers are quite slow in terms of responding to things". When asked how the vendors' experience would benefit the provision of cloud services, Council C points out that they would certainly expect cloud vendors to have more skills than their own staff which is one of the reasons for migrating.

Driving Forces

Cost Savings

As already mentioned, cost-saving is perhaps the most important factor driving local government to consider cloud computing since local authorities are currently under enormous pressure to find cost-effective ways of restructuring IT infrastructure to reduce capital, servicing and staffing costs. Although none of the participating councils has fully implemented cloud computing it is felt that moving to cloud-based platforms and services brings the potential of massive savings. This supports Korri's argument (2009) that cloud computing presents an attractive alternative to building one's own computing infrastructure, which can be extremely costly.

Having already exhausted the cost saving potential of other IT changes it may be that councils now have to embrace cloud computing to realise the further savings demanded of them. Council A reveals that, "We run at very tight margins anyway and because we've been outsourced for a number of years so we've already taken the savings where we can. We've already cut quite a number of our costs through virtualization, through outsourcing, the rationalization of systems. I don't think there's a huge pot of money that we can save just because we're putting it out on the cloud but I'm hoping there's some savings there..... we've identified £30m worth of cuts which is approximately 20% of our overall budget. So staff will go, the numbers will be dramatically reduced, so how do you reduce staff without impacting the service, is self service the way to do it"?

Council B also predicts they could realise a cost saving of around 30% through cloud. Council C suggests that the G-Cloud would be potentially cheaper than using commercial cloud, and in addition it would be more secure. Council C's also see a double cost and security advantage in the G-Cloud; it could be seen as a secure private cloud, where councils share services with other local authorities, therefore achieving savings. It is built to be secure, because it is exclusively used by the public sector, which is a key factor for encouraging local government to move to cloud computing.

Economies of Scale

If the G-Cloud is to offer a platform where public organisations and local authorities can share IT resources and key applications, then a high level of economies of scale can be expected through sharing data centres and centralising ICT facilities and expertise (Grossman, 2009; Kliazovich et al, 2013). Many local authorities have experienced savings from collaboration between IT departments and joint tendering for IT contractors. According to Council A, joined-up data centres can significantly reduce cost round data centres across government. In essence that is cloud at its most basic level providing hosted solutions. Using common applications that provide greater flexibility is another way of keeping IT costs to the minimum. Many IT initiatives and local partnership schemes have already encouraged local authorities to work together in sharing common platforms and networks.

Strategic Focus

If local authorities no longer need to make large investments in IT infrastructure including hardware, software and staff then in theory considerable internal resource can be freed up (Aymerich et al, 2008). This enables the focus of attention and limited IT and human resources on 'mission-critical' areas (Low et al, 2011; Vining & Di Maio, 2009). First of all, only Council B has specific plans to launch cloud initiatives and therefore the other three were unable to comment on this particular point. Secondly, in the current tight funding situation one intended outcome of local government's IT strategy is a conscious move to a much smaller IT infrastructure. So after downsizing it's questionable whether there will be significant resource available to strategically focus elsewhere. Thirdly, it is suggested that the staff remaining following a rationalisation process would need to be re-trained to support areas of strategic importance and their job descriptions will be significantly altered.

Resisting Forces

Security and Reliability of Data

Security and reliability of data are clearly a concern for local government when considering a move to cloud because of the confidential and sensitive nature of data being stored in the public sector (Younis and Kifayat, 2013; Buyya et al, 2009; Grossman, 2009). There is legislation in data security which impact on the adoption of cloud, for example, Council B stresses that, "… our information can't be hosted outside the country … those set of considerations have to be brought to betterment; they're just as important as the reliability of the vendor or disaster recovery report, they all have to be right otherwise you wouldn't take the service out…"

With regards to how secure the data should be and how the level of safety can be measured, Council C explains: "Microsoft 365 is certified to impact level 2, protect level status as rated by Communications-Electronics Security Group (CESG) which means that it can carry personal information which if released incorrectly to the public domain might be an embarrassment but wouldn't cause harm. ... that is in effect G-cloud solution which is rated up to a higher security, that can carry confidential, secret information … although it's fine for Data Protection Act purposes because it's inside the European Union, it means it's not likely ever to be rated more than IL2 by UK government, it's outside of their control".

Council A offers a different opinion about cloud security. The council is not worried too much about security because it is such an obvious issue that it will have to be taken care of by cloud vendors in due course, both private and G-Cloud. Security policies and disaster recovery strategies are very much dependant on the reliability of the vendor and the contract negotiations (service level agreement). This argument is supported by Council D.

Privacy and Access

In a similar way to their views on the security and reliability of data, the participating councils are not particularly concerned about privacy of and access to data. Council A explains that, "I'm not so concerned about privacy and similar issues etc. because they're so obvious. Those are sort of hygiene factors I would absolutely expect them to be taken care of". Local councils have already had policies and strategies in place to ensure individual privacy, data security and information assurance, and now have vast experience in dealing with these issues at all scales. Council D expresses the same level of confidence commenting that, "Individual privacy I see that probably more of a perception of a problem rather than a real problem ....providing that you choose your vendors well it didn't ought to be a problem, because you know it would bad for their business if it was". These are seen to be such obvious stumbling blocks for the whole concept of cloud computing that the councils assume that the technical issues will have to be solved.

Service Level Agreements

As previously discussed, realising the potential benefits of cloud services very much depends on the detail of the Service Level Agreements (SLAs) drawn up between vendor and client. Council B provides a detailed account of what should be considered and included in a SLA, which is an important task for local authorities managing IT projects of outsourcing, SaaS and cloud: "... you can make assessment based on experience and knowledge, use that as a basis... but the whole field of defining an SLA and penalty clauses is very difficult one to do in any commercial contract because of course the supplier will construct that, see the penalty clauses that will be extremely difficult to ever implement or ever come into effect... there has to be clauses and definitions within the contract which negate and define what security the data is, we have to analyze the financial viability of the vendor to make sure that the supplier of those services is financially secure and able to continue to provide those services for the length of the contract. ...what the levels of access will be for that data and how will that data be protected". Local government works in a strict regulatory framework and is required to scrutinise and audit to a high level when spending public monies. This will impact on the drafting of the SLA.

Internet-Related Issues

Internet speed and bandwidth-related issues are held to be a concern when services are provided entirely through the Internet (Grossman, 2009). As Council D comments, "… when you were looking to go to cloud route for service you would obviously be looking at your network band capabilities and you could upgrade that capability if you needed to deliver through a provider or use efficiently through cloud mechanism. So it's just a cost factor to bear in mind if you're heading down a cloud route for something which you may need to upgrade your network bandwidth capability". The attitude of the council is not so much that this could be a resisting force, but that it is certainly a technical and cost issue to be addressed in the consideration and implementation of cloud computing.

Implementation Issues

Business Process Change

A number of business process change related issues have been identified by the participating councils. In general terms, however, it is felt that moving to a different business model of public services is very much an evolutionary, rather than revolutionary process. For example, Council A believes that the IT departments in local government will inevitably be downsized due to the need to rationalise business applications. This will not happen overnight but through a planned, staged approach to business process change.

Council B gives some forecast as to what will be changed in the next five to six years,

… we're moving our infrastructure to third parties, …the CIO, the IT director, will become much more of a commissioner of services rather than runner of internal services or manager of internal services, defining those requirements and working with businesses technology partner and then procuring those services through the most cost-effective means which might mean full scale out-sourcing, through the third party, it could be considerable, substantial outsourcing and anything in-between depending on the needs of the organization.

Similarly Council D predicts the council to be of "fewer staff, ultimately... savings don't come in a sort of linear way, they come in a step way when it comes to staffing so initially I would see in the early days just a few services you'd probably make very little difference". The job descriptions of the existing IT staff would be significantly different. They would not be doing things such as storing and looking after databases. When cloud has become a commonly used platform in local government IT professionals will need to be re-trained and move to different areas and do whatever is required. Again, Council D supports the idea that the outlook and activities of the IT department will be altered but this will change gradually, not radically.

Project Management and Planning

The four councils were asked to comment on project management in relation to cloud computing, considering the role both of central government and of local authorities. Adequate project management and planning skills are held to be critical to the successful development and implementation of G-Cloud, for which the government has adopted a staged approach. According to Council A there is a history of unsuccessful IT projects and contract negotiations in the public sector (cf. Gilbert, 2009; Sandeep and Ravishankar, 2014). This explains a delay in central government advocating its G-Cloud to local authorities. Council D shares the same view, indicating that, "…I can't see that [G-cloud] happening at the moment. G-Cloud doesn't seem to be delivering anything useful yet". The issue of G-Cloud delay should also be considered in the context of reduced public funding as already discussed.

Regarding the success or failure of IT projects in local government specifically, Council C admits that failures are mostly likely for those projects where the council has attempted to develop applications in-house. As the head of IT comments, "…I doubt you'll find any development of specific coding going on, council can't afford it; too risky and incidents of projects failing are too high". The participating councils tend to agree that the success of providing cloud-based IT provision in local government relies mainly on the selection of vendors and contract negotiations. As noted already, councils have experience in managing outsourcing and SaaS contracts, but the interviewees suggest specific project management and planning skills required for the transition from traditional IT provision to cloud-based infrastructure need to be further identified.

Information Assurance and Governance

As already discussed, security and privacy will be a concern for local government when considering cloud-based services, although local authorities are very aware of information assurance and governance issues and are familiar with the relevant legislation. Council B mentions GCS6 standards where the council has encrypted laptops so that if they are lost the data will not be accessible. They emphasise that they cannot adopt cloud computing if the cloud service is not compliant with GCS6. Cloud vendors will have to provide some assurance in the SLA (Kandukuri et al, 2009; Moreno-Vozmediano et al, 2013). "If you start to house some of that data in the cloud you may have some problems with complying with that …" As regards individual privacy, Council C argues information assurance and data security "are all part of any procurement we would do, they would be key requirements for whether it was cloud, traditional hosting or in-house. They are core considerations and they would be part of the evaluation process".

Choices of Vendors, Products, and Approach

A number of issues are addressed in the conceptual framework regarding the implementation of cloud computing: selection of vendors, vendor lock-in, approach and methods. The participating councils were invited to comment on these issues. When asked how to choose a vendor Council A provided the criteria that would be adopted by the council: functionality and price. This is similar to how Council D would select a cloud provider. However, Council D indicates that there should be a different cost model used for cloud services, taking into consideration revenue, budgets and the council's own operating costs. Council C, on the other hand, advises that they would select vendors through a competitive procurement process, just like any other types of procurement. EU and UK public sector procurement rules would in any case apply to any large competitive tender for supplying cloud services.

An interesting perspective is offered by Council B: in choosing a cloud partner they would go for medium-sized service providers, "big enough to meet our needs, small enough for us to be their significant client". An explanation is given, "… So that's the key principle going forward with our vendors, as we form partnership with them and we choose vendors that are the right size and the right flexibility to meet our needs".

Vendor lock-in is a concern, shared by all four councils. As Council A raises, "what would stop the vendor from pushing their prices up because I can't walk away very easily and because I wouldn't have local infrastructure anymore. So there really has to be tight contracts negotiated there". Moving from one supplier to another can be costly (Buyya et al, 2008; Satzger et al, 2013). This includes the cost of changing the technology once a vendor discontinues the service (Foster et al, 2008). Without the IT infrastructure, a key resource, can lead to a loss of organisational control, as warned by Buyyaet al (2008). For this Council B proposes that a contract should be formulated "in the term that you want to have the right exit strategy in it… and that there are lots of protection and procedures to make migrating commoditised service from one supplier to another relatively straightforward".

Another implementation issue is integration with existing IT infrastructure, considered the biggest challenge by Council A. As previously mentioned local authorities are relatively conservative and are likely to employ a hybrid and staged approach to cloud computing (Di Maio, 2009; Leavitt, 2013). Such an attitude is evident in Council B's plans to implement cloud computing: "We'd like other people to take the risk first and depending on how they go, then we go for it" As with all public sector IT rationalisations (and also often in large private sector organisations) choice of product and supplier has to take account of the existing infrastructure and processes. There is just not the money available to go for an idealised 'everything new' strategy. Certain otherwise attractive suppliers may need to be discounted if they cannot hybridise with the authority's existing systems.

FUTURE RESEARCH DIRECTIONS

This explorative study is based around the viewpoint of four urban local authorities, each based in London, close to central government and other national resources and with large, dense and mobile populations. Future research can build on the findings from the present study to include councils with alternative geographical and demographic characteristics, whose views might be substantially different. Including views from authorities situated in rural areas would be especially relevant, as IT resources and skills might not be readily available, and the required council service outcomes may be very different. Interviewing a greater range of stakeholders such as IT directors, senior managers, IT technicians and users from different departments would also enrich the study, adding depth to the findings. A quantitative survey would be beneficial as concepts and beliefs can be generalised. The framework can also be expanded to include success/failure factors once enough local authorities have considered and implemented cloud computing.

Taking the study in a different direction, future research can adopt a longitudinal approach by undertaking an in-depth case study with a single council which has had a full experience in utilising the G-Cloud framework. In this way the issues identified in the current conceptual framework can be investigated in greater detail. This may involve looking into the physical design and implementation of a cloud-based infrastructure, the approach, type and business model used to integrate cloud with existing systems, an analysis of cost savings in financial terms, the impact of cloud on the authorities existing and future business and IT strategies, methods used by the council for monitoring and 'lessons learned', and how central government has supported the G-Cloud.

CONCLUSION

A conceptual framework is proposed by Chang (2011) to help analyse the impact of implementing cloud computing in local government. Key issues are identified in the framework, which form the basis for the present research to gauge the general attitude and perceptions of local authorities towards the application of cloud-based services. The importance of the subject area is justified by the UK government's ICT strategies and staged plans to implement the government cloud (G-Cloud) (Cabinet Office, 2010). The research attempts to investigate to what extent local authorities are aware of cloud computing and the development of G-Cloud, the main benefits, as well as constraints of adopting cloud computing to local councils and any concerns regarding implementation, in terms of business process change, relationships with cloud providers and issues relating to data security and information assurance. A case study methodology has been adopted because the subject area is relatively new. Four London-based borough councils are chosen and interviews of senior members of staff from both IT and business departments are carried out. Their views and opinions are analysed and compared which shed a light into the current strategies and future plans for cloud services and the G-Cloud.

There is no precise definition of cloud computing, a notion that has been confirmed by the case study organisations who offer views about what cloud computing is. It can be suggested that many current IT practices, such as SaaS, hosted services and virtualisation, form part of the so-called cloud computing. In fact, most local councils now do not have in-house developers. Public services are provided mostly online and much of the IT services are outsourced. There is need for clear and universally agreed definitions of cloud computing for the purposes of academic discussion and practical guidance.

There is only one council that supports the government's cloud strategy and has intentions to implement cloud computing in the near future. Other councils would prefer to wait until there is a clear evidence to suggest that all benefits of cloud computing can be realised. Such an attitude comes from local authorities being relatively cautious and conservative in adopting new ways of providing public services, and risk-adverse so that it is unwise to be the first to implement cloud computing.

Contrary to the belief that the move to cloud services is largely driven by the government's central ICT strategies, case organisations disagree that there are specific instructions from the government to implement G-Cloud. Local government are proactively seeking ways of reducing management and operational costs, due to decreasing grant and budgets, and many local councils have already undertaken measures to ensure that considerable savings can be made in the coming years. These include using the most energy-efficient data centres, providing public services online, collaborating with surrounding councils for shared IT systems and rationalising the existing IT infrastructure, whether cloud-based or not. The view from the participating organisations is clear: cloud computing has a potential in helping councils to reduce costs but it is not the only answer to the economic downturn and reduced funding. Savings on, for example energy consumption, will depend on how efficient the cloud provider is.

It has been suggested that cloud computing is driven by the government's intension to commoditise public information and services. And the development of government cloud is linked to the prevalence of social media and Internet technologies. These views are not specifically supported by the participating councils. On the other hand, local authorities have had many years of experience in outsourcing and using external service providers to customise applications based on requirements. Local authorities are aware that considerable savings can be achieved by employing virtual servers and web-based storage and recognise the importance of negotiating with vendors for a well-balanced SLA. A more serious concern, vendor lock-in, is shared by the case organisations because the promised benefits of moving to cloud could be compromised once the cloud provider is responsible for the entire IT infrastructure and demands a higher price. Local government is urged to think carefully about 'exit' strategy and rules and procedures to be included in the contract when formulating SLAs.

Cloud computing will transform the council's IT infrastructure, business processes and how the services are provided. Although not asked specifically about downsizing the participating councils admit that due to the economic downturn and the enormous pressure arising from reduced public funding local government has 'staged' plans for a much smaller-scaled IT department, self-service online facilities and collaboration between local authorities. IT directors will be more concerned about commissioning work and negotiating SLAs. The impact of such business process change to existing staff and job descriptions need to be investigated further.

One of the major concerns in cloud computing is data security, privacy and access. The requirement to host sensitive data in the country will prevent local authorities from considering cloud services because there are certain laws and regulations councils need to comply with, for example, those governed by the CESG. This concern may be overcome by the adoption of the G-Cloud which is developed by central government with adequate security measures that will satisfy legal requirements. In fact, local authorities already have strict information governance policies and strategies in place. They are not too concerned about data security and individual privacy when considering cloud because it is an obvious issue that would be taken care of by the service provider. Similarly, technical issues such as Internet speed and network capabilities should not be a problem, because they can be easily assessed and dealt with if councils are to adopt cloud services.

REFERENCES

AbdelSalam, H., Maly, K., Mukkamala, R., Zubair, M. &Kaminsky, D. (2009). Towards energy efficient change management in a cloud computing environment. *AIMS*, 161-166.

Amazon. (2010). *Amazon elastic compute cloud*, Retrieved February 15, 2010 from www.amazon.com

Armbrust, M., Fox, A., Griffith, R., Joseph, A. D., Katz, R., Konwinski, A., & Zaharia, M. (2010). A view of cloud computing. *Communications of the ACM*, *53*(4), 50–58. doi:10.1145/1721654.1721672

Aymerich, F. M., Fenu, G., & Surcis, S. (2008). An approach to a cloud computing network. In *1st International Conference on the Applications of Digital Information and Web Technologies*, (pp. 113-118). 10.1109/ICADIWT.2008.4664329

Bertot, J. C., Gorham, U., Jaeger, P. T., Sarin, L. C., & Choi, H. (2014). Big data, open government and e-government: Issues, policies and recommendations. *Information Polity, 19*(1), 5–16.

Bojanova, I., Zhang, J., & Voas, J. (2013). Cloud computing. *IT Professional, 15*(2), 12–14. doi:10.1109/MITP.2013.26

Buyya, R., Yeo, C. S., & Venugopal, V. (2008).Vision, hype and reality for delivering IT services as computing utilities. In *10th IEEE International Conference on High Performance Computing and Communications*, (pp. 5-13). IEEE.

Cabinet Office. (2010). *Government ICT Strategy: smarter, cheaper, greener*. London: Cabinet Office, January.

Catteddu, D. (2010). *Cloud Computing: benefits, risks and recommendations for information security.* Berlin: Springer.

Chang, J. (2011, October-December). A framework of analysing the impact of cloud computing on local government in the UK. *International Journal of Cloud Applications and Computing, 1*(4), 25–33. doi:10.4018/ijcac.2011100102

Das, R. K., Patnaik, S., & Misro, A. K. (2011). Adoption of cloud computing in e-governance. In *Advanced Computing* (pp. 161–172). Berlin: Springer. doi:10.1007/978-3-642-17881-8_16

Di Maio, A. (2009a, June). Cloud computing in government: private, public, both or none? *Gartner.*

Di Maio, A. (2009b, September). GSA launches Apps.gov: what it means to government IT leaders? *Gartner.*

Di Maio, A. (2009c, June). Government in the cloud: Much more than computing. *Gartner.*

Digital Britain. (2009). *Final report, presented to Parliament in June 2009.* London: The Stationery Office.

Foster, I., Zhao, Y., Raicu, I., & Lu, S. (2008). Cloud computing and grid computing 360-degree compared. In *Grid Computing Environments Workshop*. 10.1109/GCE.2008.4738445

Grossman, R. L. (2009). *The case for cloud computing*. IEEE Computer Society. Retrieved from computer.org/ITPro

Han, Y. (2013). On the clouds: A new way of computing. *Information Technology and Libraries, 29*(2), 87–92. doi:10.6017/ital.v29i2.3147

Herbst, N. R., Kounev, S., & Reussner, R. (2013, June). Elasticity in Cloud Computing: What It Is, and What It Is Not. ICAC, 23-27.

Kandukuri, B. R., Ramakrishna, P. V., & Rakshit, A. (2009). Cloud security issues. In *2009 IEEE International Conference on Services Computing*, (pp. 517-520). IEEE.

Kliazovich, D., Bouvry, P., & Khan, S. U. (2013). Simulation and Performance Analysis of Data Intensive and Workload Intensive Cloud Computing Data Centers. In Optical Interconnects for Future Data Center Networks, (pp. 47-63). New York: Springer. doi:10.1007/978-1-4614-4630-9_4

Korri, T. (2009). Cloud computing: utility computing over the Internet. Seminar on Internetworking, Helsinki University of Technology.

Leavitt, N. (2013). Hybrid clouds move to the forefront. *Computer, 46*(5), 15–18. doi:10.1109/MC.2013.168

Lewin, K. (1947). Frontiers in group dynamics: Concept, method, and reality in social science. *Human Relations, 1*(1), 5–42. doi:10.1177/001872674700100103

Low, C., Chen, Y., & Wu, M. (2011). Understanding the determinants of cloud computing adoption. *Industrial Management & Data Systems, 111*(7), 1006–1023. doi:10.1108/02635571111161262

Luis, M.V., Luis, R, Caceres, J., & Lindner, M. (2008). A break in the clouds: towards a cloud definition. *SIGCOMM Computer Communication Review, 39*(1).

Maggiani, R. (2009, November). Cloud computing is changing how we communicate. *IEEE Explore.*

Marston, S., Li, Z., Bandyopadhyay, S., Zhang, J., & Ghalsasi, A. (2011). Cloud computing—The business perspective. *Decision Support Systems, 51*(1), 176–189. doi:10.1016/j.dss.2010.12.006

McEvoy, G. V., & Schulze, B. (2008). Using clouds to address grid limitations. In *MGC '08: Proceedings of the 6th international workshop on Middleware for grid computing*, (pp. 1-6). New York: ACM.

Mell, P., & Grance, T. (2009). The NIST definition of cloud computing. *National Institute of Standards and Technology, 53*(6), 50.

Mishra, A., Mathur, R., Jain, S., & Rathore, J. S. (2013). Cloud Computing Security. *International Journal on Recent and Innovation Trends in Computing and Communication, 1*(1), 36–39.

Moreno-Vozmediano, R., Montero, R. S., & Llorente, I. M. (2013). Key challenges in cloud computing: Enabling the future internet of services. *IEEE Internet Computing, 17*(4), 18–25. doi:10.1109/MIC.2012.69

Nelson, M. R. (2009). The cloud, the crowd and public policy. *Issues in Science and Technology*, (Summer), 71–76.

O'Donnell, M., & Stewart, J. (2007). Implementing change in the public agency/leadership, learning and organisational resilience. *International Journal of Public Sector Management, 20*(3), 239–251. doi:10.1108/09513550710740634

Plummer, D.C., Smith, D.M., Bittman, T.J., Cearley, D.W., Cappuccio, D.J., Scott, D., Kumar, R., and Robertson, B. (2009, May). *Five refining attributes of public and private cloud computing.* Gartner.

Sandeep, M. S., & Ravishankar, M. N. (2014). The continuity of underperforming ICT projects in the public sector. *Information & Management, 51*(6), 700–711. doi:10.1016/j.im.2014.06.002

Satzger, B., Hummer, W., Inzinger, C., Leitner, P., & Dustdar, S. (2013). Winds of change: From vendor lock-in to the meta cloud. *IEEE Internet Computing, 17*(1), 69–73. doi:10.1109/MIC.2013.19

Scholl, H. J., & Klischewski, R. (2007). E-government integration and interoperability: Framing the research agenda. *International Journal of Public Administration, 30*(8-9), 889–920. doi:10.1080/01900690701402668

Silva, G. C., Rose, L. M., & Calinescu, R. (2013, December). Towards a Model-Driven Solution to the Vendor Lock-In Problem in Cloud Computing. In *Cloud Computing Technology and Science (CloudCom), 2013 IEEE 5th International Conference on* (pp. 711-716). 10.1109/CloudCom.2013.131

Takabi, H., Joshi, J. B., & Ahn, G. J. (2010). Security and Privacy Challenges in Cloud Computing Environments. *IEEE Security and Privacy*, 8(6), 24–31. doi:10.1109/MSP.2010.186

Thomson, R. (2009, February 24). Socitm: Cloud computing revolutionary to the public sector. *Computer Weekly*.

Tsohou, A., Lee, H., & Irani, Z. (2014). Innovative public governance through cloud computing: information privacy, business models and performance measurement challenges. *Transforming Government: People, Process, and Policy*, 8(2), 6–6.

Vaquero, L. M., Rodero-Merino, R., Caceres, J., & Lindner, M. (2008). A break in the clouds: towards a cloud definition. *SIGCOMM Computer Communication Review, 39*(1).

Vining, J. & Di Maio, A. (2009, February). *Cloud computing for government is cloudy.* Gartner.

Wyld, D. C. (2010). The Cloudy future of government IT: Cloud computing and the public sector around the world. *International Journal of Web & Semantic Technology*, 1(1), 1–20.

Yin, R. K. (2009). *Case Study Research: Design and Methods.* Sage Inc.

Younis, M. Y. A., & Kifayat, K. (2013). *Secure cloud computing for critical infrastructure: A survey. Liverpool John Moores University.*

KEY TERMS AND DEFINITIONS

Business Process Change: Business process change refers to a planned programme to redesign, update or integrate an organisation's business processes in order to achieve its business objectives. This may be in response to a specific change in the organisations business operating environment. It is an actively planned and analysed process enabling the organisation to re-think linkages between strategy, business processes and people.

Cloud Computing: Cloud computing refers to a scalable network infrastructure where consumers receive IT services such as software and data storage through the Internet on a subscription basis, like traditional utilities. Potential benefits include cost savings, simpler IT and reduced energy consumption. Areas of concern include security, access, data protection and ownership.

Data Centre: A data centre is a facility that houses and maintains computer, server and networking systems and their components as part of a company's IT infrastructure. In cloud computing the data centre is owned by the cloud service vendor.

Government Cloud (G-Cloud): The Government cloud in the UK, or G-Cloud, is an initiative developed by the central government to simplify the cloud procurement process for public organisations. The G-Cloud is a series of framework agreements with suppliers, from which public sector organisations can obtain services without needing to run a full, lengthy and complex tendering process. There is an online store called the "CloudStore" that allows public sector bodies to search for services that are approved by the G-Cloud frameworks.

IT Infrastructure: IT infrastructure refers to the set of IT hardware, software, networks and supporting facilities used by an organisation to develop, test, deliver, monitor, control or support IT services. It should be noted that users, processes and documentation are not part of the IT Infrastructure.

Outsourcing: Outsourcing is the practice whereby a business process is carried out by a vendor or service provider external to the client organisation. There are different types of outsourcing; sometimes it involves employees of the service provider working in the client company, or the other way round. It sometimes involves relocating a business function to another country to take advantage of lower labour rates. This is called offshore outsourcing. Cost savings are the main incentive to outsource business processes.

SaaS: Software as a Service, or SaaS, is a model of cloud computing in which software is licensed on a subscription basis. The term is sometimes referred as 'on-demand software'. The SaaS provider gives on-demand support to users and is responsible for software maintenance and upgrades. One of the selling points of SaaS is the client firm's reduction in IT support costs through outsourcing hardware and software maintenance to a reputable provider.

Service Level Agreements: A service-level agreement is an agreement between the client organisation and the service providers. It is the contract between two or more parties setting out the agreed services, performance measurement, timescales, warranties, disaster recovery and agreement termination procedures.

Vendor Lock-In: Vendor lock-in is a business practice whereby a service provider can make the client organisation solely dependent on them for a product or service, unable to user other vendors without paying substantial switching costs. This practice is sometimes referred as proprietary lock-in or customer lock-in. The behaviour itself encourages a monopoly in a market or industry.

Virtualisation: Virtualization is normally referred to creating a virtual, as opposed to actual version of a resource or device, such as a storage device, server, network or even an operating system. For example, server virtualization enables PCs to run multiple operating systems or applications making the IT infrastructure simpler and more efficient.

This research was previously published in Advanced Research on Cloud Computing Design and Applications edited by Shadi Aljawarneh, pages 51-72, copyright year 2015 by Information Science Reference (an imprint of IGI Global).

Section 2
Development and Design Methodologies

Chapter 9
A Multi–Dimensional Mean Failure Cost Model to Enhance Security of Cloud Computing Systems

Mouna Jouini
Institut Supérieur de Gestion, Tunisia

Latifa Ben Arfa Rabai
Institut Supérieur de Gestion, Tunisia

ABSTRACT

Cloud computing technology is a relatively new concept of offering reliable and virtualized resources, software and hardware on demand to users. It presents a new technology to deliver computing resources as a service. It allows several benefits for example services on demand, provisioning, shared resources and pay per use and suffers from several challenges. In fact, security presents a major obstacle in cloud computing adoption. In this paper, the authors will deal with security problems in cloud computing systems and estimate security breaches using a quantitative security risk assessment model. Finally, the authors use this quantitative model to solve these problems in cloud environments.

1. INTRODUCTION

Cloud Computing (CC) is an emerging technology which recently has shown significant attention lately in the word. It has several advantages like pay per use, resource pooling and scalability. The National Institute of Standard and Technology (NIST) definition defines cloud computing as a paradigm for enabling useful, on-demand network access to a shared pool of configurable computing resources (Mell & Grance, 2010; Shrivastava & Bhilare, 2015). It offers several services presented in three models: Software as Service (SaaS), Platform as Service (PaaS), and Infrastructure as Service (IaaS). Software as Service (SaaS) provides applications or software to end users, Platform as Service (PaaS) provides access to platforms and Infrastructure as Service (IaaS) offers processing storage service.

DOI: 10.4018/978-1-5225-8176-5.ch009

Cloud Computing offers many advantages. However, the biggest challenge in cloud computing is the security and privacy problems caused by its multi-tenancy nature and the outsourcing of infrastructure, sensitive data and critical applications which causes serious consequences (Sun, Zhang, Xiong, & Zhu, 2014; Kushwah & Saxena, 2013; Kushwah & Saxena, 2013; Youssef & Alageel, 2012; Aljawarneh & Bani Yassein, 2016; Mell & Grance, 2010; Ben Arfa Rabai, Jouini, Ben Aissa & Mili, 2012; Jouini, Ben Arfa Rabai, Ben Aissa & Mili, 2012; Ben Arfa Rabai, Jouini, Ben Aissa & Mili, 2013; Jouini, Ben Arfa Rabai & Ben Aissa, 2014; Sampathkumar, 2015; Shrivastava & Bhilare, 2015; Jakimoski, 2016). In fact, According to survey conducted by International Data Group (IDG) enterprise in 2014 (IDG Cloud Computing Survey, 2014), security is deeply the top concern for cloud computing. In fact, up from 61% in 2014, and higher among finance organizations (78%), 67% of organizations have concerns about the security of Cloud Computing solutions. The additional challenges are not even on the same playing field for tech decision-makers; only 43% are concerned with integration, followed by the ability of cloud solutions to meet enterprise and/or industry standards (35%) (IDG Cloud Computing Survey, 2014). Given their high security concerns, organizations are integrating strategies and tools (like cloud management and monitoring tools, and cloud security management tools) to lessen these challenges over the next 12 months.

In this paper, we show the use of a quantitative security risk analysis model to estimate security breaches for Cloud Computing systems by considering new threats perspectives. Then, we will show how to solve security problems in Cloud Computing systems using a quantitative security risk assessment model. We aim to present a generic framework that evaluate firstly cloud security by identifying unique security requirements, secondly to identify architectural components affected by this risk, thirdly to make out security threats that damage these components and finally to attempt to present viable solutions that eliminates these potential threats.

The remainder of this paper is organized as follows. Section 2 presents related work. Section 3 presents security challenges in Cloud Computing environments. Section 4 defines the Multi-dimensional Mean Failure Cost model (M^2FC) and illustrates its use to quantify security risk on a practical case study. Section 5 presents our security framework that solves security problems in CC in a quantitative way. Finally, conclusions and a direction for future work are given in section 6.

2. RELATED WORK

Literature review was illustrated that there are several works that studied cloud computing security concerns (Sun, Zhang, Xiong, & Zhu, 2014; Kushwah & Saxena, 2013; Kushwah & Saxena, 2013; Youssef & Alageel, 2012; Aljawarneh & Bani Yassein, 2016; Jakimoski, 2016; Hassan Hussein & Khalid, 2016). All works provide a qualitative discussion of security related issues in CC environments submitting a quick analysis and survey of security issues. However, in this article we develop and deploy a qualitative security management framework on CC environment by proposing some security strategies (countermeasures).

Sun et al present in (Sun, Zhang, Xiong, & Zhu, 2014) a review of security and privacy concerns in Cloud Computing systems as cloud data are stored in different locations in the world. They assess as well various security challenges from both software and hardware views for protecting data in the cloud in order to ameliorate security and privacy for customer' data. In addition, authors present a survey of data security and privacy techniques for data protection to attain highest level of data security in the cloud.

Kushwah & Saxena highlighted CC security issues and specially data privacy and confidentiality due to customers' data and application migration to the cloud (Kushwah & Saxena, 2013). It fact, the article consider that data migration to a Cloud Computing environment has many ways to exercise risk and has several serious impact to the integrity, confidentiality and auditability of the system. The paper presents the importance and motivation of security in the migration of legacy systems and carries out an approach related to security in migration processes to cloud with the aim of finding the needs, concerns, requirements, aspects, opportunities and benefits of security in the migration process of legacy systems. The approach for secure cloud data migration process uses encryption and decryption keys techniques (a set of attributes to design user's decryption keys and to encrypt simple text messages. Decryption occurs when a match occurs between the attributes held by the entity (in their Decryption key) and the attributes used to construct a simple text.)

Alemu & Omer proposed a Cloud Computing Security Framework for Banking Industry as this new technology is adopted in several area in the word (Alemu & Omer, 2014). The framework incorporates major component that addresses security, privacy, legal and compliance and regulatory issues for cloud systems and aims to preserve the availability, integrity, and confidentiality of an organization's information. The framework is inspired from Architects View of SABSA model (Sherwood, Clark, & Lynas, 2009) that it defines principles and fundamental concepts that guide the selection and organization of the logical and physical elements at the lower layers of abstraction. Accordingly, based on banking industry security requirement five basic security matrix questions (what, who, why, where, how) of Architects view

Aljawarneh & Bani Yassein study cloud computing security problems and propose an approach for secure adoption of Cloud Computing systems (Aljawarneh & Bani Yassein, 2016). The authors put a systematic survey of the current information system security issues into the cloud environment and designed a generic framework conceptually to outline the possible current solutions of software security issues. They used the concepts of fuzzy systems to solve a large numbers of issues in the cloud security on different framework levels to enhance their proposed cloud security framework.

The work dealt with security challenges in cloud environment. Authors propose a framework that identifies security and privacy challenges and highlights cloud attacks and risks and illustrates their mitigations and countermeasures (Youssef & Alageel, 2012). In addition, it proposes a generic CC security model that helps satisfy security and privacy requirements and protect them against various vulnerabilities and propose solutions that might be considered when using the cloud environment by individuals and companies.

Mukhin & Volokyta analyzed security risks in Cloud Computing systems (Mukhin & Volokyta, 2011). They identified four indicators for cloud-specific vulnerability including: core technology used by CC systems, cloud essential characteristics (mainly characteristics defined by the NIST standard (Mell & Grance, 2010), cloud innovations witch make security controls hard to implement and Cloud Computing security threats.

Several approaches have been carried out relating to security challenges in CC in a quantitative way. In fact, they do not propose a quantitative approach to analyze and evaluate security in cloud environment. This paper aims to analyze and evaluate the most known Cloud Computing security issues using a quantitative security risk analysis model called as the Multi-dimension Mean Failure Cost (M^2FC).

3. SECURITY ISSUES IN CLOUD COMPUTING SYSTEM

One of the driving forces behind the rise of Cloud Computing is the high pressure on service delivery by organization. But data security and privacy are the top concerns for CC users because data and resources in the cloud are stored and controlled in a third-party Cloud Services Providers' datacenters (CSP). Besides, cloud users utilize Internet to connect to the cloud, if they don't have an Internet connection they cannot access to their documents and applications and hence, they will lose their business.

Literature review was shown that there are many works that studied cloud security issues (Sun, Zhang, Xiong, & Zhu, 2014; Kushwah & Saxena, 2013; Kushwah & Saxena, 2013; Youssef & Alageel, 2012; Aljawarneh & Bani Yassein, 2016; Jouini & Ben Arfa Rabai, 2014). For example, in (Jouini & Ben Arfa Rabai, 2014), Jouini & Ben Arfa Rabai survey the major security concerns in Cloud Computing environments and help users and cloud service provider recognize security threats that cause these problems and security requirements associated with them. In this section, we classify security issues to in CC environments according to nine sub-categories as it is presented in (Jouini & Ben Arfa Rabai, 2014): security issues in virtualization, business services continuity, management interfaces risks, data breaches, compliance and governance, access problem, privacy problem, isolation failure, and accountability problem. Table 1 presents a detail description of security Cloud Computing problems.

Table 1. Cloud Computing security issues

Security problems	Description
Security Issues in Virtualization	Cloud computing is prone to several concerns related to the use of virtualization technology (Jouini & Ben Arfa Rabai, 2014). Virtualization lets to several security harms and several new threats appears like VM-based rootkits attack which is designed to infect both client and server machines in the cloud by abusing compromised systems by hiding files and registry keys and other operating system objects from diagnostic.
Business Services Continuity	CC systems suffer from unavailability of service because it was based on public network to let their users to get access to their applications and data (Jouini & Ben Arfa Rabai, 2014).
Management Interfaces Risks	Cloud Computing providers expose a set of software interfaces that customers use to manage and interact with cloud services. These interfaces are Internet accessible which pose a huge risk especially when combined with remote access and web browser vulnerabilities. Furthermore, cloud interfaces are prone to many threats like insecure interfaces and APIs threats, and virtual machine modification (Jouini & Ben Arfa Rabai, 2014).
Data Breaches	Cloud customers' data are stored in many places in the word using virtual machines which increase information corruption risk (Jouini & Ben Arfa Rabai, 2014). For instance, it can be difficult to determine where data is stored in the virtual cloud environment.
Compliance and Governance	Cloud service provider has to provide some assurance in service level agreements (SLA) to convince the customer on security issues (Jouini & Ben Arfa Rabai, 2014). However, this contract has several difficult to be accomplished due to the variety laws due to the variety of data locations
Access Problem: Data Location	Cloud Computing systems suffer from lack of transparency since customer' data are located in cloud provider data centers anywhere in the word, and for this reason are out of the customer's control which let many problems (Jouini & Ben Arfa Rabai, 2014).
Privacy Issues	Cloud customer's data and especially personally information can be breached more easily than if stored in users' machines. In fact, customers' private information is more risked of potential unauthorized access and exposure (Jouini & Ben Arfa Rabai, 2014).
Isolation Failure (Multi Tenancy Problem)	Infrastructure as a service (IaaS) cloud layer relies on architectural designs where physical resources are shared by multiple virtual machines and so multiple customers which cause several problems. In fact, resource sharing means that malicious activities carried out by one tenant may affect and get access to other tenant hosts (Jouini & Ben Arfa Rabai, 2014).
Accountability Problems	Cloud Computing systems uses several locations to store customers' data and thus it is difficult to keep track of actions that are related to security actions and responsibilities because of varieties of laws, locations, etc. (Jouini & Ben Arfa Rabai, 2014).

4. THE M²FC MODEL

In this section, we illustrate the use of the M²FC model on a simple case study adapted from similar cases studies found in (Ben Arfa Rabai, Jouini, Ben Aissa & Mili, 2012; Jouini, Ben Arfa Rabai, Ben Aissa & Mili, 2012; Ben Arfa Rabai, Jouini, Ben Aissa & Mili, 2013). In fact, the M²FC metrics measures the cost induced by a lack of cyber security or each stakeholder with regards to security threats dimensions. It varies depending on several factors such stakeholders, security requirements; the failure probability associated to threats dimensions. In this section, we introduce the metric of Multi-dimensional Mean Failure Cost (M²FC), and we show the use of this metric in a new practical case study.

4.1. Model Definition

Jouini et al. introduced a quantitative security risk analysis measure that quantifies this risk in terms of financial loss per unit of operation time (for example dollars per hour ($/h)) due to security threats considering several dimensions within the threat world (Jouini & Ben Arfa Rabai, 2015). The metric is called as the Multidimensional Mean Failure Cost (M²FC). The M²FC estimates the security of a system in terms of the loss that each stakeholder incurs due to security breaches considering several security threats dimensions. In fact, the world of security threats is a segmentation of this world according to each of its dimensions where a dimension can be defined as an elementary aspect or extent of the threat word. The threats world can be perceived as having several dimensions like architectural components, environmental elements, time, deployment site, laws, etc. For example, when using the architectural component dimension; we obtain the mean failure cost per component element (browser, web server…) where a security breach occurs. We consider the concept of threat perspectives to estimate security failure. For more clarification of the usage of the M²FC model, we apply on a case study to approximate the security risk of a system in terms of loss for each stakeholder (Jouini & Ben Arfa Rabai, 2015).

This model takes into account the stakeholders assessment of the cost related to their requirements with regard to the elements of two security threats dimensions. That is why, in the following model, the set H of stakeholders and the set R of their requirements are distinguished from the set of the leading dimension (where we called a leading dimension a dimension that is used to guide our decomposition of the multidimensional threat world into several slides of two dimensions each) and the set of the other considered dimension.

Model: Let S be the set of elements in the leading dimension, D be the set of elements of the other considered dimension, H be the set of stakeholders, R is a set of requirements, and T be a set of threats. For every element s ϵ S, we define the Multidimensional Mean Failure Costs M(s;D) of element s as follows (Jouini & Ben Arfa Rabai, 2015):

$$M\left(s;D\right) = V_s \circ PFR_s \circ C_s \circ P_s$$

where
We denote ∘ by the matrix multiplication operation

V_s is a matrix of size $|H| \times |R|$ that each entry $(i; j)$ represents the value of the stake that stakeholder Hi has in meeting requirement R_j. We denote by $|H|$ (resp. $|R|$) the size of the set H (resp. R).

PFR_s is a matrix of size $(|H|; |R|)$ that each entry $(i; j)$ represents the probability of failing requirement R_i due to a failure originating from element $d_j \in D$.

C_s is a matrix of size $(|D|; |T|)$ that each entry $(i; j)$ represents the probability that an element $d_i \in D$ fails once the threat t_j has materialized.

P_s is a column vector of size $(|T|)$ that each entry i represents the probability that threats materialize during unitary period of operation.

The M²FC model is a formula in the form of a hierarchical linear system composed of stakeholders, security requirements (such as confidentiality, integrity, and availability), and two perspectives (architectural components, system connectors, time, laws...). In fact, an information system has its stakeholders which have its own issues in the proper functioning of the system. The proper functioning of an information system needs certain dependability attributes which called as security requirements. If we consider the architecture of the system that has several components, a failure displaying a security requirement essentially is relative to a particular component. These components fail because of vulnerability due to a security threat. Finally, a security threat has several dimensions like source, users and location that affect information systems.

In this section, we show the application of the Multi-dimensional Mean Failure Cost model (M²FC) is a new practical application namely a Cloud Computing environment by considering a new perspective called as legal perspective.

4.2. Illustrative Case Study

We illustrate the use of our Cyber Security Model (Jouini & Ben Arfa Rabai, 2015) on a practical application, namely a Cloud Computing system. To this effect, we first identify the security requirements, then the stakeholders and their stakes in meeting these requirements. Finally, before the identification of security threats threatens the system, we categorize dimensions characterizing the security threats. In this case study we introduce a new security perspective in the literature.

We applied the M²FC model to quantify cloud systems and estimate the financial cost for each stakeholder regarding the legal and deployment site dimensions. Our assessment varies according to the stakes that each stakeholder has in meeting each security requirement per system site (or location). We opt, as well, for using the deployment dimension (i.e., sites dimension) as the leading dimension. For each site of the considered system, we have the lists of stakeholders, security requirements, legal laws, and security threats.

4.2.1. Security Requirements

We computed the M²FC model for three kinds of stakeholders (bronze, silver and gold stakeholders). Thus, we the following requirements list R = {Availability, Integrity, Confidentiality}.

Regarding Cloud Computing system confidentiality, integrity and availability are important issues of cloud security system assurance (Ben Arfa Rabai & Jouini, 2013; Jouini & Ben Arfa Rabai, 2012).

The matrix of stakes Vs is presented in Table 2.

216

Table 2. Matrix of stakes: cost of failing a security requirement in $K/h

	Security Requirement		
	Availability	Confidentiality	Integrity
Stakeholders			
Bronze	0,138	6.770 10-4	80
Silver	1,388	6.770 10-3	40
Gold	6,944	0.0338	20

4.2.2. Legal Perspective

Moving data to the CC environment rises several legal issues. In fact, in many countries throughout the world, numerous laws, and regulations require organizations to protect the privacy of personal data and the security of information and computer systems. We can cite as examples of legal issues that may arise in connection with the transfer of personal data to the cloud or the processing of personal data in the cloud (Cloud Security Alliance (CSA), 2011). We categorize legal security issues for Cloud Computing systems in four main laws (Cloud Security Alliance (CSA), 2011):

- **L1. Federal Laws:** There are several federal laws that require organizations to adopt specific privacy and security measures when processing data, and to require similar precautions in their contracts with cloud provider.
- **L2. State Laws Issues:** There are many state laws impose an obligation on companies to provide adequate security for personal data and also address that information security issues need that the company have a written contract with the service provider with reasonable security measures.
- **L3. International Regulations Issues:** Many countries have adopted data protection laws (like the European Union model). Under these laws, the data controller (typically the entity that has the primary relationship with an individual) is required to allow that any third party processing personal data on its behalf takes adequate technical and organizational security measures to preserve the data.
- **L4. Prohibition Against Cross Border Transfers:** Many laws, throughout the world, prohibit or restrict the transfer of information out of the country. In most cases, the transfer is permitted only if the country to which the data are transferred offers an adequate protection of personal information and privacy rights. This to ensure that the individual data subjects whose data are transferred across borders will be able to enjoy, in the new country where their data were transferred, privacy rights and privacy protections that are similar to, and not less than, those that were afforded to them before the transfer.

In our case study, we consider that the system is deployed on two sites. We have S = {S ite1, S ite2} and the law dimension (from legal perspective) D has the following elements which is equals to D = {l1, L2, L3}.

Table 3. Probabilities of failure requirements for sites

	Laws						
	Site 1				Site 2		
	L1	**L2**	**L3**	**No_failure**	**L1**	**L2**	**No_failure**
	Security Requirements						
Availability	0.80	0.15	0.05	0	0.8	0.2	0
Integrity	0.6	0.3	0.1	0	0.6	0.4	0
Confidentiality	0.3	0.4	0.3	0	0.5	0.5	0

4.2.3. Security Threats

Cloud Computing system is threatened by many types of attacks. We consider the security threats that are most often cited in relation with CC system (Jouini & Ben Arfa Rabai, 2012; Ben Arfa Rabai & Jouini, 2013) namely: Denial of service attack (DoS), Flood attack (FA), data loss attack (DL), and malicious insiders attack (MI). We consider that we dealing with the set $T = \{$DoS, FA, DL, MI$\}$ of threats.

Matrices PFRs and Cs are shown respectively in Tables 4 and 5.

Using this data, we compute the vector of Multidimensional Mean Failure Costs $M_{(Site,Laws)}$ (shown in Table 6) for the laws of each site.

Table 4. Probabilities of failure laws matrix for sites

Laws	Threats							
	Site 1			Site 2				
	DoS	**FA**	**No_Threat (NoT)**	**DoS**	**FA**	**DL**	**MI**	**No_Threat (NoT)**
L1	0,036	0,04	0	0,04	0,04	0,05	0,02	0
L2	0,02	0,01	0	0,036	0,04	0	0,04	0
L3	0,036	0,04	0	-	-	-	-	
No_Failure (NoF)	0,499	0,501	1	0,367	0,14	0,243	0,39	1

Table 5. Threats probabilities occurrence vector for sites

Threats	Probability	
	Site 1	Site 2
Denial of service (DoS)	14,39 10^{-4}	14,39 10^{-4}
Flooding attacks (FA)	56,44 10^{-4}	56,44 10^{-4}
Data loss (DL)	-	5,75 10^{-4}
Malicious insiders (MI)	-	6,623 10^{-4}
No Threats (NoT)	0,9929	0,9916

Table 6. Stakeholders Multidimensional Mean Failure Cost for sites considering the dimension laws

Stakeholders	M²FC	
	Site 1	Site 2
Bronze	0.0183	0.025
Silver	0.0095	0.0130
Gold	0.0063	0.0085

5. M²FC MODEL TO ENHANCE SECURITY FOR CLOUD COMPUTING SYSTEMS

In this section we introduce our new approach for secure CC systems. The main idea behind our approach is to use a quantitative security risk analysis model to solve security problems in CC. We used the Multi-dimensional Mean Failure Cost model (M²FC) presented in previous section to propose our Framework for secure CC systems.

5.1. The Proposed Approach

After introducing security problems in CC system, we propose in this section an approach that allows identifying security solutions to these problems. In fact, some investigators proposed solutions to threats but, they didn't relate solutions to security issues. Our proposed approach is based on a quantitative security risk analysis model in order to ensure that our results are more logical and efficient. We present a framework that identifies security issues in CC and highlights cloud-specific attacks and risks related to these problems to suggest their mitigations and countermeasures. Our proposed approach is modular because we consider the threats individually and seek solution for that. This helps to manage the cloud system more effectively and provide the security analysts to include the specific solution to counter the threat. For example, in some cases or for some users, confidentiality is the only requirement whereas for some users other security requirements are also required.

Figure 1 shows our framework for secure CC. It consists of four main security steps which are:

- **Identify Security Requirements for Each CC Security Issue:** For each security problem, we will choose its critical security requirement (when the problem happen the security requirement is affected).
- **Identify Security Threats Dimensions to System Requirements**: Using the matrix of probabilities of failure requirement (PFRs), we analyze, for each security requirement, the probabilities of

Figure 1. A framework for secure Cloud Computing environments

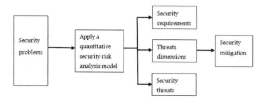

failure threats dimension (for example legal laws dimension) in order to select dimension elements D with the higher probabilities where system fails to meet this requirement.

- **Identify Security Threats to the Dimensions Elements:** Using the matrix C_s, we analyze the probabilities of failure in the matrix (C_s) and select security threats having the higher failure probability.
- **Mitigation:** For each security threats, propose appropriate countermeasures.

5.2. M²FC Model to Solve Security Problems in Cloud Computing Environment

We applied in this section our framework to an illustrative example named Cloud Computing system. We used the case study of section 3 that presents the calculation of the M²FC vector for each stakeholder regarding the legal laws and deployment site dimensions.

5.2.1. Security Requirements

This step identifies security requirements related to each CC security problem cited above. Based on our quantitative assessment security model we identified as security requirement the vailability, integrity and confidentiality.

Next, we will present security requirements associated to security problems in CC environments.

- Security issues in virtualization

Virtual machine (VM)-based malware affects the confidentiality, the integrity and the availability security requirements of CC systems (Jouini, Ben Arfa Rabai, Ben Aissa & Mili, 2012). In fact, confidentiality is at risk because the customers' data could be intercepted by malware. Integrity is at risk because the operation of the virtual machine (VM) can be changed by malware which could lead to loss of integrity of the customers' data. Availability is at risk because by malware can potentially erase, or obfuscate the customers' data.

Therefore, the security requirements related to this issue and can be affect in case of attack are integrity, confidentiality, availability

- Business services continuity

Services availability problem poses a devastating impact on the brand and the reputation of organizations by causing unavailability of cloud services. The security requirement related to this issue and can be affect in case of attack is availability.

- Management interfaces risks

Reliance on a weak set of interfaces and application programming interfaces (APIs) in Cloud Computing system exposes organizations to a variety of security issues related to confidentiality, integrity, availability, authentification and authorization and accountability (Basescu et al., 2011; Jouini, Ben Arfa Rabai, Ben Aissa & Mili, 2012).

The security requirements related to this issue and can be affect in case of attack are integrity, confidentiality and availability.

- Data breaches

Many security threats can compromise data and provide losses and corruption and it provoke a serious problems related to integrity, confidentiality and availability of data.

The security requirements related to this issue and can be affect in case of attack are integrity, confidentiality and availability.

- Compliance and governance

Finally, many threats pose risks to SLA accomplishment and give the difficulty to audit the data and verify the logs of data access which poses accountability breach.

- Access problem: data location

The security requirements related to this issue and can be affect in case of attack are integrity, confidentiality, and availability.

- Privacy issues

Privacy breaches allow confidentiality problems and data leakage which leads to serious financial implications to organization. Therefore, the security requirement related to this issue and can be affect in case of attack is confidentiality.

- Isolation failure (multi tenancy problem)

Multi tenancy problem affects the confidentiality, access control, availability, integrity and accountability of data. Thus, the security requirements related to this issue and can be affect in case of attack are integrity, confidentiality and availability.

- Accountability problems

This problem affects accountability security requirement.

5.2.2. Legal Laws

Since the failure of security requirement depends on which legal laws of cloud system, we will identify in this step using probabilities of failure requirements matrix (PFRs) for each security requirement legal laws causing this failure. Thus, we take for each security requirement the higher probability of failing this requirement Ri once a legal law has failed as show in Table 3:

- In integrity case, we find that the higher probabilities of impact of attack with the following components: L1.
- In availability case, we find that the higher probabilities of impact of attack with the following components: L1, and L2.
- In confidentiality cases, we find that the higher probabilities of impact of attack with the following components: L1, L2, and L3.

5.2.3. Security Threats

Legal laws may fail to operate properly as a result of security risk due to malicious activities. Therefore, we specify, in this step, the catalog of threats that causes components failure. We select for each component, the higher probabilities that in which a legal law fails once threat T_q has materialized (Table 5):

- **Denial of service (DoS):** L1, L2, and L3.
- **Flood attack (FA):** L1, L2, and L3.
- **Data Loss (DL):** L1.
- **Malicious insiders (MI):** Browser, web server, proxy server.

5.2.4. Mitigation

We will describe, here, threats related to security issues and we will give countermeasures to prevent against them. The aim of this step is to propose solutions to security problems.

- Denial of Service

The denial of service attack (DoS) (Ben Arfa Rabai, Jouini, Ben Aissa & Mili, 2012; Jouini, Ben Arfa Rabai, Ben Aissa & Mili, 2012) is a critical problem for virtual machines (VMs) used on cloud components. In fact, it indicates that the hypervisor software is allowing a single VM to consume all the system resources and thus starving the remaining VMs and impairing their function. Because the VMs and the host share CPU, memory, disk, and network resources, virtual machines may be able to cause some form of denial of service attack against another VM (Qaisar & Khawaja, 2012; Priyadharshini, 2013).

As a countermeasure for this attack, you can reduce the privileges of the user that connected to a server. This will help to reduce the DOS attack. Furthermore, the best approach to prevent a guest consuming all the resources is to limit the resources allocated to the guests. Current virtualization technologies offer a mechanism to limit the resources allocated to each guest machines in the environment. Therefore the underlying virtualization technology should be properly configured, which can then prevent one guest consuming all the available resources, thereby preventing the denial of service attack (Qaisar & Khawaja, 2012; Priyadharshini, 2013).

- Malicious insiders

The malicious insider threat (Ben Arfa Rabai, Jouini, Ben Aissa & Mili, 2012; Jouini, Ben Arfa Rabai, Ben Aissa & Mili, 2012) is one that gains in importance as many providers still don't reveal how they hire people, how they grant them access to assets or how they monitor them. Transparency is, in this case, vital to a secure cloud offering, along with compliance reporting and breach notification.

To confront this threat, one should enforce strict supply chain management and conduct a comprehensive supplier assessment. Another effective measure is to specify human resource requirements as part of legal contracts, and require transparency into overall information security and management practices, as well as compliance reporting. Another useful step to take is to determine security breach notification processes (Qaisar & Khawaja, 2012).

- Data loss or leak

    In (Qaisar & Khawaja, 2012), we find these solutions to confront data loss threat:
    1. Implement strong key generation, storage and management, and destruction practices.
    2. Contractually demand providers wipe persistent media before it is released into the pool.
    3. Encrypt and protects integrity of data in transit, and analyze data protection at both design and run time.

- Flooding Attacks

Flooding attacks distribute a great number of non-sense requests to a specific service. When the attacker sends a great number of requests, Cloud system will try to function against the requests by providing more resources (Qaisar & Khawaja, 2012). We can adopt counter measures for this attack like filtering the malicious requests by intrusion detection system and installing firewalls. Sometimes intrusion detection system supplies fake alerts and Could mislead administrator (Qaisar & Khawaja, 2012).

6. CONCLUSION

Cloud computing has various benefits, but the security threats embedded in cloud computing approach are directly proportional to its offered advantages. Cloud computing is a great opportunity the attackers because of the use of several technologies like virtualization. The security issues could severely affect could infrastructures. In this paper, we firstly highlight the major security problems in Cloud Computing systems and help users recognize threats associated with their uses. We use the M^2FC model to estimate security breaches for Cloud systems and we propose a framework that analyzes and evaluates security issues in CC by a quantifiable approach. Our proposed framework is modular in nature that is we consider the threats individually and seek solution for that. Our approach helps organizations managers to justify their choice by proposing the appropriate countermeasures.

We envision develop a security risk management framework as a part of Cloud Computing services to satisfy the security needs and then deploy this framework on really CC environments. Then, we envision introduce other security dimensions and perspectives in security threats classification to estimate accurately the failure cost using the dimensional Mean Failure Cost model (M^2FC).

REFERENCES

Alemu, M., & Omer, A. (2014). Cloud Computing Conceptual Security Framework for Banking Industry. *Journal of Emerging Trends in Computing and Information Sciences, 5*(12), 921-930.

Aljawarneh, SA., & Bani Yassein MO. (2016). A Conceptual Security Framework for Cloud Computing Issues. *the International Journal of Intelligent Information Technologies, 12*(2), 12-24.

Barron, C., Yu, H., & Zhan, J. (2013). Cloud Computing Security Case Studies and Research. *Proceedings of the 2013 International Conference of Parallel and Distributed Computing.*

Ben Arfa Rabai, L., Jouini, M., Ben Aissa, A., & Mili, A. (2012). An economic model of security threats for cloud computing systems. *Proceedings of the International Conference on Cyber Security, Cyber Warfare and Digital Forensic (CyberSec)* (pp. 100–105). 10.1109/CyberSec.2012.6246112

Ben Arfa Rabai, L., Jouini, M., Ben Aissa, A., & Mili, A. (2013). A cyber security model in cloud computing environments. *Journal of King Saud University-Computer and Information Sciences, 25*(1), 63–75. doi:10.1016/j.jksuci.2012.06.002

Cloud Security Alliance (CSA). (2011). Security guidance for critical areas of focus on Cloud Computing V 3.0.

Hashizume, K., Rosado, D. G., Fernandez-Medina, E., & Fernandez, E. B. (2013). An analysis of security issues for cloud computing. *Journal of Internet Services and Applications, 4*(1), 1–13. doi:10.1186/1869-0238-4-5

Hassan Hussein, N., & Khalid, A. (2016). A survey of Cloud Computing Security challenges and solutions. *International Journal of Computer Science and Information Security, 14*(1).

IDG Cloud Computing Survey. (2014). Cloud Continues to Transform Business Landscape as CIOs Explore New Areas for Hosting. Retrieved from http://www.idgenterprise.com/news/press-release/cloud-continues-to-transform-business-landscape-as-cios-explore-new-areas-for-hosting/

Jakimoski, A. (2016). Security Techniques for Data Protection in Cloud Computing. *International Journal of Grid and Distributed Computing, 9*(1), 49–56. doi:10.14257/ijgdc.2016.9.1.05

Jouini, M., & Ben Arfa Rabai, L. (2014). Surveying and Analyzing Security Problems in Cloud Computing Environments. *Proceedings of the 10th International Conference on Computational Intelligence and Security (CIS '14)* (pp. 689–493).

Jouini, M., Ben Arfa Rabai, L., & Ben Aissa, A. (2014). Classification of security threats in information systems. *Proceedings of ANT/SEIT 2014.*

Jouini, M., Ben Arfa Rabai, L., Ben Aissa, A., & Mili, A. (2012). Towards quantitative measures of information security: A cloud computing case study. *International Journal of Cyber-Security and Digital Forensics, 1*(3), 265–279.

Jouini, M., Ben Arfa Rabai, L., & Khedri, R. (2015). A Multidimensional Approach Towards a Quantitative Assessment of Security Threats. *Proceedings of ANT/SEIT 15* (pp. 507-514).

Kushwah, V. S., & Saxena, A. (2013). A Security approach for Data Migration in Cloud Computing. International Journal of Scientific and Research Publications, 3(5).

Mell, P., & Grance, T. (2010). The NIST definition of cloud computing. *Communications of the ACM*.

Mukhin, V., & Volokyta, A. (2011). Security Risk Analysis for Cloud Computing Systems. *Proceedings of the 6th IEEE International Conference on Intelligent Data Acquisition and Advanced Computing Systems: Technology and Applications.* 10.1109/IDAACS.2011.6072868

Priyadharshini, A. (2013). A survey on security issues and countermeasures in cloud computing storage and a tour towards multi-clouds. *International Journal of Research in Engineering & Technology*, *1*(2), 1–10.

Qaisar, S., & Khawaja, K.F. (2012). Cloud computing: network/ security threats and countermeasures. *Interdisciplinary journal of contemporary research in business, 3*(9), 1323-1329.

Sampathkumar, R. (2015). *Disruptive Cloud Computing and IT: Cloud Computing SIMPLIFIED for every IT Professional*. Amazon.

Sherwood, J., Clark, A., & Lynas, D. (2009). Enterprise Security Architecture (White paper). SABSA Limited.

Shrivastava, V., & Bhilare, D.S. (2015). SAFETY: A Framework for Secure IaaS Clouds, *International journal of Advanced Networking and Applications*, *6*(6), 2549-2555.

Sun, Y., Zhang, J., Xiong, Y., & Zhu, G. (2014). Data Security and Privacy in Cloud Computing. *International Journal of Distributed Sensor Networks*, *10*(7), 190903. doi:10.1155/2014/190903

Yan, L., Rong, C., & Zhao G, (2009), Strengthen Cloud Computing Security with Federal Identity Management Using Hierarchical Identity-Based Cryptography. *Proceedings of CloudCom* (pp. 167–177).

Youssef, A. E., & Alageel, M. (2012). A Framework for Secure Cloud Computing. *IJCSI International Journal of Computer Science Issues*, *9*(4), 487–500.

This research was previously published in the International Journal of Embedded and Real-Time Communication Systems (IJERTCS), 7(2); edited by Sergey Balandin, pages 1-14, copyright year 2016 by IGI Publishing (an imprint of IGI Global).

Chapter 10
Enterprise Security Framework for Enterprise Cloud Data Centres

Muthu Ramachandran
Leeds Beckett University, UK

ABSTRACT

Enterprise security is the key to achieve global information security in business and organisations. Enterprise Cloud computing is a new paradigm for that enterprise where businesses need to be secured. However, this new trend needs to be more systematic with respect to Enterprise Cloud security. This chapter has developed a framework for enterprise security to analyze and model Enterprise Cloud organisational security of the Enterprise Cloud and its data. In particular, Enterprise Cloud data & Enterprise Cloud storage technologies (Amazon s3, Drop Box, Google Drive, etc.) have now become a normal practice for almost every computing user's. Therefore, building trust for Enterprise Cloud users should be the one of the main focuses of Enterprise Cloud computing research. This chapter has developed a framework for enterprises which comprises of two models of businesses: Enterprise Cloud provider enterprise model and Enterprise Cloud consumer enterprise model.

INTRODUCTION

Enterprise Cloud computing technology has emerged to provide a more cost effective solution to businesses and services while making use of inexpensive computing solutions which combines pervasive, internet, and virtualisation technologies. Enterprise Cloud computing has spread to catch up with another technological evolution as we have witnessed internet technology, which has revolutionised communication and information superhighway. Enterprise Cloud computing is emerging rapidly and software as a service paradigm is increasing its demand for more services. However, this new trend needs to be more systematic with respect to software engineering and its related processes. For example, current challenges that are faced with cyber security and application security flaws, lessons learned and best practices can be adopted. Similarly, as the demand for Enterprise Cloud services increases and so increased importance

DOI: 10.4018/978-1-5225-8176-5.ch010

sought for security and privacy. The business of Enterprise Cloud technology can only be sustained if we can maintain balance between demand for services in-line with improved Enterprise Cloud security and privacy. Popović & Hocenski (2010) have reported an analysis of results from an IDC ranking of security challenges that 87.5% responded to demand for Enterprise Cloud security against on-demand Enterprise Cloud services. This confirms the importance of Enterprise Cloud security against Enterprise Cloud services.

Enterprise Cloud service providers such as Microsoft, Google, Sales force.com, Amazon, GoGrid are able to leverage Enterprise Cloud technology with pay-per-use business model with on-demand elasticity by which resources can be expended or shortened based on service requirements. They often try to co-locate their servers in order to save cost. There every effort by several other enterprises to establish their Enterprise Cloud efforts to build their own Enterprise Cloud (private Enterprise Clouds) on their premises but can't afford to compromise security of their applications and data which is their major hurdle in their new effort. Most important of all, they need to develop a legitimate and controlled way of establishing service-level-agreements with their clients and to embed these rules to be built-in with services.

Standardisation has been active in software development and information technology to ensure systematic use of process, methods, and to that of client's requirements. Standards include on Quality, Quality of Services (QoS), Usability, and Process such as ISO, CMMI, and others to ensure product and service quality are adhered. The emergence and adherence of standardization such as Information Technology Infrastructure Library (ITIL), ISO/IEC 27001/27002, and Open Virtualization Format (OVF 2010) are critical in establishing expected Enterprise Cloud sustainability and trust in this new technological service business. Hence, it is highly recommended OVF standard as a vendor and platform independent, open, secure, portable, efficient and extensible format for the packaging and distribution of software to be run in virtual machines (software stacks that incorporates the target applications, libraries, services, configuration, relevant data, and operating enterprise).

This paper proposes two tier enterprises for Enterprise Cloud computing: Enterprise Cloud provider as an enterprise and an Enterprise Cloud consumer as an enterprise. This will allow us to apply best practice security measures, principles, and frameworks. This chapter addresses some of the key research issues in this area such as how do we learn and adopt a decade of best practices on enterprise security to Enterprise Cloud technology transition? How we can also improve and sustain Enterprise Cloud enterprise security framework continuously?

BACKGROUND

Enterprises Engineering incorporates a systematic and comprehensive approach to modelling, designing, and developing enterprises includes software and service based enterprises. Caminao project (2013) provides a comprehensive framework for enterprises engineering methods and concepts. The internet technology has revolutionized the way we live on a daily basis. The use of internet is growing rapidly from devices, appliances and Enterprise Cloud computing, which has emerged to address a cost-effective solution for businesses. However, security is the most common security concerns of all. Therefore, security for Enterprise Cloud computing is the main aim of this chapter. The everyday Enterprise Cloud applications and apps can be protected using commonly available anti-security software packages. However, it is harder to protect us from security related attacks which emerges unexpectedly and are often hard to predict. This isn't sufficient for Enterprise Cloud service providers who offer three different types of services such as Software as a Service (SaaS), Platform as a Service (PaaS), and Infrastructure as a Service (IaaS). Therefore, there is a need for going beyond boundaries of existing security techniques such as password protection, virus checks, secured financial transaction techniques, etc. The following are categories of the broad spectrum of security related research that are undertaken:

- Application software security deals with how we can build enterprises that can automatically protect itself.
- Network (LAN, MAN, GAN), Wireless network security, and Platform Security include Operating Enterprises, Virtualisation, and other enterprise software.
- VoIP security as the application is gaining popularity.
- Convergence network security where converging multi-network media infrastructures, social networks and technologies which is one of the emerging areas of research.
- Service-oriented security where issues related to enterprise services such as denial of service attacks, distributed denial of services, and web services.
- Enterprise Cloud security deals with services security, data security and privacy so that services delivered and assets are protected.
- Open-source software security deals with issues such as trust, certification and qualification models.
- Software components and architecture security deals with building components and architectures with security can be used as plug-ins.
- Web services security is essential to ensure secure services are delivered with integrity
- Enterprises &Software security engineering deals with building security in (BSI) right from requirements. This also considers developing software applications with BSI.

Security engineering deals with many aspects of protecting assets and delivering secured services including business services and building trust. Figure 1 shows a landscape of enterprise security related areas of research which will dominate most of Enterprise Cloud computing in the forthcoming areas.

Security research is emerging as we discover and learn new forms of threats. Therefore, the research landscape shown in Figure 1 will have to be expanded. Computer security can be classified into a number of general concepts and processes such as identification which identifies objects, functions, and actions, authentication, authorisation, privacy, integrity, and durability. This is categorized and presented in Figure 2 as basic security principles. We have so far well established basic security features with identification, authentication, authorisation, and digital security encryption and decryption techniques. However, there are number challenging issues that are undiscovered to be addressed when dealing with Enterprise Cloud services. Basic security features have also been defined briefly.

- **Identification:** A basic and the first process of establishing and distinguishing amongst person/ user & admin ids, a program/process/another computer ids, and data connections and communications. Often we use alphanumerical string as user identification key and some may use your email itself as the user identification key and this can be checked against when a user login into the enterprise. Authentication and authorisation are two distinct forms of allowing users to access what they are not allowed to access any information in the enterprise.

Figure 1. Enterprise security research landscape

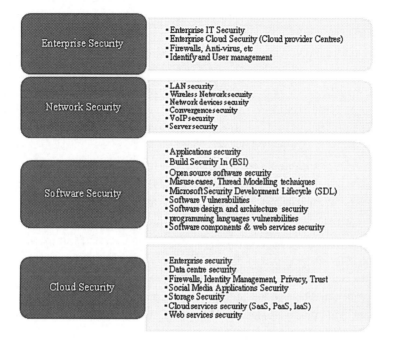

Figure 2. Basic security principles

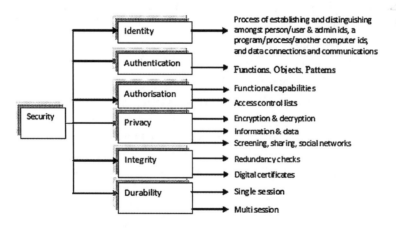

- **Privacy:** The key to maintaining the success of Enterprise Cloud computing and its impact on sharing information for social networking and teamwork on a specific project. This can be maintained by allowing users to choose when and what they wish to share in addition to allowing encryption & decryption facilities when they need to protect specific information/data/media content.

- **Integrity:** Defined as the basic feature of the human being as a process of maintaining consistency of actions, communications, values, methods, measures, principles, expectations, and outcomes. Ethical values are important for Enterprise Cloud service providers to protect integrity of Enterprise Cloud user's data with honesty, truthfulness and accuracy at all time. In Enterprise

Cloud computing terms, we can achieve integrity by maintaining regular redundancy checks and digital certification in addition to other basic security features of maintaining identification, authentication, and authorisation. *Durability* is also known as, persistency of user actions and services in use should include sessions and multiple sessions.

In general, we can emphasis on basic of security principle into three main categories as Identification, Authentication, and Authorisation (IAA). The basic process is a cyclic in nature as illustrated in Figure 3 and can be defined based on IAA steps. This is a recursive process which must be applied to every action, transactions, and service provisions.

Andress (2011) provides an excellent literature survey on the basics of information security techniques. The cyclic security principles known as IAA is not limited pattern of solution for developing secure enterprises. There are other security concepts that form a pattern of solution known as CIA (Confidentiality, Integrity, and Availability). The CIA considers more towards how well we should design supporting those three characteristics of enterprises including software and services. In addition, Andress (2011) stated the concept of *ParkerianHexad*, which consists of six principles CIA (3) + PAU (3) (Possession or control, Authenticity, and Utility).

Traditionally, security has been added and fixed by releasing security patches on a daily basis by major software vendors. This practice needs to change by systematically identifying and incorporating enterprise security right from requirements. This process is known as *Building In Security (BSI)*. Readers are urged to follow the work by McGraw (2004 & 2006) and Ramachandran (2011). This chapter contributes towards providing an enterprise engineering process for developing and deploying Enterprise Cloud services systematically. It also provides a classification system for enterprise Cloud security and Enterprise Cloud data security which are useful for developing and maintaining large scale enterprises with build in security. Finally, data security has been modelled and simulated using the business process methodology. The results show effectiveness when we develop enterprises systematically with good enterprises engineering principles and tools. Therefore, our main recommendation towards building security in (BSI) strategy is to follow one of our guidelines/recommendations:

The aforementioned processes and classification (security principles diagrams shown in Figure 2 & 3) of security attributes can be used as a framework for capturing security specific requirements supporting BSI focus by Enterprises and Software Engineers. In other words, Security requirements = principles of CIA + PAU

The following section introduces a systematic approach to developing security specific enterprise requirements for building BSI right from requirements phase of the enterprise engineering life-cycle.

Figure 3. Cyclic security principles

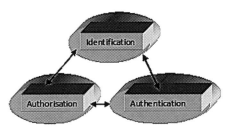

Enterprise Security Framework for Enterprise Cloud Services

Capturing and identifying requirements for security explicitly is one of challenges in software engineering. Often security is considered as one the non-functional requirements which have been considered as constraints identified during and after software has been developed and deployed. However, it has an impact on the functionality of the enterprise. Therefore, we need to be able specify security requirements explicitly throughout the security-specific life-cycle phases as part of achieving BSI (security requirements, design for security, security testing & securability testing). Tondel et al. (2008) has provided an extensive survey on security requirements methods which help to identify security requirements systematically and structure them. For example, Mead (2005) for the SEI's (software Engineering Institute) has identified a method known as SQUARE (Secure Quality Requirements Engineering) and our earlier work on SysSQUARE (Ramachandran 2014) which has been extended to address Enterprise Cloud security EC-SQUARE (Enterprise Cloud security), is shown in Figure 4, towards enterprises security engineering method. Our extended method consists of nine steps as follow:

- **Agree on Security Definition:** To define a set of acronyms, definitions, and domain-specific knowledge needs to be agreed by stakeholders. This will help identify and validate security-specific requirements clearly by stakeholders.
- **Identify Security Goals:** To clearly define what is expected by the enterprise with respect to security by the business drivers, policies, and procedures.
- **Develop Security Artifacts:** To develop scenarios, examples, misuse cases, templates for specifications, and forms.
- **Perform Security Risk Assessments:** To conduct risk analysis for all security goals identified, conduct threat analysis.
- **Select a Security Elicitation Technique:** Includes enterprise identification and analysis of security requirements from stakeholders in the forms of interviews, business process modelling and simulations, prototypes, discussion and focus groups. As part of this phase, one has also to identify level of security, cost-benefits analysis, and organisational culture, structure, and style.

Figure 4. EC-SQUARE model

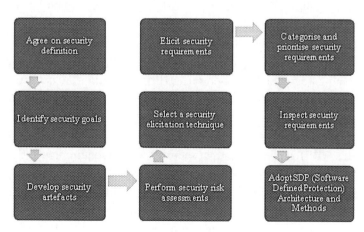

- **Elicit Security Requirements:** Includes activities such as producing security requirements document based security specific principle structure as part of our goal of developing BSI earlier, risk assessment results, and techniques, identifies for analysis such as business process modelling and simulations, threat modelling, and misuse cases, etc.
- **Categorise and Prioritise Security Requirements:** Includes activities such as classifying and categorising security requirements based on company-specific requirements specification templates and to use our recommended security principles as this will help Enterprises Engineers to apply BSI and track security-specific requirements for validation & verification at all stages of the enterprises engineering life-cycle.
- **Identify Enterprises Data Security Requirements:** Include activities on extracting and carefully identifying data security and relevant sub-enterprises such as data centres, servers, Enterprise Cloud VM, and software security, SQL security, and other types of security that are relevant to data. This separation of concerns allows enterprises engineers to integrate, track, design, and develop data security as part of enterprise wide enterprises development.
- **Prioritise Security Requirements:** Include activities of selecting and prioritising security requirements based on business goals as well as cost-benefit analysis.
- **Inspect Security Requirements:** To conduct requirements validation process using requirements inspection and review meetings.
- **Adopt SDP (Software Defined Protection):** Layers for building enterprise security blueprint.

According to our EC-SQUARE model, the first phase starts with identifying security requirements that are achievable and agreed by all stakeholders who are involved in the process. The second step focuses mainly on developing a list all possible security goals as part of the business and functional goals. Thirdly, to develop a list of artifacts that are needed to achieve those security goals. Fourthly, to conduct a detailed risk assessment for each security goal identified and assessed. Clear identification of the requirements of the whole enterprise applications and to extract security requirements for those applications. Interact with stakeholders to clarify security requirements and the technology they want to use, and cost implications. Categorisation and prioritisation of security requirements will help achieve realistic goals against business targets. For example, for a networked enterprise, we need to separate the enterprise system into two further categories of security requirements such wired and wireless security enterprises. The EC-SQUARE method elicitation of security requirements have been applied to study the behaviour of threat modelling for Enterprise Cloud data security which has been presented in the last section of this chapter.

The traditional software development life cycle (SDLC) process does not state security requirements explicitly. Software security is part of a quality requirements collection process and it consists of three different requirements sub-categories: 'confidential and privacy' builds the trust (trust is one of the basic and backbone for establishing quality), 'integrity', and 'availability'. Therefore, security needs to be identified early, designed and to be tested as part of the SDLC process explicitly. Firstly, we need to identify all the attributes of software security so that we can assess and evaluate each requirement against a set of security attributes that will enable us to extract security related requirements. Security is an essential part of the enterprise in achieving and protecting enterprises and its users. Security has several attributes that are related to a simple email enterprise (where most of the attacks, such as virus, spam, intrusions, and identity fraud occur frequently); security baselines are standards that specify a minimum set of security controls that has to be met for most organisations under normal circumstances. They also include both technical and operational security concerns. Enterprise Cloud computing has emerged to address the needs of the IT cost-benefit analysis and also a revolution in technology in terms of reduced cost for internet data and speed. Therefore, the demand for securing our data in the Enterprise Cloud has also increased as a way of building trust for Enterprise Cloud migration and to benefit business confidence in the Enterprise Cloud technology by Enterprise Cloud providers such as Amazon, Microsoft, Google, etc. Therefore, we also want to make sure our BSI model and strategies are applicable to Enterprise Cloud services as well as traditional enterprises. Figure 5 shows a detailed technical model to structure enterprise Cloud security attributes to develop and integrate BSI across the enterprise development life-cycle. This model has evolved based on further research and gain knowledge and experience of our own enterprise and therefore the model will be expanded as and when we discover new attributes.

Most of the security attributes and principles identified earlier are clearly applicable to developing Enterprise Cloud services with enterprises engineering focus. However, there are some Enterprise Cloud-specific security related issues such as security in virtualisation and server environments. Enterprise Cloud security attributes can be found in many-fold as shown in Figure 5. They belong to broadly into the following categories:

- **Confidentiality, Privacy, and Trust:** These are well known basic attributes of digital security such as authentication and authorisation of information as well protecting privacy and trust
- **Enterprise Cloud Services Security:** This includes security on all its services such as SaaS, PaaS, and IaaS. This is the key area of attention needed for achieving Enterprise Cloud security
- **Data Security:** This category is again paramount for sustaining Enterprise Cloud technology. This includes protecting and recovering planning for Enterprise Cloud data and service centres. It is also important to secure data in transactions.
- **Physical Protection of Enterprise Cloud Assets:** This category belongs to protecting Enterprise Cloud centres and its assets.

Figure 5. Enterprise cloud security attributes

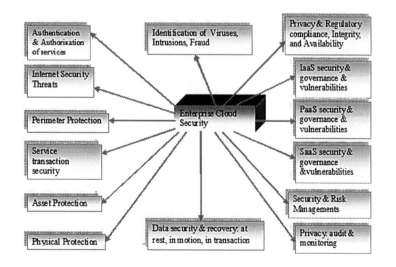

The above Enterprise Cloud security attributes/characteristics are essential and useful to understand non-functional aspects of services development and service provision. These attributes are also useful for building BSI and maintaining security. The following section will identify some of the challenges, issues, and opportunities for tackling security-specific enterprise development and how this can be applied to solve some of the key challenges that are facing Enterprise Cloud computing benefits. The following section will also use Enterprise Cloud security attributes and frameworks identified in this section as the main input for building security in (BSI) not developing security patches after Enterprise Cloud services has been delivered.

Checkpoint, a software technologies limited, more recently, has introduced the concept of a Software Defined Protection (SDP) for enterprise security blueprint by emphasising the need for a secured enterprise security for dynamic networks and infrastructures. The concept of SDP offers a pragmatic approach to building an enterprise security based on the enterprise architecture and agile methodology. The SDP architecture divides the security infrastructure into three interconnected layers (ESB 2014):

- An Enforcement Layer that is based on physical and virtual security enforcement points and that segments the network, as well as executes the protection logic in high demand environments.
- A Control Layer that analyzes different sources of threat information and generates protections and policies to be executed by the Enforcement Layer.
- A Management Layer that orchestrates the infrastructure and brings the highest degree of agility to the entire architecture.

The SDP, as shown in Figure 6, has been extended with our EC-SQUARE model as discussed in this chapter for a more systematic approach to building enterprise SDP.

In the context of our EC-QDUARE SDP framework, the management layer provides support for overall management of Enterprise Cloud security for clients as well as in-house. The various modules in this layer are componentised to provide flexibility for making changes and reuse. The control layer

Figure 6. EC-SQUARE SDP framework

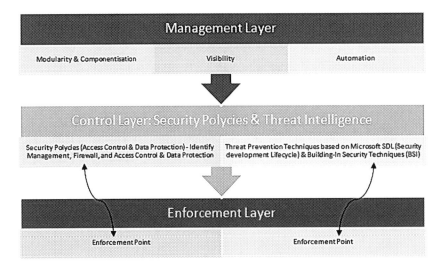

provides support for security policies for access control and data protection for the Enterprise Cloud data centres as well as client devices. This layer also supports with threat intelligence based a number of key BSI techniques including SDL. The Enforcement layer supports key enforcement points where a complete profile for each user can be created and analysed securely.

Enterprise Security Engineering for Enterprise Cloud Computing: Issues, Problems, Challenges, and Opportunities

So far we have seen in the past 20 years of unsecure applications and we have experienced the loss and recovery. We have also invented many security patches to protect against spam, viruses, id theft, and phishing. It is now time to build secure applications from start to delivery which will save cost and effort enormously. Figure 7 provides a framework for providing solution to software security challenges and provides a basic means of achieving software security: benefits such as increased trust, integrity and availability; means of achieving this are by using techniques such as requirements elicitation method for software security and by designing secured functions, objects, components, frameworks, and architectures; and its threats are lack of finding software security engineers, additional cost involved, and people's willingness to develop secured applications.

Software and Web based applications are growing fast and so the attacks such as virus, phishing, id theft, and spam. In order for us to build trust in web based application users, we need to therefore build software security (preventions) as opposed to protection (applying patches soon after attacks have happened in most cases so far in IT industry). Software security touchpoints (one of the software security methodology proposed by McGraw 2004) are a set of specific security specific activities to be applied during each software phase in the software development Lifecycle. This is discussed later in the section and also has shown in Figure 10 (identify security requirements and apply abuse cases during Requirements and use cases (phase 1), employ risk analysis during Architecture and design (phase 2), identify risk-based security tests during test plan, conduct tools-based code reviews during coding, conduct risk analysis and adopt penetration testing techniques during the test phase, and observe security operations during feedback/release phase. Risk analysis should be conducted across the phases and need to feedback knowledge gained from attacks and exploitations on a regular basis.

The notion of taxonomy is the practice and science of classification. Taxonomy helps to identify new categories to shelve and retrieve easily when needed. We know where to find. Gonzalez-Castillo (2004)

Figure 7. Enterprise security challenges solution framework

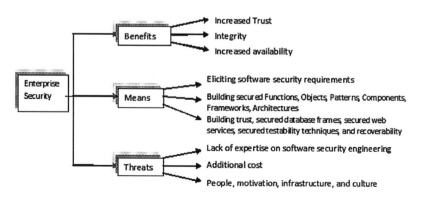

defines security as a set of knowledge and tools obtained and developed by means of the observation and the reasoning, systematically structured and of which general principles and laws are deduced to protect the human life and the existing resources. Taxonomy of software security helps to classify techniques and methods, therefore the relevant technique can easily be identified for use. We can also develop a set of specific guidelines which can be used as a checklist for security validation. A kingdom of security considered as a highest group or a top group in the hierarchy. The parameters that affect the kingdom of security are:

- Economical;
- Political;
- Social;
- Functionality.

Gonzalez-Castillo (2004) defines further classify software security engineering and its implementation into two major groups: software acquisition security (includes the security specifications in all processes to buy, rent, or interchange software to use in an enterprise) and enterprises & software development security (includes the security specifications in all processes to develop information enterprises), as shown in Figure 8.

As shown in Figure 8, software acquisition deals with the COTs (component off-the-shelves), packages, and buy-in tools. Information enterprises development has been divided further into two main categories known as static and dynamic enterprises. Static enterprises security includes compilers (involves specification to develop compilers), assemblers, Programming Languages (PLs), and Operating Enterprises (OS). Dynamic enterprise security deals with enterprise business management (take control of business process information), enterprise administration (security specs to develop applications which objective is to provide control of administrative process information), Manufacturing enterprises, database enterprises, and end user enterprises which deal with developing applications for daily activity tools for end users.

In this section we have seen a generic taxonomy and software security taxonomy, which will help us to identify and organise new security categories. It helps to organise information and contents for many useful purposes. The software security challenges framework (shown in Figure 7) and enterprise security taxonomy (shown in Figure 8) together provides a solution to identify security threats and ap-

Figure 8. Enterprises security taxonomy

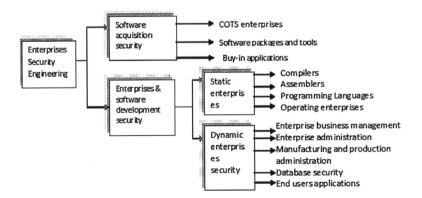

plying security-specific development right from the upfront of the enterprise engineering development life-cycle for successfully completing our goal of BSI.

Information security is the overall security for the whole enterprise and its network environment. Network security is to make sure the secured transactions and communications take place. Whereas application security is to make sure software enterprises as a whole is secured in its environment. Figure 9 shows a distinction between classical software engineering (SE) Lifecycle vs. enterprises security engineering Lifecycle (SSE). The SSE extracts and specifies security requirements using specific methods in addition to the usual functional modelling conducted during requirements engineering phase of SE Lifecycle.

Design for security is part of a design phase where specific design artifacts are created for handling security requirements purposefully. Design for security calls for specific design rationale and features supporting security explicitly. We can also distinguish furthermore in defining security design where functional design artifacts are created as usual with security. McGraw (2004) has identified a number of security techniques against each stage in the software development Lifecycle (SDLC). Figure 10 illustrates a set of these techniques. For example, abuse cases, security inspection and security modelling should be conducted as part of the RE process, security risk analysis should be conducted during design phase, external review and risk based security test analysis should be done during test planning stage, static analysis for security at the code level (this may include code inspection or automated code analysis tools equipped with security), and penetration testing & security breaks should be conducted during operational and field testing.

Figure 9. Enterprises security engineering life cycle

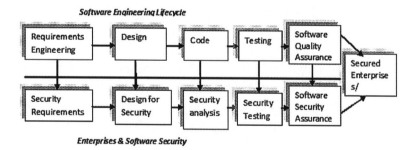

Figure 10. Software security techniques (build-in security)

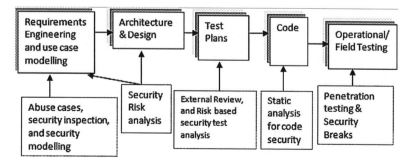

The processes shown in Figure 9 & 10 illustrates how we can use security-specific techniques from analysis, modelling, integrating data security, designing, developing, and testing enterprises development with build in security. The techniques are applicable to traditional enterprises development as well as Enterprise Cloud services. There are also a number of methods have been developed for addressing security-specific enterprises development, such as Microsoft security development life-cycle (SDL), McGraw's security touchpoints (shown in Figure 10) and others (CLASP, UMLsec, VGCs, S2D-ProM).

Microsoft Security Development Lifecycle (SDL)

In 2004, Microsoft introduced its own security development Lifecycle as strategic based method to be adapted for all its product development. Therefore Windows Vista enterprise has been developed according to the SDL process. The process consists of a very specific set of activities to be followed for each stage in the software development Lifecycle as shown in Figure 11 (Howard & Lipner 2006). This illustration is based on SDL v4.1. The process consists of seven stages: Training, Requirements, Design, Implementation, Verification, Release, and Response. Each stage is focused on a specific set of activities that are tailor-made for software security.

SDL has added value for security modelling as it comes with a threat modelling tool which is comprehensive for analysing requirements and generates threats and risks (Ramachandran 2011; Chang and Ramachandran, 2015). Some of the benefits of SDL are:

- Complete Lifecycle support for security based development;
- Have been used in Windows Vista and SQL server development;
- Reducing the number of software vulnerabilities;
- Reducing the total cost of development (it is possible to save 30 times if security vulnerabilities are fixed early).

Some of the terms used for activities are based on Microsoft in-house such as bug bars and quality gates. The idea is to start identifying and providing security-specific skills before even identifying security requirements. During the requirements phase start gathering quality goals and conduct risk analysis. Conduct threat modelling and attack analysis during the design phase. During implementation conducts static analysis and identify banned functions that are known. During verification phase conduct dynamic and threat analysis. During release phase conduct security review plan.

Figure 11. Microsoft's Security Development Lifecycle (SDL)

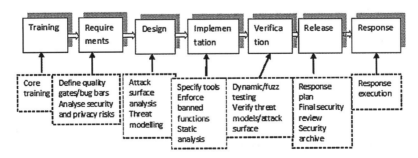

We conclude this section with a comparison table of security processes that are most popular such as Microsoft SDL the security development Lifecycle (Howard & Lipner 2006), McGraw's Touchpoints (McGraw 2004 & 2006), CLASP (Owasp 2006), VCGs (Byers & Shahmehri 2007), S2D-ProM (Essafi, Labed, & Ghezala 2007), and UMLsec (Jurgen 2005). The process methods feature comparison is shown in Table 1.

As we have seen, a number of software security specific processes have emerged and provide a systematic approach to developing and integrating security requirements right from business analysis to build security in. The following section focuses mainly on our approach on how do we apply and customise SSE specific process towards Enterprise Cloud computing.

Software Engineering has been well established for the past 30 years with high end methods, techniques, and tools. We have also seen a good number of well established guidelines and best practices ranging from management to software development. It is time to make use of it all for new emerging applications and technologies when delivering new services such as Enterprise Cloud paradigm. Ramachandran (2008) has captured such good practices in the form of software guidelines across software development, reuse, and component based software engineering (CBSE). Software as a Service provides new abstraction for developing and delivering business application as part of the Enterprise Cloud. Service implementation is based on software component for implementing their core logics. Ramachandran (2012) has produced a number of service component models for implementing services with build in security. In this section, we need clearly to distinguish amongst general security principles discussed in the earlier section such as information security, business security, etc.; software security is a means of developing software with build in security (BSI) whereas Enterprise Cloud security, which is a process of developing Enterprise Cloud services with BSI.

Software engineering has established techniques, methods and technology over two decades. However, due to the lack of understanding of software security vulnerabilities, we have been not successful in applying software engineering principles when developing secure software enterprises. Therefore, software

Table 1. Software security process comparison

Methods \ Features	Microsoft SDL(Howard and Lipner2006)	McGraw's Touchpoints (McGraw 2004 & 2006)	OWASP's CLASP (2006)	VCGs (Byers & Shahmehri 2007)	S2D-ProM (Essafi, Labed, & Ghezala 2007)	UMLSec (Jurjen 2005)
Process Stages/ Activities	Full set of activities supported	Range of activities	A set of activities	VCG based	Risk based	UML based profiling and formalism
Risk Management	Part of	Aspect of	Aspect of	Not explicitly	Risk based	Aspect of
Security Techniques	Threat modelling	Threat modelling	Threat modelling	Process is based on specifically to Vulnerability Cause Graphs (VCGs)	Attack tree and labelled directed graph with goals/ intentions(state transitions diagrams)	UMLsec
Lifecycle Support	✓	✓	✓	✓	✓	✓
Iterative	✓	✓	✓	✓	✓	✓
Strengths	Applied to Windows Vista internal experience	Experience over years and other companies	consortium	evolving	evolving	evolving
Weaknesses	internal					

security can't be just added after a enterprise has been built as seen in today's software applications. SSE (software security engineering) has emerged to address various software security vulnerabilities right from requirements to testing.Security is a major concern for Enterprise Cloud service providers because both the program and customer data are residing on the Enterprise Cloud service provider's premises. Furthermore, Open Enterprises Architectures have higher levels of security vulnerabilities therefore security is an important factor to be addressed continuously by the Enterprise Cloud service providers.

Srinivasan, et al. (2012) discusses a number of key security taxonomies and challenges for Enterprise Cloud computing. They have divided Enterprise Cloud security into two broad areas:

1. Architectural and Technological Aspects were issues of logical storage segregation and multi-tenancy security issues, identity management, insider attacks, virtualisation and cryptography issues are highlighted; and
2. Process and Regulatory-related issues where governance, insures APIs, SLAs and Trust Management, and Enterprise Cloud Migration issues are identified.

These two categories are the key to Enterprise Cloud security challenges. This chapter has devoted to addressing Enterprise Cloud data security as the key factor for determining Enterprise Cloud technology. This chapter highlights most of the issues and have also provided a number of systematic approaches and solutions to address some of these issues. This section proposes a comprehensive framework for Enterprise Cloud security and discusses an important issue of Enterprise Cloud data security and some protection mechanisms.

Security-specific enterprises development process methods and techniques shown in this section helps to achieve BSI to traditional enterprises as well as Enterprise Cloud computing applications which needs to be engineered to reap benefits of Enterprise Cloud technology. The following section considers Amazon Enterprise Cloud services as an example for studying the performance of Enterprise Cloud data security. The main reason for choosing Enterprise Cloud data security is that there is little research on this very important issue and data is one of the main reason that hinders Enterprise Cloud users with respect to building trust.

A MODEL AND PROCESS FOR BUILD-IN ENTERPRISE CLOUD DATA SECURITY: PROPOSED SOLUTIONS AND RECOMMENDATIONS

This section emphasises a rule of thumb to categorise Enterprise Cloud design principles at the heart of Enterprise Cloud computing as a core principle of service design when dealing with developing Enterprise Cloud services. Figure 12 shows a model of the pillars of Enterprise Cloud computing with a triangular model. The central focus is Enterprise Cloud security and data security with corner one as scalability, availability, elasticity, and discoverability of Enterprise Cloud services, corner two for service reuse and integrity, and corner three for measuring and continuously improving security and performance assessments of Enterprise Cloud services.

This model provides a framework for integrating data security and developing build-in Enterprise Cloud security systematically. For example, how do we develop a continuous monitoring strategy for Enterprise Cloud identify management and how do improve from failures? This is one the key aim of this model to build on from experience and user feedback and trails in order for Enterprise Cloud pro-

Figure 12. Pillars of enterprise cloud computing

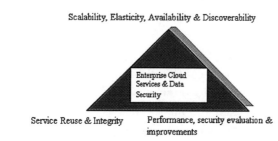

viders to be in a sustainable business of Enterprise Cloud computing. We also need a process by which this model can be established when developing and delivering Enterprise Cloud services. In particular, our aim is to build security in (BSI) right from beginning of service development. The Figure 13 shows a process model for developing Enterprise Cloud services with BSI simultaneously when developing Enterprise Cloud services.

As shown in Figure 13, Enterprise Cloud service development are classified into a number of phases:

1. Requirements engineering for Enterprise Cloud services during which time we can identify security related requirements from various stakeholders,
2. Conduct business process modelling and simulations (BPM) for each Enterprise Cloud services during which time we can also simulate security aspects and study performance related measures and also introduce a possible number of intrusion and conduct simulations before actual service implementation take place,
3. Identify SLAs identifies a number of service level agreements and regulatory and governance related compliances during this time we should be able to separate out security related SLAs and risks,
4. Design and develop services during this phase we can actually implement security related threads that have been carried continuously from all phases, and finally
5. Test and deploy services that are developed with BSIs.

Also, we can:

Figure 13. Enterprise cloud security-based service development and integrating data security process with build-in security

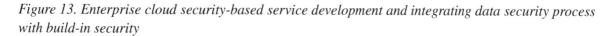
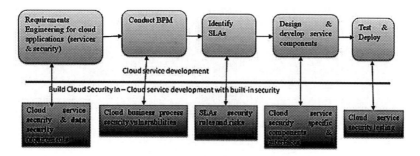

- Apply software security engineering techniques all identified Enterprise Cloud services. This includes using security analysis tree and various other techniques specified by Ramachandran (2011).
- The second step is on identifying BPM (Business Process Modelling) which should include software security analysis for each business process identified to allow us to identify potential security threats which start with service requirements and business requirements as the input to conduct service security analysis using techniques such as Enterprises Secure Quality Requirements Engineering (EC-SQUARE), and Microsoft Secure Development Lifecycle (SDL). The outcome of this process should yield a set of Enterprise Cloud services security requirements with clear indication of software security issues.

We also need to use a framework for classifying Enterprise Cloud securities and policies as shown in Figure 14. Enterprise Cloud security is the key to business sustainability and hence we need to structure security related aspects into a simple framework that helps us to evolve and improve over a time period.

The Enterprise Cloud framework is based on specifying securities into five classes such as data security, services security, infrastructure security, platform security, and security policies (SLAs). This provides a clear guidance and mechanisms for Enterprise Cloud providers to monitor and improve their Enterprise Cloud security related concerns.

Enterprise Cloud Data Security Classification

There is almost not much work found in the literature on Enterprise Cloud data security currently. This is a key issue for Enterprise Cloud computing for its sustainability. Data security address most of the Enterprise Cloud computing security challenges either you consider architectural and technological concerns nor process and regulatory security challenges; all of them comes down to data in many forms such as information (deals with identity management), data in transition and transaction, data in modification, privacy of user's data, and data at rest on servers and storages. However, Oracle (2012) has identified about eight key data security issues that are:

- **Data Tampering:** Issues of unauthorised modification to a transaction. For example, if you add 100 times to a simple transaction of £/$1000.00 this equals to £/$100K. Oracle (2012) also says there 80% of security breaches caused by insider attacks than any other forms of security attacks.

Figure 14. Enterprise cloud security framework

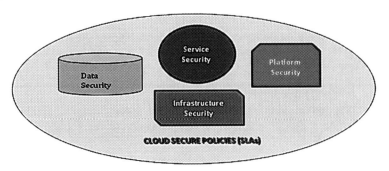

- **Eavesdropping and Data Theft:** Stealing critical personal data (personal and financial information such as credit card, etc.) during data transmission. Network and packet sniffers can be used to steal such information.
- **Falsifying User Identities:** Identity theft by gaining access to data and can also threaten digital signatures with non-repudiation attacks
- **Password-Related Threats:** Stealing passwords
- **Authorised Access to Tables, Columns, and Rows:** Security at the database level
- **Lack of Accountability:** Enterprise administrators for monitoring and protecting data access and user account management
- **Complex User Management Requirements:** User account management strategies.
- **Multitier Enterprises:** Providing access to other services and application layers.
- Scaling the security administration of multiple Enterprises poses extra complexity for managing Enterprise Cloud security as it deals with providing multiple access to multiple applications.

Although these are primitive security loopholes that are well known and have been addressing on a daily basis. However, these issues provide important lessons for Enterprise Cloud data centres and servers and other forms of Enterprise Cloud security issues. CSA (2010) provides a clear and detailed guidance for Enterprise Cloud providers to manage and maintain Enterprise Cloud identity management.

For protecting Enterprise Cloud data, we need to distinguish different states of transitions that can occur in the Enterprise Cloud. This will allow us to employ appropriate data security techniques. An example model for different classes/states for Enterprise Cloud data is shown in Figure 15. Our notion of Enterprise Cloud data security concept is to "Divide Enterprise Cloud data transactions into six possible ways:

- **Data at Rest:** Enterprise Cloud storage servers and all types of storage on the Enterprise Cloud.
- **Data in Change:** All types of data creation and modification processes, from file creation/deletion of folders.
- **Data in Use:** A file or a program that has being used currently at this point in time for a single or a multiple session.
- **Data in Privacy:** Users' data that are protected which needs to be respected by Enterprise Cloud service providers.

Figure 15. Enterprise cloud data security model

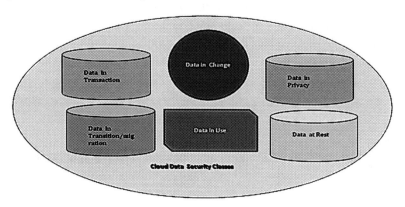

- **Data in Transaction:** A process where a Enterprise Cloud service uses users data or applications.
- **Data in Transition or Migration:** A process where data have been physically re-located or moved to a different server or a storage which needs to transparent to Enterprise Cloud users and to make sure privacy is protected.

We have seen different states in the user's data which must be protected and managed logically and consistently. How do we achieve data security in these circumstances with different scenarios that exist? How do we ensure a business process will provide that expected return on investment (ROI) before actually investing in implementing an Enterprise Cloud business or a service process? Therefore, we have created a number of BPMN (Business Process Modelling Notation) models (BPMN2 2012) for each of those scenarios and run a number of possible simulations with various business variability using an open source simulation tool, known as Bonita Soft (2012) BOS 5.8.

BEST PRACTICE RECOMMENDATIONS

In the context of the work being carried out in the area of enterprise cloud security, this chapter summarises a key set of best practices on enterprise security:

- Always ensure to establish the basic security triad (The essential security principles of confidentiality, integrity, and availability applies to most systems).
- Always establish and allow a flexible provision for legal and regulatory constrains and governance, as these are likely to change internationally based on political policies and cultural constraints.
- Always ensure physical security. This includes protecting against natural disaster, preparedness, and recovery planning. This should also look at availability of services by building resiliency. The scope of issues in physical security is significant, and it involves a range of measures to avoid, prevent, detect, and respond to unauthorized access to the facility or to resources or information on the facility.
- Establish enterprise cloud security standards and policies which are consistent with appropriate standards, such as International Organization for Standardization (ISO) 27001 and ISO 27002.
- Develop and apply a set of guidelines for enabling security in the development of infrastructure software, infrastructure management processes, and operational procedures.
- Develop a set of security standards for access control, incident response and management, system and network configuration backups, security testing practices such as penetration testing, resilience testing, disaster recovery testing, emergency-response testing, firewall testing, data and communication encryption techniques such as encryption algorithms used, etc., password standards, and continuous monitoring.
- Establish enterprise architecture for security and its infrastructure services.
- Establish a consistent identify management, which is the key element of an enterprise security. Controls must be implemented to protect the confidentiality, integrity, and availability of identity information.
- Establish Access Management, where access controls use identity information to enable and constrain access to an operating cloud and its supporting infrastructure.

- Apply a consistent encryption and decryption key management requirements. In an enterprise cloud, encryption is a primary means to protect data at rest (storage) and between storage and processing phases.
- Establish a regular system for auditing system and networking practices in place, which should include presenting and reviewing all event logs for all devices and systems on the network and on the infrastructure, all virtual machines (VM), user logs, operational logs, security logs, reviewing archiving policies, etc.
- Establish a regular Security Monitoring process in place. Security monitoring is predicated on audit logs, network security monitoring (using traffic inspection such as snort and so on), and environmental data. This service should be available on premises as well as remotely.

These are, as we believe, are a critical and essential set of best practices for all enterprises and in particular enterprise cloud services. These are not fixed and it is continue to grow as we learn from systematic literature and also in discussion with key experts in the area of enterprise security.

FUTURE RESEARCH DIRECTIONS

This chapter provided our approach to developing Enterprise Cloud services systematically with build in security. We have developed a number of security-specific components that can be reused and customised because they are components with message interfaces. We have also developed a number of business processes with simulation to pre-inform us about their performances and security measures that can be taken before service implementation and deployment. As we discussed in this chapter, to make Enterprise Cloud computing as a new technological business model that is highly successful, profitable, and sustainable, we need to ensure Enterprise Cloud security and privacy can be maintained and trusted. Therefore, most of the future research will focus mainly on Enterprise Cloud security related issues, in particular:

- Control of Enterprise Cloud resources where it is being used and shared and their physical security if this is a hardware resource. In other words, security concerned with sharing resources and services.
- Seizure of a company because it has violated the local legislative requirement. Concerns of client's data when it has also been violated. Therefore, forensic investigation of Enterprise Cloud services and Enterprise Cloud data recovery and protection issues will dominate much of the future research.
- Consumer switching to price competition. Storage services provided by one Enterprise Cloud vendor may be incompatible with another vendor's service if user decides to move from one to the other (for example, Microsoft Enterprise Cloud is currently incompatible with Google Enterprise Cloud).
- Security key encryption/decryption keys and related issues. Which is suitable technique for a specific service request and for a specific customer data? Who should control? Consumers or providers?
- Enterprise Cloud service development paradigm. What is the suitable development paradigm for this type of business driven delivery model?

- Service security vs. Enterprise Cloud security vs. data security will dominate most of the future research.
- Privacy related issues. Who controls personal and transactional information?
- Audit and monitoring: How do we monitor and audit service provider organisations and how do we provide assurance to relevant stakeholders that privacy requirements are met when their Personally Identifiable Information (PII) is in the Enterprise Cloud?
- Engineering Enterprise Cloud services. How do we develop, test, and deploy Enterprise Cloud services? Can we continue to follow traditional methods and process?
- Business process modelling integrated with Enterprise Cloud service development will emerge and can address business related issues.
- Integrating data security as part of the enterprises, software, and service engineering processes.
- Improvement model for enterprise security.
- Software defined security framework.
- Resilient cloud architecture which is able to sustain all types of security attacks.

As we discussed in this chapter, there are a number of issues, problems, and challenges need to be addressed if want to create sustainable and successful business paradigm for Enterprise Cloud computing. We also discussed a number of research challenges and areas of research focus in the coming years on Enterprise Cloud security in section of this chapter. To summarise some of the research issues & challenges are:

- What can we learn from different paradigms of SDLC? How do we address Enterprise Cloud security? Security vs. Software security vs. Enterprise Cloud Services Security.
- How do we address service reuse as opposed to component reuse? Composability is the main characteristics of Enterprise Cloud computing (to build Enterprise Cloud applications with component parts). Here we want to compose Enterprise Cloud applications with built-in security.
- Are existing design principles can address service composition? Learning the autonomic nature of service-oriented computing when applying design principles.
- How do we customise and apply SE principles to Enterprise Cloud application development? Software component models vs. Service component models.
- How do we learn and reuse best practices? Service component characteristics to match Enterprise Cloud characteristics. Building large scale Enterprise Cloud architectures that are scalable.
- Two major challenges: applying SE principles and best practices; applying SSE principles and best practices.
- How do we address Enterprise Cloud data security and how do we protect Enterprise Cloud centres? Are there data recovery planning that has been continuously monitored and improved?

CONCLUSION

Enterprise Cloud computing has established its businesses and software as a service paradigm is increasing its demand for more services. However, this new trend needs to be more systematic with respect to software engineering and its related processes. For example, current challenges that are witnessed today with cyber security and application security flaws are important lessons to be learned. It also has provided best practices that can be adapted. Similarly, as the demand for Enterprise Cloud services increases and so increased importance sought for security and privacy. We can build Enterprise Cloud application security from the start of the Enterprise Cloud service development. Enterprise Cloud computing is a multi-disciplinary that includes social engineering, software engineering, software security engineering, distributed computing, and service engineering. Therefore, a holistic approach is needed to build Enterprise Cloud services. Use Business process modelling and simulation to study service and business performances before implementation.

REFERENCES

Andress, J. (2011). *The basics of information security: Understanding the fundamentals of infosec in theory and practice, syngress*. USA: Elsevier.

BPMN2. (2012). *BPMN 2.0 handbook* (2nd ed.). Future Strategies Inc.

Bonita Soft. (2012) BOS 5.8, Open source BPMN simulation software. Retrieved from http://www.bonitasoft.com/resources/documentation/top-tutorials

Caminao Project. (2013) Caminao's way: Do enterprises know how symbolic they are? *Modelling Enterprises Engineering Project*. Retrieved June 21, 2014, from http://caminao.wordpress.com/overview/?goback=%2Egde_3731775_member_251475288

Chang, V. & Ramachandran, M., Towards achieving Big Data Security with the Cloud Computing Adoption Framework, IEEE Transactions on Services Computing.

CSA. (2010) Enterprise Cloud Security Alliance, domain 12: Guidance for identity & access management. Retrieved from https://EnterpriseCloudsecurityalliance.org/guidance/csaguide-dom12-v2.10.pdf

ESB. (2014) Software defined protection – Enterprise security blueprint. Retreived April 18, 2014, from https://www.checkpoint.com/press/2014/check-point-introduces-software-defined-protection.html

Iaa, S. (2010), Enterprise Cloud computing world forum. Retreived from http://www.EnterpriseCloudwf.com/iaas.html

McGraw, G. (2004). *Software security: Building security in*. IEEE Security & Privacy.

McGraw, G. (2006). *Software security: building security in*. USA: Addison Wesley.

Mead, N. R., Hough, E., & Stehney, I. I. T. (2005). Security quality requirements engineering (SQUARE) methodology. TECHNICAL REPORT, CMU/SEI-2005-TR-009. Retrieved from http://www.sei.cmu.edu/library/abstracts/reports/05tr009.cfm

OVF. (2010) Open virtualization format (OVF). Distributed Management Task Force. Retrieved from http://dmtf.org/sites/default/files/standards/documents/DSP0243_1.1.0.pdf

Oracle. (2012) Data security challenges. Oracle9i security overview release number 2(9.2), retrieved November 4, 2012, from http://docs.oracle.com/cd/B10501_01/network.920/a96582/overview.htm

Popović, K., & Hocenski, Z. (2010) *Enterprise cloud computing security issues and challenges*. Paper presented at MIPRO 2010, May 24-28, Opatija, Croatia

Ramachandran, M. (2008). *Software components: Guidelines and applications*. NY: Nova Publishers.

Ramachandran, M. (2011). Component-based development for cloud computing architectures. In Z. Mahmmood & R. Hill (Eds.), *Cloud computing for enterprise architectures*. Springer.

Ramachandran, M. (2011). *Software security engineering: Design and applications,*. New York: *Nova Science Publishers*.

Ramachandran, M. (2012) Service component architecture for building enterprise cloud services. *Service Technology Magazine, 65*. Retrieved from http://www.servicetechmag.com/I65/0812-4

Ramachandran, M. (2014) Enterprises engineering processes for the development and deployment of secure enterprise cloud applications. In M. Khosrow-Pour (Ed.), Encyclopedia of Information Science and Technology. Hershey, PA: IGI Global.

Srinivasan, M. K., Sarukesi, K., Rodrigues, P., Manoj, M. S., & Revathy, P. (2012) *State-of-the-art enterprise cloud computing security taxonomies: A classification of security challenges in the present enterprise cloud computing environment*. Paper presented at ICACCI '12, August 03 - 05 2012, Chennai, India

Tondel, I. A., Jaatun, M. G., & Meland, P. H. (2008). *Security requirements for rest of us: A survey. IEEE Software, 25*(1).

KEY TERMS AND DEFINITIONS

Build Security in (BSI): A process of identifying service security requirements right from beginning of the service identification to the complete life cycle.

Business Process as a Service (BPaaS): A set of process related to managing process related activities of a service business.

Enterprise Cloud Data Security: Security of maintaining and preserving client's data that are kept in the Enterprise Cloud.

Security Attacks: Injected against normal working of software systems with the intention to destroy or collect data for misuse.

Service Reuse: A process of reusing services when composing new services.

Software Security Engineering (SSE): A new discipline of applying engineering principles to develop security requirements to engineer software applications including Enterprise Cloud services such as SaaS is essentially a software application which is delivered as a service.

Software Security: Resilience of software against security attacks.

This research was previously published in Delivery and Adoption of Cloud Computing Services in Contemporary Organizations edited by Victor Chang, Robert John Walters, and Gary Wills, pages 435-458, copyright year 2015 by Information Science Reference (an imprint of IGI Global).

Chapter 11
A Security Framework for Secure Cloud Computing Environments

Mouna Jouini
Institut Supérieur De Gestion De Tunis, Tunisia

Latifa Ben Arfa Rabai
Institut Supérieur De Gestion De Tunis, Tunisia

ABSTRACT

Cloud computing technology is a relatively new concept of providing scalable and virtualized resources, software and hardware on demand to consumers. It presents a new technology to deliver computing resources as a service. It offers a variety of benefits like services on demand and provisioning and suffers from several weaknesses. In fact, security presents a major obstacle in cloud computing adoption. In this paper, the authors will deal with security problems in cloud computing systems and show how to solve these problems using a quantitative security risk assessment model named Multi-dimensional Mean Failure Cost (M^2FC). In fact, they summarize first security issues related to cloud computing environments and then propose a generic framework that analysis and evaluate cloud security problems and then propose appropriate countermeasures to solve these problems.

1. INTRODUCTION

Cloud computing is an emerging technology which recently has shown significant attention lately in the word. It provides services over the internet: users can utilize the online services of different software instead of purchasing or installing them on their own computers. The National Institute of Standard and Technology (NIST) definition defines cloud computing as a paradigm for enabling useful, on-demand network access to a shared pool of configurable computing resources (Mell & Grance, 2010). It offers several services presented in three models: Software as Service (SaaS), Platform as Service (PaaS), and Infrastructure as Service (IaaS). Software as Service (SaaS) provides services existing in the cloud or

DOI: 10.4018/978-1-5225-8176-5.ch011

applications to end users, Platform as Service (PaaS) provides access to platforms and Infrastructure as Service (IaaS) offers processing storage and other computing resources.

Cloud computing offers many advantages. But as more and more information on individuals and companies are placed in the cloud, concerns are beginning to grow especially about security. In fact, data users' externalization makes hard to maintain data integrity and privacy, and availability which causes serious consequences. Security is the big challenge in cloud computing systems (Zissis & Lekkas, 2012; Ukil, Jana & De Sarkar, 2013; Sun, Chang, Sun, Li & Wang, 2012; Malik & Nazir, 2012; Mell & Grance, 2010; Ben Arfa Rabai, Jouini, Ben Aissa & Mili, 2012; Jouini, Ben Arfa Rabai, Ben Aissa & Mili, 2012; Ben Arfa Rabai, Jouini, Ben Aissa & Mili, 2013; Jouini, Ben Arfa Rabai & Ben Aissa, 2014; Sampathkumar, 2015). In fact, according to survey conducted by International Data Group (IDG) enterprise in 2014 (IDG Cloud Computing Survey, 2014), security is deeply the top concern for cloud computing. In fact, up from 61% in 2014, and higher among finance organizations (78%), 67% of organizations have concerns about the security of cloud computing solutions. The additional challenges are not even on the same playing field for tech decision-makers; only 43% are concerned with integration, followed by the ability of cloud solutions to meet enterprise and/or industry standards (35%) (IDG Cloud Computing Survey, 2014). Given their high security concerns, organizations are integrating strategies and tools (like cloud management and monitoring tools, and cloud security management tools) to lessen these challenges over the next 12 months.

In this paper, we will show how to solve security problems in cloud computing systems using a quantitative security risk assessment model. We aim to present a generic framework that evaluate firstly cloud security by identifying unique security requirements, secondly to identify architectural components affected by this risk, thirdly to make out security threats that damage these components and finally to attempt to present viable solutions that eliminates these potential threats.

The remainder of this paper is organized as follows. Section 2 presents related work. Section 3 presents security issues in cloud computing environments. Section 4 illustrates a quantitative security risk model that we will use in our new approach. Section 5 presents our security framework that solves security problems in Cloud Computing environments in a quantitative way. Finally, conclusions and a direction for future work are given in section 6.

2. RELATED WORK

Literature review was shown that there are many works that studied cloud security issues (Zissis & Lekkas, 2012; Ukil, Jana & De Sarkar, 2013; Hu, Wu & Cheng, 2012; Sun, Chang, Sun, Li & Wang, 2012; Sun, Chang, Sun, Li & Wang, 2012). All works provide a qualitative discussion of security related issues in CC environments submitting a quick analysis and survey of security issues. In fact, they develop and deploy a qualitative security management framework on cloud computing environment by proposing some security strategies (countermeasures).

Arijit Ukil et al, have analyze in (Ukil, Jana & De Sarkar, 2013) security problems in cloud computing. They proposed a framework for satisfying cloud security ensuring the confidentiality, integrity and authentication of data. In fact, they provide security architecture and necessary security techniques for cloud computing infrastructure. The presented architecture incorporates different security schemes, techniques and protocols for cloud computing, particularly in Infrastructure-as-a-Service (IaaS) and

Platform-as-a-Service (PaaS) systems. This would facilitate to manage the cloud system more effectively and provide the administrator to include the specific solution these security problems.

Hu et al present in (Hu, Wu & Cheng, 2012) a Law-as-a-Service (LaaS) model for automatic enforcing of legal policies to handle queries for cloud service providers (CSPs) and their customers. The law-aware super-peer acts as a guardian providing data integration as well as protection. In fact, they provide Law-as-a-Service (LaaS) for CSPs on our law-aware semantic cloud policy infrastructure. The semantic legal policies in compliance with the laws are enforced automatically at the super-peer to enable LaaS. This allows CSPs to deploy their cloud resources and services without worrying about law violations. After that, users could query data from the law-aware super-peer within a super-peer domain. Each query is also compliant with the laws.

Sun et al present in (Sun, Chang, Sun, Li & Wang, 2012) the pay-as you go business model of cloud infrastructure where they put forward the urge of providing high security for cloud computing as this is going over publicly accessible internet domain. The proposed model was based on the new definition of the security trust term and its properties in order to compute trust in cloud systems. In fact, they believe that we need to better define and established trust means term to better security of cloud platforms. The proposed model includes a time-variant comprehensive evaluation multi-dimensional method for expressing direct trust and a space-variant evaluation multi-dimensional method for calculating recommendation trust.

Kevin et al present in (Sun, Chang, Sun, Li & Wang) a dynamic multidimensional trust model with time-variant comprehensive evaluation multi-dimensional method. With this backdrop, we present our proposed architecture and security model towards better protection of confidentiality, privacy in a public domain cloud infrastructural backbone.

Zissis et al., identify in (Zissis & Lekkas, 2012), firstly security requirements that can be damage when a security problem rises. Then, they present a security strategy based on encryption technique to eliminate security threats in cloud systems. The proposed solution ensures the authentication, integrity and confidentiality of involved data and communications. The solution presents a horizontal level of service available to all implicated entities and maintains a trust between customers and cloud providers.

In (Malik & Nazir, 2012), Malik et al., list the most common security threats that damages cloud computing environments and develop a methodology for cloud providers that will protect users' data and information. They provide simple countermeasures to protect users' data, messages, information against various attacks that are the major issue for anyone when they want to adopt cloud services for their work. They study the major threats arising in cloud environments, and then propose countermeasures to them. In fact, it provides security solutions to insecure application programming interfaces threat and data loss/leakage threats.

The work of Wang et al, presented in (Wang, Wang, Ren, Lou & Li, 2011), studied the integrity problem of data storage in Cloud Computing. In particular, the authors considered the task of allowing a third party auditor (TPA), to cloud client, in order to verify the integrity of the dynamic data stored in the cloud. The TPA allows eliminating the involvement of the client through the auditing of whether his data stored in the cloud are indeed intact. The work aims to ensure remote data integrity that supports public auditability and dynamic data operations. The authors constructed a verification scheme for the integration of these two salient features in their protocol design. In particular, to achieve efficient data dynamics, they improved the existing proof of storage models by manipulating the classic Merkle Hash Tree construction for block tag authentication. To support efficient handling of multiple auditing tasks, they explored the technique of bilinear aggregate signature to extend their main result into a multiuser setting, where TPA can perform multiple auditing tasks simultaneously.

In (Basescu et al., 2011), Basescu et al proposed a generic security management framework allowing providers of cloud data management systems to define and enforce complex security policies. They designed a framework to detect and stop a large number of attacks defined through an expressive policy description language and to be easily interfaced with various data management systems. They showed that they can efficiently protect a data storage system by evaluating their security framework on top of the BlobSeer data management platform.

Several frameworks have been carried out relating to security issues in cloud computing in a quantitative way. In fact, they do not propose a quantitative approach to analyze and evaluate privacy, and security in cloud computing environment. This paper primarily aims to analyze and evaluate the most known cloud computing security issues using a quantitative security risk analysis model called as the Multi-dimension Mean Failure Cost (M^2FC).

3. SECURITY ISSUES IN CLOUD COMPUTING SYSTEM

One of the driving forces behind the rise of cloud computing is the high pressure on service delivery by organization. But data security and privacy are the top concerns for cloud computing users because data and resources in the cloud are stored and controlled in a third-party Cloud Services Providers' datacenters (CSP). Besides, cloud users utilize Internet to connect to the cloud, if they don't have an Internet connection they cannot access to their documents and applications and hence, they will lose their business.

Literature review was shown that there are many works that studied cloud security issues (Ukil, Jana & De Sarkar, 2013; Hu, Wu & Cheng, 2012; (Sun, Chang, Sun, Li & Wang, 2012; Sun, Chang, Sun, Li & Wang, 2012; Jouini & Ben Arfa Rabai, 2014). For example, in our previous work (Jouini & Ben Arfa Rabai, 2014), we survey the major security issues in present existing cloud computing environments and help users and cloud service provider recognize security threats that cause these problems and security requirements associated with them. In this section, we classify security issues to in cloud computing environments according to nine sub-categories as it is presented in our previous work (Jouini & Ben Arfa Rabai, 2014): security issues in virtualization, business services continuity, management interfaces risks, data breaches, compliance and governance, access problem, privacy problem, isolation failure, and accountability problem. The detailed survey of cloud security problems are presented in our previous work in (Jouini & Ben Arfa Rabai, 2014).

3.1. Security Issues in Virtualization

Cloud computing is prone to several concerns related to the use of virtualization technology (Jouini & Ben Arfa Rabai, 2014). In fact, CC systems are based on several technologies like distributed systems, utility computing and virtualization. This last technology allows several security harms in this system and lets many new security threats like VM-based rootkits attack which is designed to infect both client and server machines in the cloud. It abuses compromised systems by hiding files and registry keys and other operating system objects from diagnostic.

3.2. Business Services Continuity

CC systems suffer from service unavailability due to many reasons (Jouini & Ben Arfa Rabai, 2014). In fact, as it was based on public network to let their users to get access to their applications and data, Internet connectivity due to natural circumstances causes unavailability of cloud computing services. We can mention as well that this system is prone to distributed denial of service (DDoS) attacks which led to the unavailability of services.

3.3. Management Interfaces Risks

Cloud computing providers expose a set of software interfaces that customers use to manage and interact with cloud services (like provisioning, and monitoring) which are prone to several security risks (Jouini & Ben Arfa Rabai, 2014). These interfaces are Internet accessible which pose a huge risk especially when combined with remote access and web browser vulnerabilities. Furthermore, cloud interfaces are prone to many threats like insecure interfaces and APIs threats, virtual machine modification, and placement of malicious VM images on physical systems.

3.4. Data Breaches

Cloud systems offer several services to their users like storage. In fact, customers' data are stored in many places in the word using virtual machines (in data centers) which increase information corruption risk (Jouini & Ben Arfa Rabai, 2014). For example, it can be difficult to determine where data is stored in the virtual cloud environment, the robustness the cloud provider's security, and even in some cases whether the cloud provider is handling data in a lawful way.

3.5. Compliance and Governance

Cloud service provider (CSP) has to provide some assurance in service level agreements (SLA) to convince the customer on security issues (Jouini & Ben Arfa Rabai, 2014). The SLA must contain a comprehensive list of regulations that govern the system and associated services and how compliance with these items is executed. However, this contract has several difficult to be accomplished. In fact, the variety laws due to the variety of data location in many sites may cause data replication.

3.6. Access Problem: Data Location

Cloud computing systems suffer from a problem of access to the data view that data is stored in different locations in the world (Jouini & Ben Arfa Rabai, 2014). This environments suffer from lack of transparency since customer' data are located in cloud provider data centers anywhere in the word, and for this reason are out of the customer's control which let many problems.

3.7. Privacy Issues

Privacy presents a big security problem in cloud computing environments (Jouini & Ben Arfa Rabai, 2014). In fact, CC customer's data and especially personally information can be breached more easily than if stored in users' machines. Indeed, in the shared cloud computing infrastructure, customers' private information is more risked of potential unauthorized access and exposure.

3.8. Isolation Failure (Multi-Tenancy Problem)

Infrastructure as a service (IaaS) cloud layer relies on architectural designs where physical resources are shared by multiple virtual machines and so multiple customers. This characteristic causes several problems in cloud use (Jouini & Ben Arfa Rabai, 2014). In fact, resource sharing means that malicious activities carried out by one tenant may affect and get access to other tenant host.

3.9. Accountability Problems

It is difficult to keep track of actions that are related to security actions and responsibilities in cloud computing systems (Jouini & Ben Arfa Rabai, 2014). In fact, in this environment, we have several locations, several lows, and several cloud services providers.

4. THE M²FC MODEL

In (Jouini & Ben Arfa Rabai, 2015), Jouini et al., introduced a quantitative security risk assessment measure that quantifies this risk in terms of financial loss per unit of operation time (for example dollars per hour ($/h)) due to security threats considering several dimensions within the threat world. The measure is called as the Multidimensional Mean Failure Cost (M²FC). The M²FC is a stakeholder based security threats assessment model. It estimates the security of a system in terms of the loss that each stakeholder incurs due to security breaches considering several dimensions within the threat world. In fact, the world of security threats is a segmentation of this world according to each of its dimensions where a dimension can be defined as an elementary aspect or extent of the threat word. The domain or world of threats can be perceived as having several dimensions like architectural components, environmental elements, time, deployment site…For example, when considering the deployment dimension; we give the mean failure cost per deployment site where a security breach occurs. The basic idea is to consider threat perspectives to estimate security failure. To better explain the usage of the proposed M²FC model, we apply on a case study to estimate the security of a system in terms of loss incurred by each stakeholder.

The M²FC model takes into account the stakeholders assessment of the cost related to their requirements with regard to the elements of two security threats dimensions. That is why, in the following model, the set H of stakeholders and the set R of their requirements are distinguished from the set of the leading dimension (where we called a leading dimension a dimension that is used to guide our decomposition of the multidimensional threat world into several slides of two dimensions each) and the set of the other considered dimension.

Model: Let S be the set of elements in the leading dimension, D be the set of elements of the other considered dimension, H be the set of stakeholders, R is a set of requirements, and T be a set of threats. For every element s ε S, we define the Multidimensional Mean Failure Costs M(s;D) of element s as follows (Jouini & Ben Arfa Rabai, 2015):

$$M(s;D) = V_s \circ PFR_s \circ C_s \circ P_s$$

where:

- We denote $\circ$ by the matrix multiplication operation;
- V_s is a matrix of size $|H| \times |R|$ that each entry $(i; j)$ represents the value of the stake that stakeholder Hi has in meeting requirement R_j. We denote by $|H|$ (resp. $|R|$) the size of the set H (resp. R);
- PFR_s is a matrix of size $(|H|;|R|)$ that each entry $(i; j)$ represents the probability of failing requirement R_i due to a failure originating from element $d_j \in D$;
- C_s is a matrix of size $(|D|;|T|)$ that each entry $(i; j)$ represents the probability that an element $d_i \in D$ fails once the threat t_j has materialized;
- P_s is a column vector of size $(|T|)$ that each entry i represents the probability that threats materialize during unitary period of operation.

The M²FC model is a formula in the form of a hierarchical linear system composed of stakeholders, security requirements (such as confidentiality, integrity, and availability), and two perspectives (architectural components, and environmental entities). In fact, an information system has its stakeholders which have its own issues in the proper functioning of the system. The proper functioning requires certain attributes of dependability which called as security requirements. If we consider the architecture of the system that has several components, a failure exhibiting a security requirement essentially is relative to a particular component. These components fail because of vulnerability due to a security threat. Finally, a threat has several dimensions like source, users and location that affect information systems.

We applied the Multi-dimensional Mean Failure Cost model (M²FC) is a practical applications namely a Cloud Computing environment (Jouini & Ben Arfa Rabai, 2015). We computed the M²FC model for three kinds of stakeholders (bronze, silver and gold stakeholders) considering the following threats dimensions: partner application, time, components and connectors.

5. METHODOLOGY

We show in this section how to use a quantitative security risk analysis model to suggest our framework for secure Cloud Computing environment. We used the Multi-dimensional Mean Failure Cost model (M²FC) presented in previous section to propose an approach for secure CC systems.

5.1. The Proposed Framework

After introducing security issues in cloud computing system, we need to make approach that allows analyzing and making relation between security problems and their solutions. We notice that some investigators proposed solutions to threats but, they didn't relate solutions to security issues. We propose, in this section, an approach that uses quantitative analysis in order to ensure that our results are more logical and efficient. We will present framework that identifies security and privacy challenges in cloud computing. It highlights cloud-specific attacks and risks and clearly illustrates their mitigations and countermeasures. Our proposed architecture is modular because we consider the threats individually and seek solution for that. This helps to manage the cloud system more effectively and provide the security analysts to include the specific solution to counter the threat. For example, in some cases or for some users, confidentiality is the only requirement whereas for some users' other security requirements are also required. Based on the requirement like security strength, latency, bandwidth, the administrator can choose the appropriate primitives.

Figure 1 shows our framework for secure cloud computing. It consists of four main security steps which are:

- **Associate security requirements to security problems:** For each issue, we will choose the security requirement affected by this problem;
- **Associate security threats dimensions to system requirements:** For each security requirement, we analyze the probabilities of failure threats dimension matrix (PFR_s) in order to select dimension elements with the higher probabilities where system fails to meet this requirement if an element of the dimension D fails;
- **Associate threats to the dimension elements:** For each dimension element D, we analyze the probabilities of failure in the matrix (C_s) to choose security threats having the higher failure probability when an element of D is compromised;
- **Mitigation:** For each security threats, propose appropriate countermeasures.

Figure 1. A framework for secure cloud computing environments

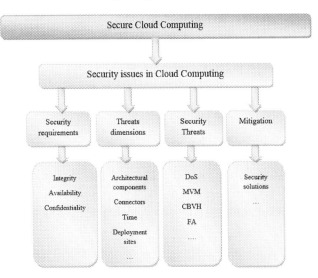

5.2. Using Methodology to Solve Security Problems in Cloud Computing Environment

We applied in this section our framework to an illustrative example named cloud computing system. We applied the M²FC model to quantify cloud systems and estimate the financial cost for each stakeholder regarding the architectural component and deployment site dimensions. In fact, we take into account the deployment sites dimension and the architectural components dimension. Our assessment varies according to the stakes that each stakeholder has in meeting each security requirement per system site (or location). We opt, as well, for using the deployment dimension (i.e., sites dimension) as the leading dimension. For each site of the considered system, we have the lists of stakeholders, security requirements, components, and threats as we mentioned above.

5.2.1. Security Requirements

This step identifies security requirements related to each cloud computing security problem cited above. Based on our quantitative assessment security model (Jouini & Ben Arfa Rabai, 2014; Jouini & Ben Arfa Rabai, 2015), we identified in previous work the following security requirement:

- Availability;
- Integrity;
- Confidentiality.

Next, we will present security requirements associated to security problems in CC environments:

- **Security issues in virtualization:** Virtual machine (VM)-based malware affects the confidentiality, the integrity and the availability security requirements of cloud computing systems (Basescu et al., 2011; Jouini, Ben Arfa Rabai, Ben Aissa & Mili, 2012). In fact, confidentiality is at risk because the customers' data could be intercepted by malware. Integrity is at risk because the operation of the virtual machine (VM) can be changed by malware which could lead to loss of integrity of the customers' data. Availability is at risk because by malware can potentially erase, or obfuscate the customers' data.

Therefore, the security requirements related to this issue and can be affect in case of attack are integrity, confidentiality, availability:

- **Business services continuity:** Services availability problem poses a devastating impact on the brand and the reputation of organizations by causing unavailability of cloud services. The security requirement related to this issue and can be affect in case of attack is availability;
- **Management interfaces risks:** Reliance on a weak set of interfaces and application programming interfaces (APIs) in cloud computing system exposes organizations to a variety of security issues related to confidentiality, integrity, availability, authentication and authorization and accountability (Basescu et al., 2011; Jouini, Ben Arfa Rabai, Ben Aissa & Mili, 2012).

The security requirements related to this issue and can be affect in case of attack are integrity, confidentiality and availability:

- **Data breaches:** Many security threats can compromise data and provide losses and corruption and it provoke a serious problems related to integrity, confidentiality and availability of data.

The security requirements related to this issue and can be affect in case of attack are integrity, confidentiality and availability:

- **Compliance and governance:** Finally, many threats pose risks to SLA accomplishment and give the difficulty to audit the data and verify the logs of data access which poses accountability breach;
- **Access problem: data location:** The security requirements related to this issue and can be affect in case of attack are integrity, confidentiality, and availability;
- **Privacy issues:** Privacy breaches allow confidentiality problems and data leakage which leads to serious financial implications to organization. Therefore, the security requirement related to this issue and can be affect in case of attack is confidentiality;
- **Isolation failure (multi tenancy problem):** Multi-tenancy problem affects the confidentiality, access control, availability, integrity and accountability of data. Thus, the security requirements related to this issue and can be affect in case of attack are integrity, confidentiality and availability;
- **Accountability problems:** This problem affects accountability security requirement.

5.2.2. Architectural Components

For architectural component in the Cloud system, we will consider data extracted from our previous work given in (Jouini & Ben Arfa Rabai, 2015). Thus, we will consider in this illustration two dimensions in cloud computing systems namely deployment sites and architectural components. As well, we consider as a leading dimension the deployment site dimension. Thus, to illustrate our secure framework, we will consider mainly these two dimensions. Therefore, we consider that the considered system is deployed on two sites. We have S = {S ite1, S ite2} and the component dimension D has the following elements which is equals to D = {Browser, Web server, Proxy server}. We identify as well two stakeholders for this example namely: local user and external user. We consider that this system is prone to four kind of security threats hence the set T = {Virus, Data Bases Attacks, Denial of service}. Finally, as we mention in the illustrative example in (Jouini & Ben Arfa Rabai, 2015) that we consider the following requirements R = {Availability, Integrity, Confidentiality}.

Since the failure of security requirement depends on which component of the system architecture is operational, we will identify in this step using probabilities of failure requirements matrix (PFRs) for each security requirement components causing this failure.

We take for each security requirement the higher probability of failing this requirement Ri once component Ck has failed as show in Table 1:

- In **integrity** case, we find that the higher probabilities of impact of attack with the following components: Browser, proxy server and web server;

Table 1. Probabilities of failure requirements for sites (Jouini & Ben Arfa Rabai, 2015)

	Components							
	Site 1				Site 2			
	Browser	Web_ server	Proxy_ server	No_failure	Browser	Web_ server	Proxy_ server	No_failure
Security Requirements								
Availability	0,2	0,1	0,3	0,4	0,2	0,3	0,3	0.5
Confidentiality	0,1	0,1	0,2	0,6	0,3	0,3	0,3	0.7
Integrity	0,1	0,2	0,4	0,3	0,2	0,2	0,2	0.6

- In **availability** case, we find that the higher probabilities of impact of attack with the following components: Browser, proxy server and web server;
- In **confidentiality** cases, we find that the higher probabilities of impact of attack with the following components: Browser, proxy server and web server.

5.2.3. Security Threats

Components of the architecture may fail to operate properly as a result of security breaches due to malicious activities. Therefore, we specify, in this step, the catalog of threats that causes components failure. We select for each component, the higher probabilities that in which a component C_k fails once threat T_q has materialized. We will present threats that affected components above, through an analysis of probabilities of failure components matrix (Table 2) (Jouini & Ben Arfa Rabai, 2015):

- **Denial of Service (DoS):** Browser, proxy server, web server;
- **Account, Service and Traffic Hijacking:** Web server, proxy server;
- **Malicious Insiders (MI):** Browser, web server, proxy server.

We will make synthesis of our analysis in the three steps. For example, we take "Regulatory compliance" has seven security requirements: integrity, confidentiality, and availability. Each security requirement related to some components. The components are: browser, web Server, proxy server.

Each component affected by some threats. The threats are: denial of service (DoS), malicious insiders, and account, service and traffic hijacking.

According to the analysis, we can conclude that all threats presented by M²FC are the cause of security issues, because of the threats' distribution which is uniform for cloud computing system. We propose to focus on each threat and suggest solutions. These threats are: denial of service (DoS), malicious insiders, and account, service and traffic hijacking.

Table 2. Probabilities of failure components matrix for sites (Jouini & Ben Arfa Rabai, 2015)

	Threats						
	Site 1			Site 2			
	Virus	Data_Bases _Attacks	No_Threat (NoT)	Virus	Data_Bases _Attacks	Denial_of_Ser vive (DoS)	No_Threat (NoT)
Components							
Browser	0 .2	0 .5	0 .3	0 .2	0 .2	0 .1	0 .5
Web_Server	0 .5	0 .4	0 .1	0 .2	0 .35	0 .1	0 .35
Proxy_Server	0 .3	0 .6	0 .1	-	-	-	-
No_Failure (NoF)	0 .1	0 .3	0 .6	0 .11	0 .2	0 .09	0 .6

5.2.4. Mitigation

In this part, we will describe threats related to security issues and we will give countermeasures to prevent against them. The aim of this step is to propose solutions to security problems:

- **Denial of Service:** The denial of service attack (DoS) (Ben Arfa Rabai, Jouini, Ben Aissa & Mili, 2012; Jouini, Ben Arfa Rabai, Ben Aissa & Mili, 2012) is a critical problem for virtual machines (VMs) used on cloud components. In fact, it indicates that the hypervisor software is allowing a single VM to consume all the system resources and thus starving the remaining VMs and impairing their function. Because the VMs and the host share CPU, memory, disk, and network resources, virtual machines may be able to cause some form of denial of service attack against another VM (Qaisar & Khawaja, 2012; Priyadharshini, 2013).

As a countermeasure for this attack, you can reduce the privileges of the user that connected to a server. This will help to reduce the DOS attack. Furthermore, the best approach to prevent a guest consuming all the resources is to limit the resources allocated to the guests. Current virtualization technologies offer a mechanism to limit the resources allocated to each guest machines in the environment. Therefore, the underlying virtualization technology should be properly configured, which can then prevent one guest consuming all the available resources, thereby preventing the denial of service attack (Qaisar & Khawaja, 2012; Priyadharshini, 2013).

- **Malicious Insiders:** The malicious insider threat (Ben Arfa Rabai, Jouini, Ben Aissa & Mili, 2012; Jouini, Ben Arfa Rabai, Ben Aissa & Mili, 2012) is one that gains in importance as many providers still don't reveal how they hire people, how they grant them access to assets or how they monitor them. Transparency is, in this case, vital to a secure cloud offering, along with compliance reporting and breach notification.

To confront this threat, one should enforce strict supply chain management and conduct a comprehensive supplier assessment. Another effective measure is to specify human resource requirements as part of legal contracts, and require transparency into overall information security and management practices, as well as compliance reporting. Another useful step to take is to determine security breach notification processes (Qaisar & Khawaja, 2012).

- **Account, Service and Traffic Hijacking:** Account service and traffic hijacking (Ben Arfa Rabai, Jouini, Ben Aissa & Mili, 2012; Jouini, Ben Arfa Rabai, Ben Aissa & Mili, 2012) is another issue that cloud users need to be aware of. These threats range from man-in-the-middle attacks, to phishing and spam campaigns, to denial-of service attacks. Account hijacking (Barron, Yu & Zhan, 2013) is usually carried out with stolen credentials. Using the stolen credentials, attackers can access sensitive information and compromise the confidentiality, integrity, and availability of the services offered.

As solution, (Qaisar & Khawaja, 2012) one should prohibit the sharing of account credentials between users and services. Another effective measure is to leverage strong two-factor authentication techniques where possible, and employ proactive monitoring to detect unauthorized activity. Another useful step to take is to understand cloud provider security policies and SLAs (Qaisar & Khawaja, 2012; Priyadharshini, 2013).

In (Hashizume, Rosado, Fernandez-Medina & Fernandez, 2013) we find a presentation of two approaches to confront this threat. The first is identity and access management guidance. However, the second is dynamic credentials (Hashizume, Rosado, Fernandez-Medina & Fernandez, 2013). It presents an algorithm to create dynamic credentials for mobile cloud computing systems. The dynamic credential changes its value once a user changes its location or when he has exchanged a certain number of data packets.

6. CONCLUSION

Security problems present a major issue in information systems adopting and especially in cloud computing environments in which sensitive applications and data are moved into the cloud data centers. Cloud computing poses many novel vulnerabilities like virtualization vulnerabilities, data vulnerabilities and software vulnerabilities.

Furthermore, with advancement of cloud computing technologies and increasing number of cloud users, security dimensions will continuously increase. In this paper, we primarily classify and highlight the major security problems in cloud computing systems and help users recognize threats associated with their uses. We propose a framework that analyzes and evaluates security issues in cloud computing environment by a quantifiable approach. Our proposed framework is modular in nature that is we consider the threats individually and seek solution for that. This helps to manage the cloud system more effectively and provide the administrator to include the specific solution to counter the threat.

We envision develop a complete security evaluation and management framework as a part of cloud computing services to satisfy the security demands and then deploy this framework on really cloud computing environments. Then, we envision control the multi-dimensional Mean Failure Cost model (M²FC) by analyzing the cost of various countermeasures that one can deploy in Cloud Computing systems to improve security, and match these costs against the benefits that result from these measures in terms of reduced multi-dimensional mean failure costs (M²FC).

REFERENCES

Barron, C., Yu, H., & Zhan, J. (2013). Cloud Computing Security Case Studies and Research. *Proceedings of the 2013 International Conference of Parallel and Distributed Computing.*

Basescu, C., Carpen-Amarie, A., Leordeanu, C., Leordeanu, C., Costan, A., & Antoniu, G. (2011). Managing Data Access on Clouds: A Generic Framework for Enforcing Security Policies. *Proceedings of the International Conference on Advanced Information Networking and Applications (AINA)*. 10.1109/AINA.2011.61

Ben Arfa Rabai, L., Jouini, M., Ben Aissa, A., & Mili, A. (2012). An economic model of security threats for cloud computing systems. *Proceedings of the International Conference on Cyber Security, Cyber Warfare and Digital Forensic (CyberSec)* (pp. 100–105). 10.1109/CyberSec.2012.6246112

Ben Arfa Rabai, L., Jouini, M., Ben Aissa, A., & Mili, A. (2013). A cyber security model in cloud computing environments. *Journal of King Saud University-Computer and Information Sciences, 25*(1), 63–75. doi:10.1016/j.jksuci.2012.06.002

Hamlen, K., Kantarcioglu, M., Khan, L., & Thuraisingham, B. (2010). Security Issues for Cloud Computing. *International Journal of Information Security and Privacy, 4*(2), 36–48. doi:10.4018/jisp.2010040103

Hashizume, K., Rosado, D. G., Fernandez-Medina, E., & Fernandez, E. B. (2013). An analysis of security issues for cloud computing. *Journal of Internet Services and Applications, 4*(1), 1–13. doi:10.1186/1869-0238-4-5

Hu, Y., Wu, W., & Cheng, D. (2012). Towards law-aware semantic cloud policies with exceptions for data integration and protection. *Proceedings of the 2nd International Conference on Web Intelligence, Mining and Semantics.* 10.1145/2254129.2254162

IDG Cloud Computing Survey. (2014). Cloud Continues to Transform Business Landscape as CIOs Explore New Areas for Hosting. Retrieved from http://www.idgenterprise.com/news/press-release/cloud-continues-to-transform-business-landscape-as-cios-explore-new-areas-for-hosting/

Jouini, M., & Ben Arfa Rabai, L. (2014). Surveying and Analyzing Security Problems in Cloud Computing Environments. *Proceedings of the 10th International Conference on Computational Intelligence and Security (CIS 2014)* (pp. 689–493).

Jouini, M., Ben Arfa Rabai, L., & Ben Aissa, A. (2014). Classification of security threats in information systems. *Proceedings of ANT/SEIT '14.*

Jouini, M., Ben Arfa Rabai, L., Ben Aissa, A., & Mili, A. (2012). Towards quantitative measures of information security: A cloud computing case study. *International Journal of Cyber-Security and Digital Forensics, 1*(3), 265–279.

Jouini, M., Ben Arfa Rabai, L., & Khedri, R. (2015). A Multidimensional Approach Towards a Quantitative Assessment of Security Threats. *Proceedings of ANT/SEIT '15* (pp. 507-514).

Malik, A., & Nazir, M. M. (2012). Security Framework for Cloud Computing Environment: A Review. *Journal of Emerging Trends in Computing and Information Sciences, 3*(3).

Mell, P., & Grance, T. (2010). The NIST definition of cloud computing. *Communications of the ACM, 53*(6), 50.

Priyadharshini, A. (2013). A survey on security issues and countermeasures in cloud computing storage and a tour towards multi-clouds. *International Journal of Research in Engineering & Technology, 1*(2), 1–10.

Qaisar, S., & Khawaja, K.F. (2012). Cloud computing: network/ security threats and countermeasures. *Interdisciplinary journal of contemporary research in business, 3*(9).

Sampathkumar, R. (2015). *Disruptive Cloud Computing and IT: Cloud Computing SIMPLIFIED for every IT Professional.* Amazo.

Sun, D., Chang, G., Sun, L., Li, F., & Wang, X. (2012). A dynamic multi-dimensional trust evaluation model to enhance security of cloud computing environments. *International Journal of Innovative Computing and Applications*, *3*(4), 200–210. doi:10.1504/IJICA.2011.044529

Ukil, A., Jana, D., & De Sarkar, A. (2013). A security framework in cloud computing infrastructure. [IJNSA]. *International Journal of Network Security & Its Applications*, *5*(5), 11–24. doi:10.5121/ijnsa.2013.5502

Wang, Q., Wang, C., Ren, K., Lou, W., & Li, J. (2011). Enabling Public Auditability and Data Dynamics for Storage Security in Cloud Computing. *IEEE Transactions on Parallel and Distributed Systems*, *22*(5), 847–859. doi:10.1109/TPDS.2010.183

Zissis, D., & Lekkas, D. (2012). Addressing cloud computing security issues. *Future Generation Computer Systems*, *28*(3), 583–592. doi:10.1016/j.future.2010.12.006

This research was previously published in the International Journal of Cloud Applications and Computing (IJCAC), 6(3); edited by B. B. Gupta and Dharma P. Agrawal, pages 32-44, copyright year 2016 by IGI Publishing (an imprint of IGI Global).

Chapter 12
Information Security Innovation:
Personalisation of Security Services in a Mobile Cloud Infrastructure

Jan H. P. Eloff
SAP Innovation Center Pretoria, South Africa & Department Computer Science, University of Pretoria, South Africa

Mariki M. Eloff
University of South Africa, South Africa

Madeleine A. Bihina Bella
SAP Innovation Center Pretoria, South Africa

Donovan Isherwood
University of Johannesburg, South Africa

Moses T. Dlamini
University of Pretoria, South Africa

Ernest Ketcha Ngassam
University of South Africa, South Africa

ABSTRACT

The increasing demand for online and real-time interaction with IT infrastructures by end users is facilitated by the proliferation of user-centric devices such as laptops, iPods, iPads, and smartphones. This trend is furthermore propounded by the plethora of apps downloadable to end user devices mostly within mobile-cum-cloud environments. It is clear that there are many evidences of innovation with regard to end user devices and apps. Unfortunately, little, if any, information security innovation took place over the past number of years with regard to the consumption of security services by end users. This creates the need for innovative security solutions that are human-centric and flexible. This chapter presents a framework for consuming loosely coupled (but interoperable) cloud-based security services by a variety of end users in an efficient and flexible manner using their mobile devices.

DOI: 10.4018/978-1-5225-8176-5.ch012

INTRODUCTION

The increasing demand for cost-effective always on connectivity on all types of end-user computing devices (e.g. desktop computer, laptop, MP3 player, tablet, smartphone) results in the need for new business models (mobile, cloud, services, platforms) that increase the level of exposure to a company's assets. This creates new security challenges for networked businesses as a number of 3rd-party services and infrastructures within complex ecosystems are integrated. For instance, many actors are involved in the service provisioning ranging from the customer, the service provider, the content provider, the network provider, the cloud provider and the electronic or mobile payment provider. Each of these actors has an entry point to the service and therefore is a potential security risk.

Investigating a security breach thus requires the collection of data from all these different sources. In addition, the existence of various mechanisms to access the network (e.g. wired, wireless, 3G, modem, VPN) creates many access points that can be exploited for unauthorized access to and misuse of the company's information.

Detecting such events requires the continuous exchange of information between all service elements and network devices (Bihina Bella, Eloff, & Olivier, 2009). Furthermore, entities involved in the service provisioning can have conflicting security policies that need to be aligned to the company's policy.

In this collaborative environment, security risks shifts from the IT system as a whole to the services it offers to a multitude of independent users and to the data that travel across systems (e.g. in cloud computing applications hosted on public infrastructures). For example applications hosted on public cloud infrastructures are not only open to the general public but are also open to malicious individuals. Such applications become a public good and are susceptible to excessive and malicious use. Malicious or disgruntled individuals may decide to flood such applications with targeted distributed denial of service (DDoS) attacks so that the general public could not have access to them.

Maintaining a secure configuration in such heterogeneous IT landscapes is complex a security requirements are multi-lateral and diverse. This creates the need for innovative security solutions that are human-centric, flexible and also robust. Potential avenues for innovation within the information security domain include, amongst others, the following:

1. The definition of data-centric policies that travel with the services as well as the data.
2. The usage of privacy-preserving computing (Wang, Zhao, Jiang, & Le, 2009) to ensure the privacy of all parties involved.
3. Access control policies and mechanisms that take care of conflict management (Cuppens, Cuppens-Boulahia, & Ghorbel, 2007) between the members of an ecosystem.
4. The possible aggregation of different access control approaches such as usage and optimistic based access control (Padayachee, 2010).
5. Simple and basic authentication services on mobile devices.
6. Forensic tools for mobile-cum-cloud environments (Ruan, Carthy, Kechadi, & Crosbie, 2011) services utilization, using mobile devices.

This is an opportunity to capitalize on the advantages offered by cloud computing for accessing value-added business services, by end-users. In general, end-users are not concerned by the complexity of the technical infrastructure required to set up cloud-based services for large consumption but rather the intended business outcome offered by exposed services.

This paper presents an innovative framework for accessing loosely coupled (but interoperable) cloud-based security services by a variety of end-users, in a secure, elective and flexible manner, anywhere and anytime, using their mobile devices. The remaining part of this paper is structured as follows: the next section provides some background information discussing the concept of innovation within the domain of information security.

Furthermore, background information is provided on the current state-of-the-art in information security services and existing approaches to services oriented architectures. In the next section, a generic SiYP (Security-In-Your-Pocket) platform is presented from a Service Oriented Architecture (SOA) point of view. The following section presents a conclusion and future work.

BACKGROUND AND RELATED WORK

From the previous section it is clear that various technologies, tools and devices will form part of this proposed framework in order to provide the required flexibility, efficiency and security. In this section the different terms and technologies will be discussed as well as how they relate to each other. IDC (Christiansen, 2008) identified the importance of leveraging the strengths of both innovation and security in order to gain a competitive advantage over companies who do not do it. However, no extensive research was found that addresses how information security can strengthen innovation and vice versa. In this section these terms will be defined as well as their interrelationship. Some well-known terminologies are associated with information security such as information security services, privacy and trust. However, it is important to understand how, for example, trust, relates to service oriented architecture and innovation.

Innovation

For any organization to gain and maintain a competitive advantage and be an economic leader, being innovative is of utmost importance. Innovation should not be confused with invention, which is only the idea or model for a new or improved product, process, device or system, whereas innovation is bringing this idea to market as a real product, process, system or device that is part of the economic system (Roth, 2009). Innovation is only accomplished with the first commercial transaction involving this new invention. Schumpeter said, in as far back as 1943, that Economic change revolves around innovation, entrepreneurship and market power (Schumpeter, 1943).

Information Security Services

According to the ISO 7498-2 standard, produced by The International Standards Organization (ISO) information security can be defined in terms of the five security services, namely identification & authentication, authorization, confidentiality, integrity and nonrepudiation (ISO, 1989). These services are required to ensure that information are protected and secured at all times, whether in storage of any nature, during transmission or usage. A definition for each of these services follows:

The identification and authentication of any subject who wants to access any computer system is the first step towards enforcing information security. A subject requesting access needs to present a user-id that uniquely identifies it. On presentation of such a user-id, the user-id should be verified to ensure that it does, in fact, belong to the subject who presented it.

The next step is to determine if the authenticated subject has the right to access the computer facilities in question. In terms of the authorization process, control is, therefore, exerted over the access rights of all authenticated subjects. All information must be strictly accessible to authorized parties only. Protecting the confidentiality of information, therefore, gives the assurance that only authorized parties will have access to the information in question.

Information should not only be kept confidential, but its integrity should also be guaranteed. Only authorized parties should be able to change the content of protected information. In other words, unauthorized changes to information must be prevented, ensuring that the information can be deemed accurate and complete. The last step is to ensure that no action is performed to affect information security, for example, changing some of the content of information that could be denied at a later stage. This process is referred to as non-repudiation. It may be argued that the security services are not applicable in current computing applications; however, various authors have proven through research that these services are essential, especially in mobile and cloud computing (Chetty & Coetzee, 2011; Huang, Ma, & Li, 2010).

Privacy

Privacy, which is closely related to information security, is defined as the right of an individual or a group to isolate information about themselves from others. This ability allows individuals to reveal themselves selectively. The Oxford English Dictionary refers to privacy as the condition of free from public attention, undisturbed, or the freedom from interference or intrusion (Proffitt, 2012).

Trust

Trust is in principle a human action. A person may trust another to behave in a certain manner, where trust is based on past experience, recommendation or the reputation of the other person. The Oxford English Dictionary (Proffitt, 2012) defines trust as the confidence in or reliance on some quality or attribute of a person or thing, or the truth of a statement. This definition of trust does not take all aspects of trust into consideration nor does it satisfy the requirements of trust as required in the Web 2.0 environment (OReilly, 2007). . Trust is bi-directional with mainly two parties involved, namely the truster and the trustee. The truster is the party who trusts, confides, or relies on the other party; he/she is the one who believes or credits; the one that gives credit, a creditor. The trustee is, on the other hand, the party who is trusted, or to whom something is entrusted; a person in whom confidence is put (Proffitt, 2012). Josang, Ismail, and Boyd (2007) go further and distinguish between reliability trust and decision trust. Reliability trust implies that trustee will act as expected, while decision trust refers to the situation where the truster depends on the trustee, even though some risks may be involved.

Service Oriented Architecture and Cloud Computing

Service oriented architecture (SOA) developed from older concepts such as distributed computing and modular programming into cloud computing. Cloud computing can be seen as a service-oriented architecture (SOA) exploring almost every computing component including, but not limited to distributed computing, grid computing, utility computing, on-demand, open source, Peer-to-Peer and Web

2.0 (Weinhardt, Anandasivam, Blau, & Stosser, 2009). It is a natural next step from the grid model to a supply and demand utility model. In minimizing potential security and trust issues as well as adhering to governance issues facing Cloud computing, prerequisite control measures are required to ensure that a concrete Cloud computing Service Level Agreement (SLA) is put in place and maintained when dealing with mobile applications.

Mobile Computing

Mobile computing refers to any computing device that possesses processing and storage capabilities and that can connect to other computing devices, preferably through wireless connections. Devices include, but are not limited to cellular phones, tablets, PDAs, laptops, notebooks etc.

Security in Mobile and Cloud Computing

Trust is a key element of security in cloud computing. If one party is not trustworthy, it is clear that this party's security, even if claimed to be strong, is not security at all (Masnick, 2011). One of the most important protocols in ensuring transparency and security within Cloud computing is the SLA. The SLA is the only legal agreement between the service provider and client and its importance should not be under estimated (Balachandra, Ramakrishna, & Rakshit, 2009). The only means that the cloud provider can gain the trust of clients is through the SLA; therefore the SLA has to be standardized. The following are the main aspects as a guideline for SLA:

1. Services to be delivered and performance.
2. Tracking and Reporting.
3. Problem Management.
4. Legal Compliance.
5. Resolution of Disputes Customer Duties.
6. Security Responsibility.
7. Confidential Information Termination.

However, ensuring mobile and cloud security is still a serious challenge as identified and addressed by various research studies (Leavitt, 2011; Lin, 2011; Oberheide, & Jahanian, 2010). From the above discussions it is clear that for the proposed framework it will be important that the existing security services should be embedded in the SOA as well as in the mobile-cloud infrastructure. The user will play an important part in these security services. The mobile applications, being loosely coupled, propose unique security challenges.

A GENERIC SERVICE MODEL FOR THE SECURITY IYP PLATFORM

As alluded to in previous sections, the intended purpose of a user centric security platform is to supply the user with the ability to bind available apps to be consumed as service. This requires a range of security services for ensuring that all transactions performed during the consumption of cloud-based services are secured and guaranteed, not only for good quality of services, but also to adhere to prescribed service level agreements amongst interoperable services.

In general, the SiYP platform is regarded as a container of apps grouped together and supported by a range of loosely coupled, security-based, services deployed in the cloud. Security-based services will be implemented and deployed in the cloud for consumption based on the various constraints required for ensuring that any app consumed by end-users adhered to the prescribed security standard. However, the approach adopted in this new paradigm provides the flexibility for the end-user to wrap the business app with the minimum necessary security app (and therefore service) required for an effective consumption without any security breach. For illustration purpose, an end user who would like his device to be secured based on its location while using a given business app would configure the business app such that the location service provided in the platform is activated. This approach provides interested users, to only rely on the consumption of security services that are necessary while consuming a given business app through the cloud. Equally, the end-user would have the ability to enforce the traceability of all its operations while consuming the service, provided that he has activated the secured security app in the platform, dedicated to such a role. Of course, one may argue that security enforcement would require that all security-based services are activated (ISO, 1989). However with the limited computational resources available on mobile devices as well as the complexity that could arise if all those services are invoked, it makes perfect sense to adopt the approach of delivering those services on-demand, to be consumed by end-users on an as-needed basis.

It follows that the overall structure of the platform would reflect the manner in which apps are usually grouped together based on the kind of services being rendered by any given app. In the app world, each app as presented to end-users contains the necessary functionality that reflects the service to be provided to the consumer. As such, there is a range of services at the lower level of the hierarchy that are invoked and aggregated in order to meet end-user's expectation. Therefore two different apps may share many services although their end-result appears different to the end-users. This is a true reflection of the principles of loosely coupling and interoperability that make up a service model following modern Service Engineering (and therefore SOA) paradigm (Bullingera, Fhnrichb, & Meirena, 2003) . As such the conceptualization of our proposed SiYP platform would equally be based on current trends, as reflected in the state-of-the-art of Services Engineering (Bullingera et al., 2003).

We perceive the SiYP service model, therefore, as a four-tier architecture, see figure 1. As a naming convention, all the apps are called "My" followed by "App name" and the term security is implied. For instance My Device indicates that this is the app for the user device security. The description of each layer of the architecture as well as components thereof follows.

The Presentation Layer

This layer represents the entry-point to the security innovation platform by end-users using the necessary computational medium for the consumption of any given business app. For instance, the Business in Your Pocket (BiYP) interface available on the end-user's device would enable him/her to consume business services in the cloud anywhere and anytime. In order to do so, the edit-ability of the platform would allow the user to personalize a range of security apps required for the secure consumption of all business services attached to the app. Discussion on those business services are beyond the scope of this work. Since the end user might require that security, with respect to the device being used for service consumption, be enforced, he/she then has to "wrap-on" the business app, the appropriate security app

Figure 1. An extract SiYP security service model

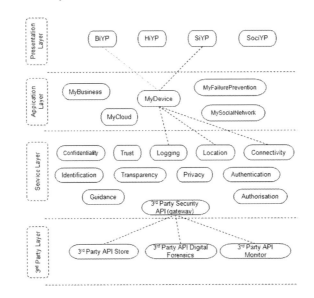

available from the lower layer in the hierarchy. This security app also invokes a range of security services from lower layers as well as required security services for interaction with third party API's that are not part of the SiYP platform. The presentation layer is therefore the environment used by consumers to personalize their required security services in order to ensure that security is enforced during the consumption of a given business app.

The Application Layer

This layer provides a pool of security apps that can be added to and removed from a business service based on the user requirements. Examples of some possible security apps are described below. They are My Device, My Failure Prevention, My Cloud and My Social Network.

My Device App

This application enables users to select the level of security for the specific device they are using to connect to the corporate network. Security levels will differ from one computing device to another based on the device features and usage profile of the user. To this effect, MyDevice will use services such as Location, Connectivity and Logging. For instance, one user may use his laptop and smartphone mainly in the office but his iPad and iPod mainly out of the office.

The laptop is mostly used for processing power intensive usage such as creating and editing documents, running and installing applications while the iPad is used primarily to read documents as well as to read and write emails. The iPad may be used for Wi- Fi access to his corporate emails. This information could be recorded in his corporate user profile along with identifiers of all the devices he/she uses. This can allow single sign-on with his corporate user credentials on all devices. The security level for a device will be defined in terms of various services such as Location, Connectivity, and Logging.

The Location service recognizes whether the user is in a trusted familiar environment (e.g. home, office, regular coffee shop) and adjusts the security features accordingly. In an unknown location, security will be tighter (e.g. 2- step authentication) and geo-location data will only be sent to authorized recipients.

The Logging service keeps a record of the user's activity and the data stored on the device that is not linked to any application (e.g. multimedia le, software and hardware identifiers). This is used to specify the level of security for the user data according to the selected device (e.g. encryption of transmitted data). This is also applicable to the SIM card data. If one SIM card is transferred from one device to another, security policies applicable to this device can be enforced on the SIM card as well.

The Connectivity service specifies the security level required based on the connection channel used (e.g. 3G, Wi-Fi or VPN). For instance, accessing the corporate network from a public non-encrypted Wi-Fi access point will require tighter controls than access through a more secure VPN.

My Failure Prevention App

This application will monitor the service consumed to detect unsafe events and situations that can lead to a failure. The application will use the Logging service to log such events and any associated data for a possible future root cause analysis and to prevent the recurrence of such events. An example of such an event, referred to as a near miss, is the near exhaustion of critical resources (e.g. memory or battery power). The user will have the choice to specify a near miss threshold that indicates how close the near miss is to cause a failure to generate an alert (Bihina Bella, Olivier & Eloff, 2012).

This app can also be used to prevent misuse of the business service by creating a service profile. The service profile specifies how the business service is normally used by the average user. It can thus help detect suspicious activity that deviates significantly from the normal usage pattern and which can indicate that the service is being misused. The profile will provide information such as the average spending and the usual time and duration of the service usage.

My Cloud App

My Cloud app uses the cloud infrastructure to deliver security services to customers and other cloud service providers. This is referred to as Security as a Service (SECaaS) (Cloud Security Alliance, 2011). SECaaS is defined as the on-demand provisioning of cloud-based security services either to hosted cloud infrastructure and software or to clients on premise private systems (Cloud Security Alliance, 2011). My Cloud leverages a cloud-based model to deliver security service-based offerings which include end point protection, on-demand transparency-enhancing technology, identity as a service, risk-based authentication etc.

Cloud-based end point protection leverages the SECaaS model to provide cost effective anti-virus and anti-spyware services to all types of end point devices (desktop, laptops, tablets and smartphones) that each user employs when connecting to corporate resources. This service also maintains and manages all updates to each of these end points.

On-demand transparency-enhancing technology leverages the auditing and logging capability of cloud based systems. It provides customers with a clear indication of all the data centers where their data is hosted and/or replicated and who is accessing it and for what purposes. The customers can query their cloud service providers for the exact location of where their data sits at any particular time. And they could also query the cloud service provider for all access to their resources within a given time period, for example over the past 12 months. Providing the customer with such transparency can help ensure that customer data can only be stored in data centers in approved geographical locations. The cloud security app will help solve most of the jurisdictional compliance challenges.

Nowadays, organizations are faced with a workforce that is highly mobile. This type of a workforce constantly require access to corporate resources from wherever they are (on-premise or hosted), at all times, from any location, using a plethora of devices (Dlamini, Venter, Eloff, & Mitha, 2012). This raises concerns on how to keep corporate resources available to only those who must have access. How to ensure that the right people, systems, and end point devices have the necessary access privileges to both on-premise and hosted cloud services. Cloud computing through Identity as a Service (IDaaS) presents a platform that does exactly that. It decouples the provisioning, de-provisioning, maintaining and managing users from the apps. This app provides digital identity as a service. IDaaS provides an API that authenticates users from different directories (e.g. Active Directory, LDAP or Web Service) on cloud-based apps and supports cross-domain authentication.

My Social Network App

My Social Network app monitors and manages all social media accounts of a user from one place. This app offers social network Single Sign-On portal. You sign-in on one Social Network and gain access to everything you need. For a first time user, he/she will register once and then choose from a wide pool of all the social networks that he/she wishes to gain access to. The app will then use the provided registration information to register the user on all the other social network sites. For those users who are already registered with different Social Networks and have different credentials, this app integrates all their accounts and put them under one umbrella called My Social Network app. The user can use this app to log on supplying it with his/her credentials for one Social Network where he/she is registered e.g. Facebook and then gain access to all his/her social media accounts.

This app use federated identity to authenticate the user only once and then share the credentials in assertions across all registered Social Networks. It provides the user in real-time with all the RSS feed updates happening in all of the social networks where he/she is registered, all in one place. This app ensures that the users are no longer required to manage multiple user accounts for multiple Social Networks. When the user logs out of the My Social Network app it automatically logs him/her out in all of the social networks.

Furthermore, this app uses a mobile devices built-in GPS to determine a user's location at any given time. After picking the user's location, it then scans the friend lists on each of his/her registered social media accounts to see if any one of them is in the same area. It then notifies the user of all friends who are within his/her vicinity giving their distance, time it will take to reach them, a detailed route plan and a good restaurant where they could meet and have coffee after a day's long work.

The Services Layer

In this layer, loosely coupled (but interoperable) security services required for consumption by apps in the application layer are available. These services should be designed in such a way that they can be consumed, depending on the needs of the user within the context of selecting an appropriate business app. For example it will not make sense for a security service such as authentication to be used by the MyDevice app in that it is supporting an application as opposed to a device. Therefore, although services in this layer are loosely coupled, interoperability will only be applicable amongst those services that are deemed to be interoperable according to security standards at both hardware and software levels. We briefly describe a selected number of services in this layer along the following lines.

3rd Party Security API (Gateway)

This service is a specialized service required for interaction with a 3rd party application. In order to facilitate integration with other third party applications foreign to the platform, a range of API would be necessary for facilitating such interactions. This justifies the presence of this specialized service that is made available for ensuring that there is no breach in the security of the application being invoked outside the platform. Equally, third party applications would also want to prevent any security breach in their system, hence the importance of this specialized service in the platform.

Furthermore, the monitoring of operation in the platform might be necessary if such a service has not yet been implemented in the platform. This is equally true when some forensic tools are required for enforcing the security in the platform should a breach arise. Hence the importance of the 3rd party gateway that is used for interaction with other security services not yet available in the platform.

Trust

The Trust service is an important security service that has the function of providing a truster with information that will assist in determining whether the trustee can be trusted. Such information would be derived from past experiences as well as the trustees reputation according the general public or community, based on the trust model used. This service would make use of existing data, feedback from users, 3rd party data, and social position to determine the trustworthiness of stakeholders in the iYP ecosystem. This Trust service would be consumed by apps such as My-Business and MySocialNetwork, where personal relationships and business collaborations are established. For example, a user of the BiYP application, wrapped with the MyBusiness security app, would like to collaborate with another user, for business purposes. The collaboration could be in the form of bulk-buying, selling products on credit, or customer recommendations.

The MyBusiness app would be able to provide trust ratings and recommendations to the parties involved through the use of the Trust service, therefore facilitating trustworthy collaborations. Similarly, the MySocial-Network security app could consume the Trust services functionality to facilitate trusting personal relationships.

The 3rd Party Layer

This layer is the extension of the API services gateways mentioned above. But the layer is physically situated in the service providers' environment (e.g. suppliers, banks, etc.) and has the purpose of uploading and/or receiving information from the specialized API services in the third layer, for further processing. In summary, the service model forms the basis for the decision of an appropriate generic cloud-based technical infrastructure required for implementing and deploying the SiYP platform. However, discussions on the architectural model are beyond the scope of this paper.

CONCLUSION AND FUTURE WORK

The Security-in-Your-Pocket (SiYP) platform is innovative in the sense that it provides a user-centric approach towards the personalization of security services with specific reference to mobility within cloud infrastructures. SiYP, as discussed in this paper, also highlights the acute need for new security services that will support apps such as MyBusiness, MyDevice, and the like. Interesting examples of such services, amongst others, include a Transparency service and a Trust service. Future work will focus on the construction and usability aspects of the proposed SiYP platform.

ACKNOWLEDGMENT

The support of SAP Research Pretoria and Meraka CSIR towards this research is hereby acknowledged. Opinions expressed and conclusions arrived at are those of the authors and not necessarily to be attributed to the companies mentioned in this acknowledgement.

REFERENCES

Balachandra, R. K., Ramakrishna, P. V., & Rakshit, A. (2009). Cloud Security Issues. In *Proceedings of the Services Computing* (pp. 517-520). Bangalore, India: IEEE.

Bihina Bella, M. A., Eloff, J. H. P., & Olivier, M. S. (2009). A fraud management system architecture for next-generation networks. *Forensic Science International, 185*(1-3), 51–58. doi:10.1016/j. forsciint.2008.12.013 PMID:19168299

Bihina Bella, M. A., Olivier, M. S., & Eloff, J. H. P. (2012). Near miss Detection for Software Failure Prevention. In *Proceedings of the Southern African Telecommunication Networks and Applications Conference* (SATNAC 2012) (pp. 165-170). George, South Africa: Telkom.

Bullingera, H., Fhnrichb, K., & Meirena, T. (2003). Service engineering methodical development of new service products. *International Journal of Production Economics, 85*(3), 275–287. doi:10.1016/S0925-5273(03)00116-6

Chetty, J., & Coetzee, M. (2011). Information Security for Service Oriented Computing: Ally or Antagonist. In *Proceedings of the Availability, Reliability and Security conference (ARES)* (pp. 460-465). Vienna: IEEE.

Christiansen, C. A. (2008). *Innovation and Security: Collaborative or Combative*. International Data Corporation (IDC) White Paper. Retrieved from http://www.techrepublic.com

Cloud Security Alliance. (2011). SecaaS: Defined categories of Service. Retrieved from https://cloudsecurityalliance.org

Cuppens, F., Cuppens-Boulahia, N., & Ghorbel, M. B. (2007). High level conflict management strategies in advanced access control models. *Electronic Notes in Theoretical Computer Science, 186*, 3-26.

Dlamini, M. T., Venter, H. S., Eloff, J. H. P., & Mitha, Y. (2012). Authentication in the Cloud: A Risk-based Approach. In *Proceedings of the Southern African Telecommunication Networks and Applications Conference* (SATNAC 2012) (pp. 469-478). George, South Africa: Telkom.

Huang, Y., Ma, X., & Li, D. (2010). Research and Application of Enterprise Search Based on Database Security Services. In *Proceedings of the Second International Symposium on Networking and Network Security* (ISNNS '10) (pp. 238-241). China: Academy Publisher.

ISO 7498-2. (1989). *Information processing systems Open systems Interconnection Basic Reference Model Part 2: Security architecture.*

Josang, A., Ismail, R., & Boyd, C. (2007). A Survey of Trust and Reputation Systems for Online Service Provision. *Decision Support Systems, 34*, 618–644. doi:10.1016/j.dss.2005.05.019

Leavitt, N. (2011). Mobile Security: Finally a Serious Problem? *Computer, 44*(6), 11–14. doi:10.1109/MC.2011.184

Lin, X. (2011). Survey on cloud based mobile security and a new framework for improvement. In *Proceedings of the International Conference on Information and Automation* (ICIA) (pp. 710-715). Shenzen: IEEE.

Masnick, M. (2011). Innovation. In Security: It's All About Trust. Retrieved from http://www.techdirt.com

Oberheide, J., & Jahanian, F. (2010). When mobile is harder than fixed (and vice versa): Demystifying security challenges in mobile environments. In *Proceedings of the Eleventh Workshop on Mobile Computing Systems & Applications* (pp. 43-48). Annapolis, MD: ACM.

OReilly, T. (2007). What Is Web 2.0: Design Patterns and Business Models for the Next Generation of Software. *Communications & Strategies, 1*, 1738.

Padayachee, K. (2010). *An aspect-oriented approach towards enhancing Optimistic Access control with Usage Control.* (PhD thesis). University of Pretoria, Pretoria, South Africa.

Proffitt, M. (2012). *The Oxford English Dictionary.* Oxford University Press.

Roth, S. (2009). New for whom? Initial images from the social dimension of innovation. *International Journal of Innovation and Sustainable Development, 4*, 231–252. doi:10.1504/IJISD.2009.033080

Ruan, K., Carthy, J., Kechadi, T., & Crosbie, M. (2011). Cloud Forensics. In Advances in Digital Forensics VII, (pp. 35-46). Orlando, FL: Springer.

Schumpeter, J. A. (1943). *Capitalism, Socialism, and Democracy.* Routledge.

Wang, J., Zhao, Y., Jiang, S., & Le, J. (2009). Providing Privacy Preserving in cloud computing. In *Proceedings of the International Conference on Test and Measurement* (pp.213-216). Hong Kong: IEEE.

Weinhardt, C., Anandasivam, A., Blau, B., & Stosser, J. (2009). Business Models in the Service World. *IT Professional, 11*(2), 28–33. doi:10.1109/MITP.2009.21

ADDITIONAL READING

Dinh, H. T., Lee, C., Niyato, D., & Wang, P. (2013). A survey of mobile cloud computing: architecture, applications, and approaches. *Wirel. Commun. Mob. Comput*, *13*, 1587–1611. doi:10.1002/wcm.1203

Fernando, N., Loke, S. W., & Rahayu, W. (2013). Mobile cloud computing: A survey. *Future Generation Computer Systems*, *29*(1), 84–106. doi:10.1016/j.future.2012.05.023

Garg, S. K., Versteeg, S., & Buyya, R. (2013). A framework for ranking of cloud computing services. *Future Generation Computer Systems*, *29*(4), 1012–1023. doi:10.1016/j.future.2012.06.006

Grobauer, B., Walloschek, T., & Stöcker, E. (2011). Understanding Cloud Computing Vulnerabilities. *IEEE Security & Privacy*, *9*(2), 50–57. doi:10.1109/MSP.2010.115

Huang, D. (2011). Mobile cloud computing. *IEEE COMSOC Multimedia Communications Technical Committee (MMTC). E-Letter*, *6*(10), 27–31.

Khan, A. N., Kiah, M. L., Khan, S. U., & Madani, S. A. (2013). Towards secure mobile cloud computing: A survey. *Future Generation Computer Systems*, *29*(5), 1278–1299. doi:10.1016/j.future.2012.08.003

Kshetri, N. (2013). Privacy and security issues in cloud computing: The role of institutions and institutional evolution. *Telecommunications Policy*, 373–386.

Li, L., Huang, D., Shen, Z., & Bouzefrane, S. (2013). A cloud based dual-root trust model for secure mobile online transactions. In *Proceedings of IEEE Wireless Communications and Networking Conference (WCNC): SERVICES & APPLICATIONS* (pp. 4404-4409). Shanghai, China: IEEE.

Subashini, S., & Kavitha, V. (2011). A survey on security issues in service delivery models of cloud computing, *Journal of Network and Computer Applications archive*, 34(1), 1-11.

Xiao, H., Ford, B., & Feigenbaum, J. (2013). Structural cloud audits that protect private information. In *Proceedings of ACM Cloud Computing Security Workshop* (pp. 101-112). Berlin, Germany: ACM.

Zhou, Z., & Huang, D. (2012). Efficient and secure data storage operations for mobile cloud computing. In *Proceedings of Network and Service Management conference* (pp. 37-45). Las Vegas, U.S.: IEEE.

Zissis, D., & Lekkas, D. (2012). Addressing cloud computing security issues. *Future Generation Computer Systems*, *28*(3), 583–592. doi:10.1016/j.future.2010.12.006

KEY TERMS AND DEFINITIONS

Cloud Computing: Is a model for enabling on-demand network access to a shared pool of configurable IT capabilities and resources (e.g., networks, servers, storage, applications, and services) that can be rapidly provisioned and released with minimal management effort or service provider interaction.

Cloud Computing Architecture: Refers to the components and subcomponents required for cloud computing. These components typically consist of a front end platform (fat client, thin client, mobile device), back end platforms (servers, storage), a cloud based delivery, and a network (Internet, Intranet, Intercloud). Combined, these components make up cloud computing architecture.

Cloud Service Provisioning: Is through three service delivery models (Cloud Software as a Service (SaaS), Cloud Platform as a Service (PaaS), and Cloud Infrastructure as a Service (IaaS)) (CNSSI, 4009)

Information Security: The protection of information and information systems from unauthorized access, use, disclosure, disruption, modification, or destruction in order to provide confidentiality, integrity, and availability. (CNSSI No. 4009)

Innovation: This is the process of bringing an idea to market as a real product, process, system or device that is commercially marketable involving new inventions. The process of translating an idea or invention into a good or service that creates value or for which customers will pay.

Mobile Cloud: Is Internet-based data, applications and related services accessed through smartphones, laptop computers, tablets and other portable devices.

Mobile Computing: Is a generic term used to refer to the use of a variety of mobile devices such as laptops, cell phones and tablets that allow people to access data and information from where ever they are.

Security Services: Are the capabilities that support one, or more, of the security requirements (Confidentiality, Integrity, Availability). Examples of security services are key management, access control, and authentication.

This research was previously published in Information Security in Diverse Computing Environments edited by Anne Kayem and Christoph Meinel, pages 303-315, copyright year 2014 by Information Science Reference (an imprint of IGI Global).

Chapter 13
Intelligent Techniques for Providing Effective Security to Cloud Databases

Ar Arunarani
Anna University, India

D Manjula Perkinian
Anna University, India

ABSTRACT

Cloud databases have been used in a spate of web-based applications in recent years owing to their capacity to store big data efficiently. In such a scenario, access control techniques implemented in relational databases are so modified as to suit cloud databases. The querying features of cloud databases are designed with facilities to retrieve encrypted data. The performance with respect to retrieval and security needs further improvements to ensure a secured retrieval process. In order to provide an efficient secured retrieval mechanism, a rule- and agent-based intelligent secured retrieval model has been proposed in this paper that analyzes the user, query and contents to be retrieved so as to effect rapid retrieval with decryption from the cloud databases. The major advantage of this retrieval model is in terms of its improved query response time and enhanced security of the storage and retrieval system. From the experiments conducted in this work, proposed model increased storage and access time and, in addition, intensified the security of the data stored in cloud databases.

INTRODUCTION

Cloud databases have provided efficient storage and retrieval services to cloud users in recent years. In such a scenario, the use of cloud databases to store transactions as well as machine-generated big data pertaining to organizations is gaining traction. Owing to the volume of growth, security attacks on cloud databases have also proliferated, culminating in a need for encrypted storage in cloud databases. In the past, researchers proposed new methods to retrieve encrypted data from relational databases. However,

DOI: 10.4018/978-1-5225-8176-5.ch013

retrieving encrypted data from cloud databases was not considered an important research challenge. In recent years, the volume of data stored in cloud databases has multiplied considerably, and big data analytic techniques are applied on such data to ascertain interesting patterns that can help organizations in decision making.

Storage structures used in relational databases, including the B-Tree and related indexing techniques, are unsuited to the storage and retrieval of cloud databases. A cloud database stores data in the form of key and value pairs in which the value can be represented as a vector so it is possible to provide a mapping between relational databases and the Not Only SQL (NoSQL) format of cloud databases. In relational databases, users are grouped into database administrators, application programmers, query language users and end users. Each is given a set of privileges that include the right to write, read, update, delete and insert records. Database administrators are provided the highest privileges and end users the least. The chief difference between transactions in relational databases and cloud databases is that the former insists on atomicity, consistency, isolation and durability (ACID) properties, while the latter insist on BASE properties.

Big data analytics and cloud databases are two major areas of research popular among researchers in the area of cloud computing. Big data grows at enormous speed with respect to velocity, variety and volume. Therefore, tackling the challenges of the growing quanta of data with respect to secured storage and retrieval is a key task to be undertaken so big data can be stored safely in cloud databases and retrieved just as easily. The existing query languages for relational databases provide only a facility to retrieve records which are not encrypted. Certain recent works attempted to provide a facility to retrieve encrypted data from relational databases through a query language in which new keywords were introduced to enhance the SELECT statement feature of the Structured Query Language (SQL). Moreover, the GRANT and REVOKE commands of the SQL have been used to perform access control in relational databases. However, cloud databases lack such facilities and hence secured storage and retrieval call for greater attention.

In this paper, a new querying model based on a query generator through a user interface which provides an integrated feature for storage and retrieval, along with access control techniques to store data in an encrypted form and retrieve them in a decrypted form, is proposed. The query generator allows for query creation through a user interface in which database objects and user requirements can be specified either using English words or SQL queries. These queries, converted by the proposed system into cloud database queries, are executed by the cloud databases themselves. Validation is provided by the system, during database creation and insertion of new records, through the use of rules. Given that the rules systems validate tasks, the cloud database manager is relieved of the business of verifying integrity and security. In addition, authentication is carried out based on user credentials and queries. Intelligent agents are deployed in each cloud network site so the distributed cloud database system is able to coordinate and perform storage and retrieval operations - in encrypted form for storage and decrypted form for retrieval - with different types of cryptographic algorithms used for the effectual encryption of data. In this model, the Caesar cipher is used to store ordinary data, while the Advanced Encryption Standard (AES)-based encryption is used to store and retrieve valuable user data and, finally, the RSA algorithm is utilized to store the confidential data that can be accessed only by managers. The primary advantage of the proposed model is that it classifies users, data and queries suitably by applying rules and makes intelligent decisions with respect to fast and secured storage and retrieval.

The remainder of the paper is organized as follows: Section 2 discusses the related work on access control, encrypted storage and retrieval techniques and querying. Section 3 depicts the architecture of the proposed intelligent storage and retrieval model for cloud databases. Section 4 explains the proposed work. Section 5 shows the results obtained from the experiments conducted in this work and discusses them. Section 7 concludes the work and suggests possible future developments.

RELATED WORK

Access control technology for web and cloud databases has become a crucial area of research in recent years, with a number of researchers contributing ideas and work in the literature in this area. Of these, Damiani et al. (2000) proposed a new access control technique for web databases. On the other hand, several researchers including Damiani et al. (2002) and Bhatti et al. (2003) suggested new methods for access control to web documents by providing new rules for restricting access directly on both the schema and content of web documents. Nevertheless, most of these studies have focused more on securing web databases rather than cloud databases. Huang et al. (2006) advanced new access control policies for web databases that used regular path expressions to specify database objects for applying access control policies. Their work is better suited to providing access control to web databases that use XML-based queries. Mohan et al. (2006) propositioned a model for access control to secure web documents by specifying access constraints that enforce access privileges using query rewrite operations.

He et al. (2000) recommended a new type of Role-based Access Control (RBAC) model to provide secured web information management. In this access control scheme, it is necessary to provide a path to access information. This scheme is more appropriate for web databases and hence can be extended to service cloud database environments. Liu et al. (2005) submitted a new access control model based on an analysis of applications to assess access control requirements for web applications. They discussed the limitations of current access control models for web services and proposed a new attribute-based RBAC model for web applications. He et al. (2006) proposed a new web security model by implementing the RBAC in a web services environment. Their work focused more on applying RBAC policies to protect e-learning applications. In spite of these, researchers in this area have proposed no complete access control model for cloud databases yet. Moreover, the inclusion of rules and spatio-temporal constraints intelligently handled by intelligent agents can be most effective at securing cloud databases.

Sandhu et al. (1996) presented a type of RBAC model based on users, roles and operations. Interest in the RBAC has led to the use of roles at the application level to control access through applications that use web data. Li et al. (2006) offered new security methods to maintain a desirable level of security by assigning privileges. Barker[19] introduced a generalized RBAC model called the Action Status Access Control model for web database security, built on an automatic changing of access control policies based on events as triggers. Further, the authors provided implementation details for their model and evaluated it using performance metrics. Bertino et al. (2001) put forward a Temporal-RBAC (TRBAC) model by providing temporal extensions to the RBAC. The principal advantage of this model is that it supports dynamic enabling/disabling of roles and actions using events and triggers. The use of triggers in this model enhanced its decision-making control using intelligent production rules.

Joshi et al. (2005) projected a new TRBAC model with the use of temporal constraints for role assignment. It also allows the addition of a new set of temporal constraints at any time. Cui et al. (2007)

presented an Extended RBAC by appending identity and integrity constraints for a mobile environment, alongside new assignment rules for handling privileges and roles. Vijayalakshmi et al. (2007) introduced an effective location-dependent query processing algorithm to access information in distributed mobile database environments using mobile agents. Li et al. (2010) made a comparative analysis of the action-based access control model with the other existing access control models and proved that the former is better for distributed systems. Zhou et al. (2015) advocated a new trust model to secure stored data in cloud database systems. Their trust model provides a facility for the owners and roles to decide on the trustworthiness of individual roles for users. The authors presented a security model that shows how trust models are integrated with cryptographic access control schemes. The foremost advantage of this model is that it helps provide security to cloud databases.

Jung et al. (2015) presented a semi-anonymous privilege control scheme to address data privacy and user identity privacy in the existing access control schemes. Muthurajkumar et al. (2015) developed a cloud security model using transaction logs. According to these authors, log management is a key activity in the cloud. In any cloud-based database application, the real challenge lies in the maintenance of log records securely over an interval of time. Besides, such a log is both helpful for recovery operations and maintaining integrity, security and effective audits. They divided their work into different phases, each identified by a time interval. They proposed a new algorithm for the log-based recovery of transactions in cloud databases that maintains log records in tandem with the history of data records. They use cryptographic encryption and decryption techniques to store data with the kind of security in which keys are generated using primary key attributes and temporal information. Their temporal model for log management is a new contribution in the area of cloud database recovery with security. In addition, their model is more powerful than the role-based access control model, since they use keys with the time interval as a component for encryption and decryption.

Yao et al. (2015) propounded a lightweight cipher text sharing scheme that uses an anonymous authorization credential to simplify access control, ensure user anonymity and support decryption key reconstruction. Baig et al. (2016) proffered a novel and reactive approach based on a rate limit technique, with low overhead, to detect and mitigate EDoS attacks against cloud-based services. Through this reactive scheme, limited access permission for cloud services is granted to each user. Liu et al. (2014) posited a new scheme called the k-times attribute-based anonymous access control, particularly designed for supporting a cloud environment. They also provide a k-times limit for anonymous access control. That is, the server may limit a particular set of users from accessing the system for a maximum k-times within a period or an event. Zhou et al. (2015) proposed new trust models to reason about and improve security for stored data in cloud storage systems that use cryptographic RBAC schemes. The trust models provide an approach for owners and roles to determine the trustworthiness of individual roles and users, respectively, in the RBAC system. Their trust models consider role inheritance and hierarchy in the evaluation of the trustworthiness of roles. They present a design of a trust-based cloud storage system, showing how trust models can be integrated into a system that uses cryptographic RBAC schemes. They also considered practical application scenarios and illustrated how trust evaluations can be used to reduce risks, enhance the quality of decision-making by data owners and underscore the role of cloud storage services.

Ficco et al. (2015) suggested a strategy to orchestrate stealthy attack patterns, which exhibit a slowly-increasing intensity trend designed to inflict the maximum financial cost to the cloud customer, while respecting the job size and service arrival rate imposed by detection mechanisms. They described how to apply the proposed strategy and deliberated on its effects on the target system deployed in the cloud.

Mehmood et al. (2015) advanced a unique security scheme called the Distributed Intrusion Detection System using Mobile Agents in Cloud Computing (DIDMACC) to detect distributed intrusions in the cloud. They used mobile agents to carry out intrusion alerts from consumer virtual machines to the management server where the correlation takes place. Their system can detect intrusions on virtual machines, identify vulnerable ports, and correlate malicious events to detect distributed intrusions in a cloud-based network. Mobile agents are used to update the signature database at the virtual machines being monitored. Mobile agents, being lightweight and flexible software programs, reduce the network load by carrying the intrusion-related data and code. Their scheme provides a scalable and robust intrusion detection system, which is a key requirement for cloud networks.

Ye. (2016) propositioned a scheme that allows cloud users to delegate their access permission to other users easily so as to facilitate resource sharing. Their scheme uses cryptographic techniques to obscure access control policies and users' credentials to ensure the privacy of cloud users. They used data encryption to guarantee the confidentiality of the data. Ma et al. (2016) identified certain error in the existing anonymous attribute-based encryption scheme which calculates the system-wide master key. The attribute-based encryption scheme focused on data content privacy and access control with limited attention being paid to problems with privilege control and privacy identification. Liu et al. (2016) introduced a new fine-grained two-factor authentication access control system for web-based cloud computing services. Specifically, their system was based on an attribute-based access control mechanism implemented with both a user secret key and a lightweight security device. Their system enables the cloud server to restrict access to users with the same set of attributes, while still preserving user privacy.

A lot of work on intrusion detection for cloud security is found in the literature reviewed. Among these, Mansour et al. (2010) recommended a machine learning-based method called the Growing Hierarchical Self-Organized Map for effective intrusion detection in the cloud. Their system reduces false positive and false negative rates significantly for enhanced security. Hussain et al. (2013) submitted anew anomaly-based intrusion detection system using soft computing techniques for virtual machines on cloud computing. Their model is best-suited to cloud environments.

Baig et al. (2013) offered a new intrusion detection system which classifies network data into normal and abnormal groups using two types of techniques, monolithic and ensemble-based, for intrusion detection. Louvieris et al. (2013) put forward an intrusion detection technique which detects attack networks by identifying their contributory features. Elbasiony et al. (2013) projected a new network intrusion detection system using the random forests algorithm, which detects insider and outsider attacks, for classification. Koc et al. (2012) used the Naive Bayes classifier in their work on the detection of Denial-of-Services (DoS) attacks.

Hasani et al. (2014) introduced a new wrapper-based model built on genetic programming and the bees algorithm for a feature selection algorithm to build an IDS. Kim et al. (2014) advocated a new hybrid intrusion detection model capable of finding misuse and anomaly intrusions. Xiao et al. (2013) systematically presented security and privacy issues in cloud computing and identified the most representative security/privacy attributes for cloud security. They also discussed attacks and prevention models for cloud data security. Ganapathy et al. (2013) surveyed the use of techniques from artificial intelligence and soft computing for effective feature selection and better classification to develop efficient intrusion detection systems to be deployed in computer networks. Their survey focused on different areas of artificial intelligence such as intelligent agents, neural classifiers, genetic algorithm-based classification, neuro-genetic modeling for classification, the use of fuzzy logic and rough sets to handle uncertainty in classification, and the application of particle swarm optimization to develop intelligent intrusion detection systems. According to them, the proposed techniques collected from different studies are of use in effectively identifying attacks and preventing network intrusions. Their survey, which focuses on the existing models in the IDS, provided suggestions on improving performance by proposing a new model. Yan et al. (2016) explained the causes for Distributed Denial of Service (DDoS) attacks and their growth in cloud computing environments. In addition, they discussed the sound features of the Software Defined Networking (SDN)-based cloud for preventing DDoS attacks. Ahmadian et al. (2017) introduced a descriptive language-based notation, a new tool to create and parse a security plan comprising cryptographic modules, data elements and mappings of cryptographic methods to data fields, alongside the introduction of a query and data validation mechanism based on the security plan. Sharma et al. (2016) propounded a new security framework to manage and detect a range of cloud intrusions. Eric Totel et al. (2016) demonstrated the possibility of a distributed cloud application behaviour model for intrusion detection, relying only on a partial ordering of events.

SYSTEM ARCHITECTURE

The overall architecture of the proposed system is shown in Figure 1. It comprises nine major components: a user interface module, query generator, cloud database manager, rule manager, rule base, cloud database, agent system, storage and retrieval sub-system and security sub-system. The user interface module collects the necessary user queries from the user and forwards them to the query generator. If the user is not familiar with writing XML and SQL queries, the user interface calls the query generator to provide assistance in generating a query. The query generator checks the available database objects and the constraints on them using the cloud database manager and is able to provide the user details of the data available. However, the cloud database manager validates user credentials with the security manager before providing users details about database objects. The agent system creates intelligent agents and deploys them at each cloud network site to undertake communication and coordination during transaction processing. For this purpose, it uses the intelligent rules stored in the rule base through the cloud database manager.

Figure 1. System architecture

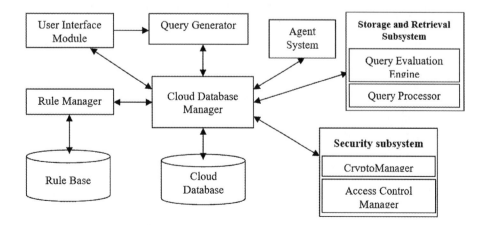

The overall control of the proposed system is with the cloud database manager, which interacts with all the eight components responsible for query generation, validation, security checking and query processing. The rule manager performs rule firing, rule matching and rule execution tasks to maintain integrity and security. It manipulates the rule base by adding new rules, modifying existing rules and deleting unused rules. The rule base comprises IF...THEN rules created and maintained by the rule manager. The cloud database consists of indexes, keys and values with validation rules so that it retains only valid data. The storage and retrieval subsystem consists of two major components: a query evaluation engine and a query processor. The query evaluation engine parses the query, optimizes it and checks for the presence of indexes. The query processor executes the query and performs data definition or data manipulation operations, based on the user's query. The security subsystem is responsible for providing secured storage and retrieval techniques after discussions with the cloud database manager. Finally, the cloud security subsystem consists of a module for access control checking and another module for managing encryption and decryption activities.

PROPOSED WORK

The proposed system has been implemented with Amazon cloud and MangoDB databases along with Java programming language, Java. To this end, Anna University's student database has been utilized to collect data, and is indexed with the system's owner so as to monitor security. The central contribution of this paper is in a user interface design with a query generator facility on the user's side. The query generation module validates the user, based on his HELLO message. Once validated, the user's credentials - including password setting for application systems - are used with the permission of the administrator to store the data collected from different users and other components of the database system.

The query generator approaches the cloud database manager to start a transaction, and the latter calls the intelligent agent system to create independent agents to be deployed at different cloud network sites. The user query is analyzed by the query evaluation engine and the query is transformed into an optimized query, executed by the query processor. Before executing the query, the cloud database manager calls the security subsystem where access permissions for the user are checked by the access control manager. In addition, the crypto manager decides the type of algorithm to be used for encryption and decryption, based on the nature of the data, which is analyzed for user details and query contents. Finally, the results obtained from the query execution are forwarded to the cloud database manager for final validation and transfer to the user interface.

Query Generation

User queries are in the form of natural language or an XML / SQL formats. The queries are subjected to a syntax analysis and divided into tokens. For example, the query, "Find the details of all employees in Anna University, Chennai" is divided into tokens, as follows:

- Find - Verb
- The - Determiner
- Details - Object
- Of - Preposition

- All employees - Noun phrase
- In - Preposition
- Anna University, Chennai - Noun phrase

For all these tokens in a natural language format, a dictionary is maintained so that their validity can be checked. For an SQL query such as "SELECT * FROM EMPLOYEES", the tokens are:

- SELECT - Keyword
- * - All attributes
- FROM - Keyword
- EMPLOYEES - Table name

A similar type of query analysis is carried out for XML queries as well. The queries are checked for syntax, based on the grammar developed for all types of queries. The syntax analyzer checks the query by carrying out a left-most derivation of the query using the bottom-up parsing algorithm, LALR. Intelligent agents are created by launching a CREATE AGENT command to create a root agent which finds network sites, and is helped by the cloud database manager to create a number of intelligent agents. Each agent is deployed at a particular site of the cloud network.

Access Control

The access control technique is used both implicitly and explicitly. The implicit access control procedure is given by the access control matrix shown in Table 1.

Based on Table 1, it is observed that the DBA has the highest level of privileges and the end user the least. Each query is subjected to access control for the user providing the query.

Encryption and Decryption

For encryption and decryption, the keys are first generated. To this end, user details and the type of data accessed by the said user are analysed. Caesar cryptography is used for simple types of data with the encryption formula $C = (P + K) \bmod 26$ for encryption and $P = (C-K) \bmod 26$ for decryption, with the value of $K = 3$ where P is the plain text, C is the cipher text. If the contents are medium-level important, the AES algorithm is used to carry out symmetric encryption. Here, the first-round key is generated by running a random number generator algorithm to generate a 128-bit random number, known only to the

Table 1. Access control matrix

User Level/ Privileges	CREATE	SELECT	INSERT	DELETE	UPDATE	GRANT/ REVOKE	USER MANAGEMENT
DBA	Yes	Yes	Yes	Yes	Yes	Yes	Yes
Query developer	Yes	Yes	Yes	Yes	Yes	No	No
Application programmer	Yes	Yes	Yes	Yes	Yes	Yes	No
End user	No	Yes	No	No	No	No	No

person storing the data. Therefore, when the user wants to retrieve the data in decrypted form he must provide the key along with the query. The key, already stored in the cloud database, can be verified by the cloud database manager. Finally, the RSA algorithm is used to store the most important data in encrypted form. Here, two prime numbers, P & Q, are generated by the cloud database manager and communicated to the cryptographic manager. The cryptographic manager generates a public key for the database manager, along with a private key for the owner of the data, and the RSA algorithm is used for both encryption and decryption during storage and retrieval.

Query Processing

In the query processing algorithm, the query processor decomposes the query into a number of sub queries and each is given to an intelligent agent present in the relevant site of the cloud network. These intelligent agents perform data manipulation operations at their own site and despatch the result to the coordinator agent, which applies the rules and checks the validity of the results and transfers them to the query processor. The root agent present in the query processor performs decryption, helped by the cryptographic manager, and finally provides the query results to the user using directions from the cloud database manager.

For retrieval, the distributed access plan algorithm is as follows:

- **Input** : User query
- **Output:** Query access plan
- Algorithm Access_Plan (Key, value, query, user)
- Begin
- Create root_agent (Site 1).
- For each site i varying from 1 to n, do
- Begin
- Create sub_agent (site[i]).
- Check_level (User, database, algorithm).
- Read data (DB_name, query, content).
- Decrypt (Key).
- Return (Records).
- End
- //   Collect results from each site.
- Segment = NULL
- For i = 1 to n, do
- Begin
- Segment = Segment U records[i].
- Convert_format (User).
- End
- Return results to the cloud database manager.
- End

Similar to retrieval, a distributed processing algorithm is developed for each operation carried out on the database including database creation, insertion, deletion and updates.

Rule Management Algorithm

The rule management algorithm is used to perform rule firing, rule matching and rule execution. Rules are used for user authentication, data validation and maintenance of integrity. The steps of the rule management algorithm are as follows:

- **Input**   : Rules
- **Output**: Constraints obtained from rules in the IF part of the rule
- Step 1: Read rules R1, R2 … Rn, relevant to the particular operation.
- Step 2: For each rule Ri, perform the following:
  o 2. a) Divide IF and THEN parts of the rule separately.
  o 2. b) Check for rule conflicts.
  o 2. c) Find rule priorities.
  o 2. d) Check for rule chaining.
  o 2. e) Check for rule exceptions.
- Step 3: Constraints = Union of results from 2a to 2e.
- Step 4: Return constraints to the rule manager.

Query Matching Algorithm

- **Input**: Query constraints and data records
- **Output**: Matched constraints
- Step 1: Read the query constraints.
- Step 2: Read the first data record.
- Step 3: While not EOR, do
  o Begin
  ▪ Apply constraint1.
  ▪ If constraint satisfied, then
  ▪ return.
  ▪ Else
  ▪ Apply constraints2, 3… etc., one by one.
  ▪ If constraint satisfied, then
  ▪ return.
  ▪ Else
  ▪ Read the next record.
  o End
- Step 4: Return failure.

Rule Execution Algorithm

- **Input**   : Rules and constraints
- **Output**: Validated query results
- Step 1: Read the results from the rule firing and rule matching algorithms.

- Step 2: Form a discrimination network.
- Step 3: Apply the constraints.
- Step 4: Retrieve the data or perform data manipulation.
- Step 5: Consolidate the results.
- Step 6: Send the results to the cloud database manager.

In this model, the query is given to the cloud database manager by the query generator or user interface. Next, the query is forwarded to the security manager and the rule manager for checking integrity and security. Finally, the query evaluation engine evaluates the query and executes it. The distributed access plan is used to execute the query. The rule firing, rule matching and rule execution algorithms are used to check integrity and security constraints most effectively.

RESULTS AND DISCUSSION

The experiments were carried out with Anna University's faculty information system, student information system and administrative information system databases, alongside business applications such as the sale of books, mobiles, computers and food. The results obtained on these applications are discussed in this section.

Figure 2 shows the security analysis based on the cryptographic methods proposed in this model and the use of other cryptographic encryption provided in the existing models.

From Figure 2, it is observed that the performance of the proposed system is better, when compared with the other existing ones. This is largely due to the use of effective multiple cryptographic methods and intelligent rules.

Figure 3 depicts the access control analysis of access control for user-level data management when the applications were executed using cryptographic methods, log management techniques and the proposed algorithm.

Figure 2. Security analysis

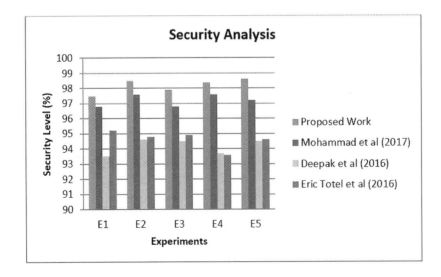

Figure 3. Access control analysis

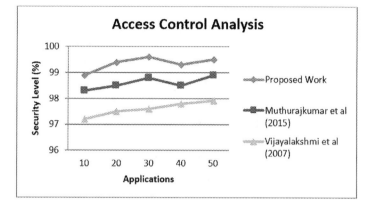

From Figure 3, it is noticed that the security level of the database log maintenance is higher when compared to the role-based access control model used in the existing database management systems. This is owing to the fact that the existing relational databases follow the access control hierarchy based on user roles. The proposed algorithm, on the other hand, considers user roles as well as trust values, key values and application types for enhanced security.

Figure 4 shows the query processing time analysis for the proposed system. We have used different types of queries to evaluate the proposed system by conducting five different experiments.

From Figure 4, it is seen that the performance of the proposed system, in terms of response time, is above 99 milliseconds for all the experiments with different kinds of queries.

Figure 5 shows a comparative analysis between the proposed system with rules and without. The proposed system is a combination of two methods, access control and encryption.

Figure 5 makes it clear that the performance of the proposed system with rules is better than the one without. This is because of the use of intelligent rules that reduce the time taken for executing different types of queries.

Figure 4. Query processing time analysis

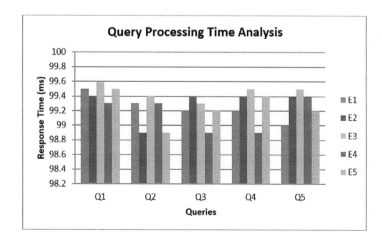

Figure 5. Comparative analysis

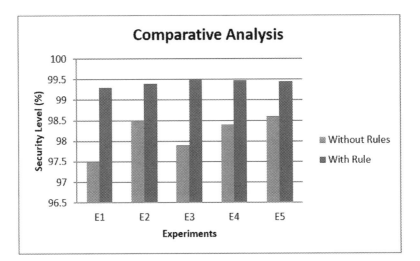

CONCLUSION

This paper analyzed the user, query and contents retrieved to enable fast retrieval with decryption from cloud databases. The proposed retrieval model improved query response time and enhanced the security level of the storage and retrieval system. The experimental results demonstrated that the performance of the proposed model, in terms of response time and security level, is superior. It reduces response time for query processing and increases the systems. Security level. Further work in this direction can incorporate the inclusion of security-proof methods that use mathematical analyses to provide effective methods for cloud security.

REFERENCES

Ahmadian, M., Plochan, F., Roessler, Z., & Marinescu, D. C. (2017). Secure NoSQL: An approach for secure search of encrypted NoSQL databases in the public cloud. *International Journal of Information Management, 37*(2), 63–74. doi:10.1016/j.ijinfomgt.2016.11.005

Anand, K., Ganapathy, S., Kulothungan, K., Yogesh, P., & Kannan, A. (2012). A rule based approach for attribute selection and intrusion detection in wireless sensor networks. *Procedia Engineering, 38,* 1658–1664. doi:10.1016/j.proeng.2012.06.202

Baig, Z. A., Sait, S. M., & Binbeshr, F. (2016). Controlled access to cloud resources for mitigating Economic Denial of Sustainability (EDoS) attacks. *Computer Networks, 97,* 31–47. doi:10.1016/j.comnet.2016.01.002

Baig, Z. A., Sait, S. M., & Shaheen, A. R. (2013). GMDH-Based networks for intelligent intrusion detection. *Engineering Applications of Artificial Intelligence, 26*(7), 1731–1740. doi:10.1016/j.engappai.2013.03.008

Barker, S. (2008). Access Control by Action Control. *Proceedings of the 13th ACM Symposium on Access Control Models and Technologies (SAGMAT)* (pp. 143-152). 10.1145/1377836.1377858

Barsoum, A., & Hasan, A. (2013). Enabling Dynamic Data and Indirect Mutual Trust for Cloud Computing Storage Systems. *IEEE Transactions on Parallel and Distributed Systems*, 24(12), 2375–2385. doi:10.1109/TPDS.2012.337

Berger, S., Caceres, R., Goldman, K., Pendarakis, D., Perez, R., Rao, J. R., ... Valdez, E. (2009). Security for the cloud infrastructure: Trusted virtual data center implementation. *IBM Journal of Research and Development*, 53(4), 1–12. doi:10.1147/JRD.2009.5429060

Bertino, E., Bonatti, P. A., & Ferrari, E. (2001). TRBAC: A Temporal Role-Based Access Control Model. *ACM Transactions on Information and System Security*, 4(3), 191–233. doi:10.1145/501978.501979

Bhatti, R., Joshi, J. B. D., Bertino, E., & Ghafoor, A. (2003). Access Control in Dynamic XML-Based Web-Services with XRBAC. *Proceedings of the First International Conference on Web Services*, Las Vegas (pp. 23-26).

Cui, X., Chen, Y., & Gu, J. (2007). Ex-RBAC: An Extended Role Based Access Control Model for Location-Aware Mobile Collaboration System. *Proceedings of Second International Conference on Internet Monitoring and Protection* (pp. 36-41). 10.1109/ICIMP.2007.17

Damiani, E., Vimercati, S. C., Paraboschi, S., & Samarati, P. (2000). Securing XML Documents. *Proceedings of the International Conference on Extending Database Technology* (pp. 121-135).

Damiani, E., Vimercati, S. C., Paraboschi, S., & Samarati, P. (2002). A Fine-Grained Access Control System for XML Documents. *ACM Transactions on Information and System Security*, 5(2), 169–202. doi:10.1145/505586.505590

Elbasiony, R. M., Sallam, E. A., Eltobely, T. E., & Fahmy, M. M. (2013). A hybrid network intrusion detection framework based on random forests and weighted k-means. *Ain Shams Engineering Journal*, 4(4), 753–762. doi:10.1016/j.asej.2013.01.003

Ficco, M., & Rak, M. (2015). Stealthy Denial of Service Strategy in Cloud Computing. *IEEE Transactions on Cloud Computing*, 3(1), 80–94. doi:10.1109/TCC.2014.2325045

Ganapathy, S., Kulothungan, K., Muthurajkumar, S., Vijayalakshmi, M., Yogesh, P., & Kannan, A. (2013). Intelligent feature selection and classification techniques for intrusion detection in networks: A survey. *EURASIP Journal on Wireless Communications and Networking*.

Ganapathy, S., Vijayakumar, P., Yogesh, P., & Kannan, A. (2016). An Intelligent CRF Based Feature Selection for Effective Intrusion Detection. *International Arab Journal of Information Technology*, 13(1), 44–50.

Ganapathy, S., Yogesh, P., & Kannan, A. (2012). Intelligent Agent based Intrusion Detection System using Enhanced Multiclass SVM. *Computational Intelligence and Neuroscience*, 2012, 1–9. doi:10.1155/2012/850259 PMID:23056036

Hasani, S. R., Othman, Z. A., & Kahaki, S. M. M. (2014). Hybrid feature selection algorithm for intrusion detection system. *Journal of Computer Science*, 10(6), 1015–1025. doi:10.3844/jcssp.2014.1015.1025

He, F., & Le, J. (2006). Apply the Technology of RBAC and WS-Security for Secure Web Services Environment in Campus. *Proceedings of IEEE International Conference on Machine Learning and Cybernetics* (pp. 4406 – 4411). 10.1109/ICMLC.2006.259093

He, H., & Wong, R. K. (2000). A Role Based Access Control Model for XML Repositories. *Proceedings of the First International Conference on Web Information Systems Engineering* (Vol. 1, pp. 138-145). 10.1109/WISE.2000.882385

Huang, X., Wang, H., Chen, Z., & Lin, J. (2006). A Context Rule and Role Based Access Control Model in Enterprise Pervasive Computing Environment. *Proceedings of the International Symposium on PC and Applications* (pp. 497 – 502). 10.1109/SPCA.2006.297443

Hussain, A., Sabyasachi, B., & Jena, P. D. (2013). Machine learning approach for intrusion detection on cloud virtual machines. *International Journal of Application or Innovation in Engineering & Management, 2*(6), 57–66.

Hwang, K., & Li, D. (2010). Trusted Cloud Computing with Secure Resources and Data Coloring. *Proceedings of IEEE Internet Computing* (pp. 14-22). 10.1109/MIC.2010.86

Joshi, J. B. D., Bertino, E., Latif, U., & Ghafoor, A. (2005). A Generalized Temporal Role-Based Access Control Model. *IEEE Transactions on Knowledge and Data Engineering, 17*(1), 4–23. doi:10.1109/TKDE.2005.1

Jung, T., Li, X., Wan, Z., & Wan, M. (2015). Control Cloud Data Access Privilege and Anonymity with Fully Anonymous Attribute-Based Encryption. *IEEE Transactions on Information Forensics and Security, 10*(1), 190–199. doi:10.1109/TIFS.2014.2368352

Khorshed, T. A. B. M., Ali, S., & Wasimi, S. A. (2011). Trust Issues That Create Threats for Cyber Attacks in Cloud Computing. *Proceedings of IEEE 17th International Conference on Parallel and Distributed Systems* (pp. 900-905).

Kim, G., Lee, S., & Kim, S. (2014). A novel hybrid intrusion detection method integrating anomaly detection with misuse detection. *Expert Systems with Applications, 41*(4), 1690–1700. doi:10.1016/j.eswa.2013.08.066

Koc, L., Mazzuchi, T. A., & Sarkani, S. A. (2012). Network intrusion detection system based on a hidden naive bayes multiclass classifier. *Expert Systems with Applications, 39*(18), 13492–13500. doi:10.1016/j.eswa.2012.07.009

Kulothungan, K., & Ganapathy, S., IndiraGandhi, S., Yogesh, P., & Kannan, A. (. (2011). Intelligent secured fault tolerant routing in wireless sensor networks using clustering approach. *International Journal of Soft Computing, 6*(5), 210–215. doi:10.3923/ijscomp.2011.210.215

Li, F., Wang, W., Ma, J., & Su, H. (2010). Action-Based Access Control for Web Services. *Journal of Information Assurance and Security, 5*, 162–170.

Li, N., & Tripunitara, M. V. (2006). Security Analysis in Role-Based Access Control. *ACM Transactions on Information and System Security, 9*(4), 139–420. doi:10.1145/1187441.1187442

Li, X., & Du, J. (2013). Adaptive and Attribute-Based Trust Model for Service Level Agreement Guarantee in Cloud Computing. *IET Information Security*, *7*(1), 39–50. doi:10.1049/iet-ifs.2012.0232

Lin, G., Wang, D., Bie, Y., & Lei, M. (2014). MTBAC: A Mutual Trust Based Access Control Model in Cloud Computing. In *China Communications* (pp. 154-162).

Liu, J. K., Au, M. H., Huang, X., Lu, R., & Li, J. (2016). Fine-Grained Two-Factor Access Control for Web-Based Cloud Computing Services. *IEEE Transactions on Information Forensics and Security*, *11*(3), 484–497. doi:10.1109/TIFS.2015.2493983

Liu, J. K., Yuen, T. H., Au, M. H., Huang, X., Susilo, W., & Zhou, J. (2014). K-Times Attribute-Based Anonymous Access Control for Cloud Computing. *IEEE Transactions on Computers*, *64*(9), 2595–2608.

Liu, M., Guo, H., & Su, J. (2005). An Attribute Based Access Control Model for Web Services. *Proceedings of the International Conference on Machine Learning and Cybernetics*, *18*(21), 1302-1306.

Louvieris, P., Clewley, N., & Liu, X. (2013). Effects based feature identification for network intrusion detection. *Neurocomputing*, *121*, 265–273. doi:10.1016/j.neucom.2013.04.038

Ma, H., Zhang, R., & Yuan, W. (2016). Comments on Control Cloud Data Access Privilege and Anonymity with fully Anonymous Attribute-Based Encryption. *IEEE Transactions on Information Forensics and Security*, *11*(4), 866–867. doi:10.1109/TIFS.2015.2509865

Mansour, N., Chehab, M., & Faour, A. (2010). Filtering intrusion detection alarms. *Cluster Computing*, *13*(1), 19–29. doi:10.100710586-009-0096-9

Mehmood, Y., Shibli, M. A., Kanwal, A., & Masood, R. (2015). Distributed Intrusion Detection System using Mobile Agents in Cloud Computing Environment. *Proceedings of the Conference on Information Assurance and Cyber Security*. 10.1109/CIACS.2015.7395559

Mohan, S., Sengupta, A., & Wu, Y. (2006). A Framework for Access Control for XML. *ACM Transactions on System and Information Security*, *5*, 1–38.

Muthurajkumar, S., Ganapathy, S., Vijayalakshmi, M., & Kannan, A. (2015). Secured Temporal Log Management Techniques for Cloud. *Procedia Computer Science*, *1*(46), 589–595. doi:10.1016/j.procs.2015.02.098

Noor, T. H., Sheng, Q. Z., Maamar, Z., & Zeadally, S. (2016). Managing Trust in the Cloud: State of the Art and Research Challenges. *Computer*, *49*(2), 34–45. doi:10.1109/MC.2016.57

Noor, T. H., Sheng, Q. Z., Yao, L., Dustdar, S., & Ngu, A. H. H. (2015). Cloud Armor: Supporting Reputation-Based Trust Management for Cloud Services. *IEEE Transactions on Parallel and Distributed Systems*, *27*(2), 367–380. doi:10.1109/TPDS.2015.2408613

Sandhu, R. S., Coynek, E. J., Feinsteink, H. L., & Youmank, C. E. (1996). Role-Based Access Control Models. *IEEE Computer*, *29*(2), 38–47. doi:10.1109/2.485845

Sharma, D. H., Dhote, C. A., & Potey, M. M. (2016). Implementing Intrusion Management as Security as-a-Service from Cloud. *Proceedings of the International Conference on Computational Systems and Information Systems for Sustainable Solutions* (pp. 363-366). 10.1109/CSITSS.2016.7779387

Shen, H., & Liu, G. (2014). An Efficient and Trustworthy Resource Sharing Platform for Collaborative Cloud Computing. *IEEE Transactions on Parallel and Distributed Systems*, *25*(4), 862–875. doi:10.1109/TPDS.2013.106

Sindhu, S. S. S., Geetha, S., & Kannan, A. (2012). Decision tree based light weight intrusion detection using a wrapper approach. *Expert Systems with Applications*, *39*(1), 129–141. doi:10.1016/j.eswa.2011.06.013

Stallings, W. (2013). *Cryptography and Network Security* (5th ed.). Pearson Education.

Totel, E., Hkimi, M., Hurfin, M., Labiche, Y., & Leslous, M. (2016). Inferring a Distributed Application Behaviour Model for Anomaly Based Intrusion Detection. *Proceedings of the 12th European Dependable Computing Conference* (pp. 53-64).

Vijayalakshmi, M., & Kannan, A. (2007). Processing location dependent continuous queries in distributed mobile databases using mobile agents. *Proceedings of the IET-UK International Conference on Information and Communication Technology in Electrical Sciences (ICTES 2007)* (pp. 1023-1030). 10.1049/ic:20070760

Xiao, Z., & Xiao, Y. (2013). Security and Privacy in Cloud Computing. *IEEE Communications Surveys and Tutorials*, *15*(2), 843–859. doi:10.1109/SURV.2012.060912.00182

Yan, Q. F., Yu, R., Gong, Q., & Li, J. (2016). Software-Defined Networking (SDN) and Distributed Denial of Service (DDoS) Attacks in Cloud Computing Environments: A Survey, Some Research Issues, and Challenges. *IEEE Communications Surveys and Tutorials*.

Yao, X., Liu, H., Ning, H., Yang, L. T., & Xiang, Y. (2015). Anonymous Credential-Based Access Control Scheme for Clouds. *IEEE Cloud Computing*, *2*(4), 34-43.

Ye, X. (2016). Privacy Preserving and Delegated Access Control for Cloud Applications. *Tsinghua Science and Technology*, *21*(01), 40–54. doi:10.1109/TST.2016.7399282

Zhou, L., Varadharajan, V., & Hitchens, M. (2015). Trust Enhanced Cryptographic Role-Based Access Control for Secure Cloud Data Storage. *IEEE Transactions on Information Forensics and Security*, *10*(11), 2381–2395. doi:10.1109/TIFS.2015.2455952

This research was previously published in the International Journal of Intelligent Information Technologies (IJIIT), 14(1); edited by Vijayan Sugumaran, pages 1-16, copyright year 2018 by IGI Publishing (an imprint of IGI Global).

Chapter 14
A TPM-Based Secure Multi-Cloud Storage Architecture Grounded on Erasure Codes

Emmy Mugisha
Nanjing University of Science and Technology, China

Gongxuan Zhang
Nanjing University of Science and Technology, China

Maouadj Zine El Abidine
Nanjing University of Science and Technology, China

Mutangana Eugene
Nanjing University of Science and Technology, China

ABSTRACT

In cloud storage systems, data security management is becoming a serious matter. Big data and accessibility power is increasingly high, though the benefits are clear, such a service is also relinquishing users' physical possession of their outsourced data, which inevitably poses new security risks toward the correctness of the data in cloud. As a result, cloud storage security has become one of the driving components in Cloud Computing regarding to data manipulation trust on both hosting center and on-transit. This paper proposes a TPM-Based Security over Multi-Cloud Storage Architecture (MCSA) grounded on Erasure Codes to apply root of trust based on hardware authenticity. An erasure codes such as Reed-Solomon, is capable of assuring stability in storage costs with best practice to guarantee data accessibility failure recovery. A Multi-Cloud Control Node manages other Control Nodes evolved in the cloud; this work introduces TPM-Based Security functions per Control node in the architecture. This concept will resolve a number of storage security issues, hence Cloud Computing adoption.

DOI: 10.4018/978-1-5225-8176-5.ch014

INTRODUCTION

Nowadays, the volume of data produced to be stored is growing higher as detailed in Sakr, Liu, Batista, & Alomari (2011). The growth is revealed when the volume of data is so huge to manage on available systems. The content of large daily weather radar reports, traffic surveillance equipment records, commercial transactions, medical daily reports, and distributed sensor reports are classic examples. Cloud storage providers play a significant role handling these advancement records of other organs flexibly with cost effectiveness, compared to constructing their own infrastructure.

A pay-as-you-go model was introduced for economic realm (Armbrust, Fox, Griffith et al., 2009). The model suggests a user to pay when the service is available (on-demand concept). As a result, users are at the mercy of their cloud service providers (CSP) for the availability and integrity of their data (Trust, Cloud, & With, 2009; Ren, Wang, & Wang, 2012). Although the cloud infrastructures are much more powerful and reliable than personal computing devices, broad range of both internal and external threats for data integrity still exist.

On the other hand, since users may not retain a local copy of outsourced data, there is still room for providers to behave unfaithfully toward the cloud users regarding the status of their outsourced data. For example, to increase the profit margin by reducing cost, it is possible for provider to discard rarely accessed data without being detected in a timely fashion (Juels & Kaliski, 2007). Similarly, CSP may even attempt to hide data loss incidents so as to maintain a reputation (Ateniese, Burns, Curtmola et al., 2007; Shah, Baker, Mogul, & Swaminathan, 2007; Swaminathan & Baker, 2008). Therefore, although outsourcing data into the cloud is economically attractive for the cost and complexity of long-term large-scale data storage, it's lacking of offering strong assurance of data integrity and availability may impede its wide adoption by both enterprise and individual cloud users.

Recent works based on this idea has been revised; RACS which uses a proxy server as a broker to manage transactions between customers and cloud storage providers (Abu-Libdeh, Princehouse, & Weatherspoon, 2010).

STRATOS is another implementation of Multi-Cloud. It focuses on automatic cloud provider selection for resource allocation to process running on multiple cloud providers (Pawluk, Simmons, Smit, Litoiu, & Mankovski, 2012). To achieve various data management strategies, it separates data control and execution. This data management is robust and elastic (Ghoshal & Ramakrishnan, 2012).

In order to achieve the assurances of cloud data integrity, availability and enforce the quality of cloud storage service, plus efficient methods that enable on-demand data correctness verification on behalf of cloud users, have to be designed. This work considered erasure coding as a method for distributing data over multiple cloud storage providers. Nevertheless, there is no comprehensive security analysis of the capabilities and potentials of this method in the context of Multi-Cloud storage services. This research provides a general architectural concept for applying erasure coding in-combination with hardware TPM-Based security in Multi-Cloud Storage Architecture. The idea is to introduce TPM-Based Security solutions to vulnerable nodes, impacting data accessibility across multiple cloud storage providers based on hardware root of trust.

The Trusted Platform Module (TPM) is a hardware chip designed to enable commodity computers to achieve greater levels of security than was previously possible. There are 100

million TPMs currently in existence (Ryan, 2009). These are commonly in high-end laptops made by HP, Dell, Sony, Lenovo, Toshiba, and others. The TPM stores cryptographic keys and other sensitive data in its shielded memory, and provides ways for platform software to use those keys to achieve security goals. The TPM offers three kinds of functionality: secure storage, platform measurement and reporting and platform authentication. For secure storage, user processes can store content that is encrypted by keys only available to the TPM. In platform measurement and reporting; a platform can create reports of its integrity and configuration state that can be relied on by a remote verifier. In platform authentication, a platform can obtain keys by which it can authenticate itself reliably.

The rest of the paper is organized as follows: Section 2 introduces the Erasure Codes, comparison to replication, our design goal on Cloud Storage Security. A detailed description of our scheme and implementation are provided in Sections 3 and 4 respectively. Section 5 gives a conclusion the whole work.

Erasure Coding Technique

In recent years, erasure codes have moved to a fore data failure prevention over storage systems with segmented multiple storage disks. In the storage disks, a k-of-n systematic Maximum Distance Separable (MDS) erasure codes takes k *data blocks* and produces n − k *parity blocks m*, such that any subset of k blocks can reconstruct the k data blocks (original data) (Plank, Jianqiang & Schuman, 2009).

Moreover, redundant blocks are considered as linear combinations of data blocks. *Stripe* is the set of the *k* data blocks and *m* parity blocks i.e., If *a* & *b* are data blocks *{D0, D1, ..., Dk-1}*, then, two parity blocks can be produced; *a+b* and *a−b*, {P0, P2, P3, ..., Pm-1}.

Given a stripe consisting of the four blocks *{a, b, a+b, a−b}*, any subset of two blocks can reconstruct *a* & *b* (Figure 1);

That is to say, *a+b* & *b* subsets can obtain a by subtracting b from *a+b*. Therefore, there is a 2-of-4 erasure code, which can tolerate the loss of any 2 blocks in the stripe (Figure 2);

Figure 1. Erasure Coding Storage System where n =4, m=2, k=2

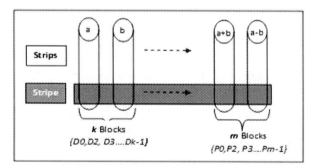

Figure 2. Replication and Erasure Codes Data reconstruction comparison

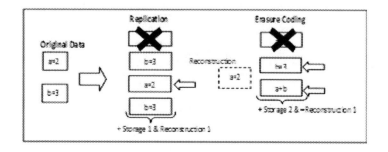

In comparison with replication technique, this is more powerful than *2-way* replication with the same space overhead; its logic is as if we replicate *a & b, {a, b, a, b}* is produced; thereafter, given that a failure occurred from any of, let' say *a*, it cannot be reconstructed anymore.

Cloud Storage Security Problem

Active systems accessibility of huge data, cloud storage is one of the best alternatives in the world of computerized systems. In that, cloud vendors/providers guarantee high availability and reliability of data. In this case, there are states where clients may fail to access their data/services due to internal or external data threats and leakages. Therein, data insecurity problem occurs.

Cloud storage concept, data insecurity occurs when data accessibility is impossible or its behavior is unknown by the owner. Meanwhile, cloud storage is not just a third party data warehouse. The data stored in the cloud may not only be accessed but also be frequently updated by the users including insertion, deletion, modification, appending, etc. (Ateniese, Di Pietro, Mancini et al., 2008; Wang, Wang, Li et al., 2009; Erway, Küpçü, Papamanthou, & Tamassia, 2015). Thus, it is also imperative to support the integration of this dynamic feature into the cloud storage correctness assurance, which makes the system design even more challenging. Also, the deployment of cloud computing is powered by data centers running in a simultaneous, cooperated, and distributed manner (Trust, Cloud, & With, 2009). It is more advantageous for individual users to store their data redundantly across multiple physical servers so as to reduce the data integrity and availability threats. Thus, distributed protocols for storage correctness assurance will be of most importance in achieving robust and secure cloud storage systems. However, such important area remains to be fully explored in the literature.

Cloud computing is provided to be a game changer as the back end of the enterprise; however, there are still a number of major issues that need to be resolved before the cloud approach can be adapted as a secure infrastructure. With Cloud computing, your data could literally be stored on the same server as that of your competitors or adversaries. Individuals, corporations and governments are handing over their most protected corporate data to essentially an outsourced storage provider, or relying on another party's server processing or software for their business applications. The decision of putting critical data on a server that you don't physically control turns traditional security paradigms on their head.

Traditional Secure Access Control for sensitive information is accomplished through first identifying the person or entity that is requesting the information by means of authentication of user to end system and end system to the enterprise. The second step is to review the current policies that govern the data, and the requestor and the locations where that data is allowed to be shared. Finally, considering specified data and examines all the attributes that are available including such information as: source, sensitivity, and location, to determine if that information is sharable with the requesting entity, based on the metadata. The current approaches to access control vary and include such methods like Policy Based Access Control (PBAC) and Attribute Based Access Control (ABAC) (Karp, Haury, & Davis, 2010).

In addition, we introduce TMP-Based security to cloud storage nodes to authenticate itself and external accessibility based on hardware attestation and pre-measured parameters. Trusted Platform Module offers facilities for the secure generation of cryptographic keys, and limitation of their use, in addition to a random number generator (Suciu & Carean, 2010; TCG, 2007a). It also includes capabilities such as remote attestation and sealed storage.

Remote attestation creates a nearly un-forgeable hash key summary of the hardware and software configuration. The program hashing the configuration data determines the extent of the summary of the software. This allows a third party to verify that the software has not been changed.

Binding encrypts data using TPM bind key, a unique RSA key descended from storage key (TCG, 2007b). Sealing encrypts data in a similar manner to binding, but in addition specifies a state in which TPM must be in order for the data to be decrypted (unsealed) (TCG, 2011). The TPM is anticipated to be used for device identification, authentication, encryption, measurement, and device integrity (Hackney, Livingood, & Reed, 2011). Software can use a TPM to authenticate hardware devices. Since each TPM chip has a unique and secret RSA key burned in at manufacture time. It is capable of performing platform authentication.

Generally, pushing the security down to the hardware level in conjunction with software provides more protection than a software-only solution. However even where a TPM is used, a key would still be vulnerable while a software application that has obtained it from TPM using it to perform encryption/decryption operations, as has been illustrated in the case of a cold boot attack. This problem is eliminated if key(s) used in TPM are not accessible on a bus or to external programs and all encryption/decryption is done in TPM.

The primary scope of a TPM in combination with other TCG implementations is to assure the integrity of a platform. In this context 'integrity' means 'behave as intended' and a 'platform' is generically any computer platform – not limited to PCs or a particular operating system: start the power-on boot process from a trusted condition and extend this trust until the operating system has fully booted and applications are running.

Together with the BIOS, TPM forms a 'root of trust': TPM contains several Platform Configuration Registers (PCRs) that allow a secure storage and reporting of security relevant metrics. These metrics can be used to detect changes to previous configurations and derive decisions how to proceed. Good examples can be found in Linux Unified Key Setup (LUKS), (LUKS, 2013) and in Microsoft's BitLocker Drive Encryption and PrivateCore vCage memory encryption. Therefore, the BIOS and the operating system have the primary responsibility to utilize TPM in order to assure platform integrity. Only then can applications and users running on that platform rely on its security characteristics, such as secure I/O 'what you see is what you get', uncompromised keyboard entries, memory and storage operations.

CLOUD STORAGE STRUCTURE

Most current cloud storage architecture displays distributed nodes from remote datacenters; nodes are organized in the datacenters. Data centers are connected together forming a storage cloud. The cloud storage, composed of multiple datacenters is controlled by a single entry point, termed as control node. This node, as the main entry point for a Client Computer to access or gain the cloud services; defines all storage policies, data management and technical aspects, to which cloud users should practice before and after requesting storage services from the cloud vendor. Different cloud storage vendors are independent with self-own-based cloud policies and technical management which makes them differ from each other in terms of data accessibility and storage security.

TPM-Based Security Over MSAE

Trust rooted on hardware level predicts a brighter future in the world of cloud computing data storage security. The concept of Trusted Computing deals with authenticity between communicating ends, here a node is expected to behave in a way it is expected to behave, and if not, the node will react otherwise and if meets expected matches, the computation will be executed allowing communication between trusted ends.

Most current cloud storage vendors, cloud storage architectures are grounded on replication technique to extend data to datacenters. This paper considers Erasure Codes to eliminate storage inefficiency apparent in most current cloud storage vendors. Integrating both TPM-Based Security and Erasure Codes into a Multi-Cloud system, will improve trustworthiness between CSP and Clients. TPM-Based Security will be embedded into Control Nodes described in Figure. 4.

Figure 3. Single cloud storage architecture

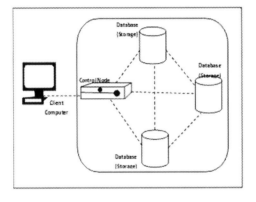

Figure 4. Multi-cloud storage architecture grounded on erasure codes

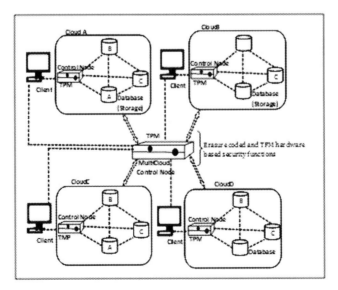

A cloud storage user, having direct access session to the cloud services through a control node, which provides an interface to access remote databases (datacenters) distributed across distinct geographical locations, i.e. Database Storage A, B, C and more depending on cloud distributed datacenters. These geographical remote databases or datacenters, grounded on erasure codes, A TPM-Based Security Control Node is proposed to distribute client's data into datacenters under the concept of Trusted Computing, avoiding inefficiency in data accessibility and insecurity trends from the hosting cloud storage, hence promoting trust between cloud nodes and external/internal tenants.

Moreover, during the process of distributing client's data based on erasure codes, the hosting cloud Control Node will transfer or distribute the same copy to a Multi-Cloud Control Node. In the same sense, the current Control Node will automatically push this copy to all connected Cloud Storage Control Nodes. We continue the same process, these Control Nodes; excluding the hosting Node will also automatically disperse the data to all its datacenters or databases. Thereafter, all Control Nodes connected to the main Multi-Cloud Control Node should agree on the same erasure codes settings while distributing data to their datacenters.

This architecture, Multi-Cloud Storage Architecture grounded on erasure codes together with TPM-Based Security guarantee a client in that when traces data inaccessibility, unavailability and data leakages in due time from the hosting cloud storage, data can still be accessible and available from co- Cloud Storage on the same network of Clouds flexibly through Multi-Cloud Control Node underlying on hardware security levels from TPM functions.

TPM-Based Security Concept

This study roots for Trusted Computing based on Trusted Platform Module (TPM), whereby TPM functions are proposed over this architecture. It composed of Shielded Locations and Protected Capabilities. For Shielded location, data is protected against any interference from the outside exposure, the only functions that can access [read or write] a shielded location is a protected capability. Lastly, Protected Capabilities, only correct operation is necessary in order for the operation of the TCG subsystem to be trusted. Both Shielded Locations and Protected Capabilities are implemented in hardware and therefore resistant against software attacks.

The TPM is a platform component, not a platform all by itself. It becomes a permanent component of the platform when its functions are applied to a platform. The TPM is not an active component, always a responder to a request and never initiates an interrupt or other such operation. It cannot alter execution flow of system (e.g. booting, execution of applications).

Figure 5. Multi-cloud control node network

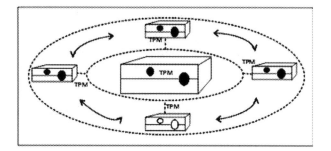

TPM functions outlines feature; TPM must be in Hardware, has a unique and signed Endorsement Certificate, bound (= soldered) to the platform. TPM provides secure storage for Platform metrics, SHA-1 for platform integrity measurements, with keys/certificates physically and cryptographically bind secrets to a platform. User keys/certificates supports an owner and user-separation role model. Moreover, TPM allows Sealing and binding data/keys/applications to the platform.

According to TPM functionalities underlying on Platform Configuration Registers, essentially internal memory slots, sealed storage can be used by an application or a process. At TPM boot time, PCR is assigned to its known values, and the only possible means of altering PCRs values is by invoking the TPM operation:

$$PRCExtend(Index, data)$$

When this operation is invoked, it updates the value of PCR indicated by index with a SH-1 (H) of the previous value of that PCR concatenated with the data provided.

$$PRC_{index} \leftarrow H\left(PCR_{index}\right) || data)$$

Data must be 20 bytes; therefore larger DAT A values must be hashed $H(DAT\ A) \rightarrow data$ before invoking PCRExtend.

For sealed storage, the TPM presents a simple interface for binding data to the current PCR through a PTM operation;

$$Seal\left(indices, data\right) \rightarrow \left[C, MAC_{K_{root}}\left(\left(index_0, PCR_{index0}\right), \left(index_1, PCR_{index_1}\right), \dots\right)\right]$$

$$Unseal\left[C, MAC_{K_{root}}\left(\left(index_0, PCR_{index0}\right), \left(index_1, PCR_{index_1}\right), \dots\right)\right] \rightarrow data$$

The Seal operation takes a set of PCR indices as input, encrypting data provided using its Storage Root Key (K_{root}), a key that never leave the TPM. It outputs the resulting ciphertext (encrypted data) C, accompanied with an integrity-protected list of indices given and the values of the corresponding PCRs at the time Seal was invoked.

For instance, to Seal a secret key $\left(K_{root}\right)$ under the values stored in PCRs 1, 3 and 17.

$$Seal\left(1, 3, 17, K_{root}\right) \rightarrow \left[C, MAC_{K_{root}}\left(\left(1, PCR_1\right), \left(3, PCR_3\left(17, PCR_{17}\right)\right)\right)\right]$$

On the Unseal command, takes in a ciphertext C and PCR list created by Seal command. The TPM verifies the integrity of the PCR's list values, and compares them against the current values of those

PCRs. If they match, TPM encrypts C and outputs the resulting data. And if no matches, the TPM returns an error. Based on the above example, invoking Unseal command

$$Unseal\left(C, MAC_{K_{root}}\left((1, PCR_1),(3, PCR_3),.(17, PCR_{17})\right)\right)$$

Will output data if;

$$PCR_1' = PCR_1$$

$$PCR_3' = PCR_3$$

$$PCR_{17}' = PCR_{17}$$

Where PCR_1', PCR_3' and PCR_{17}' represents the current values of PCRs.

Implementation

TPM-Based security can be implemented over Multi-Cloud Storage Architecture through Control Nodes level. Figure 6 shows the logic;

where 1 is measurement process, 2 denotes Extending PCR, 3 returns log event and 4 allows Transfer control process.

On the side of our Multi-Cloud Control Node, the main Node will authenticate itself and allow itself to give access to another after passing control which will activate the next node based on pre-measured logs in the TPM shielded storage.

Figure 6. TPM Chain of Trust Capabilities

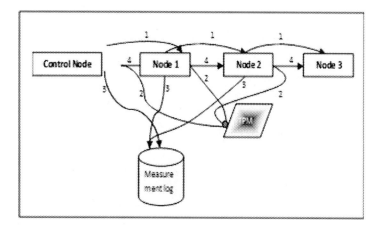

A process to be executed over the overall cloud architecture; must first pass control to confirm if the application still behaves as expected. Control and measurement process will proceed until all predefined control levels are revisited. If control returns false, the process is rejected, and if true the process will migrate to another process.

On Control nodes, pre-measured parameters will be extended into TPM's PCRs to which each request made by a remote node or user must satisfy its integrity before handing storage service or response to a requestor. This will improve trust between cloud providers and their users or clients.

Performance Analysis

TPM-Based Security performance analysis on our Multi-Cloud Storage Architecture or elsewhere that had been implemented before, data leakages and threats have improved apparently. TPM keys responsible to TPM operations never leaves TPM chip.

TPM chip in our concept will be powered on when a request is prompted to it, it will be responsible for responding for a request otherwise will be off to not be intercepted by any intruder managed to phish into our architecture in case. TPM resists consistently for any mismatch of supplied TPM operation. For instance based on our above example;

$$Unseal\left[C, MAC_{K_{root}}\left(\left(1, PCR_1\right), \left(3, PCR_3\right), .\left(17, PCR_{17}\right)\right)\right]$$

Unseals data only if;

$$PCR_1' = PCR_1$$

$$PCR_3' = PCR_3$$

$$PCR_{17}' = PCR_{17}$$

where PCR_1', PCR_3' and PCR_{17}' represents the current values of PCRs.

Figure 7. TPM root of trust Architecture

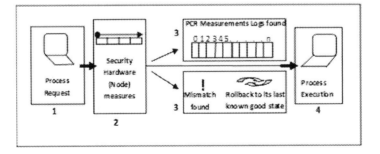

Given that, TPM chip is stolen or detached from the platform, data or any credential information on it plus keys cannot be accessed on another platform, to which it can perform its own integrity to prove if it is working on the same known platform as before. In addition, having no information about its performance might end with nothing due to its authentication data (authData) or blob supplied in by the owner during different TPM operations, to which it compares often for its security intelligence to move to the next operation.

TPM-Based Security on our designed Multi-Cloud Architecture will be implemented in Cloud Control Nodes. A Node will never operate any task until it attests itself based on its previous known good state.

CONCLUSION

This work introduced TPM-Based Security over Multi-Cloud storage architecture grounded on erasure coding capabilities of distributing large data in distributed systems. This will improve cloud user's trust based on hardware level. Hardware, the TPM chip, will be embedded in every node on cloud network. Communicating ends will authenticate each other to trigger access privileges related to storage services on the cloud.

To improve user's trust based on TPM functions, TPM's PCRs pre-measured logs of a requesting end are called at first for comparison to the current state of the requestor state. The request is granted only when match is found, if not found an error will be prompted out denying service privileges. Credential data or service will be sealed or signed by TPM commands and stored in it encrypted, and the encryption process is done inside the TPM and the encryption private key never leave TPM. When TPM chip is detached from the node, pre-measured logs and stored data, i.e. blobs, keys, etc. will stay on it and can only be used on the same TPM.

This work guarantees user's or service level of trust in the cloud computing trends using TPM functions. Generally, pushing the security down to the hardware level in conjunction with software provides more protection than a software-only solution. This will lead small and big business enterprises adopt cloud storage services with trust based on their cloud provider's architecture.

ACKNOWLEDGMENT

The authors appreciate the entire Department of Computer Science & Engineering in particular, as well as Nanjing University of Science and Technology (NJUST) for giving us the opportunity and facilities to work on this paper.

REFERENCES

Abu-Libdeh, H., Princehouse, L., & Weatherspoon, H. (2010). RACS: a case for cloud storage diversity. *Proceedings of SoCC* (pp. 229–240). doi:10.1145/1807128.1807165

Armbrust, M., Fox, A., Griffith, R., Joseph, A. D., Katz, R., Konwinski, A., ... Zaharia, M. (2009). Above the Clouds: A Berkeley View of Cloud Computing Cloud Computing. *Computing, 53*, 7–13. Doi:10.1145/1721654.1721672

Ateniese, G., Burns, R., Curtmola, R., Herring, J., Kissner, L., Peterson, Z., & Song, D. (2007). Provable data possession at untrusted stores. *Proceedings of the ACM Conference on Computer and Communications Security CCS '07, 1*, 598. Doi:10.1145/1315245.1315318

Ateniese, G., Di Pietro, R., Mancini, L. V., & Tsudik, G. (2008). Scalable and efficient provable data possession. *Proceedings of the 4th International Conference on Security and Privacy in Communication Networks SecureComm '08*. http://doi.org/10.1145/1460877.1460889

Erway, C. C., Küpçü, A., Papamanthou, C., & Tamassia, R. (2015). Dynamic Provable Data Possession. *ACM Transactions on Information and System Security, 17*(4), 1–29. doi:10.1145/2699909

Ghoshal, D., & Ramakrishnan, L. (2012). FRIEDA: Flexible robust intelligent elastic data management in cloud environments. *Proceedings - 2012 SC Companion: High Performance Computing. Networking Storage and Analysis, SCC, 2012*, 1096–1105. doi:10.1109/SC.Companion.2012.132

Hackney, D. W. G., Livingood, R., & Reed, W. A. (2011). A Study of Change Acceptance and Past-Performance-Based Outsourcing. The Department of Defense Information Security Process. *ProQuest, LLC*, 1–115.

Juels, A., & Kaliski Jr., B. S. (2007). Pors: Proofs of retrievability for large files. *Proceedings of the ACM Conference on Computer and Communications Security* (pp. 584–597). http://doi.org/10.1145/1315245.1315317

Karp, A. H., Haury, H., & Davis, M. H. (2010). From ABAC to ZBAC: The Evolution of Access Control Models. *ISSA Journal*, April, 22–30.

LUKS, (2013). Support for storing keys in TPM NVRAM

Pawluk, P., Simmons, B., Smit, M., Litoiu, M., & Mankovski, S. (2012). Introducing STRATOS: A cloud broker service. *Proceedings of the 2012 IEEE 5th International Conference on Cloud Computing CLOUD '012*, 891–898. http://doi.org/10.1109/CLOUD.2012.24

Plank, J. S., & Schuman, C. D. (2009). A performance evaluation and examination of open-source erasure coding libraries for storage. *Fast, 9*, 253–265.

Ren, K., Wang, C., & Wang, Q. (2012). Security challenges for the public cloud. *IEEE Internet Computing, 16*(1), 69–73. doi:10.1109/MIC.2012.14

Ryan, M. (2009). Introduction to the TPM 1. *Trusted Computing Group*, 1–17.

Sakr, S., Liu, A., Batista, D. M., & Alomari, M. (2011). A Survey of Large Scale Data Management Approaches in Cloud Environments. *IEEE Communications Surveys and Tutorials, 13*(3), 311–336. doi:10.1109/SURV.2011.032211.00087

Shah, M., Baker, M., Mogul, J., & Swaminathan, R. (2007). Auditing to Keep Online Storage Services Honest. In *HotOS* (pp. 236–243).

Suciu, A., & Carean, T. (2010). Benchmarking the True Random Number Generator of TPM Chips.

Swaminathan, R., & Baker, M. (2008). Privacy-Preserving Audit and Extraction of Digital Contents.

TCG. (2007a). TPM Main Part 1 Design Principles. TCG Published.

TCG. (2007b). *TCG Software Stack (TSS) Specification*. Trusted Computing Group.

TCG. (2011). TPM Main Part 3 – Commands and Specification v1.2. TCG Published.

Trust, B. C., Cloud, I. N., & With, C. (2009). *Building Customer Trust in Cloud Computing*. Framework.

Wang, Q., Wang, C., Li, J., Ren, K., & Lou, W. (2009). Enabling Public Verifiability and Data Dynamics for Storage Security in Cloud Computing Computer Security ESORICS '09. *IEEE Transactions on Parallel and Distributed Systems, 5789*(5), 355–370. doi:10.1007/978-3-642-04444-1_22

This research was previously published in the International Journal of Information Security and Privacy (IJISP), 11(1); edited by Mehdi Khosrow-Pour, D.B.A., pages 52-64, copyright year 2017 by IGI Publishing (an imprint of IGI Global).

Chapter 15
Modeling the Ranking of Evaluation Criteria for Cloud Services:
The Government Organization Perspective in India

Kshitij Kushagra
Guru Gobind Singh Indraprastha University, India

Sanjay Dhingra
Guru Gobind Singh Indraprastha University, India

ABSTRACT

The cloud market has become increasingly dense as vendors of all size compete for customers who have gravitated to technology as a way to run their operations. Today traditional players, as well as new vendors, are showing greater agility in the cloud business of India. At present, there are limited industry standards for the cloud-related businesses to assess their services. End-user government departments are puzzled as to which CSP is best suited for their requirements. An evaluation of cloud service providers should not only be driven by cost, but importance should also be given towards service provider ability and commitment to deliver the services. The absence of a common framework to assess the evaluation criteria of CSPs, combined with the fact that no two CSPs are the same, complicates the matter of CSP selection. This article proposes a framework for ranking of evaluation criteria for CSPs. The framework leverages the capability analysis of CSPs, measurable metrics and ranks the evaluation criteria for assessing the best CSP suitable for end-user government organizations.

INTRODUCTION

At present in India where the government wants everything to be digital by default in its ambitious 'Digital India' programme, there is drive in the government organizations to utilize and harness the benefits of cloud. A favorable cloud first policy, digital savvy government, huge IT talent pool can drive India to

DOI: 10.4018/978-1-5225-8176-5.ch015

the hot seat of cloud. The cloud landscape in India has a promising future. The Figure 1 illustrates the forecast for India public cloud services.

However, the journey to the cloud is not straightforward. With many dissimilarities and variants of cloud services, procurement of cloud is a confusing task. The cloud computing presents a complex scenario to the end user departments with the issues related to technology, security issues, data hosting, business models and pricing mechanism making it even more complicated. Cloud service providers have large number of baffling attributes and characteristics which is difficult for the end user departments to assess and evaluate.

Also, as the user base for the cloud adoption is increasing in the government departments, therefore to meet the requirements newer CSPs are making entry into the cloud market. The concern is that not all of them are first hand owners of cloud infrastructure and lacks inherent capability of a true CSP. In such cases it becomes difficult for the end user departments to gauze the capabilities of these new middleman or distributor who are selling the customized cloud services. Also, many organizations are seeking the validation of their strategy and need assistance in finalizing the evaluation criteria for CSPs. End user departments tend to struggle with this dilemma while finalizing the procurement. As per Bardsiri and Hashemi (2014) cloud providers offers similar products at different cost and different capabilities making it difficult for end user to make proper cloud selection. Duan (2017) stated that different cloud services are offered with different terminologies resulting in opacity and blurred picture for cloud services. As per Liu et al. (2016) the criteria parameters for cloud services are complex in nature which results in digression of cloud services. Therefore, in the absence of a common framework to assess the capabilities of CSPs, it becomes difficult for the end user departments to select the right CSP meeting their requirements with the underlying fact that no two CSPs are same. Even though the end user department is aware of the service characteristics, but is not confident of final checklist of evaluation criteria and which criteria are the most important ones. It is the need of the hour that a comprehensive framework for identification and ranking of evaluation criteria for CSPs, may be devised which an end user department can utilize to assess the right CSP suitable for its cloud requirements.

With this objective, this paper tries to identify and rank the evaluation criteria on which a CSP can be assessed with respect to the services offered, inherent capabilities and services metrics measurement.

Figure 1. Public cloud services market value in India (millions of USD) (Source: Statista 2018)

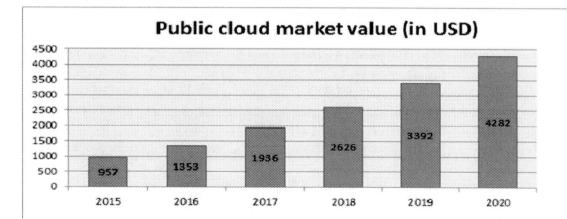

The contribution of this paper is to simplify the cloud journey of the end user government department in India by reducing the confusion, and complexity that department faces as they adopt cloud.

The paper is organized as follows- the background section provides the detail on the review of cloud evaluation criteria and the usage of Henry Garrett ranking technique. The theoretical section details framework for ranking of evaluation criteria, cloud market assessment, identification of CSPs capabilities, and metrics measurement methodology. The research methodology has been illustrated using the flowchart detailed in the relevant section. The methodology section comprises of ranking of cloud evaluation criteria based on Henry Garrett ranking technique and expert opinion. A survey is conducted for the ranking of the evaluation criteria and the ranking of the criteria is thus obtained by leveraging Henry Garrett ranking technique. The results obtained are discussed in the findings section.

BACKGROUND

The cloud computing was investigated and examined thoroughly from different evaluation criteria perspective in the various paper, journals, reports and websites. A systematic literature review was done using the approach as mentioned by Webster and Watson (2002). The review was done in two steps where first step was for determination of evaluation criteria of cloud service provider and the second step was review of the literatures which have applied Henry Garrett method for ranking of criteria. It was made certain that all the relevant literature was reviewed regarding CSPs' evaluation, cloud service measurement and metrics. By virtue of literature review it was observed that most cited criteria for the evaluation are- availability, audit, compliance, cost reduction, data center, elasticity, flexibility, metering, performance, quality of service, reliability, scalability, security, service capabilities, SLA, trust.

Bardsiri and Hashemi (2014) identified availability as the non-functional aspect and described as the capability to present redundancy for provider and information. Wagle et al. (2015) proposed the model for ranking the cloud providers in terms of availability, reliability, performance and cost. They subdivided the availability criteria into downtime and load balancing. Abbadi and Alawneh (2012) recognized availability as an important contributor to trust which is an important criterion to assess the cloud provider. Wang et al. (2016) proposed a trustworthy cloud selection framework suggesting availability as an important criterion. Naldi (2017) devised a methodology for evaluation of cloud availability, as an important yardstick for cloud performance.

Armbrust et al. (2009) identified audit as an important benchmark when data is to move to cloud. Repschlaeger et al. (2013) developed a classification framework for IaaS services wherein audit is recognised as a dimension for cloud evaluation. Ouedraogo et al. (2015) propounded audit as a prime factor for protecting confidentiality and security of cloud services. Martens et al. (2011) proposed a reference model to meet the compliance requirements which is crucial to cloud services and key performance indicators. As per Habib et al. (2012) cloud providers are gauged on compliance to audit standards and the report can be obtained by user from auditors or from provider himself.

Barnwal and Vidyarthi (2014) analysed that number of data centres their inter-distance and the area must be criteria for cloud service evaluation.

The list of evaluation criteria and the associated authors is detailed in Table 1.

Review of Evaluation Criteria

A graph derived from Table 1 illustrating the most cited criteria is described in Figure 2. The objective is to bring out the top most cited criteria by the maximum number of authors. Here as illustrated in Figure 2, the criteria which have citations more than or equal to five have been taken into consideration under this work. Hence as evident from the Figure 2 the following ten evaluation criteria was taken into consideration which are: Availability, audit, compliance, data center capabilities, performance, reliability, scalability, security, SLA and service capabilities.

Table 1. List of evaluation criteria and associated authors

Criteria	Author
Availability	Bardsiri and Hashemi (2014); Li et al. (2012); Wagle et al. (2015); Abbadi and Alawneh (2012); Wang et al. (2016); Tang et al. (2017); Fan and Perros (2014); Lin et al. (2014); Lynn et al. (2016); Leitner and Cito (2016); Naldi (2017); Ma et al. (2012)
Audit	Armbrust et al. (2009); Repschlaeger et al. (2013); Ouedraogo et al. (2015); Martens et al. (2011); Habib et al. (2012); Ghosh et al. (2015); Wagle et al. (2015)
Compliance	Bardsiri and Hashemi (2014); Martens et al. (2011); Diogo et al. (2013); Lang et al. (2016); Repschlaeger et al. (2013); Lübbecke and Lackes (2015); Gupta et. (2013)
Cost reduction	Bardsiri and Hashemi (2014); Wagle et al. (2015); Kornevs et al. (2012); Repschlaeger et al. (2012); Coutinho (2015)
Data Center	Calheiros et al. (2010); Barnwal and Vidyarthi (2014); Martens et al. (2011); Armbrust et al. (2009); Limbani and Oza (2012); Zhang et al. (2010); Buyya et al. (2009)
Elasticity	Bardsiri and Hashemi (2014); Coutinho (2015)
Flexibility	Repschlaeger et al. (2012)
Metering	Bardsiri and Hashemi (2014)
Performance	Li et al. (2012); Wagle et al. (2015); Duan (2017); Repschlaeger et al. (2012); Diogo et al. (2013); Lang et al. (2016); Chang et al. (2012); Khanghahi and Ravanmehr (2013)
Quality of service	Bardsiri and Hashemi (2014); Coutinho (2015); Habib et al. (2010)
Reliability	Bardsiri and Hashemi (2014); Li et al. (2012); Wagle et al. (2015); Abbadi and Alawneh (2012); Wang et al. (2016); Tang et al. (2017); Fan and Perros (2014); Lin et al. (2014); Lynn et al. (2016); Repschlaeger et al. (2012); Garg et al. (2013)
Scalability	Li et al. (2012); Abbadi and Alawneh (2012); Wang et al. (2016); Fan and Perros (2014); Lin et al. (2014); Kim and Park (2013); ExpóSito et al. (2013); Coutinho (2015); Abbadi and Martin (2011)
Security	Li et al. (2012); Wagle et al. (2015); Abbadi and Alawneh (2012); Wang et al. (2016); Tang et al. (2017); Fan and Perros (2014); Lin et al. (2014); Lynn et al. (2016); Repschlaeger et al. (2012); Yu et al. (2017); Habib et al. (2010); Subashini and Kavitha (2011)
Service capabilities	Li et al. (2012); Leitner and Cito (2016); Garfinkel (2007); ExpóSito et al. (2013); Repschlaeger et al. (2012); Garg et al. (2013); Srinivisan et al. (2012),
SLA	Meland et al. (2014); Habib et al. (2011); Balachandra et al. (2009); Martens et al. (2011); Diogo et al. (2013); Gopal and Koka (2012); Patel et al. (2009)
Trust	Chiregi and Navimipour (2017); Repschlaeger et al. (2012)

Review of Studies Using Henry Garrett Ranking Method

Henry Garrett ranking technique is a statistical technique used to rank the evaluation criteria for the CSP by the respondents. This technique is useful as it considers both the qualitative and the quantitative attributes while ranking criteria. It aids in finding out the most significant factor which influences the respondent. As per this method, respondents are required to assign the rank for all evaluation criteria and the outcome of such ranking has been converted into score value with the help of this technique.

The Table 2 summarizes the studies using Henry Garrett ranking method.

THEORETICAL SECTION

This section details the framework for the ranking of cloud evaluation criteria which has subsection of cloud market assessment, identification of CSP capabilities, cloud evaluation criteria and metrics measurement.

Framework for Ranking of Cloud Evaluation Criteria

Based on the model proposed by Garg et al. (2013) and Zibin et al. (2013) a framework is proposed as illustrated in Figure 3 which comprises of four stages which are identification of CSP and the cloud services to be procured, identify the service characteristics, identification of metrics, measurement and rank the cloud.

Cloud Market Assessment

The cloud market assessment comprises of identification of cloud service provider and their service capabilities. Extensive market survey, review of papers/journals and internet research was done for relevant CSPs' regarding their profile, types of services, deployment model, pricing structure, security issues, technical capabilities, service level agreement (SLA) and certifications.

Figure 2. Graphical representation of most cited criteria

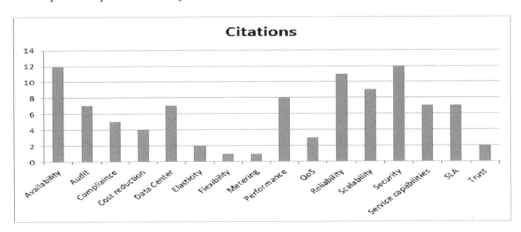

Identification of CSPs and Cloud Services

The first and foremost requirement of cloud user /government organization is to identify the CSPs offering the cloud services in India. It a vital task to assess the reliability and capabilities of CSP before engaging them for hosting one's organization data and application. By market research and business reports/publications available it was identified that currently there are twelve CSPs at present which are highly active in the cloud market of India, having significant market share and have been into existence for more than three years in Indian cloud business (MeitY, 2018). The list of such CSPs are- Amazon, BSNL, Ctrl S, ESDS, IBM, Microsoft, Netmagic, Nxtra data, Sify technologies and Tata communications. This paper has limited to the study of these CSPs only. The deployment model and the cloud service offerings of the CSPs' operating in India are mentioned in Table 3.

Identification of CSP Capabilities

Currently, there are different cloud service providers (CSPs); each has its own characteristics, service offerings and capabilities. To better understand these CSPs, an analysis in detail has been bought out and gives a comparison from their different capability aspects. The capability matrix of various CSPs' is summarized in Table 4.

Table 2. Review on studies using Henry Garrett ranking method

Author Name	Variables/Factors	Industry	Significant Factors
Jins and Radhakrishnan (2013)	Physical, psychological, behavioural	Manufacturing	Physical
Suganya and Hamsalakshmi (2017)	Brand Image & Reputation, No Chemical Product, Easy Availability of the Products, Convenience of Usage, Quality of the Product, Reasonable Price, Value for Money, Awareness from advertisements	Health	No Chemical Product
Manimegalai and Sathyapriya (2014)	Initial claim formalities, Delay in the settlement of claim amount, Ambiguity in the terms & conditions of the policy, Benefits of insurance policy is not clear, Delay in the claim due to legal formalities,	Insurance	Initial claim formalities
Devianbarasi and Mathivanan (2015)	Television, Radio, Newspaper, Banner	Media	Television
Ganesan and Chandramohan (2015)	Better performance, Emotional value, Better performance, more features, competitive price, gives social status	Consumer Electronics	Better performance
Jayaraj and Dharmaraj (2016)	Quality Products, Convenient Location, Committed Sales Force, Personalized Customer Service, Modern Equipments, Low Cost Products, Customer Base	Retail	Personalized Customer Service

Figure 3. Framework for cloud evaluation criteria ranking

Table 3. Cloud deployment model and service offerings

	Public Cloud			Private Cloud			Community Cloud		
	IaaS	**PaaS**	**SaaS**	**IaaS**	**PaaS**	**SaaS**	**IaaS**	**PaaS**	**SaaS**
Amazon	✓	✓	X	X	X	X	X	X	X
BSNL	✓	✓	✓	✓	✓	✓	✓	✓	✓
Ctrl S	✓	✓	✓	✓	✓	✓	✓	✓	✓
ESDS	✓	✓	✓	✓	✓	✓	✓	✓	✓
IBM	✓	✓	✓	✓	✓	✓	✓	✓	✓
Netmagic	✓	✓	✓	✓	✓	✓	✓	✓	✓
Microsoft	✓	✓	✓	X	X	X	✓	✓	✓
Nxtra Data	✓	X	✓	✓	X	✓	✓	X	✓
Sify	✓	✓	✓	✓	✓	✓	✓	✓	✓
Tata Comm.	✓	✓	✓	✓	✓	✓	✓	✓	✓

Source: MeitY, (2018)

Table 4. Capability matrix of cloud service providers

	Availability	Audit	Compliance (Legal/ Regulatory)	Data Center		Security Certification	Service Capability	SLA
				Data Centre Tier	No. of Data Centre in India			
Amazon	99.99	3rd party audited	IT Act 2000, CERT–IN/MeitY guidelines,	Tier 3+	3	ISO27001, ISO 27017, ISO, SSAE 16	Public cloud, VPC, Compute, storage, network, DB, analytics, appl. Services, deployment, management	<=99.95%
BSNL	99.982	3rd party audited	IT Act 2000, CERT–IN/ MeitY guidelines	Tier 3	6	ISO27001, SSAE 16	CPU, Memory, Storage, Bandwidth, IP address, firewall, VPN	<=99.99%
Ctrl S	99.995	3rd party audited	IT Act 2000, CERT–IN/MeitY guidelines	Tier 4	3	ISO 27001, SSAE 16	Private cloud, Cloud VPS, Enterprise cloud, dedicated hosting	<=99.995%
ESDS	99.982	3rd party audited	IT Act 2000, CERT–IN/MeitY guidelines	Tier 3	2	ISO 27001, SSAE 16	SAP/ERP Hosting, DR platform hosting, Hybrid cloud hosting, Private cloud	<=99.99%
IBM	99.95	3rd party audited	IT Act 2000, CERT–IN/MeitY guidelines	Tier 3	2	ISO 27001, SSAE 16	Public, private, hybrid cloud, IaaS, PaaS, SaaS	For each 30 min. continuous outage, SLA credit of 5%
Netmagic	99.99	3rd party audited	IT Act 2000, CERT–IN/MeitY guidelines	Tier 3	9	ISO 27001, SSAE 16	IaaS based Public/Private/ Hybrid cloud, DR on cloud, Object/performance tiered storage, DBaaS	<=99.95%
Microsoft	99.9	3rd party audited	IT Act 2000, CERT–IN/MeitY guidelines	Tier 3	3	ISO27001, ISO 27017, SSAE 16	Compute, storage, data management, Media services, CDN, Developer	<=99.95%
Nxtra Data	99.98	3rd party audited	IT Act 2000, CERT–IN/MeitY guidelines	Tier 3	2	ISO27001, ISO 27017, SSAE 16	Public, private, hybrid, back up, disaster recovery, choice of connectivity,	<=99.95%
Sify	99.982	3rd party audited	IT Act 2000, CERT–IN/MeitY guidelines	Tier 3	2	ISO 27001, SSAE 16	Public, private, enterprise cloud, data protection, migration	<=99.9%
Tata Comm.	99.98	3rd party audited	IT Act 2000, CERT–IN/MeitY guidelines	Tier 3+	7	ISO 27001, SSAE 16	Private cloud, storage, managed services, security solutions,	<=99.95%

Source: MeitY, (2018)

Cloud Evaluation

The cloud evaluation consists of evaluation criteria and the metrics for measuring the evaluation criteria.

Evaluation Criteria

1. **Availability:** Availability of cloud is the major considered criteria for cloud user. Availability is the proportion of time a system in functioning condition. An organization/user migrates to cloud in anticipation that it will be available, stable and as good as they have experienced with their traditional IT infrastructure. All major CSPs claim that their availability is at least equal to or greater than 99.9%, but the actual picture is different from the proclaimed availability figures. The outages were caused by a technical glitch, human error or malicious attacks. As per Ma et al. (2012), it is the percentage of service uptime measured as total uptime against total time, it is expressed in percentage:

$$Availability = \frac{Uptime}{Uptime + Downtime}$$

2. **Audit:** Auditability of CSP plays a very important role in building the trust component. CSP can have the Third Party Audit Certification at regular interval indicating the conformance to the requirements. As per Ouedraogo et al. (2015) CSP can easily decline to physical audit of infrastructure hence it become crucial that prior to the selection of CSP, the auditability of CSP may be verified thoroughly by end user government organizations. The various types of audits which CSP are subjected to can be infrastructure audit, security audit, SLA audit;
3. **Compliance:** As per CSMI Index (2014), compliance is defined as the cloud service provider following the committed standards, process and policies. It is important for the end user government organizations to understand the risk involved while moving to cloud environment. Before migrating to cloud it is crucial to check the compliance adherence of CSP. Adherence to all applicable laws, ordinances, rules, regulations and lawful orders of government of India should be complied. All the regulations like PCIDSS, IT Act 2000, CERT IN guidelines should be complied by CSPs;
4. **Data Center Capabilities:** The data center facilities cater for the space, power and physical infrastructure. The data centres are classified on basis of standardized methodology used to define the uptime of the data centre. To ascertain the data center capabilities the following metrics for data center should always be considered-number of data center of CSP, location of data centers in different seismic zones, distance between location of data center and end user, age of data center (CA Technologies, 2014);
5. **Performance:** Performance is more than a classic concept, and many factors can affect the performance of cloud computing and its resources. As per CSMI index (2014), the performance is contributed by accuracy, functionality, suitability, interoperability and service response time. As per Khanghahi and Ravanmehr (2013) factors which can affect performance are throughput, response time, delay in service, average waiting time, load balancing and number of requests;
6. **Reliability:** Reliability is related to the success in which a service functions. High end-to-end service reliability implies a service always provides correct results and guarantees no data loss. As per Garg et al. (2013) reliability can be expressed as:

$$\text{Reliability} = \left(1 - \frac{f}{n}\right) \times P_{mttf}$$

where f is the number of users who experienced a failure in a time interval less than promised by the cloud service provider, n is number of users, and p_{mttf} is the promised mean time to failure Garg et al (2013).

7. **Scalability:** Scalability refers to the idea of a system in which every application or piece of infrastructure can be expanded to handle increased load. As per Abbadi and Martin (2011) scalability at the virtual layer can be horizontal scalability, vertical scalability, or combination of both. Horizontal scalability is about the amount of instances that can be increased or decreased on demand. Vertical scalability is about increasing or decreasing the size of instances themselves to maintain increase or decrease in demand. The factors affecting scalability can be mean time to invoke, mean time to procure hardware resources, mean time to deploy. The vertical scalability can be given as:

$$\text{Vertical scalability} = \sum_{i}^{p}\sum_{j}^{q_i}$$

where r_{ij} be resource j that needs to be enhanced on cloud service i. Let q and p be the number of resources assigned to a particular cloud service and the number of cloud services used by the user, respectively.

8. **Security:** Security is the major concern for the cloud user/organization. Moving to cloud is not straight forward. There are a number of security challenges and lot of risks involved while migrating to cloud. It was identified by (Catteddu & Hogben, 2010) stating that the loss of governance as one of the top risks of cloud computing. Subashini and Kavitha (2011), surveyed different security issues that has developed due to the characteristics of the cloud service delivery model. Yu et al. (2017) highlights the security challenges where encryption is becoming a standard practice for both cloud users and cloud service providers, as a tool against unauthorized surveillance as well as malware. Certifications are the important benchmark used around the globe for measuring the security standards. The approach to mitigate the security risk is that a CSP should be compliant to the certifications like ISO27001 for information security, ISO 27017 for security in cloud, ISO 27018 for privacy in cloud, NIST security standards;

9. **Service Capabilities:** Garg et al. (2013) stated that it is becoming difficult for the cloud customer to decide which CSP can fulfil their IT needs as each CSP offers similar services at different prices. End user government organizations can have different cloud requirements which can be relate to infrastructure, platform or software. An end user can assess and evaluate the performance of the services being offered by prospective CSP as per the capability matrix shown in Table 5;

10. **SLA:** SLA is the major evaluation criteria for the cloud service providers. As the cloud computing market is still evolving there can be mismatch between the expectations of customer and the CSP's terms and conditions. As per Patel et al. (2009) the dynamic character of cloud it is crucial to have the robust SLA. Large cloud providers can be inflexible with their service agreements while small cloud providers may seem to be more flexible in order to increase their customer base. This is the possible case that in order to provide economical cloud offerings and services the CSP can compromise on SLA, and can offer a degraded SLA. Most CSP design SLA in such a way that they tend to protect providers against any legal action for their minimum assurance of cloud offerings.

Metrics

Various organizations/departments often use the same cloud computing terms with slightly different or even contradictory meanings, leading to confusion among cloud service providers and customer. Many organizations have trouble in quantifying and tracking end-user experience for their cloud applications. Choosing the right cloud metrics is essential and this cloud metrology provides an opportunity to the end user departments/organizations to make informed choices and to expand their understanding of the services being delivered by cloud service provider.

When it comes to keep cloud service providers accountable, the name of the game is tracking end-user experience and its impact on business performance. The evaluation criteria and the metric measurement is shown in Table 5.

METHODOLOGY

The primary objective of this paper is to come up with a framework to identify and the rank the evaluation criteria of CSPs. Figure 4 illustrates the flowchart for the methodology.

Literature review was done in two folds – one on the evaluation criteria and the second on the studies which have leveraged Henry Garrett ranking method. The literature reviewed for evaluation criteria and Henry Garrett ranking method is delineated in Table 1 and Table 2 respectively. Prior to the literature review, market survey of CSPs was conducted to analyse the cloud service offerings of CSPs, SLA offered, services offerings, certifications and compliances. This was done to have strong awareness of the cloud service ecosystem. Post literature review and market survey, the finalized ten evaluation criteria was shared with the cloud industry experts and their opinion was taken to rank the evaluation criteria as per the Table 8 in the Appendix. The experts were chosen from cloud computing domain comprising of

Table 5. Metrics measurement methodology (Source: Wagle et al. 2015; Bardsiri, 2014)

Criteria	Measurement Methodology
Availability	Uptime, downtime, outage frequency, flexibility, accuracy, response time
Audit	Third party certification
Compliance	Legal compliance, privacy compliance, regulatory compliance,
Data Center	Tier types, uptime certification, disaster recovery, recovery time objective, recovery point objective
Performance	Throughput, latency, data restoration time, packet loss frequency, connection error rate, computation, CPU load, instance efficiency, memory, response time, computation time
Reliability	Load balancing, recoverable, MTBF, service constancy, accuracy, fault tolerance, maturity
Scalability	Average of assigned resources, effective scalable range, effective system scalability, mean time to procure hardware resources, mean time to deploy
Security	Authentication, encryption, physical location of data, security certifications, vulnerability assessment
Service Capability	IaaS- VM Size, number of cores, flexible VM, v CPU speed/frequency, VM provisioning time PaaS- support for customer applications, rapid deployment mechanism, support for middle ware capabilities, security capabilities, tools to assist developers SaaS- scaling up capability, scaling out capability, scalability cost
SLA	Violation rate, service performance report frequency, accuracy, accessibility, reliability, timeliness, scheduled downtime

Figure 4. Flowchart for research methodology

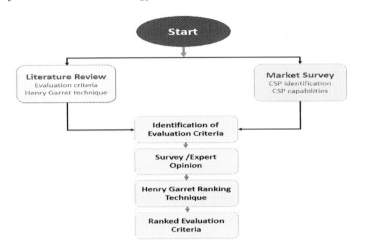

Table 6. List of officials interviewed

Stakeholders	Organizations	Designations	Officials Interviewed
Cloud Service Provider	Amazon, Microsoft, IBM, ESDS, Netmagic, Ctrl S, Sify, BSNL, MTNL, TCIL, ESDS, Nxtra Data, Reliance IT park	Director, DGM, Sr. system Manager Senior Manager, AVP, Solution Architect	36
User departments	NIC, STQC, STPI, CERT IN Ministry of Electronics and IT, AICTE, Health, Agriculture, Road transport, Shipping, Tourism	Sr. Technical Director, Additional Director, Scientist	83
System Integrator	TCS, WIPRO, Infosys	Solution Architect, Manager-Technical	27
Consultancy agency	PwC, KPMG, E&Y, Deloitte	Associate Director, Principal consultant	45

officials from government, CSPs, system integrators, consulting agencies. A total of 191 officials were asked to fill in the questionnaire placed at Table 8 in the Appendix. The list of the officials is shown in Table 6.

After the completion of expert opinion, Henry Garrett ranking technique was applied as described in the subsequent subsection.

Ranking of Evaluation Criteria

The ranking of evaluation criteria has been accomplished using Henry Garrett with the help of the following formula:

$$\text{Percent Position} = 100 * \frac{\left(R_{ij} - 0.5\right)}{N_j}$$

where:

R_{ij} = Rank given for the ith variable by j[th] respondents

N_j = Number of variable ranked by j[th] respondents

Then for each factor, the scores of each individual are added and then total value of scores and mean values of score is calculated. The factors having highest mean value is considered to be the most important factor.

The percentage score for each rank from 1 to 10 is calculated. With the help of Garrett Table, the percent position estimated is converted into scores using the table given by Henry Garrett. The scale value from 1st rank to 10th rank is 82, 70, 63, 57, 52, 47, 42, 36, 29 and 18, respectively.

The score value (fx) is calculated for each criterion by multiplying the number of respondents (f) with respective scale values (x). The total scores are found by adding the score values (fx) of each rank for every criteria. The mean score is then calculated to know the order of preference given by the respondents for the criteria. Based on the mean score, the overall ranks are assigned for each evaluation criteria.

FINDINGS

The following ten evaluation criteria were taken into consideration which are- availability, audit, compliance, data center capabilities, performance, reliability, scalability, security, SLA and service capabilities.

The ranking analysis of the criteria for selection of CSP influencing the end user through Garrett Ranking Technique is shown in Table 7.

The highest score is secured by the security criteria which is 70.5 and stood at rank 1. The scores of remaining criteria in the order of decreasing ranks i.e availability and scalability, reliability, service capabilities, performance, service level agreement (SLA), compliance, data center capabilities, and audit are 56.3, 53.5, 53.4, 49.95, 47.63, 46.56, 42.075, 40.13 and 38.71, respectively.

DISCUSSION

This paper examined and ranked the evaluation criteria of cloud service providers. This work has identified the ten vital factors i.e availability, audit, compliance, data center, performance, reliability, scalability, security, service capability, service level agreement as evaluation criteria for CSPs. Henry Garrett ranking technique was leveraged for the ranking of evaluation criteria. Officials working in cloud domain were interviewed to fill in the questionnaire and rank the evaluation criteria. Post application, of Henry technique it was inferred that the most important evaluation criteria is security followed by availability and scalability which an end user government department must consider while finalizing the evaluation criteria for CSP selection.

Security is the biggest challenge for cloud computing. Security of the cloud services has many dimensions which are hard to quantify and guaranteeing the security of data in the cloud is difficult as every service provided by CSP has its own security issues. CSP can compromise on security in order to provide a cheaper solution and to stay competitive in the market. The characteristic and nature of cloud computing introduces the possibility of new security breaches that can wipe out any gains made by switching to cloud. Careful decision and planning is required at user/organization end to assess the CSP security strengths. Efforts should be made at the user end to demand for robust security certifications, its compliance, strong encryption standards, authentication and authorization mechanism. Security can be enriched by implementing advanced authentication tools, limited access to critical data, know where the data is stored, and back up data regularly.

Availability of the cloud services was the second most critical criteria to be considered while deciding the evaluation criteria of CSP. Despite advances in IT infrastructure and robustness organizations still face hardware, software downtime and outages. As the organization host, strategically important data on cloud outage can cause loss of business, reputation. A clear-cut strategy to mitigate such availability issues can be had by having a robust SLA, disaster recovery services, CSPs offering the services through multiple zones and multiple cloud vendors should be selected.

Scalability of the cloud was discovered to be the third most critical evaluation criteria as it has the ability to expand and contract as per the IT needs of the organizations and they don't have to wait for plan to scale. Being fastened to the physical limitations of storage space, CPU, memory and bandwidth are the restrictions of traditional IT hosting. But with cloud computing, focus is on building the infrastructure for success rather than worrying about whether the in-house infrastructure can handle the constraints of success. Scalability allows more granular control of the organization resources.

Other criteria in the order of ranking wise in the decreasing order are reliability, service capability, performance, service level agreement compliance data center and audit are significant criteria to consider for CSP evaluation.

CONCLUSION

As more and more IT systems are externalised in the organization and the cloud demand on the rise. It becomes important to make a right selection of CSP by choosing the appropriate set of evaluation criteria. As the cloud market has myriad of CSP offering a vast number of services it is becoming increasingly difficult to choose the precise cloud providers for their cloud requirements and long-term success. This work has bought out the list of such criteria for CSP evaluation and has distilled the top ten key evaluation criteria for CSP and which have been ranked. It is established that security is the top most criteria followed by availability, scalability, reliability, service capability, performance, service level agreement compliance data center and audit. Security issues are the major impediment and many organizations are struggling with the security related implications. Effective security is a constant challenge, and cloud brings a new dimension of risks along with the opportunities they provide. Weaknesses in a provider's security can have a critical impact on the security concern for the end user department. Therefore, a careful and precise evaluation of security is a 'must to do' exercise by the end user departments. This study has focused as a decision support system for end user government organizations as a quick guide for deciding on the evaluation criteria of CSPs.

Table 7. Ranking analysis of criteria for CSP

Rank Criteria		I 82	II 70	III 63	IV 57	V 52	VI 47	VII 42	VIII 36	IX 29	X 18	Total	Mean Score	Rank
Services Capabilities	f	4	5	13	18	4	14	2	6	5	9	80	49.95	5
	fx	328	350	819	1026	208	658	84	216	145	162	3996		
Reliability	f	3	6	21	7	14	12	8	4	2	3	80	53.4	4
	fx	246	420	1323	399	728	564	336	144	58	54	4272		
Service Level Agreement (SLA)	f	4	7	6	3	4	17	15	13	5	6	80	46.56	7
	fx	328	490	378	171	208	799	630	468	145	108	3725		
Security	f	44	16	6	1	2	3	2	1	2	3	80	70.5	1
	fx	3608	1120	378	57	104	141	84	36	58	54	5640		
Availability	f	1	36	13	3	4	2	3	4	8	6	80	56.3	2
	fx	82	2520	819	171	208	94	126	144	232	108	4504		
Scalability	f	15	7	4	5	12	8	3	23	2	1	80	53.5	3
	fx	1230	490	252	285	624	376	126	828	58	18	4287		
Data Centre capabilities	f	1	3	9	12	10	2	3	3	14	23	80	40.13	9
	fx	82	210	567	684	520	94	126	108	406	414	3211		
Compliance	f	3	8	1	4	7	6	11	19	9	12	80	42.075	8
	fx	246	560	63	228	364	282	462	684	261	216	3366		
Audit	f	3	2	4	4	6	5	12	13	14	17	80	38.71	10
	fx	246	140	252	228	312	235	504	468	406	306	3097		
Performance	f	7	4	6	3	11	16	10	9	8	6	80	47.63	6
	fx	574	280	378	171	572	752	420	324	232	108	3811		

FUTURE WORK

For now, our framework is limited to the ranking of the evaluation criteria which can be enlarged to classification of cloud service provider. The future research work can be concentrated upon the classification of CSP based on the key performance indicators, criteria and characteristics, which can assist government departments in adoption of cloud. Compare and ranking of cloud service providers can also be done in future. More CSP can be accommodated by considering the startups in cloud domain. Also, the weightage can be implemented to accommodate the difference between the varied government organizations and testing the framework based on the real case study. There are other decision models and ranking techniques which can be used, however this study has the limitation of using Henry Garrett technique.

REFERENCES

Abbadi, I. M., & Martin, A. (2011). Trust in the Cloud. *Information Security Technical Report, 16*(3-4), 108–114. doi:10.1016/j.istr.2011.08.006

Abbadi, M., & Alawneh, M. (2012). Preventing information leakage between collaborating organisations. *Journal of Computers and Electrical Engineering*, *38*(5), 1073–1087. doi:10.1016/j.compeleceng.2012.06.006

Balachandra, R. K., Ramakrishna, P. V., & Rakshit, A. (2009). Cloud security issues. In *IEEE International Conference on Services Computing*, Banglore, India. IEEE.

Baranwal, G., & Vidyarthi, D. P. (2014). A framework for selection of best cloud service provider using ranked voting method. In *IEEE International Advance Computing Conference 2014*. Gurgaon, India: IEEE; . doi:10.1109/IAdCC.2014.6779430

Baranwal, G., & Vidyarthi, D. P. (2014, February). A framework for selection of best cloud service provider using ranked voting method. In *2014 IEEE International Advance Computing Conference (IACC)* (pp. 831-837). IEEE. Retrieved from http://www.ca.com/in/media/files/whitepapers

Bardsiri, A., & Hashemi, S. (2014). QoS metrics for cloud computing services evaluation. *International Journal of Intelligent Systems and Applications*, *12*(12), 27–33. doi:10.5815/ijisa.2014.12.04

Buyya, R., Yeo, C. S., Venugopal, S., Broberg, J., & Brandic, I. (2009). Cloud computing and emerging it platforms: Vision, hype, and reality for delivering computing as the 5th utility. *Future Generation Computer Systems*, *25*(6), 599–616. doi:10.1016/j.future.2008.12.001

Calheiros, R. N., Ranjan, R., Beloglazov, A., Rose, C. A., & Buyya, R. (2010). Cloudsim: a toolkit for modeling and simulation of cloud computing environments and evaluation of resource provisioning algorithms. In *Software: Practice and Experience*. New York: Wiley Press.

Catteddu, D., & Hogben, G. (2010). Cloud computing risk assessment European network and information security agency. Retrieved from https://www.enisa.europa.eu/.../cloud-computing-risk-assessment.pdf

Chang, S. I., Yen, D. C., Ng, C. S. P., & Chang, W. T. (2012). An analysis of IT/is outsourcing provider selection for small-and medium-sized enterprises in Taiwan. *Journal of International Management*, *49*(5), 199–209.

Chiregi, M., & Navimipour, N. J. (2017). Cloud computing and trust evaluation: a systematic literature review of the state of the art mechanisms. *Journal of Electrical Systems and Information Technology*.

Coutinho, E. F., de Carvalho Sousa, F. R., Rego, P. A. L., Gomes, D. G., & de Souza, J. N. (2015). Elasticity in cloud computing: A survey. *Annales des Télécommunications*, *70*(7-8), 289–309. doi:10.100712243-014-0450-7

CSMI, Cloud Services Measurement Initiative Consortium. (2014). *Service measurement index*. California: Carnegie Mellon University.

Devianbarasi, R., & Mathivanan, M. (2015). Impact of non-commercial advertisements on television viewers with reference to Mayiladuthurai town. *International Journal of Multidisciplinary Research and Development*, *2*(3), 299–303.

Duan, Q. (2017). Cloud service performance evaluation: status, challenges, and opportunities – a survey from the system modeling perspective. Digital Communications and Networks, 3(2), 101–111. doi:10.1016/j.dcan.2016.12.002

Expósito, R. R., Taboada, G. L., Ramos, S., Touriño, J., & Doallo, R. (2013). Performance analysis of HPC applications in the cloud. *Future Generation Computer Systems*, *29*(1), 218–229. doi:10.1016/j. future.2012.06.009

Fan, W., & Perros, H. (2014). A novel trust management framework for multi-cloud environments based on trust service providers. *Journal of Knowledge Based Systems*, *70*(3), 392–406. doi:10.1016/j. knosys.2014.07.018

Fernandes, D. A., Soares, L. F., Gomes, J. V., Freire, M. M., & Inácio, P. R. (2013). Security issues in cloud environments: A survey. *International Journal of Information Security*, *13*, 113–170.

Fox, A., Griffith, R., Joseph, A., Katz, R., Konwinski, A., Lee, G., & Stoica, I. (2009). *Above the clouds: a Berkeley view of cloud computing*. UC Berkeley Reliable Adaptive Distributive Systems Laboratory.

Ganesan, M., & Chandramohan, S. (2015). A study on consumer brand preference and satisfaction of household electronics products in Sivaganga district. *International Journal of Advanced Research in Management and Social Sciences*, *4*(12), 99–112.

Garfinkel, S. L. (2007). *An evaluation of Amazon grid computing services: EC2, S3, and SQS. Center for Research on Computation and Society*. Cambridge: Harvard University.

Garg, S., Versteeg, S., & Buyya, R. (2013). A framework for ranking of cloud computing services. *Future Generation Computer Systems*, *29*(4), 1012–1023. doi:10.1016/j.future.2012.06.006

Ghosh, N., Ghosh, S. K., & Das, S. K. (2015). SelCSP: A framework to facilitate selection of cloud service providers. IEEE Transactions on Cloud Computing, 3(1), 66–79. doi:10.1109/TCC.2014.2328578

Gopal, A., & Koka, B. R. (2012). The asymmetric benefits of relational flexibility: Evidence from software development outsourcing. *Management Information Systems Quarterly*, *36*(2), 553–576.

Gupta, P., Seetharaman, A., & Raj, J. R. (2013). The usage and adoption of cloud computing by small and medium businesses. *International Journal of Information Management*, *33*(5), 861–874. doi:10.1016/j. ijinfomgt.2013.07.001

Habib, S., Ries, S., & Muhlhauser, M. (2011). Towards a trust management system for cloud computing. In *IEEE 10th International Conference on Trust, Security and Privacy in Computing and Communications*, Washington, USA. IEEE.

Habib, S. M., Hauke, S., Ries, S., & Mühlhäuser, M. (2012). Trust as a facilitator in cloud computing: a survey. *Journal of Cloud Computing: Advances. Systems and Applications*, *1*(1), 19.

Habib, S. M., Ries, S., & Muhlhauser, M. (2010). Cloud computing landscape and research challenges regarding trust and reputation. In 7th International Conference on Autonomic Trusted Computing. Xian, China: IEEE; . doi:10.1109/UIC-ATC.2010.48

Jayaraj, A., & Dharamraj, A. (2016). Competitive advantage strategies adopted by rural retailers in Coimbatore district. *Journal of Arts Science and Commerce*, *7*(3), 102–107.

Jins Joy, P., & Radhakrishnan, R. (2013). A study on causes of work stress among tile factory workers in Kannur district in Kerala. *International Journal of Scientific and Research Publications*, *3*(9), 1–9.

Khanghahi, N., & Ravanmehr, R. (2013). Cloud computing performance evaluation: Issues and challenges. *International Journal on Cloud Computing: Services and Architecture*, *3*(5), 29–41.

Kim, M., & Park, S. O. (2013). Trust management on user behavioural patterns for a mobile cloud computing. *Journal of Cluster Computing*, *16*(4), 725–731. doi:10.100710586-013-0248-9

Kornevs, M., Minkevica, V., & Holm, M. (2012). Cloud computing evaluation based on financial metrics. Information Technology and Management Science, 15(1), 87–92. doi:10.2478/v10313-012-0013-8

Lang, M., Wiesche, M., & Krcmar, H. (2016). What are the most important criteria for cloud service provider selection? a delphi study. In *European Conference on Information Systems*, Istanbul, Turkey. AIS.

Leitner, P., & Cito, J. (2016). Patterns in the chaos study of performance variation and predictability in public iaas clouds. *ACM Transactions on Internet Technology*, *16*(3), 15–23. doi:10.1145/2885497

Li, Z., Brien, O. L., Zhang, H., & Cai, R. (2012). On a catalogue of metrics for evaluating commercial cloud services. In *2012 ACM/IEEE 13th International Conference on Grid Computing (GRID)*. Beijing: IEEE Computer Society.

Limbani, D., & Oza, B. (2012). A proposed service broker policy for data center selection in cloud environment with implementation. *International Journal of Computer Technology & Applications*, *3*(3), 1082–1087.

Lin, G., Bie, Y., Lei, M., & Zheng, K. (2014). ACO-BTM: A behavior trust model in cloud computing environment. *International Journal of Computational Intelligence System*, *7*(4), 785–795. doi:10.1080 /18756891.2013.864479

Liu, Y. W., Esseghir, M., & Boulahia, L. M. (2016). Evaluation of Parameters Importance in cloud service selection using rough sets. *Applied Mathematics*, *7*, 527–541.

Lübbecke, P., & Lackes, R. (2015). Drivers and inhibitors for the adoption of public cloud services– an empirical study. In *Twenty-first Americas Conference on Information Systems*. Puerto Rico: AIS; . doi:10.4236/am.2016.76049

Lynn, T., van der Werff, L., Hunt, G., & Healy, P. (2016). Development of a cloud trust label: A Delphi approach. *Journal of Computer Information Systems*, *56*(3), 185–193. doi:10.1080/08874417.2016.11 53887

Ma, K., Sun, R., & Abraham, A. (2012). Toward a lightweight framework for monitoring public clouds. In *Fourth International Conference on Computational Aspects of Social Networks*. Sao Carlos: IEEE; . doi:10.1109/CASoN.2012.6412429

Manimegalai, V., & Sathyapriya, P. (2014). Examining the major problems faced by the life insurance policy holders revealed with Henry Garrett ranking technique. *International Journal of Engineering and Management Research*, *4*(3), 1–7.

Martens, B., Teuteberg, Frank. & Gräuler, Matthias. (2011). Design and implementation of a community platform for the evaluation and selection of cloud computing services: a market analysis. In *19th European Conference on Information Systems (ECIS)*. Helsinki, Finland. AIS.

Meland, P., Bernsmed, K., Jaatun, M. G., Castejón, H. N., & Undheim, A. (2014). Expressing cloud security requirements for SLAs in deontic contract languages for cloud brokers. *International Journal of Cloud Computing, 3*(1), 69–93. doi:10.1504/IJCC.2014.058831

Ministry of Electronics and Information Technology. MeitY. (2017). *GI Cloud Meghraj.* Retrieved March 12, 2018, from http://meity.gov.in/content/gi-cloud-meghraj

Naldi, M. (2017). ICMP-based third party estimation of cloud availability. *International Journal of Advances in Telecommunication, Electrotechnics. Signals and Systems, 6*(1), 11–18.

Ouedraogo, M., Mignon, S., Cholez, H., Furnell, S., & Dubois, E. (2015). Security transparency: The next frontier for security research in the cloud. *Journal of Cloud Computing, 4*(1), 12. doi:10.118613677-015-0037-5

Patel, P., Ranabahu, A., & Sheth, A. (2009). Service level agreement in cloud computing. In Cloud computing workshops at OOPSLA09, Orlando, FL.

Repschlaeger, J., Wind, S., Zarnekow, R., & Turowski, K. (2012). A reference guide to cloud computing dimensions: infrastructure as a service classification framework. In 45th Hawaii International Conference on System Science. IEEE; . doi:10.1109/HICSS.2012.76

Repschlaeger, J., Wind, S., Zarnekow, R., & Turowski, K. (2013). Decision model for selecting a cloud provider: a study of service model decision priorities. In *Proceedings of the Nineteenth Americas Conference on Information Systems*, Illinois. AIS.

Repschlaeger, J., Zarnekow, R., Wind, S., & Turowski, K. (2012). Cloud requirement framework: requirements and evaluation criteria to adopt cloud solutions. In ECIS 2012 Proceedings, Barcelona, Spain. AISeL.

Srinivasan, M. K., Sarukesi, K., Rodrigues, P., Manoj, M. S., & Revathy, P. (2012). State-of-the-art cloud computing security taxonomies -a classification of security challenges in the present cloud computing environment. In *Proceedings of the International Conference on Advances in Computing, Communications and Informatics*, Chennai, India. ACM.

Subashini, S., & Kavitha, V. (2011). A survey on security issues in service delivery models of cloud computing. *Journal of Network and Computer Applications, 34*(1), 1–11. doi:10.1016/j.jnca.2010.07.006

Suganya, R., & Hamsalakshmi, R. (2017). A study on customer buying behavior of selected ayurvedic healthcare products. *International Journal of Advanced Research and Development, 2*(2), 13–18.

Tang, M., Dai, X., Liu, J., & Chen, J. (2017). Towards a trust evaluation middleware for cloud service selection. *Future Generation Computer Systems, 74*(3), 302–312. doi:10.1016/j.future.2016.01.009

Wagle, S., Guzek, M., Bouvry, P., & Bisdorff, R. (2015). An evaluation model for selecting cloud services from commercially available cloud providers. In *IEEE 7th International Conference on Cloud Computing Technology and Science,* Vancouver, Canada. CPS.

Wang, Y., Chandrasekhar, S., Singhal, M., & Ma, J. (2016). A limited-trust capacity model for mitigating threats of internal malicious services in cloud computing. *Journal of Cluster Computing, 19*(2), 647–662. doi:10.100710586-016-0560-2

Webster, J., & Watson, R. T. (2002). Analyzing the past to prepare for the future: Writing a literature review. *Management Information Systems Quarterly*, *26*(2), 13–23.

Yu, Y., Miyaji, A., Au, M. H., & Susilo, W. (2017). Cloud computing security and privacy: Standards and regulations. *Computer Standards & Interfaces*, *54*, 1–2. doi:10.1016/j.csi.2017.03.005

Zhang, Q., Cheng, L., & Boutaba, R. (2010). Cloud computing: State-of-the-art and research challenges. *Journal of Internet Services and Applications*, *1*(1), 7–18. doi:10.100713174-010-0007-6

Zheng, Z., Wu, X., Zhang, Y., Lyu, M. R., & Wang, J. (2013). QoS ranking prediction for cloud services. *IEEE Transactions on Parallel and Distributed Systems*, *24*(6), 1213–1222. doi:10.1109/TPDS.2012.285

This research was previously published in the International Journal of Electronic Government Research (IJEGR), 14(2); edited by Vishanth Weerakkody, pages 64-82, copyright year 2018 by IGI Publishing (an imprint of IGI Global).

APPENDIX

Ranking of evaluation criteria of cloud service provider (CSP) as per the format detailed out in Table 8. Kindly rank the evaluation criteria in the order which you would prefer, for CSPs evaluation (1 being the highest rank and 10 is the lowest).

Table 8. Ranking the evaluation criteria

S No.	Evaluation Criteria	Rank
1	Service Capabilities	
2	Reliability	
3	Service Level Agreement (SLA)	
4	Security	
5	Availability	
6	Scalability	
7	Data Center	
8	Compliance	
9	Audit	
10	Performance	

Chapter 16
A Framework to Secure Medical Image Storage in Cloud Computing Environment

Mbarek Marwan
Chouaib Doukkali University, Morocco

Ali Kartit
Chouaib Doukkali University, Morocco

Hassan Ouahmane
Chouaib Doukkali University, Morocco

ABSTRACT

Nowadays, modern healthcare providers create massive medical images every day because of the recent progress in imaging tools. This is generally due to the increasing number of patients demanding medical services. This has resulted in a continuous demand of a large storage space. Unfortunately, healthcare domains still use local data centers for storing medical data and managing business processes. This has significant negative impacts on operating costs associated with licensing fees and maintenance. To overcome these challenges, healthcare organizations are interested in adopting cloud storage rather than on-premise hosted solutions. This is mainly justified by the scalability, cost savings and availability of cloud services. The primary objective of this model is to outsource data and delegate IT computations to an external party. The latter delivers needed storage systems via the Internet to fulfill client's demands. Even though this model provides significant cost advantages, using cloud storage raises security challenges. To this aim, this article describes several solutions which were proposed to ensure data protection. The existing implementations suffer from many limitations. The authors propose a framework to secure the storage of medical images over cloud computing. In this regard, they use multi-region segmentation and watermarking techniques to maintain both confidentiality and integrity. In addition, they rely on an ABAC model to ensure access control to cloud storage. This solution mainly includes four functions, i.e., (1) split data for privacy protection, (2) authentication for medical dataset accessing, (3) integrity checking, and (4) access control to enforce security measures. Hence, the proposal is an appropriate solution to meet privacy requirements.

DOI: 10.4018/978-1-5225-8176-5.ch016

1. INTRODUCTION

In the field of medicine, medical imaging constitutes an essential element in the diagnostic process. This is due mainly to the continuous development of biomedical imaging technology. In fact, these tools are considered as a clinical Diagnostic Support Tool (DST) to improve the quality of medical services. That is, hospitals and imaging centers produce large quantities of digital data to meet increasing demands. Therefore, scalable platforms along with software are required to manage patients' medical data. Traditionally, healthcare organizations build and maintain local data centers to achieve this objective. Although Electronic Medical Record (EMR) systems are very beneficial for healthcare domain, they necessitate large investments in in-house applications and computational resources. Unfortunately, this has a negative impact on operating costs related to maintenance and license. To remedy this problem, cloud storage is a new way of delivering on-demand computing resources over the Internet. The primary aim of this concept is to facilitate the implementation and usage of the storage systems. More precisely, this model is designed to deliver a shared pool of configurable computing resources via the Internet. With this technology, the needed storage systems are provisioned and released to the clients with minimum management effort (Mell et al., 2009). At the same time, cloud storage relies on pay-per-use pricing model in which the consumers are charged based on cloud services utilization. Hence, cloud storage is an adequate solution to cut costs and increasing profits.

For these reasons, there has been a continuous demand for cloud services in the healthcare domain. Though cloud storage has many advantages, the adoption of this technology brings several security problems (Fabian et al., 2015; Anuja et al., 2015; Diago et al., 2014). In this regard, ensuring the confidentiality of medical data in the cloud environment is the major challenge facing this new paradigm, especially in healthcare sector. For instance, many frameworks and solutions have been proposed recently to meet security requirements. The main contribution of this paper is twofold. First, we present the state-of-the-art cloud storage implementation as well as techniques involved in data security. Second, we propose a framework that uses segmentation and watermarking techniques to secure medical images. Additionally, we use ABAC model to enforce data security policies.

The rest of this paper is organized as follows: Section 2 and 3 are meant to present and discuss existing solution to ensure the security of cloud storage. Section 4 and 5 provide a deep insight into privacy-preserving requirements to meet healthcare needs, especially data security. In section 6 and 7, we present the proposed framework as well as method used in data protection process. We end this paper in section 8 and 9 by concluding remarks and future work.

2. RELATED WORK

Bastião et al. (2012) develop a novel architecture to safely implement an outsourcing solution of PACS (Picture Archiving and Communication System). The proposal is designed to support a multi-cloud system, which incorporates more than one cloud providers. Typically, two major components of a common PACS are used in this framework, i.e., DICOM object, Repository and Relational Database (RDBMS). In the same line, blobsore and database are commonly used for storing and archiving medical records. It uses three additional components to address security risks: Gateway, MasterIndex and Cloud Slaves. The MasterIndex module protects the patient's information, especially name and referring physician in order to ensure anonymity. Furthermore, it keeps different keys that are used during encryption and decryption process. In parallel, the Cloud Gateway seeks to ensure interoperability between organizations and public cloud providers. To this aim, it mainly provides two DICOM services for facilitating the exploitation of cloud computing: C-STORE for data storage and C-FIND or C-MOVE for data exchange. In this framework, the cloud Gateway is meant to address privacy concerns by splitting data into many portions. It also uses AES (Advanced Encryption Standard) and SSL (Secure Socket Layer) connection to enforce security. The last module offers needed storage system to safeguard medical data.

Yang et al. (2010) present an application used mainly to boost collaboration between healthcare organizations and their patients. In this respect, this cloud solution uses Medical Image File Accessing System (MIFAS) for building and deploying an Electronic medical record system (EMRS). For this reason, the proposal uses Hadoop platform to enhance reliability and availability. Indeed, medical data are often replicated across many nodes. The main objective of this solution is to facilitate more efficient and effective storage systems use. Moreover, co-allocation mechanism is implemented to improve data transfer rate and enable parallel downloading for enhancing system performance. Although this application uses password for authentication, it still has several limitations in terms of data security and privacy.

Arka et al. (2014) suggest a secure repository infrastructure that allows collaboration among clients. In this case, a mobile device is used to set up remote connections to cloud services. Technically, this application is hosted on a cloud infrastructure and composed of four blocks, i.e., the picture creation device, the image viewer, the web image database and the storage server in the cloud. To protect data, the proposal uses cryptography techniques along with lossless compression functions. Hence, compression algorithms reduce the image size, and hence, minimize the amount of storage space. Next, it uses encryption with a secret key to encode medical images to enhance privacy. In addition, users email is used for access control purpose, especially authentication.

Yang et al. (2014) propose a method to maintain privacy of medical information and facilitate data sharing over cloud computing. To this end, the authors propose a hybrid technique that uses cryptography techniques and statistical analysis technologies for multi-level privacy. In the same line, the medical data are classified into multiple categories to create different security levels. In such an approach, the identifying information of patients is encrypted using the symmetric encryption. Meanwhile, medical data are saved on the cloud in a plain text format. Additionally, medical records are vertically partitioned to meet security requirements. This guarantees that only authorized users can retrieve the partitioned data by using decryption keys to reconstruct the secret image. The primary goal of this approach is to protect medical information while maintaining the unlinkability and anonymity.

Boiron et al. (2011) present a cloud solution to promote collaboration among healthcare institutions and archive medical records. Particularly, the proposed platform is based on two popular systems, i.e., PACS (Picture Archiving and Communication Systems) and RIS (Radiological Information Systems). This architecture allows healthcare organizations to manage their clients' data, especially prefetching, acquisition and viewing of medical images. Moreover, it is designed to allow users to add new records in the Personal Medical Record (PMP). In this case, digital certificates are used for authentication and restricting system access to authorized users only.

Yang et al. (2015) illustrate an image sharing framework, which is used to boost data exchange and enhance interoperability among healthcare organizations. In this regard, the authors rely on Hadoop framework and Open Nebulla, particularly Medical Image File Accessing System (MIFAS). Technically, the proposal is deployed on three separated nodes to enhance performance. In this case, co-allocation mechanism is used in this architecture to enable parallel downloading and to address network issues. In this framework, medical records are split into different parts before transmitting those files to the cloud storage. After successful authentication, a user can search a patient's information and medical records, and then, can retrieve or view medical images. Additionally, the study presented herein compares the performance of MIFAS and PACS. Accordingly, MIFAS reduces the single point failure and enables multi-user concurrency for improving performance.

Castiglione et al. (2015) present a secure cloud application to process 3D medical images. In this case, the proposed technique relies on adaptive lossless compression of 3D medical images algorithm. To this aim, it uses a hybrid approach based on predictive technique to compress data and Least Significant Bit (LSB) for embedding a digital watermark in an image. So, each bit of the watermark string is embedded into a pixel by using LSB method. Meanwhile, it processes those pixels using lossless compression algorithms. The proposed engine offers two prediction models: slice and inter-slice prediction models. Hence, it offers an efficient method for compression with secure embedded watermarks of 3D images as well as data ownership. Technically, the architecture has mainly four modules: virtual cloud, compression and digital watermark, storage and front-end interface. In this regard, the virtual cloud is responsible for locating and transferring medical records. In parallel, other modules provide both compression functionality and storage systems as a service. The proposed solution is deployed on Microsoft Azure platform using MySQL as a database. For security purpose, the proposed framework relies on passwords to ensure access control and authentication.

Fabian et al. (2015) proposed a solution based on multi-cloud environment to improve collaboration between healthcare organizations. To ensure the privacy of medical data, the authors suggest the role based access control using Ciphertext Policy Attribute Based Encryption (CP-ABE). Hence, only legitimate clients can have access to specified attributes. Additionally, the medical records are signed using DSA signature through SHA1. Next, users encrypt them according to Role Based Access Control Policy (RBACP) to ensure the integrity and confidentiality of medical images. On the Multi-Cloud Proxy (MCP) side, medical records are split into multiple portions using a secret sharing scheme in order to store them at different cloud providers' locations. As a result, the proposed method has a dual purpose; it guarantees that privacy of data is not compromised and also avoids unlinkability. In this proposed solution, it uses hash functions to identify a medical record in multi-cloud environment. Unfortunately, the system has some limitations regarding access revocation and management of emergency exceptions.

Bastião et al. (2012) presented a secure cloud architecture for facilitating exchange of medical image between multiple healthcare institutions. It is designed to provide secure connection and shared repositories to support multi-center systems. To this end, the proposal has two components: DICOM Cloud Router, DICOM Bridge. The former is responsible for handling and forwarding ciphered images. The latter offers a relay mechanism across different DICOM Cloud Router modules, which are implemented over different healthcare organizations. Also, it manages the session keys used to encrypt and decrypt digital data. Consequently, the proposed framework uses C-STORE, C-FIND and C-MOVE commands to offers the two common DICOM services, i.e., storage and query/retrieve. Nevertheless, this system has limitations on its security mechanism and measures.

Mohanty et al. (2012) propose a secure framework that performs both volume rendering and data visualization of 3D medical images. For security purpose, the secret sharing method is used for a distributed control of medical images. Meanwhile, the proposal uses pre-classification volume ray-casting for performing data rendering technique. Following this, medical records are split into multiple portions and distributed over different cloud providers to guarantee security of medical data. To get the secret image, a cloud provider has to perform the rendering operation on each share. Consequently, the authorized client relies on secret sharing method to reconstruct the original medical image. However, this solution has several limitations regarding privacy and security, especially access control.

Rostrom et al. (2011) illustrate a solution that uses cloud storage for storing medical images. In this concept, Transport Layer Security (TLS) two-way algorithm is used for authentication and establishing a secure communication between cloud provider and client. More precisely, the system uses certificate exchange for access control and encryption purpose. So, the Certificate Authority (CA) creates a unique certificate, which is distributed to all clients and cloud provider. In such a scheme, a user possesses two keys, i.e., private and public certificate. The private certificate contains a public key to encrypt data and private key to decrypt data. In this same line, the public certificate is devoted to the authentication process. This architecture is developed using Net framework and deployed on Windows Azure Platform. To sum up, this prototype ensures authentication and provides a secure method of transferring data among healthcare professionals.

Gitanjali et al. (2011) suggest a cloud application that helps patients and doctors manage and access their medical data through a mobile device. The proposed solution uses mobile cloud to store and manage medical records. Technically, the server module uses XML files and oracle 10i express edition and implemented on EyeOS platform. In parallel, the client module is developed using Java Eclipse and Android SDK. For privacy reason, it uses client's ID for authentication and access control. Moreover, data are compressed through JPEG2000 technique to enhance security and to improve performance.

Patel et al. (2012) illustrate a novel approach to process medical images. In this regard, it uses remote rendering over the cloud computing to enhance diagnostic radiology. Basically, this architecture takes advantage of cloud computing, especially virtualization technology. In this regard, the proposal offers two kinds of radiology services: software and platform to help healthcare organizations. So, it proposes software as a service to process 3D medical images using cloud services. Furthermore, cloud technology can be used as a remote infrastructure to store medical images and to exchange data between different institutions. To meet security requirements, clients' data are encrypted, and then, transferred over the Internet using Secure Socket Layer (SSL) protocol. Nevertheless, this solution has limitations relating to authentication.

Pan et al. (2015) presented a cloud platform to facilitate medical images exchange between two healthcare organizations. For this reasons, the authors describe the proposed public platform use case and then evaluate risk and security objectives for digital content. To protect medical data, they use reversible watermarking to ensure integrity and authentication. In this architecture, a Central Authority (CA) and Organization Based Access Control model (OrBAC) are used to restrict access to cloud resources and traceability. Additionally, Advanced Encryption Standard (AES) maintains the confidentiality of content medical. In this regard, this solution is built using Java and SQLite.

Teng et al. (2010) use DICOM standard to build a cloud application for providing medical image archive services. In this respect, the proposed solution is composed of three modules, including DICOM server to perform DICOM standard requests, DICOM indexer to improve the search efficiency and User Interface (UI) to view medical images. Typically, this platform is implemented on Microsoft Azure and based on the open source project DICOM#. Furthermore, both DICOM server and DICOM indexer are implemented using C# language. Meanwhile, the UI module is built using Microsoft Sliver light and ASP.NET to ensure interoperability with other systems. But, this application relies only on IP filtering mechanism and security provided by Microsoft Azure to meet security requirements.

Kanagaraji et al. (2011) present a solution that uses Open Nebula 3.0 platform to simplify and speed-up medical data storage. Also, it seeks to promote collaboration between healthcare organizations. Indeed,

Open Nebula is an efficient system to ensure interoperability, security and scalability. To enforce data security, the proposal uses Access Control List (ACL) and external authentication to prevent malicious data disclosure, such as LDAP, X509, SSH. Besides, this open source relies on Secure Socket Layer (SSL) to protect internal and external communications.

3. DISCUSSION

Over the last few years, the healthcare domain has started to take some steps towards implementing the cloud computing. The primary objective of this concept is to store medical images and to promote data exchange between different healthcare organizations. Currently, a collaborative work system has greatly grown thanks to many technological developments in information flow and cost saving. To this objective, the cloud providers offer scalable storage systems and remote services to facilitate inter-institutional communication. Consequently, there have been important efforts from both research and industry to meet the healthcare's demand. In response, there are several implementations that aim at offering secure platforms for outsourcing e-health system as they see the advantages of doing so. Although cloud computing is an affordable alternative to local data centers, there are significant challenges that obstruct the implementation of cloud storage solution in healthcare sectors. As discussed above, security problems are the key factors affecting the existing frameworks and current implementation efforts. In reality, multiple architectures and applications that are based on various encryption techniques have been used to meet privacy-preserving needs. More precisely, numerous cryptographic techniques are suggested to address security problems, including confidentiality, anonymity, unlinkability and integrity. But, ensuring privacy of medical images in cloud storage sill requires more improvements and sophisticated security measures. Indeed, the majority of those frameworks rely on conventional cryptography techniques, like AES, RSA, etc. Nevertheless, these methods are not appropriate for medical records. Particularly, a medical image is a sensitive data used during diagnosis procedure. In this case, any modifications or degradations of image quality can cause misdiagnosis. Accordingly, cryptographic methods should be lossless and reversible to prevent data loss. To this end, we suggest a hybrid solution that uses segmentation along with watermarking techniques to fulfill security and privacy requirements, especially image quality. For this objective, it is essential to define privacy requirements that need to consider when designing and developing a framework to secure cloud storage.

4. PRIVACY REQUIREMENTS IN CLOUD COMPUTING

Unlike normal data, to keep medical records safe necessitates much more security requirement than a regular model CIA (confidentiality, integrity and availability). Basically, it is mandatory to ensure proper handling of patients' data for complying with regulations and laws. In this regard, this section seeks to enlighten many factors involved in data security and privacy. The following parameters have been collected from different earlier literature surveys (Ali et al., 2015; Marwan et al., 2016; Abbas et al., 2015).

4.1. Confidentiality

Confidentiality of medical records refers to the process that keeps medical data and patients' information secret, and hence, prevents data loss and unauthorized access. To prevent insider threats and attacks, medical records should be protected against not only external clients but also against the cloud provider. Typically, clients encrypt their data before sending them to the cloud storage to avoid data disclosure.

4.2. Integrity

Basically, the original medical images need to be preserved and intact during transmission and storage in the cloud. Obviously, any change to the content when using cloud storage would affect image quality, and hence, diagnostic accuracy. In the same line, it is difficult to maintain and monitor integrity of medical record because all data are remotely saved on cloud servers. On this point, data integrity checking in cloud computing is still at its early stage, and hence, is a challenging problem.

4.3. Availability

Broadly speaking, it is mandatory that all medical data are available and accessible anywhere and anytime. In other words, cloud storage system must be available and connected to the Internet. Unfortunately, deletion of patients' records by illegitimate users or malware can bring electronic medical data offline or render service unavailable. In a matter of fact, special consideration needs to be given to this factor because of the importance of digital records in modern medicine.

4.4. Data Ownership

It is basically the procedure that allows one to determine and maintain the rightful owner of medical records. In this regard, the owner can grant and revoke access rights for other users to a specific object using access control tools. In a cloud storage system, this parameter identifies client who has the right and ability to create, edit, modify, share and restrict access to the medical images. In practice, encryption and watermarking methods are widely used to carry out this mission.

4.5. Authentication

In general, this technique plays a vital role in control access procedure. The aim is to identify users who would like to access and use cloud storage. More formally, the authentication system entails consumers to provide their identity. Typically, user's login has to be identical to the stored credentials for a successful authentication. the key idea of this mechanism is to guarantee that only authorized users can gain access to medical images stored on cloud computing.

4.6. Anonymity

According to acts regulating healthcare domain, personal health information should be kept private and confidential. In other words, the name and the social security number of patient are also sensitive data that must be protected against unauthorized entity, especially cloud providers. Currently, various techniques are used attempting to infer the real identity of a user, including pseudonyms method, K-anonymity and K-map model.

4.7. Unlinkability

For security purposes, it is important to ensure that unauthorized internal or external entities are not able to deduce the relation between medical records and their ownership. Hence, security considerations are also applied to patients' information, such as the name, address and social security number.

4.8. Auditing Capability

In the cloud computing, all actions executed by users or nominated third party need to be audited and logged. Moreover, the system can, by default, monitor all users' transactions. The primary objective of this technique is to ensure that all manipulations meet privacy requirements for complying with policies and standards.

5. CLOUD SERVICES REQUIREMENTS

Using cloud storage offers the possibility to safeguard clients' data on remote cloud servers instead of local data centers. However, this raises security challenges related to data protection. Moreover, conventional security tools are not sufficiently well-suited to highly flexible and dynamic environments, especially cloud computing. Hence, it is necessary to adopt and extend existing models to meet cloud requirements. In fact, cloud is a distributed system that delivers resources and services with high dynamicity and scalability. In this section, we provide a comprehensive taxonomy for cloud features that must be taken into consideration when designing or implementing security mechanisms in cloud environments. This aims to comply with cloud storage constraints. In addition, e-Health services necessitate data exchange between healthcare providers. In general, we can classify them into six main parameters.

5.1. Dynamic Environment

In general, existing security tools need to take into consideration that cloud resources are often dynamic and scalable to automatically adapt to changes occurred in cloud computing.

5.2. Distributed System

Cloud computing usually refers to a distributed environment. In this concept, applications and computational resources are hosted at different locations.

5.3. Scalability

Broadly speaking, cloud providers serve an arbitrary number of users that belong to different organizations. Hence, security policies have to be scalable to meet security requirements for each entity. In other words, these mechanisms are not designed for local domain, but they should support global agreement of attributes.

5.4. Heterogeneity

Cloud computing relies on a variety of diverse technologies. However, current security mechanisms are usually designed for a specific application or architecture. Following this, they are not universally suitable to all cloud providers.

5.5. Simplicity

The primary aim of cloud computing is to deliver IT services to clients with minimum management efforts. Also, it ensures ubiquitous access to cloud services. For this reason, techniques and tools involved in data protection should be simple and efficient to reduce computational complexity.

5.6. Access Revocation

In healthcare domain, patients have the ability to revoke the access right granted to other users. In this approach, the owners can revoke permissions that have been set on their objects.

5.7. Fine-Gain Access

After a successful authentication, a set of authorizations are affected to the users according to their identity. This enable authorized users accessing and modifying their health records in cloud storage.

6. PROPOSED FRAMEWORK

In essence, cloud storage is a model that aims at outsourcing images storage and computations to an external provider. For these reasons, healthcare professionals use this new paradigm to take advantage of IT services without investing in local platforms. Beside its numerous advantages, the usage of cloud computing brings about security problems. To this end, various frameworks are proposed to address privacy issues. Unfortunately, protecting medical records needs more improvement to prevent security breaches. In this study, we propose a novel method based on segmentation and watermarking approach to secure cloud storage. The proposal aims at meeting privacy requirements and avoiding disclosure of medical data.

6.1. The Fundamentals of the Proposed Framework

As discussed above, ensuring security and privacy is the key factor affecting adoption of cloud storage in the healthcare domain. For this reason, we introduce a third party called CloudSec. In this architecture, the latter is a secure interface between healthcare organizations and cloud providers. To enforce data security, the proposed architecture will be implemented in a multi-cloud environment for reducing the disclosure risk and enabling parallel upload and download of medical data. Figure 1 presents an overview of our proposed architecture and its main components. In general, it relies on two modules to address data security and enhance performance, i.e., CloudSec and Cloud Slave. The latter is a multi-cloud environment that offers remote scalable storage systems to the clients via the Internet. In this section, we discuss the fundamentals of the proposed solution, particularly the role of each module. Furthermore, we present techniques involved in data security process and their key advantages.

In such scenario, clients use SSL protocol to secure data exchange, and then, send medical records to CloudSec. For security measures, CloudSec keeps patient's identifying information in a local database. In doing so, it ensures data privacy, especially unlinkability and anonymity. At the same time, CloudSec performs segmentation techniques to divide an image into several regions to enhance confidentiality. In this regard, we rely on the Graph-Cut scheme, described in (Delong et al. 2009), to carry out multi-region segmentation. As a result, the secret image is broken up into small parts to prevent malicious data disclosure and achieve a high security level, as shown in Figure 2.

Meanwhile, using segmentation would enhance image processing and system performance. In reality, this technique plays a crucial role in data preparation and pre-processing step. Consequently, this proposed framework is designed to enable parallel data storage and processing of large amounts of data.

Figure 1. Architecture of the proposed framework

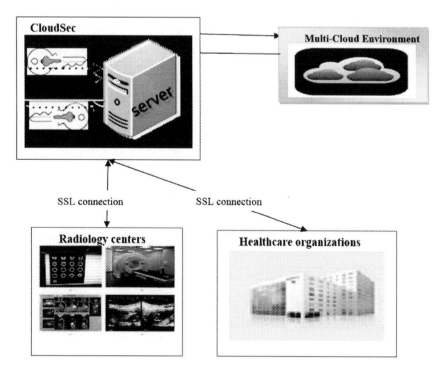

Figure 2. The principle of multi-region segmentation

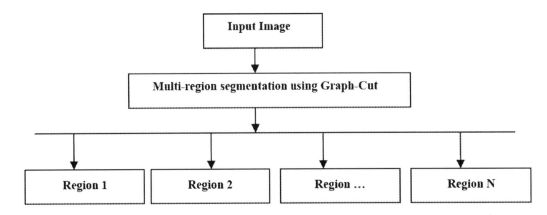

For further security measures, we use reversible watermarking technique to ensure authentication and integrity checking. More precisely, we rely on the Thodi algorithm (Thodi et al., 2004; Thodi et al., 2007) for embedding a digital watermark in each portion. The main reason for choosing this type of algorithm is twofold (Khan et al., 2014). First, is designed to survive normal image processing operations. Second, it is an efficient algorithm and easy to implement scheme. Technically, the social security number (SSN) is used as a patient identifier (ID) to maintain data ownership and ensure authentication. In this study, we use digital signatures along with lossless watermarking for verifying the integrity of medical images, especially in the retrieval process. Figure 3 below presents the fundamentals of the proposed solution to address security issues in cloud storage.

Figure 3. The fundamentals of the proposed technique

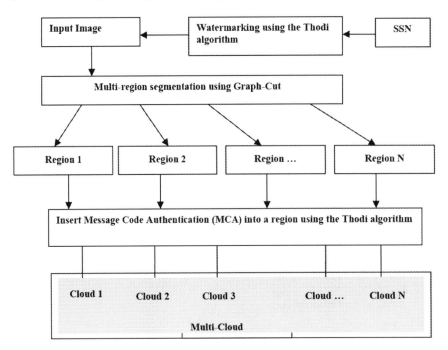

Similarly, the secret image is divided into many regions using Graph-Cut method. After that, we generate the digital signatures for each region through hash function, which is based on Secure Hash Algorithm SHA-256, especially Message Code Authentication (MCA). To monitor data integrity, we insert the digest or resume into those created regions using the Thodi algorithm. To sum up, this proposed technique is an efficient solution to control medical images integrity in the cloud storage, as illustrated in Figure 4.

In this approach, CloudSec offers also access control as a service. In other words, it decides who can use specific system, resources and applications. For this objective, a set of criteria are defined in advance, which need to comply with a security policy. In doing so, it guarantees that only authorized clients can access the medical records. Meanwhile, it monitors and records all attempts made to access a cloud storage system. Typically, various elements are defined to implement a security strategy, including subject, rights, objects, authorization, obligation and conditions. In this regard, subjects refer to users or organizations, while objects refer to medical images. In such a scheme, authentication is a process that determines decision making. The latter is influenced by two parameters: rights and obligations. The first one is the set of actions that a user can perform on cloud resources. The second one clearly indicates whether requirements to fulfill users' requests are satisfied. Figure 5 illustrates the principle and an overview of an access control mechanism.

Figure 4. The principle of the integrity checking (Pan et al., 2009)

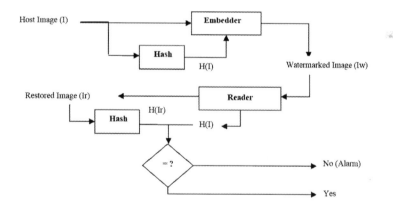

Figure 5. An overview of an access control mechanism

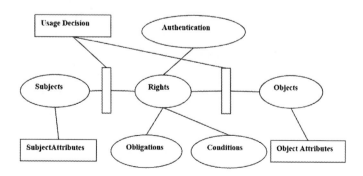

Based on this choice, the proposed framework is an appropriate solution to boost the utilization of cloud storage in the healthcare domain. This is achieved by improving both medical data security and system performance.

7. USED TECHNIQUES

As outlined above, the proposed framework uses mainly four techniques and technologies to significantly reduce security risks in cloud storage. In this section, we will discuss in detail these solutions, particularly the advantages of these techniques.

7.1. Reversible Watermarking

Basically, this technique is meant to insert digital watermark into an image in a lossless manner. Often, we use patient ID or digital signature as a watermark. Obviously, it is essential to reduce any distortion and negative impacts caused by this technique to avoid wrong interpretation. To this aim, we rely on reversible watermarking algorithms. In practice, the watermark is extracted from the medical image, and then, used for authentication and integrity checking purposes. In reality, these types of algorithms are based on various approaches, including compression, histogram modification, quantization and expansion. Hence, there are diverse reversible watermarking algorithms. Following this, it is difficult to choose the best scheme that meets all requirements. According to Khan et al. (2014), reversible watermarking algorithms that use expansion methods are often effective and easy to implement. More precisely, a practical implementation of these algorithms (Khan et al., 2014) shows that the Thodi algorithm (Thodi et al., 2004; Thodi et al., 2007) is most suitable for medical images. This is mainly due to the fact that the Thodi algorithm is rapid and efficient.

7.2. Multi-Region Segmentation

The primary objective of this mechanism is to divide an image into many segments. In this context, existing methods are classified into two types: region-based and edge-based segmentation. The first category is meant to group pixels with similar values in a region. In the second class, it is mainly based on edge pixel classification to determine boundaries between regions. In this work, we use multi-region segmentation to enhance data privacy, especially confidentiality. In this regard, we opt for Graph-Cut techniques, particularly the scheme developed by Delong (Delong et al. 2009). Technically, this method relies on single Graph-Cut and multi-region energy to globally optimize multi-region objects. At the same time, it encodes geometric interactions between distinct regions and boundary models. Accordingly, an image is split into many regions. Thus, it helps CloudSec to store medical images on different storage systems. This would dramatically reduce the risk of data disclosure and support parallel access. Hence, this approach is an appropriate solution to meet both security and performance goals.

7.3. Access Control

It generally refers to a set of methods and procedures aimed at determining the legitimate individuals who can execute some actions on specific cloud resources. Currently, several methods, models, technologies have been suggested for designing and implementing an access control model to fulfill security requirements in cloud computing. In practice, six models are widely used to ensure data security, i.e. Mandatory Access Control (MAC), Discretionary Access Control (DAC), Attribute Based Access Control (ABAC), Role Based Access Control (RBAC), Organization-Based Access Control (OrBAC) and Identity Based Access Control (IBAC) (Younis et al., 2014). The first one focuses on restricting access to sensitive data. Accordingly, a central administrator determines authorized users who can use a specific medical record. In DAC, an access control list (ACL) is defined to restrict access of objects. In general, this model uses the principle of object ownership. Hence, data owner has complete control over specific cloud resources. However, ABAC model relies on users' attributes for decision making, which reflects the identity of a user within an organization. So, this solution ensures fine graininess and data confidentiality for data access. For security reason, the Role Based Access Control (RBAC) model uses often the job role of each user to define security policy. For this objective, each role contains a number of permissions, transactions and functionalities, which are necessary in a specific job. For scalability purposes, the OrBAC model is suggested to take into account the context of situation. In other words, the security policy is designed for an abstract entity. In IBAC, the identity of a user is considered important for access decision making. For this reason, it uses access control matrix to define the authorization policy. Basically, attribute associated for subject, action and object should be configured in advance.

According to parameters and criteria defined above, ABAC model is the most appropriate solution for a cloud environment. In fact, this model is meant to guarantee both flexibility and dynamicity. For this reason, we suggest ABAC model to secure access to the cloud storage.

7.4. Multi-Cloud

This concept is designed to support distributed storage system by saving data on various nodes. Broadly speaking, this architecture seeks to minimize cloud computing security risk and avoid vendor lock-in issues. Meanwhile, it is meant to enhance performance, reliability and availability. Currently, many frameworks have been developed to implement this new concept, including Byzantine Fault tolerance, DepSky, Redundant Array of Cloud Storage (RACS), High Availability and Integrity Layer (HAIL) and Intercloud Storage (IC Store). In this regard, DepSky is the most widely used model to build a multi-cloud environment (Tebaa et al., 2014). Basically, this system relies on two algorithms: DEPSKY-A (Available DepSky) to support data replication and DEPSKY-CA to protect data by using secret sharing technique. Hence, it guarantees confidentiality, integrity and availability. Besides, DepSky offers scalable virtual resources using four distinct clouds, as illustrated in Figure 6.

8. SECURITY ANALYSIS OF THE PROPOSED FRAMEWORK

As outlined above, implementing cloud storage in healthcare domain is still facing a number of security concerns. In this respect, we propose a framework to address these problems. To this purpose, we use CloudSec as a trusted third party to meet security requirement using a local database to store metadata.

Figure 6. The principle of DepSky architecture (Bessani et al., 2013)

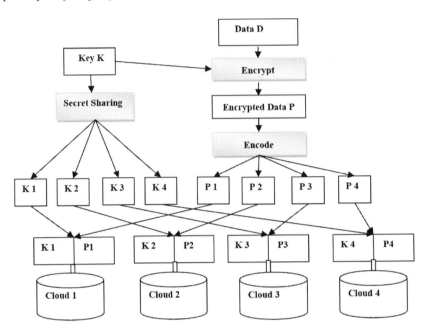

For example, it ensures collusion-resistant, anonymity and unlinkability. In this approach, segmentation and watermarking are used to protect medical data, especially confidentiality, integrity and authentication. In addition, these proposed techniques are reversible to prevent data loss. To enforce security, we use ABAC access control model to restrict and limit access to medical data stored on the cloud storage.

The proposed framework is implemented in a multi-cloud environment, particularly DepSky model, to reduce cloud computing threats and vulnerabilities. This is achieved by storing each generated region in different cloud storages. Accordingly, medical images are split into various regions using the Graph-Cut algorithm before uploading them to the cloud storage. In the same line, we use the Thodi algorithm to ensure data integrity and authentication. To summarize, the proposal divides the secret data to enhance both security and availability of cloud storage.

9. CONCLUSION AND FUTURE WORK

Healthcare industry is continuously looking for ways to improve medical services. This has led to a rapid growth and widespread use of imaging tools in the healthcare domain. Traditionally, each hospital must build a local data center and develop its in-house applications to handle medical data. However, this approach would increase operating costs linked to maintenance, license, etc. For this reason, cloud-based medical image storage is introduced to fulfill client's demands. In such a model, an external party delivers powerful and scalable storage solutions to the healthcare institutions. In addition, on-demand resources model promises cost saving and availability. In this regard, it helps healthcare organizations to concentrate on their core business by outsourcing some peripheral activities, i.e., IT services. At the same time, cloud computing is an appropriate concept to boost collaboration between healthcare professionals by sharing computational resources. Even though cloud storage offers many advantages, the implementation of this model in the healthcare sectors faces security challenges. In particular, to maintain data privacy is still the major issue that need to be addressed. For instance, various techniques are used to secure cloud storage. Unfortunately, the majority of them are basically classical cryptography techniques, including AES, RSA and DES. Therefore, they are not suitable for practical medical image encryption because of the large volume of data. For this objective, we suggested an approach based on segmentation for security purpose. Accordingly, the secret image is divided into many segments using Graph-Cut algorithm. In this context, DepSky model is selected as a storage system to ensure reliability and availability. Meanwhile, the watermarking technique is used to maintain data integrity and authentication. This is achieved by using the digital signatures for preventing unauthorized modification of medical images. For security purpose, we suggested ABAC to control and restrict access to the cloud storage. In our future work, we will implement this proposed framework using Java. Moreover, we plan to implement ABAC as an access control mechanism to improve data protection.

REFERENCES

Abbas, A. (2015). E-Health Cloud: Privacy Concerns and Mitigation Strategies. In *Medical Data Privacy Handbook* (pp. 389–421). Springer. doi:10.1007/978-3-319-23633-9_15

Ali, M., Khan, S. U., & Vasilakos, A. V. (2015). Security in Cloud Computing: Opportunities and Challenges. *Information Sciences, 305*, 357–383. doi:10.1016/j.ins.2015.01.025

Anuja, M., & Jeyamala, C. (2015). A Survey on Security Issues and Solutions for Storage and Exchange of Medical Images in Cloud. *International Journal of Emerging Trends in Electrical and Electronics, 11*(6).

Arka, I. H., & Chellappana, K. (2014). Collaborative Compressed I-Cloud Medical Image Storage with Decompress Viewer. *Procedia Computer Science, 42*, 114–121. 10.1016/j.procs.2014.11.041

Bastião, L. (2012). DICOM Relay Over the Cloud. *International Journal of Computer Assisted Radiology and Surgery, 8*(3), 323–333.

Bastião, L., Costa, C., & Oliveira, J. L. (2012). A PACS Archive Architecture Supported on Cloud services. *International Journal of Computer Assisted Radiology and Surgery, Springer, 7*(3), 349–358. doi:10.100711548-011-0625-x PMID:21678039

Bessani, A., Correia, M., Quaresma, B., Andre, F., & Sousa, P. (2013). DEPSKY: Dependable and Secure Storage in a Cloud-of-Clouds. *ACM Transactions on Storage, 9*(4), 12. doi:10.1145/2535929

Boiron, P., & Dussaux, V. (2011). Healthcare Software as a Service: the Greater Paris Region Program Experience the So-called "region sans film" Program. In *Proceedings of the 15th IEEE International Enterprise Distributed Object Computing Conference Workshops* (pp. 247-251). 10.1109/EDOCW.2011.38

Castiglione, A., Pizzolante, R., De Santis, A., Carpentieri, B., Castiglione, A., & Palmieri, F. (2015). Cloud-based Adaptive Compression and Secure Management Services for 3D Healthcare Data. Future Generation Computer Systems, 43, 120-134.

Delong, A., & Boykov, Y. (2009). Globally Optimal Segmentation of Multi-region Objects. In *Proceedings of the IEEE 12th International Conference on Computer Vision* (pp. 285-292). 10.1109/ICCV.2009.5459263

Fabian, B., Ermakova, T., & Junghanns, Ph. (2015). Collaborative and Secure Sharing of Healthcare Data in Multi-Clouds. *Information Systems, 48*, 132–150. doi:10.1016/j.is.2014.05.004

Fernandes, D. A. B., Soares, L. F. B., Gomes, J. V., Freire, M. M., & Inacio, P. R. M. (2014). Security Issues in Cloud Environments: A Survey. *International Journal of Information Security, Springer, 13*(2), 113–170. doi:10.100710207-013-0208-7

Gitanjali, S., Govardhani, T. C., Lakshmi Priya, G., & Somasundaram, M. (2011). Medical Image Data Management System in Mobile Cloud Computing Environment. In *Proceedings of the International Conference on Signal, Image Processing and Applications.*

Kanagaraji, G., & Sumathi, A. C. (2011). Proposal of an Open-Source Cloud Computing System for Exchanging Medical Images of a Hospital Information System. In *Proceedings of the 3rd International Conference on Trends in Information Sciences and Computing (TISC)* (pp. 144–149). 10.1109/TISC.2011.6169102

Khan, A., Siddiqa, A., Munib, S., & Malik, S. A. (2014). A Recent Survey of Reversible Watermarking Techniques. *Journal of Information Science, 279*, 251–272. doi:10.1016/j.ins.2014.03.118

Majumder, A., Namasudra, S., & Nath, S. (2014). *Taxonomy and Classification of Access Control Models for Cloud Environments. In Continued Rise of the Cloud, LNCS* (pp. 23-53). Springer.

Marwan, M., Kartit, A., & Ouahmane, H. (2016). Cloud-Based Medical Image Issues. *International Journal of Applied Engineering Research, 11*, 3713–3719.

Mell, P., & Grance, T. (2009). "The NIST Definition of Cloud Computing," National Institute of Standards and Technology. *Technical Report, 15*, 1–3.

Mohanty, M., Atrey, P., & Ooi, W. T. (2012). Secure Cloud-Based Medical Data Visualization. In *Proceedings of the 20th ACM international conference on Multimedia* (pp. 1105-1108). 10.1145/2393347.2396394

Pan, W., Coatrieux, G., Bouslimi, D., & Prigent, N. (2015). Secure public cloud platform for medical images sharing. *Studies in Health Technology and Informatics, 210*, 251–255. PMID:25991144

Pan, W., Coatrieux, G., Cuppens-Boulahia, N., Cuppens, F., & Roux, C. (2009). Medical Image Integrity Control Combining Digital Signature and Lossless Watermarking. In *Data Privacy Management and Autonomous Spontaneous Security, LNCS* (Vol. 5939). Springer.

Patel, R. P. (2012). *Cloud Computing and Virtualization Technology in Radiology (Technical Report).* In Clinical Radiology (pp. 1095–1100). Elsevier.

Rostrom, T., & Teng, C. C. (2011). Secure Communications for PACS in a Cloud Environment. In *Proceedings of the 33rd Annual International Conference of the IEEE, EMBS* (pp. 8219-8222). 10.1109/IEMBS.2011.6092027

Tebaa, M., & Hajji, S. E. L. (2014). From Single to Multi-Clouds Computing Privacy and Fault Tolerance. *IERI Procedia, 10*, 112-118. 10.1016/j.ieri.2014.09.099

Teng, C. C., Mitchell, J., & Walker, C. (2010). A Medical Image Archive Solution in the Cloud. In *Proceedings of the IEEE International Conference on Software Engineering and Service Sciences* (pp. 431-434). 10.1109/ICSESS.2010.5552343

Thodi, D. M., & Rodriguez, J. J. (2004). Prediction-error Based Reversible Watermarking. In *Proceedings of the International Conference on Image Processing* (pp. 1549–1552).

Thodi, D. M., & Rodríguez, J. J. (2007). Expansion Embedding Techniques for Reversible Watermarking. *IEEE Transactions on Image Processing, 16*(3), 721–730. doi:10.1109/TIP.2006.891046 PMID:17357732

Yang, C. T., Chen, L. T., Chou, W. L., & Wang, K. C. (2010). Implementation of a Medical Image File Accessing System on Cloud Computing. In *Proceedings of the IEEE 13th International Conference in Computational Science and Engineering (CSE)* (pp. 321-326). 10.1109/CSE.2010.48

Yang, C. T., Shih, W. C., Chen, L. T., Kuo, C. T., Jiang, F. C., & Leu, F. Y. (2015). Accessing Medical Image File with Co-Allocation HDFS in Cloud. *Future Generation Computer Systems, Elsevier, 43*(C), 61–73. doi:10.1016/j.future.2014.08.008

Yang, J. J., Li, J. Q., & Niu, Y. (2014). A Hybrid Solution for Privacy Preserving Medical Data Sharing in the Cloud Environment. *Future Generation Computer Systems, 43*(C), 74–86.

Younis, Y.A., Kifayat, K. & Merabti, M. (2014). Access Control Model for Cloud Computing. *Journal of Information Security and Applications, 19*(1), 5–60.

This research was previously published in the Journal of Electronic Commerce in Organizations (JECO), 16(1); edited by Pedro Isaías, pages 1-16, copyright year 2018 by IGI Publishing (an imprint of IGI Global).

Chapter 17
A Security–By–Distribution Approach to Manage Big Data in a Federation of Untrustworthy Clouds

Jens Kohler
University of Applied Sciences Mannheim, Germany

Christian Richard Lorenz
University of Applied Sciences Mannheim, Germany

Markus Gumbel
University of Applied Sciences Mannheim, Germany

Thomas Specht
University of Applied Sciences Mannheim, Germany

Kiril Simov
Bulgarian Academy of Sciences, Bulgaria

ABSTRACT

In recent years, Cloud Computing has drastically changed IT-Architectures in enterprises throughout various branches and countries. Dynamically scalable capabilities like CPUs, storage space, virtual networks, etc. promise cost savings, as huge initial infrastructure investments are not required anymore. This development shows that Cloud Computing is also a promising technology driver for Big Data, as the storage of unstructured data when no concrete and defined data schemes (variety) can be managed with upcoming NoSQL architectures. However, in order to fully exploit these advantages, the integration of a trustworthy 3rd party public cloud provider is necessary. Thus, challenging questions concerning security, compliance, anonymization, and privacy emerge and are still unsolved. To address these challenges, this work presents, implements and evaluates a security-by-distribution approach for NoSQL document stores that distributes data across various cloud providers such that every provider only gets a small data chunk which is worthless without the others.

DOI: 10.4018/978-1-5225-8176-5.ch017

INTRODUCTION

No other trend has changed the entire Information Technology during the last decade as Cloud Computing actually has done. Slowly, the hype about this buzzword abates and enterprises recognize the true added value of renting computing resources from the cloud. Cloud Computing in the context of this work is defined by the five essential characteristics listed in Mell and Grance (2011), with the on-demand self-service where customers are able to rent computing capabilities by themselves whenever they need them, followed by the requirement of a broad network bandwidth access. Furthermore, resources from the cloud are pooled together with the usage of virtualization from a provider perspective, which enables a rapid elasticity to provide requested resources. Finally, all provided resources are monitored (i.e. measured) by both, the providers and the consumers to have a provable accounting model. For most enterprises, the essential benefit is the dynamic scalability of computing resources along with cost advantages from the pay-as-you-go billing models (Furht et al., 2010). But also other benefits like working independently from any location, the fast deployment of resources and the development of new business models and markets with high-dynamic (i.e. elastic) IT infrastructures were key drivers for the development of Cloud Computing (Gens & Shirer, 2013).

Moreover, a new business case regarding Cloud Computing is now emerging: Big Data. Here, huge amounts of unstructured data at a great velocity must be managed, i.e. stored, analyzed, interpreted, corrected, etc. The notion of Big Data was firstly introduced by Pettey and Goasduff (2011) in 2011 where the three above-mentioned properties volume, variety and velocity are explained in greater detail. With respect to this, Cloud Computing is able to offer dynamically scalable resources to address these three challenges: instead of huge initial or new investments in better hardware, the required capabilities can be rented on-demand. Then, they can be used for a certain time, be dynamically scaled according to the data volume and velocity, and finally just turned off when they are not required anymore. Thus, two of the three Big Data properties are addressed, but variety is still a challenging issue. Here, NoSQL (not only SQL) databases offer promising features to efficiently store unstructured data. These new kinds of databases are considered in more detail in this chapter and are therefore defined in the following section.

Additionally, it is a fact that the more data are collected, the more important becomes privacy and security for enterprises as well as for end-customers. This becomes even more challenging, if data are managed in the cloud at an external provider. Therefore, the increasing usage of cloud services is accompanied by concerns regarding security, compliance, and privacy and customers depend on the security measures of the service providers. Moreover, for customers it is not transparent, which security measures are implemented by the provider Neves, Correia, Bruno, Fernando, and Paulo (2013), Sood (2012), and Cloud Security Alliance (2013). Hence, challenges of data privacy and compliance still are the most significant obstacles for an increased usage of Cloud Computing (Gens & Shirer, 2013).

To address these challenging security concerns and to ensure data privacy, several different approaches exist, e.g. encryption with digital signatures. A different approach is developed with SeDiCo at the University of Applied Sciences in Mannheim. SeDiCo (A Secure and Distributed Cloud Data Store) is a framework for distributed and secure data storage. With this framework, sensitive data can be segregated from non-sensitive data and stored at physically different places such as different cloud providers. Thus, the actual place of the data is disguised, as every chunk of data is worthless without the others. For example, bank accounts can be stored separately from the owners' names and thus, even if an attacker gets access to one of the partitions, the compromised data does not contain useful information. A simplified example that illustrates this basic principle is shown in Figure 1.

Figure 1. Security-by-distribution example

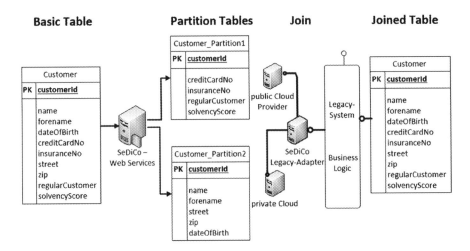

The example illustrates that when data from Customer_Partition1 is stolen or accidentally made publically available, the data (e.g. the credit card number or the insurance number) cannot be misused, as the data from the corresponding Customer_Partition2 (e.g. the corresponding name or address, etc.) is still secure and unknown to the thief or the public.

Currently, the SeDiCo framework supports relational database architectures. In widely distributed systems – particularly with respect to Big Data – those database architectures reach their limits. Here scalable databases which can be distributed to many computing nodes are considered adequate. This requirement entailed a new generation of database architectures, which can be summarized under the NoSQL umbrella. These databases were designed for a wide horizontal distribution and allow the processing of large amounts of data. In combination with that, Cloud Computing is considered suitable for those heavily distributed systems due to its cost advantages (pay as you go), but also with respect to the above-mentioned security risks. Considering this demand of data privacy with Big Data applications, this work enhances the current relational SeDiCo framework with NoSQL document stores. As this term covers much (also very different) database architectures, the focus of this work is limited to document stores. According to NoSQL Archive (2016), these architectures are mostly applied in today's practical use cases. As the existing relational SeDiCo prototype is implemented in Java and uses Hibernate as persistence framework (Kohler & Specht, 2012); Kohler, Simov, & Specht, 2015a), this work transfers the approach with the usage of Hibernate OGM (Object Grid Mapper) (RedHat, 2015) and MongoDB (2016) as the underlying document store. Finally, the prototype is evaluated with respect to its data access performance.

The contribution of this chapter to the current state-of-the-art is stated as follows:

- The conceptualization and definition of a security-by-distribution approach for NoSQL document stores.
- The creation of a framework that enables the processing of Big Data with dynamically scalable cloud capabilities, while security and privacy is maintained according to the security-by-distribution approach.

- A prototypical implementation of the framework that uses NoSQL document stores to manage unstructured data in different document stores and clouds.
- An evaluation of the implementation that compares the performance of the security-by-distribution approach to a non-distributed implementation.
- A detailed discussion and interpretation of the achieved performance measurements and their impact on other NoSQL databases.

TYPES AND EXAMPLES OF NOSQL DATABASES

First and foremost, some foundations have to be outlined to reach a common understanding about the used notions. Hence, this section provides a brief overview of NoSQL architectures and Hibernate OGM. Furthermore, this chapter introduces the concept of vertical partitioning within the SeDiCo framework.

NoSQL

The term NoSQL initially interpreted as no SQL but later interpreted as not only SQL and finally accepted by the NoSQL community was firstly proposed by Emil Eifrem of Neo4J (Neo Technology Incorporation, 2016). Hence, the term NoSQL refers to a whole generation of new database architectures and emerged as a countermovement to relational databases. Moreover, it covers a lot of database architectures and it appears to be difficult to find common features, which apply to all NoSQL architectures. Edlich, Friedland, Hampe, Brauer, and Brückner (2011) take the plethora of definitions and conclude that NoSQL databases show the following common characteristics:

- The underlying data model is not relational.
- They focus on horizontal scalability.
- Simple data replication mechanisms are used.
- They are Open Source.
- They are schema-free or have only weak schema restrictions.
- They provide a simple API but less powerful query possibilities (compared to SQL).
- They use a different model of consistency: BASE (Basically Available, Soft State, Eventual Consistency) vs. ACID (Atomicity, Consistency, Isolation, and Durability) (Edlich et al., 2011).

Especially the latter property requires a more detailed consideration. The hypothesis of BASE is based on the CAP-Theorem (Consistency, Availability, Partition Tolerance), which proves that in distributed systems always only two out of the three properties can be fulfilled simultaneously (Gilbert & Lynch, 2002; Brewer, 2000). Figure 2 illustrates this correlation.

While the ACID properties focus on consistency and availability, NoSQL databases have in common that they break up with the solid consistency property and accept a weaker one. Thus, these databases achieve a much better availability and partition tolerance at cost of consistency for certain periods of time. With respect to Big Data scenarios, this higher availability and the partition tolerance offer appealing benefits in terms of velocity and veracity.

Generally, NoSQL databases can be divided into four basic architectures: key-value, document stores, column stores, and graph databases (NoSQL Archive, 2016). Key-value stores store values with specific

Figure 2. CAP-theorem including the classification of popular NoSQL databases

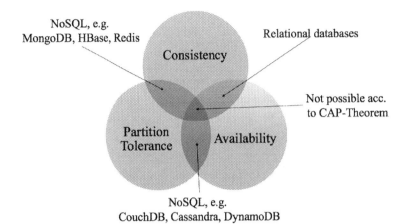

identifying keys, document stores store data in JSON (JavaScript Object Notation) (Crockford, 2006). The primer use case of these two architectures is a fast read and write access due to simple data schemes. Column stores are similar to relational databases; however, they persist data In-Memory and moreover, in columns instead of rows. This results in a good data analytical performance (i.e. read operations), as they are executed column wise and not row by row or tuple by tuple. Therefore, this architecture is used mainly in data warehouses with only few data manipulations but complex and long-lasting queries. Finally, graph databases use graphs as the underlying data model. Hence, benefits arise in special use cases where data are described as graphs with relationships. Figure 3 illustrates the data structure of the 4 NoSQL architectures schematically in which objects of a type customer are persisted. The attributes are displayed shortened due to better readability.

Figure 3. Structure of customer data in different NoSQL architectures: 1) key-value store, 2) column store, 3) document store, and 4) graph database

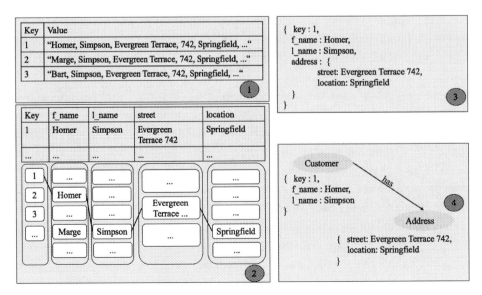

A good starting point for a general overview and detailed statistics about the current usage of NoSQL architectures is provided by (NoSQL Archive, 2016). According to these statistics, document stores are the most popular NoSQL architectures at the moment. These statistics also show that MongoDB as a concrete document store implementation currently plays a major part in the NoSQL area. In document stores, data are stored in different so-called documents and one or more documents are stored in files. The most common used notation for these files is JSON at the moment. A typical use case for document stores are highly unstructured data where a tremendous performance loss is experienced when these data are stored in a relational database in 3rd normal form. Above that, the other 3 architectures are also represented within the top 20 and these include Cassandra (Lakshman & Malik, 2010) and HBase (Apache Software Foundation, 2016a) as examples for column stores, which store data similar to relational data, but column-wise, i.e. columns are placed directly after each other in the storage engine. This improves the query performance when data is analyzed with complex queries (that include e.g. aggregate or sum functions, etc.) because data is not iterated (slowly) row by row but columns are analyzed as a whole. Hence, a typical use case for such column-based data stores is a data warehouse with a lot of analytical queries but only few write operations. Furthermore, Redis (Redislab, 2016) as a key-value store, that store data in key-value pairs, which improves read and write performance in simple data structures, as the entire data set can be regarded as a hash set has to be mentioned. A common use case for such kinds of architectures are data caches. Last but not least, Neo4J (Neo Technology Incorporation, 2016) as an example for a graph database that stores data in a set of nodes with connecting edges that represent relations between the nodes can be mentioned as one of the 4 basic NoSQL architectures. Here, traditional and well-investigated graph algorithms can be used to analyze the data. This architecture is mostly used in highly related data, such as social networks or recommendation systems (e.g. customers that bought this article also bought this one). However, it has to be mentioned that compared to relational ones, these NoSQL databases are still comparatively rarely used. Based on these figures, this work focuses on document stores and therefore a more detailed overview of the general architecture is outlined in the following section.

Above all, it has to be noted that all 4 basic architectures and their respective database implementations and systems, are intended to improve the overall read and write performance and are focused on highly distributed system architectures where data is shared, distributed or replicated among many different heterogeneous nodes. Therefore, a lot of different use cases are thinkable for each architecture. A few examples are mentioned above, besides e.g. high-availability clusters, dynamically scalable distributed cloud architectures, etc. However, data security and privacy are not in the main focus of current implementations. A survey of different documentations (Mongo DB, 2016 ;Apache, 2016a;2016b; Neo4j, 2016) show that security is mainly dealt with in the sense of losing data if one or another node breaks down. Hence, applying one or another architecture is a weighing between performance and security. Thus, this work aims at introducing a security-by-distribution principle that minimizes the gap between security and performance and deals with security and privacy from an end user's point of view. Hence, data is logically partitioned and distributed vertically in a way, such that every node only stores a small chunk of the data and one chunk is worthless without the others. Finally, this distribution requires new investigations concerning the data access performance, as data first have to be joined again before it actually can be accessed. All in all, this work demonstrates such a security-by-distribution principle and shows an evaluation that uses the most commonly known database benchmark: TPC-W (TPC, 2003).

Document Stores

As already briefly mentioned above, document stores persist data in single structured data elements so called documents. A single document is a composition of key-value pairs and several documents are treated as a collection of documents, each accessible by a specific unique key called document id. Finally, document stores do not define a concrete schema for its documents except basic key-value pairs. Consequently, an application is able to change or enhance the underlying data model (i.e. documents) with little effort. However, this schema-free approach has drawbacks in cases where a normalized data model (3rd Normal Form according to Codd (1970) is already defined or referential integrity (and therefore hard consistency according to the ACID principles) has to be ensured. Despite the major importance of document stores, only few concrete implementations are available at the moment and the most popular among these are MongoDB and CouchDB (NoSQL Archive, 2016). These two are similar in their basic architecture. In both, a database instance contains one or more databases, each database contains collections of documents, and every document is assigned to a specified document collection, as sketched in Figure 4.

Compared to relational database architectures the collection corresponds to a table and the concrete document to a tuple (or a row) respectively. Table 1 illustrates this comparison in a broader overview.

Figure 4. Structure of a document store instance

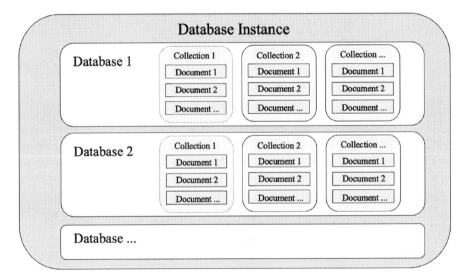

Table 1. Comparison of relational and document oriented database architectures

Relational Architecture	Document-Oriented Architecture
Database Instance	Database Instance
Database	Database
Table	Collection
Row (Tuple)	Document

Moreover, MongoDB and CouchDB have in common, that both use JSON as the basic data structure. A JSON object consists of key-value pairs, where the keys uniquely identify their corresponding value. A value can be one of the following datatypes: a (generic) object, an array, a character string, a boolean value or null. Figure 5 shows an example of such a JSON object, illustrated by an exemplified customer object in order to stick with the motivating example in Figure 1.

Here, JSON and its key-value pairs are illustrated with the attribute name followed by a colon and the actual value of the attribute (e.g. C_LNAME: Simpson). Above that, Figure 5 shows a nested structure with the attribute (C_BANKACCOUNT) which stores an array of (IBAN, BIC, and CREDITCARD attributes). Furthermore, it has to be noted that the types of the data (string, integer, etc.) are implicitly specified by the respective attribute values. Besides that, both MongoDB and CouchDB are schema-free databases. This basically means, that the schema – the concrete structure of persisted data – is created at runtime by the database and has not to be defined at the design time of the data model. This concept implies that documents within a collection not necessarily have the same structure. This is a major difference to relational models, as in relational tables the schema is predefined by the columns of the tables.

Lastly, both databases support the basic CRUD (create, read, update, delete) operations. Yet, also queries with higher complexity, such as complex joins over various document collections are possible with MapReduce functions (Moniruzzaman & Hossain, 2013). However, in order to not lose the focus of this work, the interested reader is referred to Apache Software Foundation (2016b) for concrete examples and further information about MapReduce.

Vertical Partitioning

This concept is not primarily focused on performance improvements but aims at creating a secure data store by using several database instances. Vertical partitioning in the context of this work is the logical separation of a tuple. As a result, 2 or more partitions logically contain the same tuple, but every partition contains only a part of it.

The basic concept of this approach is to identify relationships between data attributes, which bear a high potential risk when they are stored together. To ensure proper and consistent queries, the primary key is replicated in every partition and the tuple is joined during a query via its reference to the primary key. Finally, the vertical partitioning and distribution approach is considered as an appropriate solution

Figure 5. A customer JSON object stored as a document

```
1  {
2      $id :          "Customer:04b24313-f210-4f0-989c",
3      $type :        "entity",
4      $table :       "Customer",
5      C_ID :         "04b24313-f210-4f0-989c",
6      C_FNAME :      "Homer",
7      C_LNAME :      "Simpson",
8      C_BANKACCOUNT : {
9          IBAN :            "987654321000123456",
10         BIC :             "BICXXX",
11         CREDITCARD:       "123456"
12     }
13  }
```

to meet the above-mentioned Cloud Computing challenges: data compliance, privacy, security, and anonymization.

CRUD Operations for Vertically Partitioned Data

Generally, the idea of persisting objects from an application logic in a database is based on the underlying data model. Object-oriented programming languages operate with objects of specific types, created from classes. These objects contain attributes as well as methods which are in essence executable program code. On the contrary, relational databases use predefined data models with tables, columns, and rows. This shows that the mapping of tables to object-oriented classes turns out to be a non-trivial problem and this challenge is known as the Object Relational Impedance Mismatch (Ireland et al. 2009). Table 2 illustrates this mismatch in more detail and considers relational as well as NoSQL architectures.

Object Grid Mapping Frameworks

To overcome these challenges, so called Object Relational Mappers (ORM) have been and currently are developed. Figure 6 shows a typical architecture from an application to its database that uses such an ORM. The most popular example for such a framework in Java is Hibernate ORM.

Finally, ORMs implement logic that abstracts from a concrete database system and thus, they provide a unique interface that encapsulates all CRUD methods. Using this interface then allows exchanging databases without modifying the actual program logic. With respect to Figure 6, similar architectures for the other NoSQL architectures (key-value, column stores, and graph databases) apply.

Above that, it can be stated that documents in a document store do not differ so drastically from the object-oriented concepts with methods and attributes as the relational model does. Yet, a key difference is e.g. relationships between different objects. They have to be embodied as nested objects in the documents. This shows that specific aspects of the Impedance Mismatch like inheritance or encapsulation are still challenging aspects. Furthermore, the document stores discussed above use JSON to store Java objects and as a consequence, a mapping between Java and JSON is necessary. Above that, it has to be mentioned that for NoSQL architectures other mapping frameworks are available: e.g. Hibernate OGM (RedHat, 2015), Kundera (Impetus, 2016), DataNucleus (DataNucleus, 2016) and each of these mapping frameworks provides support for the mapping of several different NoSQL architectures.

Finally, another challenge is the still emerging market of NoSQL database implementations. In contrast to generic relational database drivers, e.g. JDBC (Java Database Connectivity) (Oracle, 2014) which are able to communicate with various different relational databases, in NoSQL, drivers are database-specific and cannot be used for different NoSQL databases generically. This means that persisting objects in different document stores, requires the encapsulation of different document store drivers into a single interface that acts as a generic database driver similar to JDBC.

As an exemplary mapping framework for document stores, Hibernate OGM (Object Grid Mapper) (RedHat, 2015), is outlined in more detail now. The framework aims at being compliant to the Java persistence interface JPA and Hibernate ORM (Object Relational Mapper). Hence, it uses well-known interfaces which facilitates and enables a simple change from relational to NoSQL architectures. Hibernate OGM reuses the Hibernate ORM engine to persist objects in NoSQL databases. To be precise, Hibernate OGM reuses the entire Object-Lifecycle-Management from the relational ORM implementation (RedHat, 2016b). Thus, the inbound requests of the application are processed by the Hibernate ORM

Table 2. Impedance mismatch of relational and NoSQL architectures

Impedance Mismatch Challenge	Object-Oriented Class	Relational Database Table	Key-Value Store	Document Store	Column Store	Graph Database
Structure	Attributes and methods explicitly describe semantic of a class	Only implicit semantics with table attributes (i.e. columns)	Only implicit semantics with values that are stored with corresponding key	Only implicit semantics with documents that are stored with a corresponding document id	Only implicit semantics with table attributes (i.e. columns)	Only implicit semantics with values and their relationships that are stored in a graph
Inheritance	A class/object is part of an inheritance hierarchy	Not available	Not available	Not available	Not available	Implicit with an is-a relationship
Instance	Object represents behavior	Tuple represents a statement of truth (Codd, 1970)	Key-value pair represents a statement of truth	Document represents a statement of truth	Column represents a statement of truth	Nodes and their relationships represent statements of truth
Encapsulation	Attributes are encapsulated by methods (Information Hiding)	Table attributes are directly accessed	Values are accessed by their key	Documents are accessed by their document id	Columns are directly accessed	Graph with nodes and their relationships are directly traversed
Identity	Every object is uniquely identified by its object id	Every tuple is uniquely identified by its primary key	Every value is uniquely identified by its key	Every document is uniquely identified by its document id	Every tuple is uniquely identified by its primary key	Every node is uniquely identified by its node id
Data access	Discrete	Set-oriented	Discrete	Discrete	Set-oriented	Discrete
Maintenance	Developer	Database administrator	Database administrator	Database administrator	Database administrator	Database administrator

Figure 6. ORM general, relational, and non-relational high-level architecture

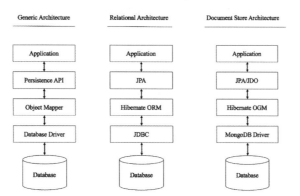

core first and are then forwarded to the Hibernate OGM core. The abstraction from a single database is realized by DatastoreProvider and GridDialect. The DatastoreProvider abstracts the connection to the database including transactions and sessions. The GridDialect abstracts from the actual architecture of the database (i.e. key-value, document, column store, or graph database). Moreover, accessing data with CRUD operations is realized with a Query Parser which abstracts from SQL as the standard relational query language. So, every query is translated to a query suitable for the respective database architecture. Finally, this abstraction fosters the above-mentioned database abstraction and enables the exchange of the underlying database architecture without modifying the application logic.

PERFORMANCE HANDLING

On the one hand, data storage in public cloud scenarios offer enormous cost advantages for enterprises, due to the dynamic scalability, pay as you go models, etc. On the other hand, public clouds cannot guarantee data security and privacy. Hence, SeDiCo offers an approach for an enhanced level of security and privacy by vertically distributing database data (Kohler & Specht, 2012;Kohler, Simov, & Specht, 2015b).

The entire SeDiCo framework is based on a security-by-distribution principle. This notion is inspired by traditional principles like security-by-compromise which is known to delay the authentication process by an incrementing timer if an authentication attempt was proven false, e.g. in the case of a misspelled password. Other principles with respect to this are e.g. security-by-analysis, where an application or an entire environment is tested against certain attacks by penetration testers, or security-by-design, where already at the design time of an application or environment security measures are taken into consideration. According to these principles, security-by-distribution aims at establishing a certain level of security and privacy with the separation of logically coherent data and their storage at different locations (in the context of this work in different clouds).

Persisting objects in relational databases requires a mapping of a table to a class containing the table's attributes (i.e. columns) as object variables. Thus, each object (or so-called entity) represents a row of in the corresponding database table. In contrast to that, document stores persist objects in documents in JSON format and each document contains all attributes of the entity (or object) as key-value pairs. Figure 7 illustrates this, again with a customer example.

At this point two major differences of document stores to relational databases can be clearly recognized:

Firstly, document stores do not define a concrete schema despite the key-value pairs. This leads to the fact that a collection of documents may also contain documents with different structures (see Figure

Figure 7. Persisting a Java object in a document store

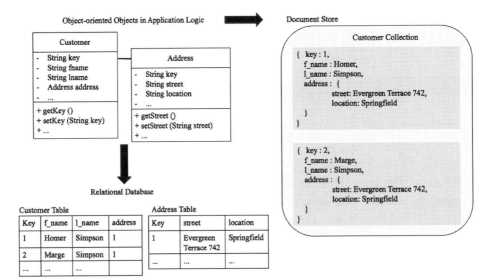

7). This schema-freedom implies two questions regarding the vertical partitioning and distribution approach of SeDiCo:

- How can data of a child-object be vertically partitioned?
- How can an array of data in a document be vertical partitioned?

With respect to these challenges, it has to be noted that the properties in JSON may also contain other JSON objects or even arrays. These key differences have to be considered in the vertical partitioning and distribution approach presented in this work and are therefore elaborated in more detail now.

To transfer the basic security-by-distribution approach from the relational model to a document store, the following 5 scenarios have to be considered.

Scenario 1

In order to outline the first scenario in more detail, Figure 8 illustrates a simple use case.

In the first level, there are simple properties ($id, $type, $table, C_ID, etc.), whereas the property C_BANKACCOUNT contains an entire object, called child-object. This C_BANKACCOUNT forms the second level of properties containing IBAN, BIC, and CREDITCARD. In the following, the first level will be referred to as level 0 and the second, nested level will be referred to as level 1.

Considering this basic example, it might be the case that the relationship of a property of level 0 (e.g. C_LNAME) contains a high security and privacy risk if it is stored together with another level 0 property (e.g. CREDITCARD).

Scenario 2

A second scenario is a relationship with a high potential risk between the name (forename and last name) of the customer (C_FNAME and C_LNAME) and its bank account number (IBAN) (see Figure 8). Regarding this scenario, it differs from the first one, as here different attributes from level 0 but not the entire attribute with all child objects from level 1, but only a single level 1 attribute (IBAN) are involved.

Figure 8. Scenario 1 and 2: basic security-by-distribution approach, based on a NoSQL document store

```
1   {
2       $id :           "Customer:04b24313-f210-4f0-989c",
3       $type :         "entity",
4       $table :        "Customer",
5       C_ID :          "04b24313-f210-4f0-989c",
6       C_FNAME :       "Homer",
7       C_LNAME :       "Simpson",
8       C_BANKACCOUNT : {
9           IBAN :          "9876543210000123456",
10          BIC :           "BICXXX",
11          CREDITCARD:     "123456"
12      }
13  }
```

Scenario 3

In this scenario, a set of properties of level 1 (IBAN and BIC) and another property at the same level and in the same child object (CREDITCARD) have a high potential risk if they are stored together (see Figure 8).

Scenario 4

Another scenario that has to be considered is the case where a property of a JSON object is an array, as depicted in Figure 9.

Figure 9 shows a customer, who owns 2 bank accounts (line 8, Figure 8) and each bank account has the same data schema (IBAN, BIC, and CREDITCARD). In contrast to the relational model, where such a one-to-many relationship has to be resolved with at least two tables, in document stores, the array elements are persisted in the same document as the parent-object. This case bears a high potential risk if all properties of all bank accounts (IBAN, BIC, and CREDITCARD) are stored together in just one single document.

Scenario 5

Additionally, it has to be noted that JSON permits that two objects in the same array have a different schema (i.e. different properties). Here, the schema-free approach of document stores becomes perceivable and this should not be restricted by the vertical partitioning and distribution approach of SeDiCo. An example for this is illustrated in Figure 10.

Figure 9. Scenario 4: advanced security-by-distribution approach of a NoSQL document store

```
1  {
2     $id :          "Customer:04b24313-f210-4f0-989c",
3     $type :        "entity",
4     $table :       "Customer",
5     C_ID :         "04b24313-f210-4f0-989c",
6     C_FNAME :  "Homer",
7     C_LNAME :  "Simpson",
8     C_BANKACCOUNT : {
9        {
10          IBAN :         "987654321000123456",
11          BIC :          "BICXXX",
12          CREDITCARD:    "123456"
13       },
14       {
15          IBAN :         "123456789",
16          BIC :          "BICYYY",
17          CREDITCARD:    "9999999"
18       }
19    }
20 }
```

Figure 10. Scenario 5: advanced security-by-distribution approach of a NoSQL document store

```
1  ▾ {
2        $id :           "Customer:04b24313-f210-4f0-989c",
3        $type :         "entity",
4        $table :        "Customer",
5        C_ID :          "04b24313-f210-4f0-989c",
6        C_FNAME :  "Homer",
7        C_LNAME :  "Simpson",
8  ▾    C_BANKACCOUNT : {
9  ▾        {
10              IBAN :             "9876543321000123456",
11              BIC :              "BICXXX",
12  ▾        },
13  ▾        {
14              CREDITCARD:   "9999999"
15  ▾        }
16  ▾    }
17  ▾ }
```

This time, the different bank accounts are stored in the C_BANKACCOUNT array in single elements but with different data schemes, e.g. one bank account has only an IBAN and a BIC and the other one has just a CREDITCARD number.

Finally, these challenges show that persisting objects according to the security-by-distribution approach of SeDiCo is more complex compared to relational databases. Therefore, the following sections address these challenges and outline possible approaches to solving them.

APPROACH

The previous section showed that it is necessary to specify which attributes of an object have to be persisted in which partition. This information is defined in an XML file (an exemplified excerpt can be found in Figure 11) and this so-called specification file builds the foundation for the vertical data partitioning and distribution approach.

Scenario 1

With respect to the first scenario depicted above, the user has to specify the distribution accordingly. Compared to the relational approach, the partitioning of the child-objects (and all grandchild objects, and so forth) have also to be specified. Transferred to a document store, this is done by extending the XML schema as illustrated in Figure 11

Although objects in documents do not have columns but properties, here the tag column was retained to be compatible to the previously used nomenclature from the relational approach. Moreover, in this case, the separation of both properties is relatively simple. The property of level 0 (e.g. C_LNAME, line 8 in Figure 11) is stored in one partition and the property containing the entire child-object (all properties of C_BANKACCOUNT from the JSON in Figure 8 in scenario 1) is stored in the other partition (lines 15-18 in Figure 11).

Figure 11. XML configuration file for scenario 1

```
1    ...
2    <targets>
3      <target isPrimary="true">
4        ...
5        <dbType>MongoDB</dbType>
6          <partition>
7            <column name="C_FNAME"></column>
8            <column name="C_LNAME"></column>
9          </partition>
10     </target>
11     <target>
12       ...
13       <dbType>MongoDB</dbType>
14         <partition>
15           <column name="C_BANKACCOUNT">
16             <column name="IBAN"></column>
17             <column name="BIC"></column>
18             <column name="CREDITCARD"></column>
19           </column>
20         </partition>
21     </target>
22   </targets>
23 </config>
```

Scenario 2

To vertically partition and distribute the data from scenario 2, the properties C_FNAME and C_LNAME (lines 7 and 8 in Figure 8) have to be persisted in one partition and the IBAN (line 16) has to be stored in another partition. In this scenario, all documents have the same schema. Thus, the partitioning and distribution schema from scenario 1 with the nested structure can be reused partly (Figure 12).

Scenario 3

To distribute data in this scenario, a separation on level 0 is not sufficient because the data has to be separated on the level of the child-object (here level 1). Again, the approach used in scenario 1 and 2 can be applied, but with a different nested structure and this is depicted in Figure 13.

Scenario 4

Just like in the previous case the relationship between IBAN, BIC and CREDITCARD is identified as a high potential risk relationship. Therefore, each of the array objects has to be vertically partitioned and distributed. As the schema of the array is homogeneous in this case, the partitioning and distribution from the previous scenarios can also be reused here, again with a different nested structure which is illustrated in Figure 14.

Figure 12. XML configuration file for scenario 2

```
1    ...
2    <targets>
3      <target isPrimary="true">
4        ...
5        <dbType>MongoDB</dbType>
6          <partition>
7            <column name="C_FNAME"></column>
8            <column name="C_LNAME"></column>
9          </partition>
10       </target>
11       <target>
12         ...
13         <dbType>MongoDB</dbType>
14         <partition>
15           <column name="C_BANKACCOUNT">
16             <column name="IBAN"></column>
17           </column>
18         </partition>
19       </target>
20     </targets>
21   </config>
```

Figure 13. XML configuration file for scenario 3

```
1    ...
2    <targets>
3      <target isPrimary="true">
4        ...
5        <dbType>MongoDB</dbType>
6          <partition>
7            <column name="C_BANKACCOUNT">
8              <column name="IBAN"></column>
9              <column name="BIC"></column>
10           </column>
11         </partition>
12       </target>
13       <target>
14         ...
15         <dbType>MongoDB</dbType>
16         <partition>
17           <column name="C_BANKACCOUNT">
18             <column name="CREDITCARD"></column>
19           </column>
20         </partition>
21       </target>
22     </targets>
23   </config>
```

Scenario 5

To partition and distribute these data vertically, the property IBAN is stored in one partition and the properties BIC and CREDITCARD are stored in another partition. However, in this case, the array has a heterogeneous schema and the array elements are different. Hence, in the specification file, the partitioning and distribution for each array element has to be done separately. This is addressed by extending the schema of the specification file and here, two approaches are viable:

- Identification via attribute is Array.

An option for specifying all necessary information for the distribution of each array element is to explicitly specify the distribution of every single element in the specification file. In this case, the indi-

Figure 14. XML configuration file for scenario 4

```
1   ...
2   <targets>
3     <target isPrimary="true">
4       ...
5         <dbType>MongoDB</dbType>
6         <partition>
7           <column name="C_LNAME"></column>
8           <column name="C_BANKACCOUNT">
9             <column name="IBAN"></column>
10            <column name="BIC"></column>
11          </column>
12        </partition>
13      </target>
14      <target>
15        ...
16        <dbType>MongoDB</dbType>
17        <partition>
18          <column name="C_FNAME"></column>
19          <column name="C_BANKACCOUNT">
20            <column name="CREDITCARD"></column>
21          </column>
22        </partition>
23      </target>
24    </targets>
25  </config>
```

vidual array elements are referenced by their index position. To distinguish arrays from simple properties, the keyword isArray is used. This strategy is considered feasible if the exact size of the array and the positions of the array elements can be determined in advance. Figure 15 illustrates the specification of an array with the isArray keyword in line 8 and in line 23 respectively.

Figure 15. Specification of a vertical distribution of a homogeneous array in a document store

```
1   ...
2   <targets>
3     <target isPrimary="true">
4       ...
5         <dbType>MongoDB</dbType>
6         <partition>
7           <column name="C_LNAME"></column>
8           <column name="C_BANKACCOUNT" isArray="true">
9             <column name="0">
10              <column name="IBAN"></column>
11            </column>
12            <column name="1">
13              <column name="BIC"></column>
14            </column>
15          </column>
16        </partition>
17      </target>
18      <target>
19        ...
20        <dbType>MongoDB</dbType>
21        <partition>
22          <column name="C_FNAME"></column>
23          <column name="C_BANKACCOUNT" isArray="true">
24            <column name="2">
25              <column name="CREDITCARD"></column>
26            </column>
27          </column>
28        </partition>
29      </target>
30    </targets>
31  </config>
```

In this example, the property C_BANKACCOUNT holds an array containing different elements. The element at index 0 holds the IBAN, the element at index 1 contains the BIC, and the array element at index 2 the CREDITCARD (lines 8, 12 and 24 in Figure 15, respectively). Note that if a property exists in several arrays, the property is replicated, which possibly might contradict the entire security-by-distribution approach.

- The storage of associations as typed descriptions.

A second option is to assign object types to the array elements and to specify the distribution of these properties. To facilitate this, the XML schema of the specification file has to be extended, too. Here, an additional node type is used which holds 0, 1 or n nodes as its children. Thus, all necessary information can be provided for the partitioning and distribution of the objects to multiple different partitions. Figure 16 (lines 7, 10, 19, 22) shows an excerpt of such a specification file which uses this typed description. Thus, every array element belongs to such a typed description, and here again, if an array element is defined for several types, it is also replicated. Finally, this approach is recommended if the schema of the array is not predefined and is likely to be changed, i.e. in scenarios where the array elements are not known in advance.

Figure 16. Specification of a vertical distribution of a heterogeneous array in a document store

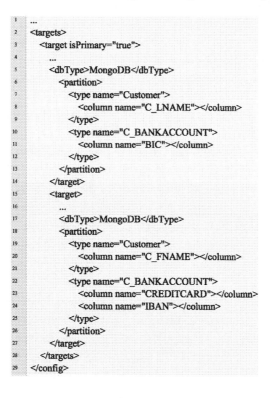

```
1    ...
2    <targets>
3      <target isPrimary="true">
4        ...
5        <dbType>MongoDB</dbType>
6          <partition>
7            <type name="Customer">
8              <column name="C_LNAME"></column>
9            </type>
10           <type name="C_BANKACCOUNT">
11             <column name="BIC"></column>
12           </type>
13         </partition>
14       </target>
15       <target>
16         ...
17         <dbType>MongoDB</dbType>
18           <partition>
19             <type name="Customer">
20               <column name="C_FNAME"></column>
21             </type>
22             <type name="C_BANKACCOUNT">
23               <column name="CREDITCARD"></column>
24               <column name="IBAN"></column>
25             </type>
26           </partition>
27       </target>
28     </targets>
29  </config>
```

IMPLEMENTATION

The relational SeDiCo implementation uses the Object Relational Mapper Hibernate. Therefore, the usage of Hibernate OGM as the mapping layer is considered adequate for the NoSQL document store approach. Above that, compared to the other mapping frameworks (sec. related work), Hibernate OGM supports all popular NoSQL architectures and a plethora of concrete implementations of them. Above that, the framework is currently developed by RedHat has an active user community which facilitates and supports the development process. These reasons substantiate the wide distribution of Hibernate OGM and explain (to a certain extent) its current state as the mostly applied mapping framework in the Java community nowadays.

In the relational version of SeDiCo, the framework interrupts the execution of the CRUD methods with the so-called Hibernate Lifecycle Events. The respective CRUD operation is canceled and instead, the tuples are processed in a virtual table which either realizes the join (in the case of a query) or the partitioning and distribution (in the case of a manipulation).

Unfortunately, it is not possible to use this relational approach for the vertical partitioning and distribution of documents in document stores for the following reasons:

- The usage of a virtual table is not suitable in the context of document stores. In fact, technologically this would be possible, but then the schema-freedom of document stores would also be restricted to a virtual table schema.
- Another drawback is the heterogeneity of NoSQL architectures (key-value, document, column stores and graph databases) in general. Distributing data vertically on the basis of the respective NoSQL architecture would result in the development of single implementations for every respective architecture. Furthermore, this would entail the translation of every query language of each database architecture. With respect to this, it must be noted that even MongoDB and CouchDB (as 2 document stores) already implement different query languages and above that, the integration of only one database driver would not be sufficient for a generic NoSQL solution.

Finally, it can be concluded that although the usage of a virtual table is technologically possible, it is not recommended.

Taking a closer look at this problem it is obvious, that the challenges for a vertical partitioning and distribution approach for NoSQL databases are caused by the heterogeneity of those data stores. Yet, these issues are already partly solved by Object Grid Mapper frameworks (OGMs), as they abstract from those different architectures. In general, these frameworks map the structure of objects to the data schema of the respective NoSQL architecture and integrate the necessary database drivers for the connection to the respective database system.

A further advantage of OGMs is the independency from the underlying database system. With these frameworks, the vertical distribution can be performed on the data model defined by the application logic and the OGM is used to translate the partitioning and distribution to the concrete underlying database system. This abstraction also enables to simply exchange the underlying NoSQL database, or expressed the other way around: All databases supported by Hibernate OGM can be used with the vertical partitioning and distribution approach of this work.

Finally, the challenge of joining data from the cloud partitions arises. Joining the partitioned and distributed data is done on the OGM layer via the document returned from the document store. In general, the partitioned objects are joined based on their document id, similar to the join via primary keys in the relational implementation. For the implementation of this work, this approach was chosen to achieve an independency from the underlying NoSQL database architecture. However, a drawback of this design is that data which are joined on the basis of the documents are stored as character strings because of the JSON format. Yet, this means that the join of the partitioned objects is not type-safe, as type-safety cannot be ensured during the runtime of the application. Yet, the actual object (in the context of this work it is a Java object) is already instantiated before the actual join has taken place. Thus, it must be concluded that as soon as child-objects with different attributes are vertically partitioned and distributed (see scenario 5), the join of these child-objects cannot be guaranteed to be type-safe anymore. The use cases depicted in the other scenarios are not affected by this, as there, the data schemes are homogenous.

EVALUATION

For the evaluation, MongoDB (MongoDB, 2016) as the most prominent and most widespread document store was used (NoSQL Archive, 2016). The performance analysis was done with an adapted version of the database benchmark TPC-W (TPC, 2003), to establish comparability between this work and results of previous works within the SeDiCo framework, e.g. (Kohler & Specht, 2012; Kohler, Simov, & Specht, 2015b). Thus, in this work also the customer table from the TPC-W benchmark was used. However, compared to the previous SeDiCo works, the evaluation scenario was slightly changed, such that the influence of cascading an object graph could be evaluated too. Therefore, the TPC-W address table that references the customer table (1 customer can only have 1 address) was introduced.

All following measurements were performed with the SeDiCo document store implementation (SeDiCo Document Store) and the following statistics show the comparison to a non-distributed and non-partitioned NoSQL document store (NoSQL Document Store). For the latter case, a typical Hibernate OGM implementation was used as described in RedHat (2016a).

To eliminate side-effects like network bandwidth, unpredictable workloads of the cloud servers, all measurements were conducted exclusively with locally installed MongoDB instances (version 3.0). All measurements were performed 3 times and the average of these measurements is presented in the following figures (Figure 17-20). Finally, the used hardware environment was a standard PC with an Intel Core i5-4200 CPU with 2,3 GHz, 8GB DDR3 RAM with 1600 MHz and Microsoft Windows 8.1 Pro 64bit.

CONCLUSION

Compared to a traditional non-partitioned and non-distributed setup, the performance degrades by factor ~11 for create operations, by factor ~20 for read operations, by factor ~3 for update operations, and by factor ~2 for delete operations. These performance losses show that the security-by-distribution approach is an outweigh between security and performance. Especially, in the context of Big Data when the velocity attribute is the crucial factor, further performance improvements, e.g. query rewriting and optimization or In-Memory caching have to be taken into consideration. All in all, it can be stated that the approach proves to be a technologically feasible solution for the given problem definition. It can

Figure 17. Create performance comparison

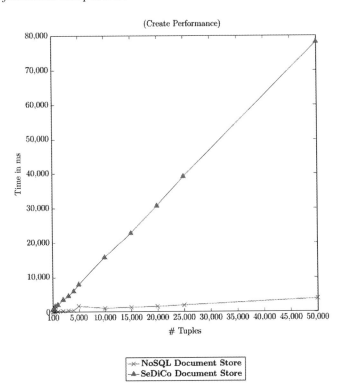

Figure 18. Read performance comparison

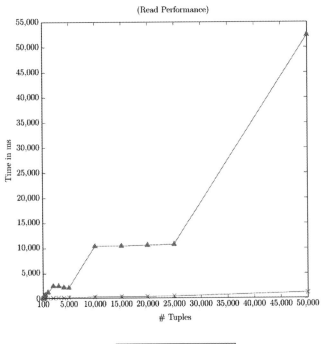

Figure 19. Update performance comparison

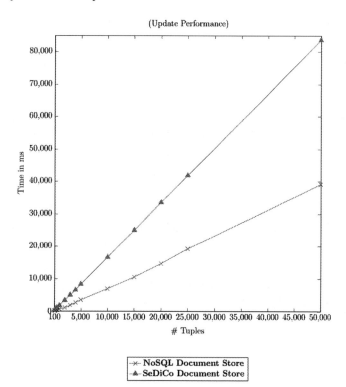

Figure 20. Delete performance comparison

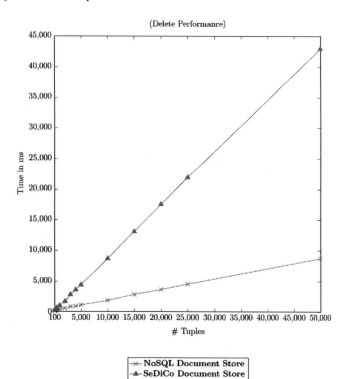

also be stated that the developed approach is able to realize security-by-distribution (to different clouds) in the context of NoSQL document stores. Evidence for this technological feasibility is given by the prototype of this work.

However, during the implementation and evaluation, the following restrictions have to be considered. Currently, it was not possible to show the feasibility of vertically distributing the attributes of different child-objects within an array for document stores (scenario 5). This was mainly caused by the choice of Hibernate OGM as the mapping framework. In Java, the concept of having objects of different types in an array is realized by inheritance. Assuming for example three classes A, B, and C, with the inheritance hierarchy, in which B contains other attributes as C. In Java (as a statically typed language) an array of type A might reference different objects of classes B and C.

Unfortunately, Hibernate OGM does not support different inheritance relationships. Only the strategy table per concrete class (RedHat, 2016a), which creates individual documents for each class instead of storing all array objects in one single document is supported. Thus, creating classes with defined object data types at runtime is not possible. In order to overcome this challenge, a non-type-safe, i.e. a script-based programming language (e.g. Groovy, which is similar to Java and is able to execute Java code) that is able to instantiate variable types of classes and objects at runtime could be used.

Finally, the benefits and drawbacks of the implementation can be summarized as follows in Table 3.

RELATED WORK

The problem definitions regarding IT security in Cloud Computing are manifold. Accordingly, (Yildiz, Abawajy, Ercan, & Bernoth, 2009) developed an approach to increase the security of a cloud infrastructure based on defined guidelines for participating parties referring to network, process, and system access. Other works like C. Wang, Chow, Wang, Ren, and Lou (2013); Juels and Oprea (2013), and B. Wang, Chow, Li, & Li, 2013 aim at increasing trust in public cloud services by assessing the integrity of the service via automated frameworks. For example, C. Wang et al. (2013) proposes a framework where the assessment of a cloud service is possible without gaining knowledge of the concrete data stored in the cloud. In B. Wang et al. (2013), this concept is enhanced by a security mediator, which minimizes the computing complexity and network overhead of the framework. Other works mentioned below study the use of encryption of data, stored in the cloud. Those technologies are applied to protect data from unauthorized access. Such an unintentional access by third parties might happen not only by external but also internal parties – for example, the cloud provider itself (so-called Insider Jobs). Further research like Sood (2012) and Saleh and Meinel (2013) show that encryption is actually a very effective protection for data in public clouds. Finally, other works e.g. (Banerjee et al., 2013; Sang, 2013) demonstrate attempts to detect attackers, to block them or allow better forensic investigations. Above these works, Tchepnda, Moustafa, Labiod, and Bourdon (2009) provide a broad overview about current security threads and challenges in today's heterogeneous networks. Further interesting security and privacy-related topics with a special focus on Cloud Computing and Big Data (e.g. the introduction of watermarks in multimedia data) are discussed in Dey and Santhi (2017).

The presented related work so far illustrates the wide range of this research field. According to Juels & Oprea, 2013) and Sood (2012), cloud providers offer a high level of security even if different well-known technologies (e.g. databases, network topologies, applications, etc.) are used in Cloud Computing. Accordingly, the authors suggest to distributing data according to their sensitivity. (Sood, 2012) also propose an algorithm for evaluating the sensitivity of information and the classification of information security in confidentiality, integrity and availability, also known as the CIA principle. A similar distribution of data is also proposed by the framework HPISecure (Saleh & Meinel, 2013). There, data is separated in encrypted data blocks and is stored distributed and thus, HPISecure offers an approach to the distributed storage of data in a Software as a Service model in an encrypted way. Comparatively, this work presents an approach which is focused on database data and thus, applicable in all service (IaaS, PaaS, and SaaS) and deployment (public, private, hybrid, and community) models according to the NIST (National Institute for Standardization and Technology) definition in Mell and Grance (2011).

Furthermore, regarding the approach proposed in this work Sood (2012) and Saleh and Meinel (2013) have to be emphasized, as those approaches also foster a vertical distribution of data in different cloud services. But in contrast to the approach of SeDiCo, those studies do not cover concrete database data but file systems.

Yet, in the context of Big Data and with respect to the conceptual database view of this work, there are numerous applications, use cases, and analytical scenarios thinkable. Current research work shows examples of not only analyzing huge amounts of data to receive a detailed overview about the past, but also to predict the future with artificial intelligence approaches. Interesting works in the field of professional sports was conducted by Jain et al. (2016). In the academic environment an approach with ambient intelligence is presented by Mikulecký, Olševicová, Bures, and Mls (2011) for the management of academic institutions (e.g. student data, research capabilities, etc.). Another application domain are recommendation systems, in which recommendations for a customer are presented based on other customers' orders. Here an interesting example can be found in Jain et al., 2016). Interestingly, such analyses require logic that is able to deal with fuzzy, incomplete and uncertain data sets. Here, Ripon et al. (2016) provide an overview about different classification methods (i.e. K-nearest neighbor, Naive Bayes and an Apriori algorithm) for such data sets, which they call rough sets. Classic examples of Big Data come from social networks like Facebook, Twitter, or the like. Analyzing these kinds of data also requires new methods and algorithms and a good example for such algorithms (based on Twitter data) is presented in Baumgarten et al. (2013). Above these new challenges, which also provide a lot of opportunities, security and privacy are issues that have been hardly dealt with so far. Nevertheless, there are further research works that take these also challenging concerns into account. Mohanpurkar et al. (2016) for example present an approach which integrates fingerprints into the underlying data set. Thus, data integrity, i.e. the fact that data is not altered by unauthorized entities can be preserved and so data manipulations can be eliminated. Besides these works, collecting such huge amounts of data is another interesting topic. As already mentioned above, nowadays social networks provide a good foundation, if there is a critical mass of users achieved. With respect to this, Zappi et al. (2010) outlined a framework that shows a sensor-based data collection approach from the cradle to the grave. Another issue with respect to Big Data is the collection of huge data amounts. Here, especially user-specific data which are used to predict future behaviors and enables enterprises to draw conclusions on specific users are challenging. Here, a good overview about the current discussion and methodologies how such data are collected and what further implications come with such collections can be found in Odella et al. (2016), Bhatt, Dey, and Ashour, 2017), and Saleh et al. (2016). Moreover, Big Data not only focuses on user data, but also provides a huge data store for machine intelligence. As an example for building an intelligent agent, Mason et al. (2015) provides a framework for building a robot that is able to mimic emotions based on collected data.

Finally, other OGM frameworks besides Hibernate OGM have to be mentioned. Here, Kundera developed by Impetus Labs (Impetus, 2016) which is also able to persist objects in many different NoSQL architectures via JPA is an example of another OGM. Furthermore, DataNucleus (2016), a framework that supports a plethora of relational as well as NoSQL architectures via JPA and JDO can be mentioned as a viable alternative to Hibernate OGM.

SUMMARY, OUTLOOK, AND FUTURE PERSPECTIVES

According to Kohler, Simov, and Specht (2015a), and Kohler and Specht (2012, 2015b), the presented security-by-distribution approach is a suitable solution to address concerns regarding security, compliance and data privacy in Cloud Computing. This work showed that the approach is also viable with NoSQL document stores. Moreover, the implemented prototype showed the feasibility of the approach in practice. Yet, the evaluation of this work revealed an inferior performance compared to a traditional non-partitioned and non-distributed Hibernate OGM implementation. In particular, create and read operations suffer from severe performance losses (factor ~11 and factor ~20 respectively), but also update and delete operations are affected (factor ~3 and factor ~2 respectively). This shows that further research work is necessary. Here already applied strategies from the relational approach like caching or query rewriting as outlined in Kohler and Specht (2015a)and Kohler, Simov, Fiech, & Specht (2015) seem to be promising.

Furthermore, it has to be stated that this work also showed the necessity of further research work to adapt the security-by-distribution approach to NoSQL architectures. First and foremost, this work was restricted to document stores and the transfer to key-value, column stores, and graph databases are still open challenges. Addressing these challenges might reveal further challenging aspects which are not obvious at first sight. This was the case in scenario 5 of this work, where the vertical partitioning and distribution approach yield to problems with the schema-freedom concerning type-safe datatypes in the application logic. Hence, as a final conclusion it can be noted that this work built the foundation to transfer the SeDiCo concept to NoSQL architectures, but also revealed further open research questions which have to be addressed in the near future to fully exploit the advantages of these architectures, especially in nowadays Big Data scenarios.

Table 3. Benefits and drawbacks of the proposed implementation

Benefits	Drawbacks
Feasible implementation of the security-by-distribution approach	In case of heterogeneous data schemes, type-safety of the objects cannot be guaranteed
Independence from the underlying NoSQL or relational data store	Performance losses because of the vertical partitioning and distribution approach

REFERENCES

Apache. (2016a). *Apache HBase Reference Guide*. Retrieved January 3, 2017, from https://hbase.apache.org/book.html

Apache. (2016b). *Cassandra Documentation*. Retrieved January 3, 2017, from http://cassandra.apache.org/doc/latest/

Apache Software Foundation. (2016a). *Apache HBase Website*. Retrieved October 1, 2016, from http://hbase.apache.org/

Apache Software Foundation. (2016b). *Hadoop MapReduce Tutorial*. Retrieved October 1, 2016, from https://hadoop.apache.org/docs/r1.2.1/mapred_tutorial.html

Banerjee, C., Kundu, A., Basu, M., Deb, P., Nag, D., & Dattagupta, R. (2013). A service based trust management classifier approach for cloud security. *2013 15th International Conference on Advanced Computing Technologies (ICACT)*, 1–5. http://doi.org/10.1109/ICACT.2013.6710519

Baumgarten, M., Mulvenna, M. D., Rooney, N., Reid, J., Jansen, B. J., Zhang, M., ... Hoffmann, P. (2013). Keyword-Based Sentiment Mining using Twitter. *International Journal of Ambient Computing and Intelligence*, 5(2), 56–69. doi:10.4018/jaci.2013040104

Bhatt, C., Dey, N., & Ashour, A. S. (2017). *Internet of Things and Big Data Technologies for Next Generation Healthcare*. Springer-Verlag New York Inc. doi:10.1007/978-3-319-49736-5

Brewer, E. A. (2000). Towards robust distributed systems. In *Proceedings of the nineteenth annual ACM symposium on Principles of distributed computing - PODC '00* (p. 7). http://doi.org/10.1145/343477.343502

Cloud Security Alliance. (2013). *Cloud Computing Vulnerability Incidents: A Statistical Overview : Cloud Security Alliance*. Retrieved June 17, 2015, from https://cloudsecurityalliance.org/download/cloud-computing-vulnerability-incidents-a-statistical-overview/

Codd, E. F. (1970). A relational model of data for large shared data banks. *Communications of the ACM*, 13(6), 377–387. doi:10.1145/362384.362685

Crockford, D. (2006). *IETF JSON RFC 4627*. Retrieved April 20, 2015, from http://tools.ietf.org/html/rfc4627

DataNucleus. (2016). *DataNucleus Website*. Retrieved October 1, 2016, from http://www.datanucleus.com/

Dey, N., & Santhi, V. (Eds.). (2017). *Intelligent Techniques in Signal Processing for Multimedia Security* (Vol. 660). Cham: Springer International Publishing. doi:10.1007/978-3-319-44790-2_16

Edlich, S., Friedland, A., Hampe, J., Brauer, B., & Brückner, M. (2011). *NoSQL (2nd ed.)*. Hanser Publishing. doi:10.3139/9783446428553

Furht, B., Escalante, A., Jin, H., Ibrahim, S., Bell, T., Gao, W., ... Wu, S. (2010). Handbook of cloud computing. In B. Furht & A. Escalante (Eds.), Handbook of Cloud Computing (pp. 3–19). Springer US. http://doi.org/ doi:10.1007/978-1-4419-6524-0

Gens, F., & Shirer, M. (2013). *IDC Forecasts Worldwide Public IT Cloud Services Spending to Reach Nearly $108 Billion by 2017 as Focus Shifts from Savings to Innovation.* Retrieved February 1, 2016, from http://www.idc.com/getdoc.jsp?containerId=prUS24298013

Gilbert, S., & Lynch, N. (2002). Brewers conjecture and the feasibility of consistent, available, partition-tolerant web services. *ACM SIGACT News, 33*(2), 51–59. doi:10.1145/564585.564601

Impetus. (2016). *Kundera Website.* Retrieved October 1, 2010, from https://github.com/impetus-open-source/Kundera

Ireland, C., Bowers, D., Newton, M., & Waugh, K. (2009). A Classification of Object-Relational Impedance Mismatch. In *2009 First International Conference on Advances in Databases, Knowledge, and Data Applications* (pp. 36-43). IEEE. 10.1109/DBKDA.2009.11

Jain, A., Bhatnagar, V., Al-Jarrah, O. Y., Yoo, P. D., Muhaidat, S., Karagiannidis, G. K., ... Misra, R. K. (2016). Olympics Big Data Prognostications. *International Journal of Rough Sets and Data Analysis, 3*(4), 32–45. doi:10.4018/IJRSDA.2016100103

Jain, A., Bhatnagar, V., Chen, M., Mao, S., Liu, Y., Frings, S., ... Santhi, V. (2016). Movie Analytics for Effective Recommendation System using Pig with Hadoop. *International Journal of Rough Sets and Data Analysis, 3*(2), 82–100. doi:10.4018/IJRSDA.2016040106

Juels, A., & Oprea, A. (2013). New approaches to security and availability for cloud data. *Communications of the ACM, 56*(2), 64–64. doi:10.1145/2408776.2408793

Kohler, J., Simov, K., Fiech, A., & Specht, T. (2015). On The Performance Of Query Rewriting In Vertically Distributed Cloud Databases. *Proceedings of The International Conference Advanced Computing for Innovation ACOMIN 2015.*

Kohler, J., Simov, K., & Specht, T. (2015a). Analysis of the Join Performance in Vertically Distributed Cloud Databases. *International Journal of Adaptive, Resilient and Autonomic Systems, 1*(2). doi:10.4018/IJARAS

Kohler, J., Simov, K., & Specht, T. (2015b). Analysis of the Join Performance in Vertically Distributed Cloud Databases. *International Journal of Adaptive, Resilient and Autonomic Systems, 6*(2), 65–87. doi:10.4018/IJARAS.2015070104

Kohler, J., & Specht, T. (2012). SeDiCo - Towards a Framework for a Secure and Distributed Datastore in the Cloud. *Proceedings of Chip-to-Cloud Security Forum 2012.*

Kohler, J., & Specht, T. (2015a). Analysis of Cache Implementations in a Vertically Distributed Cloud Data Store. *Proceedings of the 3rd IEEE World Conference on Complex System.* 10.1109/ICoCS.2015.7483294

Kohler, J., & Specht, T. (2015b). Performance Analysis of Vertically Partitioned Data in Clouds Through a Client-Based In-Memory Key-Value Store Cache. In *Proceedings of the 8th International Conference on Computational Intelligence in Security for Information Systems.* Burgos, Spain: Springer. 10.1007/978-3-319-19713-5_1

Lakshman, A., & Malik, P. (2010). Cassandra: A decentralized structured storage system. *Operating Systems Review, 44*(2), 35. doi:10.1145/1773912.1773922

Mason, C., Benson, H., Lehmann, J., Malhotra, M., Goldman, R., Hopkins, J., ... Ochsner, K. N. (2015). Engineering Kindness. *International Journal of Synthetic Emotions, 6*(1), 1–23. doi:10.4018/IJSE.2015010101

Mell, P., & Grance, T. (2011, September). *The NIST Definition of Cloud Computing.* Retrieved February 1, 2016, from http://csrc.nist.gov/publications/nistpubs/800-145/SP800-145.pdf

Mohanpurkar, A. A., Joshi, M. S., Agrawal, R., Haas, P., Kiernan, J., Blayer, O., ... Waghmode, V. V. (2016). A Traitor Identification Technique for Numeric Relational Databases with Distortion Minimization and Collusion Avoidance. *International Journal of Ambient Computing and Intelligence, 7*(2), 114–137. doi:10.4018/IJACI.2016070106

MongoDB. (2016a). *MongoDB Documentation.* Retrieved January 3, 2017, from https://docs.mongodb.com/

MongoDB. (2016b). *MongoDB Website.* Retrieved October 1, 2016, from https://www.mongodb.org/

Moniruzzaman, B. M., & Hossain, S. A. (2013). NoSQL Database: New Era of Databases for Big data Analytics - Classification, Characteristics and Comparison. *CoRR, 6*(4), 14.

Neo4j. (2016). *Neo4j Documentation.* Retrieved January 3, 2017, from https://neo4j.com/docs/

Neo Technology Incorporation. (2016). *Neo4J Website.* Retrieved October 1, 2016, from https://neo4j.com/

Neves, B. A., Correia, M. P., Bruno, Q., Fernando, A., & Paulo, S. (2013). DepSky: Dependable and secure storage in a cloud-of-clouds. *ACM Transactions on Storage, 9*(4), 31–46. doi:10.1145/2535929

NoSQL Archive. (2016). *NoSQL Archive Website.* Retrieved February 1, 2016, from http://nosql-databases.org/

Odella, F., Adamic, L., Adar, E., Adkins, B., Smith, D., Barnett, K., ... Wigg, J. M. (2016). Technology Studies and the Sociological Debate on Monitoring of Social Interactions. *International Journal of Ambient Computing and Intelligence, 7*(1), 1–26. doi:10.4018/IJACI.2016010101

Oracle. (2014). *JSR 221: JDBCTM 4.0 API Specification.* Retrieved February 1, 2016, from https://jcp.org/en/jsr/detail?id=221

Pettey, C., & Goasduff, L. (2011). *Gartner Says Solving "Big Data" Challenge Involves More Than Just Managing Volumes of Data.* Retrieved from http://www.gartner.com/newsroom/id/1731916

RedHat. (2015). *Getting started with Hibernate OGM.* Retrieved February 1, 2016, from http://hibernate.org/ogm/documentation/getting-started/

RedHat. (2016a). *Hibernate OGM Documentation.* Retrieved October 1, 2016, from http://hibernate.org/ogm/documentation/

RedHat. (2016b). *ORM Hibernate Documentation*. Retrieved February 1, 2016, from http://hibernate.org/orm/documentation/5.0/

Redislab. (2016). *Redis Website*. Retrieved October 1, 2016, from http://redis.io/

Ripon, S., Kamal, S., Hossain, S., Dey, N., Abraham, H. O. A., Ashrafi, M., ... Gao, W. (2016). Theoretical Analysis of Different Classifiers under Reduction Rough Data Set. *International Journal of Rough Sets and Data Analysis*, *3*(3), 1–20. doi:10.4018/IJRSDA.2016070101

Saleh, E., & Meinel, C. (2013). HPISecure: Towards data confidentiality in cloud applications. In *Proceedings - 13th IEEE/ACM International Symposium on Cluster, Cloud, and Grid Computing, CCGrid 2013* (pp. 605–609). http://doi.org/10.1109/CCGrid.2013.109

Saleh, M. A., Awada, A., Belnap, N., Perloff, M., Bonnefon, J.-F., Longin, D., ... Casacuberta, D. (2016). A Logical Model for Narcissistic Personality Disorder. *International Journal of Synthetic Emotions*, *7*(1), 69–87. doi:10.4018/IJSE.2016010106

Sang, T. (2013). A log-based approach to make digital forensics easier on cloud computing. In *Proceedings of the 2013 3rd International Conference on Intelligent System Design and Engineering Applications, ISDEA 2013* (pp. 91–94). http://doi.org/10.1109/ISDEA.2012.29

Sood, S. K. (2012). A combined approach to ensure data security in cloud computing. *Journal of Network and Computer Applications*, *35*(6), 1831–1838. doi:10.1016/j.jnca.2012.07.007

Tchepnda, C., Moustafa, H., Labiod, H., & Bourdon, G. (2009). Vehicular Networks Security. *International Journal of Ambient Computing and Intelligence*, *1*(1), 39–52. doi:10.4018/jaci.2009010104

TPC. (2003). *TPC Benchmark W (Web Commerce) Specification Version 2.0r*. Retrieved February 1, 2016, from http://www.tpc.org/tpcw/default.asp

Wang, B., Chow, S. S. M., Li, M., & Li, H. (2013). Storing shared data on the cloud via security-mediator. In *Proceedings - International Conference on Distributed Computing Systems* (pp. 124–133). http://doi.org/10.1109/ICDCS.2013.60

Wang, C., Chow, S. S. M., Wang, Q., Ren, K., & Lou, W. (2013). Privacy-preserving public auditing for secure cloud storage. *IEEE Transactions on Computers*, *62*(2), 362–375. doi:10.1109/TC.2011.245

Yildiz, M., Abawajy, J., Ercan, T., & Bernoth, A. (2009). A layered security approach for cloud computing infrastructure. In *I-SPAN 2009 - The 10th International Symposium on Pervasive Systems, Algorithms, and Networks* (pp. 763–767). http://doi.org/10.1109/I-SPAN.2009.157

Zappi, P., Lombriser, C., Benini, L., Tröster, G., Baldauf, M., Dustdar, S., ... Starner, T. E. (2010). Collecting Datasets from Ambient Intelligence Environments. *International Journal of Ambient Computing and Intelligence*, *2*(2), 42–56. doi:10.4018/jaci.2010040103

KEY TERMS AND DEFINITIONS

JDO: Java Data Objects is a commonly known persistence framework that abstracts from an implementation-specific database dialect such that concrete database systems can be exchanged without modifying the application logic.

JPA: Java Persistence Application Programming Interface is a commonly known persistence framework that abstracts from an implementation-specific database dialect such that concrete database systems can be exchanged without modifying the application logic.

JSON: Java Script Object Notation is a key:value notation that is used as a successor to XML as a meta and description language.

Security-By-Distribution: Aims at establishing a certain level of security and privacy with the separation of logically coherent data and their storage at different locations.

This research was previously published in Privacy and Security Policies in Big Data edited by Sharvari Tamane, Vijender Kumar Solanki, and Nilanjan Dey, pages 92-123, copyright year 2017 by Information Science Reference (an imprint of IGI Global).

Chapter 18
Enhanced Trust Path Between Two Entities in Cloud Computing Environment

Usha Divakarla
National Institute of Technology Karnataka, India

K. Chandrasekaran
National Institute of Technology Karnataka, India

ABSTRACT

Trust is the common factor of any network security. In cloud, trust is the major factor as this trust develops a relation between the user and resource of the service provider. To develop a strong trust there has to be a strong trust path between two entities. The model proposed builds a strong trust path between two important entities in cloud namely user and resources of the service provider. The trust path thus built strengthens the security of the resources as well as the authentication of the user. The implementation proved that trust model developed is more efficient in terms of computation time.

INTRODUCTION

The major influence of any human interaction is Trust. In technology trust has no definite meaning. It is defined as the degree of trustworthiness. The lesser the degree of trustworthiness the more is the risk to the system. Trust is often measured/related to terms like cooperation, confidence and predictability. According to (Gambetta, D. G., 1988) trust is the probability that an entity will perform an action that is beneficial or at least not detrimental to us is high enough for us to consider engaging in some form of co-operation with it.

The basic principle for any successful relationship is the base value of trust among the entities involved. Trust is one of the obligatory qualities in any relationship. It is due to this trust that any entity could cooperate beyond a system of formal and legal rules.

The basic nature of trust is found as the tension between depending upon another and instituting controls to make sure that other performs. The higher the risk the higher would be the loss. In human

DOI: 10.4018/978-1-5225-8176-5.ch018

science or information technology the trust plays a vital role in reconciling away fears and the willingness to become vulnerable to the other without controlling the other (Habib, S. M., Ries, S., & Mühlhäuser, M., 2011, November).

TRUST IN CLOUD ENVIRONMENT

Cloud is the emerging technology for the users to easily work with minimum effort and minimized cost. In every cloud, service is tendered with as pay-as-use term. So users can use the cloud technology to maximize their profit with minimum cost and effort. To ensure proper and efficient secured usage of resource users as well as cloud providers need to trust each other.

Trust being belief of human interaction has many definitions to it. Several researchers have studied the role of trust and reputation in e-commerce, peer to peer networks, grid computing, semantic web, web services, and mobile networks. The valuable information available on trust in various fields is of great benefit to computer scientists and it also has the drawback of presenting a complex notion for trust as there is no common agreement on a single definition of trust. Various researchers have defined trust as attitude, belief, probability, expectation, and honesty and so on. Due to the adoption of cloud computing in the industry, a significant challenge is being raised in managing trust among cloud service providers and cloud service consumers. Several solutions have been proposed to assess and manage trust feedbacks collected from participants (Conner, W., Iyengar, A., Mikalsen, T., Rouvellou, I., & Nahrstedt, K., 2009, April) (Hwang, K., & Li, D., 2010) due to high significance to the trust management. Due to malicious behavior of user's Trust management experience a setback. Due to confusion in trust definition, trust has been evaluated in very different ways. Some schemes employ linguistic descriptions of the trust relationship, such as Policy Maker, distributed trust model, trust policy language and public-key infrastructure. On the other hand, the quality of trust feedbacks differ from one person to another, depending on how experienced he/she is.

Various models are developed to ensure quality of trust with respect to the domain. The drawbacks like centralized architecture concept, private cloud for security of data, problems with keys due to changed configuration, problems in integration of the proposed layer with the existing configuration likewise. Though these models address security aspects, an improvement with respect to trust models is desirable.

LITERATURE REVIEW

In any network Trust is the eminent factor that plays a vital role in the security of the network. The more the degree of trustworthiness the less is the risk. Though extensive research has taken place on this trust factor, trust is still the most concentrated factor for any research in distributed networks.

EXISTING TRUST MODELS

Trust is an eminent factor in any network. Trust management comprises collecting the information necessary to establish a trust relationship and to dynamically supervise the existing trust relationship. The various models for describing trust and trust establishment in Cloud Environment are listed below.

Authors (Khan, K. M., & Malluhi, Q., 2010) have analyzed the trust in the cloud system in terms of security and privacy. The authors have forecast that remote access control of the resources, transparency in cloud provider's actions and providing security for users would enhance the trust of users in the services and service providers.

Authors (Sato, H., Kanai, A., & Tanimoto, S., 2010, July). have proposed a trust model of cloud security in terms of social security. The social security is divided into three sub areas, namely; multiple stakeholder problem, open space security problem, and mission critical data handling problem. The multiple stakeholders are the client, the cloud service providers, and third parties. The client assigns the operations to cloud providers as written in the Service Level Agreement (SLA). A cloud provider gives the trust to a client based on the contract that is made up of three documents known as Service Policy/Service Practice Statement (SP/SPS), Id Policy/Id Practice Statement (IdP/IdPS) and the contract. A cloud system, thus installed is called a secure cloud by the authors.

Authors (Li, W., Ping, L., & Pan, X., 2010, August) proposed a domain-based trust model to ensure the security and interoperability of cloud and cross-cloud environment. They also suggested some trust based security strategies for the safety of cloud customers and providers.

The family gene based cloud trust model (Wang, T., Ye, B., Li, Y., & Yang, Y., 2010, June), (Wang, T., Ye, B., Li, Y. W., & Zhu, L., 2010, July) proposed is basically based on the study of various basic operations such as user authentication, authorization management and access control, and proposed a Family-gene Based model for Cloud Trust (FBCT) integrating these operations.

CARE resource broker integrated trust model (Manuel, P. D., Selvi, S. T., & Barr, M. E., 2009, December) calculates trust based on three components, namely, Security Level Evaluator, Feedback Evaluator and Reputation Trust Evaluator. Security level evaluation is carried out based on authentication type, authorization type and self-security competence mechanism.. Feedback evaluation has three different stages, namely feedback collection, feedback, verification and feedback updating. The reputation, trust evaluator computes the trust values of the cloud resources based on the capabilities of computational parameters and network parameters.

Authors (Shen, Z., Li, L., Yan, F., & Wu, X., 2010, May), (Shen, Z., & Tong, Q., 2010, July) have proposed a system of integrating Trusted Computing Platform (TCP) into the cloud computing system which improves the security and dependability of cloud. The TCP is used in authentication, confidentiality and integrity in a cloud computing environment.

SLA based trust model (Alhamad, M., Dillon, T., & Chang, E., 2010, September) consists of the SLA agents, cloud consumer module, and cloud services directory. The SLA agent groups the consumers to classes based on their requests, designs SLA metrics, negotiates with cloud providers. Cloud consumer module requests the execution of services. Cloud services directory advertises the cloud provider's services and helps consumers find the appropriate providers.

Multi-tenancy trusted computing environment model (MTCEM) (Li, X. Y., Zhou, L. T., Shi, Y., & Guo, Y., 2010, July) is a two-level hierarchy which supports the security duty separation and also supports three types of stakeholders namely, CSP, customers and auditors. CSP responsibility is to keep infrastructures trusted while the customer assumes responsibility starting from the guest OS, which are installed by the customer on the Virtual Machines provided by the CSP. The auditor monitors the services provided by the CSP.

Authors (Yang, Z., Qiao, L., Liu, C., Yang, C., & Wan, G., 2010, April) study states that the existing trust models ignore the existence of a firewall in a network. The authors have proposed a firewall based trust model in the Cloud. Their paper gives the detailed design calculations of the proposed trust model and practical algorithms of measuring and updating the value of dynamic trust.

Watermark-aware trusted environment (Fu, J., Wang, C., Yu, Z., Wang, J., & Sun, J. G., 2010, July) model is made up of two components, namely the administrative center and the cloud server environment. The administrative center inserts watermark and tailors the Java Virtual Machines (JVM) and the trusted server platform includes a series of cloud servers deployed with the customized JVMs and is used to handle security due to running software on a cloud.

Authors (Ranchal, R., Bhargava, B., Othmane, L. B., Lilien, L., Kim, A., Kang, M., & Linderman, M., 2010, October) have proposed a system without the involvement of a trusted third party based on the study conducted on identity management in the cloud. The proposed system is based on the use of predicates over encrypted data and multi-party computing.

Security framework model (Takabi, H., Joshi, J. B., & Ahn, G. J., 2010, July) consists of three main entities, namely cloud customers, service integrators and service providers. The Service Integrator acts like a bridge between the customers and service providers. The Service Integrator module consists of security management module, trust management module, service management module and heterogeneity management module. The heterogeneity management module manages the heterogeneity among the service providers.

LIMITATIONS OF EXISTING TRUST MODELS

Though various Trust Models are developed to solve the trust issue still trust is a major concern. An extensive literature survey reveals some of the drawbacks found in the various trust models explained in the above section. The issues are listed as below.

Trust calculated by model(Sato, H., Kanai, A., & Tanimoto, S., 2010, July) is internal to the organization. The Cloud Service Provider(CSP) has nothing to do with the security of the resources. So the organization has to have a private cloud to secure its data which is not possible with small/medium organizations.

In Family Gene based trust models (Wang, T., Ye, B., Li, Y., & Yang, Y., 2010, June), (Wang, T., Ye, B., Li, Y. W., & Zhu, L., 2010, July) the trust model is just proposed for authentication and is tested by simulation. The model does not deal with security aspects either of data or of resources. A real time implementation is not done.

In CARE (Manuel, P. D., Selvi, S. T., & Barr, M. E., 2009, December) resource model conventional scheduling is done through FIFO. So computation/process starves for the necessary resources. The priority of resources for the critical jobs is not taken care.

Authors (Shen, Z., Li, L., Yan, F., & Wu, X., 2010, May), (Shen, Z., & Tong, Q., 2010, July) have proposed trusted computing technology for trust evaluation. The basic disadvantage of this model is that the underlying architecture is based on Trusted Computing Platform [TCP] which is difficult to integrate cloud computing with respect to hardware.

Authors (Alhamad, M., Dillon, T., & Chang, E., 2010, September) have proposed SLA based trust model and no implementation or evaluation has been developed or described. This model is a reputation based trust that has a disadvantage that the user with high scores for reputation can cheat user in fewer transactions even though they receive negative feedback. This model has a centralized architecture, so all the services and reputation information has a single point of failure.

In the Role Based Trust model the trust is based on the roles, ID used for TCP, standard certificate for assurance. The hardware maintains a master key for each machine and it uses master keys to generate unique sub key for every configuration of the machine. The data encrypted for one configuration cannot be decrypted in another configuration of the same machine. If the configuration of the machine changes the session key of the local machine will not be useful.

The Active Bundle Scheme (Ranchal, R., Bhargava, B., Othmane, L. B., Lilien, L., Kim, A., Kang, M., & Linderman, M., 2010, October) proposed based on Identity Management model approach is independent of a third party, it is less prone to attack as it reduces the risk of correlation attacks and side channel attacks, but it is prone to a denial of service as an active bundle may also be not executed at all in the remote host.

Though a lot of work is done in trust area still no researcher has proposed any trust model for trusting the resources in the cloud. As resources are the entities in cloud, the security of these entities is very essential. Though the security as a whole is taken care by the service provider still security of the resources in the cloud is at stake. It is noted from the Existing Models that trust plays an important part of the security in the cloud, but trust as a whole in terms of services provided is taken into account. When an entity enters the cloud the trust is calculated by the service provider in accordance with the other resources.

From the above details it is very clearly known that researchers have till now not considered the availability/non-availability of resources for any transaction. Thus a strong Trust model is needed to calculate Trust in Cloud Environment based on the availability of resources as the resources are the main basis for any transaction in the Cloud. Hence a new Trust Model is proposed in the next section to handle this problem.

PROPOSED TRUST MODEL

Trust is the belief of one entity to another entity to work in coordination or to complete a specific task successfully. Though this trust to date is not standardized, researchers define this trust in their own way. Based on this trust value the basic security shield is formed though not completely. For users to distinguish between cloud providers in terms of offered trust, there should be some mechanism to evaluate trust services by independent third parties.

Cloud is distributed system where the two systems are connected with each other to talk. The predominant end points in the cloud are user and resources. A strong security measure is required for the check of unauthorized users. Between two endpoints in any network, we need careful measures and these measures are extremely costly and complex in the real world. For example: for a file transfer between two systems in a network, the file initially reaches the sender's server is then passed to the receiver's server and later reaches the receiver.

Here the file goes through numerous intermediate points to reach the destination. Likewise, in cloud platform also the resources are allocated to the user using an intermediate path like memory stored in a different physical location and is converted to virtual machines and this virtual machine is allocated to user in the network. So the security of the resources becomes crucial and so is the authentication of the user too. So 'being careful' for resources as well as customer is of more priority. Careful design implies constructing checks, recovery policies for all ends in the path.

The function in question can completely and correctly be implemented only with the knowledge and help of the application standing at a point where it can be trusted to do its job in a trustworthy fashion.

A market place of providers and subscribers, gives the end-user the choice to select the provider who is trustworthy based upon their past performance. Thus a trust-trust path is generated between two stakeholders in the cloud.

A trustworthy access control mechanism for the end-user will handle the trust of users and the feedback mechanism of Service Provider (SP) in the market place will generate the trust of SP and a path, thus established between SP and end-user will generate trust-trust path between SP and end-user.

A discretionary control of access of services by the user, thus finds more trustworthy of resource usage by the SP (see Table 1).

But the major disadvantage of a discretionary trust is user has the choice to become good-guy or bad-guy. Good-guy follows the trustworthy path between user and SP whereas bad-guy has the option to manipulate the path without the knowledge of the SP.

The probable solution for the bad-guy problem is to interact with trustworthy third party who is trusted by the user as well as SP. Thus an intermediate trust path is generated.

CONCEPTUAL DIAGRAM OF THE PROPOSED MODEL

To ensure a strong trust value in cloud environment, we have proposed a Trust Model (Figure 1).

The trust is computed by Trust Computation as explained in Figure 2.

The detailed description of these components are given below:

- **Trust Admin:** Basic Trust value is needed to enter any domain. Trust Admin initializes the minimum/basic trust required to enter the system. Trust Admin also administers the overall basic trust of the user/ resources in the system. In migration also Trust Admin plays an important role in calculating the basic trust of the user/resources using the Trust Feedback component;
- **Trust Calculative Model:** Many Trust models are developed, but are always very specific for a specific scenario. Our trust model is a generic model. Here trust is calculated mathematically. The mathematical detail is as given below.

We propose to calculate the trust value based on usage values which in turn are calculated in terms of availability and non-availability.

The trust value calculation is briefly described as below:

1. Trust relationship established between two entities is based on usage and the entities are represented as customer and resources. The notation for the relationship is given as {Customer: resource, usage};

Table 1. Trust model

Mandatory trust	SP decision	Monopoly of Provider
Discretionary trust	User Trust	Based on choice user can change trustworthy path of computation

Figure 1. Trust path model is a conceptual diagram of the proposed trust path model. The User interacts with the trusted computation which calculates the trust value of the user and thus based on the calculated trust value user is connected to the CSP. Now CSP calculates the trust of the resources requested by the user in the cloud and if satisfied allocates the requested resource to the user. Thus a trust path is established between two end points in the cloud between the user and the resource.

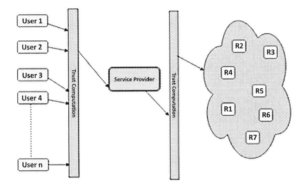

Figure 2. Conceptual model of proposed trust model is the expanded version of the trust computation which consists of trust admin, trust feedback, dynamic trust calculator, trust selection algorithm, trust calculative model, effective trust value and trust moderator

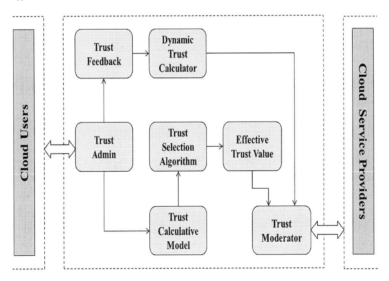

2. Trust is a collaboration of certainty and uncertainty. If the resource is available it is allocated to the customer and the customer performs the action else if not available the trust of the customer on the resource is minimized;

3. The degree of the trust can be represented by a real number called Trust Value. The trust value represents availability/non-availability;

4. Customer may have a variation of trust values based on the availability of the resources.

Principle-1: Trust Using Entropy

Thus, by the basic understanding of the trust, we further define the trust value based on usage. If the trust value is calculated based on availability that the resource is allocated to the customer for his action to be performed, then T{customer: resource, usage} denotes that the trust of the customer on the requested resource is based on the availability/non-availability. Then the probability P{customer: resource, availability} will be the availability of the resource to the customer for some action to be performed. Using entropy model (Cover, T. M., & Thomas, J. A., 1991) of the Information theory the new trust value thus defined is as:

$$T\{customer:resource,\ usage\} = \begin{cases} 1-H(p), for\ 0.5<p<1 \\ H(p)-1, for\ 0<p<0.5 \end{cases} \tag{1}$$

where $H(p)=-p\log_2(p)-(1-p)\log_2(1-p)$ and $p=P${customer: resource, usage}. When $p=1$ the customer is allocated the available resources and the trust value is high. When $p=0$ the customer is not allocated the resources due to unavailability and the trust is very low.Trust value is positive when the resource is available for usage ($p>0.5$), and is negative when the resource is not available for usage ($p<0.5$).

Let us consider a simple example. In the first case, let the probability value be increased from 0.5 to 0.509 and in second case, let the probability value be increased from 0.99 to 0.999. T probability value increases by the same amount in both cases, but the trust value increases by 0.00023 in first case and 0.07 in second case. Thus it is understood that the trust value is not a linear function of probability.

Proof

Let us assume that there are three nodes (A,B,C) in linear chain and node B observes behavior of node C and makes recommendations to node A as T_{BC} ={B:C, usage}. Node A trusts node B with T{A: B, on feedback}= F_{AB}.

Therefore:

$$T_{ABC}=F_{AB}T_{BC} \tag{2}$$

If node B has no idea about node C then T_{BC}=0or if node A has no idea about node B then T_{AB}=0, then the trust between A and C will be zero i.e., T_{ABC}=0. From (2) it is understood that trust increases or decreses with increase or decrese in feedback.

Principle-2: Dynamic Direct Trust Value

Evaluating Trust in the dynamic cloud environment is a necessary factor as cloud is dynamic in nature. Here trust is calculated based on the number of successful transactions made so as to take into account the availability of resources for every successful transaction. Initial Trust i_t is calculated as:

$$i_t = \sum_{n=0}^{n=1} (rn * cn) \tag{3}$$

where:

- r_n is initial resource trust value;
- c_n is initial customer trust value.

After successful transactions, the new trust value will be:

$$D_t = i_t \sum_{i=0}^{i=n} t_i \, / \, total \ No. \ of \ transactions \tag{4}$$

where t_i is No. of successful transactions and D_t must always be greater than the initial trust value as i_t is the initial trust required to perform any transaction.

Principle-3: Trust Value for Migration

The new trust value calculated for the customer on resources is stored in central table which can be retrieved by all Cloud Service providers (CSP).

When a customer wants to migrate to a different service provider the initial trust of the customer with the new CSP is calculated as:

$$M_t = (i_t + D_t)/0.5 \tag{5}$$

where:

$0 < Mt$ for availability

$Mt < 0$ for non-availability

i_t is initial trust by principle-1

D_t is the dynamic trust by Principle-2

0.5 is the minimum trust required by any entity for a successful transaction

Thus, in the Trust Calculative Model trust is calculated using any of the above defining principles and thus a trust value is arrived which is forwarded to Trust Selection Algorithm to check for the accurateness.

Trust Selection Algorithm

It is known from the previous researchers that Genetic Algorithm (Noraini, M. R., & Geraghty, J., 2011) is the best selection algorithm which gives near optimal solutions which are suitable for many practical problems where input data are approximate, but the basic disadvantage of genetic algorithm is it does not yield exact optimal solutions when the population size is considerably larger. So the algorithm used for trust selection is the Family Gene Genetic Algorithm (Jianhua, L., Xiangqian, D., Sun'an, W., & Qing, Y., 2006). The algorithm adapted is as shown in Algorithm 1.

Algorithm 1. Adapted family gene genetic algorithm

Input: population, Trust value

Output: Best trust value in the form of IP address retrieved, System Computation time

Method

1: Initialize P population of n elements.

2: Use a fitness function to evaluate the current solution.

3: Use genetic operators (Cross over, Mutation, Selection) to create new generations.

Go to 2 until the population does not pass the fitness criteria

4: Incorporate the Trust Model developed in the new population along with the new fitness function.

5: Find the best population from the newly incorporated population.

Effective Trust Value

The trust values generated by the Trust Calculative Model and Justified by Trust Selection algorithm are finalized here so as to assign the trust value required to allocate resources based on availability for the transactions to be performed by the customer/user. Once the thus calculated trust is assigned the user can access the resources that are termed available due to the trust value for any transaction as required by the user.

Trust Moderator

Trust Moderator assigns the final trust value to the existing customer who has requested for the specific resources and during migration the trust value of the customer.

Trust Feedback

In case the customer wants to shift his cloud service provider, then his current trust value is stored in central table called Trust Feedback.

Dynamic Trust Calculator

In case of migration the new trust value is calculated using the Principle-3 of the Trust calculative Model and the new trust by migration is sent to the Trust Moderator for the assignment of the trust.

EXPERIMENTATION

To evaluate the correctness of the proposed Trust Model proposed, the mathematical components were implemented using platform like MATLAB and the effectiveness of the mathematical model on a cloud platform was tested using the Aneka Software. The following two sub-sections give a brief description of the platforms used for evaluation.

USING ANEKA

Aneka (n.d) is a Cloud Computing platform rendering Platform-as-a-Service for developing distributed applications on the Cloud. Aneka provides developers with a rich set of APIs for exploiting resources and expressing the business logic of the application.

The Aneka based computing cloud is a collection of physical and virtualized resources connected through a network, either from the Internet or private intranet. One of the key features of Aneka is the ability of providing different ways for expressing distributed applications by offering different programming models; execution services are mostly concerned with providing the middleware with an implementation for these models. Using Aneka Platform we have created 3 users and one server. The users are treated as clients. We have implemented our Trust Model using Family Gene Genetic Algorithm in .NET framework. The Project runs from client machine using the thread concept supported by Aneka.

USING OPEN NEBULA

Open Nebula (n.d.) is a flexible solution to create public, private or hybrid Iaas Cloud. It provides a comfortable easy platform to create private cloud for self use. Open Nebula is mostly used when there is a necessary for data center virtualization and dat management. Open Nebula easily integrates with any one the leading hypervisors to provide a complete control of the virtual resources.

RESULTS AND ANALYSIS

We conducted our experiment using two cloud platforms using the Genetic Algorithm (GA) and Family Gene Algorithm (FGA) in Aneka Cloud Platform and Open Nebula Cloud Platform. Our experiment concluded that the time taken for completing the GA process was more when compared to FGA process.

Figures 3 and 4 shows the comparative results of the genetic algorithm and family gene algorithm respectively, which tells that Family Gene Algorithm gives better performance results.

From Figure 5 it is clearly shown that even in Open Nebula FGA has better CPU time than compared to GA.

From Figure 6 it is evident that as the population size increases the System time decreases in Open Nebula For FGA where as it increases for GA. From this its evident that Family Gene Algorithm is the best algorithm for optimal solution when the population size is large.

From Figure 7 it is also evident that even in Aneka as population increases the CPU Time increases for GA and decreases for FGA. From these experiments it is concluded that irrespective of any platform the proposed model is platform independent.

Figure 3. Aneka computation time

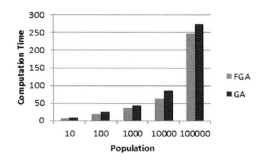

Figure 4. Open Nebula computation time

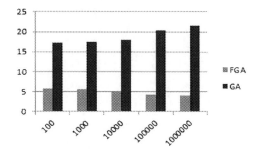

Figure 5. CPU time taken by FGA and GA in open nebula

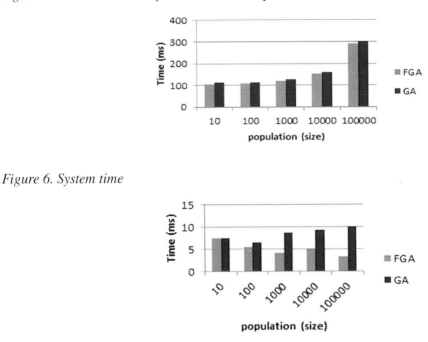

Figure 6. System time

In the CPU usage graph (Figure 8) the X-axis consists of the timestamp with weight and Y-axis consists of the timestamp and the processes running are system, Aneka Manager, Aneka UI(User Interface). In the storage graph the X-axis Consists of Disk Service Time and Y-Axis Consists of Complete time. It is clearly evident from the figure that when the system is in idle state the basic usage of CPU and Storage is minimal.

From the performance analysis in Figure 9 it is clearly evident that the system CPU and Stoarge are well utilized optimally.

We also conducted experiment to check the correctness of the proposed model.

From the experiment (Figures 10-13) we found that our trust model when incorporated gives better results as compared to results when trust is not implemented in the system.

Figure 7. CPU time

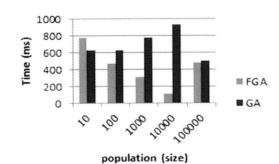

Figure 8. Performance analysis in terms of CPU (Central Processing Unit) usage and storage usage

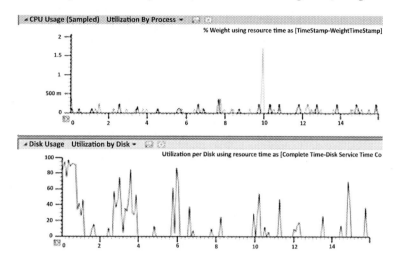

Figure 9. Performance analysis of system after implementing proposed trust model represents the performance analysis of the proposed model with regard to CPU usage and storage

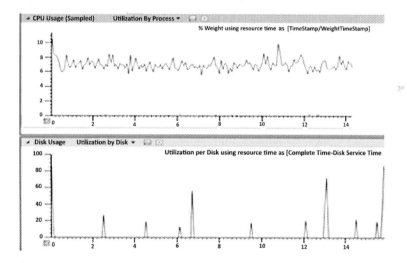

Figure 10. Process time in Aneka

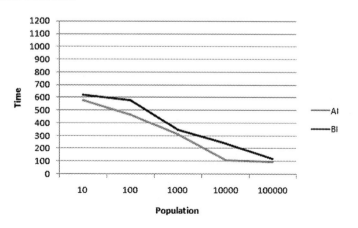

Figure 11. Process time in Opennebula represent the process time in Aneka and Opennebula platforms as before implementation of Trust (BT) and After implementation of Trust(AT)

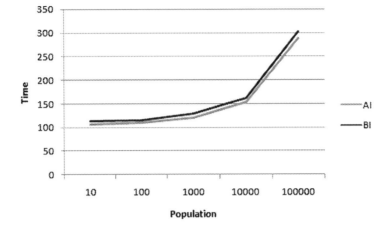

Figure 12. Compute time in Aneka

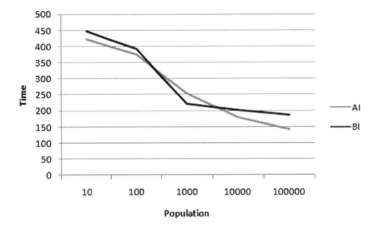

Figure 13. Compute time in Opennebula represent the compute time in Aneka and Opennebula as before implementation of Trust(BT) and After implementation of Trust(AT)

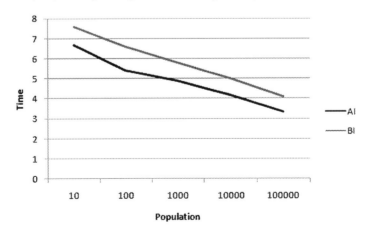

CONCLUSION

A strong Trust is build only when there is a strong trust path between two entities. In any network building trust path is still an issue when security is considered. A strong Trust model is needed to signify the importance of trust. Our model proposes a strong trust value to build a trust path between user and resources in the cloud. The implementation of the trust using the enhanced algorithm has proved that trust when implemented in any system can yield better results. Our model aslo proposes a trust value during migration.

Our future work includes implementing the proposed trust for migration in federated cloud, which would help in migrating from one cloud platform to another with minimum effort.

REFERENCES

About Us. (n.d.). Opennebula.org. Retrieved from http://opennebula.org/about/technology

Alhamad, M., Dillon, T., & Chang, E. (2010, September). Sla-based trust model for cloud computing. *Proceedings of the 2010 13th International Conference on Network-Based Information Systems (NBiS),* (pp. 321-324). IEEE.

Aneka Architecture. (n.d.). Manjrasoft.com. Retrieved from http://www.manjrasoft.com/aneka_architecture.html

Conner, W., Iyengar, A., Mikalsen, T., Rouvellou, I., & Nahrstedt, K. (2009, April). A trust management framework for service-oriented environments. *Proceedings of the 18th international conference on World wide web* (pp. 891-900). ACM.

Cover, T. M., & Thomas, J. A. (1991). *Elements of information theory.* New York. doi:10.1002/0471200611

Fu, J., Wang, C., Yu, Z., Wang, J., & Sun, J. G. (2010, July). A watermark-aware trusted running environment for software clouds. *Proceedings of the 2010 Fifth Annual ChinaGrid Conference (ChinaGrid)* (pp. 144-151). IEEE. 10.1109/ChinaGrid.2010.15

Gambetta, D. G. (1988). In D. G. Gambetta (Ed.), *Can We Trust Trust?* (pp. 213–237). Trust, New York: Basil Blackwell.

Habib, S. M., Ries, S., & Mühlhäuser, M. (2011, November). Towards a trust management system for cloud computing. *Proceedings of the 2011 IEEE 10th International Conference on Trust, Security and Privacy in Computing and Communications (TrustCom)* (pp. 933-939). IEEE. 10.1109/TrustCom.2011.129

Hwang, K., & Li, D. (2010). Trusted cloud computing with secure resources and data coloring. *IEEE Internet Computing, 14*(5), 14–22. doi:10.1109/MIC.2010.86

Jianhua, L., Xiangqian, D., Sun'an, W., & Qing, Y. (2006). Family genetic algorithms based on gene exchange and its application. *Systems Engineering and Electronics. Journalism, 17*(4), 864–869.

Khan, K. M., & Malluhi, Q. (2010). Establishing trust in cloud computing. *IT Professional, 12*(5), 20–27. doi:10.1109/MITP.2010.128

Li, W., Ping, L., & Pan, X. (2010, August). Use trust management module to achieve effective security mechanisms in cloud environment. *Proceedings of the 2010 International Conference On Electronics and Information Engineering (ICEIE)* (*Vol. 1*, pp. V1-14). IEEE. 10.1109/ICEIE.2010.5559829

Li, X. Y., Zhou, L. T., Shi, Y., & Guo, Y. (2010, July). A trusted computing environment model in cloud architecture. *Proceedings of the 2010 International Conference on Machine Learning and Cybernetics (ICMLC)* (Vol. 6, pp. 2843-2848). IEEE. 10.1109/ICMLC.2010.5580769

Manuel, P. D., Selvi, S. T., & Barr, M. E. (2009, December). Trust management system for grid and cloud resources. *Proceedings of the First International Conference on Advanced Computing ICAC '09* (pp. 176-181). IEEE. 10.1109/ICADVC.2009.5378187

Noraini, M. R., & Geraghty, J. (2011). Genetic algorithm performance with different selection strategies in solving TSP.

Ranchal, R., Bhargava, B., Othmane, L. B., Lilien, L., Kim, A., Kang, M., & Linderman, M. (2010, October). Protection of identity information in cloud computing without trusted third party. *Proceedings of the 2010 29th IEEE Symposium on Reliable Distributed Systems* (pp. 368-372). IEEE. 10.1109/SRDS.2010.57

Sato, H., Kanai, A., & Tanimoto, S. (2010, July). A cloud trust model in a security aware cloud. *Proceedings of the 2010 10th IEEE/IPSJ International Symposium on Applications and the Internet (SAINT)* (pp. 121-124). IEEE. 10.1109/SAINT.2010.13

Shen, Z., Li, L., Yan, F., & Wu, X. (2010, May). Cloud computing system based on trusted computing platform. *Proceedings of the 2010 International Conference onIntelligent Computation Technology and Automation (ICICTA)* (Vol. 1, pp. 942-945). IEEE. 10.1109/ICICTA.2010.724

Shen, Z., & Tong, Q. (2010, July). The security of cloud computing system enabled by trusted computing technology. *Proceedings of the 2010 2nd International Conference on Signal Processing Systems (ICSPS),* (Vol. 2, pp. V2-11). IEEE. 10.1109/ICSPS.2010.5555234

Takabi, H., Joshi, J. B., & Ahn, G. J. (2010, July). Securecloud: Towards a comprehensive security framework for cloud computing environments. *Proceedings of the 2010 IEEE 34th Annual Computer Software and Applications Conference Workshops (COMPSACW)* (pp. 393-398). IEEE. 10.1109/COMPSACW.2010.74

Wang, T., Ye, B., Li, Y., & Yang, Y. (2010, June). Family gene based cloud trust model. *Proceedings of the 2010 International Conference on Educational and Network Technology (ICENT)* (pp. 540-544). IEEE.

Wang, T., Ye, B., Li, Y. W., & Zhu, L. (2010, July). Study on enhancing performance of Cloud Trust model with Family Gene technology. *Proceedings of the 2010 3rd IEEE International Conference on Computer Science and Information Technology (ICCSIT)* (Vol. 9, pp. 122-126). IEEE.

Yang, Z., Qiao, L., Liu, C., Yang, C., & Wan, G. (2010, April). A collaborative trust model of firewall-through based on Cloud Computing. In *Computer Supported Cooperative Work in Design (CSCWD), 2010 14th International Conference on* (pp. 329-334). IEEE.

This research was previously published in the International Journal of Cloud Applications and Computing (IJCAC), 6(3); edited by B. B. Gupta and Dharma P. Agrawal, pages 15-31, copyright year 2016 by IGI Publishing (an imprint of IGI Global).

Chapter 19
Architectural Design of Trusted Platform for IaaS Cloud Computing

Ubaidullah Alias Kashif
Shah Abdul Latif University Khairpur - Shikarpur Campus, Pakistan

Zulfiqar Ali Memon
National University of Computer and Emerging Sciences (FAST-NUCES), Pakistan

Shafaq Siddiqui
Sukkur IBA University, Pakistan

Abdul Rasheed Balouch
Sukkur IBA University, Pakistan

Rakhi Batra
Sukkur IBA University, Pakistan

ABSTRACT

This article describes how the enormous potential benefits provided by the cloud services, made enterprises to show huge interest in adopting cloud computing. As the service provider has control over the entire data of an organization stored onto the cloud, a malicious activity, whether internal or external can tamper with the data and computation. This causes enterprises to lack trust in adopting services due to privacy, security and trust issues. Despite of having such issues, the consumer has no root level access right to secure and check the integrity of procured resources. To establish a trust between the consumer and the provider, it is desirable to let the consumer to check the procured platform hosted at provider side for safety and security. This article proposes an architectural design of a trusted platform for the IaaS cloud computing by the means of which the consumer can check the integrity of a guest platform. TCG's TPM is deployed and used on the consumer side as the core component of the proposed architecture and it is distributed between the service provider and the consumer.

DOI: 10.4018/978-1-5225-8176-5.ch019

INTRODUCTION

Businesses are looking forward to Cloud computing model for outsourcing IT services as a utility through internet. Though, it evolves from distributed computing such as, cluster and grid computing yet the internet centric requirement for the cloud computing distinguishes it from cluster and grid computing.

As the name implies, the word cloud denotes the internet that hides the underlying abstraction for the users of cloud computing and yields a problem free thought for adopting the IT services from cloud service provider (CSP). Broadly speaking in cloud computing there may be the involvement of three entities: Cloud Infrastructure, Cloud Service Provider and Cloud consumer (Aboudi, 2017), (Bani-Mohammad, 2017), (Gupta, 2017), (Wang, 2017). The cloud computing demands some new paradigms to share the responsibilities of the provider.

In the literature, authors find some trust models for enhancing trust in the cloud infrastructure i.e. (Panneerselvam, 2017), (Nurmi, 2009), (Paladi, 2013), (Ristenpart, 2009), (Strasser, 2004), but these all models are based on the infrastructure of cloud service provider. Though in these model's, tamper proof trusted hardware such as Trusted Platform Module (TPM) chip is exploited; yet these can't be considered as trusted because, TPM is under physically control of the provider. So, if the provider is untrusted, how the devices through which trust is said to be established can be trusted. An alternative approach is required to fill this gap. It has been considered that trust of a consumer can be established by allowing the consumer to handle and implement security counter measures (Paladi, 2013), (Ruchika, 2016), (Bosse, 2017).

This article presents the architectural design of a trusted platform. In the proposed platform, consumer can exploit its infrastructure in performing security counter measures to check integrity and confidentiality of the Virtual Machine (VM). The core component of the proposed research work is Trusted Computing Group's (TCG's) tamper proof hardware chip known as Trusted Platform Module (TPM), by incorporating the provisions of TCG. The authors in (Bertholon, 2011) states that above-mentioned chip i.e. TPM, will be the essential hardware component for every computer in near future. Their prediction is becoming true and today almost every computer comes with TPM. Microsoft has also declared it as an essential component for every computer (Gupta, 2017), (Bosse, 2015). Keeping these facts, it can be argued that availability of the TPM is not an issue and authors are utilizing the very important component of computers to entrust the consumer in cloud computing.

The proposed solution provides an architecture to share the security responsibilities among the provider and consumer. As in traditional cloud architecture the sole responsible for security management and service hosting is provider; whose trustworthiness is difficult to validate. The aim of the proposed solution is to give some control to consumer side. The aim of this manuscript is not to provide complete isolation between provider and host VM, but rather divide the responsibilities among provider as well as consumer (Hoogendoorn, 2013).

Supporting from the literature, "trust" seems to be big problem in cloud computing. There are different techniques proposed in the literature (Khoshkholghi, 2017), (Nurmi, 2009), (Paladi, 2013), (Ristenpart, 2009), (Strasser, 2004), (Bosse, T., 2012) at different levels, i.e., SPI (Software, Platform, Infrastructure) of cloud computing to enhance the trust of consumer. IaaS is the fundamental layer that supports other layers of cloud computing i.e. SaaS and PaaS. This article is focused on IaaS model, where consumers rent Virtual Machines (VMs) on the infrastructure of Cloud Service Provider (CSP). All models presented in literature are absolutely reliant on the collaboration of provider. According to the models proposed in the literature, consumer requires to trust in provider's infrastructure. Trusted Computing Groups (TCG) has specified a hardware chip i.e. Trusted Platform Module (TPM) for ensuring the trustworthiness of platform. In the models mentioned in Section 4, the core component of trusted computing i.e. TPM is under the physical control of service provider and virtual instances of TPM i.e. Virtual TPM (vTPM) are in the control of management VM. As consumer's VM is hosted at Virtualized Environment (VE) of the cloud and it indicates that consumer has no any access to hardware tamper proof chip. As for as vTPM is concerned, it exists at Virtualized Environment (VE); yet it is accessible to the service provider. If service provider itself is corrupt and untrusted; how the services and security counter measures can be trusted? Any malicious activity in the cloud environment may tamper computations or data of cloud consumer. These models are only workable if and only if provider is trusted. As an alternative choice, there should be a distributed trusted cloud computing model that no longer depends on the infrastructure of the service provider for enhancing the trust in the cloud computing (Bosse & Hoogendoorn, 2012). In this research work, problem of trust is intervened by presenting a novel consumer centric trust model for cloud computing (Bosse, 2011).

GENERALIZED ARCHITECTURE

The proposed architectural design for trusted platform provides the opportunity to consumer to take part in securing the VM. This model is distributed between the provider and the consumer. In this presented platform consumer can exploit his/her infrastructure in performing security counter measures to check integrity and confidentiality of the Virtual Machine (VM). The core component of our research work is a tamper proof hardware chip called Trusted Platform Module (TPM). Work is incorporated with the specifications of Trusted Computing.

Figure 1 depicts the scenario of the presented Trusted Cloud Platform. On the left side of the Figure 1, model for cloud consumer is given which is comprises of software and hardware layers. Software layer

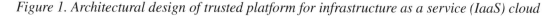

Figure 1. Architectural design of trusted platform for infrastructure as a service (IaaS) cloud

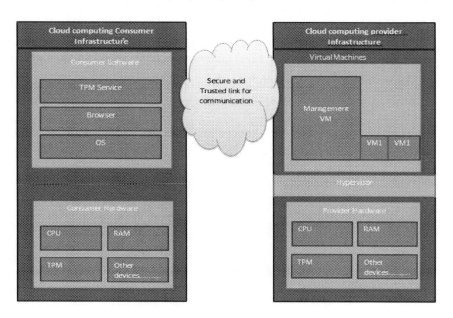

of consumer comprises of operating system supported by trusted computing services. Trusted computing services are essential with the proposed architecture and are meant to be run all the time. Hardware layer of consumer comprises of a complete computer system of the consumer with TPM chip embedded on it. TPM is the actual place where all credentials of guest user will be stored. In this cloud computing environment, consumer has a tamper proof hardware known as Trusted Platform Module (TPM). The whole platform is distributed across the network and shares the responsibility of security between consumer and provider. The proposed solution provides an architecture to share the security responsibilities among the provider and consumer. As in traditional cloud architecture the sole responsible for security management and service hosting is provider; whose trustworthiness is difficult to validate. The aim of the proposed solution is to give some control to consumer side. The aim of this manuscript is not to provide complete isolation between provider and host VM, but rather divide the responsibilities among provider as well as consumer (Bosse & Memon, 2011).

ARCHITECTURE OF TRUSTED CLOUD PLATFORM AT PROVIDER SIDE

This article presents an architectural design of Trusted Cloud Platform. Trusted Cloud Platform aims to utilize the infrastructure of cloud service consumer. Figure 2 illustrates the architectural design of Trusted Cloud Platform (TCP) of Cloud Service Provider (CSP). Here cloud computing environment is consistent of hardware, software and other resources that are usually under the control of CSP.

Left side of the Figure 2, shows zoomed view of Virtualized Environment (VE), it has mainly two components i.e. (a) Management VM and (b) User VM. In XEN hypervisor, the Management VM and User VM is known as Dom 0 and Dom U respectively. All user VMs are connected with Dom 0 via the Front End Driver of Dom U with the Back End Driver of Dom 0. Management VM of CSP is privileged VM and is responsible for all the management of user VMs and underlying resources of the environment.

According to the need and nature of particular environment, there may exist different components in the architecture of management VM. In our presented architecture, two components of management VM are specifically designed with regards to open source system, that will be defined later on in the Section 3. First, is VM Manager that is responsible for the management of user VMs. Second, is Security Manager that is responsible for synchronizing and measuring the security (authentication, integrity, confidentiality) of the user VM. The design of architecture is based on XEN (Barham, 2003; Memon, 2010) as a hypervisor and Ubuntu as a host operating system. This architecture is further mapped with open source cloud computing platform i.e. EUCALYPTUS (Vaquero, 2011) as a cloud computing platform.

Figure 2. Architecture of trusted cloud platform at provider side

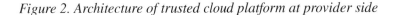
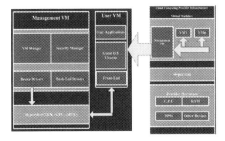

ARCHITECTURE OF TRUSTED CLOUD PLATFORM AT CONSUMER SIDE

Our presented cloud computing model aims to utilize the consumer infrastructure for the security of user virtual machine, that is hosted or running on provider infrastructure. This section, describes the architectural design of the infrastructure of cloud service consumer, as illustrated in Figure 3.

Here, cloud service consumer is having a simple computer machine running operating system having Trusted Platform Module (TPM) chip attached to it which is a pre-requisite for the system to function according to the proposed model. It is worth mentioning with reference (Krautheim, 2010; Memon & Treur, 2010), that 250 million TPM chips are embedded with notebooks, personal computers (PCs), server computers, mobile phones, and other devices. So, it can be convincingly claimed, that TPM will be the de facto rule for every computing machine in near future. Keeping this de facto rule in the mind, this article presents such a consumer centric trusted cloud computing platform.

Here, infrastructure of consumer consists of computer system, operating system, TPM chip and services of trusted computing running and supporting the system architecture. As shown in Figure 3, the lowest level is the hardware layer and the highest level there is software layer. At the software layer, the consumer needs to run trusted computing service i.e. TSS (Trusted Software Stack) Core Service (TCS) and TSS Service Provider (TSP) etc. that support the operation of the TPM device. According to the design both types of resources i.e. software and hardware of the consumer will be utilized. As these resources are under the physical control of the consumer hence the consumer will be very confident to secure cloud computing environment.

PROTOTYPE IMPLEMENTATION

The presented architecture is distributed between cloud consumer and provider. This concept does not let the customer to feel alone in cloud environment. In this Section, we present the prototype implementation of the model. Figure 4, illustrates the components required for the cloud consumer. In the prototype implementation of consumer infrastructure, we have used Ubuntu (Strasser, 2004) of Canonical (Kivity, 2007), (Mouna J, 2016), (Laeeq, 2018) as an operating system configured with trusted computing APIs. PKCS#11 (Wang, 2014) is a Public-key Cryptography Standard No. 11. It's a platform independent API to support cryptographic operation at software level. A Software based TPM Emulator (Graz, 2010) is

Figure 3. Architecture of trusted cloud platform at consumer side

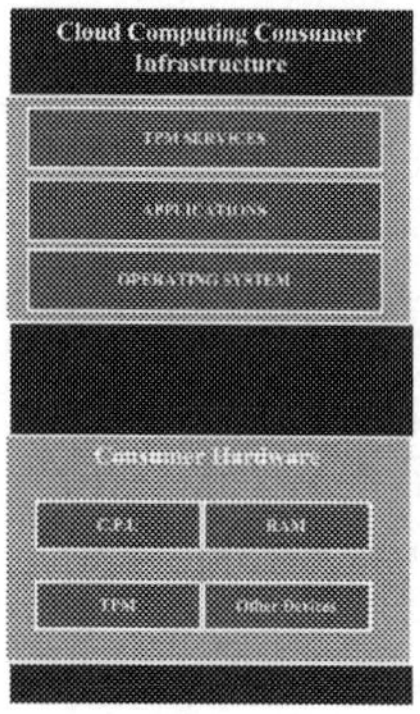

Figure 4. Requirements for consumer infrastructure

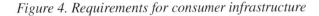

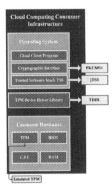

installed in the machine of consumer and java based implementation of Trusted Software Stack (TSS) i.e. IAIK jTSS - TCG Software Stack for the Java (tm) Platform (Aboudi, 2017) is used to communicate with emulated TPM. TCG device driver library TDDL is meant for the low-level communication with TPM. In emulated TPM, simulation of hardware tpm driver is done by a linux kernel module i.e. tpmd_dev and provide the device "/dev/tpm" and also forwards commands to daemon service i.e. tpmd. This daemon is actual implementation of TPM Emulator.

The prototype implementation of provider infrastructure utilizes the virtualized environment (VE) and is partially under control of provider. Typically, it seems that both parts i.e. User VM and Management VM are under the physical control of provide, but, according to the presented platform, consumer has direct access to its virtual machine and can perform integrity checking by using its own infrastructure. This ultimately means, being geographically distant, the consumer can remotely check the integrity of VM by the proposed VM integrity checking protocol. Credentials or integrity report of user VM is directly transferred to the consumer.

In this architecture, the main role is played by initiating Core Root of Trust for Measurement (CRTM) that is supported by each user VM, hosted at provider's platform. Likewise, for the platform attestation process of TPM where Quote_TPM() operation is used, here TPM_Extend() operation is used to record the integrity value of VM components. Figure 5, shows all the components of user VM that forms the Trusted Building Blocks (TBB). Here, user VM is embedded with all the components that supports

Figure 5. Requirements for provider infrastructure

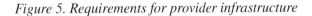

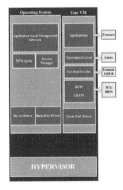

trusted boot of complete virtual machine. These components mainly involve the CRTM, TCG BIOS, TrustedGRUB and Operating System. CRTM is executable immutable code that remains constant in the platform invoked by the CPU of the platform. Actually, CRTM is the part of the BIOS that measures all the bootstrapping components of the system. In virtualized environment of our system, support of trusted computing is available. After CRTM is invoked by the CPU, it then initializes the process of trusted boot by computing the SHA-1 of the BIOS and returns the hashed value to user and it is extended by PCR_EXTEND () function into the TPM of the user. After the BIOS, TrustedGRUB is measured and given control to execute. TrustedGRUB is the enhancement of GNU GRUB and it supports to implement SHA-1 in the software. It consists of two stages during boot process i.e. stage1 and stage2. Stage 2 is more importance, because in this stage OS kernel is loaded. In this architecture, the chain of trust also exists at this level and TrustedGRUB measures the Operating Systems in the Stage2 and extends the PCR value to the user TPM.

All this communication that involves measurement of Hash, loading of components and Extension into PCRs is carried out via the component of management/host VM, i.e., TPM Agent. Actually, TPM Agent orchestrates with the support of guest VM, host VM and consumer program that is communicating with the cloud environment.

INTEGRATION WITH EUCALYPTUS: AN OPEN SOURCE CLOUD COMPUTING PLATFORM

This Section presents the integration of the proposed architecture with open source cloud computing platform EUCALYPTUS (Vaquero, 2011), (Fahad Samad, 2018) which is designed to support and promote academic research in the field of cloud computing. It is simple to use and its modular approach attracts users and administrators to itself. EUCALYPTUS supports state of the art hypervisors such as XEN (Barham,2013), KVM (Li, X.-Y., 2010), (Memon, 2017), etc.

The prototype integration of the architecture with EUCALYPTUS uses kernel based virtual machine KVM (Neisse, 2011) as hypervisor and Ubuntu Enterprise Cloud (UEC) (Wang, 2017). UEC is a complete setup that is packaged with Ubuntu (Strasser, 2004), (Fahad Samad, 2017) of Canonical and has built in support for cloud computing environment.

In Figure 6, three components of EUCALYPTUS i.e. Node Controller (NC), Cluster Controller (CC) and Cloud Controller (CLC) are shown. Whereas, fourth component i.e. Storage Controller (SC) is not shown because, storage of VM is outside the scope of the presented architecture in this article. Node Controller is responsible for hosting user VMs. Cluster Controller exists in between the NC and Cloud Controller. CC performs scheduling task for running VMs. CLC is at front side of the other components of EUCALYPTUS. Cloud Controller can be used to query the node manager of NC for VM resources. In this presented architecture, integrity of user VM that is hosted at NC is measured. For the measurement, it is required for this complete setup to support or incorporate Trusted Computing Group (TCG) specifications. As shown in Figure 6, all the components of EUCALYPTUS are configured with TCG support tools. Main idea of this article is to measure the hash SHA-1 of VM components and store the values in the tamper proof locations of TPM that is under the physical control of consumer. To accomplish this task, the user VM is enabled by trusted computing technology. In order to measure all the components of VM, following steps are crucial to be taken:

Figure 6. Integration of trusted platform with EUCALYPTUS

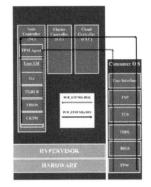

1. Chain of trust is started from the core component of the VM i.e. CRTM that enables the support of TPM operation in the BIOS. It is also necessary for measuring the initial state of machine;
2. TrustedGRUB is used to bootstrap and measure the other components of VM;
3. Additionally, Checkfile functionality of the TrustedGRUB can be used to check the integrity values in the next boot time.

Starting Steps for the Process From the Consumer

1. First step will be to establish a Secure and Trusted communication link. For the time being this link is secured with IPsec Tunnel. (After establishing secure communication, second step for consumer will be to procure a VM on the provider's infrastructure. In case of Amazon Web Service (AWS), Elastic Cloud Compute (EC2) consumer selects an instance type (m1 small, medium, large, extra, large etc.), location and payments);
2. Request from the user is well entertained by the CLC, CC and NC. In this process, user VM is created inside the NC upon executing describeInstance and RunInstance operation by NC. Afterwards, underlying hypervisors creates virtual CPUs, virtual memories and other computing resources that are required to form a complete VM;
3. Third step will be the booting of user VM. In this process, NC instructs the hypervisor to boot the instance. According to our architecture, the boot process is not a typical process but it is a trusted boot process;
4. Dashed arrow shows the flow of instruction from consumer to provider and solid line arrow shows the flow of instruction from provider to consumer. In the process of Trusted Boot, root of trust is created by measuring the hash of each component of VM. This root of trust is initiated from CRTM. It is also known as transitive trust, here CRTM measures hash SHA-1 of BIOS and the result is extended via PCR_Extend() operation to the specified PCR of the TPM. By the same way BIOS measure the hash of Boot loader and this process continues up to the operating system.

During the calculation of SHA-1 of each component, digest values are recorded into the platform Configuration Registers (PCRs) of the consumer TPM:

$$PCR[n] -> SHA - 1(PCR[n] \| measured\ data)$$

Storage of TPM is tamper proof and is in the control of consumer that gives the confidence to the consumer that he may never lose the platform configurations and credentials that are used between the consumer and the provider.

VIRTUAL MACHINE INTEGRITY CHECKING ALGORITHM

Trusted Platform Module (TPM) is tamper proof chip that can generate random numbers, create session keys and perform some cryptographic operation. TPM Endorsement Key (EK) is a 2048-bit RSA key that is generated by the manufacturer of the TPM. This EK causes the platform to be uniquely identified during the operation of TPM this some raise the privacy concern of the users of the systems. To mitigate this privacy concern Attestation Identity Key (AIK) of 2048-bit is created as an alias of EK. It is used to sign data generated from TPM. TPM has capability to generate almost unlimited number of AIKs.

To make the communication safe we are using IPsec communication that is assumed to be safe without making any concern over here. Here communication starts with sharing credentials with each other. In this connection, we have used some keys that are generated from a valid TPM.

Below is a list of keys with symbols used in our protocol:

- Public Part of Attestation Identity Key (AIK_{pub});
- Private part of EK (Endorsement Key) i.e. (EK_{pr});
- Session Key (S);
- {} AIK_{pub} Encrypted with AIK_{pub};
- Number Once Generated (nonce N);
- Public Key of Provider K_{pub};
- Private key of Provider K_{pr}.

Assumptions

1. Consumer has valid certificate of AIK from privacy CA;
2. Consumer knows the public Key of provider:
   STEP1 Consumer->Provider: $\{AIK_{pub}, N, \{(N)\} AIK_{pub}\}P_{pub}$
   STEP2 Provider->Consumer: $\{\{N, P_s\}AIK_{pub}, \{N\}P_s\}P_{pr}$
   STEP3 Provider->Consumer: $\{N, Hash (VM_i)\} P_s\}AIK_{pub}$

In step 1 of the above described protocol, consumer initiates communication by sending nonce N and his public part of his Attestation Identity Key (AIK_{pub}) and this complete message is encrypted with the public key of provider (P_{pub}). In the next step session key is encrypted with the AIKpub so that the session should be dedicated to the consumer, and the whole message is encrypted with the private key of provider (P_{pr}). So that it can be said that this message has come from the provider. In the third step digest value of the component calculated at the provider side is sent to the consumer by encrypting the message with the AIK_{pub}. After the second step Node controller starts to create and launch VM for the consumer and digest values are computed and sent during the boot process of VM. Algorithm 1 calculates and sends the digest values to the user.

Algorithm 1. Guest VM integrity checking protocol

```
Input: Boot components i.e. CRTM, BIOS, Boot_Loader, Operating_System of guest
VM hosted at provider.
Output: Result of Extend_TPM operation (SHA-1 hashed values) stored inside TPM
at provider side.
while execute (1)
load (CRTM) & measure (BIOS)
Extend_TPM(PCRi)
load (BIOS) & measure (Boot_Loader)
Extend_TPM(PCRi)
load (Boot_Loader) & measure (Operating_System)
Extend_TPM(PCRi)
end
```

COST-BENEFIT ANALYSIS

Cost of Computation

The following parameters have been considered to measure the cost of computation:

1. Integrity measurement of VM's components;
2. Transferring hashed values to the TPM of the consumer.

This article follows the process described in (Krautheim, 2010), (Memon & Ahmed, 2017) for consumer VM hosted at provider side. Trusted Boot process takes the hash SHA-1 of all the booting components of VM and stores the measurement (hashed values) in the TPM at consumer side. Following two steps have been taken to measure the cost of computation:

1. **Integrity measurement of VM's components:** SHA-1 is cryptographic hash function designed by National Security Agency (NSA) and published by National Institute of Standard Technology (NIST) as U.S. Federal Information Processing Standard (FIPS). SHA-1 produces Output (O) (message digest) of 160 bits of any Message (M) having maximum size of 264 - 1 bits. The Message (M) is composed of various blocks. The input block, of 512 bits, is divided into total 80 of 32-bit words, denoted as, one 32-bit word for each computational round of the SHA-1 algorithm. Every round comprises of various operations like additions and logical operations, and bitwise logical operations and bitwise rotations to the left. Calculation of algorithm depends on the round being executed, as well as the value of the constant (Wallom, 2011; Asad Abbasi, 2017). The SHA-1 takes 80 iterations that are split into four groups of 20 iteration, each with different values for the applied logical functions;
2. **Transferring Integrity Measurement values to the Consumer (Cost of Network):** As each component at boot time is measured by SHA-1 algorithm and in a result, it produces a 160 bit (20-bytes) of hash values, so to calculate IPsec overhead, this article uses IPsec Packet Size Calculator. IPsec

is a Tunnel Model having ESP of AES-256, esp-md5-hmac and AH of Ah-sha-hmac (Wang, 2017), (Rehman, Laghari & Memon, 2015).

As illustrated in Table 1, measurement values are not in big size but, these are the encrypted values in some hundreds of bytes:

- Total No. of bytes are denoted by S;
- Hash Value is denoted by h;
- IPsec Transformation is denoted by t.

Whereas, i is the initial value and n is the final value that shows the number of VM component at boot time:

Total No. of Bytes (S) =

Hash Value (h) + IPsec Transformation (t)

$$S = \sum_{i=1}^{i=n}(i)(h+t) \tag{1}$$

Cost of Network

Following parameters have been considered to measure the cost of Network:

1. Bandwidth Consumption CB;
2. Total Bandwidth B;
3. Total Size of packet S:

$$C_B = \frac{S}{B} \tag{2}$$

Table 1. Cost of network

VM Components	Size After Calculating SHA-1 Hash	Size After IPsec Transform in Tunnel Mode	
		Encapsulating Security PayLoads (ESP) AES-256, esp-md5-hmac	Authentication Header (AH) Ah-sha-hmac
BIOS	160-bits (20-Bytes)	112-Bytes	
Boot Loader	160-bits (20-Bytes)	112-Bytes	
Operating System	160-bits (20-Bytes)	112-Bytes	

Benefit of the Proposed Architecture

In comparison to the architectures studied in the literature review the proposed architecture does not add any significant additional cost on the consumer side but it, gives control of the partial security to the consumer. As the TPM chip is the de facto hardware module chip in every computer. To make the full advantage of TPM, consumer can take security measures to secure the guest platform of cloud by checking its integrity through our integrity checking protocol initiated through the TPM. By incorporating such protocol cloud service provider can also enhance the trust of consumers.

Complexity Measurement and Other Overheads

As our proposed architecture is can be implemented on an open source cloud computing platform like EUCALYPTUS as discussed in section 6. Its full implementation is left for future work. As for as its complexity and overhead is concerned our proposed architecture would be desirable to be used. As the guest VM is hosted at provider side. The components that are being considered for VM are BIOS, Boot Loader and operating System. As the measurement of VM components will be taken place at provider side and then will be transferred and stored at the consumer side. All such details are discussed in section 5 and 6.

RELATION TO OTHER WORK

In cloud computing, consumer has no any direct access to physical parts of the provider's platform. So, in cloud environment, transitive trust is started from OS loader rather than from TPM. In cloud environment, virtualization is a key technique at IaaS layer. To use TPM in cloud environment, TPM has been virtualized (Wardley, 2009), to meet the demand of hundreds of VMs. Trusted Cloud Computing Platform (TCCP) proposed in (Strasser, 2004) and implemented in (Perez, 2006) lets the IaaS provider to provide, closed box for execution of VMs and it also allows the consumer to attest the platform and decide whether to launch VM or not on the hosted platform. The core components of (TCCP) includes, Trusted Virtual Machine Monitor (TVMM), Trusted Node Controller (TNC), External Trusted Entity (ETE) and Trusted Coordinator (TC). TVMM prevents privileged users to gain access to the user VMs and also provide isolation among the VMs that are running under the node. External Trusted Entity (ETE) manages the TC and TC manages the set of nodes. The Core Root of Trust Management (CRTM) is provided by the TPM embedded at nodes. The protocol also helps to determine whether VM is launched on trusted node or not. IBM presented Trusted Virtual Datacenter (TVDc) (Berger, 2008) that consists of TPM, vTPM, sHype and cloud management software to incorporate a complete system for strong isolation and to assure integrity guarantee. Cloud Security Alliance states that the service provider should have less responsibility of security in IaaS model (Alliance, 2013).

Trust in cloud computing can also be enhanced by letting the client to securely launch VM in the service provider's infrastructure. Allowing the user to verify the infrastructure at provider side by using Trusted Computing is most recommended and viewed in the literature. Authors in (Aslam, 2012) proposed a launch protocol for VM hosted at IaaS cloud computing. Protocol allows service consumer to bind the VM to trusted computer configuration VM image used in this model which is not the one which is provided by the provider rather it is a pre-packaged selected and uploaded by consumer to the infrastructure of the provider. It is suitable for enterprise fashion of cloud computing but in general scenario, VM image is provided by the service provider so, for this general scenario another technique is proposed in (Wallom, 2011) which lets the consumer to securely launch VM.

THREAT MODEL SPECIFIC TO THE PROPOSED RESEARCH

In (Berger, 2008), (Clulow, 2015), (Vaquero, 2011) researchers have stated that VM of consumer hosted at IaaS cloud computing has major threats of being tampered. This statement reasons barrier in trend of cloud computing adoption. So, to protect the user VM, researchers have designed such platforms in which cloud (user VM and host VM) is protected. VM integrity measurement (Ristenpart, 2009) and (Santos, 2009) are among the significant protection technique among others (Nurmi, 2009), (Paladi, 2013), (Ristenpart, 2009), (Strasser, 2004), (Wallom, 2011). Currently integrity measurement and reporting is done solely by the provider. Moreover, at the layer of IaaS cloud computing, consumer has no access to report or to measure the integrity of user VM by using his own infrastructure. Table 2, describes few threats that a VM in cloud may come across, along with the description of how the proposed model handle these threats. The different threats are on the vertical axis and the description of threat along with the approach with which the proposed model is addressing the threat is on the horizontal axis.

Figure 7, illustrates that at IaaS layer of cloud computing, TPM used with physical infrastructure and vTPM (Virtualized TPM) at Virtual Machine Monitor (VMM) layer is under control of the provider.

Table 2. Threats for VM in IaaS cloud along with the approach of proposed model addressing

Threat	Description	Proposed Model
Rootkit BIOS (Heasman, 2006)	"Root is a UNIX/Linux term that's the equivalent of Administrator in Windows. The word kit denotes programs that allow someone to obtain root/admin-level access to the computer by executing the programs in the kit -- all of which is done without end-user consent or knowledge" [http://www.techrepublic.com/blog/10-things/10-plus-things-you-should-know-about-rootkits/]	As in the process of Trusted Boot of VM, this tampering can be detected. In the process of Trusted Boot, integrity of BIOS to OS is measured and on the next boot time of VM, integrity values will be matched and detected.
Cross VM Attack (Ristenpart, 2009)	Cross-VM side-channel is a type of attack to steal information from a target VM being on the same node.	NO
Inserting Virtual Device (Wardley, 2009)	A virtual device is attached that is used to access random memory locations. By doing so, kernel or one of its modules can be changed too. Finally, stream of data to and from the disk can also be accessed.	As in the process of Trusted Boot of VM this tampering can be detected. In the process of Trusted Boot, integrity of devices from BIOS to OS is measured.

Figure 7. IaaS cloud and consumer access

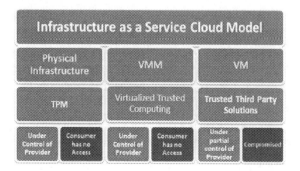

Whereas, at the VM layer there exists, Trusted Third Party (TTP) solution (Neisse, 2011) in which consumer is not involved. To secure the VM, there also exist some techniques based upon TCG's Remote Attestation (Ristenpart, 2009), (Clulow, 2003) but, in these systems provider's TPM is used and again consumer is not involved.

To address this threat, the proposed architecture follows the principle of security duty separation to enhance trust of consumer in cloud environment. This can be accomplished by involving the consumer to take part in securing the procured virtual environment, in our case procured VM.

COMPARISON WITH THE RELATED WORK

In the literature, security duty separation principle for cloud computing paradigm is discussed in (Neisse, 2011). According to this principle, security responsibility boundaries are to be set between the cloud of consumer and provider and this boundary depends on the architecture and service delivery model cloud computing.

Researchers have used TCG's two core techniques that includes Platform Attestation Technique and Platform Integrity Checking Technique. Platform Attestation technique is used in (Aslam, 2012) and Platform Integrity Checking Technique is used in (Ristenpart, 2009).

This article proposes an alternative way by following the principle of security duty separation. In the cited techniques, consumer is getting closer to provider to secure the platform. To continue this approach of getting the consumer closer to provider, this article proposes a technique in which consumer can use its infrastructure to secure the cloud platform. Table 3 compares the state of the art techniques with the technique proposed in this article. Our proposed architecture is different, unique and naïve with regards to TPM chip used by the cloud consumer for the security of its guest VM hosted at cloud consumer side. Because integrity report generated by the cloud provider in combination consumer is stored at the safest place of consumer's TPM. The tamper proof hardware chip TPM has platform configuration registers (PCRs) where integrity values of VM are actually stored. In this comparison, authors did not find any system that lets the consumer to secure the platform by using his own infrastructure.

CONCLUSION AND FUTURE PLAN

Many trust mechanisms have been exercised at different layers of IaaS model, such as Service Level Agreement (SLA) based, feedback based, Trusted Computing Group's (TCG's TPM), Virtual TPM (vTPM) based etc. In some research articles, authors have separated cloud infrastructure between consumer and provider and in some techniques researchers have exposed some part of cloud infrastructure to consumer for remote attestation.

This article devises a naïve technique for enhancing trust in cloud infrastructure where consumer can use its infrastructure to measure the integrity of VM that is hosted at provider side. For this task, a Trusted Cloud Computing Platform is presented that is distributed between consumer and provider. Means, the upper layer (VM layer) of the cloud platform is integrated with the consumer infrastructure and consumer can incorporate his/her TPM to secure the VM. Authors also mapped presented architecture with open source cloud computing platform: i.e. EUCALYPTUS. After presenting architectural design

Table 3. Comparison of proposed architecture with others architecture

Parameters	(TCCP) (Wallom, 2011)	(TVEM) (Landry, 2011)	Implementing Trust in Cloud Infrastructures (Nurmi, 2009)	(PVI) (Krautheim, 2010)	Trusted Launch of Virtual Machine Instances in Public IaaS Environments (Ristenpart, 2009)	Securely Launching Virtual Machines on Trustworthy Platforms in a Public Cloud (Aslam, 2012)	myTrusted Cloud (Clulow, 2011)	Proposed Architecture
Client can Verify Procured Platform	X	X	X	X	X	√	√	√
Host Platform Verification	√	√	√	√	X	X	X	√
Host Platform Measurement	√	√	√	X	√	√	√	√
Consumer Centric	X	X	X	X	√	√	√	√
Hardware TPM Based Security by Provider	√	√	X	√	X	√	√	√
vTPM Based Security	X	X	√	X	√	X	X	X
Measurements are Reported to Client	X	X	X	X	X	√	√	√
Measurements are stored at provider side	√	√	√	X	√	√	√	√
Consumer TPM is used	X	X	X	X	X	X	X	X
Security Duty Separation	X	√	√	X	√	√	√	√
Trusted Boot of user VM	X	X	X	X	X	X	X	X

of Trusted Platform, authors presented Distributed Trust Protocol for checking the integrity of VM. This distributed trust protocol is crucial in securing the VM in cloud environment.

It is worth mentioning that the proposed architecture is ideal for developing distributed trusted security systems for cloud computing. Though, our proposed architecture is limited to only IaaS cloud computing yet this distributed type of approach can also be applied for other types of cloud services i.e. PaaS and SaaS. As it is the proposed architecture, authors aim to fully implement the proposed architecture and perform detailed analysis and evaluation in future. The proposed architecture can also be extended as a further work in some other respects. Pervasiveness, ubiquitous and always on are likely features of cloud computing services. By keeping such features in view, centralized accessibility of VM for distributed trusted cloud computing environment can be devised. Another future aspect of the research work is run time verification of vital software parts or applications of guest VM running at provider side can be achieved.

REFERENCES

Jouini, M., & Rabai, L. B. A. (2016). A Security Framework for Secure Cloud Computing Environments. *International Journal of Cloud Applications and Computing, 6*(3), 32–44. doi:10.4018/IJCAC.2016070103

Abbasi, Asad, & Memon, Zulfiqar A., Jamshed, M., Tahir Q. Syed, Rabah A. (2017). Addressing the Future Data Management Challenges in IOT: A Proposed Framework. *International Journal of Advanced Computer Science and Applications, 8*(5), 197–207.

Aslam, M., Gehrmann, C., Rasmusson, L., & Bjorkman, M. (2012). Securely Launching Virtual Machines on Trustworthy Platforms in a Public Cloud - An Enterprise's Perspective. In F. Leymann, I. Ivanov, M. van Sinderen, & T. Shan (Eds.), *CLOSER, SciTePress* (pp. 511–521).

Bani-Mohammad, S. (2017). An Efficient All Shapes Busy List Processor Allocation Algorithm for 3D Mesh Multicomputers. *International Journal of Cloud Applications and Computing, 7*(2), 10–26. doi:10.4018/IJCAC.2017040102

Barham, P., Dragovic, B., Fraser, K., Hand, S., Harris, T., Ho, A., ... Warfield, A. (2003). Xen and the art of virtualization. In *SOSP '03: Proceedings of the nineteenth ACM symposium on Operating systems principles* (pp. 164–177). New York, NY: ACM. 10.1145/945445.945462

Berger, S., Cáceres, R., Pendarakis, D., Sailer, R., Valdez, E., Perez, R., ... Srinivasan, D. (2008, January). TVDc: Managing Security in the Trusted Virtual Datacenter. *Operating Systems Review, 42*(1), 40–47. doi:10.1145/1341312.1341321

Bertholon, B., Varrette, S., & Bouvry, P. (2011). Certicloud: A Novel TPM-based Approach to Ensure Cloud IaaS Security. In *Proceedings of the IEEE International Conference on Cloud Computing (CLOUD)* (pp. 121-130). 10.1109/CLOUD.2011.71

Bosse, T., Duell, R., Memon, Z. A., Treur, J., & van der Wal, C. N. (2015). Agent-Based Modelling of Emotion Contagion in Groups. *Cognitive Computation Journal, 7*(1), 111–136. doi:10.100712559-014-9277-9

Bosse, T., Duell, R., Memon, Z. A., Treur, J., & van der Wal, C. N. (2017). Computational Model-Based Design of Leadership Support Based on Situational Leadership Theory. *Simulation: Transactions of the Society for Modeling and Simulation International, 93*(7), 605–617. doi:10.1177/0037549717693324

Bosse, T., Hoogendoorn, M., Memon, Z. A., Treur, J., & Umair, M. (2012). A Computational Model for Dynamics of Desiring and Feeling. *Cognitive Systems Research Journal, 19*(1), 39–61.

Bosse, T., Memon, Z. A., Oorburg, R., Treur, J., Umair, M., & de Vos, M. (2011). A software environment for an adaptive human-aware software agent supporting attention-demanding tasks. *International Journal of Artificial Intelligence Tools, 20*(5), 819–846. doi:10.1142/S0218213011000310

Bosse, T., Memon, Z. A., & Treur, J. (2011). A recursive BDI-Agent model for theory of mind and its applications. *Applied Artificial Intelligence Journal, 25*(1), 1–44. doi:10.1080/08839514.2010.529259

Bosse, T., Memon, Z. A., & Treur, J. (2012). A cognitive and neural model for adaptive emotion reading by mirroring preparation states and Hebbian learning. *Cognitive Systems Research Journal, 12*(1), 39–58.

Clulow, J. (2003). On the security of PKCS# 11. In *Cryptographic Hardware and Embedded Systems-CHES* (pp. 411–425). Springer.

El Aboudi, N., & Benhlima, L. (2017). Parallel and Distributed Population based Feature Selection Framework for Health Monitoring. *International Journal of Cloud Applications and Computing*, 7(1), 57–71. doi:10.4018/IJCAC.2017010104

Rehman, W. U., Laghari, A., & Memon, Z. (2015). Exploiting Smart Phone Accelerometer as a Personal Identification Mechanism. *Mehran University Research Journal of Engineering Technology*, 34(S1), 21–26.

Gupta, S., & Gupta, B. B. (2017). Detection, Avoidance, and Attack Pattern Mechanisms in Modern Web Application Vulnerabilities: Present and Future Challenges. *International Journal of Cloud Applications and Computing*, 7(3), 1–43. doi:10.4018/IJCAC.2017070101

Hashizume, K., Rosado, D. G., Fernndez-Medina, E., & Fernandez, E. B. (2013). An analysis of security issues for cloud computing. *Journal of Internet Services and Applications*, 4(1). doi:10.1186/1869-0238-4-5

Heasman, J. (2006). Implementing and Detecting an ACPI BIOS Rootkit. Presented at Black Hat Federal.

Hoogendoorn, M., Klein, M. C. A., Memon, Z. A., & Treur, J. (2013). Formal specification and analysis of intelligent agents for model-based medicine usage management. *Computers in Biology and Medicine*, 43(5), 444–457. doi:10.1016/j.compbiomed.2013.01.021 PMID:23566391

jTSS – Java TCG Software Stack. (n.d.). Retrieved from http://trustedjava.sourceforge.net/

Kay, R. L. (2006). *How to implement trusted computing*. Endpoint Technologies Associates.

Khoshkholghi, M. A., Derahman, M. N., Abdullah, A., Subramaniam, S., & Othman, M. (2017). Energy-Efficient Algorithms for Dynamic Virtual Machine Consolidation in Cloud Data Centers. *IEEE Access: Practical Innovations, Open Solutions*, 5, 10709–10722. doi:10.1109/ACCESS.2017.2711043

Kivity, A., Kamay, Y., Laor, D., Lublin, U., & Liguori, A. (2007). KVM: The Linux Virtual Machine Monitor. In *Proceedings of the Linux Symposium* (pp. 225-230).

Krautheim, F. J. (2009). Private virtual infrastructure for cloud computing. In *Proceedings of the Hot-Cloud'09*. Berkeley, CA: USENIX Association.

Krautheim, F. J., Phatak, D. S. & Sherman, A.T. (2010). Introducing The Trusted Virtual Environment Module: A New Mechanism For Rooting Trust In Cloud Computing. In Trust And Trustworthy Computing (pp. 211-227). Springer.

Laeeq, K., Memon, Z. A., & Memon, J. (2018). The SNS-based e-learning model to provide smart solution for e-learning. *International Journal of Educational Research and Innovation*, 10(1), 2018.

Landry, K.N., Babajide, J.-C., Olufunke, S.O., Gharaibeh, Z. & Harold, B.K. (2011). Implementing trusted cloud computing platform using virtual tpm to achieve confidentiality and integrity. case study: Amazon Ec2.

Li, X.-Y., Zhou, L.-T., & Shi, Y. & Guo, Y. (2010). A trusted computing environment model in cloud architecture. In *Proceedings of the 2010 International Conference On IEEE Machine Learning And Cybernetics (ICMLC)* (pp. 2843-2848).

Memon, Z. A. (2010). Designing human-awareness for ambient agents: A human mindreading perspective. *Journal of Ambient Intelligence and Smart Environments, 2*(4), 439–440.

Memon, Z. A., Ahmed, J., & Siddiqi, J. A. (2017). CloneCloud in Mobile Cloud Computing. *International Journal of Computer Science and Network Security, 17*(8), 28–34.

Memon, Z. A., & Samad, F. (2017). CPU-GPU Processing. *International Journal of Computer Science and Network Security, 17*(9), 188–193.

Memon, Z. A., & Treur, J. (2010). On the reciprocal interaction between believing and feeling: an adaptive agent modelling perspective. *Cognitive Neurodynamics Journal, 4*(4), 377–394. doi:10.100711571-010-9136-7 PMID:21139709

Neisse, R., & Holling, D. & Pretschner, A. (2011). Implementing Trust In Cloud Infrastructures. In *Proceedings of the 2011 11th IEEE/ACM International Symposium On Cluster, Cloud And Grid Computing* (pp. 524-533). IEEE Computer Society.

Nurmi, D., Wolski, R., Grzegorczyk, C., Obertelli, G., Soman, S., & Youseff, L. & Zagorodnov, D. (2009). The Eucalyptus Open-Source Cloud-Computing System. In *Proceedings of the 9th IEEE/ACM International Symposium on IEEE Cluster Computing and the Grid CCGRID'09* (pp. 124-131).

Paladi, N., Gehrmann, C., & Aslam, M. & Morenius, F. (2013). Trusted launch of virtual machine instances in public IAAS environments. In Information Security And Cryptology ICISC 2012 (pp. 309-323). Springer.

Panneerselvam, J., Liu, L., Hardy, J., & Antonopoulos, N. (2017). Analysis, Modelling and Characterisation of Zombie Servers in Large-Scale Cloud Data centres. *IEEE Access: Practical Innovations, Open Solutions, 5,* 15040–15054. doi:10.1109/ACCESS.2017.2725898

Perez, R., & Sailer, R. & Van Doorn, L. (2006). Vtpm: Virtualizing The Trusted Platform Module. In *Proc. 15th Conf. On Usenix Security Symposium* (pp. 305-320).

Reed, A., Rezek, C., & Simmonds, P. (Eds.). (2011). *Security guidance for critical areas of focus in cloud computing v3.0.* Cloud Security Alliance.

Ristenpart, T., Tromer, E., & Shacham, H. & Savage, S. 2009. Hey, You, Get Off Of My Cloud: Exploring Information Leakage In Third-Party Compute Clouds. In *Proceedings of the 16th ACM Conference On Computer And Communications Security* (pp. 199-212). ACM. 10.1145/1653662.1653687

Ruchika, A., & Rajarathnam, N. (2016). Healthcare SaaS Based on a Data Model with Built-In Security and Privacy. *International Journal of Cloud Applications and Computing, 6*(3), 1–14. doi:10.4018/IJCAC.2016070101

Samad, F., & Memon, Z. A. (2017). A New Design of In-Memory File System based on File Virtual Address Framework. *International Journal of Advanced Computer Science and Applications, 8*(9), 233–237. doi:10.14569/IJACSA.2017.080933

Samad, F., & Memon, Z. A. (in press). The Future of Internet: IPv6 Fulfilling the Routing Needs in Internet of Things. *International Journal of Future Generation Communication and Networking, 11*(1).

Santos, N., & Gummadi, K. P. & Rodrigues, R. (2009). Towards Trusted Cloud Computing. In Proceedings Of The 2009 Conference On Hot Topics In Cloud Computing.

Strasser, M., & Sevnic, P. E. (2004). *A Software-based TPM Emulator for Linux*. Zurich: Department of Computer Science, Swiss Federal Institute of Technology.

Vaquero, L. M., Rodero-Merino, L., & And Morán, D. (2011). Locking The Sky: A Survey On Iaas Cloud Security. *Computing, 91*(1), 93–118. doi:10.100700607-010-0140-x

Wallom, D., Turilli, M., Taylor, G., Hargreaves, N., Martin, A., & Raun, A. & Mcmoran, A. (2011). Mytrustedcloud: Trusted Cloud Infrastructure For Security-Critical Computation And Data Managment. In *Proceedings of the 2011 IEEE Third International Conference On Cloud Computing Technology And Science (Cloudcom)* (pp. 247-254).

Wang, H., & Wang, J. (2014, November). An effective image representation method using kernel classification. In *Proceedings of the 2014 IEEE 26th International Conference on Tools with Artificial Intelligence (ICTAI)* (pp. 853-858). IEEE. 10.1109/ICTAI.2014.131

Wang, W., & Qin, Y. & Feng, D. (2014). Automated Proof For Authorization Protocols Of Tpm 2.0 In *International Conference On Information Security Practice And Experience* (pp. 144-158). *Springer*.

Wardley, S., Goyer, E., & Barcet, N. (2009). Ubuntu Enterprise Cloud Architecture (Technical White Paper).

This research was previously published in the International Journal of Cloud Applications and Computing (IJCAC), 8(2); edited by B. B. Gupta and Dharma P. Agrawal, pages 47-65, copyright year 2018 by IGI Publishing (an imprint of IGI Global).

Chapter 20
An Adaptive Enterprise Architecture Framework and Implementation:
Towards Global Enterprises in the Era of Cloud/Mobile IT/Digital IT

Yoshimasa Masuda
Keio University, Japan

Seiko Shirasaka
Keio University, Japan

Shuichiro Yamamoto
Nagoya University, Japan

Thomas Hardjono
Massachusetts Institute of Technology, USA

ABSTRACT

Considering the relation between Enterprise Architecture (EA) and IT is a prerequisite when promoting the uptake of IT by societies. In this paper, the authors propose an "Adaptive Integrated EA framework," based on the results of a survey, to support the strategy of promoting cloud/mobile IT. They considered a unique advanced case and provide details and the structure/mechanism of building this EA framework in a global pharmaceutical company. Moreover, the authors revealed the effectiveness of the proposed EA framework by evaluating/analyzing the problems caused by the rapid shift to cloud/mobile IT in divisions in the US and Europe. Furthermore, they compared the characteristics of The Open Group Architecture Framework (TOGAF) and the "Adaptive Integrated EA framework" (global deployment) in building EA frameworks while evaluating the effectiveness of this framework to achieve digital transformation. Finally, the authors clarify the challenges, benefits, and critical success factors of the framework to assist EA practitioners with its implementation.

DOI: 10.4018/978-1-5225-8176-5.ch020

1. INTRODUCTION

Many global corporations have experienced a variety of changes resulting from the emergence of new technologies, globalization, shifts in customer needs, and the implementation of new business models. Significant changes in cutting-edge IT technology due to recent developments in cloud computing and mobile IT (such as progress in big data technology), in particular, have arisen as new trends in IT. Furthermore, major advances in the abovementioned technologies and processes have created a "digital IT economy," introducing both business opportunities and business risks, forcing enterprises to innovate or face the consequences (Boardman & KPN 2015). Enterprise systems (ES) are complex application software packages that contain mechanisms capable of supporting the management of the entire enterprise and of integrating all areas of its functioning (Davenport 1998, p.121). This requires Enterprise Architecture (EA) to be effective because contributing to the design of such large integrated systems would in future represent a major technical challenge toward the era of cloud/mobile IT/digital IT. From a comprehensive perspective, EA encompasses all enterprise artifacts, such as business, the organization, applications, data, and infrastructure, which are necessary to establish current architecture visibility and future architecture to produce a roadmap. EA frameworks need to embrace change in ways that adequately consider new emerging paradigms and requirements that affect EA, such as enterprise mobile IT/cloud computing (Buckl et al., 2010/ Alwadain et al., 2014). However, specific EA frameworks, e.g., The Open Group Architecture Framework (TOGAF), are criticized for their size, lack of agility, and complexity (Gill et al., 2014). Masuda et al. (2016) found existing EA frameworks to be inappropriate to achieve digital transformation. On the other hand, the necessity of implementing EA in parallel in the mid-/long term (roadmaps and target architectures, etc.) in the era of cloud/mobile IT/digital IT should be emphasized in terms of promoting the alignment of IS/IT projects with management strategy/IT strategy.

In consideration of the above background information, the purpose of this paper is to propose an "Adaptive Integrated EA framework" to meet the requirements of the digital transformation in relation to the above agility-related aspects. The proposed EA framework should support an IT strategy promoting cloud/mobile IT/Digital IT on the basis of what our prior research suggested. The paper also presents the results of our investigation of an example case in a global healthcare enterprise (GHE), where the abovementioned EA framework is built and practically implemented. This is the only case study of related up-to-date EA toward the era of digital IT and enables us to clarify the effectiveness, adaptability, benefits, and critical success factors of this EA Framework in the era of cloud/mobile IT/digital IT.

2. DIRECTION OF ENTERPRISE ARCHITECTURE

2.1 Related Work

In the past ten years, EA has become an important method for modeling the relationship between the overall image of corporate and individual systems. In ISO/IEC/IEEE42010:2011, an architecture framework is defined as "conventions, principles, and practices for the description of architecture established within a specific domain of application and/or community of stakeholders." Furthermore, in the TOGAF (2011) technical literature, it is defined as "a conceptual structure used to develop, implement, and sustain an architecture." In addition, EA visualizes the current corporate IT environment and business landscape to promote a desirable future IT model (Buckl et al., 2010). EA is required as an essential element of corporate IT planning; it is not a simple support activity (Alwadain, 2013), and it offers many benefits to companies, such as coordination between business and IT, improvement in organizational communication, information provision, and reduction in the complexity of IT (Tamm et al., 2011). In order to continue to deliver these benefits, EA frameworks need to embrace change in ways that adequately consider the new emerging paradigms and requirements that affect EA, such as the paradigm of cloud computing or enterprise mobility (Alwadain et al., 2014).

Mobile IT computing is an emerging concept that uses cloud services provided over mobile devices (Muhammad & Khan, 2015). In addition, Mobile IT applications are based on web services. The literature does not contain many reports that discuss EA integration with Mobile IT and the relationship between the two; however, integration with SOA has been discussed greatly. Many organizations have invested in SOA as a crucial approach to achieve agility to ensure the organization can manage rapid change (Chen et al., 2010). In the meantime, there has been a recent focus on microservices architecture, which allows rapid adoption of new technologies such as Mobile IT applications and cloud computing (Newman, 2015). This paper considers both perspectives.

In terms of cloud computing, mobile devices also have cloud-computing capabilities, and many Mobile IT applications also operate with SaaS cloud-based software (Muhammad & Khan, 2015). A few studies concerning the integration and relationship between EA and cloud computing have also been reported. Although there are three general cloud-computing formats—SaaS, PaaS, and IaaS—the current EA framework merely models this computing format and the business components managed by the company. Considering recent dynamic moves in business and the characteristics of cloud computing, it is necessary for companies to link the service characteristics (those similar to the above mobile IT characteristics) of EA and cloud computing (Khan & Gangavarapu, 2009). It is said, when the traditional EA approach is used, it requires months to develop an EA that allows cloud technology to be implemented to realize a cloud adoption strategy. In addition, the same researchers suggested that organizations will demand adaptive enterprise architecture to iteratively develop and manage an EA adaptive to cloud technology (Gill et al., 2014).

Moreover, according to previous research based on a survey (Masuda, Shirasaka, & Yamamoto, 2016), when promoting Cloud/Mobile IT in a strategic way, a good approach for companies that have implemented frameworks such as TOGAF or the Federal Enterprise Architecture Framework 2013 (FEAF) is to adopt an integrated framework. This framework should be an Adaptive EA framework that supporting elements of cloud computing. Henceforth, this previous research (Masuda, Shirasaka, & Yamamoto, 2016) is referred to as "the prerequisite research" of this paper.

2.2 Directions of Cloud/Mobile IT

2.2.1 Cloud Architecture

The NIST definition of cloud computing emphasizes three cloud service models: namely, SaaS, PaaS and IaaS. PaaS is an IaaS platform that includes both system software and an integrated development environment. SaaS is a software application that is developed, implemented, and operated on a PaaS foundation. The SaaS interface is accessed through the client and API interface. IaaS accommodates PaaS and SaaS by offering infrastructure resources such as computing the amount of memory required for network storage through specific centers (Gill, 2015). The Open Platform 3.0 standard (developed by the Open Group) presents the basic architecture models by focusing on trends in cutting-edge technology that create new business models such as those based on cloud / mobile IT.

2.2.2 SOA and Microservice

SOA and microservice vary greatly from the viewpoint of service characteristics (Richards, 2015). SOA is a cooperative design method in which multiple services provide different functions and has been used in large-scale, monolithic applications (Newman, 2015). The SOA architecture pattern defines the four basic forms of business service, enterprise service, application service, and infrastructure service (Richards, 2015). OASIS, a public standards group (MacKenzie et al., 2006), introduced an SOA reference model that presents elements and interfaces for each service.

Microservice is an approach for dispersed systems and is defined by the two basic forms of functional services through an API layer and infrastructure services, and promotes the use of granular services through their respective lifecycles. Since these services operate cooperatively by integrating newly emerging technology, they resolve many problems that existed in SOA implementation (Newman, 2015). Microservice enables the early adoption of new technologies such as Mobile IT and cloud computing (Newman, 2015). Multiple microservices cooperating to work together enable implementation as a Mobile IT application (Familiar, 2015).

2.3 EA Frameworks

What follows is an explanation of EA frameworks that were the subject of a comparative survey in preliminary research for this study.

- **TOGAF (The Open Group Architecture Framework), other**

TOGAF is a framework for the development of EA and was developed and maintained by the Open Group. The framework includes detailed methods and support tools. The Architecture Development Method (ADM) is at the center of TOGAF and is a tiered approach for EA development (Garnier, Bérubé, & Hilliard, 2014). TOGAF is the most widely used framework in companies, and Gill et al. (2014) also discussed TOGAF from the perspective of mobile IT / cloud / SOA integration.

Other EA frameworks are FEAF (Federal Enterprise Architecture Framework 2013), the most widely used framework in government organizations, in particular DoDAF (Department of Defence Architecture Framework), which is most widely used in the network and security domains, and MODAF (British Ministry of Defence Architecture Framework), used by the UK government. These have been discussed by the Federal CIO, the U.S. Department of Defense, and Gill (2014) from the viewpoint of Mobile IT / Cloud / SOA integration (Federal CIO Council, 2008; US Department of Defense, 2009; UK Ministry of Defence, 2010).

- **Adaptive Enterprise Architecture Framework**

The Adaptive EA framework (known as the Gill framework) is a meta-framework that enables support by specifying the situation and tailoring an adaptive EA function and framework. It is based on adaptive enterprise service system logic expanding on the SoS (System of Systems) and Agility, service science approach (Gill, 2013). This adaptive EA framework is defined from the viewpoint of integrating cloud-computing elements, and broadly speaking is composed of two main layers: an external layer (Context, Assessment, Rationalization, Realization, and Un-realization) and an internal layer (Defining, etc.) (Gill et al., 2014).

2.4 EA Framework Analysis

2.4.1 Integrating the Elements of Mobile IT/Cloud Into EA

The mobile IT / cloud-computing elements identified in the EA framework selected in the preliminary research of this study are presented in Table 1.

First, concerning the integration of mobile IT elements, the preliminary research of this study identified mobile IT-related elements in all subject EA frameworks, as shown in Table 1. Mobile devices are identified in TOGAF, DoDAF, MODAF, and adaptive EA frameworks and are also seen in FEAF meta-models. A description of the API is seen in TOGAF and applied EA framework documentation as well as in FEAF meta-models. However, no description of mobile device managers or mobile application controllers is seen in any subject EA frameworks.

Next, concerning the integration of cloud-computing elements, according to the preliminary research on which this study is based, many cloud-computing elements including SaaS, PaaS, and IaaS are identified in the adaptive EA framework as shown in Table 1. In addition, all of SaaS, PaaS, and IaaS are seen in the FEAF document IRM and DoDAF documents. However, the description of a cloud interface is only seen in the adaptive EA framework.

Gray areas: the results of further prior research (Alwadain, 2014); yellow areas: resurveying results in the preliminary research accompanying the FEAF 2013 model definition change; * denotes written content, and ** denotes a meta-model viewpoint architecture process existing in a layer in the framework.

According to the preliminary research of this study, mobile IT and cloud architecture models and guide process elements that are effective in promoting EA are rarely found in the subject EA framework. On the other hand, the cloud interface indispensable in a hybrid cloud-based implementation is important to companies and is only identified in the adaptive EA framework. Based on prior research and an observation we made, an analysis of this EA framework suggests a method that integrates an adaptive EA framework that provides further support to cloud elements in corporate entities already implementing EA. This is suggested to be possible by applying frameworks such as TOGAF and FEAF along with a TOGAF mobile IT / cloud guide and adaptive EA framework mobile IT / microservice architecture meta-model for additional effectiveness.

3. RESEARCH METHODOLOGY

In this paper, as an "EA Framework fitting to the strategy of promoting cloud/mobile IT," we first propose an "Adaptive Integrated EA framework" on the basis of previous research in this field. The propose framework needs to include the necessary EA elements for the era of cloud/mobile IT/digital IT.

Moreover, we present research questions to verify this "Adaptive Integrated EA framework" toward the requirements in the era of cloud/mobile IT/digital IT and to ensure the effectiveness of this proposed

Table 1. Mobile IT/Cloud elements in EA frameworks

EA Frameworks		TOGAF 9			FEAF					DoDAF v2.0		MODAF		Adaptive EA	
Layers (views) / Mobile IT/Cloud elements		Business	Information	Technology	BRM	DRM	ARM	IRM	SRM	Capability V	Services V	Strategic V	Service V	Enterprise Service	Cloud EA Capability
Mobile IT Category (TA)	Mobile Device			*	*		*	**	**	*		*			*
	API		*	*		*	**								*
	Mobile Device Manager														
	Mobile Application Controller														
Mobile IT-related Cloud Category (TA)	SaaS							*		*	*				**
	PaaS							*		*					**
	IaaS							*		*					**
	Cloud Interface								*	*					*
	Other						*	**	*	*	**		**		**
Services Category (AA)	Service				**	*				*	**		**	**	**
	Business Service (micro service)	**			**	*	*				*			**	**
	Application Service (functional service)		**				*			*	*		*	**	**
	IS Service (functional service)		**											**	**
	Enterprise Service (functional service)				*									*	
	Infrastructure Service (infrastructure service)			*				*						**	*
	Platform Service (functional service)			**										**	**
	(Service based) Mobile Application														*

EA framework. Next, we evaluate two research questions corresponded to the case study of a Global Healthcare Enterprise (GHE), which is a research-based global company with primary focus on pharmaceuticals. Being the largest pharmaceutical company in Asia and an industry leader, this GHE prioritizes the future direction of Digital Healthcare as an important element of corporate strategy; therefore, this case study of the GHE is among the only advanced cases of EA implementation toward the era of Digital IT, especially in the field of digital healthcare.

RQ1: How is an "Adaptive Integrated EA framework" developed to meet the requirements in the era of cloud/mobile IT/digital IT?

RQ2: How can our proposing EA framework solve problems in the era of cloud/mobile IT/digital IT?

Then, the author who actually led the project to build and implement this EA, carried out the case study within a global pharmaceutical company, where we built and implemented the "Adaptive Integrated EA framework," by focusing on real developments and progress histories. Moreover, we evaluate the aforementioned research questions using this case study of the global pharmaceutical company.

On the basis of the above research, we clarify the challenges, benefits, and critical success factors of this EA framework for EA practitioners.

4. PROPOSAL OF ADAPTIVE INTEGRATED EA FRAMEWORK ALIGNED WITH IT STRATEGY PROMOTING CLOUD/MOBILE IT/DIGITAL IT

4.1. Necessary Elements in EA Frameworks for the Era of Cloud/Mobile IT/Digital IT

When considering the necessary elements of the EA framework for the era of cloud/mobile IT/digital IT, the EA should have the ability to accommodate agility-related elements. However, the TOGAF is criticized for its size, lack of agility and complexity (Gill et al. 2014). Table 2 contains the results of efforts to identify the elements defined in each of the architecture domain categories and agility-related elements in all subject EA frameworks below. In Table 2, TOGAF9, FEAF, MIT EA, and our proposed "Adaptive Integrated EA framework" are included as all-subject EA frameworks. DODAF and MODAF were excluded from this table because these frameworks do not contain a specific description of agility-related elements.(US Department of Defense, 2009; UK Ministry of Defence, 2010a/2010b) In addition, because the Gartner framework is limited to commercial use, complete access is not possible and it is therefore outside of our scope (Franke et al. 2009). Moreover, because the Zachman framework does not provide an enterprise architecture process for implementing and operating an enterprise architecture capability (Gill 2015), this is also out of our scope at this time. Moreover, when describing the review criteria of "elements in each Architecture Domain Category" in the table, we referred to the definitions of each element in the EA framework development project (in this case the global pharmaceutical company) because there were no specific definitions for these elements in existing EA frameworks. On the other hand, regarding the review criteria of "agility-related elements" we referred to the definitions of agility elements published by Gill (2014).

First, all the elements of each architecture domain such as Business Architecture (BA), Application Architecture (AA), Data Architecture (DA), and Technology Architecture (TA) are identified in TOGAF9

Table 2. Elements of each Architecture Domain and Agility in EA frameworks

EA Frameworks		TOGAF 9	FEAF	MIT EA	Adaptive Integrated EA framework
Necessary elements of EA for Cloud/Mobile IT/Digital IT	Review Criteria				
BA – High level	Business process policy	○ (definable)	○ (definable)	○ (definable)	○ (definable)
BA - Detailed level	Business function chart, Business Process flow	○ (definable)	○ (definable)	× (none)	○ (definable)
AA – High level	Application optimization policy	○ (definable)	○ (definable)	○ (definable)	○ (definable)
AA – Detailed level	Application function chart, Application user location & Communication diagram	○ (definable)	○ (definable)	× (none)	○ (definable)
DA – High level	Data Integration Policy	○ (definable)	○ (definable)	○ (definable)	○ (definable)
DA – Detailed level	Standard Logical Data model, Standard Interfaces, BI DWH Specifications	○ (definable)	○ (definable)	× (none)	○ (definable)
TA – High level	Technology Platform Integration Policy	○ (definable)	○ (definable)	○ (definable)	○ (definable)
TA - Detailed level	Technology Standard, Technology Reference Model, Logical diagram	○ (definable)	○ (definable)	× (none)	○ (definable)
Speed	Rapid flexible response of enterprise in timely manner	Extensible with IT4IT RA (Requirement to Deploy)	× (none) No specific description	-Faster develop in stage 4 (Business Modularity)	○ (definable) -Accommodates expected or unexpected changes rapidly by short-term cycle
Responsiveness	Appropriate responses to deal with changes while sensing situations	Extensible with IT4IT RA (Detect to Correct)	- Service Responsiveness in Performance Reference Model	-IT responsiveness improve in stage 2(Standardize) & 4	○ (definable) - scans, senses and reacts properly to expected and unexpected changes by short-term cycle
Flexibility	Adapt to changing complex business demands in defining Principles in EA	Extensible with IT4IT RA (Requirement to Deploy)	Extensible with SOA (Service Oriented Architecture)	-"Foundation for execution" is this base.	○ (definable) -Able to define Principles flexibly
Leanness	EA operation with optimal /minimal resources without compromising quality	× (none) No description	× (none) No description	-Optimal core business process and data in stage 3	○ (definable) -With optimal EA deliverables, focus on reducing waste and cost without compromising on quality
Learning	EA using up-to-date knowledge/experience with continuous growth/adaptation	× (none) No description	× (none) No specific description except for education systems	-Management Practice in stage 4 accelerate learning	○ (definable) -With knowledge sharing, focuses on enterprise fitness, improvement, transformation and

(The Open Group, 2009c). On the other hand, agile-related elements can be realized by extension by IT4IT, although there is no specific description regarding agile-related elements such as "leanness" and "learning" in TOGAF9 itself.

IT4IT can be used to cover the agile-related elements that would extend the capabilities of TOGAF, whereas the logical service model defined in IT4IT should be equivalent to parts of the adaptive EA framework (The Open Group, 2017).

Second, all the elements of each architecture domain (BA, AA, DA, and TA) are also identified in FEAF (Federal Enterprise Architecture Framework 2013). However, in terms of agile-related elements, there is no specific description regarding "speed," "leanness," and "learning" defined in Table 2. "flexibility," which may be realized by extending SOA and "responsiveness," is identified in the PRM (Performance Reference Model) in FEAF itself (Federal Enterprise Architecture Framework 2013).

Third, all high-level elements of each architecture domain, such as the "business process policy" in BA, "application optimization policy" in AA, "data integration policy" in DA and "technology platform integration policy" in TA, are identified in the MIT EA (Ross et al., 2006). However, almost none of the detailed elements in each architecture domain (BA, AA, DA and TA) are found in the MIT EA (Yamamoto, 2017). On the other hand, descriptions regarding the agility-related elements of "speed," "learning," and "responsiveness" are found in stage 4 of the "business modularity" section in the MIT EA, and a description of "responsiveness" is also found in stage 2 of "technology standardization." A description concerning the agility-related element of "leanness" is found in stage 3 of "optimized core" and the description of the agility-related element of "flexibility" is found in the "foundation for execution" in the MIT EA (Ross et al., 2006)

Forth, all the elements of each architecture domain (BA, AA, DA, and TA) should be identified in the Adaptive Integrated EA framework proposed in this study, because this EA framework is designed to include long-term principles and target architectures in addition to an adaptive EA framework. Moreover, descriptions regarding all the agility-related elements of "speed," "responsiveness," "flexibility," "leanness," and "learning" are identified in both the adaptive EA framework (Gill, 2015) and the proposed Adaptive Integrated EA framework.

Based on the above comparison, the "Adaptive Integrated EA framework" we propose in this study should have capabilities for all the elements of each of the architecture domain categories and all of the agility-related elements defined in Table 2, to address the limitations of TOGAF9, FEAF, and MIT EA.

4.2. Overview of Adaptive Integrated EA Framework

The preliminary research of this study promoted the strategic use of cloud / mobile IT. This suggests that corporate entities that implement EA by having applied frameworks such as TOGAF and FEAF, could adopt a framework that enables the integration of an adaptive EA framework to provide further support for cloud elements as one possible solution. Accordingly, this study proposes an Adaptive Integrated EA Framework based on this suggestion for an EA framework that can even be used by corporate entities to promote a cloud / mobile IT strategy. Figure 1 illustrates the proposed model of the Adaptive Integrated

Figure 1. Adaptive Integrated EA framework proposed model (ex:TOGAF and Adaptive EA framework, etc.)

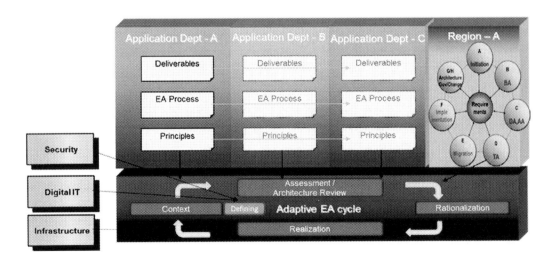

EA Framework. The proposed model is an EA framework integrating an adaptive EA cycle in the lower part of the diagram with TOGAF or a simple EA (framework)[1] for different business division units in the upper part of the diagram.

The adaptive EA cycle in the proposed model makes provision for initiation documents (including conceptual architecture designs) for new cloud / mobile IT related projects that are continuously drawn up on a short-term basis (monthly, etc.). This begins with the Context Phase, which is prepared for referencing the Defining Phase (architecture design guidelines related to all types of security / cloud / mobile IT consistent with the IT strategy) in line with the needs of business divisions. In the next phase of the assessment / architecture review, the architecture committee / organization reviews the architecture by focusing on the conceptual design portion of the initiation documents for this IT project. In the Rationalization Phase, the stakeholders and Architecture Board differentiate/decide upon information systems that will be replaced by the proposed new information system structure or that are no longer necessary and can be abandoned. In the Realization Phase, this project team begins to implement the new IT project agreed upon as a result of deliberating these issues/action items. This enables the corporate entity to adopt an EA framework capable of flexibly adapting to new cloud / mobile IT projects that continuously occur, and which are composed of these four phases.

Moreover, the "TOGAF" and "simple EA (framework)" based on an operational division unit in the top part of the figure is able to respond to differing policies and strategies in business divisions from a mid-long-term perspective. This part of the framework has a structure that can select the above EA framework in line with the characteristics of business division unit operational processes and future architecture. This part also enables application. Further, the framework should align EA guiding principles with the definitions of these principles for business divisions to ensure consistency between the adaptive EA cycle in the lower portion of this figure and the "TOGAF" and "simple EA (framework)" in the upper portion. Furthermore, in the defining phase, the architecture committee / organization promotes the appropriate architectural design of each of the new cloud/mobile IT related systems by developing/ publishing the architectural guidelines for security/cloud/mobile IT, etc. to achieve alignment with the IT strategy.

5. CASE OF EA FRAMEWORK BUILDING IN A GLOBAL PHARMACEUTICAL COMPANY

Here we present a case of EA framework building by the global pharmaceutical company featured in this paper. This global pharmaceutical company, which is headquartered in Japan, has the largest Asian pharmaceutical market share in terms of sales volume, and is smoothly advancing its global deployment of EA by implementing strategic cloud/mobile IT projects and systems at its divisions especially in the US and Europe. The author is actually responsible for all phases of building and implementation of this EA framework and provides background and details of how the EA framework was built.

5.1. Building an EA Framework Through TOGAF at Japan Headquarters

The global pharmaceutical company featured in this paper engaged in several mergers and acquisitions with US research institutes and European pharmaceutical companies in the aftermath of 2008. Consequently, the information system environment at each of its bases in Japan/Asia, the US, and Europe was separated. Therefore, in order to promote the deployment and coordination of IT architecture according to its global IT strategy, from the end of 2013 the company first commenced an EA framework building project at its Japan headquarters, and proceeded to adopt TOGAF, an internationally recognized EA framework for corporations. The company proceeded with the actual building of its EA framework at Japan headquarters according to the TOGAF9 ADM phase. First, the company verified existing IT architecture documentation at its Japan headquarters and set EA project objectives as the Preliminary Phase. Thereafter, the company formulated an IT vision according to its 2020 management vision strategy under Phase A: Architecture Vision, and defined about 12 EA guiding principles necessary to realize this vision. Next, in parallel phases B: Business Architecture, C: Information System Architecture, and D: Technology Architecture, the company visualized its current architecture, prepared a current business function map/chart for its business architecture (BA). At this time the company also produced current application maps of the application architecture (AA) within that information system architecture, current high-level data flowcharts of its data architecture (DA), and a current TA map (execution environment/operating environment/development environment/infrastructure) of the technology architecture (TA). Thereafter the company formulated a future image of each of the BA/AA/DA/TA architectures, envisioning the next five years of the parallel implemented Phase B, Phase C, and Phase D. In addition, the company formulated technology standards for some TA target architecture prepared in Phase D, referencing and utilizing the TOGAF9 TRM (Technology Reference Model).

Furthermore, in the parallel implemented Phase E: Opportunities and Solutions, a gap analysis was performed between each of the current architectures (BA/AA/DA/TA) visualized in phases B/C/D, and global pharmaceutical industry benchmarking information/best practices. Opportunities for transformation to promote EA in each BA/AA/DA/TA were identified, and incorporated into the respective target architectures of each of the aforementioned BA/AA/DA/TA.

Next, in Phase F: Migration Planning, the company selected and organized various IT projects for each of the BA/AA/DA/TA target architectures and each in-progress global IT initiative, and then prepared an architecture roadmap for business application areas and each technology area. In addition, in the parallel implemented Phase G: Implementation Governance, each EA governance process (target architecture formulation and updating process, standard architecture management process, etc.) and the structure of each EA deliverable were defined for BA/AA/DA/TA, and related tasks were incorporated into the architecture roadmap prepared in Phase F. Finally, in Phase H: Architecture Change Management, and Requirements Management, it was determined whether the tasks needed to be defined globally depending on their nature, and then they were defined and the timing of their implementation earmarked for global deployment of EA at a later phase.

5.2. Problems With EA Implementation in Cloud/Mobile IT/Digital IT Strategy

After EA framework building according to TOGAF9 ADM at the Japan headquarters as described above, the company initiated coordination among overseas information system departments (US/Europe), and started global EA training and meetings in July 2014. These meetings with US and European information system departments clarified that, at that time, there were not many information systems at Japan headquarters that were based on SaaS and IaaS-based cloud services and mobile IT. It was established that these information systems actually exceeded half of the new information systems and projects planned for the US and Europe, and thus already constituted the mainstream. Therefore, this global pharmaceutical company faced the following problems in terms of the further global deployment of EA.

1. The inclusion of information system departments in the US and Europe complicated the definition of each principle/standard for the global organization.

2. New European and US IS/IT system projects in the cloud (SaaS and IaaS-based)/mobile IT/digital IT fields constitute more than half of the total, and it was no longer possible for conventional SOA-based reference architecture to be used for architecture guidelines.

3. There exist areas in which BPR projects intended to define standard global business processes (BA) and MDM projects to design and build global master data management platforms (DA) have stalled, and no progress is being made in the formulation of target architecture (BA/DA).

4. Even under the above circumstances, global architecture committees hold meetings for the Architecture reviews on a flexible basis, and there has been demand for reducing architecture risks in each new IT project, and the promotion of a solution based on sound architecture design.

5.3. Building and Application of an Adaptive Integrated EA Framework in Global Deployment of EA

In the latter half of 2014, after 10 or more global EA training sessions and meetings had been held with the overseas US and European information system departments of this global pharmaceutical company, it was decided to pursue global deployment of the EA from 2015. On the other hand, at that time the company was not in a position to globally pursue the formulation of target architecture in BA/DA. There were many new AA related projects in the cloud (SaaS and IaaS-based)/mobile IT/digital IT fields in Europe and the US, and conventional SOA-based architecture guidelines were often inapplicable; thus, the company started each task in the area of TA (technology architecture) for global EA. These TA tasks for global EA included determining and drafting global technology standards organized along the lines of a global IT infrastructure integrated system building project, and the formulation of the target architecture and guidelines in each IT infrastructure area.

Thereafter, this global company initiated a global architecture board in July 2015 (facilitated and coordinated by the author from 2016), started architecture reviews for each new IT/information system project, and realistically pursued the global deployment of EA. Specifically, the company first proceeded to build an EA framework as part of the global deployment of EA according to the steps (Figure 2) of the adaptive EA cycle (framework) presented in the lower part of the Adaptive Integrated EA framework in Figure 1. This would allow them to flexibly introduce new cloud (SaaS and IaaS-based)/mobile IT/digital IT projects successively in each overseas region. First, in the Context Phase, the company embarked upon each project team's short-term (monthly) drafting of new successive cloud/mobile IT/digital IT-based IT system projects (including conceptual architecture design) based upon business department needs, by referencing the security/cloud/mobile IT-related architecture guidelines. When architecture guidelines were drafted in the Defining Phase, the company's architecture teams defined principles conforming to IT strategy elements, and established consistency with global IT strategy by linking the guidelines to various architecture patterns.

In the subsequent Assessment/Architecture Review Phase, each of these new system planning drafts were submitted to the monthly global architecture committee, and thus received architecture reviews, mainly of the conceptual design sections of IT project planning drafts. Altogether, the company's Architecture Board distinguished "replaced systems" and "unnecessary, eliminable information systems" according to the implementation of these proposed new information systems, and determined the positioning of new information systems at the Rationalization Phase. Here, application portfolio management was

Figure 2. Adaptive EA cycle built and implemented during global deployment of EA (created by the author and partially acknowledging Gill (2013), "Proceedings of the 19th Americas Conference on Information Systems (AMCIS 2013), 2013, Figure-1")

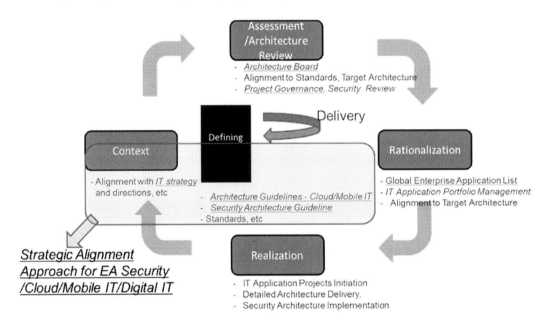

started mainly by sales finance departments. Thereafter, as a result of these phases, endorsed/approved new IT system projects were initiated in the Realization Phase and implemented. Moreover, in the latter half of 2016, the author (EA team) worked towards the development of a digital platform to enhance the efficiency of Architecture Review and to improve communications among Architecture Board members using tools such as the enterprise portals and social tools. Thus, the global pharmaceutical company globally adopted adaptive EA cycles, and built flexibly applicable EA mechanisms for successive new cloud (SaaS and IaaS-based)/mobile IT projects.

On the other hand, from the latter half of 2015, in an attempt to facilitate global deployment of EA in terms of mid- to long-term cycles (global principle and target architecture formulation, etc.), the company promoted the EA framework built around business division units. More specifically, Application Dept-A in Figure 1 was defined as a manufacturing supply chain department, Application Dept-B as a sales marketing finance department, and Application Dept-C as a research and development/quality/personnel department in the proposed Adaptive Integrated EA framework in the upper part of Figure 1, in a form integrated with the Adaptive EA cycle (framework). Specifically, as proposed in this paper, mechanisms were arranged for selecting and applying an EA framework matching the characteristics of business processes and future architecture in business divisions (TOGAF and simple EA (framework)). Thus, it would be possible to respond to different policies/strategies in each business department from the mid- to long-term perspective.

For example, in global manufacturing supply chain departments, referencing the EA deliverables based on TOGAF9 deployed at Japan headquarters (principle and target architecture, etc.), a simple EA framework was built matching the characteristics of the business applications of manufacturing supply chain departments (MES, supply chain systems). In addition, target architectures were formulated by defining principles conforming to global manufacturing supply chain department strategies and policies, by considering coordination of the annual processes for the scheduled acquisition of IT project budgets. Altogether, the company coordinated against the Adaptive EA cycle in the lower part of Figure 1, and for each EA guiding principle that was defined according to IT strategy, they defined conforming global manufacturing supply chain department principles. Furthermore, by referencing the security/application/cloud/mobile IT/integration-related architecture guidelines drafted and proposed in the Defining Phase, they instructed each IT project team to design new IT/information systems for the manufacturing supply chain departments. In addition, other global sales marketing finance departments, and each of the research and development/quality/personnel departments, also selected and formulated EA frameworks matching the characteristics of business processes and future architecture in terms of business division units from TOGAF and the simple EA (framework). These departments are considering the application of the above EA framework in forms coordinated against the adaptive EA cycle in the lower part of Figure 1.

6. EVALUATION AND ANALYSIS OF CASE STUDY

In the case study described in this paper, we evaluated when and how the various problems (1) to (4) presented prior to the start of global deployment of EA were addressed. The responses to each of these problems are structured in Table 3.

As described in Table 3, the initial three problems (1), (2), and (4) have either been solved or are being solved by promoting the use of an Adaptive Integrated EA framework during the global deployment of EA. Regarding problem (3), BA/DA had the same direction at the commencement of each architecture committee, while it is possible to consider problem (3) as resolved based on architecture reviews based on the most realistic solutions. The current study verifies that our proposed "Adaptive Integrated EA framework" can solve problems occurring in the era of Cloud/Mobile IT/Digital IT to address RQ2.

7. DISCUSSIONS

7.1. Valuation for Agility-Related Elements

In this case study, first, the EA team involving the author built an EA framework on the basis of TOGAF9 in Japan headquarters of this GHE. Moreover, the author and each architecture team promoted/proceeded with global EA based on the proposed "Adaptive Integrated EA framework," to address the rapid shifts to cloud/ mobile IT in US and Europe. We compare both TOGAF and the "Adaptive Integrated EA framework" in terms of agility-related elements. Table 4 presents a comparison of valuations for agile-related elements between TOGAF and the "Adaptive Integrated EA framework," from the standpoints of qualitative/quantitative analysis, as a result of the Case Study. The review criteria are the same as in Table 2; additionally, quantitative criteria have been added as defined by the authors. The authors have referred to the definitions of agility elements published by Gill (2014).

First, in terms of speed, EA members (the author) performed EA tasks corresponding to mid- or long-term IT strategy/business unit policies on the basis of TOGAF9 at the Japan headquarter of the GHE in those days. On the other hand, to ensure improvement under the global EA deployment based

Table 3. Status of responses to each problem in the global deployment of EA

Problem number and details	Building and deployment status of each EA	
	Status at time of EA framework building at Japan headquarters through TOGAF	Status of resolution after global deployment of EA through Adaptive Integrated EA framework
Issue (1) **Definition of each principle/ standard for global organization**	- About 12 EA guiding principles defined based on the direction of global IT at Japan headquarters. Thereafter, from 2014 to 2015, a request was made to mainly sales finance business application departments in Europe and mainly IT infrastructure departments and research development departments in the US in order to promote definition of architecture and principles conforming to EA guiding principles, but the obligation to define each principle was temporarily stopped without being determined globally. - Global definition of each standard based on global organizational agreement was difficult. As of 2015, the global IT infrastructure system building project has already made progress, and the definition and formulation of TA standards (technology standards) conforming to this direction is occurring with the agreement of the global IT infrastructure.	- Each principle role and responsibility is being clearly defined globally, and progress is being made in defining each principle involving the areas of Applications, Digital IT and Security, by building an EA framework matching the system characteristics of each area within each business application department. - The role of standard definitions for AA in each area is clarified within each business application department, and presently definitions for each AA standard are being established. BA/DA standards require time for definition due to Problem (3) "Global business process standardization (BA) and delayed progress in MDM platform building (DA)."
Issue (2) **Architecture guidelines for handling new cloud/mobile IT-related projects**	- Drafting began for guidelines related to application architecture, but the external reference architecture available at the time (hereinafter, RA0 was mainly based on SOA, and there was no external RA based on cloud interface and microservice needed in mobile IT application development and SaaS/PaaS implementation.	- At the Defining Phase, the departments responsible for the areas of security, cloud and mobile IT are developing a security/cloud/mobile IT-related architecture guide to handle each area, including microservice, in the form of a service catalog, and are promoting it as a reference when new cloud/ mobile IT-related systems are drafted by each project team.
Issue (3) **Delays in global business process standardization and MDM system building (DA)**	- No global standard business (BA) formulation or master data management platform building started at the time.	- No progress in the definition of global standard business processes (BA) or master global data management system building (DA), and target architecture (BA/DA) not formulated. - On the other hand, new IT/information system projects drafts were reviewed by the architecture committee at the Assessment/Architecture Review Phase of the adaptive EA cycle. In actual reviews, the direction of BA/DA at the time was the same, while architecture review was performed based on the most realistic solution at the time. Efforts were made to promote design quality improvements for each new system and conformance with global IT strategy to address Problem (3).
Issue (4) **Convening of global architecture committee and performing architecture review**	- Architecture committee/architecture reviews consisted mainly of reviews related to TA in Europe and US regional units, but there was a demand for activity to conform to IT strategy covering the promotion of Digital IT on a global level.	- The global architecture board was set up according to definite objectives and the EA implementation process, architecture review conforming to IT strategy of each new IT/information system project involving Cloud/Mobile IT/Digital IT was gradually spread globally, and global deployment of EA was fully promoted.

on the "Adaptive Integrated EA framework," EA members (the author) corresponded to new short-term cycle cloud/mobile IT/digital IT systems. At the same time, mid- or long-term IT strategy/business unit policies were also considered. Quantitatively, in the Case Study analysis, the timeline of one EA-cycle based on TOGAF ADM was 1 year at the Japan headquarter of the GHE. During global EA deployment, the timeline of one EA-cycle based on Adaptive EA was 1 month (or 2 weeks), a notable improvement.

Second, from the standpoint of responsiveness, the technology scan could accommodate changes while sensing situations when updating the technology standard on the basis of TOGAF9 at the Japan headquarter of the GHE in those days. However, the scope of responsiveness was limited to technology architecture. On the other hand, a considerable improvement under global EA deployment based on the "Adaptive Integrated EA framework" would enable the monthly Global Architecture Board to correspond to new systems of cloud/mobile IT/digital IT that occur frequently with changes. Quantitatively, the Case Study analysis, the frequency corresponding to the introduction of new IS/IT systems and new projects on the basis of the TOGAF technology scan was once a year at the Japan headquarter of the GHE and

Table 4. Comparison of valuations for agile-related elements between TOGAF and the Adaptive Integrated EA framework

EA Frameworks		TOGAF 9 (At time of EA framework building at Japan headquarters)	Adaptive Integrated EA framework (After global deployment of EA, Our proposing)
Necessary elements of EA for Cloud/Mobile IT/Digital IT	Review Criteria		
Agility related Elements — Speed	[Qualitative] Rapid flexible response of enterprise in timely manner	Basically, performed EA tasks corresponding to the mid- or long-term of IT strategy/Business Unit policies	Correspond to new systems of cloud/mobile IT/digital IT occurring short-term cycle based, while addressing the mid- or long-term IT strategy/Business Unit policies as well
Speed	[Quantitative] Timeline of one-EA cycle	1 year (TOGAF ADM cycle)	1 month or 2 weeks (Adaptive EA cycle)
Responsiveness	[Qualitative] Appropriate responses to deal with changes while sensing situations	Technology Scan can overcome changes while sensing situations in updating Technology Standard	Monthly Global Architecture Board can correspond to new systems of cloud/mobile/IT/digital IT occurring frequently with changes
Responsiveness	[Quantitative] Frequency of corresponding to new IS/IT systems and projects	Once per year in Japan Once per several months in some locals	Once or twice a month in global
Flexibility	[Qualitative] Adapt to changing complex business demands in defining Principles in EA.	Especially no such kinds of adaptation	Each Architecture team can define Architecture Principles in each domain flexibility while adapting to changing complex business demands
Flexibility	[Quantitative] The number of accepted new IS/IT project planning documents (Architecture Requirements)	Five acceptable new IS/IT planning documents per year (10 Architecture Requirements per document)	Twenty-four acceptable new IS/IT planning documents per month (5-10 Architecture Requirements per document); 288 acceptable new documents per year
Leanness	[Qualitative] EA operation with optimal/ minimal resources without compromising quality	Visualize the current Architecture at the global level, each domain, after that, developing Target Architecture at the global level and each domain (the fields of Business Applications/Technology/Data, etc.)	Establish Project Governance and hold Global Architecture Board monthly, where can perform architecture reviews for new IS/IT projects. Develop Target Architecture in the fields of each Application, Digital IT, Security, while visualizing only necessary current Architecture.
Leanness	[Quantitative] The number of Governance issues and time required to resolve Governance issues	Four kinds of Governance issues exist; 1) No short-term demand-based correspondence; 2) No global architecture board; 3) No global architecture review; 4) No project portfolio management	In particular, no governance issue and four Governance issues were resolved. 1) issue was solved in 1 month 2) issue was solved in 1.5 months 3) issue was solved in 3 months; 4) issue was solved in 2 months
Learning	[Qualitative] EA using up-to-date knowledge/experience with continuous growth/adaptation	Mainly publish SOA-based guidelines of reference architecture, and focus on defining, compliance to standards	Publish service-catalog-based guidelines covering security to accommodates cloud/mobile IT with microservices as well as SOA, while defining the necessary standards.
Learning	[Quantitative] The number of Architecture Deliverables generated on the learning base / The cycle speed of learning	No Architecture Deliverables generated on the learning base.	3 Architecture Guidelines generated on the learning base with 3-month update cycles for Learning – cloud with microservices, mobile IT, cloud security involving microservices.

once in several months in some local regions. However, during global EA deployment the frequency at which the global Architecture Board introduced new IS/IT systems and new projects on the basis of the "Adaptive Integrated EA framework" was once or twice per month.

Third, in terms of Flexibility, there was no such kind of adaptation to changing complex business demands on the basis of TOGAF9 at the Japan headquarter of the GHE in those days. On the other hand, global EA deployment based on the "Adaptive Integrated EA framework" was improved by defining the architecture principles in each domain flexibly by each architecture team, while adapting to changing complex business demands. Quantitatively, in the Case Study analysis, five new IS/IT project planning documents (Architecture Requirements) in the TOGAF ADM were accepted (10 Architecture Requirements per document) at the Japan headquarter of the GHE per year. However, the Flexibility improved during global EA deployment in that the number of accepted new IS/IT project planning documents (Architecture Requirements) in the "Adaptive Integrated EA framework" was 24 per month (5-10 Architecture Requirements per document), which was equivalent to 288 acceptable new ones per year.

Fourth, from the standpoint of Leanness, the EA team visualized the current architecture at the level of global and each of the four domains, after which the target architecture was developed at these levels (the fields of business applications /technology/data, etc.) on the basis of the TOGAF9 ADM at the Japan headquarter of the GHE in those days. On the other hand, a significant improvement in the Leanness was achieved during global EA deployment based on the "Adaptive Integrated EA framework." This was accomplished by the EA team established by project governance. The global Architecture Board convened monthly to perform architecture reviews for new IS/IT projects, and developed target architecture in each of the fields of application, digital IT, and security, while visualizing only the necessary current architecture. Quantitatively, in the Case Study analysis, four governance issues were found in the TOGAF ADM (no short-term demand-based correspondence, no global Architecture Board, no global architecture review, no project portfolio management) at the Japan headquarters of the GHE, which were not solved in those days. However, in terms of Leanness, a considerable improvement for time taken to resolve Governance issues was achieved; during global EA deployment, there were no governance issues especially in the "Adaptive Integrated EA framework," because the 1st issue of "no short-term demand-based correspondence" was solved in 1 month, the 2nd issue of "no global Architecture Board" was solved in 1.5 months, the 3rd issue of "no global architecture review" was solved in 3 months, and the 4th issue of "no project portfolio management" was solved in 2 months, as described in issue(3) of Table 3.

Finally, in terms of Learning, the EA team published the guidelines of SOA-based reference architecture, and focused on defining/compliance to the standards on the basis of TOGAF9 ADM at the Japan headquarter of the GHE in those days. On the other hand, learning during global EA deployment based on the "Adaptive Integrated EA framework" was improved as a result of the EA team publishing service-catalog-based guidelines covering security to accommodate cloud/mobile IT with microservices as well as SOA, while defining the necessary standards. Quantitatively, in the Case Study analysis, no architecture deliverables were generated on the learning base in the TOGAF ADM at the Japan headquarters of the GHE. However, a considerable improvement was achieved in terms of Learning during global EA deployment based on the "Adaptive Integrated EA framework"; three architecture guidelines were generated on the learning base by updating the 3-month learning cycle– cloud with microservices, mobile IT, and cloud security involving microservices.

TOGAF is criticized for its size, lack of agility, and complexity (Gill et al., 2014). As seen in Table 4, the "Adaptive Integrated EA framework" has capabilities for the above five agility-related attributes that are lacking in TOGAF. The proposed "Adaptive Integrated EA framework" also contains all the elements of the architecture domains (BA/AA/DA/TA), thereby ensuring that the global EA deployment based on this framework in the GHE was performed in alignment with the cloud/mobile IT/digital IT approach.

The current research verifies that the "Adaptive Integrated EA framework" is developed to meet the requirements in the era of cloud/mobile IT/digital IT, which involves the five agility-related attributes of "Speed/Responsiveness/ Flexibility/Leanness/Learning," provided in Table 4 to address RQ1.

7.2. Benefits of EA Implementation Using the "Adaptive Integrated EA framework"

This paper proposed the "Adaptive Integrated EA framework" to promote an IT strategy towards cloud/mobile IT/digital IT. The Case Study in the GHE confirmed that our proposed EA framework could be expected to introduce the following benefits:

1.   Reducing Risks for Digital Transformation

In the Assessment/Architecture Review Phase of the adaptive EA cycle in Figure 1 and Figure 2, the Architecture Committee/ Board can review the solution architecture by focusing on the conceptual design portion of the initiation documents for all the new Digital IS/IT projects. The action items should be issued there. One of the authors determined the risks connected to each action item raised by the Architecture Board and defined an equivalent solution for each risk. In addition, in the following phases, they monitored the status of each risk capable of reducing the Risks for Digital Transformation in the GHE as great benefits of our proposed EA framework.

2.   Improvement of Architecture Quality

In the Context Phase of the adaptive EA cycle in Figure 1 and Figure 2, each project team drafted the project initiation documents of new cloud/mobile IT/digital IT-based IT system projects (including conceptual architecture design) based on business department needs. This was achieved by referencing the security/cloud/mobile IT-related architecture guidelines, which the EA team developed in the Defining Phase in Figure 1 and Figure 2. The company's architecture teams defined principles conforming to IT strategy elements, and established consistency with appropriate architecture patterns. Moreover, in the Assessment/Architecture Review Phase of the adaptive EA cycle in Figure1 and Figure 2, the Architecture Committee/Board can review the solution architecture in the initiation documents for all the new IS/IT projects involving Digital IT to improve the architecture quality. These activities are expected to improve the quality of the architecture in each new information system in the GHE as great benefits of our proposed EA framework.

3.   More Effective Cost Control

In the Rationalization Phase of the adaptive EA cycle in Figure 1 and Figure 2, the company's Architecture Board distinguished "replaced systems" and "unnecessary, eliminable information systems" according to the implementation of these proposed new information systems involving Digital IT, and determined the positioning of the new information systems. These activities of application rationalization should lead to optimal cost control in consideration of the appropriate "replaced systems" and "decommissioned information systems" in the GHE as benefits of our proposed EA framework.

7.3. Challenges Encountered in EA Implementation

Although this paper proposed the "Adaptive Integrated EA framework" to promote an IT strategy towards cloud/ mobile IT/digital IT, the EA implementation in the GHE could face some challenges. Based on the Case Study of this EA implementation in terms of cloud/digital IT, the following challenges were encountered in the EA implementation of the "Adaptive Integrated EA framework" in the GHE.

1.   Countermeasure for the supplements in BA and DA

The development of target business architecture and target data architectures is very important in EA implementation. However, the essential projects for the development of these target architectures, such as "business process standardization" and "master data management platform building," were delayed in the GHE in those days. Hence, the challenging tasks are the architecture review for DA and BA in the solution architectures of new IS/IT systems in alignment with an IT strategy promoting cloud/mobile IT/digital IT, without sufficient flexibility in these target architectures.

2.   Communication with Resistant Employees

This Case Study identified communication with resistant employees as one of the challenges of EA implementation for Digital Transformation. Some employees failed to understand the reason why it should be important to recognize a "replaced system" or "decommissioned system" as parts of existing IT infrastructure platforms in the IT strategy and EA especially for Digital Transformation in the GHE. Hence, the challenging task was to overcome these communication problems by utilizing effective methods or platforms such as a communication process or communication platforms in the GHE in those days.

7.4. Critical Success Factors for Implementing EA in the Era of Cloud/Mobile IT/Digital IT

On the basis of the EA implementation experience in this GHE Case Study in the era of Digital IT, we identify the following three critical success factors for EA implementation with the "Adaptive Integrated EA framework." These factors support an IT strategy promoting cloud/mobile IT/digital IT, especially in a global enterprise.

1.   Commitment from CIO and top management

The implementation of EA as well as Architecture Board formulation in a global enterprise is often resisted. One of the reasons is the inability of almost all existing EA frameworks to meet the requirements in the era of cloud/mobile IT/digital IT as suggested in this paper. Even if EA is implemented on the basis of the "Adaptive Integrated EA framework" in the enterprise, commitment from the CIO/ top management and their participation in EA are extremely important to achieve EA implementation and Architecture Board formulation especially in a global enterprise. In this Case Study in the GHE, early risk identifications and countermeasures for new IS/IT projects as a result of participation of the

Architecture Board Top Management (Global IT Executives, Regional CIOs, CISO, etc.) were also very effective. Particularly, for digital IT-related new project strategic alignment risk, countermeasures through participation of the Architecture Board Top Management are effective and strategically important.

2.   Collaboration between the architecture and PMO communities

Collaborative EA implementation among the architecture community, PMO community, and top management is another critical success factor for achieving EA implementation on the basis of the "Adaptive Integrated EA framework" and Architecture Board formulation especially in a global enterprise. In this Case Study in the GHE, it was a key element to establish project governance and hold monthly meetings of the Global Architecture Board to ensure collaboration between the architecture and PMO communities, to perform architecture reviews for new IS/IT projects. Moreover, this collaboration is very important to enable the Architecture Board to discover risks related to project management at an early stage and to devise corresponding "project scope definition" countermeasures (project scope redefinition and reconfirmation) particularly for digital IT-related projects.

3.   Effective utilization of digital platforms

Digital platforms such as the enterprise portal and social tools are very effective to overcome the aforementioned challenges of communicating with resistant employees as well as in political organizational situations. In this Case Study in the GHE, global communications on digital platforms such as the enterprise portal and social tools were conducted to overcome the barriers posed by resistant employees, those between global logical organizations, and the location barriers between countries and regions especially in the Architecture Board. Effective digital platforms are thus a critical success factor to achieve EA implementation on the basis of the "Adaptive Integrated EA framework" and Architecture Board communications especially in a global enterprise. These platforms promote communications within the architecture and PMO communities, global/local organizations, and with resistant employees effectively.

7.5. Limitations

The main limitation of this study concerns the scope of the research, which was based on data collected from a single Case Study in one GHE. The number of projects related to the areas "social/SNS," "analytics for R&D," and the "Internet of Things" was limited in this GHE. Moreover, the scope of this research in terms of data architecture and business architecture was also limited because the project related to the master data management platform and the business process redesign project were delayed in this GHE.

8. CONCLUSION

In this paper, we proposed the "Adaptive Integrated EA Framework," which comprises the necessary EA elements for the era of cloud/mobile IT/digital IT. The framework is based on preliminary research, which suggested an EA framework that can be applied to corporations to promote a cloud/mobile IT/digital IT strategy toward the digital transformation. In addition, we briefed and investigated an example case of a GHE, where the abovementioned EA framework is built and implemented in practice as the only case study of related up-to-date EA toward the era of digital IT. We evaluated the effectiveness of the "Adaptive Integrated EA framework" in the digital IT era by using a case study of a GHE. Furthermore, we clarify the challenges, benefits, and critical success factors of this EA framework for EA practitioners.

We verified that the "Adaptive Integrated EA framework" is developed to meet the requirements of the era of cloud/mobile IT/digital IT, which involves the five agility-related elements of "Speed/ Responsiveness/ Flexibility/Leanness/Learning." Furthermore, we verified that our proposed "Adaptive Integrated EA framework" can solve problems occurring in the era of cloud/mobile IT/digital IT. We are currently investigating further details of the Case Study of the GHE, with the aim of determining the extent to which our proposed EA can solve the problems associated with the era of digital IT. The main limitation of this study is the scope of the research, which was based on the data collected from a single Case Study in one GHE. Its application to other industries might be limited; however, to the best of our knowledge, this is the first and foremost useful research result for global companies that operate in a similar industry, i.e., chemical and manufacturing companies positively promoting a digital IT strategy on a global scale.

Our future research aims to further analyze the effectiveness of the "Adaptive Integrated EA framework" for systems related to digital healthcare applications, such as the "Internet of Things" and "Big data," both of which were raised during Architecture Board meetings in the global corporation. We aim to propose a new approach to achieve benefits for corporations in these areas.

REFERENCES

Alwadain, A., Fielt, E., Korthaus, A., & Rosemann, M. (2014). A Comparative Analysis of the Integration of SOA Elements in Widely-used Enterprise Architecture Frameworks. *International Journal of Intelligent Information Technologies*, *9*(2), 54–70. doi:10.4018/jiit.2013040105

Boardman, S. & KPN. (2015). Open Group Snapshot - Open Platform 3.0™. The Open Group.

Buckl, S., Matthes, F., Schulz, C., & Schweda, C. M. (2010). Exemplifying a Framework for Interrelating Enterprise Architecture Concerns. In M.-A. Sicilia, C. Kop, & F. Sartori (Eds.), *Ontology, Conceptualization and Epistemology for Information Systems, Software Engineering and Service Science, 62* (pp. 33–46). Springer; doi:10.1007/978-3-642-16496-5_3

Chen, H., Kazman, R., & Perry, O. (2014). From Software Architecture Analysis to Service Engineering: An Empirical Study of Methodology Development for Enterprise SOA Implementation. *IEEE Transactions on Services Computing*, *3*(2), 145–160. doi:10.1109/TSC.2010.21

Cruz, A. & Vasconcelos, A. (. (2015). Architecture for the CRM Domain: The Portuguese Citizen Space Case Study. *International Journal of Enterprise Information Systems*, *11*(2), 24–49. doi:10.4018/ IJEIS.2015040102

Davenport, T. H. (1998). Putting the Enterprise into the Enterprise System. *Harvard Business Review*, *76*(4), 121–131. PMID:10181586

Familiar, B. (2015). *Microservices, IoT, and Azure: Leveraging DevOps and Microservice Architecture to Deliver SaaS Solutions*. Apress Media, LLC. doi:10.1007/978-1-4842-1275-2

Federal Chief Information Officers Council. (2008). *A Practical Guide to Federal Service Oriented Architecture*, Version 1.1.

Federal Enterprise Architecture Framework (Version 2). (2013).

Franke, U., Hook, D., Konig, J., Lagerstrom, R., Narman, P., Ullberg, J., . . . Ekstedt, M. (2009). EAF2-A framework for categorizing enterprise architecture frameworks. In *Proceedings of the 10th ACIS International Conference on Software Engineering, Artificial Intelligences, Networking and Parallel/Distributed Computing* (pp. 327–332). IEEE Computer Society. 10.1109/SNPD.2009.98

Garnier, J.-L., Bérubé, J., & Hilliard, R. (2014). *Architecture Guidance Study Report 140430,* ISO/IEC JTC 1/SC 7 Software and systems engineering.

Gill, A. Q. (2013). Towards the Development of an Adaptive Enterprise Service System Model. In *Proceedings of the 19th Americas Conference on Information Systems (AMCIS 2013)* (pp. 15-17).

Gill, A. Q. (2014). Applying Agility and Living Service Systems Thinking to Enterprise Architecture. *International Journal of Intelligent Information Technologies, 10*(1), 1–15. doi:10.4018/ijiit.2014010101

Gill, A. Q. (2015). Adaptive Cloud Enterprise Architecture: Intelligent. *Information Systems, 4.*

Gill, A. Q., Smith, S., Beydoun, G., & Sugumaran, V. (2014). Agile Enterprise Architecture: A Case of a Cloud Technology-enabled Government Enterprise Transformation. In *Proceedings of the 19th Pacific Asia Conference on Information Systems (PACIS 2014)*, (pp. 1-11).

Khan, K. M., & Gangavarapu, N. M. (2009). Addressing Cloud Computing in Enterprise Architecture: Issues and Challenges. *Cutter IT Journal, 22*(11), 27–33.

Lagerstrom, R., Sommestad, T., Buschle, M., & Ekstedt, M. (2011). Enterprise architecture management's impact on information technology success. *Paper presented at the 44th Hawaii International Conference on System Sciences (HICSS).*

MacKenzie, C. M., Laskey, K., McCabe, F., Brown, P. F., & Metz, R. (2006). *Reference Model for Service Oriented Architecture 1.0. (Technical Report).* Advancing Open Standards for the Information Society.

Masuda, Y., Shirasaka, S., & Yamamoto, S. (2016). Integrating Mobile IT/Cloud into Enterprise Architecture: A Comparative Analysis. In *Proceedings of the 21th Pacific Asia Conference on Information Systems (PACIS 2016).*

Muhammad, K., & Khan, M. N. A. (2015). Augmenting Mobile Cloud Computing through Enterprise Architecture: Survey Paper. *International Journal of Grid Distribution Computing, 8*(3), 323–336. doi:10.14257/ijgdc.2015.8.3.30

Newman, S. (2015). *Building Microservices*. O'Reilly.

Qumer, A., & Henderson-Sellers, B. (2008). An Evaluation of the Degree of Agility in Six Agile Methods and Its Applicability for Method Engineering. *Journal of Information and Software Technology, 50*(4), 280–295. doi:10.1016/j.infsof.2007.02.002

Richards, M. (2015). Microservices vs. Service-Oriented Architecture (1st ed.). O'Reilly Media.

Ross, J. W., Weill, P., & Robertson, D. C. (2006). *Enterprise Architecture as Strategy – Creating a Foundation for Business Execution*. Harvard Business Review Press.

Tamm, T., Seddon, P. B., Shanks, G., & Reynolds, P. (2011). How Does Enterprise Architecture Add Value to Organizations? *Communications of the Association for Information Systems*, *28*(10).

The Open Group. (2009c). Content Metamodel. Retrieved October 15, 2010 from http://www.opengroup.org/architecture/togaf9-doc/arch/chap34.html

The Open Group (2017). Open Group Standard - The Open Group IT4IT™ Reference Architecture, Version 2.1.

UK Ministry of Defence. (2010a). MOD Architecture Framework (MODAF). Retrieved October 22, 2010, from http://www.mod.uk/DefenceInternet/AboutDefence/WhatWeDo/InformationManagement/MODAF/ModafDetailedGuidance.htm

UK Ministry of Defence. (2010b). *The MODAF Service Oriented Viewpoint*, 2010. Retrieved October 24, 2010 from http://www.mod.uk/DefenceInternet/AboutDefence/CorporatePublications/Information-Management/MODAF/TheServiceOrientedViewpointsov.htm

US Department of Defense. *DoD Architecture Framework Version 2.0*. (2009). Retrieved October 20, 2010, from http://cio-nii.defense.gov/sites/dodaf20/

Yamamoto, S. (2017, February). Operating Model: Architecture Series, Web Computer Report.

ENDNOTE

[1]   A simple EA (framework) is a simple mid- to long-term perspective EA structure composed of EA principles, EA processes, and EA deliverables (target architecture, roadmaps, etc.).

This research was previously published in the International Journal of Enterprise Information Systems (IJEIS), 13(3); edited by Madjid Tavana, pages 1-22, copyright year 2017 by IGI Publishing (an imprint of IGI Global).

Chapter 21

An Authentication Technique for Accessing De–Duplicated Data From Private Cloud Using One Time Password

Prakash Mohan
Karpagam College of Engineering (Autonomous), India

Saravanakumar Chelliah
St. Joseph's Institute of Technology, India

ABSTRACT

Objective: The main aim is to de-duplicate the redundant files in the cloud and also to improve the security of files in public cloud service by assigning privileges to the documents when it is uploaded by confidential user. Methods: To achieve the objective the authors have used the AES algorithm to encrypt the file stored after de-duplication in the cloud. De-duplication is done based on comparison of contents, file type and size. For an authorized user to access the file from the cloud, generation of OTP using SSL protocol is adopted. Findings: Files uploaded in the cloud are encrypted using traditional encryption algorithms which don't provide high levels of security. Files can be accessed by anyone who is authorized. Privileges are not considered. During de-duplication, only the name and size of the files are considered. Application: Files within the public cloud can't be viewed by everyone who has registered with the cloud. Those who have the respective privileges can only view the file. Proof of Ownership is assured. Since de-duplication is done based on the content redundancy within the cloud storage is avoided. Usage of OTP ensures that the content is viewed by the individuals who have the respective privileges related to the file. These concepts provide additional security to the files stored in the public environment.

INTRODUCTION

Cloud computing technology is used to store enormous amount of data and appear to be a virtual resource to the users. It is dynamic and can be easily accessed from anywhere provided with internet. It encapsulates the platform and execution details from the user. Instead of using costly hardware components, cloud

DOI: 10.4018/978-1-5225-8176-5.ch021

service is comparatively cheap. It is extensible, scalable and updated with ease. Ex: If the user currently has 2GB of space and is in need of further storage space (Li, 2013; Itani, 2009), he can expand it easily. Private cloud provides more security (Mohan, 2013; Popović, 2010; Prakash, 2012) with less storage space. It can be accessed easily. It is suitable to use within the organisation. Data (Annamalai, 2015) can be accessed based on privileges. The keys for the files stored in public cloud are usually stored in private cloud. On contrary, public cloud provides data storage with less security. It is mostly concerned with the private cloud. To secure the data from losing its confidentiality, privileges (Prakash, 2015; Annamalai, 2015) are given to the files, so that only specific people can access the file. Privileges can be given both the types of cloud service (Saravanakumar, 2012). Authorization to the cloud is provided based on the credentials stored in the database during registration with the cloud. De-duplication is a data compression technique used to eliminate the redundant copies in the cloud enhancing (Mell, 2009; Khan, 2016) the storage capacity. It is done at both file level and block level. In file level, it eliminates the duplicated files and at block level redundant blocks in the file are eliminated in non-identical files. The file attributes like size, content and type are checked. Privacy concerns are present due to insider and outsider attacks. Data are encrypted (Corena, 2012; Ryan, 2011) for security (Pearson, 2013; Subashini, 2011) reasons. In traditional encryption, when the same file is uploaded by different people different cipher texts are created for each individual. This makes de-duplication difficult. In convergent encryption, a convergent key is generated by calculating the cryptographic hash value of the file. This key is used to encrypt or decrypt the file. Keys are present with the user and the cipher texts thus generated are stored in the cloud. Here the cipher text produced for identical copies of file will be same and helps in de-duplication. Proof of ownership is provided to the files to ensure the user holds the file in spite of duplicate copies. When convergent encryption is used de-duplication of cipher text is possible and proof of ownership helps to enhance confidentiality. The de-duplication systems based on this fail to provide duplicate check with privileges. Issues arise when de-duplication with privileges are tried to be implemented at same time.

RELATED PREVIOUS WORK

Venkatesh, Sharma, Desai et al. (2014), aimed to minimize the data duplication along with data. Security is to protect the confidentiality of the data. The security is provided by using many encryption techniques to encrypt the data before outsourcing. The users are checked whether they are authorized or not. Encryption is symmetric. SCSP is used to reduce de-duplication. The algorithm used here is novel encryption key generation algorithm. During the process of uploading the file, a tag is generated. It helps to identify the duplicates. These tags are stored in a separate table. The project has the advantage that the system is suitable for backup storage by using authorized de-duplication. In data duplication the encrypted keys are generated by private key cloud server. But the decryption of cipher text cannot be done by private cloud server and S-CSP based on security of symmetric encryption with traditional data duplication in cloud computing is semantically secure. The proposed system is storing the authorised privileges.

Kumaresan, and Visuwasam (2015) had tried to overcome the disadvantage of traditional encryption techniques using convergent encryption. Hash calculation is done at block level. If the target device finds a duplicate, then it doesn't store a duplicate block. Instead it references to the existing block. This takes quite a longer time. Data Duplication is an important technology used in many companies to save a lot of money on storage cost and bandwidth by avoiding the replication. This paper proposed that the server will pop-up the duplication message if a file duplication is found. The security is provided by encryption algorithm. In order to protect the higher secured data, the effort made to increase the data accuracy check and hardware utilization. RSA algorithm is used to increase the security in hybrid cloud.

Walunj, Lande, and Pansare (2014). had said that the data duplication plays a vital role in eliminating the replicated data copies. This process eliminates the duplicate copy by saving only one copy and replacing the other copies with pointers. The pointers make the link to original copy. De-duplication widely used in companies for backup and disaster recovery process. The paper aimed to provide the authorized de-duplication check by combining the convergent encryption algorithm in hybrid cloud. In public cloud the data are stored securely in encrypted format. In private cloud the keys are stored with respective file no need to remember the key. Hence to access the data in public cloud the user must provide the key.

Samadhu, Rambabu, Pradeep Kumar et al. (2015) had considered differential privileges of users for duplicate check besides the data itself. The paper details about the insider and outsider attacks. Convergent encryption concept uses convergent key which is obtained by encrypting the file and tag is used to detect the duplicate copies. In IBI (Identity Based Identification) there is an authority who will have the public key and a master secret key. Based on user's identity secret key will be provided. IBS (Identity Based Signature) is a method in which user will sign the message. RevDedup is used to avoid the issue of fragmentation of images.

Li, Li, Chen et al. (2015) say that the same file may be saved in several different places by different users, or two or more files that aren't identical may still include much of the same data. De-duplication eliminates these extra copies replacing them with pointers that lead back to the original copy. The convergent encryption technique is used to encrypt the data. Proof of data is proposed by them. It is used while uploading file. If there is a copy of the uploaded file along with same privilege duplicate could be found by the user. The duplicate-check tokens of files will be generated by the private cloud server with private keys.

OUR NEW APPROACH

Cloud computing is ruling the progressing hi-tech environment. It helps to store voluminous data and access can be gained by users from anywhere. The service providers provide the storage and access to people at low costs. With more number of people started to use cloud, there can chances of redundancy. People belonging to same organisation can upload a file with same content with different names. This can occupy a lot of space. De-duplication helps to reduce the redundant copies of files in the cloud. When files with same content are found, they are de-duplicated. The data owner can assign privileges for the file so that only specific people can gain access to it. The file will not be available for others. This is one of the advancement related to security for the cloud service. Security is provided to the data in public cloud. The data stored in cloud are de-duplicated based on the content, size and type using AES algorithm. This enhances the confidentiality of the files within the cloud. When an authenticated user tries to access a file, his details are checked with the database. If the credentials match with the database, then an OTP will be sent to the client's mail. The client will be requested to enter the received OTP on the web interface. The previously generated OTP is checked with the value the client entered. If both the values match then access to the file is given to the client. Client can access the file only if his privilege is available in the list of privileges given to the file. It provides increased security to the data within the public cloud.

A FRAMEWORK FOR ACCESSING DE-DUPLICATED DATA

De-duplication helps to reduce the redundancy in the cloud. Instead of saving many copies of same file and increasing the storage space, it's better to have a single copy of file and pointing the reference to the file. Though most of the issues in cloud aren't solved yet, one of the major challenges (Wei, 2010) is providing security to the file in public cloud. When the data owner tries to upload the file, he could assign the list of privileges to the file. When an authenticated user tries to access a file, he could download it only when his privileges are available in list of privileges attached to the file when the file is uploaded. He will be sent an OTP which he should enter in the web interface. AES algorithm is used to encrypt the file within the cloud.

The entire system provides a conduit to store voluminous data with confidentiality element based on privileges. As shown in Figure 1, a new user first registers with name, password, email and designation to utilize the cloud service. All the credentials are stored in MySQL database. The designations are included by an administrator. He assigns the appropriate privileges for the designations. The new user should select one amongst the designations included by the administrator.

He is present to maintain the credentials stored in the database. Once the user registers, he can login to the cloud. The authorized users who upload the data are the data owners. These data owners can upload the file and provide privileges to the file. Based on the privileges the clients can access the file. Many data owners can upload the files with same content but different file names. Based on size, content and type the files are de-duplicated. The de- duplicated files are encrypted using AES algorithm and stored within the cloud. The client tries to access the file stored within the cloud. Validation of users is done based on the credentials stored within the database. If the credentials of client match to the details in the

Figure 1. A frame work for accessing de-duplication data

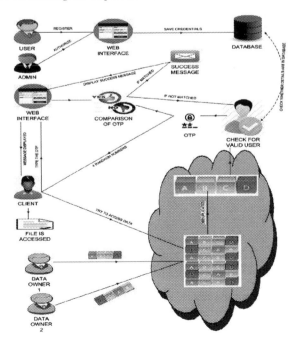

database, then an OTP is generated and sent to the client's email address. The client enters the received OTP into web interface.

The previously generated OTP which is stored in database is checked with the user entered OTP. If they are same then a success message pops up and the file can be accessed by the client. Else an error message is displayed.

Assigning Privileges to Designations

The administrator can login and include the necessary designations, the privileges. He can also assign the appropriate privileges to specific designations as in Equation 1. On the user's side, users should first register. Once they have registered, they can login with the required credentials. Based on the designation they give during registration, files will be made accessible to them:

$$Admin \leftarrow Login \cup Designations \cup Access\ Privileges \tag{1}$$

De-Duplication and Encryption

When the data owner tries to upload a file, he should include the necessary privileges to the file. On uploading the file is checked for duplication based on the content, size and type. Finally, the file is encrypted by using AES algorithm and saved in the cloud as in Equation 2 and Equation 3:

$$File\ Uploading \leftarrow File\ Privilege \cup File\ Characteristics \tag{2}$$

$$File\ Characteristics \leftarrow AES\left(Content \cup Size \cup Type\right) \tag{3}$$

OTP Generation

When an authenticated user tries to access a file within the cloud, the privileges of user are checked whether it matches with the requestor's privilege or not. If it matches an OTP is generated using SSL protocol and sent to the requestor's mail address which is given at the time of registration. The client should enter this value into the web interface. When both the values match, then the file can be accessed by the client. Else an error message is thrown to the client as in Equation 4:

$$OTP\ Generation = \begin{cases} True, File\ Characteristices == Matched \\ False, \qquad\qquad\qquad\quad Otherwise \end{cases} \tag{4}$$

ALGORITHM AND FLOW PROCESS OF PROPOSED DE-DUPLICATION

The algorithm for the de-duplication is discussed below. If the Cloud Service User request uploads the file then Checks for the Identity belongs to the same organization otherwise the map-reduce action is performed:

```
De-duplication()
begin
Cloud Service User (CSU) request the cloud service (CSU_req);
Cloud Service Provider (CSP) provides the appropriate Services (CSP_res);
if(CSUreq == "file upload")
identify the request source (Id_req)
        if(Id_req == "same_organization")
        preprocess the request;
        else
        peform map-reduce;
        goto L1;
else
        access the CSP_res from cloud
L1: Categorize the contents (Cat_content);
if(cat_content == "file content")
        identify the redundant block;
        eliminate the redundant bloc;
else
        identify the file name;
        identify the content of a file;
        perform map-reduce operation for the file content
end
```

The Figure 2 shows the De-duplication process flow that how the files are uploaded and how the OTPs are generated.

RESULTS AND DISCUSSION

Experimental Setup

The experimental setup of the proposed algorithm using Hive. It is a data warehouse tool which is used to handle structured data. This tool follows the Hadoop and Bigdata technology for analysing and summarizing the data with effective manner. This tool also uses the features like OLAP, HDFS support, HIVE QL with scalable and effective manner.

VM player (Liu, 2010; Bu, 2013; Tian, 2015) is used for creating VM's. The VM (Tanahashi, 2010) has been started with various setting by using Ubuntu 14.04 LTS. Initially the Hadoop is installed and create the cluster with one node which is act as Distributed File System. The Map Reduce program has been tested. The Hive act as a data warehouse for storing the data. The Hive directories are created in Hadoop for effective management of data. The Map-reduce programming has been implemented for identifying redundant data. The file redundancy is checked with file name along with file contents, whereas the file content with different file name is handled in different manner. There are two stages to perform redundancy check in an entire file. In first stage, it checks the file name and in second stage it applies the Map-reduce for identifying a unique content.

Figure 2. Flow chart of proposed data de-duplication process

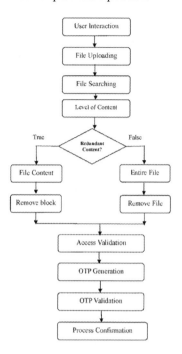

Compared to the existing system the encryption algorithm AES used in the proposed system proves to be much secured. In previous systems, privileges for accessing file are not included. In the proposed system, privileges for each file are included. New privileges can also be added and controlled by an administrator. Differential authorisation is included. The major advancement of the proposed system is the generation of One Time Password using SSL protocol for each user validation before accessing the file. De-duplication takes place based on the content, size and type. Traditional SCSP database are not used in the proposed system.

The File tag (TAG) computes the SHA-1 has of the File. The Encryption Algorithm AES with 256 bits, encrypts the different ranges of file from 10 – 500 MB of different category of files as shown in Figure 3. At the time of file initialization there won't be any duplication and the file transfer in the public

Figure 3. Breakdown for different file size

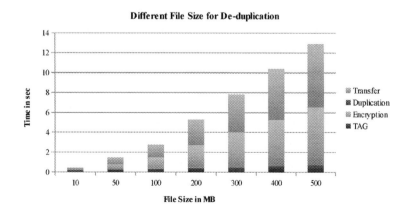

cloud also disclosed. When the data is uploaded in the cloud, if there is any duplication of the data's is identified those duplicated data can be removed. Figure 3 shows if the file size is increased then for authentication the data encrypted is also gradually increased.

If the file content or the file its duplicated then those duplicated content is removed and the same is shown in Figure 4 with De-duplication ratio with the time. The figure shows that the file tag for all the category of file with an average time of one second. For finding the duplication within the cloud it takes only a very minimal duration. The stored data in cloud is retrieved with the help of OTP and the time taken for retrieval is also minimal.

After completion of the de-duplication in Cloud storage a sample of 5 different files of different size has taken and compared its Similarity and Redundancy rate. It has absorbed clearly that for the very lesser in file size has more than 60% of Similarity Content. This shows that maximum number of user creates the file size with the lesser in file size and the File 5 as shown in Figure 5 shows that higher percentage of similarity in file contents whereas the redundancy data rate for all the file content remains very negotiable. This clearly indicates that de-duplicated content has been removed.

Figure 4. Breakdown for de-duplication ratio in percentage

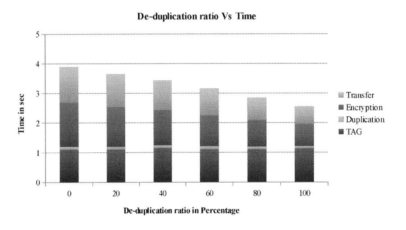

Figure 5. Comparative between similarity in file content and redundancy rate in percentage

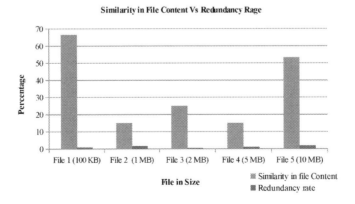

CONCLUSION

Cloud computing had emerged as a boon to the advancing world. Though most of the issues have not been solved the major concern of providing security for the data within a public cloud is solved by the proposed system by issuing differential authorization to the files uploaded into the cloud. Further access of files by the clients are authorised by OTP method. Implementation of a prototype related experiments were conducted. It is shown a minimal overhead is incurred compared to the existing systems.

REFERENCES

Annamalai, R., Srikanth, J., & Prakash, M. (2015). Accessing the Data Efficiently using Prediction of Dynamic Data Algorithm. *International Journal of Computers and Applications*, *116*(22).

Annamalai, R., Srikanth, J., & Prakash, M. (2015). Integrity and Privacy Sustenance of Shared Large Scale Images in the Cloud by Ring Signature. *International Journal of Computers and Applications*, *114*(12), 13–18. doi:10.5120/20029-1945

Bu, X., Rao, J., & Xu, C. Z. (2013). Coordinated self-configuration of virtual machines and appliances using a model-free learning approach. *IEEE Transactions on Parallel and Distributed Systems*, *24*(4), 681–690. doi:10.1109/TPDS.2012.174

Corena, J. C., & Ohtsuki, T. (2012). Secure and fast aggregation of financial data in cloud-based expense tracking applications. *Journal of Network and Systems Management*, *20*(4), 534–560. doi:10.100710922-012-9248-y

Itani, W., Kayssi, A., & Chehab, A. (2009, December). Privacy as a service: Privacy-aware data storage and processing in cloud computing architectures. *Proceedings of the Eighth IEEE International Conference on Dependable, Autonomic and Secure Computing DASC'09* (pp. 711-716). IEEE.

Khan, N., & Al-Yasiri, A. (2016). Cloud Security Threats and Techniques to Strengthen Cloud Computing Adoption Framework. *International Journal of Information Technology and Web Engineering*, *11*(3), 50–64. doi:10.4018/IJITWE.2016070104

Kumaresan, G., & Maria Michael Visuwasam, L. (2015). Enhanced In-Line Data Duplication and Secure Authorization in Hybrid Cloud. *International Journal of Innovative Research in Science. Engineering and Technology*, *4*(2), 2319–8753.

Li, J., Li, Y. K., Chen, X., Lee, P. P., & Lou, W. (2015). A hybrid cloud approach for secure authorized deduplication. *IEEE Transactions on Parallel and Distributed Systems*, *26*(5), 1206–1216. doi:10.1109/TPDS.2014.2318320

Li, N., Zhang, L. J., Xu, P., Wang, L., Zheng, J., & Guo, Y. (2013, June). Research on pricing model of cloud storage. *Proceedings of the 2013 IEEE Ninth World Congress on Services* (pp. 412-419). IEEE. 10.1109/SERVICES.2013.70

Liu, Q., Weng, C., Li, M., & Luo, Y. (2010). An In-VM measuring framework for increasing virtual machine security in clouds. *IEEE Security and Privacy*, *8*(6), 56–62. doi:10.1109/MSP.2010.143

Mell, P., & Grance, T. (2009). Effectively and securely using the cloud computing paradigm [PowerPoint]. NIST, Information Technology Laboratory.

Mohan, P., & Thangavel, R. (2013). Resource Selection in Grid Environment Based on Trust Evaluation Using Feedback and Performance. *American Journal of Applied Sciences*, *10*(8), 924–930. doi:10.3844/ajassp.2013.924.930

Pearson, S. (2013). Privacy, security and trust in cloud computing. In *Privacy and Security for Cloud Computing* (pp. 3–42). Springer London. doi:10.1007/978-1-4471-4189-1_1

Popović, K., & Hocenski, Ž. (2010, May). Cloud computing security issues and challenges. *Proceedings of the 33rd International Convention, Opatija* (pp. 344-349). IEEE.

Prakash, M., Farah Sayeed, R., Princey, S., & Priyanka, S. (2015). Deployment of Multicloud Environment with Avoidance of DDOS Attack and Secured Data Privacy. *International Journal of Applied Engineering Research*, *10*(9), 8121–8124.

Prakash, M., & Ravichandran, T. (2012). An Efficient Resource Selection and Binding Model for Job Scheduling in Grid. *European Journal of Scientific Research*, *81*(4), 450–458.

Ryan, M.D. (2011). Cloud computing privacy concerns on our doorstep. *Communications of the ACM*, *54*(1), 36-38.

Samadhu, A.A., Rambabu, J., Pradeep Kumar, R., & Santhya, R. (2015). Detailed Investigation on a Hybrid Cloud Approach for Secure Authorized Deduplication. *International Journal for Research in Applied Science & Engineering Technology*, *3*(2), 226–269.

Saravanakumar, C., & Arun, C. (2012). Traffic analysis and shaping of the cloud services over common deployment model using cloud analyst. *International Journal of Computers and Applications*, *43*(4), 33–37. doi:10.5120/6094-8281

Subashini, S., & Kavitha, V. (2011). A survey on security issues in service delivery models of cloud computing. *Journal of Network and Computer Applications*, *34*(1), 1–11. doi:10.1016/j.jnca.2010.07.006

Tanahashi, Y., Chen, C. K., Marchesin, S., & Ma, K. L. (2010, November). An interface design for future cloud-based visualization services. *Proceedings of the 2010 IEEE Second International Conference on Cloud Computing Technology and Science (CloudCom)* (pp. 609-613). IEEE. 10.1109/CloudCom.2010.46

Tian, W., Zhao, Y., Xu, M., Zhong, Y., & Sun, X. (2015). A toolkit for modeling and simulation of real-time virtual machine allocation in a cloud data center. *IEEE Transactions on Automation Science and Engineering*, *12*(1), 153–161. doi:10.1109/TASE.2013.2266338

Venkatesh, B., Sharma, A., Desai, G., & Jadhav, D. (2014). Secure Authorised Deduplication by Using Hybrid Cloud Approach. *International Journal of Innovative Research in Advanced Engineering*, *1*(10), 221–227.

Walunj, R. S., Lande, D. A., & Pansare, N. S. (2014). Secured Authorized Deduplication Based Hybrid Cloud. *International Journal of Engineering Science*, *3*(11), 34–39.

Wei, Y., & Blake, M. B. (2010). Service-oriented computing and cloud computing: Challenges and opportunities. *IEEE Internet Computing*, *14*(6), 72–75. doi:10.1109/MIC.2010.147

This research was previously published in the International Journal of Information Security and Privacy (IJISP), 11(2); edited by Mehdi Khosrow-Pour, D.B.A., pages 1-10, copyright year 2017 by IGI Publishing (an imprint of IGI Global).

Chapter 22
A Comprehensive Survey on Techniques Based on TPM for Ensuring the Confidentiality in Cloud Data Centers

Arun Fera M.
Thiagarajar College of Engineering, India

M. Saravanapriya
Thiagarajar College of Engineering, India

J. John Shiny
Thiagarajar College of Engineering, India

ABSTRACT

Cloud computing is one of the most vital technology which becomes part and parcel of corporate life. It is considered to be one of the most emerging technology which serves for various applications. Generally these Cloud computing systems provide a various data storage services which highly reduces the complexity of users. we mainly focus on addressing in providing confidentiality to users' data. We are proposing one mechanism for addressing this issue. Since software level security has vulnerabilities in addressing the solution to our problem we are dealing with providing hardware level of security. We are focusing on Trusted Platform Module (TPM) which is a chip in computer that is used for secure storage that is mainly used to deal with authentication problem. TPM which when used provides a trustworthy environment to the users. A detailed survey on various existing TPM related security and its implementations is carried out in our research work.

INTRODUCTION

Trusted platform module is considered to be the core part of trusted computing group which provides various capabilities of cryptographic possibilities which protects PC from various threats to user's sensitive information. This paper explains about the trusted platform module features which help from preventing various threats.

DOI: 10.4018/978-1-5225-8176-5.ch022

Trusted platform module (TPM) is a microcontroller which stores the passwords, key and digital certificates. It is attached to motherboard which can be used in any devices for security purposes. We can save that TPM provides a secure place for storing all types of sensitive information which provides a secure space for key operations and protect from other security attacks.TPM is attached to motherboard of our PC and that can be used in any computing devices. TPM's overview is given in Figure 1.

SURVEY ON TRUSTED PLATFORM MODULE

A trusted platform module is used for generating secure asymmetric key. Goh W, Yeo CK (2013) describes the use of a secure key generating authority in Shamir identity-based signature scheme implementation. They proposed an idea of identity-based asymmetric cryptosystems (IBC) together with an identity-based asymmetric signature. The proposed IBS scheme in this paper has itself proven secure against forgery under chosen message attacks. This paper also proposed a new concept that assigns TPM as key generating authority and list out the various merits of implementing it.

Abbadi M, Muntaha (2012) lists out the challenges for establishing the trust in the cloud and then proposes a secure framework which helps in addressing the listed challenges. This paper is actually an extension of their previous work. In their previous work, they proposed a unique framework for establishing trust in the cloud environment. By extending their previous work, the current paper addresses those issue; it clearly covers applications data and their integration with infrastructure management data. The proposed framework by Abbadi M, Muntaha (2012) has four types of software agents, each run on trusted devices. The paper also explains about the controlled content sharing between devices.

In Huang et al (2013), security is ensured using C-code-like formal modeling at the application level. As a result of this approach, security of the protocol is ensured not only at the abstract level of protocol 1, but also at the concrete level.

Figure 1. Overview of TPM

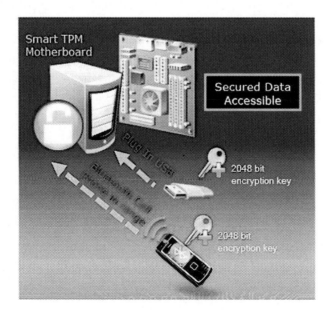

In Ramon et al. (2006), the authors propose the virtualization of trusted platform module, so that not only single machine can use the TPM but also any number of virtual machines can also use the TPM; doing so will support higher level services like remote attestation and so on. They also propose that the full TPM has been implemented in the form of software and integrate into hypervisor to make the TPM available to virtual machines also. In this environment, virtual TPM helps to establish trust using remote attestation and sealing capabilities. Establishing trust in computer platform is purely dependent upon validation. Validation allows external entity to keep up their trust on their platform based upon the specification of platform.

Schmidt et al. (2013) proposes a unique validation method to validate tree-formed data platform. This paper also uses Merkle hash tree to protect the integrity of the secure start up process of a trusted platform.

In Ali et al. (2015), a survey is done about the various security issues in cloud. This paper Ali et al. (2015) initially clearly explains about what are the security issues that are present in the various levels of cloud and suggest suitable countermeasures for resolving those issues. This also addresses some open issues and researches in cloud.

TPM usually contains a unique identity to provide security functions. This paper by Goh et al. (2011) proposes a new method of using TPM-enabled computer as client and server to detect anti-forensics. This paper presents and analyzes an anti-forensic system constructed by utilizing TPM-enabled security on a client-server system. It extends the basic system specification presented and pro- vides detailed analysis of its anti-forensic capabilities. The system design considers various vectors in which forensic examination can be conducted. Security analysis of the system showed how each component contributes to the overall objective of the system being anti-forensics capable. An important note is that the system is designed to hinder forensics, not prevent it. Therefore, as a hinderer, it works as it should. However, the system does not completely prevent forensics since human factor comes into play.

In Krautheim et al. (2010), a new mechanism is proposed for rooting trust in cloud environment called trusted virtual environment module. This paper introduces the high-level system architecture and design concepts of a necessarily somewhat TVEM system. In this paper [8], the TVEM protects information and conveys ownership in the cloud through the TEK generation process, which creates a dual rooted trust for the virtual environment and finally, when compared with other cloud computing security technologies such as private virtual infrastructure and locator bots, TVEMs enable a powerful solution to protecting information in cloud computing.

Trusted cloud computing platform provides a confidential execution of virtual machines by Santos et al (2009). Before launching their virtual machines, they allow the users to ensure whether the service is secure by VMware (2010).

The trusted computing group (TCG) claims the technology with TPMs has now reached about more than 600 million PCs by Ashford W (2012). TPM is tamper-resistant security chip that can be used for machine authentication, machine attestation, and data protection.

Though there exist a number of applications that makes use of TPM, there are number of problems that needs to be solved before we can fulfill the grand vision of trusted computing ISO/IEC-11889 (2009). In Sadeghi A-R, detailed explanation of TPM is given. It explains about the root of trust for storage (RTS), which is used for secure data storage implemented as hierarchy of keys.

TCG software stack (TSS) is the supporting software on the platform supporting the platform's TPM. TCG mainly explains with protected storage and protected capabilities. Since TPM is very expensive, the resources within the TPM should be kept in a restrictive manner BitLocker Drive Encryption Technical Overview (2012). The integration of various computing technologies into virtualized computing environments enables the protection of hardware Chen and Zhao (2012). Here, they addressed the problem of enabling secure migration in private clouds Danev et al (2011). The cloud networking (CloNe) infrastructure provides various services to virtualized network resources by Dhungana et al (2013). The framework supports AAI (authentication, authorization, and identity management) of entities in its infrastructure by Data Remanence solutions. A review on TPM usage is given in Table 1.

TPM FEATURES

Cryptographic Mechanisms and Algorithms

The following are the important features in cryptography that should be implemented in TPMs. These are explained and various cryptographic features are described in the following sections.

- Signing (RSA),
- Hashing (SHA-1),
- Keyed-Hash Message Authentication Code (HMAC),
- Random number generation (RNG),
- Asymmetric key (RSA) and nonce generation,
- Asymmetric encryption/decryption (RSA).

The specification that allows TPMs to implement various additional features or algorithms, such as elliptic curve asymmetric algorithms or DSA and there is no guarantee that these keys can migrate to

Table 1. A review on usage of TPM

Paper Details	Gist of the Paper
A framework for establishing trust in the cloud	This paper identifies the related challenges for establishing trust in the cloud and then proposes a foundation framework for identifying those challenges. Mainly focuses on IaaS. The framework presented in this paper is not enough by itself and it requires further extension as establishing trust in the cloud. Cloud provenance is not covered in this paper. It will be addressed in their future work
Design and implementation of a trusted monitoring framework for cloud platforms	In this paper, they have designed a trusted monitoring framework, which provides a chain of trust and have implemented this framework on Xen and integrate it with open nebula to improve the performance. But, this monitoring VM could crash under some circumstance. Therefore, recovering the monitoring functionality is something which is needed to be taken into consideration.
A hijacker's guide to communication interfaces of the trusted platform module	They proposed the some attacks in hijacking the trusted platform module. They have proposed active attack and implemented it. Though active attacks perform various activities, it does not allow direct retrieval of TPM protected data, like private parts of non-migratable keys. To extract this kind of information it is still necessary to resort to invasive high-effort method which directly targets the TPM chip by Winter et al (2013)
Security in cloud computing: Opportunities and challenges	This survey paper presented the security issues that arise due to the shared, virtualized, and public nature of the cloud computing paradigm. Subsequently, the counter measures presented in the literature are presented
Fine-grained refinement on TPM-based protocol applications	In this paper they formalize parts of the interfaces of TPM. Thus in their future work they try to expand our refinement framework to more general applications by formalizing all the interfaces of TPM

other TPM devices or that other TPM devices will accept signatures from these additional algorithms. A minimum key length has been specified for some uses of TPM. Storage keys, for example, must be equivalent in strength to a 2048-bit or greater RSA key.

Random Number Generator

Nonce value can be generated by the TPM's random number generator which is used in key generation, and as randomness in signatures. The specification allows the RNG to be a Pseudo Random Number Generator implementation or a generator based on some source of hardware entropy. The RNG must be capable of providing at least 32 bytes of randomness at a time.

Key Generation

The Key Generation component of the TPM is capable of creating RSA key pairs as well as symmetric keys and nonce values. RSA key generation must follow the IEEE P1363 Standard Specifications for Public-Key Cryptography. The private key is held in a shielded location and usually does not leave the TPM unencrypted. Nonce values use the next n bits from the random number generator where n is the length of the nonce.

RSA Engine and Keys

TPMs use the RSA asymmetric algorithm encryption/decryption and digital signatures. While TPMs may support other algorithms for these purposes, they must support RSA, including key sizes of 512, 768, 1024, and 2048 bits. Other key sizes are also permissible, and the specification recommends a minimum key size is 2048 bits. The specification also states that the RSA public exponent must be $2^{16}+1$. The formats defined in the PKCS #1 standard are followed, but the TPM specification does specify how RSA algorithm should be implemented. This allows TPM implementations to use the Chinese Remainder Theorem or any other method of implementing RSA.

TPMs can sign both internal items and external data. TPMs do not perform signature verification, though, because verification does not use or expose private information and is better suited for software. Key pairs must be identified as either for signing or for encryption/decryption. TPMs do not allow a signature key to encrypt or an encryption key to sign because this can lead to attacks.

Secrets can also be assigned to keys so that use of the key requires knowledge of the secret. Keys can also be tied to specific system states or configurations (specified by PCR values). All keys have a parent key, which is used to encrypt the private part of the key if it needs to be stored off the TPM for future loading.

SHA-1 Engine

SHA-1 is the only hash algorithm that TPMs are required to support as of version 1.2 of the specification. This could become a concern since there are collision attacks against SHA-1. The SHA-1 functionality is used by the TPM and via exposed interfaces. These interfaces can be used for measurement taking during boot and to provide a hash function in platforms that have limited capabilities. The functionality is not intended to provide an accelerated hash capability, and there are no specific performance requirements for TPM hash services. Therefore, this engine should only be used to compute hash values of small chunks of data. Larger chucks of data should be hashed outside the TPM if possible.

HMAC Engine

TPMs support the calculation of HMACs according to RFC 2104 with a key size of 20 bytes and a block size of 64 bytes. The contents and order of the data depend on the TPM command that uses the HMAC engine

Symmetric Encryption Engine

TPMs use symmetric encryption to encrypt data during various operations (authentication and transport sessions). In these cases, a one-time pad is XORed with the data. In some cases, the nonce is large enough to perform a direct XOR, but in others, the entropy must be expanded using the MGF1 function from PKCS #1. (The specification allows for use of AES or Triple DES in use models where it would be beneficial.) Symmetric encryption is also used to encrypt protected data that is stored outside the TPM. For this purpose, the TPM specification allows the designer to use any symmetric algorithm that is deemed to have the proper level of protection.

While TPMs use symmetric encryption internally, they do not expose this functionality or the algorithm for general data encryption. As such, the TPM can only generate, store, and protect symmetric keys. The TCG FAQ does, however, leave the door open for use of AES or other symmetric encryption algorithms in future versions of the TPM specification.

Time Stamping

TPMs provide a type of time stamping service for various pieces of data. The time stamp that TPMs provide is the number of timer ticks the TPM has counted and not a universal time clock (UTC) value. The caller must associate the tick count with the actual UTC time, and the TPM specification provides a complex protocol that can be used to accomplish this. Time stamping is further complicated by the affect of various power states on the tick count and the differences in these states on various platforms.

Platform Configuration Registers

A Platform Configuration Register (PCR) is a 160-bit register for storing integrity measurements. TPMs must have at least 16 PCRs, all of which are protected and inside the TPM. While the number of PCRs is limited, they can each represent an unlimited number of measurements. This is accomplished by cryptographically hashing all updates to a PCR such that the new PCR value is dependent on the previous value and the value to add. The ordering and one-way properties of cryptographic hashes are particularly important for this use case.

The TPM_Seal operation can be used to encrypt data such that it can only be decrypted on a specific platform. Callers of this operation may specify PCR values required to unseal the data. Future TPM_Unseal operations will reveal the sealed data only if attempted on the same platform and the PCR value(s) match. In this way, the sealed data is protected from changes in the configuration. TPM_Seal and TPM_Unseal both require "AuthData" (similar to a password). This means that data can be sealed such that only a specific user can access it on a given client under a specific configuration.

Identities

Some TCG use cases require that the platform be identifiable or prove that it has a genuine TPM. There are two types of identifying keys, the Endorsement Key (EK) and Attestation Identity Keys (AIK).

Endorsement Key

The Endorsement Key is a 2048-bit RSA key pair that is unique to the TPM and therefore the platform containing the TPM. The key pair is generated at manufacture time, and once it is set, it can never be changed. The private key is never exposed outside the TPM. The public key is used for attestation and for encryption of sensitive data sent to the TPM. Because of security reasons and privacy concerns, the EK cannot perform signatures. The EK (along with other infrastructure) is also used to recognize a genuine TPM.

Attestation Identity Keys

An Attestation Identity Key is an alias to the Endorsement Key. Like the EK, the AIK is a 2048-bit RSA key pair. Unlike the EK, there can be many (virtually unlimited) AIKs, and they can be generated at any time by the TPM Owner. Also unlike the EK, an AIK is a signature key and can perform signatures on information generated by the TPM, including PCR values, other keys, and TPM status information. AIKs cannot sign other data because this would make it possible for an attacker to create a fake PCR value.

Because many AIKs can be created, they cannot all be stored in the TPM. Therefore, AIKs may be stored on some general-purpose storage device. When stored outside the TPM, the AIK must be encrypted and its integrity must be protected.

An AIK can be used for platform authentication, platform attestation and certification of keys. A protocol known as Direct Anonymous Attestation uses zero-knowledge-proof technology to allow the EK to anonymously establish that an AIK was generated in a TPM. This allows the quality of an AIK to be confirmed without identifying which TPM generated it.

Figure 2. Keys in TPM

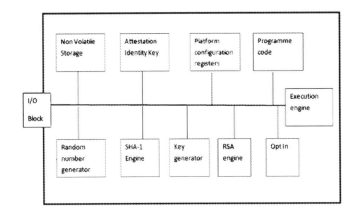

Use Models

Protecting Information

Clients contain a lot of information that should be protected from view, copying, and use by others. This includes keys, passwords, and other types of data. The first two are particularly important because some of them are used to authenticate to networks.

Protection of User Keys

Users can generate an RSA key pair in the TPM and specify that the private key never leave the chip unprotected. Even though the private key can is only known as plaintext inside the TPM, it can still be used for general signing and encryption purposes. If the private key is protected and an attacker gains control of the system, he or she may be able to execute encryption, decryption, and digital signing operations on any data he or she chooses while in control of the system, but this capability will cease once they lose control (i.e. the system is patched or powered off) because the private key cannot be copied to another system.

Additional security is possible that will prevent an attacker from even using the keys while in control of the system. Keys can be bound to specific PCR values such that use of the keys is not permitted if the PCR value is incorrect as would occur if the system has been improperly booted or the integrity of measured files has been compromised. In this way, the keys can be protected if a key logger, worm, etc. are installed.

Protection of User Passwords

Passwords can be encrypted by an RSA public key whose matching private key is protected by the TPM. If the private key requires specific a PCR value to be used, the password cannot be decrypted if a compromise has been detected. In this way, passwords cannot be obtained no matter what the attacker does. Protected storage could also be used to augment password storage programs, such as Password Safe these programs also encourage the use of strong (long, random) passwords.

Protection of User Data

The TPM can also be used to protect files and file system keys in the same way that user keys can be protected. Thus, if system compromise is detected, the TPM can prevent access to or use of the file or file system key. As a result, the encrypted files will be protected from theft or modification. Note that the user may still be able to destroy a file system depending on the file system and operating system implementation and configuration.

There are a couple options to protect large amounts of data. The easiest and quickest is to encrypt the large block of data using a one-time symmetric key then use the TPM to protect the symmetric key.

Trusted Boot

The TPM supports a trusted boot mechanism that can help detect root kits and other types of security compromises. During a trusted boot, hashes of configuration information throughout the boot sequence are stored in the PCRs. This configuration information may include the BIOS, option ROMs, Master Boot Record (MBR), OS loader, kernel, and other operating system information. Once the client has booted in a known clean state, keys and other information can be sealed – encrypted and tied to the PCR value(s). During subsequent boots, the sealed data will only be unsealed if the PCR values match. Consequently, if the configuration is changed or a virus, back door, or root kit has been installed, the PCR value(s) will be incorrect and the protected information will not be unsealed. The boot process itself is not stopped or changed by the TPM. This protects the sensitive information and any data it may protect. As a result, the user would also be informed of the compromise and could take action to address it.

The recorded measurements can also be used by multiple challengers to determine what boot process occurred and in turn whether they trust it. The TPM signs the stored measurement before sending it to challengers to prove that the measurement came from the TPM. The TPM provides the benefit that of measurement, storage, and reporting of integrity metrics in a secure manner.

Platform Authentication

Each TPM also has a unique identity (EK) that can be used to generate other identities (AIKs). Since the TPM is attached to the client and cannot be (easily) removed or replaced, the TPM can use these identities to prove that it is a specific client. This is different from user or even smart card authentication, which only proves that a specific user is using the system (or someone else is using their credentials). If a challenger, say a network, has prior knowledge about permitted clients, it is possible for the TPM to authenticate itself to the challenger. That is, it can prove that it is one of the known and permitted clients. This allows a network or server to identify the clients that are accessing or requesting to access it and only permit access to clients that it knows and trusts.

Attestation

Attestation is one of the central features of Trusted Computing. It is the process of a client declaring the current state of the platform in a way that is trusted by the challenger. The challenger can then take actions based on the state. The basis for TPM attestation is the measuring of the platform – both the hardware and software – using the PCRs and/or digital signatures. TPMs allow a platform to attest that the platform configuration is as expected and has not been changed. The "configuration" can include as much information as is required. The TPM can also attest to a trusted boot and the information collected during that process. Attestation could also be used to prove that antivirus definitions are up to date. In this case, the client could measure the antivirus definitions file and create a digital signature of the measurement. The client could then send the signed message to the challenger. Attestation allows an administrative system to check the health (security, configuration, software, etc.) of a client to confirm that it meets a security policy and has not been compromised.

Threat Model

Sensitive Information

The TPM and other elements of the TCG specifications are designed to protect against or mitigate the potential damage caused by a variety of threats and attacks. This paper focuses on those that affect PC clients (desktops and notebooks).

PC clients have a large number of vulnerabilities, known and unknown, and this is unlikely to change given the nature and practices of the software industry. In addition, keeping patches up to date for all software installed on a system is time consuming and a large percentage of systems do not have all applicable patches. While networks and servers offer the most value for attackers, they are also better protected than PC clients.

In addition, PC clients often contain information, such as keys and passwords that can be used to access and compromise networks and servers or can be used for distributed attacks, such as Distributed Denial of Service (DDoS), against them. Keys could also be used to decrypt sensitive information, steal a digital identity, or forge signatures. PC clients also contain information, such as credit card and social security numbers, that is itself valuable. As a result of these and other factors, attackers are increasingly focused on PC clients. TPMs should support preventing attackers from being able to find information on a compromised client that can be used to compromise another system for which the client or its user has access. The TPM should also enable a network administrator to prevent a compromised client from being able to compromise or disrupt the rest of the network.

The information on clients could include encryption or signing keys, passwords, and personal or proprietary information. The TPM is designed to protect sensitive information on PC clients as well as the servers and networks they may connect to. In addition, some private RSA keys never leave the TPM, so it is impossible to obtain them directly by software means. The TPM does *not* attempt to reduce the number of vulnerabilities in software or prevent an attacker from exploiting those vulnerabilities. Instead, the TPM seeks to detect when the client is compromised and limit the damage and protect sensitive information when it occurs. If the TPM and related software are configured correctly, the attacker cannot access the sensitive information regardless of what he or she does. Attacks on sensitive information should be no better than a brute force attack.

One primary attack that the TPM seeks to thwart is attack on keys when cryptographic operations are performed in software. It has been definitively proven[1] that even very good encryption is vulnerable to attack performed in the usual locations, such as memory. TPM cryptography operations are performed in a closed hardware environment, protecting the keys at their most vulnerable point.

The TPM should prevent theft (copying to another system for use there) of RSA keys as well as improper use of keys when the system has been compromised. The latter is very dependent on the system firmware (i.e. BIOS), TPM Software Stack (TSS) and how they work detect that a system has been compromised, but the TPM provides all necessary framework.

The TPM also allows multiple users to protect sensitive information on a shared client. Even if a user has permission to use the client, they still may not have access to other user's secrets.

If any encryption key-pair is compromised, the data it protects and any data protected by keys that it protects may also be compromised. Once an encryption key-pair is compromised, all data ever encrypted with it is compromised and this cannot be recovered from, except by deleting all copies of the data encrypted with that key (including ones that may have been stolen). Likewise, once a digital signature key is compromised, the attacker can sign anything they wish. If certificates are used, the certificate could be revoked. The TPM cannot detect compromises of its own keys. Instead it protects them by not letting some private keys leave the TPM, encrypting its keys when they leave the TPM, and detecting compromise of the client software.

Keys and other sensitive information may be stored outside the TPM. For data stored outside the TPM, the protection of the sensitive information is only as strong as the encryption algorithm by which it is protected. The TPM cannot increase the strength of an algorithm with respect to algorithmic (i.e. brute force and differential cryptanalysis) attacks. For example, if a large file is encrypted with DES and the DES key is encrypted with a 2048-bit RSA key and stored in the TPM, the encrypted file is still subject to attacks on the DES encryption, which should be much easier than attacking the 2048-bit RSA key.

The TPM is intended to protect sensitive information even when hardware is physically stolen. This is important because the data on stolen clients, such as notebooks, is often more valuable than the hardware. Still, the TPM spec does not require protection against physical tampering. Thus, if the client is physically stolen, it may be possible for the attacker to steal sensitive information by means such as RF analysis, but it would be difficult. These attacks are not covered in this paper.

There is debate as to whether the TPM is designed to protect against attacks on digital rights management (DRM) mechanisms, and some of it is related to the physical protections of the TPM. DRM uses and attacks on those are also not covered in this paper.

Platform Authentication and Attestation

When a compromised client is connected to a network, it can be a threat to the entire network even if the sensitive information on the client is protected. Therefore, it is important to be able to identify unauthorized or compromised clients and prevent them from connecting to the network. Software-only methods of authenticating clients can be circumvented because the authentication information, such as the computer name or MAC address, can be forged. Network administrators should be able to prevent access to the network to specific authorized client hardware. They should also be able to prevent access to properly configured and uncompromised clients before they gain access. Furthermore, an attacker or rogue client should not be able to forge its authentication as an authorized client or its configuration and current state.

If one system is compromised, it should not enable the compromise of other systems or the network. If the prevention mechanism is defeated, the entire network infrastructure, clients, and servers could be compromised or prevented from serving their purpose.

CONCLUSION

Thus TPM has a lot to do with embedding trust in any kind of application by making the chip to be placed in all the machines and also network trust can be of future research direction where the data that travel across globe are to be protected and provided trust.

REFERENCES

Abbadi, I. M., & Muntaha, A. (2012). A framework for establishing trust in cloud. *Computers & Electrical Engineering*, *38*(5), 1073–1087. doi:10.1016/j.compeleceng.2012.06.006

Ali, M., Khan, S. U., & Vasilakos, A. V. (2015). Security in cloud computing: Opportunities and challenges. *Inf Sci*, *305*, 357–383. doi:10.1016/j.ins.2015.01.025

Ashford, W. (2012). *Will this be the year TPM comes of age?*. Retrieved from: http://www.computerweekly.com/news/2240157874/Analysis-2012-Will-this-be-the-year-TPM-finallycomes-of-age

BitLocker Drive Encryption Technical Overview. (n.d.). *Microsoft TechNet*. Retrieved from: http://technet.microsoft.com/en-us/library/cc732774(v=ws.10).aspx

Chen, D., & Zhao, H. (2012). The data security and privacy protection issues in cloud computing. In International Conference on Computer Science and Electron ICS Engineering (ICCSEE, IEEE). doi:10.1109/ICCSEE.2012.193

Cloud Computing. (n.d.a). Retrieved from: https://zapthink.com/2011/05/19 /data-remanence-cloud-computing-shellgame

Cloud Computing. (n.d.b). Retrieved from: http://www.cornwallcloud services.co.uk/index.php/easyblog/categories/listings/theinternetofthings

Cloud Computing Security. (n.d.a). Retrieved from: http://searchcompliance.techtarget.com/definition/cloudcomputing-security

Cloud Computing Security. (n.d.b). Retrieved from: http://www.forbes.com/sites/netapp/2012/12/12/cloud-security-1/

Cloud Storage. (n.d.). Retrieved from: http://securosis.com/blog/securing-cloud-data-withvirtual-private-storage/

Danev, B., Masti, R. J., Karame, G. O., & Capkun, S. (2011). Enabling secure VM migration in private clouds. In *Proceedings of the ACM 27th annual computer security applications conference*. 10.1145/2076732.2076759

Data Remanence. (n.d.). Retrieved from http://elastic-security.com/2010/01/07/data-remanence-in-the-cloud/

Data Remanence. (n.d.a). Retrieved from: http://www.itrenew.com/what-is-data-remanence

Data Remanence. (n.d.b). Retrieved from: http://en.wikipedia. org/wiki/Data_remanence

Data Remanence Solutions. (n.d.). Retrieved from http://fas.org/irp/nsa/rainbow tg025-2.htm

Deqing, Z., Wenrong, Z., Weizhong, Q., & Guofu, X. (2013). Design and implementation of a trusted monitoring framework for cloud platforms. *Future Generation Computer Systems*, *29*(8), 2092–2102. doi:10.1016/j.future.2012.12.020

Dhungana, R. D., Mohammad, A., Sharma, A., & Schoen, I. (2013). Identity management framework for cloud networking infrastructure. In *IEEE International conference on innovations in information technology (IIT)*. 10.1109/Innovations.2013.6544386

Fan, K., Mao, D., Lu, Z., & Wu, J. (2013). OPS: offline patching scheme for the images management in a secure cloud environment. In *IEEE International conference on services computing (SCC)*. 10.1109/SCC.2013.57

Goh, W., Leong, P. C., & Yeo, C. K. (2011). The plausibly-deniable, practical trusted platform module based anti-forensics client-server system. *IEEE Journal on Selected Areas in Communications*.

Goh, W., & Yeo, C.K. (2013). *Teaching an old trusted platform module: repurposing a tpm for an identity-based signature scheme*. Academic Press.

Huang, W., Xiong, Y., Miao, F., Wang, X., Wu, C., Lu, Q., & Xudong, G. (2013). Fine-grained refinement on tpm-based protocol applications. *IEEE Trans Info Forensics Sec, 8*(6).

ISO/IEC-11889:2009. (2009). *Information technology – Trusted Platform Module*. ISO.

Johannes, W., & Kurt, D. (2013). A hijacker guide to communication interfaces of the trusted platform module. *Computers & Mathematics with Applications (Oxford, England), 65*(5), 748–761. doi:10.1016/j.camwa.2012.06.018

John Krautheim, F., Phatak, D.S., & Sherman, A.T. (2010). *Introducing trusted virtual environment module: a new mechanism for rooting trust in cloud computing*. Academic Press.

Ramon, S., Caceres, R., Kenneth, A., Goldman, R., Sailer, P., & Leendert, R. (2006). vTPM: Virtualizing the Trusted Platform Module. *USENIX Association, Security'06:15th USENIX Security*.

Sadeghi, A-R. (n.d.). *Trusted platform module, lecture slides for secure, trusted and trustworthy computing*. Technische Universität Darmstadt. Retrieved from: http://www.trust.informatik.darmstadt.de/fileadmin/user_upload/Group_TRUST/LectureSlides/STCWS2011/Chap3__Trusted_Platform_Module.pdf.pdf

Santos, N., Gummadi, K. P., & Rodrigues, R. (2009). Towards trusted cloud computing. In *Proceedings of the conference on cloud computing*. Berkeley, CA: USENIX Association.

Schmidt Andreas, U., Leicher, A., Brett, A., Shah, Y., & Cha, I. (2013). Tree-formed verification data for trusted platforms. *Computers & Security, 32*, 19–35. doi:10.1016/j.cose.2012.09.004

The TCG Software Stack (TSS) Specification-version 1.20 Errata A Golden Candidate 2. (n.d.). Trusted Computing Group.

VMware. (2010). *VMware vCenter Server*. Retrieved from http://www.vmware.com/products/vcenter-server/

This research was previously published in the Handbook of Research on Recent Developments in Intelligent Communication Application edited by Siddhartha Bhattacharyya, Nibaran Das, Debotosh Bhattacharjee, and Anirban Mukherjee, pages 366-379, copyright year 2017 by Information Science Reference (an imprint of IGI Global).

Chapter 23
Strategic Planning for Cloud Computing Adoption in STEM Education:
Finding Best Practice Solutions

Alan S. Weber
Weill Cornell Medical College in Qatar, Qatar

ABSTRACT

This chapter describes effective strategic analysis and implementation methods for the adoption of cloud computing services (infrastructure, platforms, and software) in Science, Technology, Engineering, and Mathematics (STEM) education. The benefits of cloud computing, including lower costs, scalability and virtualization capabilities, have been recognized and adopted by major educational, governmental and research institutions internationally during the last five years. However, the term 'cloud computing' was only recently clarified in 2011 in the NIST's standard definition published by Mell and Grance (2012) as "a model for enabling ubiquitous, convenient, on-demand network access to a shared pool of configurable computing resources (e.g., networks, servers, storage, applications, and services) that can be rapidly provisioned and released with minimal management effort or service provider interaction." Despite the increasing clarity in defining cloud computing, the deployment models can be complex, encompassing hybrid, public, community and private cloud frameworks, all with varying levels of privacy, security, and trust. Data format, integrity, and portability as well as geographical server location represent additional factors that educational institutions must weigh when they consider adopting a cloud solution for their educational needs. The chapter provides advice on how to strategically plan for the use of cloud computing services and how to identify, weigh and assess the various factors in decision-making. Just as with e-learning when it was found at the end of the 1990s that purely online technological approaches were not as effective as pedagogical models (blended learning) which took into account human factors such as student motivation, teacher training, technological illiteracy, etc., the author suggests that a holistic technology adoption process that includes needs assessment and stakeholder engagement will be the most successful.

DOI: 10.4018/978-1-5225-8176-5.ch023

INTRODUCTION

Science, Technology, Engineering, and Mathematics (STEM) education has been the focus of recent interest in the federal government in the last decade, including the White House and U.S. Department of Education. The 2013 *Federal Science, Technology, Engineering, and Mathematics (STEM) Education 5-Year Strategic Plan* issued by the National Science and Technology Council (Committee on STEM Education) identified five key STEM education investment areas:

- **Improve STEM Instruction:** Prepare 100,000 excellent new K-12 STEM teachers by 2020, and support the existing STEM teacher workforce;
- **Increase and Sustain Youth and Public Engagement in STEM:** Support a 50 percent increase in the number of U.S. youth who have an authentic STEM experience each year prior to completing high school;
- **Enhance STEM Experience of Undergraduate Students:** Graduate one million additional students with degrees in STEM fields over the next 10 years;
- **Better Serve Groups Historically Under-Represented in STEM Fields:** Increase the number of students from groups that have been underrepresented in STEM fields that graduate with STEM degrees in the next 10 years and improve women's participation in areas of STEM where they are significantly underrepresented;
- **Design Graduate Education for Tomorrow's STEM Workforce:** Provide graduate-trained STEM professionals with basic and applied research expertise, options to acquire specialized skills in areas of national importance, mission-critical workforce needs for the CoSTEM agencies, and ancillary skills needed for success in a broad range of careers. (CoSTEM, 2013, pp. vii-viii).

In each of these targeted areas, cloud computing has a role to play, as outlined in the discussion below. In this chapter, selected examples and analysis are used to demonstrate the current capabilities and potential of cloud computing in STEM education. Some of the pitfalls and potential harms and risks associated with using these technologies are also highlighted to provide potential adopters with a balanced view of benefit/risk scenarios. Although there are a number of currently available technology adoption and technology acceptance models, such as Davis, Bagozzi, and Warshaw's Technology Acceptance Model (David et al., 1989; Davis, 1989) later modified with Venkatesh (2000) as TAM2 and again by Venkatesh et al. (2003) as the Unified Theory of Acceptance and Use of Technology (UTAUT)–they are difficult to apply to real world technology adoption scenarios. The UTAUT model, for example, has over 40 variables explaining decision-making and subsequent behavior of new technology adopters. This chapter takes a common sense and practical approach to cloud computing technology adoption by identifying key factors in the process of selecting infrastructure, platforms, and services.

Cloud computing within STEM degree granting institutions is unique, since cloud technologies comprise a set of tools and a domain of knowledge that not only facilitate the production of knowledge in other fields of study, but also represent an area of research and discovery in their own right allied with each STEM discipline; for example, basic and pure sciences (information theory, physics), technology (all aspects of cloud computing), engineering (computer engineering, computer architecture, Internet infrastructure, networking) and mathematics (algorithms, chip logic, etc.). The main STEM educational areas in which cloud computing can have a serious impact are:

1. **Administration:** Many educational administrative tasks and functions can be migrated to cloud services, most notably email, database storage, and analytics. A common platform can simplify tasks and reduce complexity and enhance interoperability between departments and units.

2. **Virtual Laboratories:** Computer modeling of large and complex systems can be extremely processing intensive in the fields of theoretical physics, cosmology, climate modeling, etc. or any field that makes use of 3D visualization or graphic or satellite images such as geography and the earth sciences, for example. Also physics and engineering virtual learning laboratories that mimic digital or analog sensors and measurements can use considerable computing resources. Cloud computing provides scalability (on-demand resource allocation) to meet changing demands in research and teaching based on faculty and researcher needs. Thus, unneeded specialized hardware or software is not left over after grant periods end or if an institution changes its curricula.

3. **Educational Online Platforms:** These include Learning Management Systems (LMSs), Course Management Systems (CMSs), and routine educational activities. This area is where cloud computing has had its most significant impact on education in the form of free and low cost hosted services such as email, social networking style tools for communication (chat or bulletin board) and collaboration, spreadsheets, or mobile apps in which data processing occurs on remote cloud servers. Educational tools in addition can be seamlessly integrated into management tools, i.e. student records, library records, student services, and registration. However, privacy and security of data, specifically student-generated online behaviors that are tracked and monitored to create consumer profiles, are an area of concern if the cloud vendor reserves the right to collect these data, since the types of data collected by public cloud firms have become increasingly personal and highly detailed in nature (Weber, 2013b, pp. 401-402; Weber 2013a). Some of the records systems described above are not new; for example, campus-wide integrated computer records systems on in-house main frame computers have been available since the 1970s. In fact, many of these legacy systems are still running and viable and the large mainframe computer is still ubiquitous in business and education. In the early days of cloud computing development, many unsubstantiated, commercially-motivated statements were made by technology companies that cloud computing would be vastly superior to the mainframe ecosystem and solve all of an institution's computing needs, i.e. 'hype.' Thus cloud adopters should seriously consider whether a mature, stable and working system such as an onsite data center might meet institutional needs better than a cloud solution.

4. **Professional Workplace:** Cloud computing has become an increasing feature of the professional workplace outside of the academic environment. Many professionals are expected to be fluent in the use of online collaborative tools for creating and sharing work documents and large file storage or transfer tools such as Dropbox.com or similar services. Familiarity with cloud technologies as a student can translate to a better school to workplace transition and contributes to greater general student computer literacy.

BACKGROUND: LEARNING AND MANAGEMENT BENEFITS OF CLOUD COMPUTING FOR EDUCATIONAL INSTITUTIONS

The definition of cloud computing of the National Institute of Standards and Technology (NIST) is widely accepted: cloud computing is "a model for enabling ubiquitous, convenient, on-demand network access to a shared pool of configurable computing resources (e.g., networks, servers, storage, applications, and services) that can be rapidly provisioned and released with minimal management effort or service provider interaction" (Mell & Grance, 2012). On-demand services are available at the infrastructure, platform, and software level. These technologies rely on virtualization in which logical resources at the software level can be configured to act like hardware for creating a virtual machine (VM). This means that very different operating systems can co-function on the same system (multitenancy), and that tasks can be scheduled efficiently with maximized and optimal resource use using a software device called a 'hypervisor' that acts as a router, gatekeeper, scheduler, or overall system manager. The hypervisor opportunistically seeks out idle resources for provisioning. These resources can be scattered across the globe, and the autonomous nature of decision-making can pose serious problems in identifying where data resides at any particular moment and how secure it is.

Many valid arguments have been advanced for the superiority of cloud computing over the stand-alone desk top computing and in-house data center models. Since cloud companies run 24/7 under constant vigilance, and opportunistically seek the most efficient load balancing and task distribution, they are inherently more efficient, an important consideration as institutions are moving towards green building and operations policies. Economic efficiencies and energy savings are also a major concern of all large institutions. Koomey estimated in 2010 that between 1.1% - 1.5% of total global electricity usage could be traced to data centers (2011). Most major cloud companies such as Microsoft Azure, Amazon.com EC2, and Salesforce.com have achieved an approximately 98-99% availability rate, making resources highly reliable and available when they are needed. Every educational institution constantly battles with unused hardware, rapid obsolescence, unused hard drive space, and computers left on and unattended in offices. The greatest advantage of cloud computing for educational institutions is that the institution only pays for the services that it uses, and these can be modified rapidly to respond to changing needs (on-demand provisioning).

The scalability of cloud computing allows institutions to rapidly introduce large scale cpu-intensive research projects and learning systems, including virtual labs, without the lengthy process of needs assessment, sourcing, and approval and purchase of costly hardware. The cloud vendor normally maintains the hardware (remote data centers), takes care of updating software and fixing bugs, and maintaining data security and backups, which reduces institutional IT costs. Many vendors offer analytical services and consultation services as well that can be calculated into services packages. Cloud technologies can capture large amounts of user-generated data and runtime logs (large data sets, known as 'Big Data') that are useful for planning and optimization of systems, including human-computer interfaces. Mayer-Schönberger's and Cukier's recent popular book *Big Data: A Revolution that Will Transform How We Live, Work, and Think* (2013) illustrated the potential for big data to aid business analysis (airline ticket prices), biomedicine (flu trends tracked by Google search engine searches) and many other areas of human activity.

PRIMARY CONCERNS IN CHOOSING A CLOUD PLATFORM, SERVICES, AND SOFTWARE

Issues, Controversies, Problems

Engaging All Stakeholders

The author has witnessed in his varied career working in robotics, technical writing, education, and journalism the devastating effects of computer technology purchases that were made without consultation with the users and managers of those technologies. Problems with technology use can often be foreseen based on existing workflows. This has been a very common scenario since computer technology became a standard feature of the professional workplace in the 1970s and 80s. Some of the reasons for unnecessary and inappropriate purchases of technology are rooted in lack of interdepartmental communication, lack of employee voice and decision-making in the workplace, or competition between institutional divisions ('siloing' or 'territorialism').

In the case of very new and emerging technologies like cloud computing, institutional decision makers may be vulnerable to clever salespersons who may play on their insecurities about rapidly developing technology. Such tactics include creating fears that the educational institution will be 'left behind' in the technology advancement game, with loss of status, funding and eventually students; or they may convince purchasers they are not keeping up to date, and not providing standard tools that students will need for the future workplace. And as with all salespersons, they often overstate the capabilities of their product. Fortunately, both determining the real needs of an institution and engaging educational stakeholders can be easily accomplished with the standard strategies used in social sciences research such as public meetings, questionnaires, focus groups and interviews: not only does management gain valuable insight into the potential barriers and road blocks to the actual use of the technology in that institution (including policy and legal challenges), but stakeholders feel more invested in the final technological solution and will be more willing to help it succeed.

Regulatory / Legal Framework

Major cloud vendors often own servers which are physically located in many different parts of the world. They may wish to process and store information in countries where electricity or labor costs are lower. Servers may simply be located in specific geographic regions for closer access to point of service, or multiple backups may co-exist in different regions making a particular dataset more readily available when it is needed for processing, also guarding against central catastrophic hardware failure. These facts introduce the difficult question of legal jurisdiction. Data residing in a physical geographical location logically would be subject to that country's data regulatory regime, including data privacy. Migrating data from a country with strict data privacy laws to one with more lax regulations might violate an institution's internal data policies or statutory requirements such as maintaining the privacy of student records under the Federal Family Educational Rights and Privacy Act (FERPA) in the U.S. or another nation's data retention and destruction laws. Also, will the nature of the data and the data transfer conform to the local laws of the new jurisdiction in which it resides? These issues have sparked an ongoing dispute between Google, Facebook, and Apple (who all offer hosted services in Europe) and the European

Union's Justice Commissioner Viviane Reding, who is concerned that these technology companies' data protection policies violate European privacy protection rules.

For example, biomedical research data, or patient and health data, may need stricter privacy controls since research may be regulated and covered by the Health Insurance Portability and Accountability Act (HIPAA) which regulates protected health information (PHI) in a strict manner. Also, there may be strict confidentiality requirements for researchers undertaking Human Subjects Research (HSR) in collecting, storing and analyzing computer-based data on humans as governed by Institutional Review Boards (IRBs)–also known as Ethical Review Boards (ERBs) and Research Ethics Boards (REBs)–as mandated by Code of Federal Regulations: Title 45 Public Welfare Department of Health and Human Services Part 46 Protection of Human Subjects.

Privacy

Many technology companies who offer cloud services simultaneously collect large amounts of user generated data about Internet behaviors, such as buying patterns, websites visited, friends networks, and email and telephone contacts, all for targeted behavioral marketing. Compiling these data into profiles and analyzing it provides valuable information that corporations can use for advertizing and other commercial purposes. A prime example is Google Apps for Education, a suite of educational productivity and learning tools, which includes one of its popular products Gmail. Users of Gmail in the Apps for Education package believed that their communications were not being automatically key-word scanned to deliver targeted individualized advertisements to their computers. However, after a lawsuit in 2014, Google admitted that key-word scanning was occurring with all Gmail communications even though users of Apps for Education believed that their communications were not being analyzed; educational users were simply not served advertisements. Thus educational users of Gmail may have held a reasonable expectation of privacy with respect to their academic activities. This may seem minor since email scanning is carried out by an algorithm and not a human agent, but it is an important point since some communications in the academic environment (for example, emailing student grades, or alerting student services to a student behavioral problem) may be subject to FERPA or the The Protection of Pupil Rights Amendment (PPRA) prohibiting information disclosure to a third party without a consent process, the third party being Google corporation.

Privacy is an extremely complex issue in cloud computing. For example, simply combining different kinds of anonymized data may introduce a privacy threat, i.e. aggregation, that would identify a single user, hence rendering each of the previously disparate elements also identifiable. And although a cloud vendor may agree not to access data on its servers, it may engage in various forms of traffic or log analysis which might easily reveal private information such as an individual's current geospatial location or their actual identity. Potential cloud adopters should strongly consider seeking external disinterested professional advice on potential privacy threats and mitigation strategies when considering migrating any potentially protected private, sensitive or confidential student, faculty or employee data to the cloud.

Data Integrity: System Reliability, Security, and Vendor Lock In (Interoperability)

Institutions which are investigating cloud services or platforms should be reasonably comfortable that data will not be lost or corrupted, or that loss of services (outages) could detrimentally impact operations. For example, several serious interruptions of Gmail occurred in 2009, locking businesses out of their email functionality. Institutions should investigate what potential compensation or reimbursement might be available for outages, and what mitigation strategies the vendor employs to prevent these issues from occurring. Also, contractually, what will happen to data if a cloud vendor closes, enters receivership, or ends a particular service – will the data be accessible to the client? Some categories of data may be sold off as a business asset to another company if a vendor declares bankruptcy, so it is in the best interests of educational institutions to clarify any data ownership concerns at the beginning of service. Similar to the problem of data traversing different territorial jurisdictions, some cloud processes may migrate data from more secure to less secure environments where it would be vulnerable to attack.

As Gritzalis et al. (2014) argued in a recent special issue of the *International Journal of Information Security*, cloud computing entails placing trust in a vendor's security system as well as other forms of trust, and centralizing data makes cloud datasets profitable targets for data thieves. Data typically reside on a cloud server unencrypted. Thus, new security practices in the cloud industry are imperative: "The whole IT infrastructure is under the control of the cloud provider, and the clients have to trust the security protection mechanisms that the cloud and the service providers offer. At the same time, the centralization of resources constitutes the cloud provider a very tempting target. The cloud computing technology is evolving rapidly, and the security and privacy protection mechanisms must keep this quick pace in order to support the acceptance of the cloud model. New security solutions are required, while well-established practices must be revisited" (Gritzalis et al., 2014, p. 95). Pearson (2013) notes additionally that "it is a common requirement under the law that if a company outsources the handling of personal information or confidential data to another company, it has some responsibility to make sure the outsourcer uses 'reasonable security' to protect those data" (p. 12).

The National Cybersecurity Center of Excellence (NCCoE) has identified several major security and privacy issues with cloud computing related to the physical location and transfer of data. A cloud client would need to be assured that:

- The cloud computing platform hosting their workload has not been modified or tempered,
- Sensitive workloads on a multi-tenancy cloud platform are isolated within a logically defined environment from the workloads of competing companies,
- Workload migration occurs only between trusted clusters and within trusted data centers,
- Cloud servers are located in their preferred regions or home countries so that the cloud provider is subject to the same data security and privacy laws" (NCCoE, n.d., p. 1; 2013, pp. 2-5).

The NCCoE in partnership with Intel is developing Trusted Geolocation in the Cloud, a tamper-proof automated 'hardware root of trust' that would test for hardware integrity and manage workloads among cloud servers only within defined locations. The NIST also introduced a trusted geolocation draft framework in the cloud framework for IaaS in 2012 (Banks et al., 2012).

The Service Level Agreement

Many of the issues above could be solved by customized contracts and service level agreements (SLAs) in which customer concerns could be adequately addressed. However, a recent review of cloud computing contracts demonstrates that there is little variation in the standard contracts offered (Srinivasan, 2014, p. 120). Most cloud services are purchased online with a credit card using the standard click-through process after a purchaser reads the Terms of Service online. Also, according to Hon et al. (2012), there is little incentive for cloud providers to alter terms of service for anyone except a major customer. Srinivasan's (2014) review of cloud contracting is helpful in delineating the serious concerns that cloud adopters may encounter with a vendor. For example, clauses in SLAs can be linked to terms of service on the vendor's website and many cloud vendors such as Google reserve the right to change terms of service without notifying customers, which could void certain specially negotiated SLA terms. Some advances have been made in automating the SLA adoption process (Cuomo et al., 2013, pp. 1-25).

SOLUTIONS AND RECOMMENDATIONS

The adoption of institution-wide cloud computing solutions–whether at the level of infrastructure, platform, or software–is obviously a highly personalized decision. Cloud computing is particularly suited for STEM degree granting higher education institutions since these fields, as opposed to humanities and many social sciences that rely on qualitative data, have high throughput and high capability computing needs for research, modeling and virtual laboratories. Table 1 lists a number of practical steps which institutions might consider following in their cloud technology adoption strategy. These steps are not necessarily in order of importance or chronology, since institutions will weigh different factors in different ways.

FUTURE RESEARCH DIRECTIONS

In the future, researchers would be better served with a technology adoption model with a theoretical component but which would also output practical advice on specific adoption and implementation strategies. Ideally this would be automated, but the complete service selection process at the present time is too complex for artificially intelligent agents, although progress has been made to automate sub routines such as service level agreements. Legal, political and social constraints need to be integrated with the factors of privacy, security and trust discussed above, and also the constraints related to external vendors such as interoperability of systems should be considered. Human factors such as training, computer literacy, openness to change, and individual investment in a particular cloud service, etc. also need to be considered. Due to the proprietary nature of cloud technologies, it is extremely difficult to quantify and predict in today's rapidly moving IT ecosystems what new products and services will emerge. Often, changes in educational technology are driven more by changes in consumer electronics that are then adapted to educational uses in academic settings rather than a needs-based approach to new technology development specifically geared towards educational institutions. More holistic toolkits that take into account not only optimization of architectures and services, but also social, legal and political features of cloud adoption would be welcome. Such a proposal called OPTIMIS was published by Ferrer et al. in 2012.

CONCLUSION

The U.S. government along with many business and now academic institutions have started to embrace cloud computing technologies and services for obvious reasons: low cost, ease of use of interfaces, scalability, availability, and reduction of in-house IT costs. However, adoption of these technologies

Table 1. Summary of recommended steps towards safe and responsible cloud computing adoption in STEM education (not necessarily in chronological order)

Key Steps
Conduct an exhaustive institution-wide needs assessment survey about cloud computing needs. Focus groups and online questionnaires are effective. Stakeholders may first need to be educated about cloud computing capabilities via public presentations. Include all stakeholders: students, faculty, staff, and administration.
Identify key areas where cloud computing will have a significant and measurable institutional impact (i.e. research, administration, course management, etc.)
Determine what institution-wide training programs will be required to learn new cloud technologies and who will carry them out.
Assess complete current software, hardware, and IT personnel capabilities of the institution.
Create a transition team to move from in-house to cloud services, and a permanent management team. Identify the required skill set of these teams.
Investigate compatibility of current system with cloud systems, including any potential shifts in cloud provisioning that might render current in-house systems obsolete.
Consult with legal experts about national and international laws on data, particularly highly protected data categories such as health information, financial information, student records and data on under-13 years of age. Determine from the cloud vendor the geographical jurisdiction(s) in which data will reside and obtain copies of the data laws of those territories. Cloud vendors may not be willing or able to supply this information for technical and security reasons.
Test the network and determine required upload, download (data transfer) speeds for optimal performance.
Identify all sensitive data that would present significant risk to the institution if leaked or destroyed. Common categories include: school records, patentable material / intellectual property, health data, ground breaking research, military research, human subjects research, institutional / departmental financial documents and personnel or student files containing large amounts of personally identifiable information. Conduct worst case scenario testing to gauge potential institutional damage (punitive fines, legal action, loss of reputation of institution). Some data may not be appropriate for the public cloud. These data can be held in-house or in cloud structures in which security and access are completely controlled by the institution ('private clouds').
If possible, negotiate a comprehensive contract and Service Level Agreements with a reputable cloud vendor that meets the needs of the institution.

must constitute a planned and rational process, with the serious factors of data security, privacy, data laws, and vendor lock-in (interoperability) all taken into consideration. Cloud computing is well suited for educational institutions that offer STEM degrees since many science and engineering disciplines rely on computer modeling and computer assisted design for research and teaching, and increasingly on big datasets. However, some mission critical data and sensitive data categories may still need to be processed and stored in-house or in a cloud structure in which the data owner holds encryption keys and can monitor and control all aspects of security.

REFERENCES

Banks, E. K., Bartock, M., Fiftal, K., Lemon, D., Scarfone, K., Shetty, U., ... Yeluri, R. (2012). *Trusted geolocation in the cloud: Proof of concept implementation (Draft)*. Gaithersburg, MD: National Institute of Standards and Technology, Computer Security Division.

Committee on STEM Education (CoSTEM). (2013). *Federal science, technology, engineering, and mathematics (STEM) education 5-Year strategic plan*. Washington, DC: Executive Office of the President, National Science and Technology Council.

Cuomo, A., Di Modica, G., Distefano, S., Puliafito, A., Rak, M., Tomarchio, O., ... Villano, U. (2013). An SLA-based broker for cloud infrastructures. *Journal of Grid Computing*, *11*(1), 1–25. doi:10.100710723-012-9241-4

Davis, F. D. (1989). Perceived usefulness, perceived ease of use, and user acceptance of information technology. *Management Information Systems Quarterly*, *13*(3), 319–340. doi:10.2307/249008

Davis, F. D., Bagozzi, R. P., & Warshaw, P. R. (1989). User acceptance of computer technology: A comparison of two theoretical models. *Management Science*, *35*(8), 982–1003. doi:10.1287/mnsc.35.8.982

Ferrer, A. J., Hernandez, F., Tordsson, J., Elmroth, E., Ali-Eldin, A., Zsigri, C., ... Sheridan, C. (2012). OPTIMIS: A holistic approach to cloud service provisioning. *Future Generation Computer Systems*, *28*(1), 66–77. doi:10.1016/j.future.2011.05.022

Gritzalis, S., Mitchell, C., Thuraisingham, B., & Zhou, J. (2014). Security in cloud computing. *International Journal of Information Security*, *13*(2), 95–96. doi:10.100710207-014-0232-2

Hon, W., Millard, C., & Walden, I. (2012). Negotiating cloud contracts: Looking at clouds from both sides now. *Stanford Technology Law Review*, *16*(1), 79–129.

Koomey, J. G. (2011). *Growth in data center electricity use 2005-2010*. Stanford, CA: Analytics Press.

Mayer-Schönberger, V., & Cukier, K. (2013). *Big data: A revolution that will transform how we live, work, and think*. Boston: Houghton Mifflin Harcourt.

Mell, P., & Grance, P. (2011). The NIST definition of cloud computing. Special Publication 800-145. Washington, DC: The National Institute of Standards and Technology (NIST).

NCCoE (National Cybersecurity Center of Excellence). (n.d.). *Building block: Trusted geolocation in the cloud*. Gaithersburg, MD: National Institute of Standards and Technology, Computer Security Division.

Pearson, S. (2013). Privacy and security for cloud computing. In S. Pearson & G. Yee (Eds.), *Computer Communications and Networks* (pp. 3–41). London: Springer-Verlag; doi:10.1007/978-1-4471-4189-1_1

Srinivasan, S. (2014). Hidden Aspects of a cloud computing contract. In Cloud computing basics. New York: Springer Science+Business Media. doi:10.1007/978-1-4614-7699-3_7

Venkatesh, V., & Davis, F. D. (2000). A theoretical extension of the technology acceptance model: Four longitudinal field studies. *Management Science*, *46*(2), 186–204. doi:10.1287/mnsc.46.2.186.11926

Venkatesh, V., Morris, M. G., Davis, G. B., & Davis, F. D. (2003). User acceptance of information technology: Toward a unified view. *Management Information Systems Quarterly*, *27*(3), 425–478.

Weber, A. S. (2013a). Cloud computing in education. In G. Sampson, E. Demetrios, P. E. Isaias, D. E. Ifenthaler, & J. M. Spector (Eds.), *Ubiquitous and mobile learning in the digital age* (pp. 19–36). New York: Springer. doi:10.1007/978-1-4614-3329-3_2

Weber, A. S. (2013b). Protecting student privacy and data in the age of surveillance. In *Proceedings of the ICEE / ICIT 2013 Conference* (pp. 398-406). Cape Town, South Africa: Cape Peninsula University of Technology.

KEY TERMS AND DEFINITIONS

Cloud Computing: A model for online on-demand provisioning of rapidly scalable computing resources.

FERPA: Family Educational Rights and Privacy Act (1974). The main federal statute protecting student record privacy.

Google Apps for Education: A productivity suite of cloud software for educational purposes.

HIPAA: The Health Insurance Portability and Accountability Act (1996) governs electronic healthcare and record keeping.

Human Subjects Research: Any research, either biomedical or social science, involving humans.

Hypervisor: Software or firmware that creates and manages a virtual machine (VM).

NIST: National Institute of Standards and Technology, an agency that recommends national technology standards for cloud computing to promote interoperability and security for government adoption of the cloud.

PHI: Protected health information, an especially sensitive category of data protected by HIPAA and consisting of 18 identifiers.

PPRA: The Protection of Pupil Rights Amendment of 1978 requires parental consent before sensitive PII is collected from students.

Privacy: The ability of an individual or group to control or conceal information about themselves.

Security: The protection of computer data and systems from theft, destruction, and alteration.

Service Level Agreement (SLA): A negotiable agreement in a contract between a service provider and a service user.

TAM: Technology Acceptance Model, a model that attempts to understand how and why users adopt a particular technology.

TAM2: Modification of the Technology Acceptance Model (TAM).

UTAUT: Unified Theory of Acceptance and Use of Technology, a social psychology model used to explain why users adopt a particular technology and their consequent behavior.

Virtual Machine (VM): In full virtualization, a VM is a software emulation of a real machine.

This research was previously published in the Handbook of Research on Cloud-Based STEM Education for Improved Learning Outcomes edited by Lee Chao, pages 1-11, copyright year 2016 by Information Science Reference (an imprint of IGI Global).

Chapter 24
The Dynamic Data Privacy Protection Strategy Based on the CAP Theory

Xinwei Sun
Beijing Information Science & Technology University, China

Zhang Wei
Beijing Information Science & Technology University, China

ABSTRACT

With the rapid development of cloud storage technology, the cloud storage platform has gradually been used to store data. However, the privacy protection strategy provided by public cloud storage platform is hard to be trust by users. Moreover, they are unable to customize their own storage strategy according to their demands. This study proposed a consistency-availability-partition tolerance (CAP) theory -based data privacy protection strategy, which firstly employed CAP theory to provide privacy data protection for users and then offer users with choice to select corresponding privacy strategy to store data. Moreover, a total of three privacy protection strategies were put forward, focusing on the balance between data consistency and response time, data consistency and data availability, as well as response time and availability respectively.

INTRODUCTION

Cloud storage (Cloud Storage, 2015) refers to that the data of enterprises or individuals are outsourced to the third-party cloud storage service providers for storage and maintenance (Fox et al., 2009). It makes way for enterprises or individuals being free of the problems such as deficiency of local software and hardware resources, transferring inconvenience, as well as the failure and loss of storage equipment, etc. as long as paying for the needs. With the rapid development of cloud storage, more and more individuals prefer to store their own data into the public clouds by public APIs. At present, numerous famous IT enterprises worldwide have served users with highly reliable cloud storage environments that are ac-

DOI: 10.4018/978-1-5225-8176-5.ch024

cessible all the time, such as AmazonS3 (Amazon S3, 2006), Dropbox (Dropbox, 2014), Google Drive (Google Drive, 2014), OneDrive (OneDrive, 2014), and AliCloud (AliCloud, 2014), etc.

Cloud storage has many features such as cheap and easy to expand. These features will make cloud storage become a hot research when it appears. As cloud storage brings convenience to users in the continuous development, some problems in the cloud storage are gradually disclosed. When users upload private data to the cloud, they will lose absolute control over the data. Cloud storage system has an urgent security needs.

Part of users begins to be worried about the security of cloud storage. In a survey, forty percent of the Dropbox users indicate that they are most concerned about security (Cloud Storage User Survey, 2012). A survey suggested that about 80% of the enterprises were reluctant to save their internal data on the public cloud directly out of safety fears, and only 20% of users showed willingness of storing their private data on the private cloud (Twinstrata, 2012). To solve this problem, many cloud storage systems put forward corresponding security policies. The current mainstream cloud storage platforms include Amazon S3, Dropbox, iCloud, Google Drive, Microsoft OneDrive, and SugarSync (SugarSync, 2014). Further, Kuaipan (Kingsoft) and Baiduserve only the Chinese market. The mainstream primary storage systems have offered users with secure sockets layer (SSL) mechanism in the transmission process and advanced encryption standard (AES) (128-bit, 256-bit) encryption mechanism in the storage process (Amazon S3, 2006; Shraer et al., 2010; iCloud, 2013). However, it is hard for users to completely trust the safety security strategy provided by cloud storage system. Therefore, many users still encrypt their private data using local encryption methods and then upload the private data to the public cloud platform; in case of need of using, the data are firstly downloaded from the public cloud platform and then reduced using corresponding decryption methods. However, traditional encryption algorithm mainly depends on the key for encryption. Once the key is lost, the data is brought into an unsafe state.

Microsoft has proposed Cryptographic Cloud Storage in 2009 (Kamara & Lauter, 2010). Cryptographic Cloud Storage system uses encryption to protect the confidentiality of data. Cryptographic Cloud Storage system uses searchable encryption, attribute-based encryption and probable of data possession in the prototyping systems. It improves the performance of overall system while enhancing the effect of user experience.

Like the industry, academia also attaches great importance to the safety of cloud storage system. Shraer (Shraer et al., 2010) and other people proposed a trust system based on a core Set in Venus system. It through tripartite architecture to provide users with security features. In 2011, Bessani (Bessani et al., 2013) and other people proposed an idea of cloud-of-clouds in DEPSKY. To some extent alleviate the problem of data confidentiality and vendor data lock-in issues.

At present, in addition to the security, users also pay attention to the availability of the data saved in cloud. Thirty percent of Google Drive users believe that file loss is the biggest problem currently. In addition to file loss, the service suspension of the cloud storage system also bugs many users. Merely in 2013, many cloud storage systems around the world saw crashes in different degrees, such as the Google Drive, Microsoft's OneDrive, Apple's iCloud, Amazon S3. The crash of cloud storage system makes it impossible for users accessing to the data they upload to the public cloud and thus brings some economic loss to the user.

In order to solve the problem of the data security in cloud storage system and the application process. In 2011, BIAN (BIAN et al., 2011) and other people proposed a security structure of cloud storage based on dispersal. The mechanism of safety management and transmission of storage data are realized by layer through the use of information dispersal algorithms (IDA), distributed storage management, and data restore methods. This method can effectively ensure the security, reliability and availability of user's private data. However, to ensure the security of users' private data at the same time will lose some space and time to satisfy the requirements of safety.

Therefore, with the rapid increasing of data, user will experience a sense of decline. In view of the problems above, this study proposed a cloud storage-based customized data privacy protection model according to CAP theorem. Users can select different storage schemes for privacy protection and redundant processing on their data according to their own needs. Privacy protection technology used in this study employed the Bit Split Bit combine (BSBC) data privacy protection technology (SUN et al., 2014). Bit Split Bit Combine (BSBC) did not depend on any original encryption algorithms. Bit Spit (BS) technique will recode data and split them into multiple part files before these are upload to the different cloud storage servers. After downloading the multiple part files Bit Combine (BC) technique will recover the original data.

In this paper, we present a dynamic data privacy protection strategy based the CAP theory. There are three ways to protection user's privacy data. Due to the different requirements of users on the availability, consistency, partition tolerance of data, one model is incapable of meeting the demands of all users. Therefore, this study proposed three kinds of data privacy protection plans. By selecting suitable plan according to needs, users can protect the privacy of their data.

RELATED WORKS

CAP Theorem

The CAP theory was put forward by Brewer (Brewer, 2009) and proved by Gilbert and Lynch (Gilbert et al., 2002). In large distributed systems, the consistency, availability, and partition-tolerance of data are unavailable at the same time. Only two of them can be met at most at the same time. Figure 1 shows the relationship of the consistency, availability, and partition-tolerance of data. However, in the non-distributed system, it is needed to meet the consistency, usability, and partition tolerance simultaneously (Lomotey & Deters, 2013):

- **Consistency:** A service that is consistent operates fully or not at all. Gilbert and Lynch use the word "atomic" instead of consistent in their proof, which makes more sense technically because, strictly speaking, consistent is the C in ACID (LIN Zi-Yu et al., 2012; Pretchett D., 2008) as ap-

Figure 1. The relationship of the consistency, availability, and partition-tolerance of data

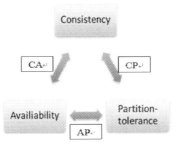

plied to the ideal properties of database transactions and means that data will never be persisted that breaks certain preset constraints. But if you consider it a preset constraint of distributed systems that multiple values for the same piece of data are not allowed then I think the leak in the abstraction is plugged (Browne, 2009). Ensuring the consistency of the storage state of the distributed system from the client (R. Royans, 2012);

- **Availability:** Being able of corresponding each reading and writing request (Pritchett, 2008);
- **Partition tolerance:** Allowing the loss of the information sent between nodes in distributed system. That is, the operation of the system was unaffected by the information loss.

CAP theorem states that the consistency, availability, and partition tolerance are unavailable simultaneously. Therefore, during processing the CAP problem, only two can be met at most at the same time. There are a few options:

- Satisfying consistency and availability simultaneously:
  - This option means that partition tolerance is given up. In case of ginning up partition tolerance, it is needed to prevent the partition problems as far as possible. Since all things are put on a machine in this condition generally, the scalability of the system is affected;
- Satisfying consistency and partition tolerance simultaneously:
  - This option means that the availability is given up. In case of giving up availability, the data are only accessible when the data in all servers are consistent;
- Satisfying availability and partition tolerance simultaneously:
  - This option means that the consistency is given up. In case of giving up consistency, users are allowed to continue the operations merely when the data are consistent finally instead of when the data in all servers are consistent.

CAP theorem is most suitable for the scalable distributed system. At present, the mainstream public cloud storage platform firstly guarantees the partition tolerance and then the consistency and availability alternatively. CAP theory has been applied in many fields of computer, especially in NoSQL database (Browne, 2009). This paper presented a CAP theory-based data privacy protection strategy, which allows users customizing different data privacy protection strategies according to different needs.

The Privacy Protection Method Basing on Mainstream Commercial Cloud Storage Platform

By reserving the data in the cloud storage system offered by cloud storage service providers, users needn't to be worried about the data loss induced by USB flash disk damage or loss and can access their data whenever and wherever as long as network is available. With the continuously elevating requirements of users on data privacy, an increasing number of cloud storage platforms began to provide data privacy protection technology for users.

AmazonS3 is a cloud storage service provided by Amazon Company. Amazon S3 makes great efforts in aspect of the security of user. AmazonS3 allows users making choice on whether or not using SSL mechanism to upload data to ensure the safety of the data uploaded. In case of using SSL mechanism, it is able to ensure that the data are free of the interception of attackers in the uploading process. In aspect of storage, Amazon S3 also provided privacy protection mechanism for users. Users can make decisions on whether or not using the data encryption method provided by Amazon Company, namely AES encryption algorithm (with key length of 256-bit), to encrypt their data.

Being similar with Amazon S3, Dropbox offers two encryption mechanisms for users:

1. **Transmission Encryption:** Using the SSL mechanism for data uploading; providing data encryption for users in the uploading process of data;
2. **Static Encryption:** Using AES encryption algorithm in data storage process (with key length of 256-bit) to encrypt users' data.

As another public cloud platform, Ali Cloud has not provided any encryption strategies for users. However, as the public cloud platform in China, its greatest advantage lies in the high transmission speed.

Currently, the public cloud storage platform in the countries out of China has begun to provide users with data privacy protection plan. However, the privacy protection strategy provided by the cloud storage platform is hard to be trusted by users. Therefore, this study employed the BSBC privacy protection technology to protect the data privacy of users.

CORE IDEA

During the usage of cloud storage system, users are mostly worried about the safety and partition tolerance of data currently. Aiming at the two properties, this study proposed a highly efficient redundant storage strategy that is applicable to the cloud storage. The detail process is indicated as follows: before data uploading, the data of users were firstly split into four parts using Bit Split technology to realize the privacy protection of data. Then using corresponding algorithms, part of the data is uploaded onto AmazonS3, Dropbox, and Ali Cloud respectively. In case of need of data, users can download the data from cloud system and combine the data using Bit Combine technology. Finally, the data can be used.

BSBC Privacy Protection Technology

Bit Split (BS) Technology

Bit Split (BS) privacy protection technology is a method of splitting users' data into multiple parts. Its main idea is to realize the privacy protection through shift and diffusion. The Bit Split (BS) method used in this study divided a file into four parts. Figure 2 shows the core technological flow:

1. **Data Reading:** The data of four bytes are read from a file;
2. **Splitting and Shifting:** A byte consists of eight bits. The data of each byte are split by a group of two bits, namely, the first and second bits, the third and fourth bits, the fourth and fifth bits, and the sixth and seventh bits are split respectively. Moreover, the data sequence is adjusted;
3. **Restructuring:** The first and second bits of each datum are combined into a new byte; then the third and fourth bits, the fifth and sixth bits, and the seventh and eighth bits are combined separately into new bytes respectively;
4. **Data Writing:** The data newly obtained are writing into file 1, file 2, file 3, and file 4 respectively;

Figure 2. Flow chart of Bit Split (BS) technique

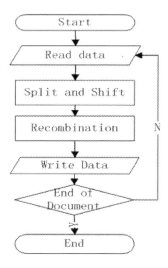

5. **Making Judgments on Whether or Not Reaching to the File End:** If having not reached to the file end, repeating the step 1-5. If having reached to the file end, the work flow ended.

Bit Split (BS) technology can realize the split of data. Using this technology, the original one data copy can be diffused into four files. Therefore, in case of attackers intending to capture users' data, the content of user's data is hardly to be cracked if attackers merely obtaining one data copy. Only obtaining all the data, can the content of the user's data can be obtained.

Bit Combine (BC) Technology

Bit Combine (BC) technology is based on Bit Split technology. It mainly purposes on combining the data split by Bit Split technology. It reduces the data so that users can use their own data. Figure 3 shows the Bit Combine (BC) technological flow of four files:

1. **Data Reading:** The data of one byte are read from four files;
2. **Splitting and Shifting:** The data of each byte is split into four copies by the unit of two bits;
3. **Combining Process:** The first and second bits, the third and fourth bits, the fifth and sixth bits, the seventh and eighth bits of the fourth byte are combined into new bytes respectively;
4. **Data Writing Process:** The data newly obtained were written into a new file in sequence;
5. **Making Judgments on Whether or Not Reaching to the File End:** If having not reached to the file end, repeating the step 1-5. If having reached to the file end, the work flow ended.

Using Bit Combine technology, the originally scattered data in the four files are combined into a new file. The whole process is actually a reverse process of Bit Split technology. It enables users to get the original data.

Figure 3. Flow chart of Bit Combine (BC) technique

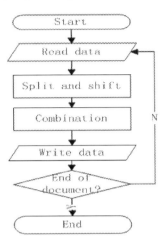

The CAP-Based Data Privacy Protection Technology

Due to the different requirements of users on the availability, consistency, partition tolerance of data, one model is incapable of meeting the demands of all users. Therefore, this study proposed three kinds of data privacy protection plans. By selecting suitable plan according to needs, users can protect the privacy of their data:

- **High Consistency and Availability:** In this case, the partition tolerance of data is poor since only one data copy is reserved and data are not backed up. Each cloud storage system merely contains one piece of data of user. In case of the failure of one data copy, the whole data would become useless. This case is applicable to the users that have high consistence requirements and need to rapidly read, write, and access the data;

- **Satisfying Availability and Partition Tolerance:** User's data are stored in two copies and backed up. Therefore, in case of the inaccessibility of the public cloud storage platform, users still have way of obtaining corresponding data from other pubic cloud platforms. In case of the cracks of multiple pubic cloud storage platforms, users may be unable to access their own data. This plan is mainly applicable to the users that have certain requirement on data availability and are unexpected to spend too much time on the consistency of data;

- **High Availability and Partition Tolerance:** In this plan, the availability and partition tolerance of data are guaranteed since user's data are stored in three copies. At present, the data in the mainstream cloud storage file systems, such as GFS (Ghemawat et al., 2003), HDFS (Shvachko et al. 2010) data, are all stored in three copies to prevent the unavailability of data. Therefore, the three copies of the data stored ensured the high availability of user's data. In this case, even if there is the missing of part data or the crash of part of cloud storage, the data of users are unaffected and remains accessible. Unfortunately, data show poor consistency in this case. Moreover, it is needed of a long time to ensure the consistency of data. This plan is merely applicable to the users with high data availability requirements.

The Dynamic and Adjustable Structure

Aiming at the different requirements of users on the availability, consistency, and partition tolerance of users, this study proposed a dynamic adjustable data privacy protection structure. User can adjust their storage plan according to their demands. The dynamic pseudo codes of adjustable structure are shown in Algorithm 1.

Users can split the file to several parts (N) according to their demands. Then users will choose several clouds where they want to upload the files (J), and set the number of redundant copies ($0 <= i <= J-1$). Finally, system will upload the data to different public cloud according to users' different demands.

CASE ANALYSIS

This study divided the data into four copies ($N = 4$) and uploaded the data into four public cloud storage platforms (Ali cloud, AmasonS3, Dropbox, and Google Drive, $J = 4$) to verify the dynamic adjustable CAP theory-based data reluctance protection strategy indicated above. The data in size of 10 M and 40 M were used for comparison. The process is indicated as follows: firstly, the data are split using BSBC privacy protection technology into four copies (2.5 M and 10 M for each copy respectively). Then the data were uploaded onto different public cloud storage platforms. The experimental environment includes a CORE i3 processor, windows 7, memory of 6 G; Network environment is provided by the campus network of Beijing Information Science and Technology University.

High Consistency and Availability Plan

If user has high consistency requirements on data and needs to rapidly read, write, and access the data, the high consistency and availability plan is suitable. That is to say, $i = 0$. According to the data above, it is calculable that which piece of data is uploaded into which the public cloud storage platforms. The upload the relationship is shown below. The first piece of data of user is uploaded to the fourth public

Algorithm 1.

```
1)  for (i; i >= 0; i--)
2)  {
3)      for (m = 1; m <= 4; m++)
4)      {
5)              for (k = 1; k <= J; k++)
6)              {
7)              if (((k + m - 1) mod N)- i == 0)
8)              Upload the M slice data;
9)              }
10) }
11)}
```

i: denotes to the redundant copies of data;($0 <= i <= J-1$)
N: represents that the number of the copies split
m: refers the current copy
J: represents the total number of clouds
k: is the current cloud

cloud storage platform (Google Drive); the second piece of data is uploaded to the third public cloud storage platform (Dropbox); the third piece of data is uploaded to the second public cloud storage platform (Amazon S3); the fourth piece of data is uploaded first public cloud storage platform (AliCloud). Figure 4 displays the file upload model.

When using high consistency and availability plan, each piece of data is merely needed to be uploaded to a public cloud storage platform. Figure 5 shows the data uploading time. It can be seen that different public cloud storage platforms present different response times.

Satisfying Availability and Partition Tolerance Plan

If users want to back up their data simply to prevent data loss while are unexpected to spend on too much time on data consistency, this plan is more favorable. In this condition, a total of two data copies were saved. One of them is the backup data, that is to say, $i = 1$. According to the formulas above, it is calculable of that the first piece of data is uploaded to the first and fourth public cloud storage platforms (AliCloud, Google Drive); the second piece of data is uploaded to the third and fourth public cloud storage platforms (Dropbox, Google Drive); the third piece of data is uploaded to the second and third public cloud storage platforms (Amazon S3, Dropbox); the fourth piece of data is uploaded to the first and second public cloud storage platforms (AliCloud, Amazon S3). Figure 6 illustrates the uploading model of specific files.

When using the satisfying availability and partition tolerance plan, each piece of data can be uploaded to two public cloud storage platforms. Figure 7 shows the data uploading time.

Figure 4. High consistency and availability plan file upload model

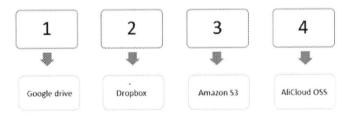

Figure 5. High consistency and availability plan response times

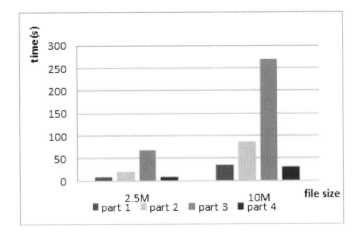

Figure 6. Satisfying availability and partition tolerance plan file upload model

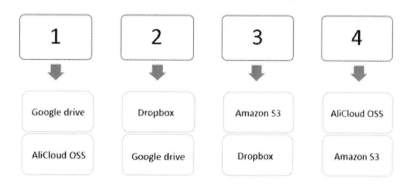

Figure 7. Satisfying availability and partition tolerance plan response times

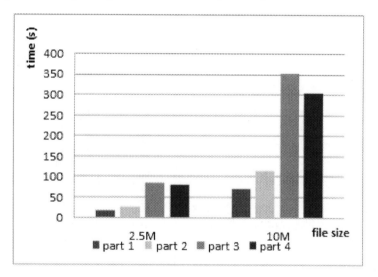

High Availability and Partition Tolerance

When user has high requirements on data availability, the data can be stored in three copies. Two of the copies are backup data, namely, i = 2. According to the formulas above, it is calculable of that the first piece of data is uploaded to the first, second, and fourth public cloud storage platforms (AliCloud, Amazon S3, Google Drive); the second piece of data is uploaded to the first, third, fourth public cloud storage platforms (AliCloud, Dropbox, Google Drive); the third piece of data is uploaded to the second, third, and fourth public cloud storage platforms (Amazon S3, Dropbox, Google Drive); the fourth piece of data was uploaded to the first, second, and third public cloud storage platforms (AliCloud, Amazon S3, Dropbox). Figure 8 illustrates the uploading model of specific files. Using this plan, user can still read and write their data at any time in case of the network failure or data loss.

When using the high availability and partition tolerance plan, every piece of data should be uploaded to three public cloud storage platforms. Figure 9 shows the data uploading time.

Figure 8. High availability and partition tolerance file upload model

Figure 9. High availability and partition tolerance response times

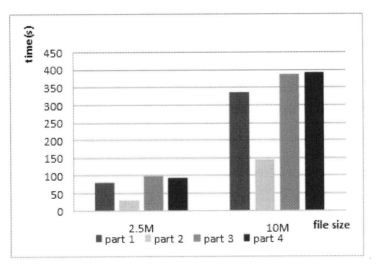

CONCLUSION

Considering the disparate data requirements of different users, this study proposed a CAP theory-based privacy protection structure, which allowed users customizing different privacy protection plans according to the demands.

In order to ensure the security of users' data. The first, we use BS privacy protection techniques to protect the users' data privacy. And split the users' data to multiple parts. When users need to use the data, we download the data and use BC technology to restore the user's data.

A total of 3 plans were proposed to meet users' different demands on the consistency, availability, and partition tolerance of data. High consistence and availability realized the rapid reading and writing responses of user on data and is applicable to the users with high reading and writing frequency on data; satisfying availability and partition tolerance plan meets the requirements of user on the rapidly reading and writing file. Meanwhile, it provides data backup to prevent the failure of the whole data induced by the inaccessibility of part of data. Although the data upload process in high availability and partition tolerance model will cost a lot of time. It can provide a good data backup capabilities for users. One part data storage 3 times, even if the data is losing on two cloud storage users will not have any impact. Dynamically adjustable strategy provides users with a new privacy policy for users to self-select. And providing different services to users based on the users' needs is the trend of the future development. Therefore, this paper proposes that dynamically adjustable privacy protection policies based on the users' demand. Using this data split privacy protection policy the rate of privacy protection will be quick, but the process of the data uploaded to the public cloud will be slow because of network bandwidth and affect the speed. Believe that with the rising speed of the network, the method can provide users worth a better experience feeling.

ACKNOWLEDGMENT

This paper was funded by the Beijing Excellent Talent Training Project (2012D005007000009), the Opening Project of Beijing Key Laboratory of Internet Culture and Digital Dissemination Research (ICDD201306), and The Project of Construction of Innovative Teams and Teacher Career Development for Universities and Colleges Under Beijing Municipality (IDHT20130519).

REFERENCES

AliCloud. (2014). Retrieved from AliCloud: http://www.aliyun.com/

Amazon S3. (2006). Using Data Encryption. Retrieved March 1, 2006, from http://docs.aws.amazon.com/AmazonS3/latest/dev/UsingEncryption.html

Bessani, A., Correia, M., Quaresma, B., André, F., & Sousa, P. (2013). DepSky: Dependable and secure storage in a cloud-of-clouds. [TOS]. *ACM Transactions on Storage*, 9(4), 12. doi:10.1145/2535929

Bian, G., Gao, S., & Shao, B. (2011). Security structure of cloud storage based on dispersal. *Journal of Xi'an Jiaotong University*, 45(4), 41–45.

Browne, J. (2009). Brewer's CAP theorem. J. Browne blog.

Cloud storage. (2015). Retrieved from Wikipedia: http://en.wikipedia.org/wiki/Cloud_storage

Cloud Storage User Survey. (2012) Cloud Storage User Survey. Retrieved December 10, 2012, from http://sec.chinabyte.com/447/12485447.shtml

Dropbox. (2014). Retrieved from Wikipedia: http://en.wikipedia.org/wiki/Dropbox

Fox, A., Griffith, R., Joseph, A., Katz, R., & Konwinski, A. Lee, Stoica, I. (2009). Above the clouds: A Berkeley view of cloud computing. Dept. Electrical Eng. and Comput. Sciences, University of California, Berkeley, Rep. UCB/EECS, 28, 13.

Ghemawat, S., Gobioff, H., & Leung, S. T. (2003, October). The Google file system. [). ACM.]. *Operating Systems Review*, 37(5), 29–43. doi:10.1145/1165389.945450

Gilbert, S., & Lynch, N. (2002). Brewer's conjecture and the feasibility of consistent, available, partition-tolerant web services. *ACM SIGACT News*, *33*(2), 51–59. doi:10.1145/564585.564601

Google Drive. (2014). Retrieved from Wikipedia: http://en.wikipedia.org/wiki/Google_Drive

Kamara, S., & Lauter, K. (2010). Cryptographic cloud storage. In *Financial Cryptography and Data Security* (pp. 136–149). Springer Berlin Heidelberg. doi:10.1007/978-3-642-14992-4_13

Lomotey, R. K., & Deters, R. (2013, March). Reliable Consumption of Web Services in a Mobile-Cloud Ecosystem Using REST. In *Service Oriented System Engineering (SOSE), 2013 IEEE 7th International Symposium on* (pp. 13-24). IEEE. 10.1109/SOSE.2013.10

OneDrive. (2014).Retrieved from Wikipedia: http://en.wikipedia.org/wiki/OneDrive

Pritchett, D. (2008). Base: An acid alternative. *Queue*, *6*(3), 48–55. doi:10.1145/1394127.1394128

Pritchett, D. (2008). Base: An acid alternative. *Queue*, *6*(3), 48–55. doi:10.1145/1394127.1394128

Royans, R. (2012) "Brewers CAP Theorem on distributed systems," Retrieved September 23, 2012, http://www.royans.net/arch/brewers-cap-theorem-on-distributedsystems/

Shraer, A., Cachin, C., Cidon, A., Keidar, I., Michalevsky, Y., & Shaket, D. (2010, October). Venus: Verification for untrusted cloud storage. InProceedings of the 2010 ACM workshop on Cloud computing security workshop (pp. 19-30). ACM iCloud (2013) iCloud Security and Privacy Overview. Retrieved February 11, 2013, http://support.apple.com/kb/HT4865?viewlocale=zh_CN&locale=zh_CN

Shvachko, K., Kuang, H., Radia, S., & Chansler, R. (2010, May). The hadoop distributed file system. In *Mass Storage Systems and Technologies (MSST), 2010 IEEE 26th Symposium on (pp. 1-10)*. IEEE. 10.1109/MSST.2010.5496972

SugarSync. (2014). Retrieved from Wikipedia: http://en.wikipedia.org/wiki/SugarSync

Sun, X., Zhang, W., Xu, T. (2014, May) High-performance Data Privacy Protection for Cloud. In Computer science, 41(5), 137-142

Twinstrata. (2012). Twinstrata. Retrieved May 10, 2012, http://twinstrata.com

Zi-Yu, L. I. N., Yong-Xuan, L. A. I., Chen, L. I. N., Yi, X. I. E., & Quan, Z. O. U. (2012). Research on Cloud Databases. *Journal of Software*, *23*(5), 1148–1166. doi:10.3724/SP.J.1001.2012.04195

This research was previously published in the International Journal of Interdisciplinary Telecommunications and Networking (IJITN), 7(1); edited by Michael R Bartolacci and Steven R. Powell, pages 44-56, copyright year 2015 by IGI Publishing (an imprint of IGI Global).

Chapter 25

A Novel Multi-Secret Sharing Approach for Secure Data Warehousing and On-Line Analysis Processing in the Cloud

Varunya Attasena
Université de Lyon, France

Nouria Harbi
Université de Lyon, France

Jérôme Darmont
Université de Lyon, France

ABSTRACT

Cloud computing helps reduce costs, increase business agility and deploy solutions with a high return on investment for many types of applications, including data warehouses and on-line analytical processing. However, storing and transferring sensitive data into the cloud raises legitimate security concerns. In this paper, the authors propose a new multi-secret sharing approach for deploying data warehouses in the cloud and allowing on-line analysis processing, while enforcing data privacy, integrity and availability. The authors first validate the relevance of their approach theoretically and then experimentally with both a simple random dataset and the Star Schema Benchmark. The authors also demonstrate its superiority to related methods.

1. INTRODUCTION

Business intelligence (BI) has been an ever-growing trend for more than twenty years, but the recent advent of cloud computing now allows deploying data analytics even more easily. While building a traditional BI system typically necessitates an important initial investment, with the cloud pay-as-you-

DOI: 10.4018/978-1-5225-8176-5.ch025

go model, users can punctually devote small amounts of resources in return for a one-time advantage. This trend is currently supported by numerous "BI as a service" offerings, with high economic stakes.

Although cloud computing is currently booming, data security remains a top concern for cloud users and would-be users. Some security issues are inherited from classical distributed architectures, e.g., authentication, network attacks and vulnerability exploitation, but some directly relate to the new framework of the cloud, e.g., cloud service provider or subcontractor espionage, cost-effective defense of availability and uncontrolled mashups (Chow et al., 2009). In the context of cloud BI, privacy is of critical importance. Security issues are currently handled by cloud service providers (CSPs). But with the multiplication of CSPs and subcontractors in many countries, intricate legal issues arise, as well as another fundamental issue: *trust*. Telling whether trust should be placed in CSPs falls back onto end-users, with the implied costs.

Critical security concerns in (especially public) cloud storage are depicted in Figure 1. User data might be deleted, lost or damaged. First, some CSPs have the policy of taking the highest profit. Therefore, unmodified or unaccessed data may be deleted to serve other customers. Second, data loss may also be caused by accidental, e.g., electrical or network failure, or intentional plans, e.g., maintenance or system backup. Moreover, virtual cloud architectures might not be sufficiently safeguarded from inside attacks. Finally, all CSPs cannot guarantee 100% data availability, although some cloud businesses must run on a 7/24 basis. Thus, data privacy, availability and integrity are major issues in cloud data security.

Encrypting and replicating data can solve most of these issues, but existing solutions are greedy in resources such as data storage, memory, CPU and bandwidth. Moreover, cloud data warehouses (DWs) must be both highly protected and effectively refreshed and analyzed through on-line analysis processing (OLAP). Thence, while CSPs must optimize service quality and profit, users seek to reduce storage and access costs within the pay-as-you-go paradigm. Thus, in cloud DWs, the tradeoff between data security and large-scale OLAP analysis poses a great challenge (Chow et al., 2009; Sion, 2007).

To address this challenge, we propose a global approach that relies on a new multi-secret sharing scheme, a family of encryption methods that enforce privacy and availability by design. Moreover, we incorporate in our approach features for data integrity verification and computation on shared data (or shares). Eventually, we minimize shared data volume. This paper expands (Attasena et al., 2013) along three axes. First, we complement the state of the art and deepen our analysis of related works. Second,

Figure 1. Cloud data security issues

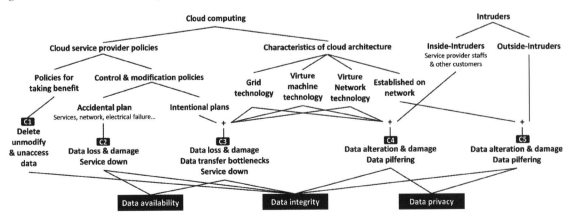

we detail the section related to sharing a DW and specify the way OLAP queries run on shares. Finally, we complement our validation effort with new experiments, especially with the Star Schema Benchmark.

The remainder of this paper is organized as follows. We first introduce and discuss previous research related to our proposal. Based on this diagnosis, we further motivate and position our work. Then, we detail our secret sharing-based approach, before providing a security analysis and performance evaluation that highlight the relevance of our proposal and demonstrates the enhancements it brings over existing methods. We finally conclude this paper and hint at future research perspectives.

2. RELATED WORKS

Existing research solve data privacy, availability and integrity issues by encrypting, anonymizing, replicating or verifying data (Figure 2).

Encryption turns original data into unreadable cipher-text. Modern encryption schemes, such as homomorphic (HE – Melchor et al., 2008; Gentry, 2009) and incremental encryption (Bellare et al., 1994), help perform computations and updates on cipher-texts without decrypting them first. Partially HE allows only one operation, e.g., addition or multiplication, whereas fully HE supports several, but still does not allow mixed-operators. Unfortunately, HE is currently too computationally expensive for practical use. An older, well-known encryption strategy is secret sharing (Asmuth & Bloom, 1983; Blakley, 1979; Shamir, 1979), which distributes individually meaningless shares of data to n participants to enforce privacy. A subset of $t \leq n$ participants is required to reconstruct the secret. Moreover, up to $n-t$ participants may disappear without compromising data availability. The drawback of this solution is the multiplication of the initial data volume by the number of participants. Modern secret sharing schemes, such as multi-secret sharing (Liu et al., 2012; Waseda & Soshi, 2012), verifiable secret sharing (Bu & Zhou, 2009), and verifiable multi-secret sharing (Bu & Yang, 2013; Eslami & Ahmadabadi, 2010; Hu et al., 2012), help reduce the volume of shares, verify the honesty of each participant, and both, respectively.

Data anonymization (Cormode & Srivastava, 2009; Kenneally & Claffy, 2010; Machanavajjhala et al., 2007; Sweeney, 2002) is also used to enforce data privacy. In a database, only keys or sensitive information are protected (Sedeyao, 2012). Thus, data anonymization straightforwardly allows data querying. There are several models (e.g., k-anonymized, l-diversity) and techniques (hashing, hiding, per-

Figure 2. Existing data security solutions

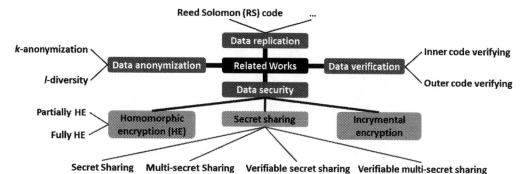

mutation, shift…) to protect keys and sensitive information, respectively. For example, the k-anonymized model transforms k distinguishable records into k indistinguishable records (Sweeney, 2002). The l-diversity model creates l different sensitive values from only one value in each key identification combination (Machanavajjhala et al., 2007). While cheap when accessing data, anonymization is not strong enough to protect against attacks such as homogeneity and background knowledge attacks (Sedeyao, 2012), and is not designed to address data availability and integrity issues.

Data replication (Padmanabhan et al., 2008) is the process of copying some or all data from one location to one or several others. Its main purposes are to improve availability, fault-tolerance and/or accessibility. A well-known data replication scheme is Reed Solomon (RS) code (Thomas & Schwarz, 2002), which is quite similar to secret sharing. RS code indeed distributes data amongst a group of participants and can reconstruct data even if some participants disappear, thus enforcing availability. RS code and secret sharing mostly differ in their driving goals, i.e., availability and privacy, respectively.

Data verification (Bowers et al., 2009; Juels & Kaliski, 2007; Shacham & Waters, 2008; Wang et al., 2009) is the process of checking data integrity, by verifying data corruption caused by either accident or intruder attack, with the help of signatures (digital signature, message authentication, fingerprint…). However, since signature creation typically involves random or hash functions, they cannot guarantee 100% data correctness. Moreover, so-called outer code verifying methods (Juels & Kaliski, 2007) allow checking encrypted data without decrypting them first.

Table 1 summarizes the features of the above security approaches, with respect to data privacy, availability, integrity and full access. No existing approach simultaneously satisfies all criteria.

Eventually, some security solutions directly relate to ours. Most apply Shamir's (1979) classical secret sharing to relational databases or data warehouses (Emekci et al., 2006; Hadavi & Jalili, 2010), thus, enforcing data privacy, availability and updating. In addition, Thompson et al. (2009), Wang et al. (2011) and Hadavi et al. (2012) also support data verification through HE, a hash function, and checksums and a hash function, respectively. Most of these methods allow computing at least one query type (aggregation, range and match queries) on shares.

As in the three last cited approaches (here after denoted TWH for brevity), our strategy is to extend one security scheme presenting interesting characteristics, namely multi-secret sharing, by integrating

Table 1. Comparison of data security solutions

Approaches	Data Privacy	Data Availability	Data Integrity	Data Access
Encryption				
• Homomorphic encryption	√			On encrypted data without decryption.
• Incremental encryption	√			On encrypted data without decryption.
• Secret sharing	√	√		Summing and averaging shares
• Multi-secret sharing	√	√		
• Verifiable secret sharing	√	√	√	
• Verifiable multi-secret sharing	√	√	√	
Data anonymization	√			On non-anonymized data
Data replication(RS code)		√		
Data verification			√	

the missing features needed in cloud DWs. However, in our approach, shared data volume is better controlled than in TWH's, i.e., it is significantly lower than n times that of the original data volume. Moreover, we also incorporate both inner and outer code data verification in our solution, whereas TWH only feature inner code data verification. Finally, we also include capabilities from homomorphic and incremental encryption that allow updating and computing basic operations on shares. Thus, to the best of our knowledge, our multi-secret sharing-based approach is the first attempt at securing data warehousing and OLAP while minimizing data volume.

3. MULTI-SECRET SHARING OF CLOUD DATA WAREHOUSES

The solution we propose is based on trusting neither CSPs nor network data transfers. It is subdivided into two schemes. Scheme-I is a new multi secret sharing scheme that transforms data into blocks (to optimize computing and storage costs), and shares data blocks at several CSPs'. Each CSP only stores part of the shares, which are not exploitable, neither by the CSP nor any intruder, because they have been transformed by a mathematical function. Though performing computations on shares is possible, i.e., data need not be decrypted, it yields meaningless results. It is only when all results are mathematically transformed back at the user's that they can be reconstructed into global, meaningful information. Individual shares and computed results being encrypted, network transfers to and from CSPs are thus safe. Hence, privacy is achieved at any point outside of the user's (network, providers). Finally, to verify the honesty of CSPs and the correctness of shares, we incorporate into Scheme-I two types of hash-based signatures. Signatures help verify data correctness in case some CSPs are not honest, and incorrect or erroneous data before decryption.

However, updating and querying data are still difficult and expensive in Scheme-I, because data pieces are dependent on the others in the same block. Thus, Scheme-II builds upon Scheme-I to actually allow sharing and querying a DW in the cloud. Assuming a DW stored in a relational database, each attribute value in each record is shared independently. We first transform each attribute value to at least one block, depending on data type and size (e.g., one block for integers, reals or characters; and l blocks for strings of length l), and encrypt each data block with Scheme-I. Then, we allow analyzing data over shares with ad-hoc queries and Relational OLAP (ROLAP) operations, without decrypting all data first whenever possible. All basic OLAP operations (roll-up, drill-down, some slice and dice, pivot and drill-across) can apply directly on shares at the CSPs', with results being reconstructed at the user's. However, other complex queries must be transformed or split first, depending on operations and functions used.

3.1. Scheme-I: (m, n, t) Multi-Secret Sharing With Data Verification

Scheme-I is an (m, n, t) multi-secret sharing scheme: m data pieces are encrypted and shared among n CSPs. t out of n shares can reconstruct the original data. The total volume of shares is only about $mn / (t-1)$. Data are organized into blocks that are encrypted and decrypted all at once. The priorities of blocks and data in the blocks are important because they directly affect the results of data access in Scheme-II. All data pieces in a block are encrypted at once by n distinct random t-variable linear equations, where variables are data and their signatures and coefficients are pseudorandom. Eventually, we introduce two types of signatures. The first, inner signature is created from all data pieces in one block. It matches with data in the reconstruction process if CSPs return correct shares. The second, outer signature is created from each share. At each CSP's, it verifies shares before transferring them back to the user for reconstruction.

Parameters of Scheme-I are listed in Table 2. $ID_{i=1..m}$ are randomly selected from distinct integers and are stored at the user's. D is split into o blocks with $o = \dfrac{m}{t-1}$. If m is not a multiple of $t-1$, the last block is padded with integer values -1 (Figure 3).

Table 2. Scheme-I parameters

Parameters	Definitions
n	Number of CSPs
CSP_k	CSP number k
m	Number of data pieces
o	Number of data blocks
t	Number of shares necessary for reconstructing original data
P	A big prime number
D	Original data such that $D = \left\{ d_1, \ldots, d_m \right\}$ and $D = \left\{ b_1, \ldots, b_o \right\}$.
d_i	The ith piece of D. in integer format such that $P - 2 > d_i \geq 0$.
b_j	The jth block of D such that $b_j = \left\{ d_{(j-1)(t-1)}, \ldots, d_{(j)(t-1)} \right\}$
ID_k	Identifier number of CSP_k such that $ID_k > 0$
$e_{j,k}$	Share of b_j stored at CSP_k
s_in_j	Signature of original data in b_j such that $P > s\_in_j \geq 0$
$s\_out_{j,k}$	Signature of share of b_j stored at CSP_k

Figure 3. Organization of data in blocks

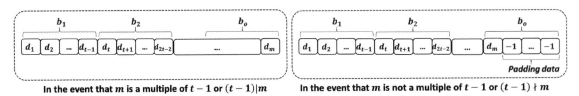

In the event that m is a multiple of $t-1$ or $(t-1)|m$ **In the event that m is not a multiple of $t-1$ or $(t-1) \nmid m$**

3.1.1. Data Sharing Process

Each data block is encrypted independently (Figure 4). Data pieces in block b_j are encrypted as follows.

1. Compute signature s_in_j from data block b_j with homomorphic function H_1: $s\_in_j = H_1(b_j)$.
2. Create n distinct random $t-1$ linear equations (Equation 1).

$$y = f_k(x_1, \cdots, x_t) = \left(\sum_{h=1}^{t-1} (x_h + 2) \times a_{k,h} \right) + (x_t \times a_{k,t}) \tag{1}$$

where x_i is positive variable, a_{kh} is the hth positive pseudorandom coefficient seeded at ID_k, $P > a_{k,h} \geq 0$ and $f_{k1} \neq f_{k2}$ if $k1 \neq k2$. These functions are used for all blocks.

3. Compute the set of shares $\{e_{j,k}\}_{k=1\ldots n}$ from data block b_j such that $e_{j,k} = f_k(b_j, s\_in_j)$, and distribute each share $e_{j,k}$ to CSP_k.
4. Compute signatures $\{s\_out_{j,k}\}_{k=1\ldots n}$ with hash function H_2 such that $s\_out_{j,k} = H_2(e_{j,k})$, and distribute each signature $s\_out_{j,k}$ to CSP_k along with $e_{j,k}$.

Thus, data and their signatures are shared among n CSPs. CSP_k stores o pairs of shares and signatures $\left((e_{j,k}, s\_out_{j,k})_{j=1\ldots o} \right)$.

Figure 4. Data sharing process

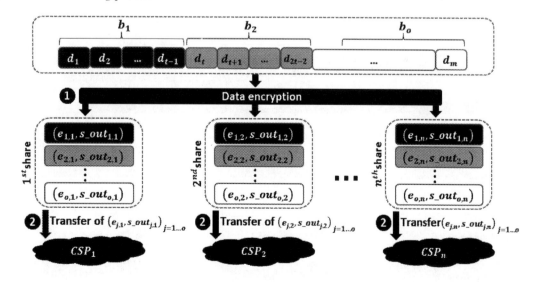

3.1.2. Data Reconstruction Process

A dataset D is reconstructed from shares and signatures $\left(e_{j,k}, s\_out_{j,k}\right)_{j=1...o}$ stored at $CSP_k \in G$, where G is any group of t CSPs (Figure 5). There are two phases to reconstruct original data: the initialization phase and the actual reconstruction phase.

Initialization phase: In this phase, share correctness is verified and a matrix C that is used in the reconstruction phase is created as follows.

1. Verify information at all $CSP_k \in G$. At each CSP's, only shares to be decrypted are verified for correctness. Share $e_{j,k}$ is correct if $s\_out_{j,k} = H_2\left(e_{j,k}\right)$. In case of error at CSP_k, then another CSP is selected and correctness is verified again.

2. At the user's, matrix A is created from ID_k of $CSP_k \in G$ such that $A = \left[a_{x,y}\right]_{t \times t}$, where $a_{x,y}$ is the yth coefficient of f_x. Then, C is computed such that $C = A^{-1}$. Let $c_{x,y}$ be an entry in the xth row and the yth column of matrix C.

Reconstruction phase: To decrypt data block b_j, share $e_{j,k}$ of $CSP_k \in G$ is transferred to the user and decrypted as follows.

1. Compute data block b_j. (Equation 2) and its signature s_in_j (Equation 3).

$$d_{(j-1)(t-1)+l} = \left(\sum_{h=1}^{t} c_{l,h} \times e_{j,h}\right) - 2; \forall [1, t-1] \tag{2}$$

Figure 5. Data reconstruction process

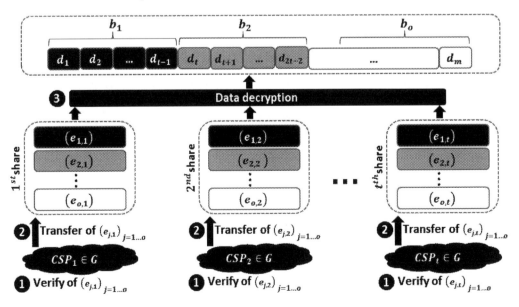

$$s\_in_j = \sum_{h=1}^{t} c_{t,h} \times e_{j,h} \tag{3}$$

2. If $s\_in_j = H_1(b_j)$, then data in block b_j are correct. In case of errors, the user can reconstruct data from shares from a new G.

3.2. Scheme-II: Sharing a Data Warehouse in the Cloud

In this section, we exploit Scheme-I to share a DW among CSPs. Databases attribute values, except NULL values and primary or foreign keys, are shared in relational databases at CSPs'. Keys help match records in the data reconstruction process and perform JOIN and GROUP BY operations. Any sensitive primary key, such as a social security number, is replaced by an unencrypted sequential integer key. Each attribute in the original tables is transformed into two attributes in encrypted tables, i.e., share and signature attributes. Figure 6 shows the example of a PRODUCT table that is shared amo three CSPs. To handle data from a shared DW, we propose solutions to encrypt data of various types, to share the customary DW logical models in the cloud, to perform loading, backup and recovery processes, and to analyze shared data through ROLAP operations.

3.2.1. Data Types

To handle the usual data types featured in databases, we encrypt and handle each data piece independently. Data pieces of any type are first transformed into integers, then split into one or several data blocks (depending on type and value), and finally encrypted with Scheme-I.

For sharing an integer, date or timestamp I, I is split into $t-1$ pieces $d_{i=1...(t-1)}$ such that $d_i = \dfrac{I}{p^{i-1}} \bmod p$, where p is a prime number and $p > \dfrac{maxint}{t-1}$ bits, where *maxint* is the size of the maximum integer value in bits. Then, $d_{i=1...(t-1)}$ is encrypted to n shares with Scheme-I.

Figure 6. Example of original data and shares at three CSPs'

ProdNo	ProName	ProdDescr	CategoryID	UnitPrice
124	Shirt	Red	1	75
125	Shoe	NULL	2	80

(a) Original data

ProdNo	ProName	SigPN	ProdDescr	SigPD	CategoryID	UnitPrice	SigUP
124	{29,18,21,22,28}	{1,4,0,1,0}	{26,20,17}	{5,6,3}	1	16	2
125	{29,18,13,20}	{1,4,6,6}	NULL	NULL	2	20	6

(b) Shares at $C\,S\,P$

ProdNo	ProName	SigPN	ProdDescr	SigPD	CategoryID	UnitPrice	SigUP
124	{29,16,19,46,52}	{1,2,5,4,3}	{26,45,42}	{5,3,0}	1	43	1
125	{29,16,37,45}	{1,2,2,3}	NULL	NULL	2	20	6

(c) Shares at $C\,S\,P$

ProdNo	ProName	SigPN	ProdDescr	SigPD	CategoryID	UnitPrice	SigUP
124	{33,22,25,39,45}	{5,1,4,4,3}	{30,37,34}	{2,2,6}	1	33	5
125	{33,22,30,37}	{5,1,2,2}	NULL	NULL	2	24	3

(d) Shares at $C\,S\,P$

For sharing a real R, R is transformed into an integer I by multiplication. For example, let R be stored in numeric format (v, s)., where v is a precision value and s a scale value. Then, R is transformed into $I = R \times 10^{|s|}$. I can then be encrypted as any integer.

For sharing a character L, L is transformed into an integer I through its ASCII code. For example, let L be 'A'. L is transformed into $I = 65$. I can then be encrypted as any integer.

For sharing a string S, S is transformed into a set of integers $\{I_j\}_{j=1...l}$ where l is the length of S, using the ASCII code of each character in S. For example, let S be 'ABC'. Then, S is transformed into $\{I_j\}_{j=1...3} = \{65, 66, 67\}$. After transformation, each character I_j is encrypted independently as any integer.

For sharing a binary string B, B is transformed into a set of integers $\{I_j\}_{j=1...\frac{l}{maxint}}$ where l is the length of B and $maxint$ is the size of the maximum integer value in bits. For example, let B=1000000 00000000000000000000000011 and $maxint = 32$ bits. Then B is split into two smaller binaries: 10 and 00000000000000000000000000000011 sizing less than $maxint$, which are then transformed into $\{I_j\}_{j=1,2} = \{2, 3\}$. After transformation, each I_j is encrypted independently as any integer.

Example of sharing an integer I follows.

1. Sharing parameters are assigned as follows: $n = 4$, $t = 3$ and $p = 13$.

2. Homomorphic and hash functions are $H_1(b_j) = \sum_{d_i \in b_j} d_i \pmod p$ and $H_2(e_{j,k}) = e_{j,k} \bmod 13$.

3. Let $I = 75$, i.e., the shirt's unit price in Figure 6(a).

4. We compute $d_{i=1,2}$ as follows: $d_1 = \dfrac{75}{13^{1-1}} \bmod 13 = 10$ and $d_2 = \dfrac{75}{13^{2-1}} \bmod 13 = 5$.

5. We compute $s\_in_1 = H_1(b_1) = (10 + 5) \bmod 13 = 2$.

6. Let four random 3-variable linear equations be:

   a. $y = f_1(x_1, x_2, x_3) = 1 \times (x_1 + 2) + 0 \times (x_2 + 2) + 2 \times x_3$,

   b. $y = f_2(x_1, x_2, x_3) = 3 \times (x_1 + 2) + 1 \times (x_2 + 2) + 0 \times x_3$,

   c. $y = f_3(x_1, x_2, x_3) = 2 \times (x_1 + 2) + 1 \times (x_2 + 2) + 1 \times x_3$.,

   d. $y = f_4(x_1, x_2, x_3) = 0 \times (x_1 + 2) + 2 \times (x_2 + 2) + 1 \times x_3$.

7. We compute $e_{1,k=1...4}$ such that

$$e_{1,1} = f_1(10, 5, 2) = 1 \times (10 + 2) + 0 \times (5 + 2) + 2 \times 2 = 16.$$

Similarly, $e_{1,2} = 43$, $e_{1,3} = 33$ and $e_{1,4} = 14$.

8. We compute $s\_out_{1,k=1...4}$ such that $s\_out_{1,1} = H_2(16) = 16 \bmod 7 = 2$. Similarly, $s\_out_{1,2} = 1$, $s\_out_{1,3} = 5$ and $s\_out_{1,4} = 0$.

9. We distribute each couple $(e_{1,k}, s\_out_{1,k})$ to CSP_k.

Then, I is reconstructed as follows.

1. Suppose CSP_1, CSP_2 and CSP_3 are selected into G.

2. We verify $s\_out'_{1,j=1,2,3}$ such that $s\_out'_{1,1} = H_2(16) = 16 \bmod 7 = 2 = s\_out_{1,1}$. Then $e_{1,1}$ is correct. After verification, all three shares $\{e_{1,1}, e_{1,2}, e_{1,3}\}$ are found correct.

3. We create matrix A from $ID_{i=1,2,3}$: $A = \begin{bmatrix} 1 & 0 & 2 \\ 3 & 1 & 0 \\ 2 & 1 & 1 \end{bmatrix}$.

4. We compute matrix $C = A^{-1} \bmod P = \dfrac{\begin{bmatrix} 1 & 2 & -2 \\ -3 & -3 & 6 \\ 1 & -1 & 1 \end{bmatrix}}{3}$

5. We compute $d_{i=1,2}$ as follows.

   a. $d_1 = \left((16 \times 1 + 43 \times 2 + 33 \times -2)/3\right) - 2 = 10$.

   b. $d_2 = \left((16 \times -3 + 43 \times -3 + 33 \times 6)/3\right) - 2 = 5$.

6. We compute $s\_in_1 = (16 \times 1 + 43 \times -1 + 33 \times 1)/3 = 2$..

7. We verify the original data. The result is correct since $s\_in'_1 = H_1(b_1) = (10+5)\bmod 13 = 2 = s\_in_1$.

3.2.2. Data Warehouse Sharing

Since each table of a shared DW is stored in a relational database at a given CSP's and each attribute value in each record is encrypted independently, Scheme-II straightforwardly helps implement any DW logical model, i.e., star, snowflake or constellation schema. Figures 7(a) and 7(b) show an example of snowflake-modeled DW that is shared among three CSPs. Each shared DW bears the same schema as the original DW's, but type and size of each attribute in each shared table differ from the original tables. All attribute types, except Booleans that are not encrypted to save computation and data storage costs, are indeed transformed into integers.

Moreover, Scheme-II supports the storage of data cubes that optimize response time and bandwidth when performing ROLAP operations. Cubes are physically stored into tables that are shared among CSPs, retaining the same structure. For example, Figure 7(c) features a shared cube named cube-I that totalizes total prices and numbers of sales by time period and by product. Shared cubes include signatures for shared aggregate measures and customarily use NULL values to encode superaggregates. Finally, indices can also be shared to improve query performance. However, they must be created from the original data before the sharing process. We envisage lazy index creation on shares in future research, though.

3.2.3. Loading, Backup and Recovery Processes

For loading data into a shared DW, each data piece is encrypted and loaded independently. New data can be loaded without decrypting previous data first, because each attribute value in each record is encrypted independently. For instance, in Figure 8, data from Figure 6 are already shared and the last record (#126) is new.

Figure 7. Example of shared data warehouse and cube

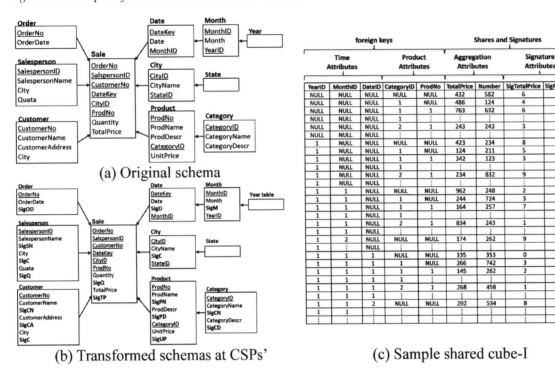

(a) Original schema

(b) Transformed schemas at CSPs'

(c) Sample shared cube-I

Figure 8. Example of sharing new data

ProdNo	ProName	ProdDescr	CategoryID	UnitPrice
124	Shirt	Red	1	75
125	Shoe	*NULL*	2	80
126	Ring	*NULL*	1	80

(a) Original data

ProdNo	ProName	SigPN	ProdDescr	SigPD	CategoryID	UnitPrice	SigUP
124	{29,18,21,22,28}	{1,4,0,1,0}	{26,20,17}	{5,6,3}	1	16	2
125	{29,18,13,20}	{1,4,6,6}	*NULL*	*NULL*	2	20	6
126	{26,21,10,26}	{5,0,3,5}	*NULL*	*NULL*	1	20	6

(b) Shares at $C\ S\ P$

ProdNo	ProName	SigPN	ProdDescr	SigPD	CategoryID	UnitPrice	SigUP
124	{29,16,19,46,52}	{1,2,5,4,3}	{26,45,42}	{5,3,0}	1	43	1
125	{29,16,37,45}	{1,2,2,3}	*NULL*	*NULL*	2	20	6
126	{26,19,34,51}	{5,5,6,2}	*NULL*	*NULL*	1	20	6

(c) Shares at $C\ S\ P$

ProdNo	ProName	SigPN	ProdDescr	SigPD	CategoryID	UnitPrice	SigUP
124	{33,22,25,39,45}	{5,1,4,4,3}	{30,37,34}	{2,2,6}	1	33	5
125	{33,22,30,37}	{5,1,2,2}	*NULL*	*NULL*	2	24	3
126	{30,25,27,43}	{2,4,6,1}	*NULL*	*NULL*	1	24	3

(d) Shares at $C\ S\ P$

However, when updating cubes, some shared aggregates may have to be recomputed. Within Scheme-II, we currently cannot apply all aggregation operations on shares. Thus, such aggregations still require to be computed on the original data. For example, maximum and minimum cannot be computed on shares because original data order is lost in the sharing process. Averaging data must be performed by summing and counting. Hence, to optimize costs, aggregates are first computed on new data, and then aggregated to relevant existing shares, which are decrypted on-the-fly.

Finally, a backup process is unnecessary in our scheme, because each share $e_{j,l}$ is actually a backup share of all other shares $e_{j,k}$, where $k \in \{1,...,l-1,l+1,...,n\}$. In case a share is erroneous, it can be recovered from t other shares.

3.2.4. Data Analysis Over Shares

Since DWs and cubes can be shared in the cloud, Scheme-II directly supports all basic OLAP operations at the CSPs' through SQL operators and aggregation functions, and helps reconstruct the result on the user's side by performing queries on shared tables. For example, query "select YearID, YearName, TotalPrice from cube-I, year where cube-I.YearID=year.YearID and MonthID=null and DateID=null and CategoryID=null and ProdNo=null" can be run at t CSPs to compute the total price of products per year.

However, although some queries apply directly onto shares, others require some or all data to be decrypted. Simple SELECT/FROM queries directly apply onto shares. All join operators, when operating on unencrypted keys, also apply directly. However, when expressing conditions in a WHERE or HAVING clause, the following routine must be followed:

1. Encrypt compared values,
2. Substitute these shares to compared values in the query,
3. Launch the query on t shares,
4. Decrypt the t results,
5. Reconstruct the global result by intersection.

For example, the query "SELECT ProdName FROM Product WHERE UnitPrice=75" would be transformed to "SELECT ProdName FROM Product WHERE UnitPrice=16" at CSP_1, where 16 is the share of 75 at CSP_1.

This routine works for many comparison operators (=, $\neq$, EXISTS, IN, LIKE…) and their conjunction, but when ordering is necessary, as in ORDER BY clauses and many comparison operators (>, <, $\geq$, $\leq$, BETWEEN…), it can no longer apply since the original order is broken when sharing data. Thus, all fetched data must be reconstructed at the client's before the result can be computed by an external program. However, some range queries can be transformed and performed on shares if comparison range is known and comparison attribute type is integer, char or string. For example, the query "SELECT ProdName FROM Product WHERE UnitPrice between 75 and 77" would be transformed to "SELECT ProdName FROM Product WHERE UnitPrice IN (16, 19, 22)" at CSP_1, where 16, 19 and 22 are the shares of 75, 76 and 77 at CSP_1., respectively.

Similarly, aggregation functions SUM, AVG and COUNT can directly apply on shares, whereas other aggregation functions, such as MAX and MIN, require all original data to be reconstructed prior to computation. Finally, grouping queries using the GROUP BY or GROUP BY CUBE clauses can directly apply if and only if they target unencrypted key attributes. Again, grouping by other attribute(s) requires all data to be reconstructed at the user's before aggregation by an external program.

Consequently, executing a complex query may require either transforming or splitting the query, depending on its clauses and operators, following the above guidelines. Figure 9 shows an example of complex query execution.

4. SECURITY ANALYSIS AND PERFORMANCE EVALUATION

In this section, we illustrate the relevance of our approach along two axes. First, we mainly theoretically study the security features of our schemes, which are our primary focus. Second, since our approach applies in the cloud, we both theoretically and experimentally study the factors that influence cost in the pay-as-you-go paradigm, i.e., computing, storage and data transfer costs, with respect to the TWH secret sharing schemes.

4.1. Security Analysis

4.1.1. Privacy

We focus here on data pilfering. Neither a CSP nor any intruder can decrypt original data from only one share, and data transferred between the user and CSPs are all encrypted. In case an intruder can steal shares from x CSPs with $x \leq t$, the probability of discovering b_j (the original data in the jth block) remains low, i.e., $\dfrac{1}{P^{2t-x-1}}$ and $\dfrac{1}{p^{2t-x-1}}$ in Scheme-I and Scheme-II, respectively (Figure 10). The probability of discovering b_j depends on the following.

Figure 9. Example of complex query execution over shares

Owner

Original query:
select Product.ProdName, count(Fact.TotalPrice)
from Fact right join Product
on Fact.ProdNo=Product.ProdNo
group by Product.ProdNo
where Product.UnitPrice = 75

1. 75 is encrypted into {16,43,33}
2. Query-I is created to perform at each CSP's
   Query-I: *select ProdNo , ProdName from Product*
   where UnitPrice=#encrypted value of 75#

5. Result is the intersection / CSPs.
   Only one row is returned.
6. {29,18,21,22,28}, {29,16,19,46,52}, and {33,22,25,39,45} are reconstructed to "Shirt"
7. Query-II is created to perform at each CSP's
   Query-I: *select Product.ProdNo, count(TotalPrice)*
   from Fact left join Product
   on Fact.ProdNo=Product.ProdNo
   group by Product.ProdNo
   where Product.ProdNo IN (124)

10. By Query-I and Query-II, result is "Shirt, 1".

CSP_1

3. Running Query-I: *select ProdNo , ProdName from Product where UnitPrice=16*
4. Result is {124, {29,18,21,22,28}}

8. Running Query-II
9. Result is {124, 1}

CSP_2

3. Running Query-I: select *ProdNo , ProdName from Product where UnitPrice=43*
4. Result is {124, {29,16,19,46,52}}

8. Running Query-II
9. Result is {124, 1}

CSP_3

3. Running Query-I: *select ProdNo , ProdName from Product where UnitPrice=33*
4. Result is {124, {33,22,25,39,45}}

8. Running Query-II
9. Result is {124, 1}

Figure 10. Probability of decrypting a data block from its shares

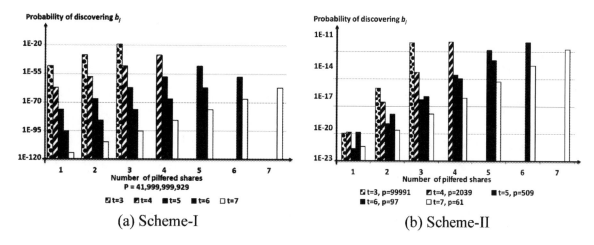

(a) Scheme-I   (b) Scheme-II

1. The size of control parameters P in Scheme-I and p in Scheme-II. In Scheme-I, the probability of breaking the secret is low because P is a big prime number. In Scheme-II, the probability of breaking the secret ranges between 10^{-22} and 10^{-10} in Figure 10's example, because p depends on t. If $p = P$, the probabilities of breaking the secret are equal in both schemes, but storage cost in Scheme-II is not controlled, which falls back to Shamir's (1979) case.

2. The user-defined value of t. The higher t, the lower the probability of breaking the secret.

3. The number of pilfered shares x. The probability of breaking the secret obviously increases with *x*. However, both our schemes are secure enough since it is difficult to retrieve shares from at least t CSPs by attacking them simultaneously.

Within Scheme-II, although some data can be decrypted, if an intruder steals all data from one CSP, s/he must discover the pattern of data blocks and generate all p^{t-1} combinations of data pieces stored at the $t-1$ other CSPs' by brute force. The complexity of Scheme-II's reconstructing process is $O\left(mt^2\right)$, since the $t \times t$ C matrix must be computed for m data pieces. Thus, with $p = 99,991$, $t = 3$ and $m = 100$ (11 KB of data), breaking the secret with a standard desktop computer would take more than 13 years. Thence, even with a botnet available, even partially decrypting a giga or terabyte-scale DW cannot be achieved in reasonable time.

4.1.2. Reliability

Reliability includes data availability and recovery, which are achieved by design with secret sharing, and data integrity and correctness. Our schemes can verify both the honesty of CSPs and the correctness of shares. Verification performance depends on the user-defined hash functions that define inner and outer signatures.

To test the reliability of our signatures, we generate random 32-bits unsigned integers and share them. Then, we generate errors in all shares with respect to a given pattern. Finally, we account the number of incorrect data pieces that are not detected as such. Figure 11 plots the ratio of false positives achieved with inner signature $s\_in_j = \sum_{d_i \in b_j} d_i \left(\bmod\ p\right)$ and outer signature $s\_out_{j,k} = e_{j,k} \bmod p_2$, where p_2 is a

Figure 11. Rate of incorrect data not being detected

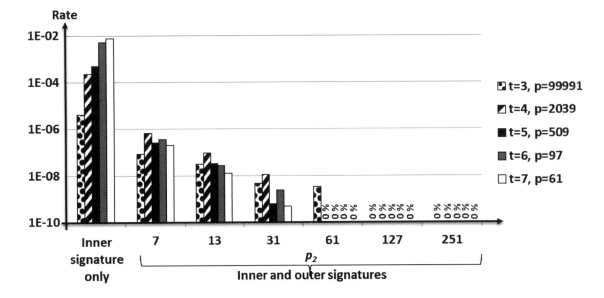

prime. If only the inner signature is used to verify data, i.e., only the honesty of CSPs is verified, the ratio ranges between 7.7E-6% and 3.2E-2%, inversely depending on p. However, all incorrect data pieces can be detected if data are verified by both inner and outer signatures (i.e., share correctness is also verified) and $p_2 > 61$.

Finally, note that sharing data on one node is a surjective function, i.e., two different initial values may have the same share value. However, since the reconstruction process is achieved by intersection from all nodes, sharing data is overall a bijective function. Thus, querying shares always results in a 100% hit rate.

4.2. Cost Analysis

In this section, we provide a cost analysis of the main factors inducing costs when storing a DW in the cloud. For this sake, in addition to theoretical considerations, we run two series of experiments. In the first series of experiments, we run 100 1 GB test cases made of 32-bits unsigned integers and vary parameters t, n and p. In the second series of experiments, we use the Star Schema Benchmark (SSB – O'Neil et al., 2009) and vary parameter p with $t = 3$ and $n = 4$. Experiments are conducted with Bloodshed Dev-C++ 5.5.3 and MySQL 5.0.51a on a PC with an Intel(R) Core(TM) i5 2.76 GHz processor with 3 GB of RAM running Microsoft Windows 7.

4.2.1. Computing Cost

The time complexity of Scheme-I's data sharing process is $O(ont)$, since n t-variable linear equations must be computed for o data blocks. Moreover, since $m = o(t-1)$, complexity can also be expressed as $O(mn)$. The time complexity of Scheme-II's data sharing process is also $O(ont)$, or $O(mnt)$ since $m = o$ here.

The time complexity of Scheme-I's data reconstruction process is $O(mt)$ or $O(ot^2)$, since the $t \times t$ C matrix must be computed for o data blocks and $o = \dfrac{m}{t-1}$. Scheme-II's is $O(mt^2)$ or $O(ot^2)$, since C must be computed for o data blocks and $o = m$.

For example, the execution time of sharing and reconstructing 32-bits unsigned integers with Scheme-II is plotted in Figure 12 with respect to t and n. The execution time of both processes increase with t when $t = n$. The execution time of the sharing process increases with n when t is fixed, whereas n does not affect reconstruction. For instance, the execution time of the data sharing and reconstruction processes are about 15 seconds (throughput is 68 MB/s) and 7 seconds (throughput is 144 MB/s) when $n = t = 3$ and $p = 99991$.

To evaluate the performance of data analysis on shares more accurately, we measure the execution time of SSB's OLAP query workload (Table 3). Quite unexpectedly, query execution is faster on shares than on the original DW. But this is because we run plain SSB queries on the original DW and MySQL does not optimize joins natively. When executing the same query on shares, we have to split the original queries and process subqueries before joining, thus implicitly optimizing join dimensionality. Query response on shares appears reasonable, though it could be further enhanced through shared indices and materialized views.

4.2.2. Storage Cost

One advantage of our schemes is that the volume of shares nears that of original data when $n = t$, t is big, and P in Scheme-I and p in Scheme-II are small. Shared data volume is only $on|P|$ in Scheme-I and $on|p|$ in Scheme-II, where $|P|$ and $|p|$ are sizes of P and p, respectively. For example, with Scheme-II, let us consider a set D of ten 32-bits unsigned integers that is shared among six CSPs, with five CSPs being sufficient to reconstruct D. The volume of D is $10 \times 32 = 320$ bits. Let $p = 9$ bits. Then, the volume of all shares is lower than $10 \times 6 \times 9 = 540$ bits ($1.69 \times D$). The volume of each share is about $10 \times 9 = 90$ bits ($0.17 \times D$).

The volume of our shared 32-bit unsigned integer dataset using Scheme-II is plotted in Figure 13. The volume of each share varies with respect to n, t and p. The volume of all shares ranges between

Figure 12. Execution time of scheme-II

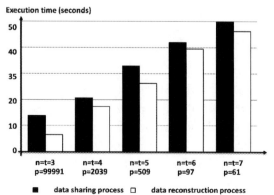

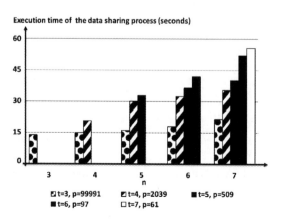

Table 3. OLAP performance with SSB

SSB Query	Query Response Time (seconds)		Query Result Size	
	Original Query	Scheme-II Query	Original Query (Bytes)	Scheme-II Query (KB)
Q.1.1	8	10	12	7,751
Q.1.2	4	4	11	176
Q.1.3	3	4	11	32
Q.2.1	80	25	6,097	930
Q.2.2	80	7	1,232	388
Q.2.3	80	4	1,232	28
Q.3.1	78	49	2,460	16,343
Q.3.2	66	8	14,400	864
Q.3.3	64	5	567	25
Q.3.4	64	4	72	5
Q.4.1	80	54	756	13614
Q.4.2	81	36	2,760	3531
Q.4.3	66	5	9,936	11
Average	**58**	**17**	**3,042**	**3,361**

Figure 13. Shared data volume

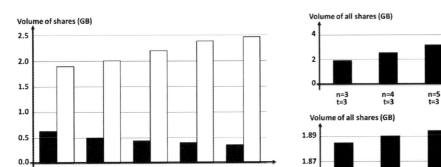

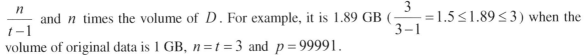

$\dfrac{n}{t-1}$ and n times the volume of D. For example, it is 1.89 GB ($\dfrac{3}{3-1} = 1.5 \leq 1.89 \leq 3$) when the volume of original data is 1 GB, $n = t = 3$ and $p = 99991$.

Finally, Table 4 shows the volume of SSB's DW, once shared with Scheme-II. The volume of each share is still smaller than that of the original DW (about 46% smaller). Therefore, this guarantees any shared DW can be stored and queried if the original DW can. If data volume is very large, a higher-performance DBMS can be envisaged, e.g., a parallel DBMS or low-level distributed storage. Although, the volume of all shares is greater than that of original data (about 185% greater), it is smaller than twice that of original data. Shared volume may be reduced to about 139% of original data if the data availability constraint is relaxed, though.

4.2.3. Data Transfer Cost

In our context, data transfer cost only relates to the size of query results, since uploads are generally free of charge at major CSPs'. SSB query result size is shown in Table 3. Since many queries do not need to decrypt data, only some parts of the shared DW are transferred when executing SSB's workload. Thus, the transferred data volume is greater than the volume of each query result, but lower than that of all shares. For example, query Q.1.3 ran on shares outputs 32 KB, which is greater the actual result size (11 bytes) but much lower than the volume of all shares (1.5 GB), thus incurring reasonable transfer costs.

4.3. Comparison of Scheme-II to Existing Related Approaches

In this section, we compare Scheme-II to the TWH approaches presented in our state of the art, with respect to security and cost. Table 5 synthesizes the features and costs of all approaches, which we discuss below.

4.3.1. Security

All approaches handle data security, availability and integrity issues, but only ours verifies both the correctness of shares and the honesty of CSPs by outer and inner code verification, respectively.

4.3.2. Computing Cost

The time complexity of Scheme-II's sharing process is equal to TH's and better than W's because m is normally much bigger than n and t. Thence, $m \log m > mnt > mn$. However, in the context of DWs, where updates are performed off-line, update performance is not as critical as in transactional databases.

The time complexity of Scheme-II's reconstructing process is again equal to TH's and better than W's. Since data decryption is part of query response time, it is critical in a DW context. However, shared data access is also part of query response time. In this regard, our approach is faster than TWH, because we can directly query shared tables, whereas TWH must perform ad-hoc queries, aggregate and reconstruct data to achieve the same result. For instance, W cannot perform any aggregation operation on shares. Thence, many shares are transferred back to the user for aggregation.

Table 4. SSB shared data warehouse volume achieved with Scheme-II

Table	Original SSB Volume (KB)	1st Share Volume (KB)	%[1]	2nd Share Volume (KB)	%[1]	3th Share Volume (KB)	%[1]	4th Share Volume (KB)	%[1]	All Shares Volume (KB)	%[1]
Customer	3,167	2,550	80.52	2,550	80.52	2,550	80.52	2,550	80.52	10,200	322.07
Date	218	205	94.04	205	94.04	205	94.04	205	94.04	820	376.15
Part	18,798	14,940	79.48	14,940	79.48	14,940	79.48	14,940	79.48	59,760	317.91
Supplier	965	768	79.59	758	78.55	758	78.55	758	78.55	3,042	315.23
Lineorder	822,929	373,610	45.40	373,610	45.40	373,610	45.40	373,610	45.40	1,494,440	181.60
All tables	846,077	392,073	46.34	392,063	46.34	392,063	46.34	392,063	46.34	1,568,262	185.36

[1]Percentage of original data volume.

Table 5. Comparison of database sharing approaches

Features and Costs	Thompson et al. (2009)	Wang et al. (2011)	Hadavi et al. (2012)	Scheme-II
Privacy	Yes	Yes	Yes	Yes
Data availability	Yes	Yes	Yes	Yes
Data integrity				
- Inner code verifying	Yes	Yes	Yes	Yes
- Outer code verifying	No	No	No	Yes
Target	Databases	Databases	Databases	Data warehouses
Data types	Positive integers	Positive integers	Positive integers	Integers, Reals, Characters, Strings, Dates, Booleans
Shared data access				
- Data updates	Yes	Yes	Yes	Yes
- Exact match queries	No	Yes	Yes	Yes
- Range queries	No	Yes	Yes	No
- Aggregation functions	Yes	No	Yes	Yes
- OLAP queries	No	No	No	Yes
Costs				
- Data storage w.r.t. original data volume	$\geq 2n + 1$ (hash tree)	$\geq n/t + n/t$ (B++ tree index) + signatures	$\geq n + 1$ (B++ tree index)	$\geq n/(t-1)$ + signatures
- Sharing process execution time	$O(mnt)$	$O(\max(m\log m, mn))$	$O(mnt)$	$O(mnt)$
- Reconstructing process execution time	$O(mt^2)$	$O(mt)$	$O(mt^2)$	$O(mt^2)$

4.3.3. Storage Cost

In addition to the storage estimations provided in Table 5, let us illustrate the storage gain achieved with our approach through an example. Let $n = 4$, $t = 3$ and V be the original data volume. Let us also assume that each share is not bigger than the original data it encrypts. For simplicity, let us finally disregard the volume of signatures that depends on user-defined parameters in all approaches. The result is shown in Table 6, with column *Improvement* displaying the storage gain achieved by Scheme-II over TWH.

4.3.4. Data Transfer Cost

Data transfer cost directly relates to the size of shares when loading data, and to the size of query results when accessing the shared database. Since all approaches allow different operations and vary in shared data volume, it is difficult to compare data transfer costs by proof. However, data transfer cost in our approach is cheaper in the sharing phase because the size of each encrypted data piece is $1/(t-1)$ smaller than that of TWH. Moreover, by creating shared data cubes, we allow straight computations on shares, and thus only target results are transferred to the user, i.e., with no additional data to decrypt at the user's.

Table 6. Comparison shared data volume in scheme-II and TWH

Approach	Shared data volume	Scope	Improvement
Scheme-II	$\dfrac{n}{(t-1)}V = \dfrac{4}{(3-1)}V = 2V$	Shares	0%
T	$2nV = 2 \times 4 \times V = 8V$	Shares	300%
W	$\dfrac{n}{t}V + \dfrac{n}{t}V = \dfrac{2n}{t}V = \dfrac{2 \times 4}{3}V = 2.67V$	Shares and indices	33%
H	$nV + V = (n+1)V = (4+1) \times V = 5V$	Shares and indices	150%

5. CONCLUSION

In this paper, we propose an original approach to share a DW in the cloud that simultaneously supports data privacy, availability, integrity and OLAP querying. Our approach is constituted of two schemes. Scheme-I exploits block cryptography and secret sharing to protect data and guarantee data privacy and availability. Moreover, Scheme-I ensures data correctness by utilizing homomorphic and hash functions as signatures. Scheme-II builds upon Scheme-I to allow sharing and querying cloud DWs. It allows analyzing data over shares without decrypting all data first. Our security and performance analysis shows that our schemes are more robust and cheaper than similar existing techniques when storing and querying data.

Future research shall run along two axes. First, we plan to further assess the cost of our solution in the cloud pay-as-you-go paradigm. Sharing data indeed implies increasing the initial data volume, and thus storage cost, as well as duplicating computing costs over CSPs. However, it also guarantees data availability. Hence, we plan to run monetary cost evaluations against classical data replication schemes. It would also be very interesting to balance the cost of our solution against the cost of risking data loss or theft. Moreover, parameter assignment affects the security of our schemes. Notably, to enforce security, big values should be assigned to primes P, p and number of CSPs needed to decrypt data t. In contrast, small values should be assigned to P, p, n and t to reduce execution time and data volume. Thus, a suitable tradeoff must be investigated.

Second, although we provide in this paper a raw framework for OLAPing shared data, more research is required to implement all operations needed in OLAP analyses, as well as incremental updates. We notably plan to reuse the strategies of Wang et al. (2011) and Hadavi et al. (2012) to achieve range and match queries, e.g., by implementing shared B+ tree indices.

REFERENCES

Asmuth, C., & Bloom, J. (1983). A modular Approach to Key Safeguarding. *IEEE Transactions on Information Theory, 29*(2), 208–210. doi:10.1109/TIT.1983.1056651

Attasena, V., Harbi, N., & Darmont, J. (2013) Sharing-based Privacy and Availability of Cloud Data Warehouses. 9th French-speaking days on Data Warehouse and On-line Analysis (EDA 2013), Blois, France: RNTI, B-9.17-32.

Bellare, M., Goldreich, O., & Goldwasser, S. (1994). Incremental Cryptography: The Case of Hashing and Signing. *Advances in Cryptology (CRYPTO'94). LNCS, 839*, 216–233.

Blakley, G. R. (1979). Safeguarding Cryptographic Keys. *1979 AFIPS National Computer Conference, Monval, NJ, USA*. 313-317.

Bowers, K. D., Juels, A., & Oprea, A. (2009). Proofs of Retrievability: Theory and Implementation. *1st ACM Workshop on Cloud Computing Security (CCSW'09)*, Chicago, IL, USA. 43-54.

Bu, S., & Yang, R. (2013). Novel and Effective Multi-Secret Sharing Scheme. *International Conference on Information Engineering and Applications (IEA'12): LNEE, 219*. 461-467.

Bu, S., & Zhou, H. (2009). A Secret Sharing Scheme Based on NTRU Algorithm. *International Conference on Wireless Communications, Networking and Mobile Computing (WiCom'09)*, Beijing, China. 1-4. 10.1109/WICOM.2009.5302743

Cormode, G., & Srivastava, D. (2009). Anonymized Data: Generation, Models, Usage. *ACM SIGMOD International Conference on Management of Data (SIGMOD'09)*, Providence, Rhode Island, USA. 1015-1018. 10.1145/1559845.1559968

Emekci, F., Agrawal, D., El Abbadi, A., & Gulbeden, A. (2006). Privacy Preserving Query Processing Using Third Parties. *22nd International Conference on Data Engineering (ICDE'06), Atlanta, Georgia, USA*. 27-37.

Eslami, Z., & Ahmadabadi, J. Z. (2010). A Verifiable Multi-Sharing Scheme Based on Cellular Automata. *Information Sciences, 180*(15), 2889–2894. doi:10.1016/j.ins.2010.04.015

Gentry, C. (2009). Fully Homomorphic Encryption Using Ideal Lattices. *41st Annual ACM Symposium on Theory of Computing (STOC'09)*, Bethesda, MD, USA. 169-178. 10.1145/1536414.1536440

Hadavi, M. A., & Jalili, R. (2010). Secure Data Outsourcing Based on Threshold Secret Sharing; Towards a More Practical Solution. *VLDB PhD Workshop, Singapore*. 54-59.

Hadavi, M. A., Noferesti, M., Jalili, R., & Damiani, E. (2012). Database as a service: Towards a unified solution for security requirements. *36th Computer Software and Applications Conference Workshops (COMPSACW'12)*, Izmir, Turkey. 415–420. 10.1109/COMPSACW.2012.79

Hu, C., Liao, X., & Cheng, X. (2012). Verifiable Multi-Secret Sharing Based on LFSR Sequences. *Theoretical Computer Science, 445*, 52–62. doi:10.1016/j.tcs.2012.05.006

Juels, A., & Kaliski, B. (2007). PORs: Proofs of Retrievability for Large Files. *14th ACM conference on Computer and communications security (CCS'07)*, Alexandria, VA, USA. 584-597. 10.1145/1315245.1315317

Kenneally, E., & Claffy, K. (2010). Dialing Privacy and Utility: A Proposed Data-sharing Framework to Advance Internet Research. *IEEE Security and Privacy*, 8(4), 31–39. doi:10.1109/MSP.2010.57

Liu, Y. X., Harn, L., Yang, C. N., & Zhang, Y. Q. (2012). Efficient (*n, t, n*) secret sharing schemes. *Journal of Systems and Software*, 85(6), 1325–1332. doi:10.1016/j.jss.2012.01.027

Machanavajjhala, A., Kifer, D., Gehrke, J., & Venkitasubramaniam, M. (2007). *l*-diversity: Privacy beyond *k*-anonymity. *ACM Transactions on Knowledge Discovery from Data*, 1(1), 3, es. doi:10.1145/1217299.1217302

Melchor, C. A., Castagnos, G., & Gaborit, P. (2008). Lattice-based Homomorphic Encryption of Vector Spaces. *IEEE International Symposium on Information Theory (ISIT'08)*, Toronto, ON, Canada. 1858-1862. 10.1109/ISIT.2008.4595310

O'Neil, P., O'Neil, E., Chen, X., & Revilak, S. (2009). The Star Schema Benchmark and Augmented Fact Table Indexing. *1st Technology Conference on Performance Evaluation and Benchmarking (TPCTC'09)*, Lyon, France: LNCS, 5895. 237-252.

Padmanabhan, P., Gruenwald, L., Vallur, A., & Atiquzzaman, M. (2008). A Survey of Data Replication Techniques for Mobile Adhoc Network Databases. *The VLDB Journal*, 17(5), 1143–1164. doi:10.100700778-007-0055-0

Sedeyao, J. (2012). Enhancing Cloud Security using Data Anonymization. http://www.intel.ie/content/www/ie/en/it-management/intel-it-best-practices/enhancing-cloud-security-using-data-anonymization.html

Shacham, H., & Waters, B. (2008). Compact Proofs of Retrievability. *14th International Conference on the Theory and Application of Cryptology and Information Security: Advances in Cryptology (ASIACRYPT'08)*, Melbourne, Australia. 90-107.

Shamir, A. (1979). How to Share a Secret. *Communications of the ACM*, 22(11), 612–613. doi:10.1145/359168.359176

Sion, R. (2007). Secure Data Outsourcing. *33rd International Conference on Very Large Data Bases (VLDB'07)*, Vienna, Austria. 1431-1432.

Sweeney, L. (2002). *k*-anonymity: A Model for Protecting Privacy. *International Journal of Uncertainty, Fuzziness and Knowledge-based Systems*, 10(5), 557–570. doi:10.1142/S0218488502001648

Thomas, J., & Schwarz, E. (2002). Generalized Reed Solomon Codes for Erasure Correction in SDDS. *Workshop on Distributed Data and Structures (WDAS'02)*, Paris, France. 75-86.

Thompson, B., Haber, S., Horne, W. G., Sander, T., & Yao, D. (2009). Privacy-Preserving Computation and Verification of Aggregate Queries on Outsourced Databases. *Privacy Enhancing Technologies: LNCS, 5672*, 185–201. doi:10.1007/978-3-642-03168-7_11

Wang, Q., Wang, C., Li, J., Ren, K., & Lou, W. (2009). Enabling Public Verifiability and Data Dynamics for Storage Security in Cloud Computing. *14th European Symposium on Research in Computer Security (ESORICS'09)*, Saint-Malo, France. 355-370. 10.1007/978-3-642-04444-1_22

Wang, S., Agrawal, D., & Abbadi, A. E. (2011). A Comprehensive Framework for Secure Query Processing on Relational Data in the Cloud. *Secure Data Management: LNCS, 6933*, 52–69. doi:10.1007/978-3-642-23556-6_4

Waseda, A., & Soshi, M. (2012). Consideration for Multi-Threshold Multi-Secret Sharing Schemes. *International Symposium on Information Theory and its Applications (ISITA'12)*, Honolulu, HI, USA. 265–269.

This research was previously published in the International Journal of Data Warehousing and Mining (IJDWM), 11(2); edited by David Taniar, pages 22-43, copyright year 2015 by IGI Publishing (an imprint of IGI Global).

Chapter 26
A Secured Real Time Scheduling Model for Cloud Hypervisor

Rekha Kashyap
Inderprastha Engineering College, India

Deo Prakash Vidyarthi
Jawaharlal Nehru University, India

ABSTRACT

Virtualization is critical to cloud computing and is possible through hypervisors, which maps the Virtual machines((VMs) to physical resources but poses security concerns as users relinquish physical possession of their computation and data. Good amount of research is initiated for resource provisioning on hypervisors, still many issues need to be addressed for security demanding and real time VMs. First work SRT-CreditScheduler (Secured and Real-time), maximizes the success rate by dynamically prioritizing the urgency and the workload of VMs but ensures highest security for all. Another work, SA-RT-CreditScheduler (Security-aware and Real-time) is a dual objective scheduler, which maximizes the success rate of VMs in best possible security range as specified by the VM owner. Though the algorithms can be used by any hypervisor, for the current work they have been implemented on Xen hypervisor. Their effectiveness is validated by comparing it with Xen's, Credit and SEDF scheduler, for security demanding tasks with stringent deadline constraints.

1. INTRODUCTION

Cloud Computing is a paradigm shift which offers virtualized resources in the form of services. "A Cloud is a type of parallel and distributed system consisting of collection of interconnected and virtualized computers that are dynamically provisioned and presented as one or more unified computing resources based on service-level agreements established through negotiation between the service provider and consumers" (Buyya, Yeo, & Venugopal, 2008). Vision of cloud is possible by virtualization technologies which provide a mechanism for mapping VMs to physical resources. It is done by the virtualization management layer, termed as hypervisor which guarantees the isolation between different virtual machines and manages virtualization of physical resources (Chisnall, 2008; Liao, Guo, Bhuyan, & King, 2008;

DOI: 10.4018/978-1-5225-8176-5.ch026

Armbrust, 2009). This mapping is largely hidden from the cloud users. Users of Amazon EC2 (2014) would never know the actual location of their physical resources or their application's execution. As this hypervisor system sits between the guest and the hardware, it can control the guest's use of CPU, memory, and storage, even allowing a guest OS to migrate from one machine to another.

Like a real machine, a VM can run any application, OS or kernel without modifications. Examples of such hypervisors are Xen (Barham et al., 2003), VMware (2007), and KVM (Kivity, Kamay, Laor, Lublin, & Liguori, 2007).

By virtualization resources are decoupled from the users and it provides greater flexibility in terms of resource allocation but at the same time it brings new challenges for provisioning, optimal design and runtime management of systems. The resource allocation problem becomes challenging when the resource needs of Virtual Machines are heterogeneous because of diversity in the applications they run and vary with time as the workloads grow and shrink (Menon, Santos, Turner, Janakiraman, & Zwae-nepoel, 2005). Recently, lot of demand for supporting real time systems in virtualized environment has been witnessed. Virtualization adds a layer of technology, which definitely increases the management of security by necessitating additional security controls. Also, combining many systems into a single physical computer can cause a larger impact on security compromise. Cloud Computing preserves vulnerabilities associated with internet applications and additionally that arise from pooled, virtualized and outsourced resources (Buyya, Yeo, Venugopal et al., 2009; Dahbur, Bassil Mohammad et al., 2011). Security is very essential for cloud users as they relinquish physical possession of their computation and data. Plenty of research has been initiated in resource provisioning for hypervisors, still many problems especially for security-aware and real time tasks running on virtual machines needs more attention. Using existing security services to satisfy the applications' security needs, however, incurs security overhead in terms of computation time, which may violate the application's deadlines. The conflicting requirement of optimal real-time performance and a quality security protection imposed by security-critical real time applications introduces a new challenge for resource allocation schemes.

The first work, introduced in this paper SRT-CreditScheduler, is preferred for Real-time VMs where the VM cannot compromise on security but at the same time is not able to specify the exact security requirements. This algorithm ensures highest level of security. The second proposed SA-RT-CreditScheduler is for Real time VMs where the owners specify their range of security requirements to achieve better success rate. The algorithm tries to offer highest security from the range and compromises only when the deadline violates. Both the works are inspired by Smith's and Moore's work where preference is given to smaller processing times and approaching deadlines but proposed work differs, as in them the weightage of preference varies depending on the characteristics of Virtual Machines to be scheduled. The contribution in this work is as follows. The next section discusses the work done in this area. Section 3 depicts the terminologies and strategies used for the proposed work. Section 4 details the proposed SRT-CreditScheduler and SA-RT-CreditScheduler. Section 5 describes the experimentation results and observations and section 6 concludes the work.

2. RELATED WORK

The proposed works have been implemented on Xen hypervisor or Virtual machine monitor. Xen was developed by Barham et al., in 2003 and since then has become one of the most popular hypervisor. It is an type-1 opensource or bare metal Virtual machine monitor. It is possible to run many instances of single operating system or multiple operating systems in parallel on a single host. Xen encapsulates complete running virtual environment by running different guests in environments known as domains. The privileged VM(dom0), is the first guest to run, with enhanced privileges. Other domains or VMs are referred to as domain U (domU). Dom0 is the privileged domain as it implements the device drivers, communicates with the actual hardware and it also translates between virtual and real I/O activity. It is given the responsibility of creating and controlling other guest domains. Domains and VMs have been interchangeably used in the proposed work. Current versions of Xen include two schedulers, the Simple Earliest Deadline First (SEDF) ("SEDF Scheduler") for real-time tasks and Credit Scheduler for weighted tasks (Nishiguchi, 2008).

Each VM of Credit Scheduler is assigned a weight and a cap. Weight defines its proportional share and is distributed among its VCPUs/Tasks. Cap defines the upper limit on the execution time. Credits are awarded periodically at the beginning of the accounting period. In the default credit scheduler credits are allotted uniformly in a fair manner. As with a multitasking operating system, scheduling in Xen is a tradeoff between achieving fairness for running domains and achieving good overall throughput. Effectiveness of scheduler significantly depends upon optimal credits allocation to various VMs so an efficient scheduling strategy should consider the heterogeneous requirements of the Virtual Machines while allocating the resources in form of credits. Recently, Xen community has worked on including the support for real time VMs in the credit scheduler (Sisu, Justin, Chenyang et al., 2011; Clark et al., 2004).

Simple Earliest Deadline First (SEDF), is a real time scheduling algorithm for xen hypervisor. Each domain Dom_i specifies its CPU requirements with a tuple (s_i, p_i, x_i), where the slice s_i and the period p_i together represent the CPU share that Dom_i requests. Slice guarantees that each Dom_i will receive at least s_i units of time in each period of length p_i. It also has provision for utilizing unused time through variable x. The boolean flag x_i indicates whether Dom_i is eligible to receive extra CPU time. The time granularity in the definition of the period impacts scheduler fairness. Two additional values (d_i, r_i) are specified for each domain, where di is the deadline representing the time at which Dom_i's current period will ends and r_i denotes the remaining CPU time of Dom_i in the current period. The runnable domain with earliest deadline is picked to be scheduled next.

SEDF scheduler in Xen allowed specifications of time slices and frequency of scheduling desired by a domain. However, SEDF incurred from several deficiencies including insufficient support for SMP. Govindan et al. (2007) introduced an enhancement to the SEDF scheduler giving preference to I/O domains over the CPU intensive domains. Their algorithm attempts to preferentially schedule communication-sensitive domains over others while ensuring the bounded resulting unfairness in CPU allocation. This is achieved by noticing the total number of packets flowing in and out of each domain and then picking one with the highest count that had not yet consumed its entire slice in the current period. Without compromising on non-real-time domains Lee et al (2010) modified Xen scheduler to support soft real-time guests. There work was to improve two aspects of the VMM scheduler, managing shared caches and managing scheduling latency as a first-class resource. Jeyarani and Nagaveni, proposed a heuristic scheduler that focuses on fulfilling deadline requirements of the resource consumers as well as energy conservation requirement of the resource provider contributing towards green IT (Alhaj, 2014). The proposed work is different as it incorporates real time requirements together with security demands of cloud tasks in the scheduling policy of hypervisors.

A good amount of research is initiated to address security issues in cloud. Subashini & Kavitha (2010) presented a study on security and privacy issues of cloud environment. Yao et.al (2010) proposed a model for ensured storage security in cloud. Abdullah Alhaj, proposed Secure Data Transmission Mechanism

(SDTM) for Cloud Outsourced Data over transport layer (Jeyarani & Nagaveni, 2012), Zhao & Sakura (2013) worked on finding schedules for meeting specific reliability and deadline requirements. These mentioned works talks about security concerns but not much has been done for security of real time tasks while making resource scheduling.

Earliest Deadline First (EDF) is one of the classic and known real time scheduling heuristic based algorithms. The logic behind EDF is to schedule the tasks with approaching deadline to the fastest processor (Stankovic, Spuri, Ramamritham, & Buttazzo, 1998; Zhao, Ramamritham, & Stankovic, 1990). The other heuristic, and MinMin schedules smallest task to the fastest processor and is used by NES systems (Netsolve) as online scheduling algorithms (Casanova, Legrand, Zagorodnov, & Berman, 2000; Maheswaran, Ali, Siegel, Hensgen, & Freund, 1999). Smith's and Moore's algorithm are well known real-time scheduling algorithms, which aims at finding the schedule with minimum number of tardy jobs. Moore's algorithm is used to find a schedule with a minimum number of tardy jobs. It forms an EDF schedule of all jobs, and if no more than one job is late, the schedule is optimal. Otherwise determine the first late job, say i, and find the job scheduled no later than i that has the largest processing time, say job j. It schedules all jobs other than j, and then schedule job j last (Smith, 1956).

Smith's algorithm (1968), minimizes Mean completion over all the schedules that have minimal maximum tardiness, Tmax (which is determined by constructing an EDF schedule). It puts the job in the order of non-decreasing ratios wi/pi (wi is the weight coefficient in a min cost objective and pi gives the processing time) MinMin heuristic can be considered as a special case of Smith's rule where all tasks are having equal weights.

It is evident that Moore's and Smith's algorithms use the combination of MinMin and EDF schedules and algorithms suggested in the paper also prioritizes Virtual machines on the basis of earlier completion time and approaching deadlines. But, proposed work, SRT-CreditScheduler (Secured and Real-time and SA-RT-CreditScheduler (Security-aware and Real-time) maximizes the success rate but differs from Smith's and Moore's algorithm as preference for deadline and shorter tasks varies depending on the characteristics of Virtual Machines

3. TERMINOLOGIES AND STRATEGIES USED

3.1. Terminologies

Some of the terms and definitions used in this work have been described as follows.

- A *Virtual Machine* (*VM*) is characterized as $VM_i = (WL_i, SL_{i,max}, SL_{i,min}, DF_i)$, where, WL_i is the predicted computational workload associated with the ith *VM* in seconds, $SL_{i,max}$ to $SL_{i,min}$ is the range of security desired by i^{th} *VM* where $SL_{i,max}$ is the highest security desired by i^{th} *VM* and $SL_{i,min}$ is the lowest security level acceptable by i^{th} *VM*. *Deadline Factor, DF_i* quantifies the urgency of the ith *VM* and deadline of VM is computed on the basis of DF. $1 <= i <= m$, and *m* refers to the total nos of *VM* created.

- A compute node is characterized as $N_j = \left(\sum_{k=1}^{n} VM_{j,k}, BT_j \right)$ where, $\sum_{k=1}^{n} VM_{j,k}$ is list of all Virtual machines assigned to it and, BT_j is its begin time (execution time of the previously assigned VMs.

- $ND_{qualified,i}$ is list of all those compute nodes which are able to meet the deadline of the ith *VM*.
- CT_{ij} defines the time taken to execute i^{th} *VM* on j^{th} compute node which is calculated as in equation (1):

$$CT_{ij} = BT_j + WL_{ij} \qquad (1)$$

where, WL_{ij} is predicted workload time of ith*VM* on j^{th} compute node. Begin time of every node at the start of schedule is assumed to be zero but once the execution starts the begin time will be affected:

- *Secured Completion Time, SCT$_{ijk}$* is time taken to complete i^{th} *VM* on j^{th} compute node with k^{th} security level which is calculated as given in equation (2):

$$SCT_{ijk} = BT_j + SWL_{ijk} \qquad (2)$$

where, SWL_{ij} is predicted workload time of ith*VM* on j^{th} compute node with k^{th} Security level. BT_j is the begin time of jth VM. Begin time of every node at the start of schedule is assumed to be zero but once the execution starts the begin time will be affected. Predicted workload computation with different encryption algorithms are shown in Table 2.

3.2. Deadline Strategy

Deadline is a limit or the completion time assigned to a *VM* for its enforced completion. It is computed as shown in Equation (3):

$$D_i = CT_{iavg} \times DF_i \qquad (3)$$

Each *VM* is assigned a deadline, D_i, which is a random value in [DF x $CT_{i,avg}$, $CT_{i,avg}$]. $CT_{i,avg}$ is the predicted completion time of ith *VM* on the node with zero begin time, which is scaled up by an deadline factor *(DF)*, which ranges between 2 to *10*. This generates a mix of urgent and delayed deadline *VMs*. A *VM* with Deadline 2 is treated three times more urgent than one with value 6. Higher the Deadline less urgent is its scheduling.

3.3. Security Strategy

Cloud computing is realized through virtualization hence securing of virtual machines is key to securing cloud applications. Although majority of security concerns associated with virtual machines are similar, if not identical, to those on physical platforms, VMs do have unique potential weaknesses because of its basic nature to support multi-tenancy. Virtual machines allow users to share the resources of the host computer and provide isolation between VMs and their host. Unfortunately, due to architectural limitations, VM vendor's approach to isolation, or bugs in the virtualization software may result in the ability to compromise isolation and thus demands stringent security checks.

Because a VM consist of set of files, machine theft has become much easier as stealing a VM can be achieved by simple snapshot of the VM and copying the contents. The discussed threat can be addressed by encrypting all or part of virtual machine for VMs running in a data centre/private cloud or public cloud. Data encryption procedures are mainly categorized into two categories depending on the type of security keys used to encrypt/decrypt the secured data. These two categories are: Asymmetric and Symmetric encryption techniques. Usually, asymmetric encryption is used to exchange the secret key, symmetric encryption is then used to transfer data between sender and receiver. In the proposed work, confidentiality is implemented using symmetric encryption techniques.

3.3.1. Quantification of Security

To support security as a Quality of Service parameter there is a need for quantification of security. All participating VM owners should be given a choice of security in a similar manner, as given choice of RAM, storage or Number of cores. In this work security range is quantified as 1,2 and 3, thus instead of presenting the Security in the form of encryption algorithms, VM owners are offered security in the form of low(1), medium(2) and high(3). Security demanded by the VM is abbreviated as SD and the security offered is abbreviated as SO.

For encryption of data using symmetric keys, multiple encryption algorithms are used but Blowfish, 3DES, AES, (Rijndael)-128, AES-192, AES-256 are mostly recommended (Ahmad, Hasan, & Jubadi, 2010; Chang, Huang, Chang, Chen, & Hsieh, 2008; Gueron, 2010). The two main characteristics that identify and differentiate one encryption algorithm from another is its ability to secure the protected data against attacks and its speed and efficiency in doing so. Strength of symmetric key encryption also depends on the size of the key used. For the same algorithm, encryption using longer key is harder to break than the one done using smaller key.

For the proposed work three levels of security are offered by implementing AES-128, AES-192 and AES-256 crypto algorithms, where 128,192 and 256 specifies the size of the key used. AES crypto algorithm is based on Rijndael cipher and was developed by Vincent Rijmen and Joan Daemen to be used by U.S National Institute of Standards and Technology (NIST) in 2001 (NIST, 2001). Encryption and decryption is done on data in blocks of 128 bits with key size of 128, 192 and 256 bits. The mentioned block ciphers being symmetric in nature uses same key for encryption and decryption. There are 10, 12 and 14 rounds, for AES-128, AES-192 and AES-256 crypto algorithms respectively, where each round comprises of multiple steps which includes transposition, substitution and mixers applied on plain text to obtain the cipher text.

4. PROPOSED WORK

The two proposed algorithms, SRT-CreditScheduler(Secured and Real-time) and SA-RT-CreditScheduler (Security-aware and Real-time) implemented on Xen hypervisor though can be used for any hypervisor, are as follows.

4.1. SRT-CreditScheduler

SRT-CreditScheduler suggests a credit allocation policy for Real-time Virtual Machines. It considers computational load and deadline requirements while assigning credits ensuring highest level of security for all VMs.

SRT-CreditScheduler is the outcome of the findings while experimenting with MinMin and EDF on randomly generated heterogeneous VMs on homogeneous compute nodes (SMP). The VM were heterogeneous for their deadline and workload. Success rate of MinMin algorithm was found to be far better than Earliest Deadline First algorithm when fewer but computationally heavy VM have urgent deadline wherein EDF performed better for success rate when larger number of VMs demanded urgent deadlines. The reasoning for the same is stated below.

EDF prioritizes scheduling on the basis of approaching deadline without considering its workload. Few computationally heavy VM with urgent deadline may make many not so urgent deadlines suffer to the extent of missing the deadline. This may lead to degradation of success rate of EDF schedule. Min-Min is preferred scheduler for such workloads. When more number of VMs are having urgent deadline, it is preferred to schedule them first making EDF a preferred scheduler.

Inspired from the above findings, SRT-CreditScheduler assigns credits to VM as the weighted sum of its workload and deadline priority. VMs with small computational workload have more workload priority and higher deadline priority is assigned to VMs with small deadline value. Workload and deadline priorities are further assigned weightages on the basis of urgency value of the schedule. Higher weightage is given to the deadline priority, if more VMs are demanding urgent scheduling. Similarly higher weightage will be given to workload priority, if more VM are having relaxed deadline. Procedure to calculate priority is explained with the help of Equations (4) to (9) in the coming section. The algorithm SRT-CreditScheduler is explained in detail as follows.

4.1.1. Algorithm for SRTCreditScheduler

From the list of all *VMs* which are to be scheduled ($VM_{Complete}$), priority of each *VM* is computed using procedure *calculatePriority* and VM with highest priority as is marked as VM_{hpr}:

1. Execution time of VM_{hpr} on every compute node of $N_{complete}$ is calculated, using Equation (1). Security level is set to $SL_{hpr,,max}$ (highest security).
2. *If* there are nodes satisfying the deadline of VM_{hpr} then
    a. From $N_{complete}$ list of all compute nodes which satisfies the deadline of VM_{hpr} is created and marked as $N_{qualified,p}$
    b. From the entire list $N_{qualified,p}$, node that executes VM_{hpr} fastest is selected, and tagged as node N_{min}.
    c. VM_{hpr} is scheduled on node N_{min} and removed from the $VM_{Complete}$ list.
    d. Begin time (*BT*) of the node N_{min} is modified.
    e. Entire process is repeated till all tasks from $VM_{complete}$ are scheduled.
        Else
        Reject the VM_{hpr}

4.1.2. Procedure to Calculate Priority

The procedure to calculate different priority values are as given in equations (4) to (6):

$$Pr_i = Wt_{deadline} \ X \ Pr_{deadline} + \ Wt_{workload} \ X \ Pr_{workload, i} \tag{4}$$

$$Pr_{deadline, i} = 1 - \left(D_i \Big/ D_{max} \right) \tag{5}$$

$$Pr_{workload, i} = 1 - \left(WL_i \Big/ WL_{max} \right) \tag{6}$$

where Pr_i is the priority assigned to the ith Virtual machine. $Pr_{deadline,i}$ is the priority of ith VM calculated on the basis of its deadline and $Pr_{workload,i}$ is priority calculated on the basis of its workload. Higher priority is given to VMs with approaching deadline and smaller workload.

Deadline of the ith VM is represented as D_i and D_{max} represents the maximum deadline desired by any VM from the complete list of VMs.

WL_i is the workload of the ith VM and WL_{max} is the maximum workload of a VM in the schedule.

$Wt_{deadline}$ is the assigned weight for deadline priority and $Wt_{workload}$ is the assigned weight for workload priority. Different *VMs* will have different deadline and workload priorities. Further Weightage for deadline and workload depends on the urgency of the schedule.

As depicted in Equation (4), priorities are further assigned weights and the calculations for the same is given in equations (7) to (9):

$$Wt_{deadline} = \left(UF_{avg} \Big/ UF_{max} \right) \tag{7}$$

$$UF_{avg} = \sum_{i=1}^{n} \left(UF_i \Big/ n \right) \tag{8}$$

$$Wt_{workload} = 1 - Wt_{deadline} \tag{9}$$

UF_{avg} is overall urgency of the schedule and is decided by averaging the urgency of individual VMs within a schedule. Higher the value implies more number of VMs in the schedule require urgent scheduling. The basis of this work rests on our findings that, MinMin algorithm is better than EDF when more VMs in the schedule have urgent deadline and EDF algorithm outperforms MinMin when more VMs have not so urgent deadline.

4.2. SA-RT-CreditScheduler

The proposed SA-RT-CreditScheduler suggests a credit allocation policy for Virtual Machines which can specify their security requirement along with deadline requirements. The algorithm is called security aware as the VMs are aware of their security requirement. It considers security requirement, security overhead, computational load and deadline requirements of VM while assigning credits. It is a dual objective algorithm; one objective is to maximize the success rate of VM and other objective is to maximize the security of the VM.

It uses the combination of MinMin and EDF/ECT algorithm to allot credit to the VMs in a manner similar as SRT-CreditScheduler. It is different from SRT-CreditScheduler as it also seeks the security demand from the VM and then assigns maximum possible security as per the demand. This can be used where the VM seekers are aware of their actual security requirements and can compromise to achieve better success rate.

4.2.1. Algorithm for SA-RT-CreditScheduler

1. From the list of all *VMs* which are to be scheduled ($VM_{Complete}$), priority of each *VM* is computed using procedure *calculatePriority* (same as RTCreditScheduler) and *VM* with highest priority as is marked as VM_{hpr}.
2. Calculate Execution time of VM_{hpr} on each compute node of $N_{complete}$ using Equation (1). Security level is set to $SL_{hpr,max}$ (highest security of the desired range).
3. *If* there are nodes satisfying the deadline of VM_{hpr} then
   a. From $N_{complete}$ list of all compute nodes which satisfies the deadline of VM_{hpr} is created and marked as $N_{qualified,p}$
   b. From the entire list $N_{qualified,p}$, node that executes VM_{hpr} fastest is selected, and tagged as node N_{min}.
   c. VM_{hpr} is scheduled on node N_{min} and removed from the $VM_{Complete}$ list.
   d. Begin time (*BT*) of the node N_{min} is modified.
   e. Repeat the entire process till all tasks from $VM_{complete}$ are scheduled.
      Else
   a. Reduce the security level of the VM_{hpr} by 1
   b. *If* Security level is within the permissible security range than go to step 2.
      Else Reject the VM_{hpr}

5. EXPERIMENTAL RESULTS AND OBSERVATIONS

The experiments were carried on Sun Fire X4800 Server supporting, eight Intel 7500 series Xeon processor and 64 GB of RAM. The machine was designed to use Xen 4.1 hypervisor. Further 30 VMs/Domains were manually created in the form of para-virtualized guests. PV guests can be made Xen aware and therefore can be optimized for Xen. Each VM is assigned 2 GB RAM. Dom0 is Pinned to one of the eight processors allowing other VM to run on the remaining processors.

Security for the VM is set to the highest level for SEDF, CreditScheduler and SRT-CreditScheduler. For SA-RT-CreditScheduler security level is selected as per the scheduling policy which can be any value from the range demanded by the VM.

5.1. Computation of Predicted Workload With Security Overhead

For scheduling strategies used in the proposed algorithms, a historical trace of predicted workload is prepared for matrix multiplication operation. On each created VM, a web service capable of running complex matrix operations was installed. Using the web service interface, multiple tasks requesting for matrix multiplication operations are then created inside each VM and each workload is made to run for AES-128, AES-192 and AES-256 crypto algorithms, where 128,192 and 256 specifies the size of the key used. The security range is quantified as 1, 2 and 3 on the basis of encryption algorithm used.

Xen-top utility was used to find the computational workload used by each VM wherein each VM is made to run 5~30 of heterogeneous matrix multiplication tasks.This recording is preserved, as shown in Table 1, and is used further as the predicted workload time with security overhead to be used in Equation (1) and (2). The total predicted workload of a VM is sum of workload of each task after referring Table 1. Java Cryptography Extension is used for encryption, decryption and key generation.

Credit scheduler is designed to share the CPU's among the VMs. Each VM is assigned a weight and resources are distributed in proportion to the weight. Thus, correct weight assignment is very important for optimal utilization of resources. In SEDF, each VM or domain is set to run for an n milliseconds slice every m milliseconds, where n and m are configurable on a per-domain basis and VM with closest deadline is picked first. The proposed works, SRT-CreditScheduler and SA-RT-CreditScheduler propose a novel weight assignment policy considering the deadline, workload and security for security demanding real time tasks. For credit scheduler and SEDF scheduler, we experimented on the default settings of Xen for credit allocation and slice values.

5.2. Performance Evaluation

The performance of the proposed schedulers are compared with Credit and SEDF scheduler with success rate, security and average response time as performance objectives:

1. Success rate = k/m where, k is Number of *VMs* that meet the deadline and m is the total number of *VM* to be scheduled;

2. Total security (Average of security value of all successfully scheduled *VMs*) = $\sum_{i=1}^{k} SL_i /^k$ where, SL_i is the security level of ith VM and k is Number of *VMs* meeting the deadline;

3. Average response time= $\sum_{i=1}^{n} (CT_{ij} - ARV_i) / m$ where, ARV_i is the arrival time of ith VM, m denotes the number of *VMs* to be scheduled and completion time of ith VM on j^{th} compute node is denoted by CT_{ij}, which is calculated as shown in Equation (1).

5.3. Effect on Success Rate and Security on Varying Deadline of Schedule

First set of experimentation is done by varying the deadline of the schedule. DF_{avg} is the measure of overall urgency of the schedule which is made to vary between 2 to 10 in the experimentation. DF below 5 is considered to be urgent and above 5 as relaxed. Smaller DF value gives tighter deadline. 30 VMs are created to be scheduled over 7 processors and eighth processor is pinned to Dom0). Each VM further contains multiple matrix multiplication tasks, ranging from 1 to 30.

Table 1. Workload of matrix-matrix multiplication operations including encryption overhead

Row.	Col.	Encryption algorithm	Security Level	Computational time with encryption overhead(secs)
200	200	None	0	1.14
		AES-128	1	1.22
		AES-192	2	1.34
		AES-256	3	1.8
400	400	none	0	4.8
		AES-128	1	5.4
		AES-192	2	6.23
		AES-256	3	7.3
800	800	none	0	13
		AES-128	1	15.2
		AES-192	2	17
		AES-256	3	18.3
1000	1000	none	0	24
		AES-128	1	26.2
		AES-192	2	28.3
		AES-256	3	30.5
1200	1200	none	0	32.4
		AES-128	1	35.6
		AES-192	2	37.5
		AES-256	3	38.4

If the deadline of overall schedule is relaxed that is more number of tasks are relaxed in nature, than it is more likely for the VMs to meet the deadline as the number of processors are kept constant. This holds true for all schedulers so the success rate of all schedulers improves when the deadline become relaxed or the deadline factor increases as shown in Figure 1. But for SA-RT-Credit Scheduler it is observed that it outperforms other scheduler giving better success rate for all values of deadline. The reason being, SA-RT-CreditScheduler optimizes the security level and security overhead depending upon the deadline of VM, whereas the other three always works on highest security resulting in maximum security overhead and thus increased completion time.

SEDF is a real time scheduler for Xen hypervisor and it tries to schedule tasks with approaching deadline on priority basis. For same level of security, it is observed that SEDF gives better success rate when schedule is urgent but its success rate deteriorates significantly over SRT-CreditScheduler and SA-RT-CreditScheduler when the schedule is relaxed as shown in Figure 1.

SA-RT-CreditScheduler works for optimal security so its security is less in comparison to security of Credit, SEDF and SRT-CreditScheduler which works at highest security. Another observation for SA-RT-CreditScheduler is that, when the schedule has relaxed deadline more tasks are able to meet the deadline with higher security levels but on the tighter deadline, security is compromised. The performance of the schedulers for overall security varying the deadline can be seen in Figure 2.

Figure 1. Effect on success rate of schedule by varying the deadline of virtual machines

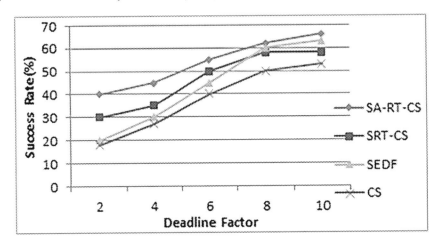

Figure 2. Effect on security of schedule by varying the deadline of virtual machines

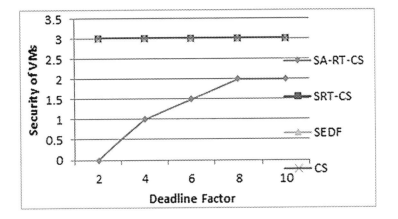

5.4. Effect on Success Rate and Average Response Time on Varying Number of VMs

Next we measured success rate and average response time on varying number of VMs to be scheduled from 15 to 30, where, VMs comprises of multiple matrix multiplication tasks. The number of compute nodes are fixed to 8 physical processors in the experiment but much more than 8 VMs can be processed with guaranteed deadlines indicating a significant improvement in service consolidation. Success rate is directly proportional to number of processors available and inversely proportional to number of VMs(tasks) to be scheduled. For same number of cores if we keep on increasing VMs, success rate will degrade for all scheduler but the degree of degradation is different for different scheduler.

It has been observed that, all the algorithms shows a increase in the number of VMs scheduled with initial increase in number of VMs but gradually it becomes constant. Once the numbers of successful VMs become constant, further increase in the number of VMs decreases the percentage of VMs scheduled, degrading the success rate for all schedulers but the degree of degradation is different for different scheduler as shown in Figure 3.

Success rate of SA-RT-CreditScheduler and SRT-CreditScheduler is better than other two for lightly loaded schedule (few and light VMs). For heavy workloads SA-RT-CreditScheduler outperforms all the three compared schedulers which behave nearly similar for heavy workloads.

Average response time is the measure of the overall wait time for the entire schedule comprising of multiple VMs. Since SRT-CreditScheduler and SA-RT-CreditScheduler considers workload of the task while assigning credits and gives fair preference to small tasks their average response time is better than other two Xen Scheduler as seen in Figure 4. It is also observed that Credit Scheduler shows better response time as compared to SEDF scheduler especially when the workload increases.

In a real cloud scenario when we have large number of VMs to be scheduled we will also have proportionately large number of processors available thus SA-RT-CS will outperform others for large number of VMs also as the ratio of number of processors over VMs to be scheduled, will be maintained in a real cloud scenario.

Figure 3. Effect on success rate of schedule by varying the number of virtual machines

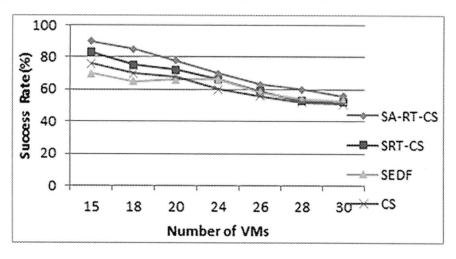

Figure 4. Effect on average response time of schedule by varying the number of virtual machines

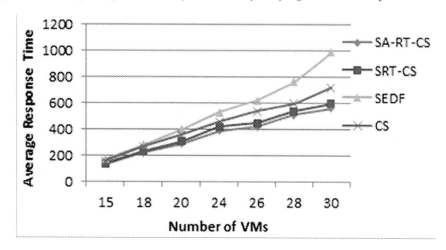

6. CONCLUSION

For any, security-aware and real time cloud environment, the job of VM scheduler is to achieve high success rate fulfilling the security demand of the VMs, without compromising on the response time of each VM. In this work, two schedulers SRT-CreditScheduler (Secured and real-time) and SA-RT-CreditScheduler (Security-aware and real-time) are proposed and implemented on Xen hypervisor. These are compared with existing Xen schedulers, i.e. SEDF and Credit Scheduler. The work also suggested a mechanism for quantifying security and proposed security overhead computation model.

The scheduling policy for the proposed schedulers prioritizes VMs on the basis of their workload and deadline requirements and shows better response time and success rate over SEDF and Credit scheduler.

The first work SRT-CreditScheduler (Secured and Real-time) maximises the success rate by dynamically prioritizing the urgency and workload of VMs but it treats all VMs with similar and highest level of security. Another work, SA-RT-CreditScheduler is a dual objective algorithm; to maximize the success rate and the security of the VM. Thus it dynamically adjusts the security as per the security and deadline requirements of the VMs. It is different from SRT-CreditScheduler as it also seeks the security demand from the VM and can be used where the VM seekers are aware of their actual security requirements. It needs to balance between the timeliness and security.

The results show that SA-RT-CreditScheduler outweighs all other studied scheduler when success rate is preferred and RTS-CreditScheduler outweighs other compared scheduler when security cannot be compromised making them much more attractive and effective scheduler for any hypervisor specifically Xen hypervisor.

REFERENCES

Ahmad, N., Hasan, R., & Jubadi, W. M. (2010, October). Design of AES S-Box using combinational logic optimization. *Proceedings of the IEEE Symposium on Industrial Electronics & Applications* (pp. 696-699). 10.1109/ISIEA.2010.5679375

Alhaj, A. A. (2014, January-March). Performance Evaluation of Secure Data Transmission Mechanism (SDTM) for Cloud Outsourced Data and Transmission Layer Security (TLS). *International Journal of Cloud Applications and Computing, 4*(1), 45–49. doi:10.4018/ijcac.2014010104

Armbrust, M. (2009, February). Above the clouds: A Berkeley view of cloud computing (Tech. Rep). *Amazon EC2*. Retrieved from http://aws.amazon.com/ec2/

Barham, P., Dragovic, B., Fraser, K., & Hand, S., *Harris, T., Ho, A., Neugebauer, R., Pratt, I., & Warfield, A.* (2003). *Xen and the art of virtualization.* ACM SOSP.

Buyya, R., Yeo, C. S., & Venugopal, S. (2008). Market-oriented cloud computing: Vision, hype, and reality for delivering it services as computing utilities. *Proceedings of the 10th IEEE International Conference on High Performance Computing and Communications HPCC '08* (p. 513). IEEE. 10.1109/HPCC.2008.172

Buyya, R., Yeo, C. S., Venugopal, S., Broberg, J., & Brandic, I. (2009). Cloud Computing and Emerging IT Platforms: Vision, Hype, and Reality for Delivering Computing as the 5th Utility. In *Future Generation Computer Systems*. Amsterdam: Elsevier Science. doi:10.1016/j.future.2008.12.001

Casanova, H., Legrand, A., Zagorodnov, D., & Berman, F. (2000). Heuristics for scheduling parameter sweep applications in grid environments. *Proceedings of the 9th Heterogeneous Computing Workshop (HCW)* (pp. 349–363). 10.1109/HCW.2000.843757

Chang, C. J., Huang, C. W., Chang, K. H., Chen, Y. C., & Hsieh, C. C. (2008, November). High Throughput 32-Bit AES Implementation in FPGA. *Proc. IEEE Asia Pacific Conf. Circuits and Systems* (pp. 1806-1809).

Chisnall, D. (2008). *The Definitive Guide to the Xen Hypervisor*. Prentice Hall.

Clark, B., & Deshane, T., Dow, E., Evanchik, S., Finlayson, M., & Herne, J. (2004). Xen and the art of repeated research. *Proceedings of the annual conference on USENIX Annual Technical Conference* (p. 47). USENIX Association.

Dahbur, K., Bassil Mohammad, J., & Tarakji, A. (2011, July-September). Security Issues in Cloud Computing: A Survey of Risks, Threats and Vulnerabilities. *International Journal of Cloud Applications and Computing*, *1*(3), 1–11. doi:10.4018/ijcac.2011070101

Govindan, S., Nath, A. R., Das, A., Urgaonkar, B., & Sivasubramaniam, A. (2007). Xen and co.: communication-aware CPU scheduling for consolidated Xen-based hosting platforms. *Proceedings of the 3rd International Conference on Virtual Execution Environments VEE '07* (pp. 126-136). 10.1145/1254810.1254828

Gueron, S. (2010). Intel Advanced Encryption Standard (AES) Instructions Set.

Jeyarani, R., & Nagaveni, N. (2012, January-March). A Heuristic Meta Scheduler for Optimal Resource Utilization and Improved QoS in Cloud Computing Environment. *International Journal of Cloud Applications and Computing*, *2*(1), 41–52. doi:10.4018/ijcac.2012010103

Kivity, A., Kamay, Y., Laor, D., Lublin, U., & Liguori, A. (2007). kvm: the Linux virtual machine monitor. *Proceedings of Linux Symposium* (pp. 225–230).

Lee, M., Krishnakumar, A., Krishnan, P., Singh, N., & Yajnik, S. (2010). Supporting soft real-time tasks in the xen hypervisor. *Proceedings of the 6th ACM SIGPLAN/SIGOPS international conference on Virtual execution environments* (pp. 97–108). ACM. 10.1145/1735997.1736012

Liao, G., Guo, D., Bhuyan, L., & King, S.R. (2008). Software techniques to improve virtualized IO performance on multicore systems. *Proceedings of the 4th ACM/IEEE Symposium on Architectures for Networking and Communications Systems ANCS '08* (pp. 161-170). 10.1145/1477942.1477971

Maheswaran, M., Ali, S., Siegel, H., Hensgen, D., & Freund, R. (1999). Dynamic mapping of a class of independent tasks onto heterogeneous computing systems. *Journal of Parallel and Distributed Computing*, *59*(2), 107–131. doi:10.1006/jpdc.1999.1581

Menon, A., Santos, J. R., Turner, Y., Janakiraman, G. J., & Zwaenepoel, W. (2005). Diagnosing performance overheads in the Xen virtual machine environment. *Proceedings of the 1st ACM/USENIX International Conference on Virtual execution environments VEE '05* (pp. 13-23). 10.1145/1064979.1064984

Moore, J. M. (1968). Sequencing *n* jobs on one machine to minimize the number of late jobs. *Management Science, 15*(1), 102–109. doi:10.1287/mnsc.15.1.102

Nishiguchi, N. (2008). *Evaluation and consideration of the credit scheduler for client virtualization.* Xen Summit Asia.

NIST. (2001). Advanced Encryption Standard (AES). Retrieved from http://csrc.nist.gov/publications/fips/fips197 fips-197.pdf

Xen Wiki. (n. d.). SEDF Scheduler. Retrieved from http://wiki.xensource.com/xenwiki/Scheduling

Sisu, X., Justin, W., Chenyang, L., & Christopher, D. (2011). *RT-Xen: towards real-time hypervisor scheduling in xen* (pp. 39–48). EMSOFT.

Smith, W. (1956). Various optimizers for single stage production. *Naval Research Logistics Quarterly, 3*(1-2), 59–66. doi:10.1002/nav.3800030106

Stankovic, J. A., Spuri, M., & Ramamritham, K. & *Buttazzo, G.C.* (1998). *Deadline Scheduling for Real time Systems – EDF and Related Algorithms.* Kluwer Academic Publishers. doi:10.1007/978-1-4615-5535-3

Subashini, S., & Kavitha, V. (2010). A survey on security issues in service delivery models of cloud computing. *Journal of Network and Computer Applications, 34*(1), 1–11. doi:10.1016/j.jnca.2010.07.006

VMware. (2007). Understanding full virtualization, paravirtualization, and hardware assist (white paper).

Yao, J., Chen, S., Nepal, S., Levy, D., & Zic, J. (2010). TrustStore: Making Amazon S3 Trustworthy with Services Composition. *Proceedings of the 10th IEEE/ACM International Conference on Cluster, Cloud and Grid Computing (CCGRID '08)*, Melbourne, Australia. 10.1109/CCGRID.2010.17

Zhao, L., & Sakura, Y. R. (2013). Reliable workflow scheduling with less resource redundancy. *Parallel Computing, Elsevier, 39*(10), 567–585. doi:10.1016/j.parco.2013.06.003

Zhao, W., Ramamritham, K., & Stankovic, J. A. (1990). Scheduling tasks with resource requirements in hard realtime systems. *IEEE Transactions on Software Engineering, 12*(3), 360–369.

This research was previously published in the International Journal of Cloud Applications and Computing (IJCAC), 6(4); edited by B. B. Gupta and Dharma P. Agrawal, pages 97-110, copyright year 2016 by IGI Publishing (an imprint of IGI Global).

Section 3
Tools and Technologies

Chapter 27
CCCE:
Cryptographic Cloud Computing Environment Based on Quantum Computations

Omer K. Jasim
Al-Ma'arif University College, Iraq

Safia Abbas
Ain Shams University, Egypt

El-Sayed M. El-Horbaty
Ain Shams University, Egypt

Abdel-Badeeh M. Salem
Ain Shams University, Egypt

ABSTRACT

Cloud computing technology is a modern emerging trend in the distributed computing technology that is rapidly gaining popularity in network communication field. Despite the advantages that the cloud platforms bolstered, it suffers from many security issues such as secure communication, consumer authentication, and intrusion caused by attacks. These security issues relevant to customer data filtering and lost the connection at any time. In order to address these issues, this chapter, introduces an innovative cloud computing cryptographic environment, that entails both Quantum Cryptography-as-service and Quantum Advanced Encryption Standard. CCCE poses more secure data transmission channels by provisioning secret key among cloud's instances and consumers. In addition, the QCaaS solves the key generation and key distribution problems that emerged through the online negotiation between the communication parties. It is important to note that the CCCE solves the distance limitation coverage problem that is stemmed from the quantum state property.

DOI: 10.4018/978-1-5225-8176-5.ch027

INTRODUCTION

In this era, computing is categorized according to their usage pattern. Parallel Computing, Sequential Computing, and Distributed Computing are a well-known form of computing technologies (Sunita & Seema, 2013). In general, distributed computing involved in many communication systems to solve a large scale communication problems. The growing of high-speed broadband networks and the rapid growth of the Internet changed the network communication way. Thus, the new trends of distributed computing technology require integration between distributed computing systems and networking communication systems (Aidan, Hans, Patrick, and Damian, 2012). This integration allows computer networks to be involved in a distributed computing environment as full participants in other sharing computing resources such as CPU capacity and memory/disk space.

Emerging trends in distributed computing paradigm include grid computing, utility computing and cloud computing (Sunita & Seema, 2013). These emerging distributed computing together with the development of networking technologies are changing the entire computing paradigm toward a new trend in distributed computing. This chapter describes the emerging technology in distributed computing which known as cloud computing.

Cloud computing is a specialized form of grid and utility computing, and that takes grid computing style when the dynamic connection service and the virtual resources service are available through the internet. In addition, any cloud architecture consisting of many layers (Service Platform Infrastructure layers-SPI) such as the infrastructure as a service (IaaS), the platform as a service (PaaS), the Software as a Service (SaaS) and some others collectively as a services (*aaS). These services layers offer numerous roles as reducing the hardware costs, providing the reliability of each consumer and provisioning resources on-demand (Chander & Yogesh, 2013; Mohammad, John, & Ingo, 2010).

SPI layers and Service Level Agreements (SLA) provide communication between cloud services provider (CSP) and consumers using cloud networks. Since cloud computing environment is a virtual and dynamic, it requires a scalable hardware that supports the virtualization technology and data transformation remotely. Data transformations remotely expose the whole cloud environment to various attacks (Faiza, 2012; Mather & Kumaraswamy, 2012). Therefore, a secure communication is an essential prerequisite for opening cloud environment as a robust and feasible solution (Kumaraswamy, 2012). Many distinct cloud security groups discussed the security vulnerabilities in the cloud computing and classified the possible vulnerabilities into cloud characteristics-related and security controls- related (Omer, Safia, El-Sayed & Abdel-Badeeh, 2014).

Despite different groups try to solve the security challenges in cloud computing, many gaps and threads are still uncovered or handled. Accordingly, the cryptographic tools are installed and developed in many cloud computing environments. These tools require a long-term secret key to guaranteeing the encryption/decryption process, which in turn, considered a valuable target for various attacks (Doelitzsch, Reich, Kahl & Clarke, 2011).

In the cloud computing environment, deploying such long-secret key for any modern encryption algorithm (symmetric or asymmetric) ensures the data confidentiality (prevention of unauthorized disclosure of information), integrity (change in the data), and availability (readiness of correctional services) (CSA, 2012, Omer, Safia, El-Sayed & Abdel-Badeeh, 2013). Despite the solvable problems based such long secret key, the key management and distribution problems still disclosed.

Quantum Key Distribution (QKD) addresses these problems in distributed computing and negotiation mechanism. It can preserve data privacy when users interact with remote computing centers remotely (Doelitzscher, Reich, Knahl & Clarke, 2011; Dabrowski, Mills, & orphan, 2011).

This chapter presents a robust cloud cryptographic environment that completely depends on quantum computations and a newly developed symmetric encryption algorithm. In addition, this chapter introduces an innovative CCCE, which poses more secured data transmission by provisioning secret key among cloud's instances based on QCaaS layer. Finally, this chapter solves the distance limitation coverage problem, by measures the randomness of qubits based on the NIST and DIEHARD test suite algorithms (Juan S., 2012; Andrew, Juan, James, Miles, Elaine and Stefan, 2013).

The rest of the chapter is organized as follows; Section 2 surveys the existing methods for cloud computing security issues such privacy, confidentiality, and key management. The background of cloud computing related-technologies, cloud security precautions, standard cloud cryptographic models, modern cloud cryptographic algorithms, and QKD technology are given in Section 3. Section 4 presents in details the CCCE development and the basic software/hardware requirements. QCaaS is explained in Section 5. Section 6 discusses in details the main building block of CCCE. CCCE phases are illustrated in Section6.

Section7 presents the CCCE characteristics and analysis. Finally, Section 8 shows the conclusion and future work.

RELATED WORKS

This section shows the literature survey correlated with the cloud data privacy, confidentiality and cloud key management.

Cloud Data Privacy and Confidentiality

Despite different studies' attempts to solve the security problem in cloud communications, many gaps and threads are still uncovered or handled. Accordingly, numerous efforts have been exerted in order overcome such gaps.

Wang et al. (2012) introduced the anonymity based method for achieving the cloud privacy. In which, the anonymity algorithm has processed the data and the output released to the cloud provider. The anonymous output is split into different tables or parts and stored on multiple service providers' storages. If the user needs to restore the meaningful information, he/she has to get all the parts or tables. Two cases have been manipulated in this study:

- **Case 1:** If one service provider aggregates the meaningful contents depending on collecting the service from other services and providing data to the consumers'. Here, there is no preservation of privacy because the aggregating service provider may read or leak the information.
- **Case 2:** If the consumers have to aggregate themselves, then they have to contact multiple service providers, which will reduce the efficiency of the service on-demand.

Itani et al. (2012) proposed the privacy-as-a-services (PaaS) model, in which, the contents are divided into two parts: sensitive and non-sensitive. Sensitive data are encrypted based on the modern encryption algorithm, but a non-sensitive data kept as plain. In general, sensitive data is decrypted by the consumer with the shared secret key between consumer and the CSP. Here, the service providers are maintaining the key in tamper-resistance device/memory with the help of the trusted third party then it is again like the standard cloud scenario.

Stephen et al. (2013) proposed the model based on obfuscation mechanism for the cloud infrastructure and ultimately based on assigned VMs. This model setups the encryption key for each trusted consumer and encrypted all the consumer-data stored in the cloud. In this model, the data goes out of the VM will be encrypted to avoid the network sniffing by CSP or others. This model is very efficient if the data are posted and accessed by a single person. Otherwise, the consumer faced the same problem mentioned in the previous model (Syam, Subramanian & Thamizh., 2010). In addition, if the consumer is posting the content as on-demand for end-users, decryption key and de-obfuscation procedure need to be setup with each one. Otherwise, it is not feasible for them to read the data. The foible of this model summarizes in case of increasing the number of end users, the key revocation and re-distribution between the data owner and end-user stilled uncover.

Emmanuel et al. (2013) described a data security system in cloud computing based DES algorithm to secure consumer and cloud server. The security architecture of the system was developed by using DES- Cipher Block Chaining (CBC), which eliminates the data stolen. However, DES algorithm hacked by many attackers such as man-in-the-middle attack, side channel attack, and Differential Power Analysis (DPA) in which the key expansion phase is exploited in the DES structure.

Doelitzscher et al. (2011) identified the abuse of cloud resources, lack of security monitoring in cloud infrastructure and the defective isolation of shared resources as focal points to be managed. They also focused on the lack of flexibility of intrusion detection mechanisms to handle virtualized environments and suggesting the use of special security tools associated with the business flow modeling through security SLAs. In addition, the analysis of the highest security concerns is also based on publications from CSA, ENISA, and NIST, without offering a detail quantitative compilation of security risks and areas of concern. Table 1 summarizes the characteristics of the surveyed cloud security studies by describing the innovative security model, cloud operating environment, security issues, and weaknesses.

Finally, we can conclude that the cryptographic mechanism is an essential field for the cloud security process. In addition, due to the dynamic characteristics of cloud technology there are many challenges regarding the securing for communications. These challenges lie in the existence of a robust security model that guarantees a trusted data transformation.

Table 1. Characteristics of the cloud data privacy studies

Authors	Innovative Model	Cloud Environment	Security Issues	Weaknesses
Wang et al. (2012)	Anonymity	Amazon EC2	data privacy, authorization, accountability	Unbalancing between the number of consumers and CSP efficiency
Itani et al. (2012)	Privacy as Services (PasS)	Hyper-V	data privacy, availability, data protection	Apt of tamper-resistance (device/memory), leakage of third trusted party
Stephen et al. (2013)	Obfuscation	Xen-Server	data privacy, key distribution, confidence	Inconvenient between the key revocation and re-distribution with no. of users
Emanuel et al. (2013)	Cryptographic Model	Hyper-V	CIA issues	Cryptographic algorithm hacked by DPA family attackers
Doelitzscher et al. (2011)	Abuse Identification	Own Cloud	Non-repudiation, integrity, digital signature	Don't offering a deeper quantitative compilation of security risks

Key Management

In order to achieve the cloud data privacy and confidentiality (mentioned above), the efficiency of key management and re-keying with consumers is vital for cloud cryptographic process. Hence, this section reviews the existing models related to the key management between consumers and CSP in order to achieve the privacy and confidentiality.

Bethencourt et al. (2011) presented an Attribute-Based Encryption (ABE) model in the cloud environment and social networks. The model allows consumers to participate in two or more groups. These groups help to assign the encryption key for each registered consumer. In order to compute and distribute the encryption key for each consumer involved in the groups, the logical expression is used. The computational cost (time and space) and rekeying to members in the same group are central weakness in the ABE model.

Mather et al. (2012) discussed the encryption mechanisms, key management capabilities and expatriated multi-entity key management mechanism in cloud computing. Also, this study examined the status of cloud computing security depending on security management, data security, and identity management. This study explored the urge for more transparency to providing the security capability in the cloud environment, therefore, the need for standardization and the creation of legal agreements reflecting the operational SLAs. However, this study does not explain the role of SLA in the security of an open cloud environment.

Cutillo et al. (2009) presented the simple shared key - consumer side storage model. The encryption key is generated based on the consumer attributes and shared with all consumers in the group. This key is given by CSP using consumer public key. In case the CSP wants to change the encryption key to revoke a particular consumer, the CSP needs to change the deployed key with a newly inherited key. In addition, the new inherited key needs to be distributed to everyone again and the decryption key is stored on the consumer machines. Consequently, the key should be transferred only to group not to all the consumers connected to the network, this is a useful advantage of this model.

Rawal et al. (2012) described the perfect alliance between cloud computing and quantum computing trends, which guarantees data safety for hosted files on remote computers or datacenter. He encrypted heavy duty of data by using the highly processing servers as a quantum computer, which hides input, processing and output data from malicious and attacks based on the quantum computations mechanism. However, the performance examination of such hybrid technique on practical cloud environment is missing.

Miao Zhou (2012) presented the tree-based key management model in cloud computing. The vital idea of this study is to design a secure and flexible key management mechanism for the data in cloud computing. The cloud database remains private and secure while some selected data and key nodes are shared with other parties in the cloud. The flexibility of key management is achieved and the security is proved in such proposed model. Finally, Table 2 summarizes the key management studies in the cloud environment by describing the innovative model, advantages and disadvantages for each one.

BACKGROUND

Cloud computing technology is a result of the integration of current computing technologies. These computing technologies, which are deployed based on the cloud functionality, are virtualization, service-oriented architecture (SOA), utility computing, grid computing, parallel computing, and cluster computing.

Table 2. Characteristics of the cloud key management studies

Authors	Innovative Model	Advantages	Disadvantages
Bethencourt et al. (2011)	Attribute-Based Encryption(ABE)	Assign keys for each registered clients into involved group	Computational cost in ABE, key assigned
Mather et al. (2012)	multi-entity key management	Defeating a passive and a side channel attacks, enhancing of identity management	Conflicted with SLA led to apt to sniffing attack
Cutillo et al. (2009)	Simple Shared Key 1-Client-side	Defeating a distributed DoS attacks, almost active attacks	Key group storage vulnerable to authentication attacks
Rawal et al. (2012)	Quantum cloud computing	Guarantees data protection for hosted files on remote computers from malicious and attacks	High costly to implement, coverage distance limitation
Miao Zhou. (2012)	tree-based key management	Design a secure and flexible key management mechanism	Leakage for key generation and distribution

Virtualization and SOA are core technologies for cloud computing (Nelson, Charles, Fernando, Marco, Tereza, Mats and Makan, 2014). Virtualization abstracts the underlying physical infrastructure, which is the most equipped component, and makes it accessible and easy to be used and managed (Syam, Subramanian and Thamizh, 2010). Whereas, SOA offers an easier way for cloud framework understanding and management (Chadwick, Casanova, 2011).

Despite most of the computing technologies trends suffered from the security issues, such as data security, cryptographic key distribution, key availability, identity, etc. Nevertheless, the major challenge in security issues addressed in data transmission, especially for cloud computing trend. Since the consumer's confidential data and business logics reside in the remote cloud servers, competitors and intruders are expected to attack such transmission process (Mandeep, Manish, 2012). This section presents in detail the cloud security precautions, classical cryptographic cloud algorithms, quantum technology features, and basic cloud encryption models.

Cloud Security Precautions

The improvement of cloud computing technology reinforced by the improvement of the security concerns. Thus, various cloud security management has been developed.

CSA security guidance (CSA, 2012, ENISA security assessment 2014, and IDC, 2014) highly focus on different security issues related to cloud computing. Such issues require further studies in order to appropriately handle and enhancing the technology acceptance and adoption. Accordingly, in order to concentrate and organize information related to cloud security next subsections shed light on the distinctive cloud security issues such as network security, cloud data security, and virtualization.

Network Security

Almost problems associated with network communications and configurations effect on cloud security infrastructures (Manpreet, Rajbir, 2013). Potential levels of cloud network security are (Nelson, Charles, Fernando, Marco, Tereza, Mats and Makan, 2014):

- **Connection Level:** distributed architectures, massive resource sharing and synchronization between cloud virtual machines require Virtual Private Network (VPN) and domain controller connection mechanisms. These mechanisms protected the cloud network environment against most types of attacks like spoofing, man-in-middle, and side channel attacks.

- **Firewalls Level:** firewalls protect the CSP (internal IaaS) against insiders and outsiders intruders (Jensen, Schwenk, Gruschka and Iacono, 2009). They also enable VM isolation, filtering the addressing mechanism, prevention of DoS, and detection external attacks by combination with sub-domain controller policy.
- **Configurations Level:** configurations help to provide a level of security and privacy without performance or efficiency compromised.

Cloud Data Security

In order to achieve a secure cloud data environment, Confidentiality, Availability, Integrity and Traceability (CAIT) requirements must be provided. So, the following mechanisms must be guarantee (William, 2012; Omer, Safia, El-Sayed and Abdel-Badeeh, 2014).

- **Cryptographic Mechanism:** a practice method to secure sensitive data by the transformation of a cloud consumer's data into ciphertext. In the cloud environment, a cryptographic data deploys as a service offered by CSP. So, the cloud consumers' must take the time to learn about the provider's policies and procedures for encryption and key management. Finally, the cloud encryption capabilities of the service provider need to match the level of sensitivity of the data being hosted.
- **Replications Mechanism:** it is essential to avoid data loss, it achieves based on many intelligent algorithms such as, Replica Location Services (RLS) (Doelitzscher, Reich, Kahl., Clarke, 2011), Quantum Evolutionary Algorithm (QEA) (Ammar,Khaled, Muneer, Eman, 2013) and others (Christain, Mario, 2011).
- **Disposal Mechanism:** elementary data disposal techniques are insufficient and commonly referred as deletion, and it is considered essential requirements for cloud datacenters. Finally, in the cloud environment the complete destruction of data including log references and hidden backup registers (Omer, Safia, El-Sayed and Abdel-Badeeh, 2014).

Cloud Computing Attacks

Despite cloud computing environments are getting more familiar, its main risk is the intrusion caused by the attackers. A most known communication attack mechanisms in a cloud computing environment which are discussed in (Omer, Safia, El-Sayed and Abdel-Badeeh, 2014).

Virtualization

According to (Syam, Subramanian and Thamizh, 2010) the main problem associated with virtualization technologies are VMs'- isolation, hypervisor vulnerabilities, data leakage, and VM identification.

- **Isolation:** Despite logically VM-isolated, all VMs share the same hardware and consequently the same resources. This act is vulnerable for allowing malicious entities to exploit data leaks and cross-VM attacks (Soren, Sven, and Hugo, 2013).

- **Hypervisor Vulnerabilities:** It is the central component of virtualization technology. However, it suffers from many security vulnerabilities like escape affords attackers, hyper-jacking (thin hypervisor) and others. The solutions of this problem are still scarce and often proprietary, demanding further studied to harden these security aspects.
- **Data Leakage:** exploit hyper vulnerabilities and lack of isolation controls in order to leak data from virtualized infrastructures, obtaining sensitive consumers data and affecting confidentiality and integrity (Omer, Safia, El-Sayed and Abdel-Badeeh, 2014).
- **VM Identification:** lack of controls for identifying VMs that are being used for executing a particular process or substantial files.

Consumer Identification

Consumer identification is an important aspect of cloud computing. Only authorized user has ability to write, access and the data contents (Omer, Safia, El-Sayed and Abdel-Badeeh, 2014). Therefore, the authorization manner with the encryption provision give a secure environment for data resident in the cloud. Without user "id" verification, the system will not allow any of the requests made to some transactions, which will ultimately help in data privacy and security.

Standard Cloud Cryptographic Models

This section illustrates the basic cryptographic mechanisms that deployed in the cloud computing environment through the last three years.

Cipher Cloud Model

Cipher cloud is a new emerging rend in encryption/decryption processes for cloud data files. It protected enterprise data using formatting and operations-preserving encryption and tokenized in any private or public cloud environment without affecting functionality, usability, or performance (Omer, Safia, El-Sayed and Abdel-Badeeh, 2014). In addition, Cipher cloud provides a unified cloud encryption gateway with award-winning technology to encrypt sensitive data in real-time before it is sent to the cloud

As shown in Figure 1, consumers probably have data stored in multiple clouds such as Google, Amazon, Azure, and many others. Cipher cloud work as a firewall security gateway that sits between users

Figure 1. Cipher cloud architecture

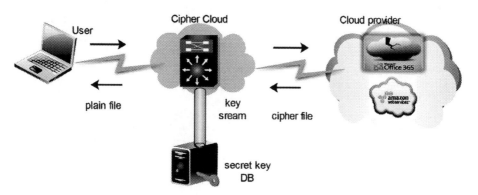

and cloud applications and it applies encryption to the data before sensitive data leave the enterprise. Furthermore, it offers multiple AES-compatible encryptions and tokenized options, including format and function-preserving encryption algorithms. Consumers see the real data when gaining access to an application through the Cipher Cloud security gateway, but the data stored in a cloud application is encrypted.

Moreover, by applying encryption in a cloud security gateway, cipher cloud eliminates the inherent security, privacy, and regulatory compliance risks of cloud computing. The cipher cloud security gateway uses flexible, configurable policies to identify sensitive data and automatically encrypt/decrypt data between users and the cloud using encryption keys that remain under the control at all times.

Finally, cipher cloud reverses the process when consumers access cloud applications over the algorithm decrypting data in real time so that users browse the actual data rather than the encrypted version that resides within the cloud datacenter.

Cryptography-as-a-Service Model

Soren et al. present a security architecture that permits establishing secure consumer-controlled-cryptography-as-a-service (CaaS) in the cloud. CaaS provides consumers to be full control of their credentials and cryptographic primitives. All these operations provided based on Trusted Platform Module (TPM) known as sub inherited domain from Xen hypervisor. Figure 2 illustrates the CaaS architecture using Xen hypervisor.

All consumers' operations run in a protected and secure execution domain that achieved by modifying the Xen hypervisor and the leveraging standard Trusted Computing Technology (TCT). Moreover, this model is legacy-compatible by installing a transparent cryptographic layer for the storage and network I/O on the VM. Finally, this type of cryptographic data cloud protects consumers from any unauthorized access that tries to extract cryptographic material from the VM – either from a privileged management domain or from outside the VM. However, this model vulnerable to authentication and side channel attacks due to all controlling mechanisms and encryption/decryption processes assigned to the consumer side.

Figure 2. CaaS Architecture

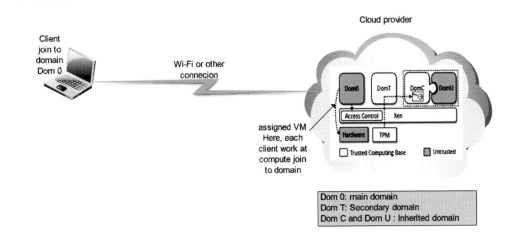

Figure 3. Cryptographic cloud storage architecture (Patil D. and Akshay R., 2012)

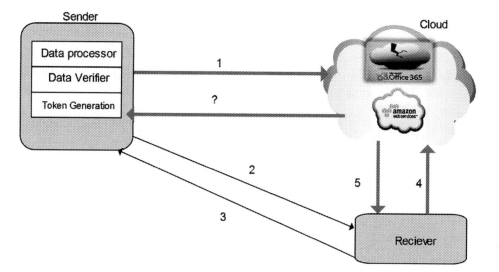

Cryptographic Cloud Storage Model

Patil D. and Akshay R proposed a virtual private storage services that would satisfy the standard requirements (Confidentiality, Integrity, Authentication, etc.).

Most of the desires are obtained by encrypting the files stored in the cloud environment, but encryption makes it very complex to search through such files or to collaborate in real time editing. This model introduced an architecture for a cryptographic storage service that would solve the security problems of "backups, archives, health record systems, secure data exchange, and e-discovery".

This architecture is based on three components see Figure 3:

- **Data Processor (DP):** Processes the data before sending it to the cloud.
- **Data Verifier (DV):** Validates the data's consistency and integrity.
- **Token Generator (TG):** Generates an indexing token allowing the service provider to retrieve files.

The consumer solution contains using a local application that has the three above mentioned components. Before uploading data to the cloud, consumers' uses the data processor to encrypt and encode the documents along with their meta-data (tags, time, size, etc.). Then, send them into the cloud environment. When consumers' wants to download some documents, he/she uses the TG to generate an index token and a decryption key. Moreover, the token is sent to the cloud storage provider to select the encrypted files to be downloaded or browsed. After that, the DV is invoked to verify the integrity of the data using a master key. The document is decrypted using the decryption key.

In general, the encryption process strategy in cloud environments mainly depends on encrypting the data in two different phases;

1. The transmission process before sending the data to the cloud and
2. The storage process after the transmission and before the storing process.

Cloud Cryptographic Algorithms (CCA)

According to cloud cryptographic models mentioned above, all of them relied on modern classical encryption algorithms (symmetric and asymmetric). In most cases, cloud computing designer and programmer use the symmetric encryption algorithm due to efficiency, scalable and easy to implementation (Omer, Safia, El-Sayed and Abdel-Badeeh, 2013). Employing an appropriate strength encryption process is essential, so, many encryption algorithms have been developed and implemented in order to provide more secure data transmission in the cloud environment. Data Encryption Standard (DES), Advanced Encryption Standard (AES), Rivest Cipher-4 (RC4), Blowfish, and 3DES fare well-known of symmetric category, while, Rivest, Shanon, Adelman (RSA) and Deffi-Hillman(DH) for asymmetric type. Table 3 summarizes the characteristics of the encryption algorithms, both symmetric and asymmetric (Winkler, 2011; Omer, Safia, El-Sayed and Abdel-Badeeh, 2013; William, 2012).

Obviously from the above table, that the symmetric encryption techniques are more popularly used than asymmetric ones in cloud computing. In a cloud environment, a cryptographic key deploys to one type of encryption algorithms to provide the encryption/decryption processes. These algorithms assist in providing the data CIAT continuously (William, 2012)

Omer K. et al. (2013) implemented the mentioned symmetric and asymmetric algorithms in order to ensure the data security in a cloud environment. In addition, they examined the performance of such algorithms, considering the time of the encryption/ decryption process and the size of the output encrypted files. Accordingly, symmetric encryption techniques are faster than the asymmetric encryption techniques, and AES algorithm guarantees more efficiency from others. Moreover, all algorithms in both categories (symmetric and asymmetric) archive the inverse proportion relation between the running time and the input file size, except the RSA algorithm. The RSA runs time changes slightly with the input file size increase (Omer, Safia, El-Sayed and Abdel-Badeeh, 2013).

Despite the encryption process uses complex techniques for random key generation based on mathematical models and computations, its encryption strategy considered vulnerable. So, if the intruder is good enough in mathematical computation field such quantum attack, he/she can easily decrypt the cipher and retrieve the original transmitted or stored documents. Furthermore, the key distribution problem ascends from the fact that communicating parties must somehow share a secret key before any secure communication can be initiated, and both parties must ensure that the key remains secret. Of course, direct key distribution is not always feasible due to risk, inconvenience, and cost factors (Winkler,

Table 3. Encryption Algorithms characteristics (S= symmetric, A= asymmetric)

Algorithm	Category	Key size (bits)	Input size (bits)	Attack apt	Initial vector size (bits)
AES	S	128; 192; 256	128	Non recognized yet	128
DES	S	56	64	Brute force attack	64
3-DES	A	112- 168	64	Brute force attack	64
RC4	S	256	256	Bit flipping attack	256
Blowfish	S	32-448	32	Dictionary attack	64
RSA	A	>1024	>1024	Timing attack	-
DH	A	n-Key Exchange	n	Ping attack	-

2011).In some situations, the direct key exchange is possible through a secure communication channel. However, this security can never guarantee. A fundamental problem remains because, in principle, any classical private channel can be monitored passively, without the sender or receiver knowing that the eavesdropper has taken place (Christain, Mario, 2010). Thus, in order to overcome this obstacle, key distribution, and mathematical computations, an unconditional secure concept must be provided. QKD system provides an unconditional security concept, because of, it ultimately depends on quantum mechanics in key generation and management (Christain, Mario, 2010; Bart De Decker, André Zúquete, 2014).

Quantum Technology

Recently, quantum technology (QT) flourished and spread rapidly in many disciplines, DNA, AI, and quantum communications are examples of such disciplines. The importance of QT is lying in its ability to solve the key challenges associated with distributed computing environments based on QKD (Ammar, Khaled, Muneer, Eman 2013; Christain, Mario, 2010). This section illustrates an unconditional QKD security scheme. As shown in Figure 4, QKD enables secret quantum keys exchanging between two different parties through two communication channels, classical and quantum channels (Omer, Safia, El-Sayed and Abdel-Badeeh, 2014). It is an alternative to the classical encryption algorithms (symmetric or asymmetric categories) and used to solve the common existing scheme problems such as key distribution, management, and defeating attacks (Omer, Safia, El-Sayed and Abdel-Badeeh, 2015).

Furthermore, in order to exchange the keys between communication parties, well-known protocols were developed such as Charles H. Bennett and Gilles Brassard-1984 (BB84) and Artur Ekert-1991 (E91). After then, these protocols are utilized by QKD for exchanging process. This chapter utilizes a BB84 protocol since it enjoys with many advantages with E91 protocol. Higher bit rate (up to 6 Mbps), secure up to 140 KM and resistance against Photon number splitting (PNS) and Man-in-the-middle attacks (Solange G., Mohammed A., 2014) are examples of these advantages. Finally, BB84 protocol utilizes four primary phases in order to generate a final secret quantum key. These phases illustrated as follows:

Figure 4. QKD architecture

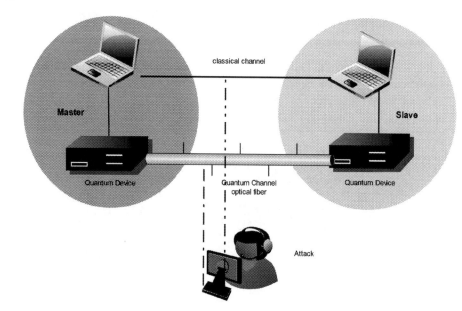

Raw Key Extraction (RKE)

The main purpose of RKE phase is to eliminate all possible errors occurred during the bits discussion (generation and transmission) over the quantum channel. Negotiated parties (i.e. Sender and receiver) compare their filter types used for each photon, unmatched polarization is eliminated otherwise, bits are considered (Omer, Safia, El-Sayed and Abdel-Badeeh, 2014).

Error Estimation (EE)

The negotiation process might occur over a noisy quantum and unsecured (public) classical channel. Such channel can cause a partial key damage or physical noise of transmission medium (Solange G., Mohammed A., 2014). In order to avoid such problems, both parties determine an error threshold value "*Emax*" when they are sure that there is no eavesdropping on a transmission medium. So as to calculate the error percentage (*Er*), the raw bits are monitored and compared with the Emax, if *Er > Emax*, then it is probably either unexpected noise or eavesdroppers.

Key Reconciliation (KR)

Key reconciliation is implemented to minimize the mentioned errors associated with the key as much as possible. It divides the raw key into blocks of K bits; then parity bit calculations are done for each block (Solange G., Mohammed A., 2014). The creating blocks and parity calculations are performed for N-rounds depending on the length of the raw key.

Privacy Amplification (PA)

Privacy Amplification is the final step in the quantum key extraction. It is applied to minimize the number of bits based on equation one that a listener might know. Sending and receiving parties apply a shrinking method to their bit sequences in order to obscure the eavesdropper ability to capture bit sequence (Solange G., Mohammed A., 2014).

$$\text{Privacy bits} = \mathbf{L} - \mathbf{M} - \mathbf{s} \tag{1}$$

$\mathbf{L}$ = bits result from RK, EE, and KR
$\mathbf{M}$ = expected values known by an eavesdropper
$\mathbf{s}$ = a constant chosen security parameter

CCCE DEVELOPMENT AND REQUIREMENTS

The cryptographic cloud computing environment (CCCE), which entails software and hardware requirements, is discussed in details next subsections.

Software Requirements

In this section, a randomness property of the qubits generation based quantum cipher system and proposed encryption algorithm(QAES) be presented associated with a simulator of QAES and quantum cipher. In general, the environment has been implemented using Visual Studio Ultimate 2012 (VC#) based Windows Server 2012 Data Center as operating system.

Quantum Key Distribution Usage

Quantum key generation mainly relies on photons' exchanging between parties over limited distances (314-kilometer) (Solange, Mohammed, 2014; Eduared, 2014,). Such distance limitation is considered as an obstacle to the vast organization and evading usage of such quantum communications based world area network. Therefore, to overcome this obstacle, NIST and DIEHARD algorithms have been implemented for testing and evaluating the randomness rates for a quantum key generation. The computation of randomness rate in the NIST and DIEHARD algorithms completely depend on p-value (Omer, Safia, El-Sayed and Abdel-Badeeh, 2014; Matthew, Caleb, Lamas, Christian, 2013). In general, the calculation for randomness of binary digits can be summarized into the following steps:

Stating the null hypothesis (assume that the binary sequence is random).
Computing a sequence test static with different test suite (based on the bit level)
Calculating the *p*-value (always P-value).
Compare the *p*-value produced to α (usually α=0.01 for all randomness testers), if the *p*-value less than 0.01, then sequence digits generated are failing (S. Juan, 2012).

In a sense, NIST and DIEHARD implemented on the output of RKE, which obtained before PA phase. After then, these algorithms are run on the output of PA phase as well. Regarding (Omer, Safia, El-Sayed and Abdel-Badeeh, 2014), Figure 5 shows the average of the P-values for five QKD-rounds with equal length (100000-bits); the P-value obtained depending on 14 tests are mentioned in S. Juan, 2012.

As shown in Figure 5, the P-value indicates the true randomness of the qubits generation and periodically changed with the rounds' contents. The randomness characteristic helps to adopt the QKD as a source to generate a random number that used with various encryption algorithms (Omer, Safia, El-Sayed and Abdel-Badeeh, 2014).

Symmetric Quantum Encryption Algorithm

This subsection describes a new trend of the symmetric quantum standard encryption algorithm (QAES). This trend incorporates both the QKD and the enhanced version of the AES in order to provide an unconditional security level (Christain, Mario, 2010) for any cipher system built on symmetric encryption algorithms. Figure 6 illustrates that the QAES utilizes the dynamic quantum S-box (DQS-boxes) that is generated from the QKD and exploits the generated key in the encryption /decryption process, instead of the ordinary used static S-boxes.

The DQS-boxes enjoy the dynamic mechanism, which in turn, the contents of each S-Box changes consequently in each round with the change of the key generation. Such dynamic mechanism aids in solving the mechanical problems associated with the traditional S-Boxes such as avoiding an off-line

Figure 5. Randomness tests for qubits generation based 5-QKD different rounds

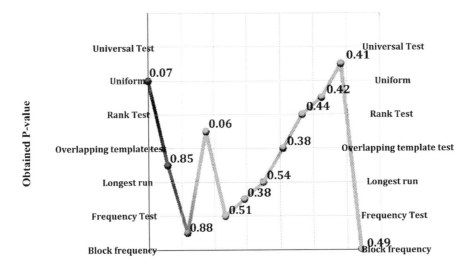

Rounds of QKD

Figure 6. Single round for QAES

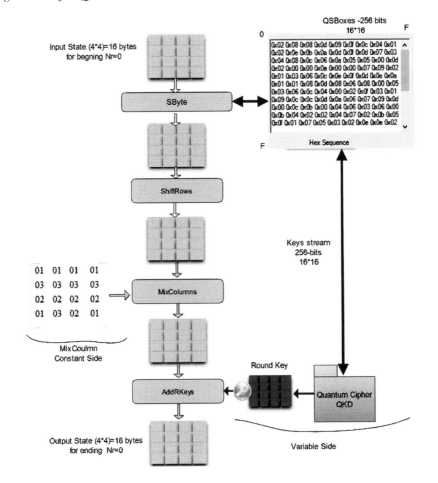

analysis attack and resistant to the quantum attack. Figure 7 shows the pseudo-code of DQS-box has been developed.

Figure 7 shows the achieving process of the DQS-box and InvDQS-box generation by choosing the index d of the bytes *b* from the quantum cipher, which depends on variables *i*, m and *l*. The operation of DQS-box generation is terminated when m equals to 256, which represents the interval value of DQS-box [0-255]. Furthermore, the number of rounds, key length, and input plain text equivalent to classical AES algorithm. Accordingly, QAES development and design do not contradict the security of the AES algorithm and all the mathematical criteria and transformation functions remain unchanged. For more details about QAES architecture and nature of work see (Omer, Safia, El-Sayed and Abdel-Badeeh, 2014). Figure 8 shows the performance examination of QAES in the CCCE considering the time of the encryption/ decryption process and the size of the output encrypted files. This examination implemented using several input file sizes: 500kb, 1000kb, 1500kb, 2000kb, 3000kb, and 4000kb and the running time is calculated in milliseconds.

Comparing the QAES with others encryption algorithms, theQAES reflects a higher security level. However, it takes longer time than others due to the time consumed in the quantum key generation process (time for quantum negotiation and time required for the encryption / decryption process).

Figure 7. Pseudo code of DQS-box

Algorithm: Generation a DQS-box and Inverse DQS-box[1]

- **Input: stream of a quantum key q from QKD cipher**
- **Output: hexadecimal numbers which are arrange in 2-D matrix [16*16].**

// Encryption Process

1. *Initial value* $(i = 0, m = 1, and\ l = 1)$
2. *while* $(m < 256$
   {
   a. $i = i + 1;$
   b. $d = 1 + (m + 1 * l)\ mod\ 176$
   c. $S(i + 1) = S(i) + b(d)mod\ 256;$
   d. $l = 0;$
3. *for j* $= 1\ to\ m\ do$
   {
   a. *If* $(S(i + 1) = S(j)$ //compare between $S(i + 1)$ and $S(j)$ and compute the elelmets
   b. *Go to step 4*
   c. *else*
   d. *Go to step 2*
   e. $J + +;$
   }
4. *if* $l = j$
   {
   a. $DQSbox(m + 1) = DQSbox(i + 1);$
   b. $m = m + 1$
   }
   } *// end for while*

// Decryption process

5. *for* $m = 1\ to\ 256\ do$
   {
   $InvDQSbox(DQSbox(m) + 1) = m - 1;$
   }

Figure 8. An efficient of QAES on Quantum Cloud environment

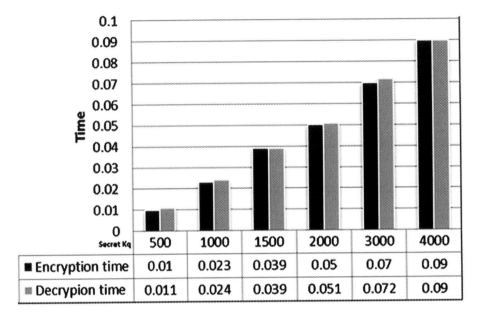

Secret Kq	500	1000	1500	2000	3000	4000
■ Encryption time	0.01	0.023	0.039	0.05	0.07	0.09
▒ Decrypion time	0.011	0.024	0.039	0.051	0.072	0.09

Hardware Requirements

CCCE utilizes many operations such as the number of VMs, quality of services (QoS), storage capacity and other features depending on the IaaS layer. This layer helps consumers to rent virtual resources like network and VMs and configure them according their needs.

Accordingly, the bare-metal Hyper-V and the System Center 2012 SP1(SCSP1) components are explained and implemented (Aidan, Hans, Patrick, Damian, 2012). System Center Virtual Machine Manager (SCVMM), System Center Operation Manager (SCOM), Application Controller (AC), and Operation Services Manager (OSM) are basic components of SCSP1. The main host server utilizes the Core i5 (4.8GHz) with 16GB of RAM with 2TB-HDD as the central hardware. As shown in Figure 9, CCCE includes the following servers:

- **Domain controller "qcloud.net":** It is the central server that manages a single sign process and offers a response multiple cloud services. It deploys a credential account for each trusted consumer and provides a trust connection among consumers and cloud instances. Moreover, it helps to defeat bot the insider attack and denial of service attack (DoS). Finally, it holds the right to access hardware resources.
- **SQL Server:** Each SCSP1 site database can be installed on either the default instance or a named instance of an SQL Server installation. The SQL Server instance can be co-located with the site server, or on a remote computer. In the CEEE, a remote SQL Server is implemented and configured as a failover cluster in either a single instance or a multiple instance configuration. It is responsible for keeping the credential of *SCVMM* and *SCOM* services and creating the report viewer for all operations.

Figure 9. CCCE servers architecture

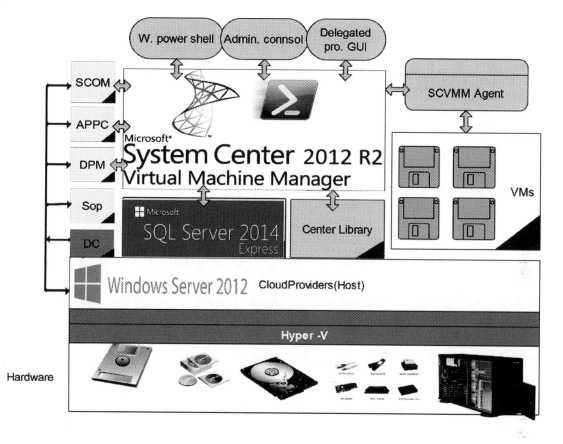

- **SCVMM Server:** it manages the virtualized data center, visualization host, and storage resources. It can integrate with other system center components (mentioned above), deploy a management console operations and cloud configuration wizards. Moreover, it creates VM templates, capability profiles (Aidan, Hans, Patrick, Damian, 2012), ISO images, private cloud objects, and self-service user roles.
- **AC server:** it mainly depends on *SCVMM* to manage applications and services, which in turn, are deployed in private or public cloud infrastructures. It provides a unified self-service portal that helps to configure, deploy, and manage VMs and services on predefined templates. Although some administrator tasks can be performed via the *APPC* console, the users for APPC cannot be considered as administrators.
- **SCOM:** A robust, comprehensive monitoring tool which provides the infrastructure that is flexible and cost-effective, helps ensure the predictable performance and availability of vital applications and offers comprehensive monitoring for datacenter and cloud.
- **StarWind (v.8) server:** it replaces the expensive SAN and NAS physical shared storage. Since it is a software-based and hypervisor-centric virtual machine, which provides a fully fault-tolerant and high-performing storage for the virtualization platform (StarWind Software, 2014). It could seamlessly be integrated into the hypervisor platforms, such as Hyper-V, Xen Server, Linux and Unix environments. In the CCCE, the SCVMM libraries, VHD file, and cloud applications are assigned to *StarWind* server after the integration through the logical unit (LUN) at the fabric panel.

CRYPTOGRAPHIC SERVICE LAYER

This section describes a proposed cryptographic service in the CCCE. This layer provides (i) the secret key provisioning to VMs' consumers, (ii) separating both consumers' cryptographic primitive and (iii) credential accounts based on trusted domain. QCaaS applied to the multiple trusted consumers, which renting the VMs, concurrently. Integrating such service achieves both confidentiality and integrity protection. Figure 10 depicts the QCaaS architecture (software & hardware resources) for single VM. Accordingly, QCaaS has the following features:

- Mini-OS is directly connected with the cloud platform and isolated from the cloud instances.
- Private network configuration and IP for each trusted consumer.
- Sub-inherited domain for each new cryptographic service.
- Special hardware resources (CPU, HDD, and memory) assigned for each service.

Consequently, it assures both the appropriate load for cloud performance optimization and the consumer controlling activities (consumer prevents the cloud administrator from gained or preserve his data). Therefore, a secured environment for each consumer's VMs, with no possibility for insiders or external attackers, is guaranteed.

Finally, after the signing in verification and the VM renting, QCaaS deploys the consumer wizard and the CSP wizard to achieve the encryption/decryption processes and connect to the Quantum Cloud environment.

Figure 10. QCaaS architecture

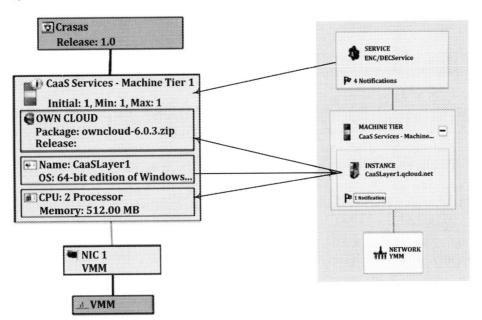

CCCE MAIN BUILDING BLOCKS

CCCE generates the encryption keys based on quantum mechanics instead of classical mathematic operations. Such quantum provide unbroken key and eavesdropper detection. Most definite criteria associated with CCCE came from the nature of the quantum mechanism. Substantially, CCCE encrypts cloud data based QAES using two implemented modes (online and offline).

- **Online Mode:** Consumers directly negotiate with QCaaS based on QKD-BB84 protocol, in order to get a final secret key, which used with QAES algorithm to encrypt files. However, a consumer and QCaaS-provider are not able to know the secret key until the negotiations of their bases are finished (PA phase).
- **Offline Mode:** According to subsection (*QKD Usage*) mentioned above, QCaaS deploys a selected random key for the particular consumer through the VPN-connection domain. Such key is exploited as a seed by QAES algorithm to provide a key session for cryptographic rounds and encrypted files. Furthermore, some classical concepts (randomness test and key session) and quantum techniques (encoding photons) are applied in order to improve the key distribution. However, BB84 cannot be used in such mode because no negotiation between connected partied are achieved.

Additionally, CCCE aims to:

- Improve the availability and the reliability of the cloud computing cryptographic mechanisms by deploying both key generation and key management techniques based on QCaaS layer.
- Manipulate massive computing processes that cannot be executed using the personal computer only.

As shown in Figure 11, CCCE consists of the cloud network that entails Windows Server 2012 Datacenter and Hyper-V installations and configurations with N- full-VMs. These VMs classified as, cloud infrastructure such SCVMM, SCOM, APPC, SQL, DC, cloud instances (VMs rented from the consumer), and VMs for cryptographic processes.

CCCE PHASES

Registration and verification, encryption/decryption, and uploading/downloading are primary phases of CCCE. It discussed based on two modes.

Registration and Verification Phase

Firstly, the end user registers as a consumer to the CSP. The CSP verifies the MAC address and assigns and generates a certificate authority (CA) to authorize the consumer via Kerberos authentication function. Secondly, the CSP checks the resources availability and picks up, depended on the Microsoft Load Balancing (MLB) (Aidan, Hans, Patrick, Damian, 2012), the lowest load VM among the others. Finally, the VM-IP address is assigned to the consumer. Accordingly, due to such assigned process, when the consumer needs to reconnect his/her VM is assigned directly after the authentication achieved.

Figure 11. CCCE main building blocks

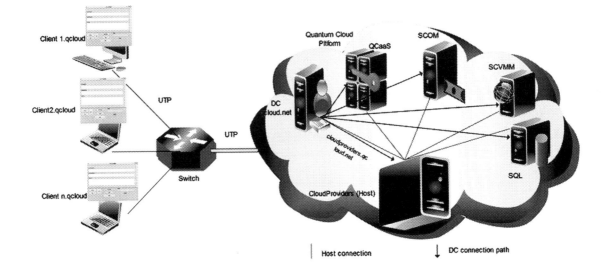

Encryption / Decryption Phase

The encryption/decryption phase entails online and offline modes. In the online mode, the final secret key is generated as a result of the negotiation between the consumer and the QCaaS. Whereas, in the offline mode, the qubits is directly sent by the QCaaS to the authenticated consumer. Finally, in order to gain a secured communication for file transmission, the QAES-256 is used in both modes during the encryption/decryption process.

- **Consumer: $E_n (P, K_q) \leftarrow P'$** // trusted client encrypts the file (P) on the own machine using QAES.
- **IQCaaS: $D (P', K_q) \leftarrow P$** // service decrypts an encrypted file (P') on CCCE using QAES.

Uploading / Downloading Phase

In this phase, necessary steps for uploading / downloading files in the CCCE are illustrated. The following is the uploading process in *the on-line* mode:

- The Consumer sends a request to CSP, (http://sharepoint2:8088/scvm_layout/request), for authentication.
- CSP sends the corresponding registered VM-IP successful authentication.
- CSP assigns a QCaaS layer and deploys a console wizard to the consumer.
- The Consumer starts the negotiation with QCaaS service.
- Consumer encrypts a file on the own machine by QAES-256-bits.
- The Consumer sends the file to the cloud environment via secure web-services.
- QCaaS decrypts the sending file and saves it.
- While, the uploading process steps in the *off-line mode* are:
- The Consumer sends a request to CSP, (http://sharepoint2:8088/scvm_layout/request), for authentication.

- CSP sends the corresponding registered VM-IP successful authentication.
- CSP assigns a QCaaS layer and deploys a console wizard to the consumer.
- QCaaS generate a pseudo-random number based quantum cipher and create a secret key.
- QCaaS deploys a secret key to the consumer.
- The Consumer encrypts a file on the own machine by QAES-256-bits.
- The Consumer sends the file to the cloud environment via secure web-services.
- QCaaS decrypts the sending file and saves it.

The steps for the downloading process are the inverse of uploading one.

DISCUSSIONS

In this section, CCCE is analyzed based on the security management, QCaaS functions, and DoS defeating.

Security Management

The rapid growth of cloud computing usage leads to more complications in the security management task that is mainly responsible for providing a secure environment to both consumer and CSP. Confidentiality is one of the security management complications that can be assured by encrypting data. However, the primary barrier of the encryption techniques is still the key management issues. CSA and NIST classify the key management as the most complex part of any security system (Juan, 2012).

Accordingly, CCCE has overcome the key availability problem by deploying a new cloud service layer (QCaaS) that combines the developed AES algorithm and the QKD technique (Omer, Safia, El-Sayed and Abdel-Badeeh, 2014). This hybrid technique:

- Supports scalability in dynamic key distribution via two implemented modes.
- Defeats the most types of attack such as (man-in-the-middle-attack, side-channel attack)
- Provides independent and trusted communication for each user.

QCaaS Main Roles

QCaaS protects the consumer's cryptographic key and file through the communication. Moreover, due to the isolation criteria for the resources, QCaaS prevents an attacker or malicious from information extraction through the cloud.

- **Securing the Consumer:** QCaaS provides the encryption/decryption process by cooperating both consumer's machine and cloud servers, this corporation defeats two types of attacks (man-in –the middle attack and authentication attack).
- **Consumer Encryption Permissions:** QCaaS helps the consumer for encrypting the flying data, which in turn, provides a higher level of security.

- **Key Protection:** Key generation and key distribution processes are critical in any cloud storage environment; therefore, keys must be carefully generated and protected. QCaaS achieves these processes by dynamic key generation based QKD (Omer, Safia, El-Sayed and Abdel-Badeeh, 2014; Rawal V., Dhamija A., Sharma, 2012). After then, keys are expired as soon as the sending or receiving files process completed.

DoS Attack Defeating

DoS attack is considered as the most critical threat to VMs environment. The threat lays in its ability to overcome the hypervisors misconfiguration. It allows a single VM to consume all available resources and causes starving for others on the same physical device. However, Quantum Cloud hypervisor prevents any VM from exploiting 100% of the shared hardware resources, including CPU, network bandwidth, and RAM. This feature provided by creating a standard Quota (see Figure 12) and controlling centralization of "qcloud.net" domain. Such quota deploys standard resources for each new VM creation. Domain controller name, number of processors and hardware resources are examples of such resources. If any VM exceeds this prevailing quote, the CSP sends alerts and destroys the connections.

CONCLUSION AND FUTURE WORKS

Cloud computing allows consumers to use applications without installing or accessing their personal files on their personal machine via the internet. In cloud computing technology, there is a set of critical security issues, such as privacy, anonymity, telecommunications capacity, and reliability. However, the most significant problem in these issues is to provide a secure environment and assure it.

Figure 12. VMs quota

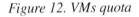

This chapter presented a CCCE, which entails both QCaaS and QAES (developed AES-based QKD) aiming to provide more flexibility and secure communication environment, improve the performance of the encryption/decryption process, and support more secure data transmission process using less computational time.

CCCE enjoys certain advantages when compared with the others, especially with respect to the secret key generation used in the encryption/ decryption process. It can be considered as the first cloud environment that integrates both the CSP principles and the QKD mechanisms. CCCE shows that the availability and the reliability of the secret key generation can be easily achieved based on two modes, On-line and off-line. CCCE poses more secure data transmission by provisioning secret keys among cloud's instances based on innovative cryptographic service QCaaS.

The QCaaS solves the key generation, key distribution and key management problems that emerged through the two implemented modes, since it is assigned to the two communication parties (consumer and CSP). Furthermore, QCaaS enjoys many advantages such as:

- Serving the consumer secure communication and protecting their sensitive data,
- Verifying and monitoring the identity of the original user depending on "qcloud.net" and Kerberos authentication function,
- deploying an encryption service with each VM,
- Achieving the encryption/decryption processes using QAES.

Generally, any privileged operations that traditionally could be done by "qcloud.net "administrators, such as building a new sub domain or forest, increasing the validity of the consumer, domain migration, and the cloud instances.

Finally, Cloud data encryption based quantum technology platform dispels all security fears through the cloud data transmission. This technology offers, a simple low-cost for the data protection, security tools for services integration, and an efficient disaster recovery.

In the future work, third trusted party (TTP) should be added to a cloud environment and consumer enterprise. This TTP works as a quantum cipher cloud and responsible for key generation and key deployment. Moreover, a secure cloud computing system that mainly depends on randomness ratio associated with the quantum system is going to be build.

REFERENCES

Aidan, F., Hans, V., Patrick, L., & Damian, F. (2012). *Microsoft Private Cloud Computing*. John Wiley publisher.

Andrew T., Juan K., James L., Miles Z., Elaine R., & Stefan S. (2013). A statistical test suite for random and pseudorandom number generators for cryptographic applications. NIST Special Publication 800-22 Revision.

Bethencourt, J., Sahai, A., & Waters, B. (2011). Ciphertext-policy attribute-based encryption, *Proceedings of the IEEE Symposium on Security and Privacy (SP '07)* (pp. 321–334).

Center for Quantum Technology. (n. d.). Retrieved from http://www.quantumlah.org/research/topic/ qcrypto,1/9/2014

Chadwick, D., & Casanova, M. (2011). *Security API for private cloud. Proceedings of the 3rd IEEE International on cloud computing technology and sciences, CloudCom* (pp. 792–798). CPS.

Chander, K., & Yogesh, S. (2013). Enhanced security architecture for cloud data security. International journal of advanced research in computer science and software engineering, 3(5).

Christain, K., & Mario, P. (2010). *Applied Quantum cryptography*. Lect. Notes Phys.: Vol. 797. Berlin, Heidelberg: Springer. Doi: doi:10.1007/978-3-642-04831-9

CSA, (2012). *Security a-a-services guidance for critical areas in cloud computing, Category 8.*

Cutillo, A., Molva, R., & Strufe, T. (2009). Safe book: A privacy-preserving online social network is leveraging on real-life trust. *IEEE Communications Magazine, 47*(12), 94–101. doi:10.1109/ MCOM.2009.5350374

De Decker, B., & Zúquete, A. (Eds.), (2014). *Communications and Multimedia Security*. Springer.

Doelitzscher, F., Reich, C., Knahl, M., & Clarke, N. (2011). *An autonomous agent-based incident detection system for cloud computing, 3rd IEEE International on cloud computing technology and sciences, CloudCom* (pp. 197–204). CPS.

Eduared, G. (2014). An Experimental Implementation of Oblivious Transfer in the Noisy Storage Model. Nature Communications Journal, 5.

Emmanuel S., Navdeep A., Parshant T., Bhanu P. (2013). Cloud Computing: Data Storage Security Analysis and its Challenges. *International Journal of Computer Applications*, 70(24).

ENISA security. (2014). Retrieved from http://www.enisa.europa.eu/

Faiza, F. (2012). Management of symmetric cryptographic keys in a cloud-based environment. *Proceedings of the 2nd IEEE international conference on cloud computing technology and science.*

Farhad, A., Seyed, S., & Athula, G. (2013). Cloud computing: security and reliability issues. Communication of the IBIMA (Vol. 1).

IDC. (2014). IDC Ranking of issues of Cloud Computing model. Retrieved from http://www.idc.com/

Itani, W., Kayassi, A., & Chehab, A. (2012). Energy-efficient incremental integrity for securing storage in mobile cloud computing. *Proceedings of the International Conference on Energy Aware Computing (ICEAC10)*. Cairo, Egypt.

Jensen, M., Schwenk, J., Gruschka, N., & Iacono, L. (2009). On Technical Security Issues in Cloud Computing. IEEE ICCC, Bangalore (pp. 109-116).

Juan, S. (2012). *Statistical testing of random number generators*. National Institute Standards Technology.

Juan, S. (2012). *Statistical testing of random number generators ", National Institute Standards Technology*. NIST.

Mandeep U., & Manish T. (2012). Implementing Various Encryption Algorithm to Enhance the Data Security of Cloud in Cloud Computing. *International Journal of Computer Science and Information Technology*, 2(10).

Manpreet, W., & Rajbir, N. (2013). Implementing Encryption Algorithms to EnhanceData Security of Cloud in Cloud Computing. *International Journal of Computers and Applications*, 70(18).

Mather, T., & Kumaraswamy, S. (2012). *Cloud security and privacy; An enterprise perspective on risks and compliance* (1st ed.). O'Reilly Media.

Matthew, G. (2013). Statistical tests of randomness on QKD through a free-space channel coupled to daylight noise. *Journal of Lightwave Technology*, 3(23).

Matthew, P., Caleb, H., Lamas, L., & Christian, K. (2008). *Daylight operation of a free space, entanglement-based quantum key distribution system*. Centre for Quantum Technologies, National University of Singapore.

Mohammad, G., John, M., & Ingo, K. (2010). An analysis of the Cloud Computing Security Problem. *Proceedings of APSE 2010 Cloud Workshop*, Sydney, Australia.

Mohammad, O.K.J., Abbas, S., El-Horbaty, E.-S.M., & Salem, A.-B.M. (2013). A Comparative Study of Modern Encryption Algorithms based On Cloud Computing Environment. *Proceedings of the 8th International Conference for Internet Technology and Secured Transactions (ICITST-2013)* (pp. 536-541).

Mohammad, O.K.J., Abbas, S., El-Horbaty, E.-S.M., & Salem, A.-B.M. (2014). Cryptographic Cloud Computing Environment as a More Trusted Communication Environment. *International Journal of Grid and High Performance Computing*, 6.

Mohammad, O.K.J., Abbas, S., El-Horbaty, E.-S.M., & Salem, A.-B.M. (2014). Statistical Analysis for Random Bits Generation on Quantum Key Distribution. *Proceedings of the 3rd IEEE- Conference on Cyber Security, Cyber Warfare, and Digital Forensic (CyberSec2014)* (pp. 45-52).

Mohammad, O.K.J., Abbas, S., El-Horbaty, E.-S.M., & Salem, A.-B.M. (2014). Advanced Encryption Standard Development Based Quantum Key Distribution, the 9th International Conference for Internet Technology and Secured Transactions (ICITST-2014), pp.446-456.

Mohammad, O.K.J., Abbas, S., El-Horbaty, E.-S.M., & Salem, A.-B.M. (2015). Quantum Key Distribution: Simulation and Characterizations. *International Conference on Communication, Management and Information Technology (ICCMIT 2015)*, Prague (pp. 78-88).

Nelson, G., Charles, M., Fernando, R., Marco, S., Tereza, C., Mats, N., & Makan, P. (2014). A quantitative analysis of current security concerns and solutions for cloud computing, Journal of cloud computing: advanced, systems and applications, 1(11).

Odeh, A., Elleithy, K., Alshowkan, M., & Abdelfattah, E. (2013). Quantum key distribution by using RSA. *Proceeding of 3rd International Conference on Innovative Computing Technology (INTECH)*.

Padmapriya, A., & Subhasri, P. (2013). Cloud Computing: Security Challenges and Encryption Practices. *International Journal of Advance Research in Computer Science and Software Engineering*, 3(3).

Patil D., & Akshay R. (2012). Data Security over Cloud Emerging Trends in Computer Science and Information Technology. International Journal of Computer Applications, pp. 123-147.

Patil D., Akshay R. (2012), "Data Security over Cloud Emerging Trends in Computer Science and Information Technology", proceeding published in International Journal of Computer Applications, pp. 123-147.

Rawal V., Dhamija A., Sharma S. (2012). Revealing New Concepts in Photography & Clouds. *International Journal of Scientific & Technology Research*, 1(7).

Solange, G., & Mohammed, A. (2014). Applying QKD to reach unconditional security in communications. European research project SECOQC. Retrieved from www.secoqc.net

Soren, B., Sven, B., & Hugo, I. (2013). Consumer –controlled cryptography-as-a-service in the cloud. *Proceedings of 11th International Conference, ACNS 2013*.

StarWind Virtual SAN- Quick Start Guide. (2014). *StarWind Software*. USA.

Sunita, M., & Seema, S. (2013). *Distributed Computing* (2nd ed.). USA: Oxford University Press.

Syam, P., Subramanian, R., & Thamizh, D. (2010). Ensuring data security in cloud computing using sobol sequence. *Proceedings of the 1st international conference on parallel, distributed and grid computing (PDGC)*.

Wang Q., Cong X., Min S. (2012). Protecting Privacy by Multi-dimensional K-anonymity. *Journal of Software*, 7(8).

William, S. (2012). *Cryptography and network security (5th ed.)*. Prentice Hall.

Winkler, J. (2011). Securing the cloud: cloud computer security techniques and tactics.

Yau, S. S., & An, H. G. (2010). Confidentiality Protection in Cloud Computing Systems. *Int J Software Informatics*, 4(4), 351.

Zhou, M., Mu, Y., Susilo, W., Yan, J., & Dong, L. (2012). Privacy enhanced data outsourcing in the cloud. *Journal of Network and Computer Applications*, 35(4), 1367–1373. doi:10.1016/j.jnca.2012.01.022

KEY TERMS AND DEFINITIONS

Advanced Encryption Standard (AES): A symmetric block cipher used 128-bit block data encryption technique developed by Belgian cryptographers Joan Daemen and Vincent Rijmen. The U.S government adopted the algorithm as its encryption technique in October 2000. AES works at multiple network layers simultaneously. In addition, such algorithm take 128; 192 or 256 bits of key size.

Cloud Computing: A type of computing that relies on sharing computing resources rather than having local servers or personal devices to handle applications and it is a general term for anything that involves delivering hosted services over the Internet. These services are broadly divided into three categories: Infrastructure-as-a-Service (IaaS), Platform-as-a-Service (PaaS) and Software-as-a-Service (SaaS).

Cloud Computing Cryptographic Algorithm: A mathematical algorithm, used in conjunction with a secret key, that transforms original input into a form that is unintelligible without special knowledge of the secret information and the algorithm. Such algorithms are also the basis for digital signatures and key exchange.

Hyper-V: A native hypervisor; it can create virtual machines on x86-64 systems and starting with Windows 8. Hyper-V supersedes Windows Virtual PC as the hardware virtualization component of the client editions of Windows NT. A server computer running Hyper-V can be configured to expose individual virtual machines to one or more networks. Hyper-V was first released along Windows Server 2008 and became a staple of the Windows Server family ever since.

Quantum Key Distribution: A new mechanisms that uses quantum mechanics to guarantee secure communication. It enables two communication parties to produce a shared random secret key known only to them, which can then be used to encrypt and decrypt messages. It is often incorrectly called quantum cryptography, as it is the most well-known example of the group of quantum cryptographic tasks. The important and unique property of quantum distribution is the ability of the two communicating users to detect the presence of any third party trying to gain knowledge of the key.

Quantum Technology: A new field of physics and engineering, which transitions some of the stranger features of quantum mechanics, especially quantum entanglement and most recently quantum tunneling, into practical applications such as quantum computing, quantum cryptography, quantum simulation, quantum metrology, quantum sensing, quantum communication, intelligent quantum system, and quantum imaging.

System Center Configuration Manager (SCCM): A Windows product that enables administrators to manage the deployment and security of devices and applications across an enterprise. SCCM is part of the Microsoft System Center 2012 systems management suite. The SCCM integrated console enables management of Microsoft Application Virtualization (App-V), Microsoft Enterprise Desktop Virtualization (Med-V), Citrix XenApp, Microsoft Forefront and Windows Phone applications from a single location.

This research was previously published in Managing Big Data in Cloud Computing Environments edited by Zongmin Ma, pages 71-99, copyright year 2016 by Information Science Reference (an imprint of IGI Global).

Index

G

H

Q

R

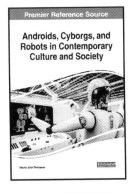

Ensure Quality Research is Introduced to the Academic Community

Become an IGI Global Reviewer for Authored Book Projects

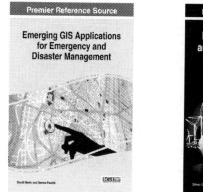

The overall success of an authored book project is dependent on quality and timely reviews.

In this competitive age of scholarly publishing, constructive and timely feedback significantly expedites the turnaround time of manuscripts from submission to acceptance, allowing the publication and discovery of forward-thinking research at a much more expeditious rate. Several IGI Global authored book projects are currently seeking highly qualified experts in the field to fill vacancies on their respective editorial review boards:

Applications may be sent to:
development@igi-global.com

Applicants must have a doctorate (or an equivalent degree) as well as publishing and reviewing experience. Reviewers are asked to write reviews in a timely, collegial, and constructive manner. All reviewers will begin their role on an ad-hoc basis for a period of one year, and upon successful completion of this term can be considered for full editorial review board status, with the potential for a subsequent promotion to Associate Editor.

If you have a colleague that may be interested in this opportunity, we encourage you to share this information with them.

Printed in the United States
By Bookmasters